STUDY GUIDE

BUSINESS LAW & THE REGULATORY ENVIRONMENT

THIRTEENTH EDITION

RONALD A. ANDERSON
Professor Emeritus, Drexel University
Member of the Pennsylvania and Philadelphia Bars

IVAN FOX
Professor of Law, Business Law Department, Pace University
Member of the New York Bar

DAVID P. TWOMEY
Professor of Law, Carroll School of Management, Boston College
Member of the Massachusetts and Florida Bars

MARIANNE M. JENNINGS
Professor of Legal and Ethical Studies, Director, Lincoln Center for Applied Ethics, Arizona State University
Member of the Arizona Bar

Prepared By
RONALD L. TAYLOR
Metropolitan State College of Denver

WEST
WEST EDUCATIONAL PUBLISHING COMPANY
An International Thomson Publishing Company

Publisher/Team Director: Jack C. Calhoun
Aquisitions Editor: Rob Dewey
Marketing Manager: Scott D. Person
Development Editor: Mignon D. Worman, J.D., Member, California and Ohio Bars
Production Editor: Marci Dechter
Team Assistant: Kristen Meere
Manufacturing Coordinator: Georgina Calderon

Copyright © 1998
by West Educational Publishing Company
I(T)P® *An International Thomson Publishing Company*
Cincinnati, Ohio

ALL RIGHTS RESERVED
The text of this publication, or any part thereof, may not be reproduced or transmitted in any form or by any means, electronic or mechanical, including photocopying, recording storage in an information retrieval system, or otherwise, without the prior written permission of the publisher.

ISBN: 0-538-86901-1

1 2 3 4 5 6 7 8 9 PN 5 4 3 2 1 0 9 8 7

Printed in the United States of America

I(T)P®
International Thomson Publishing
West Educational Publishing is an ITP Company.
The ITP trademark is used under license.

CONTENTS

1. Law and Determination of Legal Rights 1
2. Business Ethics, Social Forces and the Law 13
3. The Constitution as the Foundation of the Legal Environment 23
4. Government Regulation of Competition and Prices 31
5. Administrative Agencies 39
6. The Legal Environment of International Trade 49
7. Crimes 57
8. Torts 65
9. Nature and Classes of Contracts 75
10. The Agreement 83
11. Capacity and Genuine Assent 93
12. Consideration 103
13. Legality and Public Policy 113
14. Form of Contract 121
15. Interpretation of Contracts 129
16. Third Person and Contracts 137
17. Discharge of Contracts 145
18. Breach of Contract and Remedies 153
19. Accountants' Liability and Malpractice 161
20. Personal Property 169
21. Intellectual Property Rights 175
22. Bailments 183
23. Legal Aspects of Warehousing, Transportation, Factoring, and Hotel Keeping 191
24. Nature and Form of Sales 199
25. Risk and Property Rights 211
26. Obligations and Performance 219
27. Warranties and Other Product Liability Theories 227
28. Remedies for Breach of Sales Contracts 237
29. Consumer Protection 245

30	Kinds of Instruments, Parties, and Negotiability	253
31	Transfer of Commercial Paper	261
32	Rights of Holders and Defenses	269
33	Checks and Funds Transfers	277
34	Secured Transactions in Personal Property	287
35	Other Security Devices	295
36	Bankruptcy	303
37	Insurance	313
38	Agency—Creation and Termination	321
39	Principal and Agent	331
40	Third Persons in Agency	339
41	Regulation of Employment	347
42	Equal Employment Opportunity Law	357
43	Forms of Business Organizations	365
44	Creation and Termination of Partnerships	373
45	Partnerships, Limited Partnerships, and Limited Liability Companies	381
46	Introduction to Corporation Law	389
47	Corporate Stock and Bonds	397
48	Securities Regulation	405
49	Management of Corporations	413
50	Real Property	421
51	Environmental Law and Community Planning	431
52	Leases	437
53	Decedents' Estates and Trusts	445
	Quicken Exercises	453
	Quicken Answers	491

CHAPTER 1
LAW AND DETERMINATION OF LEGAL RIGHTS

CHAPTER OUTLINE

A. **NATURE OF LAW AND LEGAL RIGHTS**

Law consists of the principles that govern conduct and that can be enforced in court or by administrative agencies.

1. **LEGAL RIGHTS**

    (a) *The "rights of the human being" concept*:

    GENERAL RULE.   The American legal system recognizes individuals as human beings who enjoy certain legal rights.
    STUDY HINT.   Prior to the American Revolution, people in most societies were not viewed as having rights as human beings. At best, they were viewed as subjects of the ruling government.

    (b) *The right of privacy*:

    ▸ Today, Americans enjoy a fundamental right of privacy. ▸ This right was first recognized in 1890.

    (c) *Technology and privacy*:

    Even though technology enables one to invade other's privacy, persons' reasonable expectations of privacy still govern their privacy rights.

    (d) *Abolition of rights*:

    ▸ A legal right can be altered or eliminated by statute unless the right is protected by the Constitution.
    ▸ Example: Rights created by court decisions (i.e., rights created by common law), such as the typical right of minors to avoid contracts, can be changed or eliminated by statute.

2. **TECHNOLOGY AND THE LAW**
    As technology expands, new rules of law are often required to address new issues relating to the rights and obligations of individuals and businesses.

3. **WHAT ARE THE SOURCES OF LAW?**
    Important sources of the law include:

    ■ *Constitutional law*: law created by the U.S. Constitution and state constitutions. This type of law typically creates the structure of the government and its relationship to the people governed.
    ■ *Statutory law*: law created by Congress, state legislatures, and local governments, such as cities.
    ■ *Administrative regulations*: law (rules) created by federal and state administrative agencies.
    ■ *Case law*: law created by courts. Courts adopt precedents that are followed in future cases under the doctrine of *stare decisis*. This body of judge-made law is known as the common law.

4. UNIFORM STATE LAWS

▸ Uniform state laws are statutes that have been drafted and are proposed for adoption by states and that relate to various types of businesses and activities. ▸ Examples: Uniform Commercial Code (UCC) that regulates various areas of commercial transactions; Uniform Consumer Credit Code (UCCC) that establishes various credit-related protections for consumers.

5. CLASSIFICATIONS OF LAW

Law is classified in many ways. Important classifications include:

- *Legal rights and procedures*: ▸ Substantive law creates and defines the legal rights and liabilities of persons. Example: right not to have another person wrongfully injure your reputation. ▸ Procedural law specifies the steps that must be followed to enforce a person's substantive legal rights and liabilities. Example: statutes that limit the time within which you can sue another person.
- *Origin of the law*: English common law (basis for much of early American law); Roman (civil) law; law merchant.
- *Subject matter of the law*: Examples include law of contracts, property law, and tort law.
- *Nature of relief sought (law and equity)*: ▸ Principles that are used to resolve civil lawsuits may be classified by the relief sought. ▸ *Principles of law* are used if a party seeks monetary damages.
▸ *Principles of equity* are used if a party seeks a remedy other than damages, such as specific performance (order that a party perform a contract). Equitable principles are more flexible than principles of law and provide a remedy in accordance with equity and justice. Equitable relief is denied unless a party will suffer a loss that cannot be adequately remedied by damages.

B. DETERMINATION OF LEGAL RIGHTS

6. CONTRACT SELECTION OF LAW OR FORUM

GENERAL RULES. ▸ By contract, parties may specify that the law of a certain state will control a particular transaction. ▸ Contracting parties may also specify the forum, i.e., the court of a particular state or country in which a lawsuit must be brought.

LIMITATIONS. ▸ The law chosen must reasonably relate to the transaction and it cannot violate a strong public policy. ▸ The forum selected must reasonably relate to the parties or transaction.

7. COURTS

GENERAL RULE. A court is a tribunal established by a government to decide controversies, provide a remedy for persons who have been wronged, punish wrongdoers, and prevent wrongs.

STUDY HINT. Courts may be classified as: (1) courts of record (proceedings are recorded); or (2) courts not of record (proceedings are not officially recorded).

(a) *Jurisdiction*: ▸ Jurisdiction is the power to hear and decide certain types of cases. ▸ Courts may have: (1) *original jurisdiction* (power to decide cases for the first time); or (2) *appellate jurisdiction* (power to review decisions of lower courts). ▸ Courts may have: (1) *general jurisdiction* (power to decide all types of cases); or (2) *limited (special) jurisdiction* (power to decide only certain types of cases). ▸ Courts may be classified as: (1) *criminal courts* (decide cases involving crimes); or (2) *civil courts* (decide cases involving private wrongs and noncriminal public matters).

(b) *Judicial control of procedure*: ▸ Courts have the inherent power to create rules that are necessary to preserve order and to enable them to perform their duties. Examples: fine or imprison persons for contempt; refuse to allow evidence that was improperly withheld earlier in a lawsuit.

(c) *Declaratory judgment*: In a declaratory judgment procedure (action), a court is authorized to determine the rights of parties before a loss has occurred.

(d) *Mootness as a bar to court relief*: Courts cannot determine matters after the dispute has ended, i.e., the dispute is moot. Example: lawsuit to determine custody of a son who is now an adult.

(e) *Immunity for wrong decision*: A judge, juror, or arbitrator cannot be sued for making a wrong decision, although they may be criminally prosecuted if their action constitutes a crime.

8. ADMINISTRATIVE AGENCIES

Congress and state legislatures have created a number of administrative agencies, such as the Federal Trade Commission, that often have the power to make rules, enforce their rules, and conduct hearings to determine if their rules have been violated.

9. ALTERNATE MEANS OF DISPUTE RESOLUTION (AVOIDING A LAWSUIT)

(a) Arbitration

GENERAL RULES. ▸ Arbitration is typically a voluntary process by which parties agree to submit a dispute to disinterested persons called "arbitrators." ▸ The parties' agreement determines whether a particular dispute must be submitted to arbitration. ▸ The arbitrator's decision generally is final, i.e., legally binding on the parties. ▸ The decision can be set aside by a court only if it is the result of fraud, arbitrary (grossly unreasonable) conduct by the arbitrator, or serious procedural mistakes.
LIMITATION. Laws may require mandatory arbitration of some disputes. If arbitration is mandatory, then a decision can be appealed and a party is entitled to a new trial (a trial *de novo*).

(b) Mediation

Mediation is a process whereby a neutral party (mediator) delivers settlement proposals from one party to the second party, and the mediator may also make suggestions for settlement of the dispute. The mediator's suggestions are not legally binding on the parties.

(c) Other alternate means to resolve disputes

- *Reference to third person*: Parties voluntarily refer determination of a fact, such as the appraised value of a fire loss, to an impartial third party or committee. The parties usually agree that the decision will be final.

- *Association tribunals*: Panel resolves disputes between association members or between an association member and a consumer. The decision is generally binding on the association member, but not on the consumer.

- *Summary jury trial*: A mock (pretend) trial is held before a jury. The decision is *not* binding.

- *Rent-a-judge*: Parties hire a judge ("referee") to try a case. The decision is typically binding unless reversed on appeal.

- *Minitrial*: Parties submit the disputed issues to a person, such as a retired judge, for determination. The parties' agreement dictates whether the determination is legally binding.

- *Contract provisions*: Contracts often require that parties use one of the foregoing procedures.

10. DISPOSITION OF COMPLAINTS AND OMBUDSMEN

Statutes sometimes authorize appointment of an ombudsman to receive complaints and make recommendations for improvements. An ombudsman may review, but cannot legally decide, complaints.

REVIEW OF TERMS AND PHRASES

MATCHING EXERCISE

Select the term or phrase that best matches a definition or statement stated below. Each term or phrase is the best match for only one statement or definition.

Terms and Phrases

a. Administrative law
b. Appellate jurisdiction
c. Case law
d. Doctrine of *stare decisis*
e. Original jurisdiction
f. Precedent
g. Procedural law
h. Statutory law
i. Substantive law
j. Uniform state laws

Statements and Definitions

____ 1. Classification of law that defines the steps required to enforce legal rights and obligations.

____ 2. Law that is created by federal and state administrative agencies.

____ 3. Classification of law that defines legal rights and obligations.

____ 4. Jurisdiction that allows a court to hear and decide a case for the first time.

____ 5. Body of law that is created by Congress and state legislatures.

____ 6. Rule of law (principle) adopted by a court for the first time.

____ 7. Law that is created by courts.

____ 8. Rule generally requiring that precedents be followed in future, similar cases.

____ 9. Jurisdiction that allows a court to review the judgment of a lower court.

____ 10. Model statutes that have been proposed for adoption by each of the states.

COMPLETION EXERCISE

Fill in the blanks with the words that most accurately complete each statement. Answers may or may not include terms used in the matching exercise. A term cannot be used to complete more than one statement.

1. The power of a court to hear and determine certain types of lawsuits is called _____.

2. _____ _____ are courts that decide controversies involving private wrongs against individuals.

3. _____ is a voluntary, alternate means of dispute resolution by which parties agree to submit a dispute to one or more disinterested persons known as arbitrators.

4. A _____ ___ _____ is a court in which a record is kept of the court proceedings.

5. A _____ _____ procedure is a court procedure that allows a party to request a court to determine the rights of parties before a loss actually occurs.

REVIEW OF CONCEPTS

Write **T** if the statement is true, write **F** if it is false.

_____ 1. A statute cannot alter a person's legal right if the right is protected by the U.S. Constitution.

_____ 2. In most societies that existed before the creation of the United States, individuals were not regarded as human beings who possessed certain basic rights.

_____ 3. Parties to a contract may agree that a lawsuit relating to the contract must be brought in the court of any state or country they choose (forum) even if the designated forum does not bear any relationship to the parties or to the transaction in question.

_____ 4. Criminal courts hear and decide cases involving private rights and wrongs.

_____ 5. Courts generally have the inherent power to adopt rules that are necessary to assure that order is preserved in the court.

_____ 6. In general, judges, juries, and arbitrators are personally liable for any damages that are caused by their wrong decisions.

_____ 7. A court will generally hear and decide a matter even if the dispute no longer exists.

_____ 8. If a statute requires arbitration of a dispute, then the arbitration decision is generally not final and a party may obtain a court trial on all of the issues (a trial *de novo*).

_____ 9. Parties are legally prohibited from hiring a private judge or referee to hear and decide a dispute that they have with one another.

_____ 10. Ombudsmen do not generally have the power to legally hear and decide complaints.

REVIEW OF CHAPTER - APPLICATION OF CONCEPTS

MULTIPLE CHOICE QUESTIONS

_____ 1. Thomas Television Network aired a show entitled "Do It Yourself." This program instructed the viewing audience on how to manufacture certain illegal drugs and where to buy the necessary ingredients. Thomas Television was notified that it was being charged with violation of a regulation of the Federal Communications Commission, a federal agency. What type of law was Thomas Television charged with violating?
    a. Constitutional law.
    b. Statutory law.
    c. Administrative law.
    d. Common law.

____ 2. A state supreme court adopted a principle of law (precedent) that holds that a skier can sue a ski area for negligence even if the skier was skiing out of bounds (constitutional rights are not involved). This state's legislature later enacted a statute which provided that a skier could *not* hold a ski area liable if the skier was skiing out of bounds. Under these facts:
   a. The principle of law adopted by the state supreme court was statutory law.
   b. The principle of law adopted by the state supreme court was case law.
   c. The legal right of skiers to sue that was created by the state supreme court was effectively changed by the statute enacted by the state legislature.
   d. b and c.

____ 3. Raymond Inc. was sued by a government agency for violating federal antidiscrimination law. At its trial in a lower federal trial court, Raymond asserted that the law in question was unconstitutional. However, in a previous case involving other parties, the U.S. Supreme Court held, for the first time, that this law was constitutional. Under these facts:
   a. The prior decision of the Supreme Court is a precedent.
   b. Under the doctrine of *stare decisis*, the trial court in Raymond's case is generally bound to follow the Supreme Court's prior decision and find the law to be constitutional.
   c. Under the doctrine of *stare decisis*, the trial court in Raymond's case is not bound to follow the Supreme Court's prior decision and it may find the law to be unconstitutional.
   d. a and b.

____ 4. Which of the following is an example of case law?
   a. The legislature passes a statute requiring businesses with more than 10 employees to offer a maternity leave program for the employees.
   b. In resolving a legal controversy between two parties, the state supreme court adopts a rule of law that an agreement is not enforceable unless there is both a valid offer and acceptance.
   c. The President of the United States issues an executive order restricting exports to a hostile nation.
   d. The Department of Motor Vehicles changes the fee for renewing a driver's license.

____ 5. Roger and Teresa owned competing grocery stores. Roger told a group of Teresa's customers that she had previously been convicted of selling spoiled meat. Teresa claimed this statement was false, and she sued Roger for $50,000 for defamation (i.e., the wrongful injury to the reputation of another). Roger asserted two defenses: (a) He did not commit this wrong because what he said was true; and (b) the court lacked jurisdiction over him because he had never been served with process. Under these facts:
   a. Defense (a) is based on procedural law.
   b. Defense (b) is based on procedural law.
   c. Defense (b) is based on substantive law.
   d. a and c.

____ 6. Trenton Antiques contracted to sell a painting to Janis for $500. The painting is a rare antique portrait that cannot be replaced. Subsequently, Trenton Antiques refused to perform this contract and Janis sued. In this lawsuit, the relief that Janis requested was an order of specific performance that would require Trenton Antiques to perform the contract. Under these facts:
   a. Principles of law will determine whether Janis will be awarded the relief that she has requested.
   b. Principles of equity will determine whether Janis will be awarded the relief that she has requested.
   c. Janis will not be awarded the requested relief unless she first establishes that damages would not adequately remedy her loss.
   d. b and c.

_____ 7. Elkar Corp., an Iowa firm, contracted to operate a business in Kansas with P&P Corp., a Kansas firm. The contract states that Kansas law will determine all contract rights and duties and that any lawsuit regarding this contract must be brought in Kansas state court. Under these facts:
   a. The contract provisions stating that Kansas law will govern and that any lawsuit must be brought in Kansas state court are both valid.
   b. The contract provision stating that any lawsuit must be brought in Kansas state court is invalid.
   c. The contract provision stating that Kansas law will govern is valid, but the provision stating that any lawsuit must be brought in Kansas state court is invalid.
   d. The contract provision stating that Kansas law will govern is invalid.

_____ 8. Carol stole inventory from Acme, Corp., her employer. Eventually, Carol was apprehended. Under these facts:
   a. Acme may sue Carol for money damages in criminal court.
   b. The state may prosecute Carol for theft in civil court.
   c. Acme may sue Carol for money damages in civil court, and the state may prosecute Carol for theft in criminal court.
   d. Acme may sue Carol for money damages in criminal court, and the state may prosecute Carol for theft in civil court.

_____ 9. Arco Construction and Juan entered into a contract whereby Arco agreed to construct a building for Juan. A contract dispute has now arisen regarding Arco's work. The contract states that all disputes relating to the contract must be submitted to arbitration. In this case:
   a. Juan does not have to submit this dispute to arbitration. If he desires, he can instead file a lawsuit.
   b. Juan must submit the dispute to arbitration. He has given up his right to file a suit on this claim.
   c. If an arbitration is held, the arbitrator's decision is not legally binding on the parties.
   d. b and c.

_____ 10. Carol leased a shop from Rentco Inc. The parties had a disagreement and they agreed to submit their dispute to binding arbitration. Under these facts:
   a. The parties have no right to appeal the arbitrator's award (decision) to a court.
   b. The parties may appeal the arbitrator's award to a court.
   c. If the arbitrator's award is appealed, the court will set the award aside if, for any reason, the court disagrees with the award.
   d. b and c.

_____ 11. Don had a dispute with his insurance company involving a $1,000 claim. State law required arbitration of all civil disputes under $5,000. In arbitration, Don was awarded $500. Under these facts:
   a. The award is not legally binding because mandatory arbitration is unconstitutional.
   b. The award is final. Don has no right to appeal the award.
   c. The award is not final. Don may appeal the award to court and he is entitled to a trial *de novo*.
   d. The award is not final. Don may appeal the award to court, but the court will not conduct a new trial.

____ 12. Tex bought a new car from Lansing Co., a new car dealer. Tex alleges that the car is defective. The parties want to use an alternate means of dispute resolution to help resolve this matter. In this case:
   a. The parties can refer the dispute to a third person, and the parties can determine whether the third party's decision is legally binding on Tex and Lansing Co.
   b. In many states, the parties can use an association tribunal operated by new car dealers, but the decision of this tribunal will be legally binding on only the association member, Lansing Co.
   c. The parties cannot use any alternate means of dispute resolution because it is illegal to do so.
   d. a and b.

____ 13. Todd has a dispute with Carla and he wants to use some type of alternate dispute resolution that may help the parties settle their dispute, but Todd does not want to be bound by the outcome of the alternate proceeding. Which of the following would meet Todd's needs?
   a. Arbitration.
   b. Mediation.
   c. Summary jury trial.
   d. b and c.

CASE PROBLEM

Answer the following problem, briefly explaining your answer.

Roger was negligently injured by Diane. Roger is preparing to file a lawsuit against Diane in state court for $25,000 damages as compensation for the private wrong that Diane committed against him.

The state in question has these courts: (a) state supreme court that has appellate jurisdiction; (b) state district court that has original jurisdiction of all cases involving private wrongs; and (c) small claims court that has original jurisdiction of cases relating to private wrongs that involve $5,000 in damages or less.

In this case:
(a) Is Roger legally entitled to bring his lawsuit in any court that he chooses?
(b) Which court has the power to hear and decide this lawsuit for the first time?
(c) Will Roger bring his lawsuit in a civil court or a criminal court?

APPENDIX TO CHAPTER 1
COURT ORGANIZATION AND PROCEDURE

APPENDIX OUTLINE

A. **PERSONNEL OF COURTS**

   1. **OFFICERS OF THE COURT**

      ▸ *Judge*: primary officer of the court. ▸ *Attorney*: additional officer of the court who represents and is typically selected by a party to the lawsuit. ▸ *Clerk*: person who keeps the court calendar and records of the proceedings. ▸ *Sheriff*: chief executive of a county who is responsible for preserving peace and performing some functions for county courts, such as serving writs and summoning witnesses. ▸ *U.S. Marshal*: officer who performs the same functions for federal courts as sheriff does for county courts.

   2. **THE JURY**

      ▸ The jury are citizens appointed by a court to determine the facts and render a verdict in a case. ▸ From a jury list, a jury panel is picked. Jury members are then selected from the jury panel.

B. **FEDERAL COURTS**

   3. **SUPREME COURT OF THE UNITED STATES**

      ▸ The Supreme Court is the highest federal court. ▸ The Supreme Court has original jurisdiction (trial court) over a few cases including cases in which a state is a party. ▸ The Supreme Court has appellate jurisdiction over all cases brought in federal court and certain cases brought in state court. Typically, the Supreme Court has the discretion to determine whether or not it will hear an appeal.

   4. **COURTS OF APPEALS**

      ▸ Courts of appeals have only appellate jurisdiction. ▸ Courts of appeal review judgments of federal district courts, and their decisions are final unless the Supreme Court hears an appeal of the case.

   5. **DISTRICT COURTS**

      ▸ District courts have original jurisdiction to decide most cases filed in federal court including: (1) civil suits in which the U.S. is a party; (2) actions involving any federal law, such as the U.S. Constitution, federal statutes or administrative rules, or U.S. treaties; and (3) cases between parties who are residents of different states if $50,000 or more is involved.

   6. **OTHER FEDERAL COURTS**

      Examples: Tax Court, Court of International Trade, Claims Court, and Court of Military Appeals.

C. **STATE COURTS**

   7. **STATE SUPREME COURT**

      The highest court in most states is the state supreme court which generally has appellate jurisdiction. The decision of a state supreme court is typically final unless it involves federal laws or the U.S. Constitution.

   8. **INTERMEDIATE COURTS**

      Intermediate state courts generally have appellate jurisdiction. Examples: state superior or circuit courts.

   9. **COUNTY AND DISTRICT COURTS**

      These courts generally have original jurisdiction of most criminal and civil cases.

   10. **OTHER STATE COURTS**

       Courts not of record, such as municipal courts, traffic courts, and small claims courts.

D. COURT PROCEDURE

Laws of procedure determine how, when, and where a legal dispute can be brought to trial.

E. STEPS IN A LAWSUIT

11. AVOIDANCE OF LITIGATION

Attorneys often try to settle cases before trial. Federal law requires attorneys to try to settle U.S. cases.

12. COMMENCEMENT OF ACTION

A lawsuit is typically begun by filing a complaint with the clerk of the court.

13. SERVICE OF PROCESS

A defendant must be served with process (a summons and/or the complaint).

14. PLEADINGS

▸ A defendant may file initial objections to the complaint, but the defendant must file an answer if the objections do not terminate the suit. ▸ A defendant may also assert a counterclaim (cross complaint).

15. PRETRIAL PROCEDURE

- *Pretrial termination of case*: A lawsuit may end before trial if a party obtains: (1) a judgment on the pleadings (judgment is given if pleadings clearly show one party should win); or (2) a summary judgment (judgment is given if there are no important fact issues and one party is entitled to win).
- *Pretrial conference*: Meeting of the judge and attorneys to eliminate undisputed issues.
- *Discovery and depositions*: ▸ Discovery is the process by which either party can find out from the other party most information relating to a lawsuit. ▸ Depositions are one form of discovery by which testimony of a witness or party is taken outside of court.

16. DETERMINATION OF FACTS

▸ A party has a constitutional right to a jury trial if, at common law, the action would have been decided by a jury. ▸ There is no right to a jury trial for actions in equity or for actions based on new statutes, such as worker compensation actions. Factual determinations are based on testimony and real evidence.

17. CONDUCT OF THE TRIAL

Opening addresses; direct examination and cross-examination of witnesses; summations.

18. CHARGE TO THE JURY AND VERDICT

▸ In its charge to the jury, the judge sums up what happened at the trial and explains the applicable law to the jury. ▸ The jury then determines factual questions and renders its verdict (finding).

19. TAKING THE CASE FROM THE JURY AND ATTACKING THE VERDICT

A suit may conclude by: (1) voluntary nonsuit (plaintiff chooses to end lawsuit); (2) compulsory nonsuit (plaintiff fails to present sufficient case and court ends lawsuit); (3) mistrial (trial ends due to serious mistakes and case is retried later); (4) directed verdict (at end of evidence, judge enters judgment for party); (5) new trial (case is retried due to jury errors or new evidence); or (6) judgment n.o.v.

20. JUDGMENT AND COSTS

▸ A court enters a judgment in accordance with the jury's verdict except as noted in the preceding section.
▸ Generally, the winning party is awarded certain costs incurred in a civil lawsuit.

21. APPEAL

▸ Appellate courts review lower court decisions for errors of law. ▸ Appellate courts do not hear witnesses and do not generally review questions of fact.

22. EXECUTION

Money judgments are collected by: (1) a sheriff selling the losing party's nonexempt property (an execution); or (2) the winning party obtaining wages or debts owed to the losing party (a garnishment).

REVIEW OF TERMS AND PHRASES

MATCHING EXERCISE

Select the term or phrase that best matches a definition or statement stated below. Each term or phrase is the best match for only one statement or definition.

Terms and Phrases

a. Answer
b. Complaint
c. Counterclaim
d. Garnishment
e. Process (summons)
f. Verdict

Statements and Definitions

____ 1. Pleading stating a defendant's response to a plaintiff's complaint.
____ 2. Procedure to enforce money judgment by which the winning party may obtain wages or debts that are owed by a third person or employer to the losing party.
____ 3. Legal notice of a lawsuit that is served on a defendant.
____ 4. Pleading stating a defendant's claim against a plaintiff and the defendant's demand for relief.
____ 5. Jury's finding or decision in a case.
____ 6. Pleading stating a plaintiff's claim against a defendant and the plaintiff's demand for relief.

COMPLETION EXERCISE

Fill in the blanks with the words that most accurately complete each statement. Answers may or may not include terms used in the matching exercise. A term cannot be used to complete more than one statement.

1. In many courts, a party to a lawsuit may request the judge to call a _____ _____ in order to determine which issues are disputed and to eliminate undisputed issues.

2. If serious mistakes, such as jury misconduct, are committed during a trial, a judge may declare a _____ which terminates the trial to be retried at a later date.

3. A _____ is a type of discovery procedure by which an interested party can take the oral testimony of a witness outside of court.

4. _____ _____ is evidence at trial that consists of tangible matters, such as writings and computer printouts.

REVIEW OF CONCEPTS

Write **T** if the statement is true, write **F** if it is false.

____ 1. In addition to law enforcement duties, sheriffs perform many functions for courts including summoning witnesses, serving legal papers (writs), and carrying out judicial sales of property.
____ 2. A person has a constitutional right to a jury trial in civil cases involving equity or new statutes.
____ 3. A court will not shorten a lawsuit by granting a summary judgment if there are important, disputed factual issues regarding a claim or defense.
____ 4. In civil cases, a party can generally use discovery procedures to find out information from the other party that relates to the lawsuit.
____ 5. A witness must appear at a trial if the witness is served with a subpoena demanding such appearance.

APPENDIX TO CHAPTER 1

____ 6. The testimony and opinions of experts cannot be admitted as evidence at a trial.

____ 7. Direct examination is questioning of a witness by the attorney who called the witness to testify.

____ 8. In a jury trial, the jury generally resolves questions of fact and the judge resolves questions of law.

____ 9. The charge is a judge's summation of what happened at the trial and explanation of the law to the jury.

____ 10. The winning party in a civil lawsuit is generally awarded recovery of his or her costs in the action.

REVIEW OF CHAPTER - APPLICATION OF CONCEPTS

MULTIPLE CHOICE PROBLEMS

____ 1. Kevin intends to sue his employer in federal court for violation of federal antidiscrimination laws. Under these facts, the federal trial court that will first hear and decide this case is the:
   a. District court.
   b. Court of appeals.
   c. Supreme Court of the United States.
   d. Tax Court.

____ 2. Tim, a resident of Iowa, is suing Rod, a resident of New York, for $75,000. Tim is suing for breach of contract (state law). Would a U.S. district court have jurisdiction to decide this case?
   a. Yes. U.S. district courts have jurisdiction to decide all lawsuits.
   b. Yes. A U.S. district court would have jurisdiction because Tim and Rod are residents of different states and the lawsuit involves $50,000 or more.
   c. No. U.S. district courts do not have jurisdiction unless federal law is involved.
   d. No. U.S. district courts do not have jurisdiction unless $100,000 or more is involved.

____ 3. Lawrence wants to sue his former landlord in order to recover his security deposit that the landlord has wrongfully failed to return. Under these facts:
   a. Lawrence will commence the lawsuit by filing a judgment with the clerk of the court.
   b. Lawrence will commence the lawsuit by filing a complaint with the clerk of the court.
   c. The landlord is automatically subject to the power of the court upon the filing of a complaint. Nothing is required to be served on the landlord to subject him to the power of the court.
   d. b and c.

____ 4. Phyllis and Daryl are involved in an automobile accident. Phyllis properly commences a lawsuit against Daryl and process is served on Daryl. Daryl does not believe that he is liable to Phyllis. Also, Daryl believes that Phyllis is actually liable to him due to this accident. In this case, Daryl should:
   a. File an answer denying the incorrect allegations stated in Phyllis' complaint.
   b. File a counterclaim asserting Daryl's claim against Phyllis and requesting appropriate relief.
   c. Do nothing.
   d. a and b.

____ 5. Rosa sued T&S Co. for breach of contract. Based on substantial factual evidence, the jury returned a verdict in favor of Rosa for $5,000, and the judge entered judgment in favor of Rosa for this amount. If T&S Co. appeals this judgment to the court of appeals, the court of appeals:
   a. May set aside or modify the judgment if the lower court committed serious errors of law.
   b. Will not review the record of the proceedings of the lower court.
   c. Will have the witnesses testify again.
   d. Will conduct a new trial.

CHAPTER 2
BUSINESS ETHICS, SOCIAL FORCES, AND THE LAW

CHAPTER OUTLINE

A. WHAT IS BUSINESS ETHICS?

Ethics is a branch of philosophy dealing with values that relate to the nature of human conduct and the moral goodness or rightness of the motives and actions of people. In a business context, conduct and values are more complex because people are working together to maximize profit.

1. THE LAW AS THE STANDARD FOR BUSINESS ETHICS

GENERAL RULE. One set of moral standards is based on: What does positive (or codified) law require? Under this standard, any behavior is ethical if it does not break the law.
LIMITATION. The issue of fairness is not necessarily addressed under this standard.
STUDY HINT. Moral standards come from different sources, and there is no universal agreement on what moral standards are appropriate.

2. THE NOTION OF UNIVERSAL STANDARDS FOR BUSINESS ETHICS

GENERAL RULE. The natural law theory holds that behavioral standards exist universally and they cannot be changed or modified by codified laws.
STUDY HINT. ▸ Those who believe in the natural law theory feel that higher standards of behavior than those required by codified laws must be followed even if those higher standards violate the codified law. Thus, proponents of the natural law theory feel that civil disobedience may sometimes be justified.
▸ Example: Although slavery was legally permissible in the U.S. in the early 1800s, civil disobedience would have been justified to help slaves escape under the natural law principle of individual freedom.

3. THE STANDARD OF SITUATIONAL BUSINESS ETHICS OR MORAL RELATIVISM

GENERAL RULE. Situational ethics or moral relativism is a flexible standard of behavior that allows an examination of circumstances and motivation before deciding whether conduct is "right" or "wrong."
STUDY HINT. The issue in situational ethics is not whether a wrong was committed, but whether the motivation and circumstances excuse the actions.

4. THE BUSINESS STAKEHOLDER STANDARD OF BEHAVIOR

GENERAL RULE. Under the business stakeholder standard of behavior, a business must consider the interests of the various stakeholders, or those with interests in the business, to resolve ethical dilemmas.
STUDY HINTS. ▸ Stakeholders might include: (1) shareholders, who have an interest in the business's maximizing earnings and dividends; (2) members of the community where the business is located, who have an interest in preserving jobs; and (3) employees, who have an interest in job security. ▸ Views differ along the continuum of extremes of the belief that the business's sole responsibility is to make as much money as legally possible to the belief that the business exists to solve social problems. Many businesses operate by trying to respond to all stakeholders and to balance conflicting interests.

B. WHY IS BUSINESS ETHICS IMPORTANT?

▸ Values are an important part of business success.

▸ Regardless of a business's views on social responsibility, complying with the law and being fair in business transactions are widely shared concerns.

5. THE IMPORTANCE OF TRUST

Business investment, purchases and sales, hiring of employees, and growth are based on trust. Although courts provide remedies for breaches of agreements, it is the reliance on promises, not the reliance on litigation, that results in good business relationships.

6. BUSINESS ETHICS AND FINANCIAL PERFORMANCE

Studies show that companies with high standards for product quality, employee welfare, and customer service are more likely to succeed over the long term than those companies making poor ethical choices.

7. THE IMPORTANCE OF A GOOD REPUTATION

A breach of ethics can be costly to a business through: (1) drops in earnings, (2) payment of fines, and (3) loss of customer trust which may impact the business for years.

8. BUSINESS ETHICS AND BUSINESS REGULATION: PUBLIC POLICY, LAW, AND ETHICS

▸ Legislation and governmental regulation are responses to business activities that are unfair or abusive. Businesses may act voluntarily to treat customers, employees, and shareholders fairly and may thus avoid costly and intrusive legislation and regulation by government. ▸ Businesses that ignore society's views and desire for change speed the transition from businesses' value choices to enforceable law. Societal values that lead to change have one or more of these underlying goals:

(a) Protection of the state

GENERAL RULE. The need to protect the federal and state governments has given rise to many laws. ▸ Examples: treason laws; tax laws; federal law that requires a person to give his or her social security number in order to obtain a government benefit (which helps prevent false claims).
STUDY HINT. If the need to protect the state conflicts with the need to protect a person (and individual freedoms), then the law attempts to balance these social forces.

(b) Protection of the person

GENERAL RULE. Many laws have been adopted to protect the health, safety, personal rights (such as the right to privacy), civil rights, and economic interests of individuals. ▸ Examples: criminal laws; tort law; laws that generally prohibit discrimination in connection with voting, employment, education, governmental assistance programs, and hotel accommodations.
STUDY HINT. One act can be both: (1) a crime for which the wrongdoer may be imprisoned; and (2) a civil wrong (tort) for which an injured person may receive damages.

(c) Protection of public health, safety, and morals

Examples: health regulations that require food and restaurant inspections; motor vehicle laws that regulate speed limits and require car occupants to wear seat belts; obscenity laws.

(d) Protection of property: its use and title

GENERAL RULE. Those who have title to property may use the property as they see fit.
LIMITATION. Even ownership has restrictions imposed by law, such as zoning, nuisance, and environmental protection restrictions.
STUDY HINT. ▸ Types of property that may be protected include real property, personal property, and intangible or intellectual property. ▸ Examples of laws protecting property: civil law that permits an owner to exclude others from coming upon his or her private, real property; criminal law that punishes a thief who wrongfully takes another's personal property; civil law that allows recovery of lost royalties because of another's infringement of one's copyrighted intellectual property.

(e) Protection of personal rights

GENERAL RULE. Many constitutional and statutory principles are intended to protect the freedom of persons to choose how to act. ▸ Examples: constitutional rights of freedom of speech, religion, and press; in many states, right of a patient (or guardian) to refuse life-support treatment.
LIMITATION. ▸ Like other social forces that protect individual freedoms, the freedom of personal action is balanced against and limited by the need to protect society from harmful conduct and the need to prevent unreasonable interference with the rights of others. ▸ Example of balancing: freedom of speech does not permit one to wrongfully injure another's reputation.

(f) Enforcement of individual intent

GENERAL RULE. In connection with voluntary transactions, such as the making of a contract or will, the law generally enforces the intent of the parties.
LIMITATIONS. ▸ Parties' intentions are not enforced if they are not stated in the legally required manner, e.g., an oral contract or will is unenforceable if it violates a legal requirement that it be written. ▸ The intent of parties will not be enforced if the intended action is illegal.

(g) Protection from exploitation, fraud, and oppression

Examples: laws that allow minors (persons under the legal age) to set aside contracts; securities laws; antidiscrimination laws; food processing and labeling laws.

(h) Furtherance of trade

Examples: laws that establish a currency; laws that permit and regulate instruments, such as checks and promissory notes; antitrust laws that promote competition.

(I) Protection of creditors and rehabilitation of debtors

GENERAL RULES. ▸Creditors are protected by laws that make contracts binding and statutes that make it fraudulent for a debtor to conceal property from a creditor. ▸ The social force of rehabilitation of debtors is furthered by bankruptcy law that allows debtors to escape liability for certain debts and thereby achieve a new economic life.
STUDY HINT. Debtors are no longer imprisoned for not paying debts.

(j) Stability and flexibility

GENERAL RULES. ▸ Stability is important in business dealings. Also, the desire for stability causes courts to follow existing decisions (precedents) unless there is a significant reason to change.

▸ Virtually all laws can be changed. ▸ A law may be changed because the reason for the law no longer exists or because society's sense of what is just has changed.

LIMITATION. The social forces of stability and flexibility often conflict.

STUDY HINTS. ▸ If no law or former decision directly resolves a question, then courts commonly resolve the issue by making a logical extension of the reasoning stated in other similar cases. ▸ It is relatively easy to change statutes; it is difficult to change constitutions. ▸ Flexibility is often accomplished by (1) creating exceptions to a law or (2) stating legal duties in general terms (such as the reasonable person standard). ▸ The social force that seeks to maximize protection of the person will often determine whether or not a law should be changed.

C. HOW TO RECOGNIZE AND RESOLVE ETHICAL DILEMMAS

9. CATEGORIES OF ETHICAL BEHAVIOR

Business managers often find themselves confronted with the difficult task of deciding what is ethically right or wrong in a particular situation. A majority of large companies provide employees with some form of ethical training, identifying categories of conduct that may or may not be an ethical breach.

(a) Integrity and Truthfulness

Integrity is the adherence to one's values and principles despite the costs and consequences.

(b) Promise-keeping

Most business undertakings are based upon promises, some legally enforceable and others not. The strategic question is whether a firm should make promises that will realize little profit for the firm. In the long run, a firm's reputation is largely determined on the degree to which it keeps its promises.

(c) Loyalty - avoiding conflicts of interest

Employees owe a duty of loyalty to their employers, and conduct that compromises this loyalty is a conflict of interest. Some firms have a zero tolerance for conduct that may create a conflict, such as a complete ban on employees' accepting any gifts whatsoever from suppliers or clients.

(d) Fairness

One way to decide what is fair in a transaction is to evaluate this issue from both parties' perspective.

(e) Doing no harm

One basic rule of business is that you should never do anything that you know will harm others.

(f) Maintaining confidentiality

Employees owe a duty of confidentiality to their employers.

10. RESOLVING ETHICAL DILEMMAS

In addition to the earlier section on stakeholders, other models for resolving ethical dilemmas include:

(a) Blanchard and Peale three-part test

Ethical breaches may be evaluated by asking three questions: (1) Is it legal? (2) Is it balanced? (3) How does it make me feel?

(b) The front-page-of-the-newspaper test

This test simply asks: "Would you want your spouse, children, and friends read about a proposed action on the front page of your local newspaper?" If not, then the proposed action is unethical.

(c) Laura Nash model

This model asks a series of questions, examining a dilemma from all perspectives.

REVIEW OF TERMS AND PHRASES

MATCHING EXERCISE

Select the term or phrase that best matches a statement or definition stated below. Each term or phrase is the best match for only one statement or definition.

Terms and Phrases

a. Ethics
b. Flexibility
c. Minor
d. Natural law
e. Positive law
f. Situational ethics
g. Social forces
h. Stability
i. Stakeholders

Statements and Definitions

____ 1. Branch of philosophy that focuses on values relating to human conduct and the moral goodness of human motives and actions.

____ 2. Codified law or law set forth in statutes.

____ 3. Different constituencies of a business, often holding conflicting goals for the business.

____ 4. Social force that discourages changing existing laws or adopting new laws.

____ 5. Social force that supports changing laws if they become unjust or outdated.

____ 6. Social desires that influence society's ethical concepts and motivate society to adopt certain laws.

____ 7. Person under legal age.

____ 8. Flexible standard of ethics that allows an examination of circumstances and motivation before attaching a label of "right" or "wrong" to the conduct.

____ 9. Theory that higher standards of behavior than those required by codified law must be followed even if those standards are contrary to the written law.

COMPLETION EXERCISE

Fill in the blanks with the words that most accurately complete each statement. Answers may or may not include terms used in the matching exercise. A term cannot be used to complete more than one statement.

1. Consumer protection laws that protect consumers from unfair and deceptive contracts further the social force of _____ ____ _____, _____, ____ _____.

2. Contract law and laws permitting a creditor to recover property that has been fraudulently transferred by a debtor further the social force of _____ ____ _____.

3. The social force of _____ ____ _____ primarily seeks to protect the ownership rights of individuals.

4. Laws requiring compulsory military service further the social force of _____ ____ _____.

CHAPTER 2

5. Laws that prohibit trespassers from entering upon private property that belongs to others further the social force of _____ ____ _____.

6. An important evidence of integrity is doing what a person says he or she will do, or _____-_____.

7. Health regulations and fire safety codes help further the social force of _____ ____ _____ _____, _____, ____ _____.

8. The social force of _____ ____ _____ is advanced by laws that authorize and regulate the use of automated teller machines.

REVIEW OF CONCEPTS

Write **T** if the statement is true, write **F** if it is false.

_____ 1. Social forces significantly affect both the ethics and laws of society.

_____ 2. Ethics is a specialized branch of criminal law.

_____ 3. The ethical values of society may change over time.

_____ 4. The law requires a person to conform his or her conduct to all ethical values of good and bad.

_____ 5. Important, fundamental ethical values frequently give rise to and are incorporated into various laws.

_____ 6. One way for business to avoid increased government regulation is for business to voluntarily conform its conduct to the ethical values of society.

_____ 7. Capitalism succeeds because of trust.

_____ 8. Laws are intended to further only individual freedoms; laws are not intended to protect the federal or state governments.

_____ 9. The social force of protection of the person includes a desire to protect the economic interests of persons as well as their physical safety.

_____ 10. The freedom of personal action is not unlimited; this freedom cannot be exercised in such a manner that it unreasonably interferes with the rights of others or important interests of society.

_____ 11. Studies show that businesses with the strongest commitment to positive values are the most successful.

_____ 12. There is general agreement that a corporate executive's sole responsibility is to make as much money for shareholders as possible, as long as the executive's actions are legal.

_____ 13. A conflict of interest may exist if a purchasing agent accepts baseball tickets from a potential supplier.

REVIEW OF CHAPTER - APPLICATION OF CONCEPTS

MULTIPLE CHOICE QUESTIONS

_____ 1. A state is considering adopting a law that requires its police officers to take mandatory drug tests. The testing is intended to protect the state by assuring that police officers can safely carry out their duties. But, the testing will intrude upon the privacy of the officers tested. In this case:
   a. Protection of the state is not a proper social force to consider.
   b. Protection of personal rights (here the right to privacy) is not a proper social force to consider.
   c. It is proper for the state to consider both protection of the state and protection of personal rights, and to create a law that seeks to balance or synthesize these social forces.
   d. a and b.

_____ 2. Two Forks Village is considering adopting a law that prohibits selling pornographic books within the city. This law is intended to protect the public morals. Ken, who sells this type of book, objects to this law, maintaining that it will impair his freedom of personal action. In this case:
   a. Protecting public morals is not a social force that may be considered.
   b. Protecting personal rights is a social force that may be considered.
   c. The law in question should not be adopted because it is ethically wrong to adopt a law if doing so will limit anyone's personal rights.
   d. The law in question must be adopted because protection of public interests always prevails over protection of personal rights.

_____ 3. Stan has lost his job and he cannot pay his debts.
   a. In order to further debtor rehabilitation, bankruptcy laws have been adopted that may allow Stan to escape liability for certain unpaid debts.
   b. The law does not provide a procedure whereby Stan can escape liability for his debts.
   c. Under these facts, Stan will be imprisoned if he fails to pay his debts.
   d. b and c.

_____ 4. Assume that a state law generally allows a person to create a trust for the benefit of another and to give his or her property to such trust. However, this law does not permit a person to do so if the person is acting with the intent to defraud his or her creditors. Under these facts:
   a. This law furthers only the social force of enforcement of individual intent.
   b. This law furthers only the social force of protection of creditors.
   c. This law furthers only the social force of freedom of personal rights.
   d. This law represents a synthesis (combination) of the social forces of enforcement of individual intent, protection of creditors, and protection of personal rights.

_____ 5. Acme Food Corp. decided to sell to third world countries all of its out-of-date canned food products. While it is illegal to sell these products in the United States, it is not illegal to sell them elsewhere. Although these products are not very pleasing to taste, they are still edible. The Acme board of directors' reasoned that if their decision were publicized in local newspapers, they could personally justify their decision and, therefore, this course of action is ethically proper. What ethical model did the directors use to arrive at their decision?
   a. Stakeholders' model.
   b. Blanchard and Peale three-part test.
   c. The front-page-of-the-newspaper test.
   d. Laura Nash model.

CHAPTER 2

CASE PROBLEMS

Answer the following problems, briefly explaining your answers.

1. Assume that a state's law permits an employer to fire an employee at will (an employee who is not hired for a definite time) for any reason provided the firing does not involve discrimination. In order to better protect employees, the state in question has proposed changing this law and adopting a law that requires employers to have a sufficient legal reason before discharging an employee.

    (a) What social forces would be furthered if the state adopts the new law? (b) What social forces would be furthered if the state does not adopt the new law?

2. State *X* presently forbids all gambling. State *X* is considering adopting a law to permit limited gambling. This law will generate tax revenues for the state, and it will allow persons to spend their money in the manner they choose, thereby enhancing their freedom of choice. But, adoption of this law will cause an increase in crime and it will allow exploitation of persons who are habitual gamblers.

    (a) What social forces would be furthered if the state adopts the new law permitting limited gambling? (b) What social forces would be furthered if the state does not adopt this new law?

3. Bankruptcy law includes these rules: (a) in order to give debtors a fresh start, debtors may keep certain property despite filing for bankruptcy; (b) in order to protect their rights, creditors may sometimes force a debtor into bankruptcy; and (c) in recognition of common business practices, a debtor who has filed for bankruptcy can make a binding promise to pay a debt even though the debt would be terminated by the bankruptcy.

    The foregoing bankruptcy rules primarily further what social forces?

CPA REVIEW

The following questions were given on CPA examinations. The answers for these questions are the unofficial answers prepared by the American Institute of Certified Public Accountants, Inc. (AICPA). All material is reproduced with permission of the AICPA.

____ 1. Which of the following actions by a CPA most likely violates the profession's ethical standards?
   a. Arranging with a financial institution to collect notes issued by a client in payment of fees due.
   b. Compiling the financial statements of a client that employed the CPA's spouse as a bookkeeper.
   c. Retaining client records after the client has demanded their return.
   d. Purchasing a segment of an insurance company's business that performs actuarial services for employee benefit plans.

____ 2. A CPA owes a duty to
   a. Provide for a successor CPA in the event death or disability prevents completion of an audit.
   b. Advise a client of errors contained in a previously filed tax return.
   c. Disclose client fraud to third parties.
   d. Perform an audit according to GAAP so that fraud will be uncovered.

____ 3. A violation of the profession's ethical standards most likely would have occurred when a CPA
   a. Issued an unqualified opinion on the 1992 financial statements when fees for the 1991 audit were unpaid.
   b. Recommended a controller's position description with candidate specifications to an audit client.
   c. Purchased a CPA firm's practice of monthly write-ups for a percentage of fees to be received over a three-year period.
   d. Made arrangements with a financial institution to collect notes issued by a client in payment of fees due for the current year's audit.

____ 4. A violation of the profession's ethical standards least likely would have occurred when a CPA
   a. Purchased another CPA's accounting practice and based the price on a percentage of the fees accruing from clients over a three-year period.
   b. Received a percentage of the amounts invested by the CPA's audit clients in a tax shelter with the clients' knowledge and approval.
   c. Had a public accounting practice and also was president and sole stockholder of a corporation that engaged in data processing services for the public.
   d. Formed an association-not a partnership with two other sole practitioners and called the association "Adams, Betts and Associates."

___ 5. According to the profession's ethical standards, an auditor would be considered independent in which of the following instances?
   a. The auditor is the officially appointed stock transfer agent of a client.
   b. The auditor's checking account that is fully insured by a federal agency is held at a client financial institution.
   c. The client owes the auditor fees for more than two years prior to the issuance of the audit report.
   d. The client is the only tenant in a commercial building owned by the auditor.

___ 6. According to the profession's ethical standards, a CPA would be considered independent in which of the following instances?
   a. A client leases part of an office building from the CPA, resulting in a material indirect financial interest to the CPA.
   b. The CPA has a material direct financial interest in a client, but transfers the interest into a blind trust.
   c. The CPA owns an office building and the mortgage on the building is guaranteed by a client.
   d. The CPA belongs to a country club client in which membership requires the acquisition of a pro rata share of equity.

___ 7. In which of the following situations would a CPA's independence be considered to be impaired?
   I. The CPA maintains a checking account that is fully insured by a government deposit insurance agency at an audit-client financial institution.
   II. The CPA has a direct financial interest in an audit client, but the interest is maintained in a blind trust.
   III. The CPA owns a commercial building and leases it to an audit client. The rental income is material to the CPA.
   a. I and II.
   b. II and III.
   c. I and III.
   d. I, II, and III.

___ 8. Which of the following statements best explains why the CPA profession has found it essential to promulgate ethical standards and to establish means for ensuring their observance?
   a. A distinguishing mark of a profession is its acceptance of responsibility to the public.
   b. A requirement for a profession is to establish ethical standards that stress primary responsibility to clients and colleagues.
   c. Ethical standards that emphasize excellence in performance over material rewards establish a reputation for competence and character.
   d. Vigorous enforcement of an established code of ethics is the best way to prevent unscrupulous acts.

CHAPTER 3
THE CONSTITUTION AS THE FOUNDATION OF THE LEGAL ENVIRONMENT

CHAPTER OUTLINE

A. THE FEDERAL SYSTEM

The United States has a federal system of government. This means that a central government (the federal government) regulates matters of national concern and states regulate matters of local concern.

1. WHAT A CONSTITUTION IS

The U.S. Constitution establishes the structure of the government. It also establishes the fundamental powers of the federal and state governments and limitations upon those powers.

2. THE BRANCHES OF GOVERNMENT

GENERAL RULE. The Constitution created a tripartite (three-part) federal government comprised of a legislative branch (Congress) to make laws, an executive branch (President) to execute the laws, and a judicial branch (federal courts) to interpret the laws.
STUDY HINT. Congress is a bicameral (two-house) body (Senate and House of Representatives).

B. THE STATES AND THE CONSTITUTION

3. DELEGATED AND SHARED POWERS

- *Delegated powers*: Certain powers ("delegated powers") were given by the states to the federal government. These powers are stated in the U.S. Constitution.
- *Shared powers*: ▸ The federal government has the exclusive right to exercise certain delegated powers. Example: power to make war. ▸ Other delegated powers are shared with states, meaning that states can also exercise these powers. Example: power to tax.
- *State police power*: Subject to certain limits (see sections 4 and 8), states have the "police power" to adopt laws that are necessary to protect the health, welfare, safety, and morals of people.
- *Prohibited powers*: The Constitution prohibits federal and state governments from doing certain acts, e.g., making *ex post facto* laws (laws that make criminal an act that has already been done).

4. FEDERAL SUPREMACY

GENERAL RULES. ▸ The Constitution embraces the concept of federal supremacy, which makes federal law supreme over state law. If a federal law conflicts with a state law, the federal law prevails. ▸ A state law is invalid if: (1) the state law directly conflicts with federal law; or (2) the state law relates to a subject that Congress has preempted (i.e., has taken over.)
STUDY HINTS. ▸ A subject is preempted if Congress expressly or by implication indicates an intent to exclusively regulate the subject. ▸ A failure by Congress to regulate a subject may indicate an intent to preempt the subject, particularly if uniform national regulation of the subject is needed.

C. INTERPRETING AND AMENDING THE CONSTITUTION

5. CONFLICTING THEORIES (ABOUT PURPOSE/INTERPRETATION OF CONSTITUTION)

- *Bedrock view*: The Constitution states fundamental rules for all time. The Constitution should be interpreted narrowly, thereby giving the federal government only limited power.
- *Living document view*: The Constitution states only goals. It is intended to change to meet the needs of society, and it is interpreted broadly to give the federal government expansive power.

6. AMENDING THE CONSTITUTION

GENERAL RULE. The Constitution's meaning and its protections have been amended (changed): (1) expressly through constitutional amendment; (2) by judicial interpretation; and (3) by practice.

STUDY HINTS. ▸ Article V states rules for express constitutional amendments. ▸ There have been few express amendments; most constitutional changes have resulted from judicial interpretation.

7. THE LIVING CONSTITUTION

During the past century the Supreme Court has generally followed the living document view. Consequently, the Constitution has been liberally interpreted resulting in the following:

- *Strong government*: The federal government has been permitted to become a strong government.
- *Strong President*: The U.S. President is strong and is actively involved in the lawmaking process.
- *Eclipse of the states*: The federal government (not states) has the greatest power to regulate business.
- *Administrative agencies*: Agencies exercise immense power in regulating business.
- *Human rights*: The constitutional rights of individuals have expanded greatly and these rights, both express and implied, cannot be violated by the federal or state governments.

D. FEDERAL POWERS

The federal government has only the powers delegated to it by the Constitution.

8. POWER TO REGULATE COMMERCE

- *The commerce power becomes a general welfare power*: ▸ The federal government has the power to regulate interstate commerce. ▸ Today, interstate commerce is interpreted very broadly. It includes virtually all business and labor activities; it is no longer limited to goods or activities that directly cross state lines.
- *The commerce power as a limitation on states*: Although a state may regulate interstate commerce, it cannot do so if: (1) regulation is preempted by the federal government; (2) state law conflicts with federal law; (3) state law discriminates against interstate commerce (e.g., tax is imposed on only interstate commerce); or (4) state law imposes an unreasonable burden on interstate commerce (i.e., burden on interstate commerce outweighs the need for the state law).

9. THE FINANCIAL POWERS

GENERAL RULE. The federal government has the power to tax, borrow, spend, and make money.

LIMITATIONS. ▸ Direct taxes (poll taxes and federal property taxes) must be allocated among the states according to the population of the states. ▸ Indirect taxes (all other federal taxes) need not be apportioned according to population, but they must uniformly apply to all states. ▸ State and municipal governments cannot be directly taxed by the federal government. ▸ Federal and state taxes can be imposed for only public purposes.

STUDY HINTS. ▸ The federal government can tax income from state or local municipal bonds. ▸ The federal government can borrow and spend money for any purpose. ▸ State governments can tax, borrow, and spend, although state law frequently limits the amount of state borrowing.

10. THE POWER TO OWN BUSINESSES

The federal and state governments can own and operate businesses. Moreover, the federal and state governments can sell goods produced by these businesses, and they can generally compete with private businesses.

E. CONSTITUTIONAL LIMITATIONS ON GOVERNMENT

GENERAL RULE. Some of the most important constitutional limitations on government are constitutional provisions that guarantee fundamental individual rights.
LIMITATION. Constitutional limits, such as due process, only apply to government action. These limits do not apply to conduct by private parties; statutes and administrative rules limit private conduct.

11. DUE PROCESS

GENERAL RULES. ▸ The Fifth and Fourteenth Amendments to the Constitution prohibit the federal and state governments, respectively, from depriving any person of life, liberty, or property without due process of law. ▸ The "due process clause": (1) prohibits unreasonable government procedures and laws; and (2) guarantees certain fundamental individual rights and interests. ▸ Examples of due process guarantees: right to reasonable notice and an opportunity to be heard; right not to be sued in a state unless one has reasonable contacts with the state in question.
LIMITATION. Due process does not nullify a law merely because the law is of debatable value.
STUDY HINT. In general, if the government proposes to take an action that will substantially interfere with a person's fundamental personal or property rights, due process guarantees that person a right to notice and an opportunity to defend his or her rights.

12. EQUAL PROTECTION OF THE LAW

GENERAL RULE. Broadly speaking, the equal protection clause prohibits the federal and state governments from discriminating against persons because they are members of a particular class.
LIMITATIONS. ▸ The equal protection clause does not always require equal treatment for everyone. ▸ A law may treat classes of persons or businesses differently if the law is reasonably related to and furthers a sufficiently important, legitimate government purpose.
STUDY HINT. Examples of *invalid* laws (classifications): (1) laws that discriminate on the basis of race, religion, or alienage (national origin); (2) laws that are not rationally or reasonably related to accomplishing a legitimate government interest; (3) certain laws that discriminate on the basis of moral standards or cultural patterns (such as a law that would deny food stamps to a person merely because he or she is a "dead head").

13. PRIVILEGES AND IMMUNITIES

▸ The Constitution generally prohibits a state from treating residents and nonresidents of the state differently. ▸ Example: Residents and nonresidents generally have the same right to do business, practice a profession, and own property in a state.

14. PROTECTION OF THE PERSON

▸ In recent years, the Supreme Court has expanded the constitutional protection of many individual rights, including many rights that are not expressly stated in the Constitution. ▸ Examples: right to privacy; protection from unreasonable zoning. ▸ The Constitution protects only living persons.

15. DEMOCRACY AND PROTECTION OF THE PERSON

Expansion of individual rights guarantees the freedom of choice of individuals, but in certain situations this process may limit the democratic notion that the majority rules.

REVIEW OF TERMS AND PHRASES

Select the term or phrase that best matches a statement or definition stated below. Each term or phrase is the best match for only one statement or definition.

Terms and Phrases

a. Bedrock view
b. Congress
c. Constitution
d. Due process clause
e. Equal protection clause
f. *Ex post facto* law
g. Federal courts
h. Federal supremacy
i. Federal system
j. Living document view
k. Preemption
l. President

Statements and Definitions

____ 1. Belief that the Constitution states fundamental principles that apply for all time and that the Constitution should be strictly interpreted.

____ 2. Written document that generally sets forth the structure and powers of a government.

____ 3. Legislative branch of the federal government.

____ 4. Constitutional principle providing that federal law is superior to conflicting state law.

____ 5. Constitutional provision that guarantees all persons and classes the same protection of the law.

____ 6. Judicial branch of the federal government.

____ 7. Government in which a central government governs matters of national concern, and states govern matters of local concern.

____ 8. Executive branch of the federal government.

____ 9. Doctrine granting Congress the exclusive power to regulate an activity or subject matter.

____ 10. Law that retroactively makes criminal an act that has already been done.

____ 11. Constitutional provision that generally prohibits unreasonable government actions.

____ 12. Belief that the Constitution states only objectives, that the Constitution must evolve to meet society's needs, and that the Constitution should be liberally interpreted.

REVIEW OF CONCEPTS

Write **T** if the statement is true, write **F** if it is false.

____ 1. The United States has a parliamentary system of government.

____ 2. Congress is comprised of two houses, the House of Representatives and the Supreme Court.

____ 3. Federal judges are appointed by the President and generally serve for life.

____ 4. The federal government possesses only the powers delegated to it by the U.S. Constitution.

____ 5. Subject to certain limits, a matter may be regulated by both the federal government and a state.

____ 6. If a federal statute and a state statute conflict, the concept of federal supremacy generally provides that the state statute is superior and cancels the federal statute.

____ 7. A state cannot regulate an activity or subject matter that has been preempted by Congress.

____ 8. The silence of Congress and its failure to regulate a subject may indicate an intent by Congress to preempt that subject thereby preventing state regulation of that subject.

____ 9. During the past 100 years, the Supreme Court generally followed the bedrock view and strictly interpreted the Constitution.

____ 10. Most changes to the Constitution result from judicial interpretation, not express amendment.

____ 11. Interstate commerce is narrowly interpreted and includes only activities that directly involve the movement of goods or services across state boundaries.

____ 12. State and municipal governments cannot be directly taxed by the federal government.

____ 13. The Constitution prohibits a state from adopting a law that directly discriminates against interstate commerce, such as a law that imposes special restrictions on only interstate commerce.

____ 14. The federal government cannot own a business that competes against private businesses.

____ 15. The Constitution generally gives a state the privilege to discriminate against nonresidents.

REVIEW OF CHAPTER - APPLICATION OF CONCEPTS

MULTIPLE CHOICE QUESTIONS

____ 1. Some people have suggested that the federal government needs to more closely regulate the Internet. If the federal government decided to do this, then:
   a. The executive branch would adopt and carry out needed laws, and the judicial branch would enforce the laws against violators.
   b. The legislative branch would adopt and carry out needed laws, and the judicial branch would enforce the laws against violators.
   c. The legislative branch would adopt needed laws, the executive branch would carry out the laws, and the judicial branch would enforce the laws against violators.
   d. The judicial branch would adopt, carry out, and enforce needed laws.

____ 2. Assume Congress enacted a law prohibiting open-pit uranium mines. State X then passed a law allowing mining companies to operate open-pit uranium mines within the state. Under these facts:
   a. The state law is unconstitutional because it violates federal supremacy.
   b. The state law is unconstitutional because it seeks to regulate interstate commerce.
   c. The state law is constitutional because the state has the police power to regulate this activity.
   d. The state law is constitutional because the federal government cannot regulate intrastate commerce.

____ 3. Wood Inc. manufactures and sells furniture in interstate commerce. Wood's manufacturing plant is located in Chicago, Illinois. Under these facts, select the correct answer.
   a. The federal government has the power to regulate Wood's business.
   b. Subject to limits, Illinois has the power to regulate Wood's business conducted in Illinois.
   c. Illinois does not have the power to regulate any aspect of Wood's business; states do not have the power to regulate any matters that the federal government regulates.
   d. a and b.

____ 4. Federal law generally requires that certain private employers must pay time and a half for hours worked in excess of 40 hours per week. Assume that a state law directly conflicts with this federal law by requiring payment of time and a half for only those hours worked in excess of 50 hours per week. Under these facts, select the correct answer.
   a. Federal law controls.
   b. State law controls.
   c. Neither federal nor state law controls; conflicting federal and state laws cancel each other.
   d. Neither federal nor state law controls; government cannot regulate private businesses.

____ 5. Jackson Manufacturing operates a steel fabrication plant in New Jersey. Jackson is subject to various federal tax laws. New Jersey has recently passed a state law that assesses a new tax on certain manufacturing firms, such as Jackson Manufacturing, in order to help pay for state environmental clean-up operations. Jackson opposes this state law, arguing that the state lacks the power to assess this tax. Under these facts:
   a. The state law is invalid. The power to tax business is delegated solely to the federal government.
   b. The state law is invalid. Although the power to tax business is shared by the federal and state governments, states cannot use this power if the federal government has already done so.
   c. The state law is valid. The power to tax businesses is shared by the federal and state governments, and both may tax a business.
   d. The state law is valid. The power of states to tax businesses is not subject to any limits.

____ 6. Cargo Storage is in the business of storing toxic wastes. For the past 10 years, Cargo stored low-level toxic wastes in steel drums. The state has just adopted a new criminal statute that makes the past or future storage of low-level toxic wastes in steel drums a felony. Under these facts:
   a. As applied only to Cargo's past storage activities, the law is an unconstitutional *ex post facto* law.
   b. As applied only to Cargo's future storage activities, the law is an unconstitutional *ex post facto* law.
   c. As applied to both Cargo's past and future storage activities, the law is an unconstitutional *ex post facto* law.
   d. As applied to both Cargo's past and future storage activities, the law is constitutional.

____ 7. The Supreme Court has determined that the U.S. Constitution protects persons from certain unreasonable zoning of real property. Assume that the commercial real estate industry wants these constitutional protections changed to provide even greater protection for property owners. Under these facts, can the U.S. Constitution be changed to provide this increased protection for persons?
   a. Yes, but the Constitution can be changed only by constitutional amendment.
   b. Yes, but the Constitution can be changed only by judicial interpretation.
   c. Yes, but the Constitution can be changed only by practice.
   d. Yes, the Constitution can be changed by constitutional amendment, judicial interpretation, or practice.

____ 8. State health agents found evidence of illegal drug sales during a warrantless inspection of Acme Pharmacy, Inc. Criminal charges were filed against Acme. The Fourth Amendment of the U.S. Constitution expressly requires the government to have a warrant before conducting a search. However, the U.S. Supreme Court has interpreted the Constitution as not requiring a warrant in this situation. Did the state violate Acme's constitutional rights?
   a. Yes. The state violated the express terms of the Constitution.
   b. No. The Constitution does not protect business entities.
   c. No. The Constitution has been amended by interpretation and the state did not violate the Constitution, as amended.
   d. b and c.

____ 9. Roscoe owns three restaurants in one southern state. The restaurants primarily cater to local customers, but occasionally, travelers from other states stop in to have a meal. Roscoe refuses to pay the minimum wage required by federal law, arguing that he is not engaged in interstate commerce and, therefore, he is exempt from federal law. Is Roscoe engaged in interstate commerce?
   a. No. Roscoe does not sell goods across state lines.
   b. No. Roscoe does not have businesses in more than one state.
   c. No. Roscoe's business does not substantially affect interstate commerce.
   d. Yes. Roscoe's business activities fall within the broad meaning given to "interstate commerce."

____ 10. One of the primary cash crops grown in State X are apples. In order to protect its in-state apple producers, the legislature of State X enacted a law forbidding the sale of any apples grown outside the state. Without this law, many smaller in-state apple producers may be driven out of business. Under these facts:
   a. This law is constitutional. State X is properly exercising its police power.
   b. This law is unconstitutional. State X cannot regulate any aspect of interstate commerce.
   c. This law is unconstitutional. State X is discriminating against interstate commerce.
   d. b and c.

____ 11. Which of the following actions may violate the U.S. Constitution's guarantee of due process?
   a. Amy is fired by her *private* employer without being given a hearing prior to her termination.
   b. The EPA (a federal agency) imposed a fine on Dill Corp. for violating federal law. Dill Corp. was not given a hearing to determine whether it actually violated the law.
   c. Congress adopted a law. Elroy Co., which is subject to this law, asserts that the law violates due process because this law is of debatable value.
   d. Arizona law allows Carl, an Arizona citizen, to sue Acme Co., a Wyoming firm, in Arizona state court for breach of a contract that arose out of a business that Acme Co. conducts in Arizona.

____ 12. State *X* adopted a law that forbids the sale of products in plastic containers, but it does not forbid the sale of products in glass containers. This law and the distinction it makes between plastic and glass containers is rationally and reasonably related to protecting the environment because plastic containers pose a greater danger to the environment than glass containers. But assume that the class of firms that sell products in plastic containers asserts that this law violates equal protection. Does it?
   a. No, because equal protection only prohibits laws that discriminate on the basis of race or religion.
   b. No, because equal protection does not prohibit laws that distinguish between certain classes of businesses if the classification is reasonable and has a rational basis.
   c. No, because equal protection does not apply to laws adopted by state governments.
   d. Yes, because equal protection prohibits the government from adopting any law that may treat any class of persons or businesses differently from other classes.

____ 13. A state legislature enacted a law requiring adult bookstores to be located 2000 feet or more away from any school, but the law does not impose the same restriction on other businesses. The purpose of the law is to protect school children from exposure to pornographic materials. Ginger bought a building to use as an adult book store, but now she cannot use it for this purpose. Under these facts:
   a. This statute is unconstitutional. It violates Ginger's guarantee of equal protection because other types of businesses are not subject to this restriction.
   b. This statute is unconstitutional. Any law that discriminates against any person or company violates the constitutional guarantee of equal protection.
   c. This statute is constitutional. The law bears a rational (reasonable) relationship to a legitimate governmental interest.
   d. a and b.

CASE PROBLEM

Answer the following problem, briefly explaining your answer.

Amex Corp.'s manufacturing plant is located in Missouri. Amex Corp. sells its goods in several states, and it conducts a significant portion of its business in Colorado.

(a) Is Amex Corp. engaging in interstate commerce? (b) Does the federal government have the right to regulate Amex Corp.'s business? (c) In general, does Colorado have the constitutional power to regulate business conducted by Amex Corp. in Colorado? (d) What restrictions will apply if Colorado regulates Amex Corp.'s business activities?

CHAPTER 4
GOVERNMENT REGULATION OF COMPETITION AND PRICES

CHAPTER OUTLINE

A. POWER TO REGULATE BUSINESS

▸ The Constitution empowers the federal government to regulate virtually all aspects of interstate commerce. Any rule required by "the economic needs of the nation" is permitted.

▸ Subject to the federal government's power to regulate business, each state may exercise its police powers to regulate all aspects of business conducted within its boundaries.

1. REGULATION, FREE ENTERPRISE, AND DEREGULATION

GENERAL RULE. ▸ In recent years some deregulation of business has occurred. ▸ Examples: Regulation of transportation charges by airlines and trucking firms has been eliminated. Also, the Telecommunications Act of 1996 reduces regulation in the national telecommunications industry.
LIMITATION. ▸ In some industries, deregulation caused undesirable results and regulation has been reinstated. ▸ Example: Deregulation of certain aspects of the banking and savings and loan industries contributed to various unsound lending practices, prompting adoption of new regulations, such as the Financial Institutions Reform, Recovery, & Enforcement Act (FIRREA).
STUDY HINT. Government regulation directly conflicts with the concept of free enterprise.

2. REGULATION OF PRODUCTION, DISTRIBUTION, AND FINANCING

GENERAL RULES. ▸ The federal government can regulate all types of interstate activities involving transportation, production of goods, financing (such as the Farm Credit Reform Act of 1996), and communication. Examples: The federal government can regulate standards for foods and drugs, the quantity of goods that a company may produce, and the prices for which goods can be sold. ▸ By virtue of its police powers, a state can also generally regulate intrastate activities (that is, activities that occur within the state).
STUDY HINTS ▸ The power to regulate includes the power to regulate the quality of goods and the power to require parties to acquire a license in order to deal in certain goods. ▸ The federal government's power to regulate interstate commerce gives it the right to regulate all modes of communication, including cable television, and doing so does not violate the free speech guarantee of the First Amendment.

3. REGULATION OF COMPETITION

GENERAL RULES. ▸ The Federal Trade Commission Act declares illegal all "unfair methods of competition" and this Act is enforced by the Federal Trade Commission (FTC). The FTC has prohibited a wide range of activities, such as boycotting, obtaining and using confidential information of others, and false and deceptive advertising. ▸ States also commonly forbid various forms of unfair competition.
STUDY HINT. An act may be unfair competition because it is harmful to competitors or consumers.

4. REGULATION OF PRICES

(a) Prohibited price discrimination

GENERAL RULE. The Clayton Act of 1914 prohibits price discrimination in interstate or foreign commerce if the discrimination may substantially lessen competition or may create a monopoly.
STUDY HINTS. ▸ Price discrimination is charging different customers different prices for the same goods. ▸ Discriminatory pricing disguised as advertising allowances or other valuable benefits that are given to some, but not all, buyers may violate federal antitrust law.

(b) Permitted price discrimination

- Price discrimination is permitted if different prices are justified by a: (1) difference in grade, quality, or quantity of goods sold; (2) difference in the cost of goods, such as different transportation costs; (3) closeout sale of goods; (4) good faith attempt by a seller to meet the competition in a particular competitive market by lowering the price charged in that market; or (5) deterioration of goods.
- The Robinson Patman Act of 1936 allows a seller to refuse in good faith to deal with anyone provided that such refusal is not intended to restrain trade.

5. PREVENTION OF MONOPOLIES AND COMBINATIONS

(a) The Federal Antitrust Act (Sherman Antitrust Act)

- ***Prohibited conduct***:

    - *Section 1 of the Sherman Antitrust Act*: This section prohibits a conspiracy or agreement by two or more persons: (1) to unreasonably restrain trade (i.e., to unreasonably limit competition); or (2) to fix prices. Because a violation of Section 1 requires an action or agreement by two or more parties, an agreement between a corporation and its employees or officers has been held not to violate this section of the Sherman Antitrust Act. ▸ Horizontal price fixing (between competitors) and vertical price fixing (manufacturer and retailer agree on resale price of a good) are both prohibited.

    - *Section 2 of the Sherman Antitrust Act*: This section prohibits an unlawful monopolization or attempt to monopolize an industry by one or more persons.

- ***Scope of the Act***: ▸ The Act applies to: (1) most persons engaging in interstate commerce, including sellers, buyers, brokers, and professionals; and (2) most activities, including manufacturing, production, and distribution. ▸ The Act protects all persons, including consumers and competitors.

- ***Exempted conduct and parties***: ▸ The Act does not forbid: (1) a city from imposing rent limits; (2) a manufacturer's agreement to distribute goods through only one dealer; or (3) large businesses, simply because they are big. ▸ Certain industries are exempt from antitrust laws. Example: Associations of exporters, farm cooperatives, and labor unions are exempted regarding agreements between their members.

- *Penalties and remedies*: (1) Imprisonment for up to 3 years for individuals and/or fines of up to $1 million for corporations and $100,000 for individuals; (2) civil suits by persons harmed for treble damages (three times the actual damages suffered); and (3) a state may file a class action on behalf of its citizens (*parens patriae* action) who paid higher prices due to antitrust violations by others.

(b) Clayton Act

▸ The Clayton Act of 1914 is a federal law that prohibits a corporation from acquiring an interest in the assets, ownership, or control of another corporation if doing so will substantially lessen competition or may create a monopoly. Before large companies can merge, they must first give a premerger notification to the FTC so that this agency can block improper mergers before they are completed. ▸ If necessary, a court may enter a divestiture order that requires a party to give up a prohibited interest in another company or its assets.

© Takeover laws

▸ The federal government and four-fifths of states regulate takeovers (i.e., mergers or consolidations of two companies). ▸ However, a state's regulation of corporate takeovers can generally apply to only takeover activities that occur within the state's jurisdiction.

B. LIMITATIONS ON STATE POWER TO REGULATE

6. CONSTITUTIONAL LIMITATIONS

A state cannot impose a regulation upon business if the regulation: (1) violates an individual's constitutional rights; (2) discriminates against interstate commerce; or (3) imposes an unreasonable burden on interstate commerce (see Chapter 3).

7. FEDERAL SUPREMACY

GENERAL RULE. A state regulation is invalid if it: (1) directly conflicts with federal law (federal supremacy); or (2) the subject has been preempted by the federal government (preemption).
STUDY HINTS. ▸ In general, any federal law (including administrative regulations) prevails over any conflicting state law. ▸ If federal law regulates a subject, the entire subject may be preempted even if all aspects are not regulated. In this event, a state is forbidden from regulating any matters relating to that subject.

8. STATE AND LOCAL GOVERNMENTS AS MARKET PARTICIPANTS

GENERAL RULES. ▸ When a state or local government is acting as a market participant, it is not subject to constitutional limitations that normally restrict actions by a governmental body. But when a state or local government does act as a market participant, it is subject to all laws that are applicable to ordinary persons, such as the requirement to pay minimum wages.
STUDY HINT. ▸ A state is a market participant if it is only buying or selling goods for itself or it is only engaging in business activities as opposed to regulating business activities. ▸ Example: A state is merely a market participant when it is contracting to have a state building constructed or it is operating a municipal bus line.

REVIEW OF TERMS AND PHRASES

MATCHING EXERCISE

Select the term or phrase that best matches a statement or definition stated below. Each term or phrase is the best match for only one statement or definition.

Terms and Phrases

a. Clayton Act of 1914
b. Divestiture order
c. Federal Trade Commission (FTC)
d. Federal Trade Commission Act
e. *Parens patriae* action
f. Premerger notification
g. Restraint of trade
h. Sherman Antitrust Act
i. Takeover laws
j. Treble damages

Statements and Definitions

____ 1. Federal agency that enforces certain federal laws that prohibit unfair competition.
____ 2. Federal law that prohibits price discrimination that may substantially lessen competition.
____ 3. Lawsuit by a state on behalf of citizens who paid higher prices due to others' antitrust violations.
____ 4. Federal law that generally prohibits various forms of unfair competition.
____ 5. Federal law that prohibits monopolies and agreements that unreasonably restrain trade.
____ 6. Court decree compelling a party to give up a prohibited interest in a company.
____ 7. Three times the actual damages suffered.
____ 8. Federal and state laws regulating acquisition of ownership of one company by another company.
____ 9. Restriction of competition in business.
____ 10. Notice that certain larger companies must give before they merge into one company.

COMPLETION EXERCISE

Fill in the blanks with the words that most accurately complete each statement. Answers may or may not include terms used in the matching exercise. A term cannot be used to complete more than one statement.

1. The federal law that generally declares unlawful all forms of unfair methods of competition in interstate commerce is the _____ _____ _____ _____.

2. An example of _____ _____ is a manufacturer's charging different customers different prices for the same goods.

3. An agreement by two or more competitors to fix the prices that they charge for competitive goods or services is called _____ _____ _____.

4. An agreement between a manufacturer and a retailer whereby the retailer agrees not to resell the manufacturer's goods below a certain price is called _____ _____ _____.

5. A party who suffers a loss due to a violation of the Sherman Antitrust Act may sue the wrongdoer and recover _____ _____.

REVIEW OF CONCEPTS

Write **T** if the statement is true, write **F** if it is false.

_____ 1. The federal government can generally regulate any aspect of interstate commerce.

_____ 2. A state has no power to regulate business within its boundaries if the business is also regulated by the federal government.

_____ 3. The federal government comprehensively regulates the rates that are charged by airlines and trucking firms.

_____ 4. Deregulation of industry is consistent with the concept of free enterprise.

_____ 5. Deregulation of certain industries has sometimes produced negative, undesirable results.

_____ 6. Deceptive advertising in connection with interstate commerce is one form of unfair competition that is generally prohibited by the Federal Trade Commission Act.

_____ 7. In general, government may regulate the prices charged for any goods or services, including rents that are charged by a landlord and interest that is charged on loans.

_____ 8. Subject to certain exceptions, price discrimination is unlawful in connection with interstate commerce.

_____ 9. A manufacturer cannot charge different customers different prices for the same goods even if the different prices can be justified by a difference in the cost of shipping the goods to the customers.

_____ 10. The Sherman Antitrust Act only applies to conduct by sellers or buyers of goods; it does not apply to professionals or others who merely render services.

_____ 11. A state cannot regulate or restrict takeovers of corporations within the state because the federal government has preempted this entire field.

_____ 12. A state regulation cannot violate an individual's right that is guaranteed by the U.S. Constitution.

_____ 13. Federal administrative agency rules prevail over conflicting state laws of any nature.

_____ 14. A state is acting as a market participant if it merely goes out into the marketplace to buy goods or services for its own use.

_____ 15. A state is not subject to constitutional limitations if the state is acting solely as a market participant and it is not acting in its capacity as a governmental body.

REVIEW OF CHAPTER - APPLICATION OF CONCEPTS

MULTIPLE CHOICE QUESTIONS

_____ 1. The federal government has the power to adopt which of the following business regulations?
   a. Regulation that requires automobile manufacturers to install dual front seat air bags in every new automobile that is sold in the United States.
   b. Regulation that forbids the interstate sale of vitamins unless they satisfy certain quality standards.
   c. Regulation that requires interstate cable television systems to carry certain educational stations.
   d. All of the above.

____ 2. Reality+ has created a virtual-reality game that dominates the video market. Reality+ has recently entered the video rental market. In order to gain market share in the rental market and to hurt its competition, Reality+ refuses to sell its virtual-reality game to any competitors. Has Reality+ violated *Section 1 of the Sherman Act*?
   a. Yes, Reality+'s conduct is an unreasonable restraint of trade.
   b. Yes, Reality+'s conduct is an illegal tying arrangement.
   c. Yes, Reality+'s conduct is an illegal boycott.
   d. No, a single company, acting alone, cannot generally violate Section 1 of the Sherman Act.

____ 3. Which of the following actions violates the Sherman Antitrust Act?
   a. Avco Inc. is a large business that owns 50% of the oil refinery business in the United States.
   b. Manufacturer gives Oliver the exclusive right to sell Manufacturer's products in a certain area, but this agreement does not substantially lessen competition.
   c. Acme Co. manufactures earth moving equipment. Acme Co. and its distributors agree that the distributors will not resell Acme Co.'s equipment below certain minimum prices.
   d. San Francisco imposes certain residential rent limitations.

____ 4. LubeTech manufactures 1Lube, a universal lubricant that works on all engines and moving parts, in any temperature, and in all conditions. 1Lube is also cheaper than comparable lubricants. Because of 1Lube, LubeTech controls 80 percent of the lubricant market. Has LubeTech violated federal antitrust law?
   a. Yes. LubeTech controls more than 70 percent of the lubricant market.
   b. Yes. LubeTech has an illegal monopoly.
   c. No.
   d. a and b.

____ 5. Which law provides that no corporation shall acquire the assets of another corporation if the effect of such acquisition may substantially lessen competition?
   a. Section 1 of the Sherman Act.
   b. Section 2 of the Sherman Act.
   c. Robinson-Patman Act.
   d. Clayton Act.

____ 6. CompuTron manufactures the Micro Data Storage Unit (MiDSU), the hottest new data storage system that dominates the personal computer market. In order to maximize its profits, CompuTron will not sell its MiDSU unless the buyer also purchases 20 Computron disks. These disks are good, but disks made by other manufacturers work just as well in the MiDSU. Has CompuTron violated federal antitrust law?
   a. Yes, this is illegal price fixing.
   b. Yes, this is an illegal tying arrangement.
   c. Yes, this is an illegal boycott.
   d. No.

____ 7. Palisade Co. and Eagle Inc. both engage in interstate commerce and they are two of the largest makers of medical equipment in the U.S. Both firms are formed under the laws of State X. All shareholders of Eagle Inc. reside in State X, and its corporate offices and plants are also in State X. Palisade Corp. is proposing taking over and merging with Eagle Inc. Under these facts:
   a. The proposed merger of Palisade and Eagle may violate the Clayton Act if the effect of the merger is to substantially lessen competition or may tend to create a monopoly.
   b. State X cannot regulate any activity relating to this proposed takeover even if it occurs within State X because only the federal government can regulate corporate takeovers.
   c. Palisade may have to file a premerger notification with the FTC before merging with Eagle.
   d. a and c.

____ 8. Several manufacturers of brand-name vitamins were concerned about competition from generic brands. The manufacturers agreed to temporarily set prices below the price of generic brands in an effort to drive out the generic brands. Under these facts:
   a. The manufacturers' conduct is illegal horizontal price-fixing.
   b. The manufacturers' conduct is illegal vertical price-fixing.
   c. The manufacturers' conduct is legal because they are just trying to be competitive.
   d. The manufacturers' conduct is legal because consumers are benefitted by their conduct.

____ 9. ChickFry makes ready-to-eat fried chicken dinners. ChickFry and its main distributor, Poultry Pluckers, agreed that Poultry Pluckers would not resell the chicken dinners for less than $4 per dinner, a reasonable price. Under these facts:
   a. This agreement is an illegal tying arrangement.
   b. This agreement is an illegal vertical price-fixing arrangement.
   c. This agreement is a legal because the parties agreed to charge a reasonable price.
   d. This agreement is a legal because antitrust law does not apply to this type of pricing arrangement.

____ 10. Perfecto, a major apparel manufacturer, wanted to get an order from the Grant Department Store chain. Perfecto got the contract by selling its clothes to Grant for 40 percent less than it sold the same goods to other stores in the same market. As a result, Grant enjoyed a major competitive advantage over other area stores. Under these facts:
   a. Perfecto engaged in illegal price discrimination in violation of federal antitrust law.
   b. Perfecto engaged in illegal price-fixing in violation of federal antitrust law.
   c. Perfecto engaged in legal price discrimination in compliance with federal antitrust law.
   d. Perfecto acted legally because its conduct is not subject to federal antitrust law.

____ 11. Heifer Co. and other meat producers agree to fix the prices that they charge for their competitive meat products that are sold in interstate commerce. Under these facts:
   a. Heifer Co. may be liable for three times the actual damages caused by its price fixing.
   b. Heifer Co. may be subject to fines of up to $10 billion.
   c. Individuals who are guilty of this price fixing may be fined, but they cannot be imprisoned.
   d. No one can be sued, fined, or imprisoned for their conduct in this case because price fixing is generally legal under the Sherman Antitrust Act.

_____ 12. Which of the following agreements may violate the Sherman Antitrust Act?
   a. Members of Union Local 412 agree that the base wage that they charge will be $10 per hour.
   b. Members of the Iowa Farmer's Cooperative agree on a uniform, reasonable price for which the Cooperative will store corn.
   c. Ten manufacturers of sheet metal agree on a uniform price that they will charge for their product.
   d. a and c.

_____ 13. Select the correct answer.
   a. States cannot regulate antitrust matters; this area has been preempted by the federal government.
   b. States can regulate antitrust matters, but state antitrust laws are invalid if they directly conflict with federal antitrust law.
   c. States can regulate corporate takeovers that occur within their jurisdiction.
   d. b and c.

CASE PROBLEM

Answer the following problem, briefly explaining your answer.

Compu Co. manufactures computers, and it sells its computers to retail stores throughout the U.S. Compu is considering various pricing plans. Would the following plans be unlawful under federal antitrust laws?

Plan A: Compu will sell its X computer to its best customers for $1,800. It will sell the same computer to less-favored customers for $3,000. This pricing plan will substantially lessen competition.

Plan B: Compu will sell its Z computer to stores in one competitive market for $800, but it will sell the same computer to stores in a different market for $600. The lower price is charged in the second market in order to match the price that a competitor charges for a comparable computer in that market.

CHAPTER 5
ADMINISTRATIVE AGENCIES

CHAPTER OUTLINE

A. NATURE OF THE ADMINISTRATIVE AGENCY

▸ Administrative agencies are governmental bodies that are generally created by Congress and state legislatures to administer and carry out legislation. ▸ Example: Federal Trade Commission (FTC).

1. IMPORTANCE OF THE ADMINISTRATIVE AGENCY

▸ Federal and state agencies govern large segments of the economy. ▸ Examples: Environmental Protection Agency: environment; Securities and Exchange Commission: interstate sales of securities; state employment agencies: workers' compensation. ▸ Agencies are governed by administrative law.

2. UNIQUENESS OF ADMINISTRATIVE AGENCIES

GENERAL RULES. ▸ Administrative agencies are usually run by appointed officials. ▸ Important administrative agencies commonly exercise legislative, executive, and judicial powers.
STUDY HINTS. ▸ Courts generally recognize that it is both fair and constitutional for an agency to exercise a combination of the foregoing powers. ▸ But to better assure impartial administrative action, some agencies have separated their various functions. Example: Judicial function of the FTC is now performed by administrative law judges.

3. RIGHT TO KNOW

The federal Administrative Procedure Act (APA) and similar state statutes govern the procedures of many agencies. Procedures that enable the public to be informed of agency matters include:

- *Open records*: ▸ The Freedom of Information Act (FOIA) generally makes information contained in federal agency records available to the public upon request. Similar state laws also generally make state agency records available. These federal and state laws are liberally construed, and a person claiming an exemption from disclosure has the burden to establish the exemption. ▸ Limitations on disclosure: (1) a party can find out only information that relates to a legitimate concern; (2) FOIA allows inspection of only governmental records; (3) FOIA exempts certain commercial and financial information that is not ordinarily made public; and (4) state laws often exempt information that would constitute an invasion of privacy.

- *Open meetings*: ▸ The Sunshine Act of 1976 requires that meetings of most important federal agencies be open to the public. ▸ Many states have similar statutes.

- *Public announcement of agency guidelines*: The APA generally requires that each federal agency publish its rules, principles, and procedures.

B. LEGISLATIVE POWER OF THE AGENCY

4. AN AGENCY'S REGULATIONS AS LAW

GENERAL RULES. ▸ Agencies make law by adopting regulations. ▸ An agency may adopt regulations within the sphere of its authority. This power includes the right to: (1) regulate new technologies that develop within an agency's realm of authority; and (2) establish policies regarding regulated matters if such policies are not already defined by statute.

LIMITATIONS. ▸ Some state courts may require legislatures to establish "standards" (descriptions of agency powers and authority) for agencies. (The modern approach is to view an agency as having all powers necessary to carry out its duties.) ▸ An agency rule or action is invalid if: (1) it exceeds the scope of the statute that created the agency; or (2) it exceeds standards established for the agency.

STUDY HINTS. ▸ An administrative regulation is presumed to be valid until it is proven invalid. ▸ In general, courts will not review the *policy* decisions of administrative agencies.

5. PUBLIC PARTICIPATION IN ADOPTION OF REGULATIONS

▸ The FTC and other agencies may hold public hearings to gather nonbinding input from industry. ▸ The APA requires public notice and public hearings if a federal agency intends to adopt regulations.

6. PUBLIC KNOWLEDGE OF REGULATIONS

The Federal Register Act states that federal agency rules are not effective until they have been published in the *Federal Register*. Regulations are effective 30 days after publication, and publication provides sufficient notice even if a party does not know that a regulation has been published.

C. EXECUTIVE POWER OF THE AGENCY

7. EXECUTION OF THE LAW

GENERAL RULE. Contemporary administrative agencies can investigate, call witnesses, require production of documents, and bring legal actions to enforce compliance with regulations, statutes, and judicial decisions within the scope of their jurisdiction.

LIMITATION. There is a trend to require agencies to file opinions or to explain their actions.

STUDY HINT. An agency can investigate to determine: (1) if there is a need for additional regulations; (2) whether its rules or other relevant laws have been violated; (3) facts relating to an alleged violation; and (4) whether a party is complying with a final order issued by the agency.

8. CONSTITUTIONAL LIMITATIONS ON ADMINISTRATIVE INVESTIGATION

GENERAL RULES. ▸ The constitutional protections against unreasonable searches and seizures and involuntary self-incrimination do not greatly limit agency investigations. ▸ A search warrant is not needed to: (1) administratively search highly regulated businesses; (2) inspect premises if a violation endangers health or safety; or (3) inspect areas that are visible from a public place or from the air.

STUDY HINTS. ▸ The protection against unreasonable searches and seizures does not apply to subpoenas that require a person to produce papers or to testify. ▸ The guarantee against involuntary self-incrimination does not entitle a corporate officer to refuse to produce records of the *corporation*.

D. JUDICIAL POWER OF THE AGENCY

9. THE AGENCY AS A SPECIALIZED COURT

▸ Although agencies are not courts, they may be given the power to determine violations of relevant laws and agency regulations, and the courts recognize the validity of this exercise of judicial power.

10. PATTERN OF ADMINISTRATIVE PROCEDURE

Due process generally requires that a person be given notice and a hearing before an administrative agency takes an action against the person. Procedures followed generally include:

(a) Preliminary steps

▸ An action commonly begins with a written, informal complaint that alleges a violation of an agency rule. This complaint may be filed by another agency or by a private party. ▸ The modern trend is for the agency to then determine whether the informal complaint is within its authority and whether further action is warranted. ▸ If further action appears proper, a formal complaint is served on the alleged wrongdoer, who may dispute the complaint in a written answer.

(b) Administrative hearing

▸ Notice must be given to all affected parties, and an agency must generally hold a hearing at which all interested parties may be heard. Example: A civil service employee is entitled to a hearing prior to being discharged. ▸ However, an agency may reach a tentative decision without a hearing, provided the agency conducts a hearing if an interested party objects to the agency's decision.

▸ Persons who are not directly affected by a decision do not have a right to participate in administrative proceedings. Example: A company does not have a right to participate in the licensing hearing of a competitor. ▸ There is no right to a jury trial in administrative hearings. ▸ The rules of evidence do not generally apply unless an agency chooses to follow such rules.

(c) Streamlined procedure

▸ Actions may be settled by informal procedures, such as consent decrees, stipulations, or voluntary agreements. ▸ The Administrative Dispute Resolution Act of 1990 authorizes federal agencies to use means of dispute resolution other than the procedures outlined in (a) and (b) above.

(d) Rehearing and correction of administrative action

Some statutes allow certain agencies to rehear or correct their decisions within certain time limits.

11. PUNISHMENT AND ENFORCEMENT POWERS OF AGENCIES

- ▸ Agencies can enforce the law by issuing cease and desist orders and assessing penalties.
- ▸ Agencies can require companies to take various actions to prove compliance with the law.
- ▸ *To the extent authorized by statute*, agencies can order an offending party to compensate (indemnify) a party for damages that were caused by the offending party's violation of the law.

12. EXHAUSTION OF ADMINISTRATIVE REMEDY

In most cases, a party cannot appeal an agency action to the courts until all agency procedures are completed and the agency has made its final decision.

13. APPEAL FROM ADMINISTRATIVE ACTION

In general, only persons directly affected by an agency action or persons authorized by statute can appeal an agency decision to the courts.

14. FINALITY OF ADMINISTRATIVE DETERMINATION

GENERAL RULE. Courts do not reverse an agency decision unless the agency: (1) clearly abused its discretion; (2) acted arbitrarily and capriciously; or (3) made an important error of law.

LIMITATIONS. ▸ Courts do not reverse agency decisions regarding questions of fact or mixed questions of law and fact if there is substantial evidence to support the agency's decision. ▸ Courts typically uphold agency decisions relating to technical matters.

15. LIABILITY OF THE AGENCY

An agency and its officials are not liable for losses caused by actions that were taken in good faith.

REVIEW OF TERMS AND PHRASES

MATCHING EXERCISE

Select the term or phrase that best matches a statement or definition below. Each term or phrase is the best match for only one statement or definition.

Terms and Phrases

a. Administrative agency
b. Administrative Dispute Resolution Act
c. Administrative law
d. Administrative Procedure Act (APA)
e. Cease and desist order
f. Consent decree
g. *Federal Register*
h. Freedom of Information Act (FOIA)
i. Sunshine Act of 1976
j. Standards

Statements and Definitions

____ 1. Order directing a person or company to discontinue certain conduct.

____ 2. Federal law that generally permits public inspection of federal agency records.

____ 3. Governmental body typically created by Congress or a state legislature to implement legislation and to regulate a particular segment of the economy or society.

____ 4. Judicial or administrative order voluntarily agreed to by an administrative agency and a party against whom an administrative action has been filed.

____ 5. Publication that provides public notice of federal agency rules, principles, and procedures.

____ 6. Federal law that requires meetings of certain federal agencies to be open to the public.

____ 7. Body of law that generally governs administrative agencies.

____ 8. Federal law that generally establishes procedures for federal administrative agencies.

____ 9. Legislature's description of the powers and authority of an administrative agency.

____ 10. Federal law that authorizes federal agencies to use alternate means of dispute resolution.

COMPLETION EXERCISE

Fill in the blanks with the words that most accurately complete each statement. Answers may or may not include terms used in the matching exercise. A term cannot be used to complete more than one statement.

1. Major federal administrative agencies commonly exercise _____, _____, and _____ powers.

2. Administrative hearings and related judicial functions of certain agencies may be conducted by independent hearing officers called _____ _____ _____.

3. The _____ ____ _____ _____ generally guarantees parties the right to inspect certain federal agency documents.

4. Some state courts may require that a legislature establish adequate _____ when creating administrative agencies so that the agencies will not act arbitrarily.

5. The _____ _____ _____ requires federal administrative agencies to give public notice and to conduct public hearings if they intend to adopt regulations.

6. Federal regulations and procedures are generally published in the _____ _____.

7. Federal regulations generally become effective _____ days after they are published.

8. The constitutional concept of _____ _____ generally requires that a party be given notice and a hearing before an administrative agency takes an action against the party.

9. An administrative action is commonly started when a party or an agency files a _____ with an administrative agency alleging a violation of the agency's regulations.

10. If a party violates agency regulations, the agency may have a _____ _____ _____ issued, directing the party to refrain from engaging in certain prohibited conduct.

REVIEW OF CONCEPTS

Write **T** if the statement is true, write **F** if it is false.

____ 1. Administrative agencies are generally created by courts to carry out judicial orders.

____ 2. Administrative agencies do not have the power to make laws. The power to make laws can only be exercised by Congress or state legislatures.

____ 3. Administrative agencies are typically run by officials who are elected by the public.

____ 4. It is an unconstitutional violation of the concept of separation of powers for an agency to exercise legislative, judicial, and executive powers.

____ 5. The Freedom of Information Act generally entitles a member of the public to inspect the private records of other individuals and companies.

____ 6. An agency claiming that it is exempt from the disclosure requirements of the Freedom of Information Act has the burden to prove such exemption.

____ 7. The Sunshine Act of 1976 requires federal agencies to open their meetings to the public only if the agencies voluntarily choose to do so.

____ 8. An agency can adopt a regulation only if doing so is within the agency's scope of authority.

____ 9. Agency rules are effective immediately upon adoption; publication is generally not required.

____ 10. The modern view is that an agency's authority may be stated in general terms, and an agency is presumed to have the authority to do acts that are necessary to carry out the agency's duties.

____ 11. Administrative regulations are presumed to be valid until they are proven to be invalid.

____12. In general, an agency is not bound to follow recommendations that are made by individuals or companies during public hearings that are conducted prior to adoption of a regulation.

____13. The constitutional protection against unreasonable searches and seizures prevents an agency from inspecting a highly regulated business unless the agency first obtains a search warrant to do so.

____14. An administrative agency does not need to obtain a search warrant in order to conduct an administrative search from an airplane.

____15. An agency cannot exercise its judicial powers to determine a party's rights in a matter if the agency previously conducted an investigation of the same matter.

____16. An individual may file a complaint with an administrative agency alleging that someone else has violated the agency's regulations.

____17. In general, an administrative agency can make a *final* determination of a person's rights without first conducting a hearing.

____18. In an agency hearing, a person accused of violating an agency regulation is entitled to a jury trial.

____19. An agency acting in good faith is not liable to a business for its increased costs created by the agency's regulations.

____20. Anyone is entitled to judicially challenge the validity of an agency regulation or decision.

REVIEW OF CHAPTER - APPLICATION OF CONCEPTS

MULTIPLE CHOICE QUESTIONS

____1. Congress is considering adopting new regulations of leveraged buy-outs and mergers of American companies. Congress is also debating whether it can create a new federal administrative agency to administer these laws and what powers this agency may exercise. Under these facts:
   a. Congress cannot create an agency; only the President can create agencies.
   b. Congress can create an agency, but it can only authorize the agency to enforce federal statutes. Congress cannot authorize the agency to exercise legislative or judicial powers.
   c. Congress can create an agency, and Congress can generally authorize the agency to exercise legislative, executive, and judicial powers.
   d. Congress can create an agency. The agency will automatically have the power to do anything it wants, and it will not be subject to any constitutional limits regarding what it can do.

____2. North Dakota is considering creating a bureau to oversee rental of homes and apartments. The proposed agency would have executive, legislative, and judicial functions carried out by appointed officials. Under these facts:
   a. North Dakota cannot create an agency; only the federal government can create agencies.
   b. A state can create an agency and appoint officials to carry out legislative, executive, and judicial functions within the agency's specified sphere of power.
   c. North Dakota can create an agency but the agency's officials must be elected, not appointed.
   d. North Dakota can create an agency. However, the agency cannot combine executive, legislative, and judicial functions because then the agency could not be impartial.

_____ 3. The Federal Trade Commission (FTC) conducted an investigation and public hearing regarding misleading advertising by razor manufacturers. Cutting Edge, a razor manufacturer, was investigated and it filed a request under the Freedom of Information Act (FOIA) to inspect certain records relating to this matter. Pursuant to its FOIA request:
   a. Cutting Edge is generally entitled to inspect FTC records of the public hearing.
   b. Cutting Edge may require other razor manufacturers to disclose their proposed advertising campaigns to Cutting Edge for its examination.
   c. Cutting Edge is generally entitled to compel other razor manufacturers to allow Cutting Edge to inspect their financial records relating to the advertising campaigns in question.
   d. a and b.

_____ 4. To avoid problems that can arise from secret activities of government, the following federal legislation has been enacted to provide for public knowledge of administrative agency activities:
   a. The Freedom of Information Act, which provides for certain agency records to be open to public scrutiny.
   b. The Sunshine Act, which requires most meetings of major agencies to be open to the public.
   c. The Administrative Procedure Act, which requires publication of agency rules and procedures.
   d. All of the above.

_____ 5. The Federal Communications Commission (FCC), which regulates interstate telephone service, proposed a regulation affecting the manufacture of facsimile (FAX) machines.
   a. The proposed regulation would be presumed valid unless proven otherwise.
   b. The proposed regulation would be presumed invalid because, at the time the FCC was created, FAX machines were not in existence. Therefore, regulation of FAX machines would be beyond the scope of the statute that created the FCC.
   c. The proposed regulation must be approved by members of the FAX manufacturing industry before it can be adopted.
   d. The proposed regulation cannot become effective until the manufacturers which would be affected are notified by registered mail 30 days in advance of the regulation's effective date.

_____ 6. Terri owns a lawn service and she used a certain chemical fertilizer in her business in violation of a new regulation adopted by the Environmental Protection Agency (EPA), a federal agency. This regulation was published 90 days previously in the *Federal Register*. Statutes provide that violators of this regulation are subject to fines. Terri did not know that this regulation had been adopted. After an appropriate administrative hearing:
   a. Terri can be fined for violating this regulation.
   b. Terri cannot be fined for violating this regulation because publication of a federal agency regulation in the *Federal Register* does not provide sufficient public notice of a regulation.
   c. Terri cannot be fined for violating this regulation because a federal agency regulation does not become effective until one year after publication in the *Federal Register*.
   d. Terri cannot be fined for violating this regulation because federal agencies do not have the power to impose fines for violations of agency regulations.

CHAPTER 5

_____ 7. The Equal Employment Opportunity Commission (EEOC) is investigating a complaint against J & J Distributors. In this situation, the EEOC may:
a. Require employees and former applicants of J & J to appear as witnesses.
b. Require witnesses to produce relevant records.
c. Bring proceedings against J & J if the EEOC investigation shows that J & J violated employment laws.
d. Do all of the above.

_____ 8. The EPA can investigate which of the following matters?
a. Whether Toxic Co. has been illegally dumping toxic wastes in violation of EPA regulations.
b. Whether Petro Inc. has been complying with an EPA order to stop polluting a river.
c. Whether the current national clean air standards need to be revised.
d. All of the above.

_____ 9. Two agents from the Bureau of Alcohol, Tobacco, and Firearms were flying over a gun shop and they noticed what appeared to be the loading of suspicious firearms into a truck at a business next door to the gun shop. After the agents landed, they entered the gun shop and, without a warrant, conducted a search of its premises. They also obtained a warrant and searched the business next door. After investigating, the Bureau brought charges against the gun shop and the business next door to it. Under these facts, which action could the Bureau successfully defend against charges that the action was an unreasonable search and seizure?
a. The entry and search of the gun shop.
b. The search by air of the business next to the gun shop.
c. The subpoena of the businesses' records related to the investigation.
d. All of the above.

_____ 10. Susan is vice president of S & S Inc., a stock brokerage firm. The firm is required by federal securities law to keep records of all stock trades. By subpoena, the Securities and Exchange Commission (SEC) orders Susan to produce the *firm's* records for an administrative inspection. Susan is afraid that the records may expose illegal conduct on her part. Under these facts:
a. Susan must produce the records.
b. Susan can refuse to produce the records because forcing her to turn over the records would violate her constitutional protection against unreasonable searches and seizures.
c. Susan can refuse to produce the records because forcing her to turn over the records would violate her constitutional protection against involuntary self-incrimination.
d. Susan can refuse to produce the records; agencies cannot investigate suspected wrongdoing.

_____ 11. David has been getting headaches from the fumes he breathes while working at the Brighton Paint Factory. He filed a written complaint with the Occupational Safety and Health Administration (OSHA) charging that the factory has inadequate ventilation. Under typical administrative procedure:
a. David's complaint cannot be investigated, since he is a private individual and any complaints must be filed only by an agency itself.
b. Due process generally requires that Brighton be notified of the charges and that it be given a chance to present its case at some type of hearing.
c. Due process generally requires that Brighton has a right to trial by jury.
d. Due process requirements are generally fulfilled if Brighton receives a copy of the written complaint and it files an answer. No hearing is necessary.

____ 12. Lynette, a civil service employee of the Internal Revenue Service (IRS), was called into her supervisor's office and told that her employment was terminated as of that afternoon. When Lynette objected, her supervisor told her she could appeal his decision if she thought it was unfair. Under these facts:
   a. Because Lynette was given the right to appeal the termination action, her due process rights have not been violated.
   b. The formal rules of evidence used in court trials must be followed in any hearing.
   c. Because she is a civil service employee, Lynette has the right to some type of hearing before her employment is terminated.
   d. Because every employee has a significant interest in continued employment, any employee has the right to some type of hearing before his or her employment is terminated.

____ 13. Which of the following is not ordinarily within the power of an administrative agency?
   a. The power to impose a civil penalty.
   b. The power to provide unlimited indemnity to persons harmed by a defendant regulated by that agency.
   c. The power to issue a binding order for a regulated business to stop a practice the agency finds improper.
   d. The power to require a regulated business to file a detailed statement showing it is acting within agency guidelines.

____ 14. Jones Co. was accused of violating certain worker protection laws. An administrative agency having jurisdiction of this matter conducted a hearing, followed proper procedures, and entered a final decision against Jones Co. If Jones Co. appeals this decision to the courts, a court will:
   a. Reverse the decision if the decision was wrong because the agency failed to properly interpret and apply the law.
   b. Reverse the decision if it was wrong due to a clear abuse of discretion by the agency.
   c. Reverse the decision if the court disagrees with any of the agency's factual determinations even if there is substantial evidence to support the factual determinations made by the agency.
   d. a and b.

____ 15. Joseph owned a manufacturing firm. The Occupational Safety and Health Administration (OSHA) in good faith adopted new safety standards that reasonably required businesses, such as Joseph's firm, to install expensive safety devices. Joseph's firm could not afford the required equipment, and it was forced to close. Joseph sued OSHA and its administrator for damages caused by these regulations. Under these facts:
   a. Joseph can recover damages from OSHA. Agencies are liable for losses caused by their rules.
   b. Joseph can recover damages from the OSHA administrators who were responsible for these regulations. Agency officials are personally liable for losses caused by their official acts.
   c. Joseph cannot recover damages from OSHA or from the OSHA administrators.
   d. a and b.

CASE PROBLEMS

Answer the following problems, briefly explaining your answers.

1. The EPA is given broad authority by Congress to regulate all matters necessary to protect the purity of water in the U.S. Assume that the EPA proposes to adopt: (1) a new environmental policy characterizing contaminated storm water runoff as a serious threat to clean water; and (2) a new regulation requiring cities and companies to install devices to control contaminated storm water runoff.

    (a) Can the EPA establish the new policy regarding contaminated storm water runoff? (b) Under the modern view, to what extent can the EPA adopt regulations and is the proposed regulation permissible? (c) Must the EPA give notice of hearings at which it will consider this regulation? Must it hold public hearings?

2. Medco manufactures and sells a certain type of vitamin. A number of individuals and state health agencies allege that the vitamin violates regulations of the Food and Drug Administration (FDA), a federal agency. The FDA can fine Medco if the vitamin violates FDA regulations.

    (a) Is Medco entitled to notice and a hearing before the FDA imposes a fine? (b) What preliminary steps may occur in an administrative action in this case? (c) In an administrative action, is Medco entitled to have a jury determine the case? (d) What informal procedures can the parties use to resolve this matter?

3. The State Health Agency has commenced an administrative action against Sue to suspend her license as a beautician due to certain violations of state health regulations. The administrative hearing is in process. If Sue loses at the hearing, there is an internal agency appeals procedure available.

    (a) If Sue loses at the first hearing, can she immediately appeal the decision to a court? (b) Can Sue appeal a final administrative decision to a court? Can Beauty Co., an unrelated party, appeal the decision? (c) If Sue is found to have violated this regulation, how can the Agency enforce its decision?

CHAPTER 6
THE LEGAL ENVIRONMENT OF INTERNATIONAL TRADE

CHAPTER OUTLINE

A. GENERAL PRINCIPLES

1. THE LEGAL BACKGROUND

- *What law applies*: Laws of different countries frequently vary. Consequently, international contracts often contain a choice of law clause whereby the parties determine which country's law to apply in case of a dispute. Otherwise, an international treaty may determine which law controls.
- *The arbitration alternative*: To avoid lawsuits, parties may contractually agree to arbitrate disputes according to stated rules, and the arbitration is often required to be held in a neutral country.
- *Financing international trade*: There is no international currency. Thus, parties generally agree in their contract on the currency to be used for payment, and letters of credits are often required.

2. INTERNATIONAL TRADE ORGANIZATIONS, CONFERENCES, AND TREATIES

The following organizations, conferences, and treaties significantly regulate international trade:

- ***GATT (General Agreement on Tariffs and Trade) 1994 and WTO (World Trade Organization)***: ▸ GATT provides protection of domestic industries through tariffs and promotes nondiscriminatory trade through its most favored nation clause. ▸ The WTO administers the GATT. ▸ The 1994 GATT has been signed by 125 countries, including the U.S.
- ***CISG (United Nations Convention on Contracts for the International Sale of Goods)***: CISG states rules for international sales contracts between parties in countries that have adopted it.
- ***UNCTAD (United Nations Conference on Trade and Development)***: This Conference aids developing countries by creating preferences for manufactured goods from third world countries.
- ***EU (European Union), formerly EEC (European Economic Community)***: ▸ EU is an organization of western European countries that focuses on monetary and political union for member nations. ▸ EU goals are: (1) unified monetary policies; (2) common foreign and security policies; and (3) cooperation in justice.
- ***NAFTA (North American Free Trade Agreement)***: This agreement, effective 1/1/94, is between the U.S., Mexico, and Canada. It seeks to eliminate all tariffs between these countries within 15 years.
- *Other regional trading groups*: Developing countries have created many regional trading groups.
- ***IMF (International Monetary Fund) - World Bank***: ▸ IMF established a complex lending system to expand and stabilize international trade after World War II. ▸ IMF members hold "special drawing rights" by which they can borrow money to enable them to stabilize their currencies.
- ***OPEC (Organization of Petroleum Exporting Countries)***: This organization is a cartel of oil producing countries whose main goals are: (1) to raise taxes and royalties for the benefit of member countries; and (2) to take control of oil production and exploration from major oil companies.

3. FORMS OF BUSINESS ORGANIZATIONS

Foreign trade is carried out in many ways. Important methods of conducting such trade include:

- *Export sales*: U.S. company sells and exports goods directly to customers in a foreign country without maintaining a physical presence in that country.
- *Agency arrangements*: ▸ U.S. manufacturer appoints a person or firm to make contracts for the manufacturer in a foreign country. ▸ Appointing an agent subjects the U.S. firm to foreign taxation.
- *Foreign distributorships*: A seller transfers title to goods to a foreign distributor for resale.
- *Licensing*: U.S. firm licenses a foreign company to use its technology to make a product abroad.
- *Wholly-owned subsidiary*: ▸ U.S. company owns and does business through a separate company in a foreign country. ▸ Sales to a foreign subsidiary at less than fair value may allow the IRS to reallocate the parent company's income, increasing the parent company's liability for U.S. taxes.
- *Joint ventures*: U.S. and foreign companies agree to work together with each party providing separate services and contributions in order to achieve a common business objective.

B. GOVERNMENTAL REGULATION

4. EXPORT REGULATIONS

GENERAL RULES. ▸ The Export Administration Act (EAA) controls the export of goods and technical data from the United States. ▸ Under 1996 regulations, not all exported products require a license.
▸ Whether an export license is required depends on the type of product and its proposed destination.
▸ Expert assistance about export licensing is available through the U.S. Department of Commerce and through licensed foreign-freight forwarders. ▸ Persons who violate the EAA may be subject to criminal penalties.

LIMITATIONS. ▸ Special restrictions may apply to exports of strategic commodities, commodities in short supply, and certain unpublished technical data to certain countries. ▸ Exports are prohibited to some countries, such as North Korea and Cuba.

5. PROTECTION OF INTELLECTUAL PROPERTY RIGHTS

- *Counterfeit goods*: ▸ Importation of counterfeit goods, goods bearing counterfeit trademarks, and goods that infringe on U.S. patents violates various U.S. laws. ▸ Intellectual property rights (trademarks, copyrights, and patents) are also protected by various international treaties.

Gray market goods: ▸ Federal law forbids importing gray market goods into the U.S. without the written consent of the affected U.S. firm. ▸ Gray market goods bear the trademark of a U.S. firm but the goods were made in a foreign country by: (1) a foreign firm under license by the U.S. firm; or (2) an affiliate of the U.S. firm, but the goods are different from goods made in the U.S.

6. ANTITRUST

GENERAL RULES. ▸ Under the "effects doctrine," U.S. courts may apply American antitrust laws to business conducted outside of the U.S. if there is a direct, substantial, and foreseeable effect on U.S. commerce. ▸ If this effect is found, U.S. courts will then apply the "jurisdictional rule of reason" and will balance U.S. interests with those of a foreign country to decide which law controls.

LIMITATION. Defenses against U.S. antitrust laws: (1) act of state doctrine (courts will not judge acts of a foreign government that were done within its own jurisdiction); (2) sovereign compliance doctrine (no liability if an act was *compelled* by a foreign government); (3) sovereign immunity doctrine (a party cannot sue a foreign country for its *governmental* acts, but one can sue a foreign country for its *commercial* conduct).

STUDY HINT. Foreign antitrust laws frequently differ from U.S. antitrust laws.

7. SECURITIES REGULATION IN AN INTERNATIONAL ENVIRONMENT

GENERAL RULE. U.S. securities laws apply to fraudulent sales of securities if: (1) a U.S. citizen living in the U.S. suffers a loss, regardless of where the sale occurred; or (2) a U.S. citizen living abroad suffers a loss *and* the sale occurred in the U.S.

LIMITATION. Enforcement of U.S. securities laws may be hampered by: (1) secrecy laws (foreign laws forbid disclosure of bank records and bank customer names); and (2) blocking laws (foreign laws forbid disclosure of documents pursuant to orders issued by foreign officials).

8. BARRIERS TO TRADE

- *Tariff barriers*: Tariffs (import or export taxes on goods) make imported goods more expensive.
- *Nontariff barriers*: ▸ Quotas restrict the amount of imported goods that may come into a foreign country. ▸ Complex foreign customs procedures may hinder the sale of imported goods.
- *Export controls as instruments of foreign policy*: Export controls may be used to carry out foreign policy by limiting trade with a country.

9. RELIEF MECHANISMS FOR ECONOMIC INJURY CAUSED BY FOREIGN TRADE

American law provides some economic relief for losses caused by foreign competition including:

- *Antidumping laws and export subsidies*: The Trade Agreement Act of 1979 prohibits foreign firms from dumping goods in the U.S. (selling foreign goods in U.S. for less than fair value). ▸ If dumping occurs and a U.S. industry is hurt, additional duties may be imposed on the foreign goods.
- *Relief from import injuries*: The Trade Act of 1974 offers government help to communities, firms, and employees hurt by foreign competition. ▸ Assistance includes readjustment allowances and job training. ▸ This Act authorizes duties or quotas on foreign goods hurting U.S. workers.
- *Retaliation and relief against foreign unfair trade restrictions*: The Omnibus Trade and Competitiveness Act of 1988 allows economic retaliation against unreasonable, unjustifiable, or discriminatory trade acts by a foreign country ("Section 301 authority").

10. EXPROPRIATION

Expropriation (that is, nationalization of assets by a foreign country) is a significant business risk for U.S. companies doing business abroad. Firms may reduce this risk by employing political scientists to assess the risks of expropriation and by obtaining insurance from private firms or a U.S. governmental agency to insure against expropriation losses.

11. GOVERNMENT-ASSISTED EXPORT PROGRAMS

The U.S. government provides assistance to U.S. export companies. This assistance includes:

- *Export Trading Company Act of 1982*: ▸ This Act: (1) grants limited protection from antitrust laws for U.S. export trading companies; and (2) allows U.S. banks to invest in these export companies. ▸ U.S. exporters face competition from foreign trading companies, such as the Japanese *sogo shosha*. *Sogo shosha* offer many services to customers, including handling documentation, obtaining insurance, providing warehousing, and extending credit.
- *Foreign Sales Corporation Act of 1984*: ▸ This Act provides export tax incentives to U.S. foreign sales corporations. ▸ A number of requirements must be met in order to qualify for incentives.
- *United States Export-Import Bank (Eximbank)*: This bank, owned by the U.S. government, makes direct loans to foreign importers who purchase U.S. goods.
- *Other programs*: Other U.S. programs provide additional assistance regarding insurance and loans.

12. THE FOREIGN CORRUPT PRACTICES ACT

▸ This U.S. law forbids any offer, payment, or gift to foreign officials or third parties to influence trading decisions. ▸ But, payments to low-level officials to expedite routine services are allowed.

REVIEW OF TERMS AND PHRASES

Select the term or phrase that best matches a statement or definition stated below. Each term or phrase is the best match for only one statement or definition.

Terms and Phrases

a. Act of state doctrine
b. Blocking laws
c. CISG
d. Dumping
e. Effects doctrine
f. EU
g. Expropriation
h. GATT
i. IMF-World Bank
j. Most favored nation clause
k. NAFTA
l. Secrecy laws
m. Single European Act
n. Sovereign compliance doctrine
o. Sovereign immunity doctrine

Statements and Definitions

____ 1. Doctrine provides that courts will not judge acts of a foreign government done within its jurisdiction.

____ 2. Provision of GATT that forbids trade discrimination against member countries.

____ 3. Institution created after World War II to aid redevelopment and to help stabilize currencies.

____ 4. Foreign laws that forbid disclosure of banking information, including names of bank customers.

____ 5. Nationalization of assets of a U.S. company by a foreign country.

____ 6. Agreement that establishes uniform rules for international sales contracts.

____ 7. Organization comprised of the major western European trading partners.

____ 8. Sale of foreign goods in the U.S. at less than fair value.

____ 9. Agreement between U.S., Mexico, and Canada to eliminate tariffs over a 15-year period.

____ 10. Doctrine creating a defense to antitrust liability if an action is compelled by a foreign country.

____ 11. Doctrine holding that U.S. antitrust laws do not apply to conduct occurring outside of the United States unless there is a direct, substantial, and foreseeable effect on U.S. commerce.

____ 12. Trading treaty among 125 countries that promotes nondiscriminatory trade among its members.

____ 13. Doctrine that generally forbids suing a foreign government due to its governmental actions.

____ 14. Foreign laws that forbid disclosure of documents pursuant to orders issued by other countries.

____ 15. Agreement that eliminates barriers to free movement of goods and services between members of the European Union.

REVIEW OF CONCEPTS

Write **T** if the statement is true, write **F** if it is false.

_____ 1. An international contract can generally state which country's law will govern the parties' rights, but the contract cannot provide for arbitration of disputes that may arise regarding the contract.

_____ 2. A distributor takes title to U.S. goods and resells them in a foreign country.

_____ 3. A U.S. firm may be subject to foreign taxation if it appoints a foreign agent to do business for it in a foreign country.

_____ 4. Licensing allows foreign businesses to manufacture goods using the technology of U.S. firms.

_____ 5. It is not a violation of U.S. law to import gray market goods into the U.S.

_____ 6. Sovereign immunity doctrine holds that a country cannot be sued for its *commercial* activities.

_____ 7. Foreign antitrust laws are frequently different from U.S. antitrust laws.

_____ 8. In general, U.S. antitrust law does not apply to conduct occurring outside of the U.S. if the conduct does not affect commerce within the U.S.

_____ 9. The Single European Act removed trade barriers for U.S. firms doing business in Europe.

_____ 10. U.S. securities laws protect an American citizen from a fraudulent sale of securities only if the American citizen lives in the U.S. and the transaction occurs within the U.S.

_____ 11. Foreign secrecy and blocking laws make enforcement of U.S. securities laws more difficult.

_____ 12. Foreign countries are generally prohibited from imposing tariffs that may interfere with the sale of U.S. goods in foreign countries.

_____ 13. One type of trade barrier that interferes with importation of goods is complex customs procedures.

_____ 14. The U.S. does not use export controls to implement foreign policy.

_____ 15. The Trade Agreement Act of 1979 generally prohibits the dumping of foreign goods in the U.S.

REVIEW OF CHAPTER - APPLICATION OF CONCEPTS

MULTIPLE CHOICE QUESTIONS

____ 1. Micro-Tech, a U.S. corporation, entered a contract to purchase transistors from a Japanese company. A disagreement arose between the companies regarding the time in which payment had to be made without interest charges. Assume the laws of the U.S. and Japan differ on this point. Under these facts:
   a. If the parties specified in their contract whether U.S. or Japanese law applies to their contract, that contract provision would govern.
   b. A choice of law contractual clause could govern as to whether U.S. or Japanese law applies.
   c. If the parties failed to specify in their contract which law applies in case of conflict, a treaty between the U.S. and Japan could govern.
   d. All of the above.

____ 2. Xy-Cor, a U.S. company, entered a sales contract with MTR, a German company. In their contract, the companies agreed to arbitrate any disputes arising under their contract in France with an arbitrator fluent in German and English. The parties specified that in case of a dispute, full discovery would be available and that any decision of the arbitrator would be final and binding on both parties. Under these facts:
   a. The parties cannot specify that arbitration take place in France. Arbitration must take place in the country of one of the parties to the contract.
   b. The parties can specify that their arbitrator be fluent in both German and English.
   c. Full discovery is ordinarily available to the parties to an arbitration, even if they do not specify in their contract that they want full discovery available.
   d. The decision of the arbitrator would not be final and binding if the parties had not specified this in their contract.

____ 3. The World Trade Organization administers the objectives of which of the following:
   a. The former GATT organization.
   b. The CISG.
   c. UNCTAD.
   d. NAFTA.

____ 4. Uniform rules to govern international sales contracts between ratifying nations are found in:
   a. The GATT.
   b. The WTO.
   c. The CISG.
   d. The UCC.

____ 5. The European Union is made up of:
   a. The European Council, the European Commission, the European Parliament, and the European Court of Justice.
   b. The European Council, the World Court, and the International Monetary Fund.
   c. The European Commission, the European Parliament, the European Economic Cooperative, and the World Court.
   d. The European Court of Justice, the European Congress, and the European Executive Commission.

_____ 6. Tymes Corporation is considering marketing its products internationally, but it does not want to be subject to foreign taxation, to manage a foreign operation, or to transfer its technology rights to anyone else. What way of doing business abroad would best meet Tymes' objectives?
   a. Appointing an agent to represent Tymes in the foreign market.
   b. Licensing.
   c. Franchising.
   d. Export sales.

_____ 7. QTC Company found that jackets bearing its well-known trademark, but not made by QTC, were showing up in discount stores in the United States. The jackets were not up to the quality standards of QTC, and they were being sold for considerably less than the normal price of QTC jackets. QTC began losing sales of its jackets because of these foreign-made counterfeit jackets. What remedies are available to QTC?
   a. Triple damages from the counterfeiters.
   b. Seizure and destruction of the counterfeit jackets.
   c. Both a and b.
   d. None of the above. The manufacture of goods at a lower quality and price, bearing a trademark of another manufacturer, is a fair method of competition.

_____ 8. Which of the following is not a defense to the application of U.S. antitrust laws outside of the United States?
   a. The act of state doctrine.
   b. The expropriation doctrine.
   c. The sovereign compliance doctrine.
   d. The sovereign immunity doctrine.

_____ 9. The American Shoe Company has suffered severe economic losses due to competition from imported foreign shoes. The Company fears that it will be forced to lay off its workforce or to shut down entirely. What relief may be available under the Trade Act of 1974?
   a. The U.S. may impose duties or quotas on foreign shoes.
   b. The U.S. may provide readjustment allowances for workers who lose their jobs.
   c. The U.S. may provide job training for workers who lose their jobs.
   d. All of the above.

_____ 10. Franco is a U.S. congressman. A constituent farmer is complaining that the foreign sale of his corn is hindered by the unreasonable, unjustifiable, and discriminatory trade barriers of a foreign country. Which statute should Franco suggest as a possible relief mechanism?
   a. Trade Agreement Act of 1979.
   b. Omnibus Trade and Competitiveness Act of 1988.
   c. Trade Act of 1974.
   d. Foreign Corrupt Practices Act.

____ 11. Carsman Co. wants to establish a mining business in a third world country. However, Carsman Co. fears that its business may be expropriated by this country in the future. What actions can Carsman Co. take to reduce the risk of expropriation?
   a. Purchase insurance to protect it against losses resulting from expropriation.
   b. Employ political scientists to assess the degree of risk of expropriation.
   c. There is nothing that Carsman Co. can do to minimize the risk of loss from expropriation.
   d. a and b.

____ 12. John Baines is organizing an export trading company. John is studying U.S. programs that may be of some assistance to this company. Which of the following types of assistance is available?
   a. Export Trading Company Act of 1982 will allow U.S. banks to invest in the company.
   b. Foreign Sales Corporation Act of 1984 will automatically eliminate any liability for U.S. or foreign taxes for the company and any of its subsidiaries.
   c. U.S. Export-Import Bank will loan the company whatever funds it needs to do business.
   d. U.S. antitrust laws will permit the company to engage in unrestricted price fixing and other restraints of trade within the U.S. and in foreign countries.

____ 13. Kristen Jones is vice president of sales for Arnold Appliance Corporation. She wishes to expedite a sale of household appliances to a customer in a foreign country. Which of the following actions may Kristen take without violating the Foreign Corrupt Practices Act?
   a. Kristen may bribe a high government official in order to gain the official's approval.
   b. Kristen may make valuable gifts to high government officials in order to gain their approval.
   c. Kristen may pay low-level government officials to expedite routine paperwork.
   d. Kristen may not make any kind of payment to any government official.

CASE PROBLEM

Answer the following problem, briefly explaining your answer.

The BYTE Corp. designs computer parts and develops technical data that can be used for a variety of commercial or military uses. BYTE Corp. wants to export certain basic, nonstrategic computer parts to Britain and certain potentially strategic data to a country that is politically hostile to the U.S.

(a) What U.S. law primarily controls BYTE Corp.'s exportation of the computer parts and data?

(b) What does BYTE Corp. need to do to determine if a license is needed to export the computer parts to Britain?

(c) What type of sanctions could BYTE Corp. face if it falsifies information on a license application to export the technical data to the politically hostile country?

CHAPTER 7
CRIMES

CHAPTER OUTLINE

A. GENERAL PRINCIPLES

A crime is conduct that is prohibited and punished by a government.

1. **NATURE AND CLASSIFICATION OF CRIMES**

   GENERAL RULE. Crimes are classified by: (1) source (common law or statutes); (2) seriousness (treason, felony, or misdemeanor); or (3) nature of the crime (mala in se or mala prohibita).
   STUDY HINT. A crime that is a misdemeanor in one state may be a felony in another state.

2. **BASIS OF CRIMINAL LIABILITY**

   GENERAL RULE. A crime consists of (1) an act or omission (2) that is voluntarily committed.
   LIMITATION. For certain crimes, a particular mental state or a specific intent must be present.
   STUDY HINT. Knowledge that an act or omission is against the law is not necessary.

3. **PARTIES TO A CRIME**

   The trend is to abolish the principal-accessory distinction; all participants are guilty of the crime.

4. **RESPONSIBILITY FOR CRIMINAL ACTS**

   - *Employers*: An employer is liable for an employee's crime if the employer directed or required the employee to commit the crime. The employee is also responsible for his or her criminal act.
   - *Corporations*: The modern trend is to hold corporations criminally liable for their agents' crimes.
   - *Persons under incapacity*: Minors below a certain age, insane persons, and (sometimes) intoxicated persons are not criminally responsible for their crimes.

5. **ATTEMPTS AND CONSPIRACIES**

   - *Attempt*: Conduct taken to commit another crime, creating an unreasonable potential risk of harm.
   - *Conspiracy*: Parties agree to commit a crime; most states do not require any acts to be taken.
   - *Number of offenses*: ▸ One cannot be tried for attempt if the intended crime is committed. ▸ One can be tried for *both* conspiracy and the agreed-upon crime if that crime is committed.

6. **CRIMINAL FINES AND ADMINISTRATIVE PENALTIES (FINES) COMPARED**

   Fines may be imposed for violations of laws. Administrative fines often exceed criminal fines.

7. **INDEMNIFICATION OF CRIME VICTIMS**

   GENERAL RULE. For most crimes, the criminal pays a fine to the government, not to the victim.
   LIMITATION. ▸ Modern criminal laws allow victims to sue for damages and in some cases federal judges can order restitution (return) of property or damages. ▸ Federal Racketeering Influenced Corrupt Organizations Act (RICO) and similar state laws allow victims of some crimes to sue for treble damages.
   STUDY HINT. A party who is wrongly convicted of a crime may be paid damages by the state.

8. **SENTENCING**

    ‣ The trend is to establish uniform sentences for the same crime. ‣ Sentences that impose an alternative of a fine, or prison if the fine is not paid, are unconstitutional. ‣ Courts can require forfeiture (loss) of property that is used to commit a crime or property that is the fruit of a crime.

B. WHITE COLLAR CRIMES

White collar crimes do not involve the use or threat of force, and do not cause injuries or damage.

9. **CRIMES RELATED TO PRODUCTION, COMPETITION, AND MARKETING**

    The transmission of fraudulent information or transportation of prohibited goods in interstate commerce, as well as violations of federal securities laws, are typically federal crimes.

10. **RACKETEERING**

    The U.S. and many states have adopted laws to control and punish racketeering activities (i.e., repeated, unlawful conduct), including the knowing and willful participation in money-laundering activities.

11. **BRIBERY**

    ‣ Bribery is giving money or other value to wrongfully influence a public official or to procure the wrongful act of another's employee. ‣ The giving and receiving of a bribe each constitute a crime.

12. **EXTORTION AND BLACKMAIL**

    ■ *Extortion*: ‣ Traditionally: Illegal demand made by a public official appearing to act in an official capacity. ‣ Modern laws: Extortion occurs if anyone obtains anything by making an illegal threat.
    ■ *Blackmail*: Same as extortion, except crime is committed by a person who is not a public official.

13. **CORRUPT INFLUENCE**

    ■ *Improper political influence*: Government official accepts gifts, money, or other value from persons who have an interest in obtaining favorable governmental action.
    ■ *Improper commercial influence*: Federal statutes forbid business persons from gaining commercial advantages by threatening economic or physical loss or harm, or by engaging in racketeering.

14. **COUNTERFEITING**

    It is a crime to make, pass, or possess (with intent to pass) counterfeit coins, money, or securities.

15. **FORGERY**

    ‣ Forgery is signing another's name to, or altering, a legal instrument (check) creating a liability against another. ‣ Forgery includes wrongfully signing another's name to a credit card charge slip.

16. **PERJURY**

    ‣ Perjury is knowingly giving false testimony in a judicial proceeding after swearing to tell the truth.
    ‣ Giving a false answer on a governmental form may also be perjury.

17. **FALSE CLAIMS AND PRETENSES**

    ‣ Knowingly making a false statement or claim to an insurance company or to a governmental agency may be a crime. ‣ In most states, obtaining money or goods by false pretenses is a crime.

18. **BAD CHECKS**

    ‣ It is a crime to use or pass a check, knowing that the account will have insufficient funds to pay the check. ‣ The required intent to defraud is presumed if a check is not paid within a certain time.

19. CHEATS AND SWINDLES

- ■ *False weights*: Cheating through the use of improper weights, measures, or labels is a crime.
- ■ *Swindles*: Obtaining money by deception or fraud may be a criminal swindle or confidence game.

20. CREDIT CARD CRIMES

▸ It is a crime to use a canceled or counterfeit credit card, or to steal or improperly use the credit card of another. ▸ It is forgery to sign another's signature on a credit card charge slip without authorization.

21. USE OF THE MAILS TO DEFRAUD

It is a crime to use the mail for a scheme to defraud or to obtain money by false pretenses.

22. CRIMINAL LIBEL

GENERAL RULE.   Falsely injuring the reputation of another may constitute criminal libel.
STUDY HINTS.   ▸ Truth is a defense if the accused had a proper motive for communicating the damaging statement. ▸ Criminal libel does not require communication to a third party.

23. LOTTERIES AND GAMBLING

▸ A game is an illegal lottery if it involves (1) a prize (2) won by chance and (3) a price is paid for the chance to win. ▸ Gambling is illegal in many states even if it benefits a charity.

24. EMBEZZLEMENT

Embezzlement is fraudulent conversion of property or money by a person to whom it is entrusted.

25. RECEIVING STOLEN GOODS

It is criminal for a person to receive goods that he or she knows or should know are stolen.

C. CRIMES OF FORCE AND CRIMES AGAINST PROPERTY

▸ *Larceny*: taking personal property with the fraudulent intent to keep such property. Example: shoplifting. At common law, larceny is not committed if a person intends to return property. ▸ *Robbery*: taking of personal property within the presence of the victim by using force or fear. ▸ *Burglary*: breaking and entering into a structure owned by another at nighttime with the intent to commit any felony. Statutes may eliminate the nighttime, or breaking and entering elements. ▸ *Arson*: willful, malicious burning of another's residence. Burning one's own property to collect insurance is the crime of burning to defraud. ▸ *Riots and civil disorders*: rioting or inciting another to riot is a crime. A crime committed during a riot is a separate crime.

D. CRIMINAL LAW AND THE COMPUTER

▸ *What Is a Computer Crime?*: A computer crime is a crime that requires knowledge of computers. ▸ *The Computer as Victim*: Theft or destruction of hardware or software is a crime under traditional criminal law. ▸ *Unauthorized Use of Computers*: The unauthorized use of another's computer is not a crime in some states. The unlawful use of information in another's computer may be a criminal taking of property. ▸ *Computer Raiding*: The unauthorized use of confidential information that is stored in a computer may be theft of trade secrets or the crime of "computer trespass." Federal and state law make it a crime to gain unauthorized access to a computer or to its database in order to harm the computer or the computer's owner. ▸ *Diverted Delivery by Computer*: Unlawfully diverting goods or money by use of a computer is larceny, theft, or embezzlement. ▸ *Electronic Fund Transfer Crimes*: Under the federal Electronic Fund Transfers Act, it is a crime: (1) to use a counterfeit or wrongfully obtained device (e.g., a credit card) to obtain money or goods through an electronic fund transfer system; or (2) to ship or receive such forbidden devices or wrongfully obtained goods.

REVIEW OF TERMS AND PHRASES

Select the term or phrase that best matches a statement or definition stated below. Each term or phrase is the best match for only one statement or definition.

Terms and Phrases

a. Attempt
b. Conspiracy
c. Corrupt influence
d. Crime mala in se
e. Crime mala prohibita
f. Embezzlement
g. Felonies
h. Larceny
i. Lottery
j. Misdemeanors
k. Perjury
l. RICO
m. Robbery
n. Swindle
o. White collar crimes

Statements and Definitions

____ 1. Crime of knowingly lying in a judicial proceeding after taking an oath to speak truthfully.

____ 2. Broad category of business crimes that do not use or threaten the use of force.

____ 3. Conduct that is a crime only because a statute states that such conduct is forbidden.

____ 4. Crime of wrongfully taking personal property within the presence of the victim by force or fear.

____ 5. Conduct that is a crime because it is inherently evil conduct.

____ 6. Crime of intentionally obtaining money or property by fraud or deception.

____ 7. Crime by a public official who influences a government action in return for benefits from a party who is interested in the governmental action.

____ 8. Crime that is committed when two or more persons agree to commit another crime.

____ 9. Classification of minor crimes that do not include treason or felonies.

____ 10. Federal law for prosecuting racketeering that permits victims to sue for treble damages.

____ 11. Classification of serious crimes that are punishable by imprisonment or death.

____ 12. Crime that is committed when conduct is taken to commit another crime, and such conduct has progressed to the point that it creates an unreasonable potential risk of harm to others.

____ 13. Crime of wrongfully taking another's personal property with an intent to keep the property.

____ 14. Transaction in which a person pays a price for a chance to win a prize.

____ 15. Crime involving fraudulent conversion of money/property by a party to whom it was entrusted.

REVIEW OF CONCEPTS

Write **T** if the statement is true, write **F** if it is false.

____ 1. Conduct that may be a misdemeanor in one state may be a felony in another state.

____ 2. A required element for a crime is that the criminal party voluntarily commit the prohibited act.

____ 3. A person cannot commit a crime if the person does not know that his or her conduct is criminal.

____ 4. The trend is to treat both accessories and principals as having committed the crime in question.

____ 5. An employer is criminally responsible for an employee's crime if the employer directed the employee to commit the criminal act.

____ 6. If a person undertakes to commit a burglary and the person succeeds in committing the burglary, then the person can be convicted of both attempt and burglary.

____ 7. *Traditionally*, a criminal is required to pay fines to the government and not to the crime victim.

____ 8. It is unconstitutional for a court to impose an alternative sentence whereby a defendant must pay a fine or be imprisoned if unable to pay the fine.

____ 9. A court can generally order a criminal to forfeit (lose) property that was used to commit a crime.

____ 10. *Traditionally*, extortion involves wrongful demands made by public officials, whereas blackmail involves wrongful demands made by persons other than public officials.

____ 11. It may be a federal crime to gain a commercial advantage by threatening improper economic harm.

____ 12. Falsely injuring the reputation of another cannot be a crime. Such conduct can only be a tort.

____ 13. If an employee wrongfully keeps money that was entrusted to the employee by his or her employer, then the employee has committed the crime of embezzlement.

____ 14. At *common law*, a person does not commit larceny if he or she takes property with the intent to return it to the proper owner.

____ 15. Participating in a riotous mob and civil disorder cannot be a crime. This activity is protected by an individual's constitutional rights.

REVIEW OF CHAPTER - APPLICATION OF CONCEPTS

MULTIPLE CHOICE QUESTIONS

____ 1. Over a period of four years, Allen knowingly and willfully engaged in numerous transactions that entailed the fraudulent sale of worthless swampland to elderly persons who lived in various parts of the United States. Mrs. Hinton unsuspectingly bought some of this worthless land from Allen, and she paid him $10,000 for the property. Under these facts:
  a. Allen can only be criminally prosecuted for violation of RICO.
  b. Allen can only be civilly sued by the government for violation of RICO.
  c. Allen can be criminally prosecuted for violation of RICO and he can be civilly sued by Mrs. Hinton for $10,000 for violation of RICO.
  d. Allen can be be criminally prosecuted for violation of RICO and he can be civilly sued by Mrs. Hinton for $30,000 for violation of RICO.

2. Jackson Electrical, Inc. employees were repairing power lines when one of its "cherry pickers" came into contact with a power line, electrocuting a worker. Prior to this accident, the employees had complained to Jackson supervisors that operation of this equipment so near to the power lines was unsafe and exposed them a significant risk of injury. The supervisors talked this over with Jackson and they all agreed: "We can always replace one of these employees if necessary, but we can't replace the client for whom we are doing this work." The supervisors then ordered the employees to continue to work (the crime of criminal negligence). Who can be prosecuted for this crime?
   a. Only the supervisors.
   b. Only the supervisors and James.
   c. Only James Electrical, Inc.
   d. The supervisors, James, and James Electrical, Inc.

3. Jim needed money so he decided to get the money by robbing others at gunpoint. Jim bought a gun, and as he confronted his first victim, a police car pulled up to investigate the commotion, scaring off Jim. Under these facts, what crimes, if any, did Jim commit?
   a. Theft.
   b. Robbery.
   c. Attempt.
   d. All of the above.

4. Drake used his computer to run a criminal ponzi game, a violation of a state criminal statute. The criminal statute in question authorizes a sentence for up to 5 years imprisonment. Under these facts:
   a. Drake may only be sentenced to prison for up to 5 years.
   b. Drake may only be sentenced for longer than 5 years if the judge feels that a longer sentence is warranted.
   c. Drake may be sentenced to prison for up to 5 years and, in addition, he may be ordered to forfeit the computer that he used to carry out his criminal activities.
   d. Drake may be sentenced for longer than 5 years if the judge feels that a longer sentence is warranted and he may be ordered to forfeit the computer that he used to carry out his criminal activities.

5. Under *traditional rules*, in which case is the crime of *extortion* committed?
   a. Sheriff Ross demands that Ruth pay him $10,000 or he will arrest her.
   b. Ida offers to pay Judge Rye $500 if Judge Rye will dismiss a driving complaint against her.
   c. Nanny, a private person, demands that Mayor Traynor pay Nanny $5,000 or she will publicly reveal evidence of certain immoral conduct by the mayor.
   d. Fargo Securities fraudulently sold stock in violation of U.S. securities laws.

6. Which of the following is the crime of *corrupt influence*?
   a. A city council member lies while testifying during her divorce hearing.
   b. A mayor counterfeits money.
   c. A congresswoman accepts $10,000 from a developer in return for voting in favor of a bill that the developer wants passed.
   d. A state senator sells illegal drugs.

____ 7. In which case does Barbie commit the crime of *forgery*?
   a. Without permission, Barbie took a blank check belonging to Kim. Barbie then filled the check out, signed Kim's name, and cashed the check.
   b. Without permission, Barbie took a credit card belonging to Sarah. Barbie bought goods, charged the bill to Sarah's card, and Barbie signed Sarah's name to the charge card slip.
   c. Without permission, Barbie printed and passed fake $20 bills.
   d. a and b.

____ 8. In which case did Kelly probably commit a crime?
   a. Kelly cashed a personal check for $50. Unknown to Kelly, she had insufficient funds in her account and the check was not paid. When informed that her bank refused payment, Kelly immediately paid the check.
   b. Kelly shipped goods for a fee based on the weight of customers' shipments. Kelly knowingly used scales that weighed significantly heavy, enabling her to overcharge her customers.
   c. Kelly's credit card was canceled and she was informed of this fact. Nonetheless, Kelly continued to use the canceled card.
   d. b and c.

____ 9. Select the correct answer.
   a. Jerry bought a watch. The watch was stolen. Jerry did not know or have reason to know that the watch was stolen. In this case, Jerry committed the crime of *receiving stolen goods*.
   b. Bob parked his bike outside a classroom while he attended class. Unknown to Bob, Lex stole the bike while Bob was in class. In this case, Lex committed the crime of *robbery*.
   c. Aris broke into Nel's house, intending to steal Nel's TV. In this case, Aris committed the crime of *arson*.
   d. Thomas shoplifted some clothing from J&J Department Store. The store was unaware of the theft at the time it occurred. In this case, Thomas committed the crime of *larceny*.

____ 10. Roger, an employee, systematically took tools from his employer whenever he was left to lock up his employer's store. Roger was arrested one night while taking more tools. What crime has Roger committed?
   a. Larceny.
   b. Burglary.
   c. Embezzlement.
   d. Criminal fraud.

____ 11. Leo worked for Motorworks, an exclusive car dealership. Secret customer information that was unavailable elsewhere was maintained on Motorworks' computers. This information gave Motorworks a significant advantage over its competitors. When Leo quit, he printed out the computerized customer information to use when he went to work for a competing car dealer. Leo also wrongfully took a computer and software from Motorworks. In many states, which conduct by Leo is a crime?
   a. Wrongfully taking the secret customer information.
   b. Wrongfully taking the computer.
   c. Wrongfully taking the software.
   d. All of the above.

____ 12. Jeanne worked as a computer programmer. One day, Jeanne was angry at her employer, and she intentionally planted a "virus" in her employer's software with the intent to destroy the information stored in the employer's computer system. Within a week, the virus had destroyed all of the information that had been stored in the employer's computer system. In most states:
   a. Jeanne's conduct is unethical.
   b. Jeanne's conduct is a tort.
   c. Jeanne's conduct is a crime.
   d. All of the above.

____ 13. "Henry the Hacker" discovered the password for Last Bank's computer and improperly shifted $100,000 of bank funds into his personal account. Under these facts, what crimes has George committed?
   a. Larceny (theft).
   b. Criminal invasion of privacy.
   c. Criminal violation of the Electronic Fund Transfers Act.
   b. All of the above.

CASE PROBLEM

Answer the following problem, briefly explaining your answer.

Over a period of five years, Drake knowingly and willfully engaged in a pattern of criminal activity that entailed repeated fraudulent sales of worthless swampland to elderly persons. Drake advertised this land by mailing fraudulent brochures to persons in many states. Drake also paid money to government officials in order to obtain their approval of these land sales. Mrs. Hinton unsuspectingly bought some of this worthless land from Drake, and she paid him $10,000 for the property.

Under these facts: (a) What white collar crimes did Drake commit? (b) What criminal penalties may be imposed against Drake? (c) What remedies does Mrs. Hinton have against Drake?

_____

_____

_____

_____

_____

CHAPTER 8
TORTS

CHAPTER OUTLINE

A. GENERAL PRINCIPLES

▸ A tort is a private wrong against a person for which the person may recover money damages. ▸ A tort is not the same as a crime or a breach of contract.

1. TORT AND CRIME DISTINGUISHED

GENERAL RULE. A crime arises from a violation of a public duty, whereas a tort arises from a violation of a private duty that is owed to a particular person.
STUDY HINT. ▸ An act that is a crime can also constitute a tort if the act causes an injury or loss to a particular person. ▸ Example: An employee's theft of his or her employer's property that was entrusted to the employee is the crime of embezzlement and it is also the tort of conversion.

2. TORT AND BREACH OF CONTRACT DISTINGUISHED

GENERAL RULE. A tort arises from a violation of a duty created by the law, whereas a breach of contract arises from a violation of a duty that was voluntarily agreed upon by contracting parties.
STUDY HINT. ▸ One act can constitute a breach of contract and a tort. ▸ Example: A doctor's failure to properly do an operation is a breach of contract and the tort of negligence (malpractice).

3. BASIS OF TORT LIABILITY

The elements required to establish tort liability are: (1) duty; (2) voluntary act that breaches the duty; and (3) causation (the breach of duty causes harm to the plaintiff). Fundamental rules include:

- *Duty*: In general, a person has no tort liability unless the person breaches a legal duty that he or she owed to another person. However, there is a strong modern trend to ignore the duty requirement and to focus instead on whether an interest should be protected in a particular case.
- *Voluntary act*: A breach must result from a *voluntary* act or failure to act.
- *Intent*: ▸ For some torts, a person must intend to do the act or intend to harm the plaintiff. Example: Tort of false imprisonment requires that a party intend to detain another person. ▸ For other torts, liability is imposed even though harm was not intended. Example: trespass to land.
- *Motive*: A person's motive (the personal reason why a person did an act) is usually irrelevant.
- *Causal relationship (causation)*: ▸ A defendant's breach must be the legal cause of the plaintiff's harm. ▸ *Proximate cause test*: In general, an act must be the "proximate cause" of the harm, i.e., the act is the immediate ("but for") cause of the harm. Also, a modern trend finds causation if an act is a substantial cause of the harm. ▸ *Foreseeability test*: Courts find causation if a plaintiff's harm was a foreseeable consequence of a wrongful act. Example: plaintiff is injured while being rescued. ▸ *Act of third party*: A defendant may be liable even if a third party later commits a foreseeable wrong against the plaintiff. In this case, the defendant and third party are both liable. Example: landlord negligently fails to provide adequate lighting and security enabling a third party to assault a tenant.
- *Liability for tort of employee or child*: ▸ In general, a person is not liable for another person's tort. ▸ In some cases, an employer is liable for an employee's tort. ▸ A parent may be liable for a child's tort if the parent: (1) failed to control a dangerous child; (2) lent a car to a child who was known to be a reckless driver; or (3) in one-half of the states, lent the family car to the child.

4. **LIABILITY-IMPOSING CONDUCT**

   GENERAL RULE. Tort liability is usually imposed only if harm to the plaintiff is caused by a defendant's (1) intentional act or (2) negligence.
   LIMITATION. In some cases, modern law may impose liability solely because a person harms another person (see section 5 below).

5. **ABSOLUTE LIABILITY**

   GENERAL RULE. Absolute liability (liability that arises without proof of intentional harm or negligence) may be imposed in connection with: (1) inherently dangerous activities, such as dynamite blasting;
   (2) unavoidably dangerous industrial activities, such as the ultrahazardous production or storage of explosives or similarly dangerous products in populated areas; and (3) the sale of consumer foods.
   STUDY HINT. ▸ No-fault liability statutes are also a form of absolute liability. ▸ Examples: no-fault automobile laws; workers' compensation laws.

6. **NEGLIGENCE**

   - *Negligence defined*: A person is negligent if he or she acts with less care than a reasonable person would use under similar circumstances.
   - *Reasonable person standard*: ▸ A jury determines what it believes a hypothetical "reasonable person" would have done under similar circumstances. ▸ This standard varies with each case and with each jury's determination of what a reasonable person would have done in a given case.
   - *Degree of care*: ▸ A person must exercise the care and skill that would be expected in that particular case, when considered in light of the harm that might result. ▸ It may be insufficient to merely exercise the care that is practiced by others or that is practiced in an industry.
   - *Contributory negligence (defense)*: ▸ Contributory negligence means that a plaintiff's own negligence was a partial cause for his or her injuries. ▸ At common law (and in some states today), a plaintiff's contributory negligence (no matter how slight) completely bars the plaintiff from recovering anything. ▸ Example: Joe and Coni are in an accident, and Coni suffered $1,000 damages. Coni's damages were 90 percent caused by Joe's negligence, and they were 10 percent caused by Coni's own negligence. Coni can recover nothing under contributory negligence.
   - *Comparative negligence (defense)*: ▸ Today, most states do not follow the common law contributory negligence doctrine. Instead, these courts apply the comparative negligence concept whereby damages are merely reduced to the extent they are caused by the plaintiff's fault. ▸ Example: In the example above, Coni would recover $900 under comparative negligence.
   - *Assumption of risk (defense)*: ▸ Assumption of risk means a plaintiff voluntarily exposes himself or herself to a known danger. ▸ At common law, assumption of risk bars any recovery. ▸ In states that follow the comparative negligence doctrine, assumption of risk is treated as if a plaintiff had been negligent, and the comparative negligence test is applied to determine the amount of recovery.
   - *Proof of negligence*: ▸ A plaintiff has the burden to prove a defendant's negligence. ▸ This burden is met if a plaintiff proves an injury was caused by an instrument that was under the defendant's control, and an injury would not normally occur absent negligence (*res ipsa loquitur*). Example: sponge left in a patient during an operation. ▸ Proof of a violation of a statute may establish negligence if the statute was intended to avoid the harm that the plaintiff suffered.

7. **DIVISION OF LIABILITY**

   ▸ Traditionally, recovery was denied if two persons harmed another, but their respective responsibility could not be proven. ▸ Modern courts hold such wrongdoers liable for all damages.

8. **WHO MAY SUE**

‣ A party may sue for his or her damages. ‣ A spouse or parent may sometimes sue for injury to a spouse or child. ‣ A spouse or child of a person who is killed can sue for wrongful death.

9. **IMMUNITY FROM LIABILITY**

GENERAL RULES. ‣ Traditionally, governments had immunity from liability for torts that were committed by their employees. ‣ Immunities that previously barred suits against charities, between children and parents, or between spouses are quickly being eliminated.

LIMITATIONS. ‣ In some states, immunity of state and local governments has been eliminated. ‣ The Federal Tort Claims Act allows suits against the U.S. government for negligence of its employees.

B. **WHITE COLLAR TORTS**

10. **CAUSING MENTAL DISTRESS (TORT OF OUTRAGEOUS CONDUCT)**

GENERAL RULES. ‣ Most courts now allow recovery for mental distress that is intentionally caused by outrageous acts. Examples: outrageous bill collection techniques; mistreatment of a corpse. ‣ Many states also allow recovery for mental distress that is caused by another's negligence.

LIMITATION. At common law, the tort of outrageous conduct was not recognized; a person could not recover for emotional harm unless a separate tort was committed.

STUDY HINTS. ‣ A party can recover for emotional harm even if there are no physical injuries.
‣ Bystanders can recover for emotional harm suffered when they witness harm to a family member.

11. **INVASION OF PRIVACY**

GENERAL RULE. Liability for invasion of privacy may result from: (1) invasion of a person's physical privacy; (2) improper publicity of private facts about another; (3) false association of a person with a product or principle; or (4) unauthorized commercial use of one's name or likeness.

LIMITATION. ‣ Sharing information with other businesses for a bona fide commercial reason is permitted. ‣ Example: creditors sharing credit information about a debtor with a credit agency.

12. **MALPRACTICE**

Malpractice liability arises from a professional's negligent or improper performance of a duty.

13. **FRAUD**

A person who knowingly or recklessly makes a false statement may be liable for fraud.

14. **DEFAMATION BY SLANDER**

- *Defamation and slander*: ‣ Defamation is the publication (communication) of a false statement regarding another person that tends to injure that person's reputation. ‣ Slander is defamation that is communicated by spoken words.
- *Privilege (defense)*: ‣ *Absolute privilege*: public officers, such as judges and legislators, have an absolute privilege (total defense) regarding false statements made in carrying out their duties.
    ‣ *Qualified privilege*: other parties have a defense to liability if: (1) a false statement is made in good faith; and (2) the parties making and receiving the statement have a bona fide interest in the matter. Example: good faith statements made in credit reports or in letters of recommendation.

15. **DEFAMATION BY LIBEL**

The tort of libel is defamation communicated by false writings, pictures, or visual transmissions.

16. **DISPARAGEMENT OF GOODS AND SERVICES AND SLANDER OF TITLE**

A false statement regarding title to land or quality of goods or services that causes damages is a tort.

17. INFRINGEMENT OF TRADEMARKS AND SERVICE MARKS

- *Trademark and service mark*: Protected word, name, device, or symbol that is used by a seller of goods or a supplier of services to distinguish the party's goods or services.
- *Tort*: Unauthorized use or substantial copying of another's trademark or service mark is infringement.

18. INFRINGEMENT OF PATENTS

- *Patent*: Exclusive right to use an invention (utility patent) for 20 years.
- *Tort*: Unauthorized use of all or a substantial part of another's patent is infringement.

19. INFRINGEMENT OF COPYRIGHTS

- *Copyright*: Exclusive right to use or reproduce literary, artistic, dramatic, or musical works for the life of the creator plus 50 years.
- *Tort*: Unauthorized use or copying of a substantial part of a copyrighted work is infringement.

20. UNFAIR COMPETITION

▸ Certain unfair business conduct is prohibited as being unfair competition. ▸ Examples: wrongful, misleading imitation of another business' name, storefront, advertisements, or product packaging.

21. COMBINATIONS TO DIVERT TRADE

▸ A business combination (joint action by two or more parties) creates liability for conspiracy if it: (1) harms another party; and (2) the objective, or means of achieving an objective, is unlawful.
▸ Examples: illegal boycott of a business' good; boycott of a store accomplished with illegal force.

22. MALICIOUS INTERFERENCE WITH CONTRACTS

▸ It is a tort for a person: (1) to maliciously (intentionally and without legal justification) cause another party to breach a contract with a third party; or (2) to maliciously prevent others from making a contract.
▸ This conduct is a tort even if done by a competitor or the contract in question is terminable at will.

23. WRONGFUL INTERFERENCE WITH BUSINESS RELATIONS

Wrongful interference with a person's right to work or to engage in a trade is a tort.

C. TORTS AGAINST PERSON OR PROPERTY

▸ *Trespass to the person*: (1) assault (wrongful placing of a person in apprehension of a battery); (2) battery (intentional, wrongful physical contact with another); and (3) false imprisonment (intentional, unprivileged detaining of a person without permission). False imprisonment is not committed if: (1) a detained person consents to a detainment; or (2) a merchant who mistakenly detains an innocent person had reasonable grounds to think that the person was shoplifting. ▸ *Trespass to land*: unpermitted entry on, across, above, or below another person's land. ▸ *Trespass to personal property*: intentional or negligent damaging of another person's personal property. ▸ *Conversion*: wrongful taking and keeping of another's personal property.

D. TORT LAW AND THE COMPUTER

▸ *Fraud and the computer*: The use of computers to commit fraud is covered by traditional tort law.
▸ *Damage to the computer*: Wrongfully damaging or destroying another's hardware or software is a tort. Intentional or reckless harm may result in punitive damages. ▸ *Theft of the computer*: Theft of computer hardware is the tort of conversion. ▸ *The computer and the protection of privacy*: A person who wrongfully discloses personal, computerized information regarding others is liable. ▸ A firm may be liable if it negligently hires or fails to supervise an employee who releases private information regarding others. In some states, a firm may be liable if it maintains inadequate computer security, enabling an outsider to obtain private information. ▸ *Defamation by computer*: The negligent/intentional release of erroneous computerized information may be defamation by computer. In certain cases, good faith and due care may prevent liability.

REVIEW OF TERMS AND PHRASES

MATCHING EXERCISE

Select the term or phrase that best matches a statement or definition stated below. Each term or phrase is the best match for only one statement or definition.

Terms and Phrases

a. Assault
b. Assumption of risk
c. Battery
d. Conversion
e. Disparagement of goods
f. False imprisonment
g. Immunity
h. Libel
i. Malpractice
j. Negligence
k. Proximate cause
l. Slander

Statements and Definitions

____ 1. Intentional, wrongful contact with the body of another.

____ 2. Wrongful taking of another person's personal property.

____ 3. Defamation of another person that is communicated orally.

____ 4. Immediate cause of harm.

____ 5. Wrongful, intentional detainment of another person.

____ 6. Negligent or improper performance of a legal duty by a professional.

____ 7. Defamation of another person that is communicated by written word or visual communication.

____ 8. Causing another to have apprehension of an imminent battery, without making physical contact.

____ 9. Protection from legal liability for a tort.

____ 10. False statements regarding the quality of a business' goods that cause damage to the business.

____ 11. Plaintiff voluntarily exposes himself or herself to a known danger.

____ 12. Failure to act as a reasonably prudent person would act under similar circumstances.

COMPLETION EXERCISE

Fill in the blanks with the words that most accurately complete each statement. Answers may or may not include terms used in the matching exercise. A term cannot be used to complete more than one statement.

1. The standard of care that is used to determine whether a party is negligent is what a hypothetical _____ _____ would have done under similar circumstances.

2. A company that engages in an inherently dangerous activity may have _____ _____ for harm that is caused to others as a result of this activity.

3. A plaintiff's negligence that is partly responsible for the plaintiff's injuries is called _____ _____.

CHAPTER 8

4. A defendant who knowingly or recklessly makes a false statement to another party, thereby causing a loss to the other party, may be liable to the other party for the tort of _____.

5. Libel and slander are two types of _____.

6. A _____ gives an author the exclusive right to use or reproduce a written work for the life of the author plus 50 years.

7. The unpermitted entry on another party's land is the tort of _____ ____ _____.

REVIEW OF CONCEPTS

Write **T** if the statement is true, write **F** if it is false.

____ 1. One wrongful act may be both a crime and a tort.

____ 2. A person is not entitled to recover for every injury or loss that is caused by another person.

____ 3. In general, tort liability will not be imposed for an involuntary act even if the act harms another.

____ 4. A required element for all torts is that the defendant intend to cause harm to the plaintiff.

____ 5. A person's motive is generally irrelevant in determining tort liability (unless the motive helps to establish a required intent).

____ 6. In many states, a defendant may have liability for an act that substantially causes an injury to a plaintiff, even if the injury is also partially caused by a person other than the defendant.

____ 7. A parent is liable for all torts that are committed by the parent's children.

____ 8. Businesses have absolute liability for any harm they cause while they are engaging in any commercial activity.

____ 9. In a suit for negligence, the plaintiff has the burden to prove the defendant's negligence.

____ 10. In some cases, negligence may be established by proving that a defendant violated a statute.

____ 11. *Res ipsa loquitur* is a concept that may allow a jury to infer that a defendant was negligent.

____ 12. Traditionally, contributory negligence by a plaintiff did not bar recovery of damages.

____ 13. The U.S. government cannot be sued for harm caused by the negligence of federal employees.

____ 14. A child may be able to sue a defendant for wrongful death if the defendant wrongfully killed the child's parent.

____ 15. Tim and his father were waiting for a bus. Rick recklessly shoved Tim's father into the path of a bus, and the father was seriously injured. As a result of seeing this event, Tim suffered serious emotional distress. Under these facts, Tim can recover for his emotional distress from Rick.

REVIEW OF CHAPTER - APPLICATION OF CONCEPTS

MULTIPLE CHOICE QUESTIONS

____ 1. One afternoon, Carrie slipped on grapes that had fallen on the floor in the produce department of Acme Groceries, injuring herself. Acme inspected the floor once in the morning and once at closing for spilled produce, even though it knew that produce was dropped on the floor more often. Is Acme liable for negligence?
   a. No, Acme owed no duty to Carrie.
   b. No, Acme did not breach its duty to Carrie.
   c. No, Acme's conduct was not the cause of Carrie's injuries.
   d. Yes, Acme was negligent and is liable to Carrie.

____ 2. Kim was driving on a freeway and she passed under an overhead roadway that was being repaired by Acme Construction. As Kim emerged from under the overpass, a steel guard rail dropped from the roadway above, smashing into Kim's car and injuring Kim. At the time of the accident, Acme was working alone on the overhead roadway, installing steel guard rails. Under these facts:
   a. An inference of negligence by Acme can be established under the doctrine of *res ipsa loquitur*.
   b. An inference of negligence by Acme can be established under the doctrine of *res ipsa loquitur* only if it can be proved how Acme negligently dropped the steel guard rail.
   c. If an inference of negligence arises, then this is absolute proof of Acme's negligence that it cannot refute.
   d. a and c.

____ 3. John and Ken went to a baseball game at their college. They sat high up in the stands behind first base even though they knew that foul balls often landed in this area. In the third inning, a foul ball struck John in the head, causing him serious injuries. John sued the college for negligence. In all likelihood, is the college liable to John?
   a. Yes, the college was negligent in allowing spectators to watch the baseball game.
   b. Yes, the college is liable under strict liability because baseball is an ultrahazardous activity.
   c. No, John assumed the risk that foul balls would sometimes land in the stands.
   d. No, colleges owe no duty to protect students from unreasonable risks of harm.

____ 4. Maria and Barb were competing for head cheerleader. With the intent to cause emotional harm to Maria, Barb repeatedly made terrible, harassing, and obscene phone calls to Maria. Maria was so frightened by the calls that she suffered a nervous breakdown requiring her to be hospitalized. Under these facts:
   a. Maria can sue Barb for the tort of battery.
   b. Maria can sue Barb for the tort of outrageous conduct.
   c. Maria can sue Barb for the tort of slander of title.
   d. Maria can sue Barb for malpractice.

_____ 5. Which of the following is fraud?
   a. Nigel offered to sell his car to Jawan, explaining that the clutch was worn out.
   b. When negotiating to sell his car to Maureen, Jack stated that the car was "a beauty - worth every penny" of the asking price. Actually, the car was a worn-out junk heap.
   c. Sally offered to sell her car to Mark. She stated to Mark that all of the car lights worked, not knowing that one rear tail light had just burned out.
   d. Guillermo sold Kim a car that he claimed had two years left on the warranty even though he knew that the warranty had run out six months before.

_____ 6. Ken is a famous politician who is running for public office. In which situation can Ken sue for the tort of invasion of privacy?
   a. The *Evening Star*, a magazine, hid a camera in the ceiling of Ken's bedroom in order to get some exclusive photos of Ken's personal life.
   b. The *Daily News* published a story about Ken's recent behavior at a local, public nightclub.
   c. Without Ken's permission, Armco Inc. used Ken's picture to advertise its deodorant products.
   d. a and c.

_____ 7. Joe wanted to buy a car from EZ Sales on credit. EZ contacted TriCo Credit Co. from whom EZ obtained credit information regarding prospective customers. Based on information from reliable sources, TriCo in good faith furnished a written report stating that Joe was delinquent on several bills. Unknown to TriCo, this information was wrong. As a result of this report, EZ refused to sell the car to Joe. Under these facts:
   a. TriCo is liable to Joe for defamation by libel.
   b. TriCo is liable to Joe for defamation by slander.
   c. TriCo is not liable for defamation because it has a qualified privilege that protects it from liability in this situation.
   d. TriCo is not liable for defamation because defamation does not apply to business transactions.

_____ 8. Apparels Inc. sells jeans under the registered mark "Blue Jelly." A competitor began to sell jeans under the mark "Really Blue Jelly." Under these facts:
   a. The competitor is liable for trademark infringement.
   b. The competitor is liable for service mark infringement.
   c. The competitor is liable for copyright infringement.
   d. The competitor is not liable for infringement.

_____ 9. Markhams, a department store chain, has been in business for many years, and it has an excellent reputation. John wanted his clothing store to be a success, so he remodeled his store so the storefront looked the same as the unique design of Markhams' stores, he erected a sign over his store reading "Markams," and he used advertising and packaging that were identical to unique advertisements and packaging used by Markhams. In this case, John is liable for the tort of:
   a. Conspiracy.
   b. Malicious interference with contract.
   c. Unfair competition.
   d. Infringement of patent.

_____ 10. Joe was angry with a clerk and, standing a foot away from the clerk, Joe drew his arm back with a clenched fist and stated, "I am going to punch your lights out." What tort did Joe commit?
   a. Libel.
   b. False imprisonment.
   c. Battery.
   d. Assault.

_____ 11. Select the correct answer.
   a. Alex stole Jose's automobile. In this case, Alex committed the tort of conversion.
   b. An ABC Store security guard had reasonable grounds to believe that Ben stole some goods and the security guard detained Ben for a few minutes to ask him some questions. In fact, Ben was innocent. In this case, the security guard committed the tort of false imprisonment.
   c. Lenny wrongfully threatened to sexually assault Carrie. In self defense, Carrie hit Lenny to protect herself from the assault. In this case, Carrie committed the tort of battery.
   d. a and b.

_____ 12. Merit Bank keeps its customer account records on a computer. A bank employee diverted funds from Kim's account into the employee's personal account. The employee had a criminal record for this type of conduct, but Merit negligently hired the employee without conducting a background check. Merit also negligently used software that incorrectly stated customer account balances. As a result, Larry's checking account balance was incorrectly stated and several of his checks were improperly not paid, causing Larry damages. Under these facts:
   a. Merit Bank is liable to Kim and Larry.
   b. Merit Bank is liable to Kim, but it is not liable to Larry.
   c. Merit Bank is liable to Larry, but it is not liable to Kim.
   d. Merit Bank is not liable to Kim or to Larry for their respective losses.

_____ 13. Rene owned a word processing company. One day, Rene intentionally planted a virus in software of a competitive firm with the intent to destroy the information stored in the competitor's computer system. The virus soon destroyed nearly all of the information that had been stored in the competitor's computer system. Under these facts:
   a. The competitor can sue Rene for only actual damages.
   b. The competitor can sue Rene for only punitive damages.
   c. The competitor can sue Rene for actual and punitive damages.
   d. The competitor cannot sue Rene for damages. Rene's conduct is a crime, not a tort.

CASE PROBLEMS

Answer the following problems, briefly explaining your answers.

1. One rainy day, Lily was driving to work. The speed limit was 45 m.p.h. Lily was driving 45 m.p.h. as were some other drivers. But, a reasonable person would have been driving only 30 m.p.h. Paul negligently rode his bike onto the road. Due to the speed Lily was driving, she could not stop and her car struck Paul. Paul suffered $5,000 damages, which were caused 80 percent by Lily's conduct and 20 percent by Paul's conduct. (a) What duty did Lily owe to Paul? (b) Was Lily negligent? (c) If Lily was negligent, how much could Paul recover under common law contributory negligence rules? (d) If Lily was negligent, how much could Paul recover under the comparative negligence doctrine?

2. Maxco sold food products to restaurants. In connection with its business, Maxco: (a) sold a shipment of kangaroo meat, intentionally misrepresenting it as ground beef; (b) falsely told a food magazine that Juan's Cafe, a cafe that had canceled a contract with Maxco, served spoiled food, causing Juan's to lose money; customers; and (c) paid $25,000 to Queen's Cafes, a restaurant chain, in order to maliciously induce Queen's Cafes to breach a contract with a Maxco competitor and to instead buy its food from Maxco. What torts did Maxco commit?

3. Todd was an overzealous vacuum cleaner salesman. One day Todd went to the home of Mabel Jones, an elderly widow. Mabel told Todd she was not interested. In response, Todd threatened to hit Mabel, he pushed Mabel aside, and he forced his way into Mabel's home to demonstrate his product. In addition, Todd would not allow Mabel to leave. To make his sales pitch, Todd poured lead shavings on an Oriental throw rug, Mabel's favorite item of personal property. The shavings permanently stained the entire rug. Todd committed what torts against the person or property of Mabel?

CHAPTER 9
NATURE AND CLASSES OF CONTRACTS

CHAPTER OUTLINE

A. NATURE OF CONTRACTS

1. DEFINITION OF A CONTRACT

GENERAL RULE. A contract is a legally binding agreement. Stated another way, "a contract is a promise or a set of promises for the breach of which the law gives a remedy, or the performance of which the law in some way recognizes as a duty." (Restatement, Contracts, 2d)

STUDY HINT. The essence of a contract is that (1) by mutual agreement (2) parties create obligations that can be legally enforced.

2. ELEMENTS OF A CONTRACT

Elements of a valid contract are: (1) an agreement; (2) competent parties; (3) genuine assent to the contract; (4) consideration given by each party; (5) legal purpose; and (6) proper form of contract.

3. SUBJECT MATTER OF CONTRACTS

A contract may relate to virtually any type of transaction. Contracts may relate to performance of a service, sale or transfer of ownership of property, or a combination of such transactions.

4. PARTIES TO A CONTRACT

GENERAL RULES. ▸ Parties to a contract may be persons, partnerships, corporations, or governments. ▸ There may be more than two parties to a contract (e.g., a credit card transaction). ▸ With some exceptions (see Chapter 16), only the parties making a contract have rights or duties under the contract.

STUDY HINTS. ▸ Parties can have special names, such as *promisor* (party making a promise) and *promisee* (party to whom a promise is made); *lessor* (party who leases property) and *lessee* (party to whom property is leased). ▸ Privity of contract means two parties directly contracted with each other.

5. HOW A CONTRACT ARISES

GENERAL RULES. ▸ A contract is created by an agreement. ▸ An agreement is made when an offeror makes an offer, and the offeree accepts the offer by making an acceptance.

STUDY HINTS. ▸ A contract cannot be made without both an offer and an acceptance. ▸ An offer may be made to a particular person or an offer may be made to the public. ▸ Example of a public offer: an owner's offer to pay a reward to anyone who returns the owner's lost pet.

6. INTENT TO MAKE A BINDING AGREEMENT

GENERAL RULE. Formation of a contract requires that both the offeror and the offeree intend to enter into a legally binding agreement.

LIMITATIONS. A contract is not created by: (1) a preliminary agreement; or (2) an agreement that states future plans of the parties but does not obligate the parties to perform such plans; or (3) statements that merely indicate the parties' desire to do something without actually obligating them to do it.

B. CLASSES OF CONTRACTS

A contract may be classified according to: (1) the form of the contract; (2) how the contract was created; (3) the validity or binding nature of the contract or agreement; (4) the extent to which the contract has been performed; or (5) how the offer to contract may be accepted.

7. FORMAL AND INFORMAL CONTRACTS

GENERAL RULE.   Classified according to its form, a contract may be either a:

- *Formal contract*: ▸ A formal contract is a: (1) contract under seal (seal or equivalent mark is made on or attached to an agreement); (2) contract of record (agreement recorded with a court, such as an agreement to forfeit a bond if a party does not appear at a trial, or an agreement made with an administrative agency); or (3) negotiable instrument (contract that satisfies certain commercial law requirements, such as a check); or
- *Informal (simple) contract*: any contract other than a formal contract.

LIMITATION.   The UCC, for sales of goods, and statutes in some states do not recognize the binding nature of seals; i.e., agreements are not legally binding merely because they are under seal.
STUDY HINTS.   ▸ Formal and informal contracts are both legally enforceable. ▸ Unless expressly required by law, the typical contract is legally binding even if it is not sealed.

8. EXPRESS AND IMPLIED CONTRACTS

GENERAL RULE.   Classified according to how a contract is created, a simple contract may be either an:

- *Express contract*: agreement is formed by the oral or written words of the parties; or
- *Implied (implied in fact) contract*: agreement is formed by the conduct of the parties.

LIMITATIONS.   ▸ An implied contract cannot arise if an express contract relating to the subject matter in question already exists. ▸ An implied contractual duty to pay does not generally arise if a person receives a service or goods from a family member and the service or goods were intended as a gift. Example: son gratuitously brings meals to and takes care of his elderly father.
STUDY HINTS.   ▸ Express and implied contracts are both legally enforceable, and they have the same basic legal effect. ▸ An implied contract arises if a person does a service for another party with an expectation of payment, and the other party accepts the service knowing that payment is expected.

9. VALID AND VOIDABLE CONTRACTS AND VOID AGREEMENTS

GENERAL RULE.   Classified according to its validity, a contract or agreement is either a:

- *Valid contract*: legally binding contract that is made in accordance with all legal requirements;
- *Voidable contract*: contract that may be set aside by a party because of circumstances surrounding the making of the contract or because a party lacked contractual capacity (examples: a contract made by a party as the result of fraudulent conduct by the other contracting party or a minor's contract to buy a camera or clothing; or
- *Void agreement*: agreement that is of no legal effect; frequently an illegal agreement.

STUDY HINT.   A void agreement cannot be made valid by a subsequent ratification (approval).

10. EXECUTED AND EXECUTORY CONTRACTS

Classified according to the degree that it has been performed, a contract is either an:

- ***Executed contract***: contract that has been fully performed; or
- ***Executory contract***: contract that has not been fully performed by all parties.

11. BILATERAL AND UNILATERAL CONTRACTS

GENERAL RULE. Classified according to how an offeree can accept an offer, a contract is a:

- ***Bilateral contract***: contract is formed by an offeree's accepting an offer by making the requested promise; or
- ***Unilateral contract***: contract is formed by an offeree's accepting an offer by actually doing the requested act.

LIMITATION. An offeree cannot accept an offer for a unilateral contract by promising to do an act; an offer for a unilateral contract can be accepted only by performing the requested act.

STUDY HINTS. ▸ Whether an offer is for a bilateral or unilateral contract is determined by the offeror's intent; focus on what the offeror is demanding in return for his or her promise. ▸ Two types of bilateral contracts are: (1) an *option contract* which grants a person the legal right (but not obligation) to accept an existing offer; and (2) a *right of first refusal contract* which grants a party a right to accept an offer if and when the offer is made.

12. QUASI CONTRACTS

GENERAL RULES. ▸ Quasi contract is a contract implied by law (i.e., by a court) to prevent unjust enrichment. ▸ Elements generally required to establish quasi contract are: (1) plaintiff gave a nongratuitous benefit (good or service) to the defendant; (2) the defendant realized an actual benefit; and (3) it would be unfair to allow the defendant to keep the benefit without paying for it.

LIMITATIONS. ▸ Quasi contract requires a party to pay only the reasonable value for the benefit received; it does not require a party to reimburse the other party for all expenses or losses that the other party may have incurred. ▸ In general, quasi contract will *not* permit a party to recover:

- the value of every benefit that is given to another person (unjust enrichment must be proven);
- the unexpected cost of labor or materials that a party must pay in order to perform a contract;
- a greater amount than is required to be paid by an existing express contract (in other words, in an express contract, *quantum meruit* recovery for the reasonable value of a benefit that is given is not allowed; only the stated contract price can be recovered);
- the value of a benefit that is given to a third party pursuant to a contract between two other parties; or
- the value of goods or services that were given as a gift.

STUDY HINTS. ▸ Quasi contract may require payment for a benefit even though there is not a valid express or implied contract that requires payment. ▸ Recovery under quasi contract does not require proof that the defendant did anything wrong. ▸ When appropriate, quasi-contractual relief may be given if: (1) a benefit is given by mistake; (2) a benefit is given (but not paid for) in expectation of the making of a contract which is never made; or (3) a benefit is given (but not paid for) pursuant to a voidable or void contract that is subsequently set aside.

CHAPTER 9

REVIEW OF TERMS AND PHRASES

Select the term or phrase that best matches a statement or definition stated below. Each term or phrase is the best match for only one statement or definition.

Terms and Phrases

a. Bilateral contract
b. Executory contract
c. Express contract
d. Formal contract
e. Implied contract
f. Informal (simple) contract
g. Offeree
h. Offeror
i. Privity of contract
j. *Quantum meruit*
k. Quasi contract
l. Unilateral contract
m. Valid contract
n. Voidable contract
o. Void agreement

Statements and Definitions

____ 1. Contract that is formed by an offeree's accepting an offer by promising to do a requested act.

____ 2. Contract that is created by the conduct of the parties.

____ 3. Contract that may be avoided by a party because it was not properly formed.

____ 4. Contract implied in law in order to avoid unjust enrichment.

____ 5. Party who makes an offer.

____ 6. Remedy allowing a party to recover for the reasonable value of services or goods.

____ 7. Agreement that is of no legal effect.

____ 8. Contract that is created by a written or oral agreement.

____ 9. Legally binding contract that cannot be set aside by a party.

____ 10. Party to whom an offer is made.

____ 11. Contract that is formed by an offeree's accepting an offer by doing a requested act.

____ 12. Relationship between two parties who have entered into a contract with one another.

____ 13. Contract that is legally binding because of the formality with which it is executed, such as a contract under seal.

____ 14. Contract that has not been fully performed by the contracting parties.

____ 15. Any contract that is not a formal contract.

REVIEW OF CONCEPTS

Write **T** if the statement is true, write **F** if it is false.

_____ 1. Every agreement is a valid, legally binding contract.

_____ 2. Contracts may relate to virtually any type of legal transaction, including performing services.

_____ 3. Individuals and corporations can make contracts, but government agencies cannot.

_____ 4. An agreement that does not actually obligate the parties to do anything is not a binding contract.

_____ 5. In general, an agreement is not a legally binding contract unless the parties sufficiently indicate an intent to be legally bound by the terms of the agreement.

_____ 6. Statutes in some states no longer recognize the binding nature of seals.

_____ 7. Informal contracts are not legally binding.

_____ 8. An offeree cannot accept an offer for a *bilateral contract* by merely promising to do the act requested by the offeror.

_____ 9. An offeree cannot accept an offer for a *unilateral contract* by merely promising to do the act requested by the offeror.

_____ 10. An option contract is a contract that gives one party the right or choice to accept an existing offer within a stated period of time.

_____ 11. A right of first refusal contract gives a party the right to accept an offer only if another party subsequently decides to make the offer.

_____ 12. An offeree can accept an offer for a bilateral contract by promising to perform the requested act. A contract is formed when the offeree communicates this promise to the offeror.

_____ 13. In some cases, a party may have a duty under quasi contract to pay for benefits received even though the party never contractually agreed to pay for such benefits.

_____ 14. Quasi contract requires that a person must pay for any benefit that is ever received from another.

_____ 15. If a party enters into an express contract agreeing to perform services for a stated price, then that party is entitled to recover only that amount; the party is not entitled to use the remedy of *quantum meruit* to recover the reasonable value for such services.

REVIEW OF CHAPTER - APPLICATION OF CONCEPTS

MULTIPLE CHOICE QUESTIONS

_____ 1. Bruce and Seller were negotiating Bruce's proposed purchase of a grocery store from Seller. In which situation did the parties manifest the necessary intent to enter into a legally binding contract for the sale of the store?
   a. Bruce and Seller signed a complete, definite agreement whereby Bruce agreed to buy the store from Seller and Seller agreed to sell the store to Bruce upon the terms stated in the agreement.
   b. Bruce and Seller signed a preliminary agreement whereby they indicated their intention to continue to negotiate terms for the sale of the store.
   c. Bruce and Seller signed an agreement whereby Bruce indicated his desire to buy the store from Seller and Seller indicated his desire to sell the store to Bruce upon terms that the parties would later agree upon.
   d. a and c.

_____ 2. An implied contract is created in which of the following situations?
   a. Abe voluntarily helped to paint his parents' fence.
   b. Bob and Pamela entered into a complete, written contract for the sale of Bob's car to Pamela.
   c. Rosa and Nan made an oral contract whereby Nan agreed to clean Rosa's home for $70.
   d. Kim requested Pete's Pest Control to fumigate her home, and Pete's did as requested. There was no express contract, but Pete's expected payment and Kim was aware of this expectation.

_____ 3. Chris agreed to sell stolen goods to Gray, and Gray agreed to buy the goods. Under these facts:
   a. This agreement is a void agreement.
   b. This agreement is a voidable contract.
   c. This agreement is a valid contract.
   d. This agreement is legally enforceable if Chris and Gray subsequently ratify the agreement.

_____ 4. Jackie offered to pay Glen $500 in consideration for Glen's complete trimming of all trees located on Jackie's property. This offer is an offer for a unilateral contract. Under these facts:
   a. Glen can accept the offer by promising to trim the trees.
   b. Glen can accept the offer by completely trimming the trees.
   c. Glen can accept the offer by promising to trim the trees or by completely trimming the trees.
   d. Glen cannot accept the offer; offers for unilateral contracts are illegal.

_____ 5. Diane and Rick entered into a signed, written contract whereby Diane promised to sell a motel to Rick for $200,000 and Rick promised to pay Diane $200,000 for the motel. Rick then paid the $200,000 purchase price to Diane, but Diane has not conveyed title to the motel to Rick. Under these facts:
   a. This contract is a formal contract.
   b. This contract is an executed contract.
   c. This contract is a bilateral contract.
   d. There is no contract until Diane conveys title to the motel to Rick.

6. Laurie is the owner of the High Water Cafe. Laurie promised to pay a $5,000 retirement bonus to i piano player, Ike, as gratitude for his many years of music, and he accepted her gesture with gre humility. Ike did not promise anything in return. Laurie later reneged on her promise and refused t pay the bonus to Ike. Under these facts, Laurie's promise is:
   a. Legally enforceable because promises are legally binding on a promisor.
   b. Legally enforceable because Ike agreed to accept it and agreements are legally binding on the parties to the agreement.
   c. Legally enforceable because the promise was made as part of a contract and contracts are legally enforceable.
   d. Legally unenforceable because the promise was not made as part of a contract.

7. Dick offered to sell his car to Jacqueline for $2,000 and she accepted the offer by promising to pay the requested price. Both parties were competent to make a contract, and they drew up the contract in the proper form. Under these facts, this contract is:
   a. Valid.
   b. Voidable.
   c. Void.
   d. Unenforceable.

8. Kirk offered to sell his video store to Edward for $50,000 and Edward accepted. Both parties were competent and the contract was in proper form. However, Kirk fraudulently lied about the past profits of the business. Under these facts, the contract is:
   a. Valid.
   b. Voidable.
   c. Void.
   d. Unenforceable.

9. In a signed writing, Patty offered to sell her business to Carol for $50,000. In this same writing, Patty promised not to revoke this offer for 30 days in exchange for $500 paid by Carol. Under these facts:
   a. The parties have entered into a legally enforceable quasi contract.
   b. The parties have entered into a legally enforceable right of first refusal.
   c. The parties have entered into a legally enforceable option contract.
   d. The parties have entered into a legally unenforceable future agreement.

10. Which of the following agreements is a formal contract?
    a. A contract to sell an office building.
    b. An invitation to a formal wedding reception.
    c. A defendant's agreement to pay a $5,000 fine, which agreement is recorded with a court.
    d. A notarized will.

Martha promised to buy Josh, her son, a car when he graduated from college. Josh did not promise to do anything in exchange for this promise. Years later, Josh graduated from college and he demanded that Martha buy him a car as she had promised years before. Martha refused. Under these facts, did Martha have a legal obligation to purchase the car for Josh?
   a. Yes. Martha promised to buy Josh a car when he graduated from college.
   b. Yes. Martha and Josh entered into a contract regarding the purchase of the car.
   c. Yes. Martha had a quasi contractual obligation to purchase the car for Josh.
   d. No. Martha and Josh did not enter into a legally enforceable contract regarding the purchase of the car.

_____ 12. Larry owned an apartment building and he rented one apartment to Rhonda. Larry contracted with Ace Painters to have Rhonda's apartment painted. Ace painted Rhonda's unit, but Larry refused to pay Ace. Under these facts:
   a. Larry has a contractual obligation to pay Ace for painting Rhonda's apartment.
   b. Rhonda has a contractual obligation to pay Ace for painting her apartment.
   c. Rhonda has a quasi contractual obligation to pay Ace for painting her apartment.
   d. a and c.

_____ 13. Select the correct answer regarding quasi contract?
   a. Quasi contract relief is not available unless parties have entered into a legally enforceable contract.
   b. Quasi contract relief is available even though parties have not entered into a legally enforceable contract.
   c. Quasi contract relief is available whenever one party receives a benefit from someone else.
   d. b and c.

CASE PROBLEM

Answer the following question, briefly explaining your answer.

Dan drove his car to Ty's Garage and requested Ty's to fix the radio. Before leaving, Dan noticed a mechanic getting ready to work on his car's engine. Dan overheard the mechanic say that he was going to overhaul the engine. Dan did not say anything to correct this mistake. When Dan returned, Ty's had overhauled the engine. The reasonable value of this work was $500. Ty's demanded $750, which included damages for profits Ty's lost because it worked on Dan's car instead of working on other jobs.

Under these facts: (a) Should Dan be required by quasi contract to pay for the engine overhaul? (b) If Dan is required to pay, how much must Dan pay?

_____

_____

_____

_____

_____

CHAPTER 10
THE AGREEMENT

CHAPTER OUTLINE

A. REQUIREMENTS OF AN OFFER

▸ One element of a contract is a valid agreement. An agreement is comprised of a valid offer made by an offeror and a valid acceptance made by an offeree. ▸ An offer is a promise that is given in exchange for (1) an act, (2) forbearance (refraining from doing an act one can legally do), or (3) a return promise.

1. CONTRACTUAL INTENTION

GENERAL RULES. ▸ A requirement for a valid offer is that the offeror objectively (outwardly) express the intent to be bound by the offer if it is accepted by the offeree. ▸ These expressions do *not* typically indicate the required intent and they are not offers: (1) social invitations; (2) statements made in fun or excitement; (3) invitations to negotiate, such as advertisements to sell, circulars, catalogs, invitations for bids, and price quotes; (4) statements indicating only an intention to do something later; and (5) agreements to make a contract in the future or to contract upon terms that will be agreed upon later.
LIMITATION. A price quotation may be an offer due to a trade custom or due to prior dealings between the parties in which they viewed a price quotation as being an offer.

2. DEFINITENESS

GENERAL RULES. ▸ An offer must be definite and certain. To be definite and certain an offer must indicate the important terms of the proposed contract. ▸ An offer is sufficiently definite if necessary terms: (1) are stated in writings that are referred to or incorporated into the contract; (2) can be determined by reference to prior dealings between the parties or trade customs; or (3) are implied by law or by the parties' conduct. ▸ Output and requirements contracts are sufficiently definite.
LIMITATIONS. ▸ An offer may be sufficiently definite even if it contains a vague term, if the term is unimportant. ▸ An offer is sufficiently definite if it states an objective standard or formula by which terms can be determined. Example: "blue book" price for a car. ▸ If a divisible contract is partially indefinite, a court may enforce the definite portion and not enforce the indefinite portion.
STUDY HINT. An offer is invalid and cannot form a contract if important terms: (1) are missing;

(2) are so vague that their meaning cannot be determined; or (3) are left to be agreed upon later.

3. COMMUNICATION OF OFFER TO OFFEREE

GENERAL RULE. An offer must be communicated to the offeree.
STUDY HINT. ▸ A unilateral contract is not formed by a party doing an act if the party did not know of the offer at the time the act was performed. ▸ Example: Lisa returned a ring, not knowing that a reward was offered for return of the ring. In this case, a contract is not formed.

B. TERMINATION OF OFFER

An offer may be terminated in several ways. An offer cannot be accepted after it has been terminated.

...ATION OF OFFER BY OFFEROR

...ERAL RULES. ▸ An offeror can revoke an offer at any time before the offer has been accepted. ▸ A revocation may result from the words or conduct of the offeror that clearly indicate the offeror's intent to terminate the offer.

LIMITATION. An offeror's right to revoke an offer may be limited by: (1) an option contract (binding promise to keep an offer open); (2) a firm offer (signed, written promise by a merchant not to revoke an offer to buy or sell goods); or (3) detrimental reliance on the offer by the offeree.

STUDY HINTS. ▸ In most states a revocation is not effective until received. ▸ A subcontractor cannot revoke a bid that has been detrimentally relied upon by a general contractor.

5. COUNTEROFFER BY OFFEREE

GENERAL RULES. ▸ A counteroffer is a manifestation by an offeree that an offer is not acceptable and that the offeree is offering to contract on terms that are different from those stated in the offer. ▸ A counteroffer terminates the original offer, and it constitutes a new offer. ▸ A contract is formed if the original offeror accepts a counteroffer.

STUDY HINT. An attempted "acceptance" (conditional acceptance) that states terms in addition to those stated in the offer or that changes any terms of the offer is actually a counteroffer.

6. REJECTION OF OFFER BY OFFEREE

A rejection is an offeree's expression that an offer is unacceptable. A rejection terminates an offer.

7. LAPSE OF TIME

An offer that is not accepted automatically terminates upon: (1) expiration of the time stated in the offer; or (2) if no time is stated in the offer, within a reasonable time after the offer is made.

8. DEATH OR DISABILITY OF EITHER PARTY

An offer is terminated if either party dies or becomes insane before the offer is accepted.

9. SUBSEQUENT ILLEGALITY

An offer is terminated if the contract's subject matter becomes illegal before the offer is accepted.

C. ACCEPTANCE OF OFFER

10. WHAT CONSTITUTES AN ACCEPTANCE

An acceptance is a clear expression that the offeree agrees to be bound by the terms of the offer.

11. PRIVILEGE OF OFFEREE

GENERAL RULE. Ordinarily, an offeree is not legally required to accept an offer.

LIMITATION. In general, an offeree cannot reject an offer: (1) for public utilities, or public accommodations if there is room available; (2) because of the offeror's race, religion, national origin, color, or disability; or (3) for advertised goods or services if rejection is forbidden by consumer laws.

12. EFFECT OF ACCEPTANCE

GENERAL RULE. Acceptance of an offer creates a contract if all other contract elements are present.
STUDY HINT. Once a contract is made, one party cannot unilaterally terminate or change it.

13. NATURE OF ACCEPTANCE

GENERAL RULES. ▸ An acceptance is a definite, unconditional expression of intent by an offeree to agree to the terms of the offer. ▸ At common law, an acceptance must accept all terms of the offer without changing or adding any terms.

LIMITATION. An acceptance with an additional term may form a contract if the term: (1) is implied by law; (2) relates to a minor matter not affecting any rights; or (3) only requests a favor.

STUDY HINTS. ▸ An acceptance may be made by words or conduct. ▸ An offeree's intent is determined by the offeree's objective (outward) intent, not by subjective or secret intentions.

14. WHO MAY ACCEPT

An offer can be accepted by only: (1) the person to whom the offer is made; or (2) a member of a class to whom the offer is made.

15. MANNER OF ACCEPTANCE

GENERAL RULE. If an offeror states a required, exclusive manner for acceptance, the offeree must accept in this manner. Failure to accept in the required manner renders an acceptance ineffective.

LIMITATION. Failure to accept in a manner stated by the offeror does not invalidate an acceptance if: (1) the manner of acceptance stated by the offeror was a suggestion, not a requirement; or (2) the offeror acts as if a contract has been formed.

STUDY HINTS. ▸ A failure to respond to an unsolicited offer and a failure to return unordered goods received in the mail do not constitute acceptances. ▸ Silence is usually not a valid acceptance.

16. COMMUNICATION OF ACCEPTANCE

- In general, an acceptance of an offer for a unilateral contract is not required to be communicated.
- An acceptance of a bilateral contract offer must be communicated in order to form a contract.

17. ACCEPTANCE BY MAIL OR TELEGRAPH

GENERAL RULES. ▸ The UCC and the modern trend is that an acceptance can be communicated in any manner and using any method of communication that is reasonable. Thus, an acceptance generally can be sent by mail unless the offeror requires otherwise. ▸ Under the "mailbox rule," an acceptance is effective when it is properly mailed. Example: Tim deposits an acceptance in the mail on May 1, and it is received by the offeror on May 8. The acceptance was effective on May 1.

LIMITATIONS. ▸ A specific medium of communication may be expressly required by an offeror. ▸ An acceptance is not effective until it is received if: (1) the offer expressly states this; (2) the offeree is also required to send a payment with the acceptance; or (3) the acceptance is not properly mailed.

18. ACCEPTANCE BY TELEPHONE

An offer can be accepted by telephone unless a written writing is required by the offeror or by law.

19. ELECTRONIC ACCEPTANCE BY E-MAIL OR FAX

Although the law is still unsettled, it is likely that acceptances by e-mail, fax, or other electronic memos are governed by the same rules that apply to acceptances sent by mail or telephone.

20. AUCTION SALES

GENERAL RULES. ▸ Placing goods for sale at an auction is merely an invitation to negotiate. ▸ A bid at an auction is an offer. A contract is formed only when the auctioneer accepts the bid.

STUDY HINT. An auctioneer can refuse to sell any item unless the sale is conducted "without reserve." If an auction is without reserve, property must be sold to the highest bidder.

REVIEW OF TERMS AND PHRASES

MATCHING EXERCISE

...ne term or phrase that best matches a statement or definition stated below. Each term or phrase is the ...atch for only one statement or definition.

Terms and Phrases

a. Acceptance
b. Counteroffer
c. Firm offer
d. Lapse of time
e. Offer

f. Option contract
g. Output contract
h. Rejection
i. Requirements contract
j. Revocation

Statements and Definitions

____ 1. Merchant's signed, written offer to buy or sell goods that promises that the offer will not be revoked for a period of time, not to exceed three months.

____ 2. Offeree's expression that both rejects an offer and constitutes an offer by the offeree to contract upon different terms.

____ 3. Contract by which one party promises not to revoke an offer to enter into another contract for a stated period of time. Consideration must be given for the promise not to revoke.

____ 4. Offeree's manifestation that an offer is not acceptable.

____ 5. Contract to sell the entire production of a seller to a buyer.

____ 6. Termination of an offer by an offeror.

____ 7. Offeror's proposal to enter into a contract regarding a specific subject matter.

____ 8. Offeree's agreement to the terms of an offer.

____ 9. Expiration of time within which a party can accept an offer.

____ 10. Contract by a buyer to purchase goods necessary to meet the good faith needs of the buyer.

COMPLETION EXERCISE

Fill in the blanks with the words that most accurately complete each statement. Answers may or may not include terms used in the matching exercise. A term cannot be used to complete more than one statement.

1. The _____ _____ generally provides that an acceptance that is properly mailed is effective when it is deposited in the mail.

2. A _____ _____ is a contract that is comprised of two or more parts, with

3. The intent of contracting parties is determined by the parties' _____ (outward) _____.

4. An auctioneer must sell a good that is being auctioned to the highest bidder if the auction is conducted _____ _____.

5. Ajax Coal Mines contracts to sell its entire 1999 production of coal to Newark Public Service Co. This contract is an example of an _____ _____.

6. Gee Whiz Car Manufacturer contracts to buy all of the tires that it needs for its 1998 Hurricane automobile from Generic Tire Co. This contract is an example of a _____ _____.

7. An agreement is comprised of a valid _____ and a valid _____.

8. In general, if an "acceptance" states terms that are different from the terms stated in the offer, then the acceptance is actually a _____.

9. A _____ is an offeror's termination of an offer.

10. Unless otherwise stated, an offer lapses (expires) a _____ _____ after the offer was made.

REVIEW OF CONCEPTS

Write **T** if the statement is true, write **F** if it is false.

____ 1. A government agency's request for bids for a government construction project does not constitute an offer to contract.

____ 2. Absent special circumstances, price quotations are typically invitations to negotiate, not offers.

____ 3. An agreement to sell land on terms to be agreed upon by the seller and buyer at a later date is sufficiently definite to be a contract.

____ 4. An offer is sufficiently definite if the important terms of the proposed contract are stated in the offer or would be implied from the parties' conduct.

____ 5. An offer to hire an attorney to provide all of the legal services that a client may require during a specified period of time in consideration for a stated fee may be sufficiently definite to form a contract.

____ 6. An offer is not required to be communicated to the offeree.

____ 7. In general, an offeror cannot revoke an offer without first allowing the offeree a reasonable time within which to accept the offer.

____ 8. Terri offered to sell land to Ben. Terri then sold the land to Roger, and a third party informed Ben of this sale. In this situation, Terri effectively revoked her offer to sell the land to Ben.

____ 9. An option contract is not formed unless an offeree gives consideration (legal value) for the offeror's promise not to revoke his or her offer.

____ 9. An option contract is not formed unless an offeree gives consideration (legal value) for the offeror's promise not to revoke his or her offer.

____ 10. Under the UCC, a merchant cannot make a firm offer that restricts the merchant's right to revoke an offer to buy or sell goods.

____ 11. An offeree cannot accept an offer after the offer has been revoked or rejected.

____ 12. In certain situations an offeree may have a legal duty to accept an offer.

____ 13. Anyone who learns of an offer from any source is legally entitled to accept the offer.

____ 14. An acceptance may form a contract even if it contains a term that is not stated in the offer, if the term in question would be implied by law into the contract.

____ 15. An acceptance is not effective if it is made in a manner that is different from the exclusive manner of acceptance clearly required by the offeror.

____ 16. An offeree's silence, i.e., failure to respond to an offer, constitutes a valid acceptance if the offeror clearly stated in the offer that such silence would constitute an acceptance.

____ 17. An acceptance of an offer for a bilateral contract must be communicated to form a contract.

____ 18. The mailbox rule generally provides that an acceptance that is mailed is not effective until it is received by the offeror.

____ 19. If an acceptance is mailed and it is not properly addressed, then it is not effective until it is received by the offeror.

____ 20. An acceptance made by telephone is effective when and where it is spoken into the telephone.

REVIEW OF CHAPTER - APPLICATION OF CONCEPTS

MULTIPLE CHOICE QUESTIONS

____ 1. Which action manifests the necessary contractual intent to constitute a valid offer?
   a. Carlos offers to take Mandy to the movies on a date.
   b. In response to Homeowner's request, Contractor submits a signed bid to Homeowner to do certain described remodeling work for $5,000.
   c. Central City posts a notice inviting contractors to submit bids to construct a new city hall.
   d. Henry distributes circulars stating that he will shampoo carpeting for $10 per room.

____ 2. Which proposal is too indefinite to be a valid offer?
   a. Red proposes to sell a company to Melanie for a price to be mutually agreed upon in 30 days.
   b. Luis proposes to sell ten ounces of gold to Tony at a price equal to the closing bid price stated by the Bank of New York on January 1, 1999.
   c. Farmer proposes to sell his entire 1999 apple crop to Co-op for $5 per bushel.
   d. Wholesaler signs a written proposal to sell Buyer ten items of equipment for $2,000 cash. The proposal refers to and incorporates another writing that identifies the equipment.

_____ 3. In which case was Alex legally entitled to revoke his offer?
   a. Alex offered to sell a business to Will. Alex promised not to revoke the offer for 24 hours in consideration for $100 paid by Will. One hour later and before Will had accepted, Alex revoked his offer, and he offered to return the $100 to Will.
   b. Alex (a subcontractor) submitted a bid to Contractor for certain work to be done on a project for which Contractor intended to bid. Contractor detrimentally relied on Alex's bid in connection with bidding for the project. Alex then revoked his bid.
   c. In a signed writing, Alex (a merchant) offered to sell Liz a car and promised not to revoke the offer for 48 hours. One hour later and before Liz accepted, Alex revoked his offer.
   d. Alex offered to sell his condo to Ben. One hour later and before Ben accepted, Alex revoked his offer.

_____ 4. Select the correct answer.
   a. Ike offered to sell a patent to Ken. Before Ken accepted the offer, Ike died. In this case, Ike's offer was not terminated, and Ken can still accept the offer.
   b. R&R Co. offered to sell some chemicals to Lex. Before Lex accepted the offer, Congress passed a law making the sale of the chemicals illegal. In this case, the offer was terminated.
   c. Tom offered to sell a business to Jack. The offer stated that the offer would lapse on September 1. On September 2, Jack accepted the offer. In this case, a contract was formed.
   d. Vicky offered to sell a TV to Carl. Carl replied, "No, the price is too high." Then Carl reconsidered, and he accepted the offer. In this case, a contract was formed.

_____ 5. Seller offered to sell certain land to Joe for $90,000. Which of the following expressions by Joe would *not* be a valid acceptance of the offer?
   a. In writing Joe stated: "I accept the offer, provided that Seller must deliver good title to the land." (You may assume that this new term would be implied by applicable state law.)
   b. In writing Joe stated: "I accept the offer provided that the price is reduced to $89,000."
   c. In writing Joe stated: "I accept the offer. Also, I would appreciate a tour of the property."
   d. In writing Joe stated: "I accept the offer. Also, I request that I be given a copy of the signed documents for my files."

_____ 6. In which case does Tara effectively accept the offer in question?
   a. Plantco mailed Tara a box of tulip bulbs, together with an offer to sell the bulbs to Tara. Tara had not ordered the bulbs, and she did not expressly accept Plantco's offer. However, Tara did not return the bulbs to Plantco.
   b. Sam offered to sell a car to Tara. The offer stated that Tara's failure to expressly reject the offer within 24 hours would be an acceptance. Tara was silent, and she did not expressly reject the offer.
   c. Bob mailed an offer to sell a motorcycle to Tara. Immediately upon receiving the offer, Tara mailed back a definite, unconditional acceptance of the offer.
   d. All of the above.

_____ 7. On April 1, Gina mailed Oscar an offer to buy his home. Oscar received the offer on April 5. On April 6, Oscar deposited a properly addressed, stamped acceptance in the mail. Gina received the acceptance on April 10. On April 8, Gina changed her mind, and she personally delivered a written revocation of the offer to Oscar. In most states:
   a. A contract was formed on April 5.
   b. A contract was formed on April 6.
   c. A contract was formed on April 10.
   d. A contract was not formed.

CHAPTER 10

CASE PROBLEMS

Answer the following problems, briefly explaining your answers.

1. Seller advertised some land for sale. In response, Bart delivered a signed, written purchase offer to Seller. The offer appeared to be sincere, and it stated all of the contract terms, except it did not state when the price would be paid. (State law would imply that payment must be made when title is delivered.) Unknown to Seller, Bart did not actually intend to buy the land unless he first obtained certain financing. Seller accepted Bart's offer. (a) Was Seller's advertisement an offer? (b) Did Bart manifest a sufficient contractual intent to be bound by his purchase offer? (c) Was Bart's purchase offer sufficiently definite to form a contract? (d) What was the effect of Seller's acceptance?

2. Fawn offered to sell a carpet-cleaning franchise to Missy. Fawn mailed the offer to Missy via first-class U.S. mail. The offer was silent regarding the required manner of acceptance. (a) Can Missy accept the offer by remaining silent, or must she communicate an acceptance to Fawn? (b) Under modern rules, how can Missy communicate an acceptance of the offer? (c) When will Fawn's offer lapse? (d) If Missy sends an acceptance via first-class U.S. mail, when will the acceptance be effective?

3. Henry, an auctioneer, conducted an auction of certain goods. The auction was a standard auction; it was *not* conducted without reserve. At the auction the following occurred:

    (a) Henry invited bids for a table. Felix bid $25 for the table, and Henry accepted the bid. Was Henry's invitation for bids an offer to sell? Was a contract formed?

    (b) Henry invited bids for an antique chair. Rene's $300 bid was the highest bid. However, Henry was not satisfied with this bid, and he refused to sell the chair to Rene. Was Henry legally required to sell the chair to Rene?

CPA REVIEW

The following questions were given on past CPA examinations. The answers for these questions are the unofficial answers prepared by the American Institute of Certified Public Accountants, Inc. (AICPA). All material is reproduced with permission of the AICPA.

_____ 1. On February 12, Harris sent Fresno a written offer to purchase Fresno's land. The offer included the following provision: "Acceptance of this offer must be by registered or certified mail, received by Harris no later than February 18 by 5:00 p.m. CST." On February 18, Fresno sent Harris a letter accepting the offer by private overnight delivery service. Harris received the letter on February 19. Which of the following statements is correct?
    a. A contract was formed on February 19.
    b. Fresno's letter constituted a counteroffer.
    c. Fresno's use of the overnight delivery service was an effective form of acceptance.
    d. A contract was formed on February 18 regardless of when Harris actually received Fresno's letter.

_____ 2. On June 15, Peters orally offered to sell a used lawn mower to Mason for $125. Peters specified that Mason had until June 20 to accept the offer. On June 16, Peters received an offer to purchase the lawn mower for $150 from Bronson, Mason's neighbor. Peters accepted Bronson's offer. On June 17, Mason saw Bronson using the lawn mower and was told the mower had been sold to Bronson. Mason immediately wrote to Peters to accept the June 15 offer. Which of the following statements is correct?
    a. Mason's acceptance would be effective when received by Peters.
    b. Mason's acceptance would be effective when mailed.
    c. Peters' offer had been revoked and Mason's acceptance was ineffective.
    d. Peters was obligated to keep the June 15 offer open until June 20.

_____ 3. Kraft Corp. published circulars containing price quotes and a description of products which it would like to sell. Rice, a prospective customer, demands the right to purchase one of the products at the quoted price. Which of the following statements is correct under general contract law?
    a. Kraft must sell the product which Rice demands at the quoted price.
    b. Rice has accepted Kraft's firm offer to sell.
    c. Kraft has made an offer.
    d. Rice has made an offer.

_____ 4. Carson Corp., a retail chain, asked Alto Construction to fix a broken window at one of Carson's stores. Alto offered to make the repairs within three days at a price to be agreed on after the work was completed. A contract based on Alto's offer would fail because of indefiniteness as to the
    a. Price involved.
    b. Nature of the subject matter.
    c. Parties to the contract.
    d. Time for performance.

5. Nix sent Castor a letter offering to employ Castor as controller of Nix's automobile dealership. Castor received the letter on February 19. The letter provided that Castor would have until February 23 to consider the offer and, in the meantime, Nix would not withdraw it. On February 20, Nix, after reconsidering the offer to Castor, decided to offer the job to Vick, who accepted immediately. That same day, Nix called Castor and revoked the offer. Castor told Nix that an acceptance of Nix's offer was mailed on February 19. Under the circumstances,
    a. Nix's offer was irrevocable until February 23.
    b. No contract was formed between Nix and Castor because Nix revoked the offer before Nix received Castor's acceptance.
    c. Castor's acceptance was effective when mailed.
    d. Any revocation of the offer would have to be in writing because Nix's offer was in writing.

6. On September 27, Summers sent Fox a letter offering to sell Fox a vacation home for $150,000. On October 2, Fox replied by mail agreeing to buy the home for $145,000. Summers did not reply to Fox. Do Fox and Summers have a binding contract?
    a. No, because Fox failed to sign and return Summers' letter.
    b. No, because Fox's letter was a counteroffer.
    c. Yes, because Summers' offer was validly accepted.
    d. Yes, because Summers' silence is an implied acceptance of Fox's letter.

7. Opal offered, in writing, to sell Larkin a parcel of land for $300,000. If Opal dies, the offer will
    a. Terminate prior to Larkin's acceptance only if Larkin received notice of Opal's death.
    b. Remain open for a reasonable period of time after Opal's death.
    c. Automatically terminate despite Larkin's prior acceptance.
    d. Automatically terminate prior to Larkin's acceptance.

8. On September 10, Harris, Inc., a new car dealer, placed a newspaper advertisement stating that Harris would sell 10 cars at its showroom for a special discount only on September 12, 13, and 14. On September 12, King called Harris and expressed an interest in buying one of the advertised cars. King was told that five of the cars had been sold and to come to the showroom as soon as possible. On September 13, Harris made a televised announcement that the sale would end at 10:00 PM that night. King went to Harris' showroom on September 14 and demanded the right to buy a car at the special discount. Harris had sold the 10 cars and refused King's demand. King sued Harris for breach of contract. Harris' best defense to King's suit would be that Harris'
    a. Offer was unenforceable.
    b. Advertisement was not an offer.
    c. Television announcement revoked the offer.
    d. Offer had not been accepted.

CHAPTER 11
CAPACITY AND GENUINE ASSENT

CHAPTER OUTLINE

A. CONTRACTUAL CAPACITY

The law generally presumes that everyone has the capacity to contract. But if a party does lack the capacity to do so, then a contract is usually voidable and the incapacitated party may avoid the contract.

1. **CONTRACTUAL CAPACITY DEFINED**

   GENERAL RULES. ▸ Contractual capacity is the ability to understand that a contract is being made and to understand its essential terms. ▸ A person may lack capacity due to: (1) status incapacity, i.e., the person is a member of a group that is legally viewed as lacking capacity; or (2) factual incapacity, i.e., the person is in fact unable to understand the nature and terms of the contract. ▸ Examples: status incapacity: a minor; factual incapacity: a mentally incompetent person.
   STUDY HINT. With the exception of minors, virtually all classes of individuals, such as married women and aliens, now have the capacity to enter into contracts.

2. **MINORS**

   In most states, a minor is a person under the age of 18. A contract made by a minor is generally voidable, and the minor can elect to disaffirm (avoid) the contract subject to the following rules:

   - *Minor's power to avoid contracts*: ▸ Disaffirmance may be express or implied. Example of implied disaffirmance: a minor refuses to perform a contract. ▸ A minor may disaffirm while he or she is a minor, or within a reasonable time after reaching majority. ▸ In most states, a minor can disaffirm even if the minor misrepresented his or her age to the other party.

   - *Restitution by minor after avoidance*: ▸ A minor is required to return benefits only to the extent the minor still has the benefits. ▸ Traditionally: minor is not liable for depreciation to or loss of property received from adult. ▸ Trend: minor is liable if minor is guilty of gross negligence or intentional tort.

   - *Recovery of property by minor on avoidance*: Upon disaffirmance, the other party must (1) repay all money paid by a minor and (2) return all property given by a minor (or pay its fair value).

   - *Contracts for necessaries*: ▸ Necessaries are food, clothing, shelter, and other things required for the proper care of a minor in light of the minor's social status. ▸ Minors can avoid contracts for necessaries, but under quasi contract minors must pay the reasonable value for necessaries. ▸ Some recent decisions have held that goods or services needed to obtain or conduct work are necessaries.

   - *Ratification of former minor's voidable contract*: ▸ Ratification is a definite expression of an intent to be bound by a contract. ▸ A minor can ratify only after attaining his or her majority. ▸ Ratification may result from words or conduct, but some states require it to be written. ▸ A failure to disaffirm a contract within a reasonable time after attaining majority is an implied ratification. ▸ Making payments after attaining one's majority may be a ratification if payments are made with the intent to ratify. ▸ A contract cannot be avoided after it has been ratified.

   - *Contracts that minors cannot avoid*: ▸ Many states do not permit a minor to avoid contracts for education loans, medical care, bank accounts, insurance, or stock. Typically, a minor cannot avoid a contract if it was approved by a court, made in business, or if the minor is a veteran. ▸ In some states, minors can avoid employment contracts, but cannot use an employer's secret information.

- *Liability of third person for minor's contract*: ▸ Parents are not liable for a minor's contracts unless the minor is contracting for the parents, or the contract involves necessaries and the parents have abandoned the minor. ▸ A person who cosigns a contract with a minor remains liable on the contract even if the minor disaffirms the contract.

3. INCOMPETENTS

GENERAL RULES. ▸ An incompetent is a person who is mentally impaired. ▸ An incompetent who cannot understand the legal nature of a contract and its essential terms lacks contractual capacity, and a contract made by this person is generally voidable. ▸ A contract is void if made by an incompetent after a guardian has been appointed to administer the affairs of the incompetent.
LIMITATIONS. ▸ A contract is not voidable if an incompetent understands a contract is being made and the incompetent understands the general nature of the transaction. ▸ A trend forbids rescission if a contract made by an incompetent is reasonable and benefits cannot be returned.
STUDY HINTS. ▸ Incompetency may result from any physical condition or psychological disorder. ▸ An incompetent can ratify a contract once his or her disability is overcome.

4. INTOXICATED PERSONS

A person lacks contractual capacity if due to intoxication he or she cannot understand that a contract is being made. Under these circumstances, the contract is voidable and it can be rescinded.

B. MISTAKE

5. UNILATERAL MISTAKE

GENERAL RULE. A unilateral mistake (mistake by one party) does *not* render a contract voidable.
LIMITATIONS. ▸ A contract can be rescinded if one party knows or has reason to know of the other party's unilateral mistake of fact. ▸ A few courts allow rescission due to a unilateral mistake unless (1) the mistake is unreasonable or (2) the other party has detrimentally relied on the contract.

6. MUTUAL MISTAKE

GENERAL RULE. A contract is void if both parties are mistaken regarding a material fact.
LIMITATION. In most cases, a contract's validity is not affected by mistakes regarding expectations or matters of law, such as a mistake regarding the permissible, legal use of property.

C. DECEPTION

7. INNOCENT MISREPRESENTATION

GENERAL RULE. Equity permits a party to rescind a contract if he or she was induced into making the contract by the other party's innocent misrepresentation of a material fact.
STUDY HINT. An innocent misrepresentation is a false statement that is made by a party who does not know or have reason to know that the statement is false.

8. NONDISCLOSURE

In general, a party has no duty to voluntarily disclose information to the other party. However, a failure to conform to the following duties may render a contract voidable:

- *Unknown defect*: A party must disclose facts relating to important defects or other negative matters if these facts are unknown to, and cannot be readily discovered by, the other party.
- *Confidential relationship*: If the contracting parties are in a confidential relationship (a relationship of trust and confidence, such as an attorney-client or parent-child relationship), the party in the position of trust must disclose all important facts to the other party.
- *Active concealment*: A party cannot actively hide an important fact from the other party.

9. FRAUD

GENERAL RULES. ▸ The elements of fraud are: (1) a false statement of fact; (2) made by a party who knows it is false or who has no basis to believe it to be true; (3) with the intent that the other party rely on the statement; (4) the other party does rely on the statement; (5) causing harm to the relying party. ▸ Ordinarily, fraud cannot be based on statements regarding: (1) an opinion; (2) an item's value; (3) a matter of law; or (4) predictions of the future.

LIMITATIONS. ▸ False statements regarding future matters may be fraud if the speaker knows facts that clearly prove the falsity of such statements. Sometimes it is fraud to lie about your intention to do an act in the future. ▸ False statements of law by an attorney may be fraud.

STUDY HINT. Fraud cannot occur without actual reliance on a misrepresentation.

D. PRESSURE

10. UNDUE INFLUENCE

GENERAL RULES. ▸ Undue influence is: (1) domination by one party of another contracting party; (2) that deprives the weaker party of his or her free will; (3) resulting in an unfair contract. ▸ Undue influence is presumed if parties are in a confidential relationship and the dominant party benefits from the contract. To overcome this presumption, the dominant party must prove that the contract was fair.

LIMITATION. Nagging and normal persuasion are not undue influence.

11. DURESS

GENERAL RULES. ▸ Duress is: (1) a wrongful threat or wrongful act by a contracting party; (2) that deprives the other party of his or her free will; (3) forcing the other party to make a contract. ▸ Duress may be: (1) physical duress (threat of harm to a contracting party or family member); or (2) economic duress (threat of wrongful act that will cause serious financial harm, e.g., breach a contract).

LIMITATIONS. ▸ Hard bargaining or threatening to sue to collect a valid debt is not duress.
▸ Economic duress requires that one have no other alternative but to enter into the requested contract.

12. ADHESION CONTRACTS

A contract of adhesion (i.e., a take-it-or-leave-it contract) is voidable if: (1) there is gross disparity in bargaining power; (2) alternative goods or services are unavailable; and (3) the contract is unfair.

E. REMEDIES

13. RESCISSION

GENERAL RULES. ▸ In most cases, lack of capacity, mistake, fraud, innocent misrepresentation, undue influence, and duress render a contract voidable. ▸ A voidable contract can be rescinded at the option of the party who lacked capacity or who was pressured or deceived into contracting.

LIMITATION. If a voidable contract is not avoided, it becomes legally binding.

STUDY HINT. A *void* contract cannot be enforced, and no act is required to avoid the contract.

14. DAMAGES

▸ Innocent misrepresentation: some states allow ordinary damages; no one allows punitive damages.
▸ Fraud: common law allows damages *or* rescission; sale of goods: damages *and* rescission.

15. REFORMATION OF CONTRACT BY COURT

If a contract fails to correctly state the parties' agreement, a court will reform (correct) the contract.

16. LOSS OF REMEDY

A voidable contract cannot be rescinded if one waits too long or if one ratifies the contract.

REVIEW OF TERMS AND PHRASES

MATCHING EXERCISE

Select the term or phrase that best matches a statement or definition stated below. Each term or phrase is the best match for only one statement or definition.

Terms and Phrases

a. Active concealment
b. Confidential relationship
c. Contract of adhesion
d. Contractual capacity
e. Disaffirmance (rescission)
f. Duress
g. Fraud
h. Incompetent
i. Innocent misrepresentation
j. Minor
k. Mutual mistake
l. Ratification
m. Reformation of contract
n. Undue influence
o. Unilateral mistake

Statements and Definitions

____ 1. Conduct or words that manifest a person's intent to be bound by a contract.

____ 2. False statement regarding a material fact made by a party who reasonably believes it to be true.

____ 3. Misunderstanding by only one party.

____ 4. Contract offered by a dominant party to a weaker party on a take-it-or-leave-it basis.

____ 5. Relationship in which one person places complete trust in and relies upon another person.

____ 6. Act of fraudulently hiding information regarding the subject matter of a contract.

____ 7. Person who is mentally impaired due to a physical or psychological disorder or condition.

____ 8. In most states, a person under the age of eighteen.

____ 9. Wrongful threat or act that deprives a party of his or her free will thereby causing the party to make a contract.

____ 10. Avoidance or setting aside of a contract.

____ 11. Intentional misrepresentation of fact reasonably relied upon by another party to his or her harm.

____ 12. Domination by one contracting party of the other contracting party that deprives the weaker party of his or her free will causing the weaker party to enter into an unfair contract.

____ 13. Ability to understand that a contract is being made and to understand its general meaning.

____ 14. Remedy whereby a court will correct a written contract that does not accurately state the parties' agreement.

____ 15. Misunderstanding of the same fact by both contracting parties.

COMPLETION EXERCISE

Fill in the blanks with the words that most accurately complete each statement. Answers may or may not include terms used in the matching exercise. A term cannot be used to complete more than one statement.

1. The relationship between an attorney and a client, between a guardian and a ward, or between a parent and a child is called a _____ _____.

2. In most states, a minor is a person who is under the age of _____.

3. An _____ _____ is a false statement that is made by a contracting party who honestly and reasonably believed that the statement was true.

4. _____ _____ involves domination by one contracting party of the other party that deprives the other party of his or her free will.

5. Fraud, innocent misrepresentation, duress, and undue influence render a contract _____.

6. A contract is _____ if it is made by an incompetent person after a guardian has been appointed to administer the affairs of the incompetent.

7. _____ _____ is the type of duress that involves a wrongful threat against a party or his or her family, whereas _____ _____ is the type of duress that involves a wrongful threat that would cause severe financial hardship to a party.

8. Food, clothing, shelter, medical care, and other goods and services that are reasonably required for the proper care of a minor are called _____.

9. A contract between a public service company and a customer that is offered on a take-it-or-leave-it basis is an example of a _____ ___ _____.

10. Fraud and innocent misrepresentations involve a false statement of a material _____.

REVIEW OF CONCEPTS

Write **T** if the statement is true, write **F** if it is false.

____ 1. Married women and aliens generally lack the contractual capacity to contract.

____ 2. In general, a minor who misrepresents his or her age can disaffirm a contract. However, in some states misrepresentation of age will make the minor liable for damages caused to the other party.

____ 3. A minor cannot avoid a contract if the minor cannot return all of the contract benefits that the minor received from the other party.

____ 4. A party who previously lacked contractual capacity cannot avoid a contract if the party has already ratified the contract.

____ 5. Avoidance of a contract by a minor terminates the minor's contractual liability, but it does not terminate the contractual liability of a person who cosigned the contract with the minor.

_____ 6. An incompetent can rescind a contract even if the incompetent understood that he or she was making a contract and the incompetent understood the essential elements of the contract.

_____ 7. In most cases, a party cannot rescind a contract merely because the party did not read or fully understand the terms of a contract.

_____ 8. If an attorney contracts to sell an investment in a cattle ranch to her client without disclosing to the client important negative matters about the investment, then the contract is voidable.

_____ 9. There is a modern trend that requires a party to disclose an important latent (hidden) defect that is unknown to, and cannot be reasonably discovered by, the other contracting party.

_____ 10. S contracted to sell a home to B. During negotiations, S told B that the home did not have any structural problems. Unknown to S, the home was actually severely damaged by wood rot. In this situation, this contract may be voidable due to an innocent misrepresentation.

_____ 11. Statutes may require certain types of contracts or terms to be printed using a certain size print, and they may also require a contract to conspicuously state certain terms.

_____ 12. A statement that a person intends to do an act may be fraud if the person does not intend to do the act.

_____ 13. A contract is voidable whenever one party persuades another party to make a one-sided contract.

_____ 14. An unfair contract of adhesion may be voidable.

_____ 15. Seller contracted to sell land to Buyer. Unknown to the parties, there was a typographical error in the contract that incorrectly stated the legal description (boundaries) of the land. In this situation, a court will correct the mistake and will enforce the contract as corrected.

REVIEW OF CHAPTER - APPLICATION OF CONCEPTS

MULTIPLE CHOICE QUESTIONS

_____ 1. Mindy purchased a stereo when she 16 years old. Mindy has used the stereo for a year, and she now wants to avoid the contract. (For purposes of this question, you may assume that 18 is the age of majority.) Under these facts:
   a. Mindy can disaffirm the contract, but she must do so before she turns 18.
   b. Mindy can disaffirm the contract, but she must pay for any depreciation to the stereo.
   c. Mindy can disaffirm the contract, and the seller must repay all money paid by Mindy.
   d. Mindy cannot under any circumstance disaffirm the contract.

_____ 2. While Ken was a minor and living on his own without any support from his parents, Ken made the contracts described below. Select the correct answer regarding these contracts.
   a. Ken contracted to buy a motorcycle that he used for pleasure. In this case, the motorcycle is a necessary and Ken can disaffirm the contract.
   b. Ken contracted to lease an apartment. In this case, the apartment is a necessary and Ken cannot disaffirm the contract.
   c. Ken contracted to buy a raincoat. In this case, the coat is a necessary and Ken can disaffirm the contract, but he must pay the reasonable value for the coat under quasi contract.
   d. Ken contracted to buy a TV. In this case, the TV is a necessary and Ken cannot disaffirm the contract.

____ 3. Molly was a minor and living on her own without any support from her parents when she entered into the contracts described below. In some states, statutes would prohibit Molly from avoiding which of these contracts?
   a. Contract for an educational loan that she used to pay her tuition to vocational school.
   b. Contract for car insurance.
   c. Contract for medical services that were needed when Molly contracted pneumonia.
   d. All of the above.

____ 4. In which case did the party in question have the contractual capacity to make a valid contract?
   a. Reggie was judicially declared incompetent and a guardian was appointed to handle his personal and legal affairs. Reggie then contracted to buy a house.
   b. Irving contracted to buy a TV. Due to senility, Irving could not understand that the contract was a legal obligation nor could he understand the basic terms of the contract.
   c. Gary contracted to buy a VCR. Gary had been drinking, and he was intoxicated. Gary understood that he was making a contract and he understood the terms of the contract.
   d. Yin, 17 years old, contracted to buy a mountain bike.

____ 5. Traditionally, which contract is voidable or void due to mistake?
   a. Subcontractor submitted a $10,000 bid to Contractor. Contractor did not know that Subcontractor had made a mistake and that the bid should have been $11,000. Contractor accepted the bid thereby forming a contract, and Contractor detrimentally relied on the bid.
   b. Holly contracted to sell a cabin to Rob. Both parties mistakenly believed that the cabin still existed. In fact, the cabin had been destroyed by a fire the previous night.
   c. Seller contracted to sell some land to Buyer. Seller and Buyer both misunderstood the law, and they mistakenly believed that Buyer could legally use the land for commercial purposes.
   d. Wayne contracted to sell his business to Betsy. Wayne and Betsy both expected that the business would make a profit after Betsy purchased the business, but they were wrong.

____ 6. Which contract is probably voidable due to fraud?
   a. Seller intentionally misrepresented to Buyer that a car being sold was a 1977 Mustang when it was actually a 1978 Mustang. However, Buyer did not rely on this misstatement because Buyer knew that the car was a 1978 Mustang.
   b. Kate contracted to sell her car to Sue. During negotiations, Kate told Sue that, in her opinion, the car was worth at least $2,000. In fact, the value of the car was only $1,500.
   c. Ali contracted to sell a store to Buyer. During negotiations, Ali intentionally lied to Buyer about the store's past profits stating that the profits were greater than they actually were, and Buyer reasonably relied on Ali's statement.
   d. a and c.

____ 7. Select the correct answer.
   a. Robin and Tim, her son, are in a confidential relationship and Robin does whatever Tim says to do. Robin contracted to sell some corporate stock to Tim for an unfairly low price because Tim demanded that she do so. In this case, this contract can be avoided due to undue influence.
   b. Employer persuaded Ron to agree to an employment contract that paid a salary of $30,000, not $40,000 as Ron wanted. In this case, this contract can be avoided due to duress.
   c. Rex threatened to injure Ina's child unless Ina lent $10,000 to Rex. Due to these threats, Ina felt compelled to agree to loan the money to Rex. This contract is voidable due to duress.
   d. a and c.

CASE PROBLEMS

Answer the following problems, briefly explaining your answers.

1. When Nancy was 16 years old, she bought a pedigree dog on credit for $200. While Nancy was a minor she made numerous payments, paying off the entire contract price. The dog has now contracted a serious illness. Nancy has just turned 18, and she is trying to decide what to do with the dog.

    (a) Did Nancy ratify the contract by paying the contract price while she was a minor? (b) Can Nancy avoid the contract? If so, what must Nancy return, and what is she is entitled to be repaid? (c) If Nancy keeps the dog for another year to breed it, can she avoid the contract at that time?

2. Lon is selling his home that has a severely damaged foundation. This damage is obvious. The home also has asbestos inside its walls, but this condition cannot be discovered without tearing the walls apart.

    (a) Under traditional rules, does Lon have a duty to volunteer information to prospective buyers regarding the obviously damaged foundation? (b) Can Lon plaster over the damaged foundation in order to hide the damage? (c) Under modern rules, does Lon have a duty to disclose the asbestos condition to prospective buyers?

3. Seller contracted to sell an airplane to Buyer. Seller intentionally misrepresented to Buyer that the plane did not have any mechanical problems. In fact, the plane had serious defects that rendered the plane unsafe to operate. Buyer was unaware of these defects, and Buyer was induced into making this contract due to Buyer's reliance on Seller's misrepresentation.

    (a) Did Seller commit fraud? (b) Is the contract between Seller and Buyer voidable? (c) What remedies can Buyer request under the UCC in this case?

CPA REVIEW

The following questions were given on past CPA examinations. The answers for these questions are the unofficial answers prepared by the American Institute of Certified Public Accountants, Inc. (AICPA). All material is reproduced with permission of the AICPA.

____ 1. On May 1, 1985, Mint, a 16-year old, purchased a sail boat from Sly Boats. Mint used the boat for six months at which time he advertised it for sale. Which of the following statements is correct?
   a. The sale of the boat to Mint was void, thereby requiring Mint to return the boat and Sly to return the money received.
   b. The sale of the boat to Mint may be avoided by Sly at its option.
   c. Mint's use of the boat for six months after the sale on May 1 constituted a ratification of that contract.
   d. Mint may disaffirm the May 1 contract at any time prior to reaching majority.

____ 2. Egan, a minor, contracted with Baker to purchase Baker's used computer for $400. The computer was purchased for Egan's personal use. The agreement provided that Egan would pay $200 down on delivery and $200 thirty days later. Egan took delivery and paid the $200 down payment. Twenty days later, the computer was damaged seriously as a result of Egan's negligence. Five days after the damage occurred and one day after Egan reached the age of majority, Egan attempted to disaffirm the contract with Baker. Egan will
   a. Be able to disaffirm despite the fact that Egan was not a minor at the time of disaffirmance.
   b. Be able to disaffirm only if Egan does so in writing.
   c. Not be able to disaffirm because Egan had failed to pay the balance of the purchase price.
   d. Not be able to disaffirm because the computer was damaged as a result of Egan's negligence.

____ 3. Payne entered into a written agreement to sell a parcel of land to Stevens. At the time the agreement was executed, Payne had consumed alcoholic beverages. Payne's ability to understand the nature and terms of the contract was not impaired. Stevens did not believe that Payne was intoxicated. The contract is
   a. Void as a matter of law.
   b. Legally binding on both parties.
   c. Voidable at Payne's option.
   d. Voidable at Stevens' option.

____ 4. To prevail in a common law action for fraud in the inducement, a plaintiff must prove that the
   a. Defendant was an expert with regard to the misrepresentations.
   b. Defendant made the misrepresentations with knowledge of their falsity and with an intention to deceive.
   c. Misrepresentations were in writing.
   d. Plaintiff was in a fiduciary relationship with the defendant.

CHAPTER 11

____ 5. Which of the following, if intentionally misstated by a seller to a buyer, would be considered a fraudulent inducement to make a contract?
   a. Nonexpert opinion.
   b. Appraised value.
   c. Prediction.
   d. Immaterial fact.

____ 6. Miller negotiated the sale of Miller's liquor store to Jackson. Jackson asked to see the prior year's financial statements. Using the store's checkbook, Miller prepared a balance sheet and profit and loss statement as well as he could. Miller told Jackson to have an accountant examine Miller's records because Miller was not an accountant. Jackson failed to do so and purchased the store in reliance on Miller's financial statements. Jackson later learned that the financial statements included several errors that resulted in a material overstatement of assets and net income. Miller was not aware that the errors existed. Jackson sued Miller, claiming Miller misrepresented the store's financial condition and that Jackson relied on the financial statements in making the decision to acquire the store. Which of the following statements is correct?
   a. Jackson will prevail if the errors in the financial statements were material.
   b. Jackson will not prevail because Jackson's reliance on the financial statements was not reasonable.
   c. Money damages is the only remedy available to Jackson if, in fact, Miller has committed a misrepresentation.
   d. Jackson would be entitled to rescind the purchase even if the errors in the financial statements were not material.

____ 7. Paco Corp., a building contractor, offered to sell Preston several pieces of used construction equipment. Preston was engaged in the business of buying and selling equipment. Paco's written offer had been prepared by a secretary who typed the total price as $10,900, rather than $109,000, which was the approximate fair market value of the equipment. Preston, on receipt of the offer, immediately accepted it. Paco learned of the error in the offer and refused to deliver the equipment to Preston unless Preston agreed to pay $109,000. Preston has sued Paco for breach of contract. Which of the following statements is correct?
   a. Paco will not be liable because there has been a mutual mistake of fact.
   b. Paco will be able to rescind the contract because Preston should have known that the price was erroneous.
   c. Preston will prevail because Paco is a merchant.
   d. The contract between Paco and Preston is void because the price set forth in the offer is substantially less than the equipment's fair market value.

____ 8. Maco, Inc. and Kent contracted for Kent to provide Maco certain consulting services at an hourly rate of $20. Kent's normal hourly rate was $90 per hour, the fair market value of the services. Kent agreed to the $20 rate because Kent was having serious financial problems. At the time the agreement was negotiated, Maco was aware of Kent's financial condition and refused to pay more than $20 per hour for Kent's services. Kent has now sued to rescind the contract with Maco, claiming duress by Maco during the negotiations. Under the circumstances, Kent will
   a. Win, because Maco refused to pay the fair market value of Kent's services.
   b. Win, because Maco was aware of Kent's serious financial problems.
   c. Lose, because Maco's actions did not constitute duress.

102   CHAPTER 11

CHAPTER 12
CONSIDERATION

CHAPTER OUTLINE

A. GENERAL PRINCIPLES

Consideration is a required element for a contract. In general, an agreement is not a legally binding contract and it will not be enforced unless each party to the agreement gives consideration.

1. DEFINITION

GENERAL RULES. ▸ Consideration is what a contracting party demands and receives in exchange for undertaking a legal obligation. ▸ Consideration in a bilateral contract is the promise by the offeror and the promise by the offeree. ▸ Consideration in a unilateral contract is the offeror's promise and the offeree's actual performance of a requested act or actual forbearance from doing an act.
STUDY HINT. ▸ Consideration is present even if the contract benefits are given to a third party.
▸ Example: Pam promised Ed that if Ed would loan $500 to Art, then she would repay the loan if Art failed to do so. If Ed loans the money to Art, Ed has given consideration for Pam's promise.

2. EFFECT OF ABSENCE OF CONSIDERATION

GENERAL RULES. ▸ A promise or an agreement is not binding if it is not supported by consideration.
▸ A person can refuse to perform a promise or an agreement without being liable unless the promise or agreement is made pursuant to a contract that is supported by consideration.
STUDY HINTS. ▸ A promise to make a gift is not binding because consideration is not given for the promise. But, once a gift has been made, the donor cannot take back the gift. ▸ The fact that a person felt morally obligated to make a promise does not, by itself, make the promise binding.

3. LEGALITY OF CONSIDERATION

A promise to do something that is illegal and a promise not to do something that the law already prohibits are not consideration, and such promises will not form a valid contract.

4. FAILURE OF CONSIDERATION

Failure of consideration occurs when a party fails to perform his or her contractual promise.

B. WHAT CONSTITUTES CONSIDERATION

GENERAL RULES. ▸ A party gives consideration if the party: (1) undertakes a new legal obligation; and (2) the obligation is undertaken pursuant to an agreed exchange for the other party's promise, act, or forbearance. ▸ A new legal obligation is undertaken if: (1) a person promises to do or does an act that he or she is not legally required to do; or (2) a person promises to forbear (refrain) from doing or actually forbears from doing an act that he or she is legally entitled to do.
LIMITATION. Everyone has many legal obligations to do certain things and to refrain from doing certain things. Promising to perform or performing such preexisting duties is not consideration.

5. A PROMISE AS CONSIDERATION

GENERAL RULES. ▸ A promise is consideration only if it actually imposes a legal obligation on a party. ▸ A promise that imposes a legal obligation is consideration even if: (1) the obligation is conditioned on the occurrence of an event; or (2) the agreement can be canceled by giving notice.

LIMITATION. An illusory promise (a promise that imposes no actual duty) is not consideration.

STUDY HINT. Frequently, an illusory promise is a promise to do something only if the promisor decides in the future that he or she wishes to do it.

6. PROMISE TO PERFORM EXISTING OBLIGATION

GENERAL RULES. ▸ Promising to do an act that one has a legal duty to do is not consideration. ▸ A person may have a preexisting duty to do an act as a result of: (1) statutes (criminal or civil); (2) general rules of law (e.g., tort law); (3) duties relating to holding a government position (e.g., duties of elected officials or police officers); or (4) an existing contract between the parties.

LIMITATION. A party *does* give consideration if a party promises to perform a preexisting duty *and* also promises to do something else that the party is not legally required to do.

(a) Completion of contract (and contract modification)

GENERAL RULES. ▸ In general, a promise by a contracting party to complete a contract that the party already has a duty to complete is not consideration. ▸ A contract modification is effective only if both parties give consideration pursuant to the modification agreement.

LIMITATIONS. ▸ Consideration is given if a party agrees to complete an existing contract *and* the party also agrees to do something that is not required. Example: For an extra $300, Painter agrees to paint a house, as required, and also agrees to paint a barn, a new obligation. ▸ There is a trend to enforce a good faith price adjustment despite the lack of consideration if unusual, unforeseen events cause the parties to voluntarily adjust the price. ▸ Under the UCC, a good faith modification of a contract to sell goods does not need consideration to be binding.

(b) Compromise and release of claims

▸ A creditor's agreement to accept a debtor's partial payment of an undisputed (liquidated) debt in return for a release of the debtor from the balance of the debt is not supported by consideration. The creditor may accept the payment and still sue for the balance of the debt.

▸ An agreement to pay and to accept a certain amount as complete satisfaction of a disputed (unliquidated) debt or claim is supported by consideration and legally binds the parties.

(c) Part-payment checks and composition of creditors

▸ A creditor's cashing of a check that is part payment of a disputed debt constitutes a release of the debtor from the balance of the debt if the check states that it constitutes payment in full. In some states the same result may occur even if the debt is undisputed.

▸ An agreement by creditors to accept part payment as payment in full is supported by consideration and is binding if the agreement is made pursuant to a composition of creditors.

7. PRESENT CONSIDERATION VERSUS PAST BENEFITS

▸ A promise (or act or forbearance) is consideration only if it is undertaken pursuant to an agreed exchange. In other words, to be consideration a promise must be made because it is the price demanded for the other party's promise. ▸ Consequently, past consideration (benefit voluntarily given in the past) cannot be consideration, and a later promise to pay for this benefit is not binding.

8. FORBEARANCE AS CONSIDERATION

GENERAL RULE. ▸ Forbearance from doing, or a promise to forbear from doing, an act that one is legally entitled to do is consideration. ▸ Examples: (1) promise not to sue for breach of contract or for damages relating to a disputed debt; (2) promise not to sue for injuries caused by another person; (3) insurance releases; (4) promise not to assert a good faith legal claim; (5) an employee's promise not to compete against his or her employer after the employment has ended.

LIMITATION. A promise not to assert a claim is consideration only if the claim is valid or is made in good faith. A promise not to assert a bad faith claim that has no merit is not consideration.

STUDY HINT. An employee's promise not to compete is binding only if the employer gives consideration for the employee's promise. The employer gives consideration if: (1) the employee's promise is made when the employee is hired; (2) the employer gives new consideration for the employee's promise; or (3) the employee's promise is made during the course of an employment that is for only an indefinite period of time (some courts disagree with this last rule).

9. ADEQUACY OF CONSIDERATION

- ▸ Courts do not examine the adequacy of considerations exchanged.
- ▸ A contract is enforceable even if the considerations exchanged are not of equal value.

C. EXCEPTIONS TO THE LAW OF CONSIDERATION

10. EXCEPTIONS TO ADEQUACY OF CONSIDERATION RULE

- ▸ In certain cases, inadequate consideration may render a contract unconscionable and not binding.
- ▸ A significant difference between the considerations exchanged by the parties may indicate that the contract is the result of fraud, mistake, undue influence, or duress.

11. EXCEPTIONS TO REQUIREMENT OF CONSIDERATION

Consideration is not required in the following situations:

- ■ *Charitable subscriptions*: Pledges to charities are generally binding regardless of consideration.
- ■ *Uniform Commercial Code*: The following do not require consideration: (1) a firm offer (i.e., a merchant's signed, written promise not to revoke an offer to buy or sell goods); (2) a good faith modification of a contract to sell goods; and (3) a written waiver of a claim for damages for breach of a commercial contract.
- ■ *Sealed instruments*: ▸ At common law, sealed instruments are binding without consideration. ▸ Some states now require consideration for sealed contracts.

12. PROMISSORY ESTOPPEL

GENERAL RULE. Promissory estoppel permits enforcement of a promise if: (1) a promisor should expect that a promise will induce the promisee to substantially rely on the promise; (2) the promise does induce such reliance; and (3) injustice can only be avoided by enforcing the promise.

LIMITATION. Promissory estoppel does not apply unless a promisee actually relies on the promise.

STUDY HINTS. ▸ If promissory estoppel applies, a promise is enforced even if the promisee did not give consideration. ▸ A promise is essential; mere expectations do not suffice.

REVIEW OF TERMS AND PHRASES

MATCHING EXERCISE

Select the term or phrase that best matches a statement or definition stated below. Each term or phrase is the best match for only one statement or definition.

Terms and Phrases

a. Conditional promise
b. Consideration
c. Existing obligation
d. Failure of consideration
e. Forbearance
f. Illusory promise
g. Past consideration
h. Promissory estoppel

Statements and Definitions

____ 1. Party does not perform a contractual promise.

____ 2. Benefit previously given as a voluntary gesture and not because the benefit was the price demanded for another's promise or act.

____ 3. Price that is demanded and received in exchange for a promise, act, or forbearance by another.

____ 4. Doctrine that permits enforcement of a promise if a promisor should reasonably expect that the promise will induce the promisee to substantially rely on the promise, and the promise does induce reliance in such a manner that injustice can only be avoided by enforcing the promise.

____ 5. Refraining from doing (i.e., not doing) an act.

____ 6. Promise to do something only if a certain event does or does not occur.

____ 7. Promise that does not impose any legal duty.

____ 8. Legal duty that presently exists based on statutes, general rules of law, responsibilities of the promisor's office, or a current contract.

COMPLETION EXERCISE

Fill in the blanks with the words that most accurately complete each statement. Answers may or may not include terms used in the matching exercise. A term cannot be used to complete more than one statement.

1. In a _____ contract, the considerations are the promises of the offeror and the offeree.

2. The considerations in a _____ contract are the offeror's promise and the offeree's performance of a requested act or forbearance from doing an act.

3. A _____ ____ _____ involves an agreement by the various creditors of a debtor to accept partial payment of their claims as payment in full.

4. _____ reliance occurs when one party reasonably relies upon a promise made by another party, and the relying party will suffer a loss if the promise is not performed.

5. Foodco agreed to buy Farmer's 2001 winter wheat crop for $3 per bushel if Foodco decides in 2001 that it wants to buy Farmer's crop. Foodco's promise is an _____ _____.

REVIEW OF CONCEPTS

Write **T** if the statement is true, write **F** if it is false.

____ 1. An agreement is not legally binding unless each party to the agreement gives consideration.

____ 2. A party is legally obligated to perform a promise if consideration is given for the promise or the party has a moral obligation to perform the promise.

____ 3. A contracting party gives consideration if the party is required to perform a new legal obligation and this is true even if the benefit from this performance is to be given to a third person and not directly to the other contracting party.

____ 4. A promise to make a gift is not legally binding. However, once a gift has been made, a donor cannot take back the gift.

____ 5. In a bilateral contract, consideration is given only when a party performs his or her promise.

____ 6. A promise to perform an illegal act is not consideration.

____ 7. If a person agrees to pay more for something than it is worth, then the agreement is not a contract and it is not legally binding due to a failure of consideration.

____ 8. A promise cannot be consideration if it is conditioned upon the occurrence of another event.

____ 9. A promise to do something only if the promisor decides that he or she wants to do it is an illusory promise and it is not consideration.

____ 10. If a party makes several promises in a single agreement, the party gives consideration if any of the promises constitutes consideration.

____ 11. A promise not to trespass on another person's property (a tort) is consideration if the promisor does in fact refrain from trespassing on the property.

____ 12. An agreement by a government official to perform an official duty in exchange for a promise of payment by a private citizen is not enforceable because the official has not given consideration.

____ 13. *Traditionally*, a promise by a contracting party to complete an existing contract is consideration if performance of the contract is more difficult than the party anticipated it would be.

____ 14. There is a trend to uphold a reasonable, good faith price adjustment even though consideration is not given for the adjustment if extraordinary unforeseeable events justify the adjustment.

____ 15. Consideration is not required to modify a contract for the sale of goods.

____ 16. A creditor can sue to recover the unpaid balance of a debt even if the creditor received partial payment of the debt and the creditor agreed in a composition of creditors to accept the partial payment as payment in full.

____17. An employee's promise not to compete against his or her employer is not legally binding unless the employee receives consideration for the promise.

____18. A release of a good faith claim is consideration even if the claim ultimately proves to be invalid.

____19. In general, courts will not enforce contracts unless the considerations exchanged are equal.

____20. In some cases grossly inadequate consideration may render a contract unconscionable.

____21. Under the UCC, a firm offer is legally binding even if consideration is not given for the merchant's promise not to revoke his or her offer.

____22. Under the UCC, a written waiver of damages for breach of a commercial contract is not legally binding unless consideration is given in exchange for the waiver.

____23. A charitable subscription (pledge) is not legally enforceable unless the charity gives consideration for the subscription.

____24. Under promissory estoppel a court will not enforce a promise unless a party actually relies on the promise in question.

____25. Under promissory estoppel a court will enforce any promise that is relied on by another person.

REVIEW OF CHAPTER - APPLICATION OF CONCEPTS

MULTIPLE CHOICE QUESTIONS

____1. Which agreement is sufficiently supported by consideration to be a contract?
   a. Alex and Wendy entered into an agreement whereby Alex promised to name Wendy as the beneficiary under his life insurance policy. Wendy did not promise or do anything in return.
   b. Rick and Diane, a bank loan officer, entered into an agreement whereby Rick promised to pay Diane $10,000 in exchange for her promise to falsify certain loan papers, a crime.
   c. Ann agreed to pay $400 to Rod in exchange for Rod's promise to transfer title to his car to Ann's son.
   d. Hal agreed to pay $500 to Juan because Hal felt morally obligated to pay this sum because Juan had voluntarily tutored Hal the previous semester.

____2. Which promise by Penny is consideration?
   a. On March 1, Penny signed a lease agreement. Pursuant to this agreement Penny promised to rent a house on March 20 if, at that time, she still wanted to rent the house.
   b. Penny signed an agreement whereby she promised to buy a parcel of land from Seller. However, Penny's promise was conditioned on the zoning board's agreeing to rezone the land.
   c. Penny signed an agreement whereby Penny promised to lease a car. However, Penny can terminate the agreement by giving six months' prior written notice.
   d. b and c.

___ 3. Which promise by Traci is consideration?
   a. In exchange for Jack's promise to pay Traci $1,000, Traci (a police officer) promised to find and arrest the person who had vandalized Jack's store.
   b. In exchange for Kim's promise to pay Traci $500, Traci promised to refrain from publishing an article that would slander Kim (a tort).
   c. In exchange for Beth's promise to pay Traci $200, Traci promised not to breach an existing contract between Beth and Traci.
   d. In exchange for Emilio's promise to pay Traci $1,000, Traci promised to refrain from using illegal drugs, and she also promised to enroll herself in a drug rehabilitation program.

___ 4. Rob contracted to build a garage for Tim. The contract required Rob to pay for all materials and labor. Later, Tim promised to pay Rob an additional $1,000. Under *traditional* rules, Tim's promise to pay the additional $1,000 is legally binding if it is given for:
   a. Rob's promise to complete the original contract with Tim.
   b. Rob's promise to complete the original contract, if labor costs are higher than Rob expected.
   c. Rob's promise to complete the original contract with Tim and his promise to construct a shed which Rob was not obligated to build.
   d. Rob's promise not to breach the original contract with Tim.

___ 5. In which situation is the creditor entitled to sue for the unpaid balance of the debt?
   a. Alice owed Otis $500. The debt was not disputed. Alice and Otis orally agreed that Alice would pay $200 in exchange for Otis' promise to release Alice from the balance of the debt.
   b. Dan hired May to paint his home for $1,000. There was an honest dispute about whether the work was done properly. Pursuant to a compromise agreement, Dan paid $800 as payment in full.
   c. Angie contractually agreed to pay Harry $300 for a tune-up of her car. There is an honest dispute regarding the amount owed because the car still frequently stalls. Angie gave Harry a $150 check that stated that it was payment in full. Harry endorsed and cashed the check.
   d. Pursuant to a composition of creditors, Oscar (a creditor) agreed to accept $500 as payment in full of a $1,000 debt, and Debtor paid the $500 to Oscar.

___ 6. Which agreement is sufficiently supported by consideration to be a contract?
   a. Randy and Alice were in an auto accident, and there is an honest dispute regarding who was at fault. Randy agreed to pay Alice $500 in exchange for her promise not to sue him.
   b. At the time Sue was hired as general manager, she agreed not to compete against Employer after her employment ended.
   c. Jody suffered a self-inflicted injury, but she falsely blamed Stu for the injury. Stu agreed to pay $1,000 to Jody in exchange for Jody's promise not to sue Stu for her injury.
   d. a and b.

___ 7. Which promise or agreement is generally *not* binding?
   a. Lynn promised to donate $100 to a charity that operates a shelter for abused children. The charity promised nothing in return.
   b. Seller and Buyer agreed to modify a land sale contract by reducing the acreage that Seller was obligated to convey. However, the price was not reduced and Seller gave no consideration for this contract modification.
   c. In a signed writing, Seller waived a claim for damages for a breach of a commercial contract.
   d. Seller and Buyer in good faith agreed to modify a contract for the sale of a car by reducing the price from $400 to $350. Buyer gave no consideration for this contract modification.

CASE PROBLEMS

Answer the following problems, briefly explaining your answers.

1. Acme hired Sally as president for a fixed, three-year term. Sally's employment contract did not include an agreement not to compete. After Sally had worked for Acme for one year, Acme requested that Sally execute an agreement not to compete against Acme after her employment with Acme ended. Sally did as requested. Acme did not promise anything pursuant to this agreement.

    (a) Is Sally's agreement not to compete supported by consideration? (b) Is this agreement not to compete a legally binding contract? (c) What should Acme have done differently?

2. Aries Inc. took the following actions regarding its employees: (a) Aries agreed to pay Randy a $5,000 bonus for extra services Randy voluntarily performed the previous year; (b) Aries agreed to pay Fred a $1,000 bonus in exchange for his promise not to breach an existing contract with Aries; and (c) Aries refused to perform a one-year contract with Hill because Aries had contractually agreed to pay Hill $30,000 pursuant to this contract, but his services were only worth $15,000.

    (a) Is the agreement with Randy legally binding? (b) Is the agreement with Fred legally binding? (c) Is Aries entitled to refuse to perform its contract with Hill because the consideration it is receiving is inadequate?

3. Lad lived in Virginia. Ratco, a California firm, repeatedly called Lad and promised that Ratco would hire Lad if he ever lived in California. (Note: Lad and Ratco never entered into an employment contract, and Lad never gave consideration for Ratco's promise to hire him.) With Ratco's encouragement and in reasonable reliance on Ratco's promise, Lad quit his job in Virginia, sold his home, and moved his family to California. When Lad arrived in California, Ratco refused to hire him. Is Ratco's promise to hire Lad enforceable under promissory estoppel?

CPA REVIEW

The following questions were given on CPA examinations. The answers for these questions are the unofficial answers prepared by the American Institute of Certified Public Accountants, Inc. (AICPA). All material is reproduced with permission of the AICPA.

____ 1. In determining whether the consideration requirement has been satisfied to form a contract, the courts will be required to decide whether the consideration
   a. Was bargained for.
   b. Was fair and adequate.
   c. Has sufficient economic value.
   d. Conforms to the subjective intent of the parties.

____ 2. For there to be consideration for a contract, there must be
   a. A bargained-for detriment to the promisor(ee) or a benefit to the promisee(or).
   b. A manifestation of mutual assent.
   c. Genuineness of assent.
   d. Substantially equal economic benefits to both parties.

____ 3. In which of the following situations does the first promise serve as valid consideration for the second promise?
   a. A police officer's promise to catch a thief for a victim's promise to pay a reward.
   b. A builder's promise to complete a contract for a purchaser's promise to extend the time for completion.
   c. A debtor's promise to pay $500 for a creditor's promise to forgive the balance of a $600 liquidated (undisputed) debt.
   d. A debtor's promise to pay $500 for a creditor's promise to forgive the balance of a $600 disputed debt.

____ 4. Kay, an art collector, promised Hammer, an art student, that if Hammer could obtain certain rare artifacts within two weeks, Kay would pay for Hammer's postgraduate education. At considerable effort and expense, Hammer obtained the specified artifacts within the two-week period. When Hammer requested payment, Kay refused. Kay claimed that there was no consideration for the promise. Hammer would prevail against Kay based on
   a. Unilateral contract.
   b. Unjust enrichment.
   c. Public policy.
   d. Quasi contract.

_____ 5. Dye sent Hill a written offer to sell a tract of land located in Newtown for $60,000. The parties were engaged in a separate dispute. The offer stated that it would be irrevocable for 60 days if Hill would promise to refrain from suing Dye during this time. Hill promptly delivered a promise not to sue during the term of the offer and to forego suit if Hill accepted the offer. Dye subsequently decided that the possible suit by Hill was groundless and therefore phoned Hill and revoked the offer 15 days after making it. Hill mailed an acceptance on the 20th day. Dye did not reply. Under the circumstances,
   a. Dye's offer was supported by consideration and was not revocable when accepted.
   b. Dye's written offer would be irrevocable even without consideration.
   c. Dye's silence was an acceptance of Hill's promise.
   d. Dye's revocation, not being in writing, was invalid.

_____ 6. Grove is seeking to avoid performing a promise to pay Brook $1,500. Grove is relying on lack of consideration on Brook's part. Grove will prevail if he can establish that
   a. Prior to Grove's promise, Brook had already performed the requested act.
   b. Brook's only claim of consideration was the relinquishment of a legal right.
   c. Brook's asserted consideration is only worth $400.
   d. The consideration to be performed by Brook will be performed by a third party.

_____ 7. Which of the following requires consideration in order to be binding on the parties?
   a. A written promise signed by a merchant to keep an offer to sell goods open for 10 days.
   b. Material modification of a sale of goods contract under the UCC.
   c. Ratification of a contract by a person after reaching the age of majority.
   d. Material modification of a contract involving the sale of real estate.

_____ 8. Which of the following will be legally binding despite lack of consideration?
   a. An employer's promise to make a cash payment to a deceased employee's family in recognition of the employee's many years of service.
   b. A promise to donate money to a charity on which the charity relied in incurring large expenditures.
   c. A modification of a signed contract to purchase a parcel of land.
   d. A merchant's oral promise to keep an offer open for 60 days.

CHAPTER 13
LEGALITY AND PUBLIC POLICY

CHAPTER OUTLINE

A. GENERAL PRINCIPLES

An agreement is illegal if its formation or performance: (1) is a crime or tort; (2) violates public policy; or (3) is unconscionable.

1. EFFECT OF ILLEGALITY

GENERAL RULES. ▸ Illegal agreements are generally void. ▸ In most cases, parties to an illegal agreement are denied remedies of any nature. A court will not require parties to perform an illegal agreement, and a court will not award damages because a party fails to perform.
STUDY HINT. Typically, a party to an illegal agreement may keep a benefit received pursuant to the agreement, and a court will not make the party pay for or return the benefit.

2. EXCEPTIONS TO EFFECT OF ILLEGALITY

GENERAL RULE. A party to an illegal agreement may obtain an appropriate judicial remedy if: (1) the law that is violated is intended to protect that party; or (2) one party is not *in pari delicto*, in other words, one party is not as guilty as the other party.
STUDY HINT. In most cases, a legal contract is not made illegal merely because one party intends to use the subject matter of the contract in an illegal manner.

3. PARTIAL ILLEGALITY

GENERAL RULE. If a contract contains legal and illegal promises and the promises can be severed from one another, then the legal promises can be enforced but the illegal promises are void.
STUDY HINT. If a contract can be interpreted to be legal or illegal, then a court will ordinarily adopt the interpretation that makes the contract legal.

4. CRIMES AND CIVIL WRONGS

Agreements that require a party to commit a crime or a tort are illegal and void.

5. GOOD FAITH AND FAIRNESS

Broadly speaking, the law requires parties to act fairly and in good faith. Under appropriate circumstances, a contract may be unenforceable if these minimum standards are not met.

6. UNCONSCIONABLE AND OPPRESSIVE CONTRACTS

GENERAL RULES. ▸ An unconscionable agreement or clause is unenforceable. ▸ An agreement may be unconscionable if: (1) a party has no real choice but to make the agreement and it is grossly unfair; or (2) terms are shockingly unfair or oppressive. ▸ The UCC, the Uniform Commercial Credit Code (UCCC), and other statutes may declare certain agreements or terms to be unconscionable.
LIMITATIONS. ▸ A contract is not unconscionable simply because a party makes a bad bargain.
▸ Unconscionability is determined in light of the circumstances that exist at the time a contract is made.
STUDY HINTS. ▸ Fraud is not a necessary element for proving that a contract is unconscionable.
▸ If only a term is improper, courts may enforce the contract, but not enforce the improper term.

7. SOCIAL CONSEQUENCES OF CONTRACTS

▸ The effect that a contract may have on society may be an important consideration in determining whether a contract is legal. ▸ The "n factor" concept (i.e., a contract is but one of a class of many similar contracts) causes courts to consider the collective impact that an entire class of contracts may have on society in determining whether a particular contract is legal.

B. AGREEMENTS AFFECTING PUBLIC WELFARE

8. AGREEMENTS CONTRARY TO PUBLIC POLICY

GENERAL RULES. ▸ Public policy creates standards of conduct necessary to protect the government, the legal system, and fundamental social values, interests, and institutions, such as marriage. ▸ An agreement or a term in an agreement is unenforceable if it violates an important public policy.

LIMITATION. ▸ An agreement may violate public policy and be unenforceable even if it does not involve a crime or tort, or violate a statute. ▸ Example: unreasonable covenant not to compete.

STUDY HINTS. ▸ By implication, statutes may establish public policy. Thus, an agreement that violates a statute which creates a public policy may be void even if this consequence is not expressly stated by the statute. ▸ Agreements that eliminate a statutory benefit or protection are often unenforceable because they violate public policy. ▸ Whether a contract is invalidated for public policy reasons often involves balancing the interests of society with the contracting parties' interests.

9. AGREEMENTS INJURING PUBLIC SERVICE

▸ An agreement that interferes with the performance of official duties by a public official violates public policy, and such an agreement is illegal and void. ▸ Examples: bribery of a public official; illegal lobbying agreements (i.e., unlawful conduct to obtain or prevent adoption of a law).

10. AGREEMENTS INVOLVING CONFLICTS OF INTEREST

GENERAL RULE. Statutes generally prohibit public officials from having a direct or indirect financial interest in matters over which they have official responsibility or control (a conflict of interest).

STUDY HINT. An agreement that involves a forbidden conflict of interest is void, even if the agreement is fair and does not result in any actual injury to the public.

11. AGREEMENTS OBSTRUCTING LEGAL PROCESSES

▸ Agreements that interfere with the functioning of courts or the judicial system are illegal and void.
▸ Examples: bribery of a judge or juror; agreement to destroy evidence; agreement to pay a witness a greater fee than is allowed by law.

12. ILLEGAL DISCRIMINATION CONTRACTS

In general, a contract is unenforceable if it requires one of the parties not to deal with a third person because of the person's race, religion, color, or national origin.

13. GAMBLING, WAGERS, AND LOTTERIES

GENERAL RULES. ▸ Gambling contracts, wagers, and lotteries are generally illegal. ▸ Elements of a wager or lottery are: (1) for a chance; (2) to win a prize; (3) one pays consideration.

LIMITATIONS. ▸ In many states, government-sponsored lotteries are legal. ▸ In some (but not all) states, bingo games, lotteries, and raffles are legal if the proceeds go to charity.

STUDY HINTS. ▸ Promotional giveaways and games that give prizes for guessing an answer are legal if one is not required to buy anything in order to win. ▸ Bets on sporting events are illegal.

C. REGULATION OF BUSINESS

14. EFFECT OF VIOLATION

GENERAL RULE. A contract is void if it violates a statute or administrative rule that expressly states that the contract is void, or if violation of the statute or rule violates an important public policy.
LIMITATION. Some courts void a contract only if this is expressly required by a law.

15. STATUTORY REGULATION OF CONTRACTS

In general, a contract should not be held to be void if it only violates a statutory business regulation that already requires payment of a fine or imprisonment as punishment for its violation.

16. LICENSED CALLINGS OR DEALINGS

GENERAL RULES. ▸ A contract is void if performance of the contract requires a party to violate a protective licensing statute that is intended to guard against unqualified work. ▸ A contract is valid and can be enforced if the contract only requires violation of a revenue-raising licensing statute, i.e., a statute that is primarily intended to raise money for the government.
STUDY HINTS. ▸ Example of void agreement: party is not licensed to practice law or medicine or to be a real estate broker. ▸ Example of valid contract: party does not have a required license to do landscaping work and the license is merely required in order to raise money for the government.

17. FRAUDULENT SALES

A contract is void if it violates a law intended to prevent fraud in connection with the sale of goods.

18. ADMINISTRATIVE AGENCY REGULATION

A contract is void if it violates an administrative agency rule that furthers an important public policy.

19. CONTRACTS IN RESTRAINT OF TRADE

Contracts that *unreasonably* restrain (diminish) trade (competition) are illegal and void.

20. AGREEMENTS NOT TO COMPETE

GENERAL RULE. ▸ An agreement not to compete is legal if: (1) it relates to a sale of a business or employment; (2) it is necessary to protect the other party; and (3) it is for a reasonable time and area.
▸ Example: When Joan was hired as president of XYZ Co., she agreed that she would not compete against XYZ Co. in the city where XYZ Co. was located for one year after she quit.
STUDY HINT. If an agreement is unreasonable, some (but not all) courts will enforce the agreement for a reasonable time and area (the "blue pencil rule").

21. USURIOUS AGREEMENTS

▸ Most states limit the rate of interest that may be charged for certain loans. ▸ Usury is charging a rate of interest in excess of the rate permitted by law. ▸ Interest includes any fees that are charged by a lender that exceed the reasonable expenses for making the loan.

22. CREDIT SALE CONTRACTS

In most states, sales on credit and revolving charge accounts are not subject to usury laws.

REVIEW OF TERMS AND PHRASES

Select the term or phrase that best matches a statement or definition stated below. Each term or phrase is the best match for only one statement or definition.

Terms and Phrases

a. Blue pencil rule
b. Good faith
c. Illegal lobbying agreement
d. *In pari delicto*
e. N factor
f. Partially illegal contract
g. Protective license
h. Public policy
i. Revenue-raising license
j. Time-price differential
k. Unconscionable contract
l. Usury

Statements and Definitions

_____ 1. Unjustifiably unfair or oppressive contract.

_____ 2. Standard or policy that furthers or protects fundamental public and social values or interests.

_____ 3. Agreement to unlawfully influence the adoption of federal or state statutes.

_____ 4. Contract that is comprised of both legal and illegal promises.

_____ 5. Under the UCC, a standard of conduct that requires a merchant who is buying or selling goods to act honestly and to follow reasonable business standards of fair dealing.

_____ 6. License that is required in order to protect against unqualified work.

_____ 7. Concept that a contract may be but one of many similar contracts.

_____ 8. Lending money at a rate of interest greater than that permitted by law.

_____ 9. Difference between the cash price and the credit price for a good or service.

_____ 10. Doctrine that, in effect, authorizes a court to rewrite an unreasonable agreement not to compete and to enforce the agreement not to compete for a reasonable time and area.

_____ 11. Equally wrong or equally at fault.

_____ 12. License that is required in order to raise money for the governmental body requiring the license.

REVIEW OF CONCEPTS

Write **T** if the statement is true, write **F** if it is false.

_____ 1. If a contract can be interpreted to be legal or illegal, a court will ordinarily adopt the interpretation that renders the contract illegal.

_____ 2. A contract that only requires commission of a tort is generally legal and enforceable.

_____ 3. In general, a contract that is fair when it is made is not rendered unconscionable merely because subsequent events cause the contract to be unprofitable to one of the parties.

_____ 4. Unconscionable contracts are illegal and void.

_____ 5. To determine the legality of a contract, a court can consider only the rights of contracting parties; a court cannot consider the impact that a contract or class of contracts may have on society.

_____ 6. An agreement may violate public policy even if the agreement does not require a party to commit a crime or tort, or require a party to violate a statute.

_____ 7. An agreement by a public official that involves a prohibited conflict of interest does not violate public policy if the agreement does not cause any actual injury to the public.

_____ 8. An agreement to pay a witness a fee that is contingent on a favorable outcome of a suit is legal.

_____ 9. In general, an agreement that requires a party to discriminate against a third person because of the person's race or religion violates public policy and is unenforceable.

_____ 10. A contract may be valid even if it requires a party to violate a revenue-raising licensing statute.

_____ 11. A contract to sell a product that has been fraudulently weighed or labeled may be void.

_____ 12. Agreements to acquire a monopoly or to fix prices are unreasonable trade restraints and are void.

_____ 13. A covenant not to compete is illegal even if it is made in connection with the sale of a business, it is necessary to protect the buyer of the business, and it is for a reasonable time and area.

_____ 14. For purposes of determining whether a lender has committed usury, interest includes both the stated interest and all reasonable loan fees or expenses that are charged to the borrower.

_____ 15. Usury laws do not generally apply to the sale of goods or services on credit.

REVIEW OF CHAPTER - APPLICATION OF CONCEPTS

MULTIPLE CHOICE QUESTIONS

_____ 1. Chemco and Glen entered into an illegal agreement whereby Glen agreed to wrongfully acquire and copy a competitor's new chemical formula in consideration for $10,000. Performance of the agreement would be a crime. If Chemco paid the $10,000 to Glen, but Glen failed to perform:
   a. A court would not require Glen to perform the agreement.
   b. A court would make Glen repay the $10,000 to Chemco.
   c. A court would make Glen pay for any damages Chemco suffered as a result of Glen's failure to perform the agreement.
   d. All of the above.

_____ 2. Select the correct answer.
   a. J&J hired Mona, age 13, in violation of child labor laws. These laws protect children, such as Mona. If Mona works but she is not paid, Mona cannot obtain any judicial relief.
   b. Hal contracted to sell his car to Carol. Although the transaction is generally bona fide, Hal knows that Carol intends to use the car to deliver goods without having a permit to do so. Under these facts, the contract to sell the car is legal.
   c. Sonny made one contract to perform two services. One service is legal, the other service is illegal. Separate considerations are stated for each service. The illegal service does not taint or affect the legal service. Under these facts, the entire contract is unenforceable.
   d. b and c.

_____ 3. In most states, which of the following agreements would be *enforceable*?
   a. When hired, Employee contractually agreed to give up her statutory right to receive worker's compensation for any future, employment-related injury.
   b. Home buyer agreed not to resell a home to anyone of Hispanic heritage.
   c. Kyle, a city official, agreed to vote in favor of a rezoning request in consideration for $500.
   d. Merchant agreed to give a car to the contest entrant whose name was selected. It was not necessary to purchase anything in order to enter the contest.

_____ 4. U-Store-It, Inc. contracted to store certain goods for Philip. Performance of this contract requires violation of a business regulation that is created by a civil (noncriminal) statute. The statute does not state whether offending contracts are valid or void. In most states:
   a. The contract is void. Violation of any business regulation renders a contract illegal and void.
   b. The contract is void if the statute states that offending contracts are void, or if violation of the statute would offend an important public policy.
   c. The contract is valid. Violating a statute does not render a contract void unless the statute specifically says so.
   d. The contract is valid. Violating a statute does not render a contract void unless the violation constitutes a crime.

_____ 5. Neal was hired as general manager for a food distributor doing business in Pork City, U.S.A. Neal managed all important customer accounts, and he was responsible for developing the company's sales strategy. When hired, Neal agreed not to compete in the food distribution business after he quit. Under these facts, Neal's agreement would probably be:
   a. Valid, if it prohibited Neal from competing in Pork City for one year after he quit.
   b. Valid, if it prohibited Neal from competing anywhere in the state in which Pork City was located for ten years after he quit.
   c. Valid regardless of its terms. All agreements not to compete are valid.
   d. Void regardless of its terms. All agreements not to compete are illegal and void.

CASE PROBLEM

Answer the following problem, briefly explaining your answer.

Todd agreed to employ Mara as general contractor to make structural modifications to a residence. A person is legally required to be licensed to be a general contractor. To assure the competency of general contractors and to protect the public from unqualified work, this license requires extensive experience and successful completion of a comprehensive exam. Mara does not have the required license.

(a) Is the required license a protective license or a revenue-raising license? (b) Is the agreement between Todd and Mara valid or void? (c) If Mara performs the agreement but Todd fails to pay her, can Mara enforce the agreement against Todd and recover the agreed-upon contract price?

CPA REVIEW

The following questions were given on CPA examinations. The answers for these questions are the unofficial answers prepared by the American Institute of Certified Public Accountants, Inc. (AICPA). All material is reproduced with permission of the AICPA.

_____ 1. Which of the following would be unenforceable because the subject matter is illegal?
    a. A contingent fee charged by an attorney to represent a plaintiff in a negligence action.
    b. An arbitration clause in a supply contract.
    c. A restrictive covenant in an employment contract prohibiting a former employee from using the employer's trade secrets.
    d. An employer's promise not to press embezzlement charges against an employee who agrees to make restitution.

_____ 2. Tell, an Ohio real estate broker, misrepresented to Allen that Tell was licensed in Michigan under Michigan's statute regulating real estate brokers. Allen signed a standard form listing contract agreeing to pay Tell a 6% commission for selling Allen's home in Michigan. Tell sold Allen's home. Under the circumstances, Allen is
    a. Not liable to Tell for any amount because Allen signed a standard form contract.
    b. Not liable to Tell for any amount because Tell violated the Michigan licensing requirements.
    c. Liable to Tell only for the value of services rendered under a quasi-contract theory.
    d. Liable to Tell for the full commission under a promissory estoppel theory.

_____ 3. Samm, a plumber, entered into a contract for $75,000 with Orr, Inc., to perform certain plumbing services in a building owned by Orr. After Samm had satisfactorily performed the work, Orr discovered that Samm had violated the state licensing statute by failing to obtain a plumbing license. The licensing statute was enacted merely to raise revenue for the state. An independent appraisal of Samm's work indicated that the building's fair market value increased by $70,000 as a result of Samm's work. The cost of the materials which Samm supplied was $35,000. If Samm sues Orr, Samm will be entitled to recover
    a. $0
    b. $35,000
    c. $70,000
    d. $75,000

_____ 4. Todd is a licensed real estate broker in Ohio. One of Todd's largest clients, Sun Corp., contracted in writing with Todd to find a purchaser for its plant in New York and agreed to pay him a 6% commission if he were successful. Todd located a buyer who purchased the plant. Unknown to Todd, New York has a real estate broker's licensing statute which is regulatory in nature, intended to protect the public against unqualified persons. Todd violated the licensing statute by failing to obtain a New York license. If Sun refuses to pay Todd any commission and Todd brings an action against Sun, he will be entitled to recover
    a. Nothing.
    b. A fee based on the actual hours spent.
    c. The commission agreed upon.
    d. Out of pocket expenses only.

CHAPTER 13

5. Blue purchased a travel agency business from Drye. The purchase price included payment for Drye's goodwill. The agreement contained a covenant prohibiting Drye from competing with Blue in the travel agency business. Which of the following statements regarding the covenant is not correct?
   a. The restraint must be no more extensive than is reasonably necessary to protect the goodwill purchased by Blue.
   b. The geographic area to which it applies must be reasonable.
   c. The time period for which it is to be effective must be reasonable.
   d. The value to be assigned to it is the excess of the price paid over the seller's cost of all tangible assets.

6. Parr is the vice-president of research of Lynx, Inc. When hired, Parr signed an employment contract prohibiting Parr from competing with Lynx during and after employment. While employed, Parr acquired knowledge of many of Lynx's trade secrets. If Parr wishes to compete with Lynx and Lynx refuses to give Parr permission, which of the following statements is correct?
   a. Parr has the right to compete with Lynx upon resigning from Lynx.
   b. Parr has the right to compete with Lynx only if fired from Lynx.
   c. In determining whether Parr may compete with Lynx, the court should not consider Parr's ability to obtain other employment.
   d. In determining whether Parr may compete with Lynx, the court should consider, among other factors, whether the agreement is necessary to protect Lynx's legitimate business interests.

7. Wert, an employee of Salam Corp., signed an agreement not to compete with Salam during and after being employed with Salam. Wert is the director of research and has knowledge of many of Salam's trade secrets. If Wert's employment with Salam is terminated and Wert wishes to compete with Salam, which of the following statements is not correct?
   a. The agreement is only enforceable if Wert voluntarily terminates his employment with Salam.
   b. The agreement must be necessary to protect Salam's legitimate interests in order to be enforceable.
   c. The geographic area covered by the agreement must be reasonable in order to be enforceable.
   d. The court will consider Wert's ability to obtain other employment against Salam's right to protect its business.

8. Parr is a CPA licensed to practice in State A. Parr entered into a contract with Jet, Inc., to perform an audit in State B for $50,000 (including expenses). After Parr had satisfactorily performed the audit, Jet discovered that Parr had violated State B's licensing statute by failing to obtain a CPA license in State B. Parr incurred $10,000 in expenses in connection with the audit. Jet refuses to pay any fee to Parr, arguing that it could have engaged a local CPA licensed in State B to perform the same services for $35,000 (including expenses). If Parr sues Jet based on breach of contract, Parr will be entitled to recover a maximum of
   a. $0
   b. $10,000
   c. $35,000
   d. $50,000

CHAPTER 14
FORM OF CONTRACT

CHAPTER OUTLINE

A. STATUTE OF FRAUDS

1. VALIDITY OF ORAL CONTRACTS

GENERAL RULE. Broadly speaking, oral contracts are valid and courts will enforce oral contracts.
LIMITATION. An oral agreement is unenforceable if: (1) parties do not intend to be bound until a written contract is signed; or (2) the agreement is required by statute to be evidenced by a writing.

2. CONTRACTS THAT MUST BE EVIDENCED BY A WRITING

These contracts are required by the statute of frauds to be evidenced by a writing to be enforceable:

(a) Agreement that cannot be performed within one year after the contract is made

GENERAL RULE. A contract that cannot be fully performed within one year from the date it is made must be evidenced by a writing. The one-year period begins the day after a contract is made (not when the work is to begin) and concludes the day performance will be completed.
LIMITATION. A writing is not required if: (1) it is possible that a contract may be fully performed in less than one year; or (2) either party may terminate the contract at will, i.e., either party may terminate the contract whenever they desire to do so.
STUDY HINTS. ▸ A writing is not excused merely because a breach of contract by a party may terminate the contract. ▸ Ordinarily, a contract for an unspecified duration does not have to be in writing since it is usually possible to perform this type of contract in less than one year.

(b) Agreement to sell or a sale of any interest in real property

GENERAL RULE. Contracts for the sale or transfer of any interest in land must be evidenced by a sufficient writing to be enforceable. Included in this category are: (1) contracts for the sale of land or buildings affixed to the land; (2) mortgages; and (3) option to purchase real property.
LIMITATION. This particular statute of frauds does not usually require (1) contracts for title searches or (2) contracts between a real estate agent and a buyer or seller to be in writing.

(c) Promise to answer for the debt or default of another

GENERAL RULE. A promise to pay a debt or to perform an obligation of another party if that party fails to do so is required to be evidenced by a sufficient writing to be enforceable.
LIMITATIONS. ▸ A promise made to a debtor (not to the creditor) to pay the debtor's debt is not required to be written. ▸ A promise to personally pay for a good or service that the other contracting party will merely deliver to a third party is not a promise to answer for the debt of another.
STUDY HINT. The most common type of promise that is subject to this statute is a guarantee whereby one promises to pay a debtor's obligation if the debtor fails to do so.

(d) **Promise by the executor or administrator of a decedent's estate to pay a claim against the estate from personal funds**

   GENERAL RULE.   A promise by a personal representative (an executor or administrator) to personally pay a debt of an estate must be evidenced by a writing to be enforceable.
   LIMITATION.   An oral promise by a personal representative that *the estate* will do something does not fall within this rule, and the oral promise may be enforced.
   STUDY HINT.   Ordinarily, an executor is not personally liable to pay an estate's debts.

(e) **Promise made in consideration of marriage**

   GENERAL RULE.   A promise made in consideration for a person's promise to marry, or for actually marrying, another person is required by statute to be evidenced by a sufficient writing.
   LIMITATION.   This statute does not apply to promises by two persons to marry one another.

(f) **Sale of goods and miscellaneous statutes of frauds**

   ▸ The UCC requires contracts for the sale of goods for a price of $500 or more to be evidenced by a writing. ▸ In some states, statutes of frauds require agreements naming a life insurance beneficiary or employing a broker to sell land to be evidenced by a writing.

3. **E-MAIL, FACSIMILE TRANSMISSIONS, AND THE STATUTE OF FRAUDS**

   ▸ Presently, e-mail does not satisfy the writing requirement.
   ▸ Faxes satisfy the writing requirement if appropriately signed.

4. **NOTE OR MEMORANDUM (REQUIRED WRITING)**

   GENERAL RULES.   ▸ At common law, a writing must: (1) state the material contract terms (including price, subject matter, quantity, and parties); and (2) be signed by the party sought to be charged (i.e., the party who is asserting the statute of frauds as a defense for not performing a contract). ▸ More than one writing may be considered if they refer to one another or are sufficiently related to each other.
   STUDY HINTS.   ▸ Any writing may suffice; a complete written contract signed by both parties is not needed. ▸ The writing may be letters, signed minutes of meetings, or other comparable writings. In one case, a fax with the party's name printed at the top was held to satisfy the writing requirement.

5. **EFFECT OF NONCOMPLIANCE**

   GENERAL RULE.   An oral agreement that does not comply with a statute of frauds is voidable (in a few states, void) and cannot be judicially enforced if the defendant raises this defense.
   LIMITATIONS.   ▸ Parties may voluntarily perform an oral contract even though a writing was required. ▸ The statute of frauds cannot be used to rescind a fully performed oral contract.
   STUDY HINTS.   ▸ If a contract is unenforceable, quasi contract entitles a party to recover the reasonable value for contract benefits that the party has given if the other party has not paid for such benefits. ▸ Violating the statute of frauds renders a contract voidable even if all other elements for a valid contract are present and no fraud actually occurred.

6. **JUDICIAL RELIEF FROM STATUTE OF FRAUDS**

   ■ *Part performance of contract*: ▸ Land sale contracts: An oral land sale contract can be enforced if the buyer: (1) takes possession of property; and (2) makes valuable improvements, the value of which is difficult to determine. ▸ Other types of contracts: In some states, a party can enforce other types of oral contracts if the party has performed his or her obligations under the contract.

- ***Promisor benefited by promise to pay debt of another***: ▸ If the primary purpose for promising to pay another's debt is to benefit the party making the promise and not the debtor, a writing is not needed. ▸ Example: Dee owes Robert $800, but Dee cannot repay this debt. To enable Dee to repay him this debt, Robert orally promises Bank that if it lends Dee the $800 and she fails to repay the loan, then Robert will repay the loan to Bank.

- ***Detrimental reliance on oral contract (promissory estoppel)***: Some courts may enforce an oral contract if: (1) a party relied on the contract; and (2) enforcing the contract is needed to avoid causing an unjust hardship to the relying party or to avoid unjustly enriching the other party.

- ***Promise to execute writing***: Some courts will enforce an oral contract if the defendant promised to sign a written contract but failed to do so.

B. PAROL EVIDENCE RULE

7. EXCLUSION OF PAROL EVIDENCE RULE (RULE FOR COMPLETE CONTRACTS)

GENERAL RULE. The parol evidence rule provides that the terms of a final, complete written contract cannot be added to, modified, or contradicted by evidence of oral statements or writings that were made before, or at the same time, the written contract was made.

STUDY HINT. ▸ The parol evidence rule prohibits changing or adding terms even if parties previously agreed to other terms. ▸ Example: Seller and Buyer sign a final, complete written contract for the sale of a business. The contract clearly states that the business does not include a particular computer owned by Seller. In this case, the parol evidence rule would not allow Buyer to prove that Seller orally stated during negotiations that the business included the computer.

8. LIBERALIZATION OF PAROL EVIDENCE

GENERAL RULE. The modern trend in some states allows parol evidence (i.e., oral or verbal evidence) to be used: (1) to establish the parties' intentions even if there is no ambiguity; or (2) to prove events that occurred prior to the making of the contract in order to understand what the parties meant by their contract.

LIMITATION. Some states continue to follow the traditional "four corners rule" which provides that terms of a written contract are determined by referring only to the writing itself unless an exception to the parol evidence rule applies.

9. WHEN THE PAROL EVIDENCE RULE DOES NOT APPLY

(a) Incomplete contract

GENERAL RULE. If a writing is intended to be a final statement of only part of a contract (an "incomplete contract"), then the parol evidence rule permits proof of prior matters to establish terms that are not expressly stated in the written contract and that are not otherwise implied by law into the contract.

STUDY HINT. Example: Sam sold a TV to Julie pursuant to a written contract. The writing only stated the parties' agreement regarding price. In this situation, Julie can prove that during negotiations Sam orally promised to service the TV without charge for one year.

(b) Situations to which the parol evidence rule does not apply

The parol evidence rule does not prevent the use of parol evidence to:
▸ Explain the meaning of an ambiguous term, or to prove a special trade meaning for a word;
▸ Prove the existence of any contract defense, such as fraud, mistake, accident, or illegality;
▸ Prove the existence or nonexistence of a contract, or what writings are part of the contract; or
▸ Prove a contract modification that was agreed to *after* the making of the written contract.

REVIEW OF TERMS AND PHRASES

Select the term or phrase that best matches a statement or definition stated below. Each term or phrase is the best match for only one statement or definition.

Terms and Phrases

a. Ambiguous term
b. Complete (integrated) contract
c. Detrimental reliance
d. Four corners rule
e. Incomplete contract
f. Material contract term
g. Parol evidence
h. Parol evidence rule
i. Party sought to be charged
j. Statute of frauds

Statements and Definitions

____ 1. Rule of law that requires a contract to be evidenced by a sufficient writing in order to be judicially enforceable.

____ 2. Written agreement that is intended to be the final statement of only part of a contract.

____ 3. Rule of law that prohibits altering a final, complete written contract by proving evidence of oral statements that were made prior to or at the same time the written contract was made.

____ 4. Reliance on a promise of another that causes substantial harm to the relying party.

____ 5. Contract that is intended by the parties to be the entire statement of their agreement.

____ 6. Contractual term that may reasonably have more than one meaning.

____ 7. Oral or verbal evidence.

____ 8. Important contractual term, such as subject matter, price, quantity, and identification of the parties.

____ 9. Traditional doctrine (similar to parol evidence rule) that requires that the terms of a written contract be determined solely from the written contract itself unless an exception to the parol evidence rule applies.

____ 10. Person who must sign a writing in order to satisfy the statute of frauds.

REVIEW OF CONCEPTS

Write **T** if the statement is true, write **F** if it is false.

____ 1. All oral contracts are unenforceable.

____ 2. Parties are legally prohibited from performing an oral contract if the statute of frauds required the oral contract to be evidenced by a writing.

____ 3. To be legally enforceable, a promise by a personal representative to personally pay the debts of an estate must be evidenced by a sufficient writing, even if the personal representative actually intended to become personally liable for such debts.

____ 4. A signed fax may constitute a sufficient writing to satisfy the statute of frauds.

____ 5. The statute of frauds requires that a writing be signed by all parties.

____ 6. The statute of frauds (at common law) generally requires that a writing state all of the material terms of the contract.

____ 7. Only formal written contracts signed by all of the contracting parties can satisfy the writing requirement of the statute of frauds.

____ 8. In most states, violation of the statute of frauds renders a contract voidable.

____ 9. A party may usually recover the reasonable value of benefits that have been given pursuant to a contract that is unenforceable under the statute of frauds if the other party has not paid for such benefits.

____ 10. The statute of frauds does not entitle a party to rescind a fully performed oral contract even if the contract was required to be evidenced by a writing to be enforceable.

____ 11. The parol evidence rule is intended to prevent false assertions that parties orally agreed to certain terms.

____ 12. The parol evidence rule requires all contracts to be evidenced by a sufficient writing to be enforceable.

____ 13. The parol evidence rule generally forbids using evidence of prior oral agreements to modify or contradict a final and complete written contract.

____ 14. Evidence of prior oral statements may be used to prove terms that are not stated or implied in an *incomplete* contract.

____ 15. A party may use parol evidence to prove that a final and complete written contract is voidable due to fraud, mistake, duress, or undue influence.

REVIEW OF CHAPTER - APPLICATION OF CONCEPTS

MULTIPLE CHOICE QUESTIONS

____ 1. On March 1, Julie orally contracted to work for Employer from April 1 through March 30 of the following year. Under these facts:
   a. The contract violates the statute of frauds because it cannot be performed within one year from the date the contract was made.
   b. The contract violates the statute of frauds because all employment contracts must be written.
   c. The contract does not violate the statute of frauds because it can be performed within one year from when the work begins.
   d. The contract does not violate the statute of frauds because it may be terminated at any time due to a party's breach.

____ 2. Which of the following oral contracts is voidable?
   a. Biff orally contracts to sell an apartment house to Marty.
   b. Sue orally contracts to grant Finance Co. a mortgage on Sue's home.
   c. Lin orally contracts to sell some land to Ashley.
   d. All of the above.

____ 3. Phil orally contracts to sell land to Buyer. Buyer takes possession of the land, and Buyer makes valuable improvements, the value of which is hard to determine. This contract is:
   a. Enforceable because the statute of frauds does not apply to land sale contracts.
   b. Enforceable due to Buyer's part performance.
   c. Voidable and cannot be enforced because the contract violates the statute of frauds.
   d. Void and cannot be enforced because the contract violates the statute of frauds.

____ 4. Which oral promise violates the statute of frauds?
   a. Pete promises Lender that, if Lender loans $5,000 to Pete's father and Pete's father does not repay the loan, then Pete will repay the loan.
   b. Mom promises Son that if Son borrows money for college and Son is unable to repay this loan, Mom will repay the loan.
   c. Personal representative promises Attorney that an estate will pay Attorney $100 per hour for services rendered to the estate.
   d. a and c.

____ 5. Which oral contract violates the statute of frauds?
   a. Dad and Jose make an oral contract whereby Dad promises to make Jose general manager of a company in exchange for Jose's promise to marry Dad's daughter.
   b. Tom orally contracts to buy a TV for $400.
   c. Osa orally contracts to buy a car for $10,000.
   d. a and c.

CASE PROBLEM

Answer the following problem, briefly explaining your answer.

Sid bought a computer pursuant to a final and complete written contract signed by Sid and the seller. The contract states that the price is $2,000, payable on delivery. The contract also guarantees the computer to be free of "serious defects," an ambiguous term.

Can Sid use parol evidence to prove: (a) the meaning of the term "serious defects"; (b) that prior to signing the written contract, the parties had orally agreed that payment was to be 30 days after delivery; (c) that the written contract was subsequently modified to change the price to $1,900?

CPA REVIEW

The following questions were given on CPA examinations. The answers for these questions are the unofficial answers prepared by the American Institute of Certified Public Accountants, Inc. (AICPA). All material is reproduced with permission of the AICPA.

_____ 1. Which of the following statements is true with regard to the Statute of Frauds?
   a. All contracts involving consideration of more than $500 must be in writing.
   b. The written contract must be signed by all parties.
   c. The Statute of Frauds applies to contracts that can be fully performed within one year from the date they are made.
   d. The contract terms may be stated in more than one document.

_____ 2. On April 3, 1985, Fier entered into an oral employment contract with Reich, whereby Reich was hired as a sales manager for a term of one year. Although Fier and Reich did not agree to a definite starting date, Fier indicated that Reich could begin employment that same day or any time prior to April 15, 1985. Reich began working on April 10. On June 15, 1985, Reich was fired without cause. If Reich sues for breach of the employment contract and Fier asserts the statute of frauds as a defense, Reich will
   a. Prevail since the contract was capable of being performed within one year.
   b. Prevail since the UCC statute of frauds applies.
   c. Lose since the contract was not in writing and signed by Fier.
   d. Lose since Reich did not begin employment until April 10.

_____ 3. Nolan agreed orally with Train to sell Train a house for $100,000. Train sent Nolan a signed agreement and a down payment of $10,000. Nolan did not sign the agreement, but allowed Train to move into the house. Before closing, Nolan refused to go through with the sale. Train sued Nolan to compel specific performance. Under the provisions of the Statute of Frauds,
   a. Train will win because Train signed the agreement and Nolan did not object.
   b. Train will win because Train made a down payment and took possession.
   c. Nolan will win because Nolan did not sign the agreement.
   d. Nolan will win because the house was worth more than $500.

_____ 4. Payne borrowed $500 from Onest Bank. At the time the loan was made to Payne, Gem orally agreed with Onest that Gem would repay the loan if Payne failed to do so. Gem received no personal benefit as a result of the loan to Payne. Under the circumstances,
   a. Gem is secondarily liable to repay the loan.
   b. Both Gem and Payne are primarily liable to repay the loan.
   c. Gem is free from liability concerning the loan.
   d. Gem is primarily liable to repay the loan.

_____ 5. Able hired Carr to restore Able's antique car for $800. The terms of their oral agreement provided that Carr was to complete the work within 18 months. Actually, the work could be completed within one year. The agreement is
   a. Unenforceable because it covers services with a value in excess of $500.
   b. Unenforceable because it covers a time period in excess of one year.
   c. Enforceable because personal service contracts are exempt from the Statute of Frauds.
   d. Enforceable because the work could be completed within one year.

_____ 6. King sent Foster, a real estate developer, a signed offer to sell a specified parcel of land to Foster for $200,000. King, an engineer, had inherited the land. On the same day that King's letter was received, Foster telephoned King and accepted the offer. Which of the following statements is correct under the Statute of Frauds?
   a. No contract was formed because Foster did not sign the offer.
   b. No contract was formed because King is not a merchant and, therefore, King's letter is not binding on Foster.
   c. A contract was formed, although it would be enforceable only against King.
   d. A contract was formed and would be enforceable against both King and Foster because Foster is a merchant.

_____ 7. Which of the following offers of proof are inadmissible under the parol evidence rule when a written contract is intended as the complete agreement of the parties?
   I. Proof of the existence of a subsequent oral modification of the contract.
   II. Proof of the existence of a prior oral agreement that contradicts the written contract.
   a. I only.
   b. II only.
   c. Both I and II.
   d. Neither I nor II.

_____ 8. In negotiations with Andrews for the lease of Kemp's warehouse, Kemp orally agreed to pay one-half of the cost of the utilities. The written lease, later prepared by Kemp's attorney, provided that Andrews pay all of the utilities. Andrews failed to carefully read the lease and signed it. When Kemp demanded that Andrews pay all of the utilities, Andrews refused, claiming that the lease did not accurately reflect the oral agreement. Andrews also learned that Kemp intentionally misrepresented the condition of the structure of the warehouse during the negotiations between the parties. Andrews sued to rescind the lease and intends to introduce evidence of the parties' oral agreement about sharing the utilities and the fraudulent statements made by Kemp. The parol evidence rule will prevent the admission of evidence concerning the

	a. Oral agreement regarding who pays the utilities	b. Fraudulent statements by Kemp
a.	Yes	Yes
b.	No	Yes
c.	Yes	No
d.	No	No

CHAPTER 15
INTERPRETATION OF CONTRACTS

CHAPTER OUTLINE

A. RULES OF CONSTRUCTION AND INTERPRETATION

1. FUNCTION OF JUDGE AND JURY

The judge interprets the meaning of unambiguous words; the jury interprets ambiguous words.

2. INTENTION OF THE PARTIES

- *Objective intent*: ▸ A court seeks to determine what parties intended contract terms to mean so that it can enforce the contract in the manner intended by the parties. ▸ The objective (outwardly indicated) intent of the parties determines the meaning of terms. The parties' subjective (secret) intentions do not control. ▸ A court must enforce a contract according to the meaning the parties intended.

- *Meaning of words*: ▸ Rules used to interpret words include: (1) ordinary words are given their ordinary meaning; (2) technical words used in a technical setting are given their technical meaning; and (3) common meanings for words are typically used unless the parties clearly intended words to mean something else. ▸ Prior dealings between parties may be used to interpret the meaning of words.

- *Incorporation by reference*: If a contract refers to and states that it incorporates (includes) another writing, this indicates an objective intent that the writing is a part of the contract.

- *Economic realities*: When searching for the parties' interest, courts will evaluate a contract in the context of the economic realities, e.g. re new or used goods being sold.

3. ADDITIONAL PRINTED MATTER

GENERAL RULE. The following rules apply regarding additional printed material:

▸ A contract includes printed material that the contract expressly refers to and incorporates.
▸ A contract does not include material that the contract expressly excludes.
▸ A contract does not include material (or a term) that is not delivered (offered) until after the contract is made unless both parties agree that the subsequent material is part of the contract.
▸ An employee handbook may be part of an employment contract if the employer and employee intended it to be part of the contract. When the parties' intent is unclear, a jury will decide.

LIMITATION. A handbook is not part of the contract if an employee signs a card stating that it is not part of the contract and stating that the employer can change the handbook at any time.

4. WHOLE CONTRACT

GENERAL RULE. A contract should be interpreted as a whole, and every word should be given effect if it is reasonable to do so.

LIMITATIONS. ▸ Typically, letterheads are not part of a contract and are not used for interpretation. ▸ Printed materials that a party is not aware of until after the contract is made are not part of the contract, and they are not used to interpret the meaning of contract terms.

STUDY HINT. A divisible contract is (1) a contract that can be divided into separate, independent performances and (2) separate considerations are stated in the contract for each performance.

5. **CONDITIONS**

   GENERAL RULE. A condition is an event, the happening or nonhappening of which creates a duty to act or terminates a duty to act. A condition may be a:

   - ***Condition precedent***: event that must occur *before* a party has a legal duty to perform;
   - ***Condition concurrent***: event that must occur at the *same time* that another event occurs; or
   - ***Condition subsequent***: event that *terminates* an *existing legal duty* to perform.

   Duties may be subject to a variety of conditions. Examples of conditions include:

   - ***Condition precedent***: Buyer's duty to purchase a house is "subject to" (i.e., conditioned upon) Buyer's being able to obtain appropriate financing.
   - ***Condition concurrent***: Buyer's payment for goods is required when Seller delivers the goods.
   - ***Condition subsequent***: Insured's failure to give Insurance Company a required notice of a fire loss terminates Insurance Company's obligation to pay for the loss.

   STUDY HINTS. ▸ Parties' duties under a bilateral contract are typically conditions concurrent, i.e., parties must perform at the same time. ▸ If a duty is subject to a condition that is not met, then a party is not required to perform that duty and the failure to perform is not a breach of contract.

6. **CONTRADICTORY AND AMBIGUOUS TERMS**

   GENERAL RULES. A contract is ambiguous if the parties' intent is unclear and the contract is capable of more than one reasonable interpretation. ▸ If a contract contains terms that conflict with one another or it contains ambiguous terms, then the following rules are used to interpret the contract:

   ▸ Handwritten terms prevail over conflicting typed terms.
   ▸ Typed terms prevail over conflicting terms that are preprinted in a form contract.
   ▸ Figures that are written as words prevail over conflicting figures that are written as numbers.
   ▸ A contract is strictly construed against the party who wrote it. In other words, if a term can reasonably be interpreted in two ways, a court will adopt the interpretation that favors the party who did not write the contract.

   LIMITATIONS. ▸ A term is not ambiguous merely because parties disagree about its meaning, and a contract is not ambiguous just because it does not address a matter. ▸ A contract may be unenforceable if it remains ambiguous regarding an important term *after* applying all appropriate rules of interpretation.

7. **IMPLIED TERMS**

   If a contract is silent regarding a matter, a court may imply the following terms:

   - ***Duration of contract***: A contract that does not have an expressly stated duration will continue for a reasonable time. However, a party may terminate the contract at any time by giving notice.
   - ***Details of performance***: Certain terms relating to the parties' performances may be implied if not stated. Examples: (1) parties must perform within a reasonable time; (2) services are to be done using such skill as is necessary to properly do the work; (3) payment is to be made in cash.
   - ***Good faith***: ▸ A duty of good faith and fair dealing is implied by law into all contracts. Good faith requires a party: (1) to act honestly; (2) to cooperate in carrying out a contract; and (3) not to unreasonably interfere with the other party's right to perform a contract. ▸ Good faith does not obligate a party to enter into a contract. Similarly, good faith does not prevent a party from exercising an express contractual right nor does it require a party to modify a contract.
   - ***Governmental approval***: A party must cooperate in trying to obtain required government permits.
   - ***Statutory terms***: A term required by statute to be stated in a contract will be implied into the contract if the contract fails to expressly state the term.

8. CONDUCT AND CUSTOM

GENERAL RULE. A contract may be interpreted using evidence of: (1) repeated performances by one party in carrying out the contract in question if these performances have been accepted by the other party; or (2) trade or industry customs that relate to the contract in question.
LIMITATION. Trade customs cannot negate clear, express terms of a contract.
STUDY HINT. Repeated performances in carrying out a contract that are inconsistent with the terms of a contract may establish that the parties have modified the contract.

9. AVOIDANCE OF HARDSHIP

GENERAL RULE. A contract is binding even if it benefits one party more than another party.
LIMITATION. A court will interpret an ambiguous contract in a way necessary to avoid: (1) an unfair hardship to a weaker party; or (2) a forfeiture, i.e., an arbitrary loss of money or property.
STUDY HINT. To avoid a hardship, courts may sometimes: (1) imply a term; or (2) negate a contract or a contract term on the basis of unconscionability.

10. JOINT, SEVERAL, AND JOINT AND SEVERAL CONTRACTS

An interpretation problem that may arise relates to the nature of parties' respective duties to perform an obligation if two or more parties agree to perform or fulfill the same obligation. If two parties agree to perform the same obligation, their respective duties may be:

- *Several*: each party has a duty to individually or separately perform the obligation; or
- *Joint*: parties have a duty to jointly (collectively or indivisibly) perform the obligation; or
- *Joint and several*: parties have a duty to jointly or collectively perform the obligation. If one party fails to perform, the other party must individually perform the entire obligation.

B. CONFLICT OF LAWS

Frequently the formation or performance of a contract relates to more than one state. In this event, principles known as conflict of laws dictate what law will be applied to determine the parties' rights.

11. STATE COURTS

GENERAL RULES. ▸ The law of the state in which a contract is made determines whether a contract is properly formed. ▸ The law of the state in which a contract is to be performed determines the parties' obligations regarding performance, liability for nonperformance, and damages. ▸ The law of the state where a lawsuit is being heard determines matters relating to procedure or evidence.
LIMITATIONS. ▸ If a contract states what law controls, this term is generally enforced. ▸ In connection with interstate contracts, there is a trend to apply the law of the state that has the most significant contacts with the parties and subject matter of the contract.

12. FEDERAL COURTS

▸ If a federal court hears a case involving state law, the court will apply the conflict of law rules that would be applied by a state court in the state where the federal court is located. ▸ Example: A U.S. district court in Oregon that is trying a case involving state law would apply Oregon conflict of law rules.

REVIEW OF TERMS AND PHRASES

Select the term or phrase that best matches a statement or definition stated below. Each term or phrase is the best match for only one statement or definition.

Terms and Phrases

a. Conditions concurrent
b. Conditions precedent
c. Conditions subsequent
d. Conflict of laws
e. Divisible contract
f. Incorporation by reference
g. Joint and several contract
h. Joint contract
i. Objective intent
j. Several contract
k. Subjective intent
l. Usage of trade

Statements and Definitions

____ 1. Events or actions that must occur before a party has a legal obligation to act.

____ 2. Contract in which two parties have a duty to collectively perform an obligation, and each party also has a duty to individually perform the obligation.

____ 3. Events or actions that terminate an existing obligation to perform.

____ 4. Secret intent of a party.

____ 5. Technique by which an additional writing is made a part of a contract.

____ 6. Events or actions that are mutually dependent and must be performed or occur at the same time.

____ 7. Outwardly manifested intent of a party.

____ 8. Contract in which two parties each have a duty to individually perform the same obligation.

____ 9. Contract in which two parties have a duty to collectively perform the same obligation.

____10. Contract intended by the parties to be, in effect, a number of separate contracts.

____11. Principles that determine what law to apply in resolving a lawsuit.

____12. Practice or understanding in an industry or trade that is regularly followed and may reasonably be expected to apply to dealings between members of that industry or trade.

REVIEW OF CONCEPTS

Write **T** if the statement is true, write **F** if it is false.

____ 1. Eli contracted to buy a car. Unknown to Seller, Eli did not subjectively intend to buy the car unless he received a pay raise. Under these facts, Eli need not buy the car unless he gets the pay raise.

____ 2. Employee handbooks are always considered to be a part of employment contracts.

____ 3. A contract term should be interpreted without considering the other terms of the contract.

____ 4. Garage agreed to install "ABS" brakes on Jim's race car. In this case Garage must install brakes that would comply with the technical meaning for "ABS" brakes. Installing brakes that would comply with the ordinary meaning for normal car brakes would not be sufficient.

____ 5. A warranty booklet that is not shown to a buyer until after a contract is made may be used to interpret the contract.

____ 6. Conditions are not favored by courts. A court will interpret a contract in such a way that the contract does not state a condition if such an interpretation is reasonable.

____ 7. If a seller makes a bilateral contract to sell property, the law will generally hold that the buyer's duty to pay is a condition precedent to the seller's duty to transfer title to the property.

____ 8. If a contract contains conflicting handwritten and typed terms, the typed terms generally prevail.

____ 9. A term is ambiguous whenever the parties disagree regarding its meaning.

____ 10. If the duration of a contract is not stated, a party may generally terminate the contract at any time by giving notice of termination.

____ 11. Trade customs and usages of trades generally do not override clear, express contract terms.

____ 12. If reasonably possible to do so, an ambiguous contract will be interpreted to avoid a forfeiture.

____ 13. A court may interpret a contract of adhesion in the manner necessary to avoid an unreasonable hardship to the weaker party.

____ 14. In connection with interstate contracts, there is a trend to determine all questions relating to such contracts by using the law of the state where the contracts were formed.

____ 15. In a case involving state law, a federal court may apply the law of whatever state it chooses.

REVIEW OF CHAPTER - APPLICATION OF CONCEPTS

MULTIPLE CHOICE QUESTIONS

____ 1. In which case do the new or additional materials or terms become a part of the contract?
   a. Hot Wire Appliance Store sold Juan a stove. The contract incorporated by reference an additional writing entitled "Warranty."
   b. Jane was hired by Employer. Before hiring Jane, Employer had adopted a new employee handbook but Jane's employment contract did not mention the handbook and the parties did not intend for it to be part of the contract.
   c. Lou contracted to buy a business. After the contract was made, Seller sent Lou new contract terms that Seller wanted to be part of the contract. Lou never agreed to these terms.
   d. Marcel contracted to become general manager for Acme Corp. The employment contract specifically excludes additional pay schedules that the parties had previously discussed.

____ 2. NASA contracted to hire Pete as a scientist. The contract stated that NASA did not have a duty to hire Pete unless he first passed a security check. Pete failed the check. Under these facts:
   a. NASA's duty to hire Pete was subject to a condition precedent.
   b. NASA's duty to hire Pete was subject to a condition concurrent.
   c. NASA's duty to hire Pete was subject to a condition subsequent.
   d. NASA will be liable for breach of contract if it does not hire Pete.

____ 3. Select the correct answer.
   a. Seller sold Buyer a TV. The contract is a printed form. A printed term states that Seller will repair the TV for one year. A specially typed term that the parties inserted into the contract states that Seller will repair the TV for two years. In this case, the one-year term controls.
   b. A contract states a price "Ten Dollars ($11.00)." In this case, the buyer must pay $11.
   c. In a sales contract for a car, a handwritten term requires Seller to service the car for one year, but a typed term requires Seller to service the car for only three months. In this case, Seller is required to service the car for only three months.
   d. Landlord prepared a lease contract with Tenant. The lease states that Landlord will pay for "utilities." Landlord intended this to mean only electricity. Tenant thought it meant electricity and gas. In this case "utilities" will probably be interpreted to mean electricity and gas.

____ 4. Select the correct answer.
   a. Ann agreed to supply Diner with 250 pounds of carrots per month. A duration for the contract is not stated. In this case, the contract is invalid because its duration is not stated.
   b. Vick agreed to build a fence for Kim. Time for completion of the fence is not stated. In this case, it is implied that Vick must complete the work within a reasonable time.
   c. Fox Co. hired Rick as a salesman. The contract expressly gives Fox Co. the unrestricted right to terminate the contract at any time. In this case, the implied duty of good faith would prevent Fox Co. from terminating the contract unless Rick had done something wrong.
   d. Al contracted to buy a patent from Ellen. The form of payment was not stated. In this case, the law will generally imply that Al can pay by check, cash, or a promissory note.

____ 5. Subcontractor agreed to supply and install 200 "standard toilets" in an apartment house being built by Contractor. Which of the following matters can be considered in interpreting this term?
   a. In the construction industry, which includes both Subcontractor and Contractor, there is an understanding that "standard toilets" means a certain type and quality of toilet.
   b. Pursuant to this contract Plumber has supplied and installed, and Contractor has accepted, 100 toilets of identical type and quality.
   c. a and b.
   d. None of the above.

____ 6. Depending on the particular contract, a condition may be:
   a. An event or performance that must occur before a contracting party has a duty to perform.
   b. An event or performance that may suspend a contracting party's duty to perform.
   c. An event or performance that may discharge a contracting party's duty to perform.
   d. All of the above.

_____ 7. Julie contracted to buy a duplex from Nat. The contract stated that Julie's duty to purchase the property is conditioned upon her first being able to obtain $40,000 financing. Julie was unable to obtain the financing. Under these facts, must Julie purchase the duplex?
   a. Yes. Julie contracted to buy the property.
   b. Yes. Conditions are not permitted in real estate sales contracts and, therefore, Julie had a contractual obligation to buy the property.
   c. No. A contract never was formed because Julie never had a legal obligation to do anything.
   d. No. The failure of the financing condition discharged Julie's contractual obligation to purchase the property.

_____ 8. Roberto's insurance required him to give notice of a loss within seven days. On July 4, Roberto's business was vandalized, but he did not report this loss until August 10. Under these facts:
   a. The notice requirement is a condition precedent to the insurer's duty to pay.
   b. The notice requirement is a condition subsequent of the insurer's duty to pay.
   c. Once Roberto gave notice, the insurer had a duty to pay.
   d. b and c.

_____ 9. Jason agreed to purchase lumber inventory from Paul Bunyan Lumber for $2,000 cash. The law implies that Jason's duty to pay is a condition concurrent to Paul Bunyan's duty to deliver the lumber. Under these facts:
   a. Jason must pay for the lumber before it is delivered.
   b. Jason must pay for the lumber at the time it is delivered.
   c. Jason must pay for the lumber within 10 days after it is delivered.
   d. Jason does not have to pay for the lumber.

_____ 10. Which of the following matters can NOT be used to interpret a contract?
   a. Usage of trade in the industry in which both contracting parties do business.
   b. Repeated prior dealings between the contracting parties.
   c. Repeated prior dealings between one of the contracting parties and others.
   d. Repeated performances by the parties under the contract in question.

CASE PROBLEM

Laurel, who lived in State X, offered to hire Contractor to build a home for her in State X. Contractor, who lived in State Y, mailed an acceptance of the offer from State Y. Under applicable law, the acceptance was effective and formed a contract when Contractor deposited it in the mail in State Y.

Contractor built the home for Laurel in State X. Laurel has filed a lawsuit in State X requesting damages due to the alleged improper performance by Contractor.

Using traditional conflict of law rules, determine whether the law of State X or State Y controls regarding the following issues: (a) Did the parties give consideration sufficient to form a contract? (b) Did Contractor properly construct the building? (c) What evidence may be admitted at trial?

CPA REVIEW

The following questions were given on CPA examinations. The answers for these questions are the unofficial answers prepared by the American Institute of Certified Public Accountants, Inc. (AICPA). All material is reproduced with permission of the AICPA.

____ 1. Which of the following types of conditions affecting performance may validly be present in contracts?

	Conditions precedent	Conditions subsequent	Concurrent conditions
a.	Yes	Yes	Yes
b.	Yes	Yes	No
c.	Yes	No	Yes
d.	No	Yes	Yes

____ 2. Dunne and Cook signed a contract requiring Cook to rebind 500 of Dunne's books at 80¢ per book. Later, Dunne requested, in good faith, that the price be reduced to 70¢ per book. Cook agreed orally to reduce the price to 70¢. Under the circumstances, the oral agreement is
   a. Enforceable, but proof of it is inadmissible into evidence.
   b. Enforceable, and proof of it is admissible into evidence.
   c. Unenforceable, because Dunne failed to give consideration, but proof of it is otherwise admissible into evidence.
   d. Unenforceable, due to the statute of frauds, and proof of it is inadmissible into evidence.

____ 3. On June 15, 1990, Alpha, Inc. contracted with Delta Manufacturing, Inc. to buy a vacant parcel of land Delta owned. Alpha intended to build a distribution warehouse on the land because of its location near a major highway. The contract stated that: "Alpha's obligations hereunder are subject to the vacant parcel being rezoned to a commercial zoning classification by July 31, 1991." Which of the following statements is correct?
   a. If the parcel is not rezoned by July 31, and Alpha refuses to purchase it, Alpha would not be in breach of contract.
   b. If the parcel is rezoned by July 31, and Alpha refuses to purchase it, Delta would be able to successfully sue Alpha for specific performance.
   c. The contract is not binding on either party because Alpha's performance is conditional.
   d. If the parcel is rezoned by July 31, and Delta refuses to sell it, Delta's breach would not discharge Alpha's obligation to tender payment.

CHAPTER 16
THIRD PERSONS AND CONTRACTS

CHAPTER OUTLINE

A. THIRD PARTY BENEFICIARY CONTRACTS

In general, only contracting parties can enforce a contract. However, subject to certain limitations, a third party who is a third party beneficiary may sue on and enforce a third party beneficiary contract.

1. DEFINITION

GENERAL RULE. In general, a third party is a third party beneficiary if: (1) a contract directly benefits the third party; and (2) the benefit satisfies an obligation owing by one contracting party to the third party, or a contracting party intends to give the benefit as a gift to the third party.
LIMITATIONS. ▸ A third party is a third party beneficiary only if the contracting parties made a contract with the intent to directly benefit the third party. ▸ Express contractual statements that third parties cannot enforce a contract or that third parties are not third party beneficiaries prevents creation of third party beneficiaries. ▸ A person has the burden to prove that he or she is a third party beneficiary.
STUDY HINTS. ▸ The most important factor is whether the contracting parties expressly or by implication intended a person to be a third party beneficiary. ▸ A third party beneficiary may be specifically named in the contract, or the contract may designate a specific class of persons for whose benefit the contract is made.

2. MODIFICATION OR TERMINATION OF THIRD PARTY BENEFICIARY CONTRACT

GENERAL RULE. Contracting parties cannot modify or terminate a third party beneficiary contract without the consent of the third party beneficiary.
LIMITATIONS. ▸ Contracting parties can modify or rescind a contract or they can change beneficiaries without a third party beneficiary's consent if the right to do so is expressly stated in the contract. ▸ Rights of a third party beneficiary are extinguished if the contract is terminated by operation of the law. Example: a necessary party to a contract dies, thereby terminating the contract.

3. LIMITATIONS ON THIRD PARTY BENEFICIARY

GENERAL RULE. A third party beneficiary has only the same right to enforce a contract as do the original contracting parties.
STUDY HINT. A beneficiary's rights are subject to all contractual terms and defenses.

4. INCIDENTAL BENEFICIARIES

GENERAL RULES. ▸ An incidental beneficiary cannot enforce a contract. ▸ A third party is an incidental beneficiary if the contracting parties do not intend to directly benefit the third party.
▸ Incidental beneficiaries can be classified either as a:

- ■ *Direct incidental beneficiary*: Incidental beneficiary who will receive a direct benefit from a contract, i.e., the third party will definitely receive a benefit if the contract is performed even though the contracting parties did not contract with the intent to benefit that party; or

- *Contingent incidental beneficiary*: Incidental beneficiary who may be benefited by a contract only if: (1) the contract is properly performed; and (2) one of the contracting parties then takes an action that will give a benefit received under the contract to the third party.

STUDY HINTS. ▸ The fact that parties know another person may benefit from a contract is not sufficient, by itself, to prove the necessary intent to make that person a third party beneficiary. ▸ A beneficiary of a contract who fails to qualify as a third party beneficiary is an incidental beneficiary. ▸ Direct incidental beneficiaries and contingent incidental beneficiaries cannot enforce a contract.

B. ASSIGNMENTS

GENERAL RULES. ▸ An assignment transfers a contract right from one contracting party (the assignor) to a third party (the assignee). ▸ In general, an assignee can sue on and enforce an assigned right.
LIMITATIONS. ▸ The assignee's right to enforce a contract is subject to all contract defenses. ▸ An assignment does not relieve an assignor of his or her contractual duties.

5. DEFINITIONS

▸ An assignment is a transfer of legal rights. ▸ An assignor is a party who transfers legal rights to another party. ▸ An assignee is a party to whom legal rights are transferred.

6. FORM OF ASSIGNMENT

GENERAL RULES. ▸ An assignment can be oral or written. ▸ Consideration is not required to make an assignment. ▸ Any words clearly showing an intent to transfer a right may be an assignment.
LIMITATION. Statutes require certain assignments, e.g., wage assignments, to be in writing.
STUDY HINT. A party makes an assignment if the party directs the other contracting party to pay the contract price to a third person.

7. ASSIGNMENT OF RIGHT TO MONEY

GENERAL RULES. ▸ A party can assign a right to receive money that is due under a contract. The modern rule and the rule under the UCC permit an assignment of a right to money (i.e., an assignment of an account receivable) even if a contract prohibits such assignment. ▸ The modern rule is that a party can assign a right to receive money in the future even though the money has not yet been earned. ▸ An assignment is proper if the contract expressly authorizes the assignment.
LIMITATIONS. ▸ According to some courts, an assignment is invalid if the contract expressly prohibits the assignment. ▸ An assignor may assign the right to only part of a sum of money the assignor is to receive. In this event, however, the debtor can be sued on the debt only if everyone who has a right to payment of the debt joins in a single suit against the debtor.

8. ASSIGNMENT OF RIGHT TO A PERFORMANCE

GENERAL RULE. In general, a party can assign a right to receive a service from another party.
LIMITATION. A party cannot assign a right to receive a performance in the following situations:

- *Assignment increasing burden of performance*: A party cannot assign a right if doing so may significantly increase the burden or risk to the other party.
- *Personal satisfaction (contracts)*: A party cannot assign a right to have an act done to a person's personal satisfaction. This would change the nature of the duty of the other party.

- *Personal services*: In general, an employer cannot assign the right to an employee's services.
- *Credit transaction*: The right to buy on credit or the right to borrow money cannot be assigned.
- *Personal nature*: Contract of a personal nature cannot be assigned (e.g., golf club membership).

9. RIGHTS OF ASSIGNEE

GENERAL RULES. ▸ An assignee stands in the shoes of the assignor. In other words, an assignee has only the same right to enforce a contract as the assignor had. ▸ A condition, contractual defense, or set-off that can be asserted against the assignor can also be asserted against the assignee.
LIMITATION. Contracts often state that defenses cannot be asserted against an assignee. This provision is typically valid, but laws may restrict this limitation in certain consumer contracts.

10. DELEGATION OF DUTIES (DOES A DELEGATION ASSIGN CONTRACT RIGHTS?)

GENERAL RULES. ▸ In general, a party may delegate a standardized, nonpersonal contractual duty thereby authorizing a third party to perform the duty. ▸ A party who delegates a duty ordinarily remains liable to the other contracting party for the proper performance of the delegated work.
LIMITATION. A party cannot delegate a duty without the consent of the other contracting party if the duty is personal in nature and it is important that the original party performs.
STUDY HINT. A common question is whether an assignment is intended to transfer rights and also to delegate duties. A trend holds that absent contrary indications, a general assignment of "the contract" assigns rights and also delegates duties. This modern rule is followed by the UCC.

11. CONTINUING LIABILITY OF ASSIGNOR

Unless otherwise agreed by the contracting parties, an assignment does not excuse an assignor from any contractual duties. The assignor remains legally bound to perform all obligations.

12. LIABILITY OF ASSIGNEE

GENERAL RULES. ▸ Ordinarily, an assignee is not liable for a breach of the contract by an assignor. ▸ An assignment that is made "subject to" a claim means that the other claim has a right to be paid before the assignee. It does NOT mean that the assignee is obligated to pay this claim.
LIMITATION. Sometimes, federal and state consumer protection laws may make an assignee of a consumer debt repay sums received or may make the assignee liable for the assignor's misconduct.

13. NOTICE OF ASSIGNMENT

GENERAL RULES. ▸ An assignment is effective when it is made. In other words, an assignee has a legal claim to an assigned right when an assignment is made, and notice of assignment is not required. ▸ If a right to money (or any other right) is assigned and the party owing the money (the obligor) is informed of the assignment and told to pay the assignee, then payment to the assignee is legally required. Payment to the assignor does not satisfy the duty to pay the assignee.
LIMITATION. If a right to money is assigned but the obligor is not told of the assignment or is not told to pay the assignee, then payment to the assignor reduces the amount of the obligation.

14. WARRANTIES OF ASSIGNOR

GENERAL RULE. If an assignment is made for consideration, the assignor warrants to the assignee that: (1) the assignor owns the assigned right; (2) the assigned right is valid, that is, it is not subject to any defenses; and (3) the assignor will not interfere with the assignee's rights.
LIMITATION. An assignor does not impliedly warrant that an obligor will in fact perform a duty.

REVIEW OF TERMS AND PHRASES

Select the term or phrase that best matches a statement or definition stated below. Each term or phrase is the best match for only one statement or definition.

Terms and Phrases

a. Assignee
b. Assignment
c. Assignor
d. Contingent incidental beneficiary
e. Delegation of duties
f. Direct incidental beneficiary
g. Incidental beneficiary
h. Obligor
i. Third party beneficiary
j. Third party beneficiary contract

Statements and Definitions

____ 1. Third party to whom a contract right is assigned.

____ 2. In general, any third party who may directly or indirectly benefit from a contract even though the contracting parties did not intend to contract for the benefit of the third party.

____ 3. Transfer of a contract right to a third party.

____ 4. Transfer of contract duties to a third party.

____ 5. Third party whom contracting parties intend to directly benefit by entering into a contract.

____ 6. Contracting party who has an obligation to perform a duty.

____ 7. Contract made by contracting parties with the intent to directly benefit a third party.

____ 8. Incidental beneficiary who may or may not indirectly receive an unintended contract benefit.

____ 9. Contracting party who assigns a contract right to a third party.

____ 10. Incidental beneficiary who will receive a direct, but unintended, benefit from a contract.

REVIEW OF CONCEPTS

Write **T** if the statement is true, write **F** if it is false.

____ 1. A third party beneficiary contract may expressly reserve the right of the original contracting parties to change third party beneficiaries whenever the contracting parties choose to do so.

____ 2. In most cases, contracting parties can modify or terminate a third party beneficiary contract without obtaining the consent of the third party beneficiary if the contract is silent on this matter.

____ 3. The intention of contracting parties determines whether a third party is a third party beneficiary.

____ 4. A third party beneficiary can enforce a contract only in accordance with the terms of the contract.

____ 5. If contracting parties know that a contract will benefit a third party, then this fact, by itself, conclusively establishes that the third party is a third party beneficiary.

____ 6. If a contractor contracted with a university to build a gymnasium for physical education classes, students at the university would be only incidental beneficiaries of the contract.

_____ 7. If a party is legally entitled to assign a contract right, then the party may assign this right without first obtaining the consent of the other contracting party.

_____ 8. The modern rule is that a party is legally authorized to assign a right to receive money under a contract even if the contract prohibits the assignment.

_____ 9. A party cannot assign a right to be insured because the assignment may increase the risk or burden to the insurer.

_____10. An employer can generally assign the right to receive the services of an employee.

_____11. In cases not involving consumer transactions, a contract can generally eliminate an obligor's right to assert contractual defenses against an assignee of a contract right.

_____12. If an assignor assigns his or her rights under a contract, then the assignment terminates the assignor's duty to perform any obligations under the contract.

_____13. The modern trend and the rule under the UCC is that a general assignment of "the contract" acts as an assignment of all contract rights and a delegation of all contract duties.

_____14. If a debt is assigned to an assignee but the obligor (debtor) is not informed of the assignment, then the obligor's payment to the assignor will discharge (terminate) the debt.

_____15. An assignor who receives consideration for an assignment by implication warrants to the assignee that the obligor will in fact properly perform all contractual duties.

REVIEW OF CHAPTER - APPLICATION OF CONCEPTS

MULTIPLE CHOICE QUESTIONS

_____ 1. Select the third party who is a third party beneficiary entitled to enforce the contract in question.
   a. Loan Co. lent Alice $500 to pay bills. The loan contract states that the parties do not intend for any of Alice's creditors to be third party beneficiaries. Third party is a creditor of Alice.
   b. Ned contracted with Rock Insurance Co. whereby the insurance company agreed to pay $10,000 to Ned's sister (third party) upon Ned's death.
   c. Samantha contracts to sell her car to Tom for $1,000. The contract requires Tom to pay the $1,000 directly to Last Chance Bank (third party) to whom Samantha owes $1,000.
   d. b and c.

_____ 2. Bank contracted to lend Terra Construction $100 million to build a residential development. Terra is considering building the development in one of several locations. One location is near property owned by Ted. The value of Ted's property will increase if Terra builds near his property. Under these facts:
   a. Ted is a third party beneficiary of the contract between Bank and Terra.
   b. Ted is an incidental beneficiary of the contract between Bank and Terra.
   c. Ted can enforce the contract between Bank and Terra.
   d. Bank and Terra cannot modify the loan contract without Ted's consent.

_____ 3. Cody owed Don $500. Don orally told Cody and Sylvia: "I transfer to Sylvia my right to be repaid the $500; Cody pay Sylvia the $500." Sylvia did not give Don anything in exchange for Don's right to receive this money. (You may assume that there are no special statutes in this case relating to the manner in which the assignment must be made.) Under these facts:
   a. The assignment by Don is invalid because Don did not use the word "assign."
   b. The assignment by Don is invalid because the assignment is oral.
   c. The assignment by Don is invalid because Sylvia did not give any consideration.
   d. The assignment by Don to Sylvia is valid.

_____ 4. Which right can be assigned without the consent of the other contracting party? (The agreements in question do not expressly prohibit assignments.)
   a. Donna agreed to pay $100 to Bret for Bret's typewriter. Bret wants to assign the right to receive this money.
   b. Painter agreed to paint a portrait of Keri, and Painter guaranteed personal satisfaction. Keri wants to assign to her sister the right to have a portrait painted to her personal satisfaction.
   c. Deadbeat Finance Co. agreed to lend $50,000 to Fred. Fred wants to assign to Manny the right to borrow the $50,000.
   d. Central Airlines has an employment contract with Captain Buck, a pilot. Central Airlines wants to assign its right to Captain Buck's services to Air Asia, another airline.

_____ 5. Arthur sold a truck to Lucky on credit for $20,000. Arthur breached the contract with Lucky, and Lucky can claim a $5,000 set-off against Arthur. Arthur validly assigned to Stella all of Arthur's rights to receive money from Lucky. Lucky was informed of the assignment and was told to pay Stella. Lucky refuses to pay anything. Under these facts, how much can Stella collect from Lucky?
   a. $ 0
   b. $ 5,000
   c. $ 15,000
   d. $ 20,000

CASE PROBLEM

Answer the following problem, briefly explaining your answer.

Erecto Construction Co. contracted to build an office building for Owner. Without Owner's consent, Erecto delegated its duty to do the excavation work to Gopher Inc., a subcontractor. The excavation work is standard, nonpersonal work that does not require any special skill. Gopher failed to do the work properly.

(a) Was Erecto legally entitled to delegate its duty to do the excavation work to Gopher without first obtaining Owner's consent? (b) Is Erecto liable to Owner because Gopher failed to properly do the work?

CPA REVIEW

The following questions were given on CPA examinations. The answers for these questions are the unofficial answers prepared by the American Institute of Certified Public Accountants, Inc. (AICPA). All material is reproduced with permission of the AICPA.

_____ 1. Ace contracted with Big City to train and employ handicapped, unemployed veterans residing in Big City. Ace breached the contract and Bell, a resident of Big City who is a handicapped, unemployed veteran, sues Ace for damages. Under the circumstances, Bell will
    a. Lose, because Bell is merely an incidental beneficiary of the contract.
    b. Win, because Bell is a third-party beneficiary entitled to enforce the contract.
    c. Lose, because Big City did not assign its contract rights to Bell.
    d. Win, because the intent of the contract was to confer a benefit on all handicapped, unemployed veterans residing in Big City.

_____ 2. Barr entered into a contract with Gray which required Gray to construct a warehouse on land owned by Barr. The contract specifically provided for Gray to use Apex Corp. pipe fittings for all the plumbing. Gray failed to use Apex pipe fittings. Apex had learned of the contract between Barr and Gray and, in anticipation of receiving an order from Gray, manufactured additional pipe fittings. Apex is
    a. Entitled to money damages due to Gray's breach of contract.
    b. Entitled to money damages since it changed its position to its detriment by relying on the contract.
    c. Not entitled to money damages since it is merely a donee beneficiary.
    d. Not entitled to money damages since it is merely an incidental beneficiary.

_____ 3. Long purchased a life insurance policy with Tempo Life Insurance Co. The policy named Long's daughter as beneficiary. Six months after the policy was issued, Long died of a heart attack. Long had failed to disclose on the insurance application a known pre-existing heart condition that caused the heart attack. Tempo refused to pay the death benefit to Long's daughter. If Long's daughter sues, Tempo will
    a. Win, because Long's daughter is an incidental beneficiary.
    b. Win, because of Long's failure to disclose the pre-existing heart condition.
    c. Lose, because Long's death was from natural causes.
    d. Lose, because Long's daughter is a third-party donee beneficiary.

_____ 4. Wilcox Co. contracted with Ace Painters, Inc. for Ace to paint Wilcox's warehouse. Ace, without advising Wilcox, assigned the contract to Pure Painting Corp. Pure failed to paint Wilcox's warehouse in accordance with the contract specifications. The contract between Ace and Wilcox was silent with regard to a party's right to assign it. Which of the following statements is correct?
    a. Ace remained liable to Wilcox despite the fact that Ace assigned the contract to Pure.
    b. Ace would not be liable to Wilcox if Ace had notified Wilcox of the assignment.
    c. Ace's duty to paint Wilcox's warehouse was nondelegable.
    d. Ace's delegation of the duty to paint Wilcox's warehouse was a breach of the contract.

_____ 5. On February 1, Burns contracted in writing with Nagel to sell Nagel a used car. The contract provided that Bunns was to deliver the car on February 15 and Nagel was to pay the $800 purchase price not later than March 15. On February 21, Burns assigned the contract to Ross for $600. Nagel was not notified of the assignment. Which of the following statements is correct?
   a. By making the assignment, Burns impliedly warranted Nagel would pay the full purchase price.
   b. The assignment to Ross is invalid because Nagel was not notified.
   c. Ross will not be subject to any contract defenses Nagel could have raised against Bunns.
   d. By making the assignment, Burns impliedly warranted a lack of knowledge of any fact impairing the value of the assignment.

_____ 6. Egan contracted with Barton to buy Barton's business. The contract provided that Egan would pay the business debts Barton owed Ness and that the balance of the purchase price would be paid to Barton over a 10 year period. The contract also required Egan to take out a decreasing term life insurance policy naming Barton and Ness as beneficiaries to ensure that the amounts owed Barton and Ness would be paid if Egan died.

Barton's contract rights were assigned to Vim, and Egan was notified of the assignment. Despite the assignment, Egan continued making payments to Barton. Egan died before completing payment and Vim sued Barton for the insurance proceeds and the other payments on the purchase price received by Barton after the assignment. To which of the following is Vim entitled?

	Payments on purchase price	Insurance proceeds
a.	No	Yes
b.	No	No
c.	Yes	Yes
d.	Yes	No

_____ 7. One of the criteria for a valid assignment of a sales contract to a third party is that the assignment must
   a. Not materially increase the other party's risk or duty.
   b. Not be revocable by the assignor.
   c. Be supported by adequate consideration from the assignee.
   d. Be in writing and signed by the assignor.

_____ 8. On August 1, Neptune Fisheries contracted in writing with West Markets to deliver to West 3,000 pounds of lobsters at $4.00 a pound. Delivery of the lobsters was due October 1 with payment due November 1. On August 4, Neptune entered into a contract with Deep Sea Lobster Farms which provided as follows: "Neptune Fisheries assigns all the rights under the contract with West Markets dated August 1 to Deep Sea Lobster Farms." The best interpretation of the August 4 contract would be that it was
   a. Only an assignment of rights by Neptune.
   b. Only a delegation of duties by Neptune.
   c. An assignment of rights and a delegation of duties by Neptune.
   d. An unenforceable third-party beneficiary contract.

CHAPTER 17
DISCHARGE OF CONTRACTS

CHAPTER OUTLINE

A. DISCHARGE BY PERFORMANCE

- If a party's contractual duties are discharged, this means: (1) the duties no longer exist; (2) the party is not required to perform such duties if they have not already been performed; and (3) the party can enforce the contract against the other party unless the other party has also been discharged.
- A discharge may result from: (1) adequate performance of contract duties (or in some cases a refusal by the other party to accept a tender of performance); (2) action by the parties; or (3) outside events.

1. THE NORMAL DISCHARGE OF CONTRACTS

Most contracts are discharged by the parties' performance of their contractual duties, such as doing a required act or making a required payment, or by expiration of the time stated in the contract.

2. NATURE OF PERFORMANCE (AND TENDER OF PERFORMANCE)

(a) **Tender (of performance)**

GENERAL RULES. ▸ A tender is an offer to perform. ▸ A party's refusal to accept the other party's *tender to do an act* generally discharges the other party's duty to perform that act. ▸ A refusal to accept a party's valid *tender of payment*: (1) does not discharge the duty to pay; but (2) stops further interest and typically enables the debtor to avoid liability for court costs.
LIMITATION.   A valid tender of payment requires an offer to pay: (1) the entire amount due plus any interest or costs owing (2) on the date due (3) in legal tender, i.e., in cash.

(b) **Special rules regarding payment of money**

- Payments must be applied in the manner stated by a debtor. If a debtor does not specify how payments are to be applied, a creditor can apply payments to any legal debt that is presently owing.
- Payment by check is only conditional payment. A debt is not discharged until the check is paid. If a check is not paid, the creditor can sue on either the original debt or on the check.

3. TIME OF PERFORMANCE

GENERAL RULES. ▸ A common issue is whether a party has performed in a sufficiently timely fashion to entitle that party to enforce the contract. ▸ If time for performance is not stated, the law implies a duty to perform in a reasonable time. ▸ If time for performance is stated, a party should perform within the time stated. Nonetheless, late performance is sufficient to entitle one to enforce a contract if: (1) performance is done in a reasonable time; and (2) time is not of the essence. ▸ A party may waive a provision that time is of the essence.
LIMITATIONS. ▸ If time is of the essence, i.e., timely performance is essential, a party can enforce a contract only if the party performs his or her duties within the time stated.
STUDY HINTS. ▸ A term stating that time is of the essence may not control if it is obvious that timely performance is unimportant. ▸ Factors that affect whether time is of the essence: (1) the contract expressly states that time is of the essence; (2) the nature of the subject matter of the contract; and (3) there will be no significant change in value of the subject matter of the contract if performance is slightly delayed.

4. ADEQUACY OF PERFORMANCE

(a) Substantial performance

GENERAL RULES. ▸ Another common issue is whether a party has sufficiently performed to entitle that party to enforce a contract. ▸ In most cases, the rule of substantial performance enables a party to enforce a contract if the party in good faith substantially performs his or her duties. (Note: A party must pay for damages caused by his or her failure to perfectly perform.)

LIMITATION. The rule of substantial performance does not apply and complete performance is required if: (1) a party intentionally fails to perform; (2) a contract clearly requires perfect performance; or (3) an act or event must occur in order to satisfy a condition precedent.

STUDY HINT. Substantial performance means: (1) a party's performance is nearly equivalent to what was required; and (2) the benefits derived from the performance can be used by the other party for their intended purposes.

(b) Satisfaction of promisee or third person

GENERAL RULES. ▸ If a party promises to perform to the personal satisfaction of the other party regarding a matter of personal taste, then most courts hold that performance is not adequate (and the duty is not discharged) unless the other party is actually satisfied. ▸ If a contract requires that a mechanical or impersonal performance be done to the satisfaction of the other party or a third party and that performance can be objectively evaluated, then most courts hold that a performance is adequate (and the duty is discharged) if a reasonable person would be satisfied.

LIMITATION. Most courts, require that a person in good faith be dissatisfied, i.e., a party cannot falsely assert that he or she is dissatisfied with the other party's performance.

5. GUARANTEE OF PERFORMANCE

A party is not discharged from a duty merely because a third party has guaranteed the proper performance of that duty.

B. DISCHARGE BY ACTION OF PARTIES

6. DISCHARGE BY UNILATERAL ACTION

GENERAL RULE. In general, a party cannot unilaterally (i.e., on one's own) cancel a contract.

LIMITATIONS. ▸ A contract may allow one party to cancel the contract. ▸ A contract that does not have a fixed duration may be ended by a party at any time. ▸ The Consumer Credit Protection Act allows a debtor three business days to rescind a contract that imposes a lien on the debtor's home. ▸ FTC rules give a buyer three business days to rescind a home solicitation sale for more than $25.

7. DISCHARGE BY AGREEMENT

GENERAL RULE. A contract may be discharged by: (1) original contract terms (for example, a contract states that it ends on a certain date); (2) mutual cancellation (parties agree to end a contract); (3) mutual rescission (parties agree to terminate a contract and to return each other to their original positions); (4) substitution of a new contract in place of the original contract; (5) novation (a contract is replaced by a new contract between one of the original contracting parties and a new party); (6) accord and satisfaction (parties accept a new performance in place of a performance that is required by the contract, but which is now subject to a dispute between the parties); (7) release; or (8) waiver.

LIMITATIONS. ▸ *Substitution of new contract*: A contract is discharged by a new contract only if the parties intend the new contract to discharge the original contract. ▸ *Accord and satisfaction*: An accord is not valid unless it fulfills all requirements for a contract. If an accord is not performed (i.e., no satisfaction occurs), the original obligation is not discharged and it may be enforced.

STUDY HINTS. ▸ An accord is an agreement by parties to accept a new performance in place of an existing, but disputed, obligation. ▸ A satisfaction is the performance of accord.

C. DISCHARGE BY EXTERNAL CAUSES

8. DISCHARGE BY IMPOSSIBILITY

GENERAL RULES. ▸ A contract is discharged if performance is made impossible by: (1) destruction of a particular subject matter that is essential for performance of the contract; (2) a change in law that makes performance illegal; (3) the death of a party who is to perform a service involving a special skill; or (4) the death of a party or third person who is to receive a service of a personal nature. ▸ A party is also discharged if performance is made impossible due to the other party's wrongful act or failure to act in good faith. Example: Manufacturer cannot build a product for Buyer because Buyer wrongfully failed to cooperate in supplying necessary specifications for the product.

LIMITATIONS. ▸ A contract is not discharged because: (1) a party is personally unable to perform a duty (for example, a contractor cannot afford to hire necessary workers to build a house that he contracted to build); (2) performance is merely more difficult or costly than expected; (3) a law changes, but the change only makes performance more difficult or less profitable than expected; or (4) a party dies, if the party's duty is only to pay money or to sell property. ▸ Delays caused by riots, strikes, or material shortages do not discharge a contract.

9. ECONOMIC DISAPPOINTMENT

GENERAL RULE. The majority rule and traditional common law rule is that (1) commercial impracticability (an unforeseen event makes it unreasonably expensive to perform the contract) and (2) economic frustration (an unforeseen event destroys the value and purpose for the contract) do not discharge a contract.

LIMITATIONS. ▸ Some modern courts hold that a contract may be discharged by commercial impracticability or economic frustration. ▸ A contract is not discharged merely because it is unprofitable to perform. ▸ An event does not discharge a contract if a party assumed the risk that the event would occur.

10. RISK OF ECONOMIC INSTABILITY

Changes in the state of the economy do not excuse failure to perform a contract.

11. TEMPORARY IMPOSSIBILITY

GENERAL RULE. ▸ According to most courts, an event that makes performance only temporarily impossible either has no effect on the parties' duties or, at most, temporarily excuses performance.
▸ Unless otherwise agreed, acts of God, such as floods, do not excuse performance of a contract.

LIMITATIONS. Contracts often contain a "weather clause" that either expressly excuses nonperformance that is caused by weather conditions or expressly denies any special rights due to weather conditions.

12. DISCHARGE BY OPERATION OF LAW

A contract (or a party's duty) is discharged by: (1) a material, wrongful alteration of a contract by the other party; (2) destruction of a written contract by the other party with the intent to discharge it; (3) a discharge in bankruptcy of the party; (4) a running of the statute of limitations (i.e., the statutory time within which to bring a suit on a contract has expired); or (5) expiration of a contractually agreed-upon time within which a suit was required to be brought to enforce the contract.

REVIEW OF TERMS AND PHRASES

Select the term or phrase that best matches a statement or definition stated below. Each term or phrase is the best match for only one statement or definition.

Terms and Phrases

a. Accord
b. Commercial impracticability
c. Discharge
d. Economic frustration
e. Impossibility
f. Novation
g. Rescission
h. Satisfaction
i. Statute of limitations
j. Substantial performance
k. Tender
l. Time is of the essence

Statements and Definitions

____ 1. Doctrine discharging a contract because an unforeseen event has made performance impossible.

____ 2. Extinguishment of a contract resulting from performance, actions of parties, or operation of law.

____ 3. Agreement to accept an alternative performance in place of a disputed contractual obligation.

____ 4. Doctrine authorizing a party to enforce a contract if the party has almost completely performed his or her contractual obligations.

____ 5. Performance of an accord.

____ 6. Offer to perform a contractual duty.

____ 7. Termination of a contract and return of the parties to the position they were in prior to contracting.

____ 8. Agreement to replace a contract with a new contract between one original party and a new party.

____ 9. Timely performance is vital; timely performance is required to discharge a contractual duty.

____ 10. Doctrine discharging a contract because its value has been destroyed by an unforeseen event.

____ 11. Doctrine discharging a contract because an unforeseen event has made performance by one or both parties unreasonably expensive or burdensome.

____ 12. Law that limits the time within which a suit may be brought to enforce a legal right.

REVIEW OF CONCEPTS

Write **T** if the statement is true, write **F** if it is false.

____ 1. A valid tender of payment only requires an offer to pay the contract price, and it need not include an offer to pay interest or costs that are also due.

____ 2. If a party's tender of payment is refused, this refusal discharges the party's duty to pay.

____ 3. If a party's tender to do an act is wrongfully refused by the other contracting party, this refusal generally discharges the party's duty to perform that act.

____ 4. If payment is made by check, the debt is not discharged until final payment of the check is made.

____ 5. If Buyer enters into an option contract to buy property that requires Buyer to accept by June 1 and time is of the essence, then an acceptance made on June 2 would not be effective.

____ 6. Under the rule of substantial performance, if a buyer's duty to purchase a house is subject to a condition precedent that the buyer be able to obtain a $25,000 loan, then this condition would be satisfied if the buyer can obtain a loan for $24,000.

____ 7. In applying the rule of substantial performance to large construction contracts, if damages are small, then courts tend to ignore the fact that a party's failure to completely perform was intentional.

____ 8. A duty is discharged and it no longer exists if a third party guarantees performance of that duty.

____ 9. Consumers have the right to unilaterally cancel any contract if this is done within three business days after a contract is made.

____ 10. Under the Consumer Credit Protection Act, a consumer generally has three business days within which to cancel a contract that grants a mortgage against the consumer's home.

____ 11. A contract may be discharged if both parties agree to cancel or rescind the contract.

____ 12. A contract is discharged by impossibility whenever it is more difficult to perform than expected.

____ 13. A contract is discharged if performance is delayed by riots or material shortages.

____ 14. If a person enters into a contract and he or she subsequently files for and receives a discharge in bankruptcy, then the person's duties under the contract are typically discharged.

____ 15. A party's wrongful alteration of important terms of a written contract without the consent of the other party discharges the other party from the contract.

REVIEW OF CHAPTER - APPLICATION OF CONCEPTS

MULTIPLE CHOICE QUESTIONS

____ 1. Penelope agreed to reupholster Flynn's couch and chair by May 1. The contract does not state that time is of the essence, and timely performance is not vital to this contract. Penelope completed the work on May 7, a reasonable time under the circumstances. Under these facts:
   a. Time is not of the essence in this contract. Penelope can enforce the contract.
   b. Time is not of the essence in this contract. Penelope cannot enforce the contract.
   c. Time is of the essence in this contract. Penelope cannot enforce the contract.
   d. Time is of the essence in this contract. Penelope can enforce the contract.

____ 2. JR contracted to renovate an historical home for June for $50,000. The renovations were completed as required, except JR unintentionally failed to refinish one oak banister. It will cost $250 to have someone else do this refinishing. Under these facts, JR is entitled to recover:
   a. $0. JR failed to completely perform his duties. Thus, JR cannot enforce the contract.
   b. $49,750. JR substantially performed his duties. Thus, JR can enforce the contract. June must pay the contract price, less damages caused by JR's imperfect performance.
   c. $50,000. JR substantially performed his duties. Thus, JR is entitled to the full contract price.
   d. Only such amount, if any, that June may decide to pay JR.

CHAPTER 17

____ 3. Ken contracted to set up ordinary accounting books for Paul's business, and Ken guaranteed Paul's satisfaction. Ken set up the books in accordance with generally accepted accounting principles, and a reasonable person would be satisfied. However, Paul refuses to pay because he is not actually satisfied with the books. Under these facts, most courts would hold that:
   a. Ken cannot enforce the contract because Paul is not actually satisfied with the books.
   b. Ken cannot enforce the contract because personal satisfaction contracts are illegal.
   c. Ken can enforce the contract because a reasonable person would be satisfied with the books.
   d. Ken can enforce the contract because promises to perform to another person's personal satisfaction are ignored by courts.

____ 4. Patty contracted to buy a car from Cars-4-U for $5,000. A dispute arose regarding the amount that Patty must pay because the car failed to satisfy certain warranties. Patty and Cars-4-U entered into an accord whereby Patty agreed to pay, and Cars-4-U agreed to accept, $3,000 as payment in full of the $5,000 disputed debt. Under these facts:
   a. The $5,000 debt was discharged when Patty and Cars-4-U made the accord.
   b. The $5,000 debt is not discharged until Patty pays the $3,000, i.e., a satisfaction occurs.
   c. The $5,000 debt is not discharged even if Patty pays the $3,000 to Cars-4-U.
   d. The $5,000 debt is not discharged until Patty pays the entire $5,000 to Cars-4-U.

____ 5. Select the contract that is discharged pursuant to the doctrine of impossibility.
   a. Acme Corp. contracted to sell a heart medicine to Wholesaler. The contract was legal when made. Prior to performance, the FDA unforeseeably declared the sale of this medicine illegal.
   b. XYZ contracted to sell a standard Sony stereo to Bob. Prior to performance, XYZ's stereos were destroyed by fire. XYZ can obtain the required stereo elsewhere to deliver to Bob.
   c. Larry contracted to buy a house. Prior to either party's performing, Larry died.
   d. Papco Inc. contracted to overhaul an airplane for Beefsteak Airlines. Papco cannot perform the contract on time due to a shortage of necessary materials.

CASE PROBLEM

Answer the following problem, briefly explaining your answer.

Roger contracted to buy a silver mining company. After contracting, the price of silver fell sharply making it unprofitable to mine silver. Prior to contracting, Roger was aware that the price of silver could fall sharply which would negatively affect the value of the mining company, and Roger assumed this risk.

(a) In general, when is a contract discharged under the doctrine of supervening (commercial) impracticability? (b) In general, when is a contract discharged under the doctrine of economic frustration? (c) Is Roger's contract to purchase the silver mining company discharged under either of these doctrines?

CPA REVIEW

The following questions were given on CPA examinations. The answers for these questions are the unofficial answers prepared by the American Institute of Certified Public Accountants, Inc. (AICPA). All material is reproduced with permission of the AICPA.

____ 1. To cancel a contract and to restore the parties to their original positions before the contract, the parties should execute a
   a. Novation
   b. Release
   c. Rescission
   d. Revocation

____ 2. Under a personal services contract, which of the following circumstances will cause the discharge of a party's duties?
   a. Death of the party who is to receive the services.
   b. Cost of performing the services has doubled.
   c. Bankruptcy of the party who is to receive the services.
   d. Illegality of the services to be performed.

____ 3. On June 1, 1986, Nord Corp. engaged Milo & Co., CPAs, to perform certain management advisory services for nine months for a $45,000 fee. The terms of their oral agreement required Milo to commence performance any time before October 1, 1986. On June 30, 1987, after Milo completed the work to Nord's satisfaction, Nord paid Milo $30,000 by check. Nord conspicuously marked on the check that it constituted payment in full for all services rendered. Nord has refused to pay the remaining $15,000 arguing that, although it believes the $45,000 fee is reasonable, it had received bids of $30,000 and $38,000 from other firms to perform the same services as Milo. Milo endorsed and deposited the check. If Milo commences an action against Nord for the remaining $15,000, Milo will be entitled to recover
   a. $0 because there has been an enforceable accord and satisfaction.
   b. $0 because the statute of frauds has not been satisfied.
   c. $8,000 because $38,000 was the highest other bid.
   d. $15,000 because it is the balance due under the agreement.

____ 4. Which of the following statements correctly applies to a typical statute of limitations?
   a. The statute requires that a legal action for breach of contract be commenced within a certain period of time after the breach occurs.
   b. The statute provides that only the party against whom enforcement of a contract is sought must have signed the contract.
   c. The statute limits the right of a party to recover damages for misrepresentation unless the false statements were intentionally made.
   d. The statute prohibits the admission into evidence of proof of oral statements about the meaning of a written contract.

CHAPTER 17   151

5. Castle borrowed $5,000 from Nelson and executed and delivered to Nelson a promissory note for $5,000 due on April 30. On April 1 Castle offered, and Nelson accepted, $4,000 in full satisfaction of the note. On May 15, Nelson demanded that Castle pay the $1,000 balance on the note. Castle refused. If Nelson sued for the $1,000 balance Castle would
   a. Win, because the acceptance by Nelson of the $4,000 constituted an accord and satisfaction.
   b. Win, because the debt was unliquidated.
   c. Lose, because the amount of the note was not in dispute.
   d. Lose, because no consideration was given to Nelson in exchange for accepting only $4,000.

6. Parc hired Glaze to remodel and furnish an office suite. Glaze submitted plans that Parc approved. After completing all the necessary construction and painting, Glaze purchased minor accessories that Parc rejected because they did not conform to the plans. Parc refused to allow Glaze to complete the project and refused to pay Glaze any part of the contract price. Glaze sued for the value of the work performed. Which of the following statements is correct?
   a. Glaze will lose because Glaze breached the contract by not completing performance.
   b. Glaze will win because Glaze substantially performed and Parc prevented complete performance.
   c. Glaze will lose because Glaze materially breached the contract by buying the accessories.
   d. Glaze will win because Parc committed anticipatory breach.

7. Dell owed Stark $9,000. As the result of an unrelated transaction, Stark owed Ball that same amount. The three parties signed an agreement that Dell would pay Ball instead of Stark, and Stark would be discharged from all liability. The agreement among the parties is
   a. A novation.
   b. An executed accord and satisfaction.
   c. Voidable at Ball's option.
   d. Unenforceable for lack of consideration.

8. In September 1988, Cobb Company contracted with Thrifty Oil Company for the delivery of 100,000 gallons of heating oil at the price of 75¢ per gallon at regular specified intervals during the forthcoming winter. Due to an unseasonably warm winter, Cobb took delivery on only 70,000 gallons. In a suit against Cobb for breach of contract, Thrifty will
   a. Lose, because Cobb acted in good faith.
   b. Lose, because both parties are merchants and the UCC recognizes commercial impracticability.
   c. Win, because this is a requirements contract.
   d. Win, because the change of circumstances could have been contemplated by the parties.

CHAPTER 18
BREACH OF CONTRACT AND REMEDIES

CHAPTER OUTLINE

A. WHAT CONSTITUTES A BREACH OF CONTRACT

1. DEFINITION OF BREACH

A breach of contract is a failure to perform contractual duties. A party is entitled to contractual remedies if the other party breaches a contract.

2. ANTICIPATORY BREACH

GENERAL RULE. An anticipatory repudiation (i.e., a renunciation of a contract) occurs when a contracting party clearly indicates that he or she will not perform the contract when the time for performance arrives.
LIMITATION. A contracting party can retract an anticipatory repudiation if the other party has not relied on the repudiation. If the other party has relied on the anticipatory repudiation, however, then the party making the repudiation cannot retract it.
STUDY HINTS. ▸ An anticipatory repudiation may result from: (1) an express statement or (2) conduct that makes it impossible for the other party to perform the contract. ▸ An anticipatory repudiation may be treated as a breach prior to the time that performance is actually due.

B. WAIVER OF BREACH

3. CURE OF BREACH BY WAIVER

GENERAL RULE. A party may waive a breach of contract by the other party. Example: Buyer is required to pay May 1, but Buyer pays May 2. Seller accepts payment, telling Buyer it's OK.
STUDY HINT. A party who waives a breach: (1) gives up the right to damages or remedies regarding such breach; and (2) cannot use the breach as a reason for not performing the contract.

4. EXISTENCE AND SCOPE OF WAIVER

GENERAL RULE. ▸ A waiver may be express or implied. ▸ Example of implied waiver: accepting a defective performance without objection.
LIMITATION. A waiver applies only to the specific matter waived. A party is entitled to require the other party to strictly perform all other contractual obligations and all future obligations.

5. WAIVER OF BREACH AS MODIFICATION OF CONTRACT

GENERAL RULE. If a party repeatedly breaches in the same manner and the other party repeatedly waives these breaches, this conduct may indicate that the parties have modified the contract.
LIMITATION. If a clause states that a contract cannot be modified by a waiver, then waivers do not modify the contract and the original contract terms can be enforced regarding future performances.

6. RESERVATION OF RIGHT

GENERAL RULE. A party retains the right to recover damages caused by another's breach if the party expressly reserves the right to damages at the time the party accepts a defective performance.
STUDY HINT. A "reservation of rights" (to damages) is indicated by an acceptance stating that a defective performance is accepted "without prejudice" to a claim for damages or "under protest."

C. REMEDIES FOR BREACH OF CONTRACT

7. REMEDIES UPON ANTICIPATORY REPUDIATION

If a party makes an anticipatory repudiation, the other party has the following options: (1) do nothing, wait until the time for performance, and then sue if performance is not made; or (2) treat the repudiation as a definite breach and sue immediately; or (3) treat the repudiation as an offer to cancel the contract and accept the offer, thereby terminating the contract.

8. ACTION FOR DAMAGES

▸ A contracting party is entitled to damages if the other party breaches a contract. ▸ In general, damages are the sum of money necessary to put a party in the same or equivalent financial position the party would have been in had the contract been performed. ▸ Important rules include:

- *Measure of (compensatory) damages*: ▸ A party can recover compensatory damages for any actual loss that the party can prove with reasonable certainty. ▸ A party cannot recover damages for annoyance, emotional upset, or for uncertain, speculative losses. ▸ If no actual loss occurred, a court may award nominal (token) damages, such as $1.
- *Punitive (exemplary) damages*: ▸ In most cases, a party cannot recover punitive damages (damages awarded solely to punish a wrongdoer) due to a breach of contract. ▸ Consumer protection laws permit consumers to recover punitive damages for a breach of certain contracts.
- *Direct and consequential damages*: ▸ Compensatory damages include: (1) direct damages (damages necessarily caused by a breach); and (2) consequential damages (damages that occur due to the particular circumstances of the injured party). ▸ A party can recover consequential damages only if a person in the position of the breaching party could have reasonably foreseen that the injured party might suffer this type of loss if the contract was breached.
- *Mitigation of damages*: ▸ A nonbreaching party has a duty to mitigate damages, i.e., to take reasonable steps to minimize damages. A party cannot recover damages that the party could have reasonably avoided. ▸ A party does not have a duty to mitigate damages if: (1) there is no reasonable way to minimize damages; or (2) the cost of mitigation is unreasonably great.
- *Conversion of foreign currency*: U.S. courts award damages in American dollars.

9. RESCISSION

GENERAL RULES. ▸ A party may rescind a contract if the other party commits a material breach. If necessary, a party may file an action to obtain a judicial rescission of the contract. ▸ A rescinding party: (1) must return the other party to the position that the other party was in prior to contracting (i.e., the party must return all contract benefits received); and (2) is entitled under quasi contract to recover the reasonable value of money paid or other benefits already given to the other party.
LIMITATIONS. ▸ A party cannot rescind if the other party cannot be returned to his or her precontracting position. ▸ In most cases, a party can only rescind the contract *or* recover damages. But; in a contract for the sale of goods, a party may rescind the contract *and* recover damages.
STUDY HINT. If a land sale contract is rescinded, the buyer can recover the value of improvements made by the buyer, and the buyer must pay rent for the time the land was occupied.

10. ACTION FOR SPECIFIC PERFORMANCE

GENERAL RULE. A party may obtain specific performance (i.e., an order compelling performance of a contract) if: (1) a subject matter is unique; and (2) damages are inadequate to remedy the harm.
LIMITATION. Specific performance is an equitable remedy that is subject to numerous limits.
STUDY HINTS. ▸ Damages may be inadequate because: (1) it is difficult to determine damages; or (2) replacement goods are not available elsewhere. ▸ A party can generally obtain specific performance of contracts to buy: (1) land; (2) stock representing a controlling interest in a close corporation (i.e., a nonpublic corporation with few shareholders) if there is no established value for the stock; or (3) goods that are unique or cannot be purchased elsewhere. ▸ Typically, a party cannot obtain specific performance of personal service contracts or employment contracts.

11. ACTION FOR AN INJUNCTION

If a party threatens to commit an act that would cause a material breach of a contract, a court may issue an injunction (court order) that prohibits the party from doing the threatened act.

D. CONTRACT PROVISIONS AFFECTING REMEDIES AND DAMAGES

12. LIMITATION OF REMEDIES

▸ In general, a contract may limit the remedies that a nonbreaching party may obtain. ▸ Example: Troy purchases a new truck from ABC Truck Sales and the contract limits Troy's remedies to having ABC repair or replace the truck if it is defective.

13. LIQUIDATED DAMAGES

GENERAL RULE. A contract may state the amount of damages to be paid if the contract is breached. This amount is "liquidated damages." Upon a party's breach, the other party will recover this amount of damages whether actual damages are more or less than the liquidated amount.
LIMITATIONS. ▸ Liquidated damages are valid only if: (1) the amount of actual damages are difficult or impossible to foresee; and (2) the liquidated amount is a reasonable forecast of probable damages. ▸ If a liquidated damage is unreasonably large, it is called a penalty and the liquidated damage clause is void. In this event, the injured party can recover only his or her actual damages.

14. LIMITATION OF LIABILITY CLAUSES

GENERAL RULE. In general, an exculpatory (limitation-of-liability) clause that eliminates a party's liability for damages caused by a breach of contract is valid and enforceable.
LIMITATION. An exculpatory clause may be invalid if: (1) parties have unequal bargaining power and the clause is unfair; (2) the clause eliminates liability of a public utility for negligence; (3) a party is guilty of intentional or reckless conduct that harms another; or (4) the exculpatory clause was obtained by fraud or other wrongful conduct.
STUDY HINTS. ▸ Release forms signed by participants in sporting activities are generally valid.
▸ Exculpatory clauses are typically upheld if agreed to by businesses with equal bargaining power.

15. INVALID PROVISION RELATING TO REMEDIES OR DAMAGES

If a clause limiting remedies or damages is invalid, the remainder of the contract is enforced.

REVIEW OF TERMS AND PHRASES

Select the term or phrase that best matches a statement or definition stated below. Each term or phrase is the best match for only one statement or definition.

Terms and Phrases

a. Anticipatory repudiation
b. Breach
c. Compensatory damages
d. Consequential loss
e. Direct loss
f. Exculpatory clause
g. Injunction
h. Liquidated damages
i. Mitigation of damages
j. Nominal damages
k. Penalty
l. Punitive (exemplary) damages
m. Reservation of rights
n. Specific performance
o. Waiver

Statements and Definitions

_____ 1. Loss that is the natural result of a breach.

_____ 2. Damages awarded to punish a party.

_____ 3. Token damages that are awarded when a party proves a breach of contract, but the party cannot prove any actual loss.

_____ 4. Contractually agreed-upon damages to be paid if a party breaches a contract.

_____ 5. Doctrine prohibiting recovery of damages that a party can reasonably avoid.

_____ 6. Clear expression by a party that future performance of a contract will not be made when required.

_____ 7. Loss occurring because of the particular circumstances of the injured party.

_____ 8. Express or implied acceptance of a defective performance by the other party.

_____ 9. Damages awarded to compensate a party for actual losses suffered.

_____ 10. Equitable remedy requiring performance of a contract.

_____ 11. Retaining a right to damages that may be caused by another party's improper performance.

_____ 12. Contract provision stating that a party shall not be liable for damages caused by a breach.

_____ 13. Unreasonably large liquidated damage amount that is unrelated to potential damages that may result from a breach.

_____ 14. Remedy that prohibits a party from doing an act that would constitute a breach of contract.

_____ 15. Failure to perform a contract.

REVIEW OF CONCEPTS

Write **T** if the statement is true, write **F** if it is false.

_____ 1. A contracting party's wrongful act that makes performance of a contract impossible may constitute an anticipatory repudiation.

_____ 2. An anticipatory repudiation cannot be taken back even if no one has relied on the repudiation.

_____ 3. In general, a party cannot waive a breach unless the waiver is stated in a signed writing.

_____ 4. In general, repeated breaches by one party that are waived by the other contracting party do not establish a modification of contract if the contract contains an antimodification clause.

_____ 5. A party may accept a defective performance by the other party and still be entitled to sue for damages if the party reserves a right to damages at the time the performance is accepted.

_____ 6. If a party commits an anticipatory repudiation, the other party cannot sue for breach of contract until the time for performance has passed.

_____ 7. A party cannot recover damages if the damages are speculative and uncertain.

_____ 8. A party cannot get consequential damages unless that type of loss was reasonably foreseeable.

_____ 9. One party breached a contract and the other party suffered $1,000 damages. If $500 of the damages were reasonably avoidable but the injured party failed to take the necessary steps to avoid these damages, then the injured party can recover no damages whatsoever.

_____ 10. A party is not required to expend an unreasonable sum of money to mitigate damages.

_____ 11. A court may refuse to award specific performance if specific performance will cause the breaching party an unreasonable hardship.

_____ 12. A party can generally get specific performance even if damages adequately compensate for a loss.

_____ 13. An example of a contractual limitation of remedy that is generally valid is a clause that limits a buyer's remedy to having a seller repair or replace a defective good.

_____ 14. In an appropriate case, a contracting party may obtain an injunction that would prohibit the other party from committing an act that would breach the contract.

_____ 15. If a limitation of remedy clause is invalid, then the entire contract is void and unenforceable.

REVIEW OF CHAPTER - APPLICATION OF CONCEPTS

MULTIPLE CHOICE QUESTIONS

_____ 1. Gill contracted to sell pasta to Cafe each week. Gill agreed to deliver the pasta every Monday. One week, Gill breached the contract when he did not deliver the pasta until Wednesday. Cafe waived the breach resulting from this one late delivery. Under these facts:
   a. Cafe can cancel the contract due to the one late delivery.
   b. Cafe can sue Gill for damages due to the one late delivery.
   c. Cafe cannot cancel the contract or sue Gill for damages due to the one late delivery.
   d. In the future, Cafe cannot enforce the original contract term requiring delivery on Monday.

_____ 2. R&R Pesticide Co. agreed to spray Farmer's fields on July 1. On May 1, R&R told Farmer that there was a 50 percent chance that it might not be able to perform the contract. Under these facts:
   a. R&R has committed an anticipatory repudiation.
   b. R&R has not committed an anticipatory repudiation.
   c. Farmer is entitled to cancel the contract on May 1.
   d. a and c.

3. Beth agreed to repair a computer for AAA Tax Service. Beth unintentionally breached the contract. As a result of Beth's breach, the computer suffered $250 damage, and AAA lost profits of $500 because it could not complete certain tax returns without the computer. The lost profits were reasonably foreseeable, although Beth never actually thought about them. Mitigation was not possible. Under these facts, can AAA recover any damages from Beth?
   a. AAA cannot recover any damages. Beth did not agree to pay for losses caused by a breach.
   b. AAA can recover only $250 direct damages.
   c. AAA can recover $250 direct damages and $500 consequential damages.
   d. AAA can recover $250 direct damages, $500 consequential damages, and $1,000 punitive damages.

4. Lori contracted to buy a tract of land from Ken. Lori has not paid any of the purchase price. Ken has conveyed title to the land to Lori. Prior to taking possession, Lori discovered that Ken had fraudulently misrepresented to her that the property contained 100 acres when in fact it contained only 75 acres. Under these facts:
   a. Lori can rescind the contract and she can sue for all of her compensatory damages.
   b. Lori can rescind the contract, but she must return title to the land to Ken.
   c. Lori can rescind the contract and she can retain title to the land.
   d. Lori cannot rescind the contract.

5. Juan can obtain specific performance of which contract?
   a. Seller contracted to sell Juan a farm. Seller wrongfully refuses to convey title.
   b. Juan bought a bull. Seller wrongfully failed to deliver the bull. The bull is a unique, hybrid bull that is to be used for breeding and it cannot be replaced. Damages cannot be measured.
   c. Juan hired Tex to be a ranch foreman. Tex wrongfully refuses to perform.
   d. a and b.

CASE PROBLEM

Answer the following problem, briefly explaining your answer.

Mica Co. agreed to build a commercial storage building by September 1 for Pack Rat Storage. It was hard to predict Pack Rat's losses if the building was not completed on time. The parties estimated that Pack Rat would lose $200 in storage fees per day if the building was not completed on time. Thus, the contract required Mica to pay liquidated damages of $200 per day if the work was completed late. Mica finished ten days late. Pack Rat actually lost $1,800 due to the breach.

(a) Is the liquidated damage amount stated in the contract between Mica Co. and Pack Rat Storage valid, or is it an invalid penalty? (b) How much in damages can Pack Rat Storage recover from Mica Co.?

CPA REVIEW

The following questions were given on CPA examinations. The answers for these questions are the unofficial answers prepared by the American Institute of Certified Public Accountants, Inc. (AICPA). All material is reproduced with permission of the AICPA.

____ 1. Jones, CPA, entered into a signed contract with Foster Corp. to perform accounting and review services. If Jones repudiates the contract prior to the date performance is due to begin, which of the following is not correct?
   a. Foster could successfully maintain an action for breach of contract after the date performance was due to begin.
   b. Foster can obtain a judgment ordering Jones to perform.
   c. Foster could successfully maintain an action for breach of contract prior to the date performance is due to begin.
   d. Foster can obtain a judgment for the monetary damages it incurred as a result of the repudiation.

____ 2. Ames Construction Co. contracted to build a warehouse for White Corp. The construction specifications required Ames to use Ace lighting fixtures. Inadvertently, Ames installed Perfection lighting fixtures which are of slightly lesser quality than Ace fixtures, but in all other respects meet White's needs. Which of the following statements is correct?
   a. White's recovery will be limited to monetary damages because Ames' breach of the construction contract was not material.
   b. White will not be able to recover any damages from Ames because the breach was inadvertent.
   c. Ames did not breach the construction contract because the Perfection fixtures were substantially as good as the Ace fixtures.
   d. Ames must install Ace fixtures or White will not be obligated to accept the warehouse.

____ 3. Which of the following remedies is available to a party who has entered into a contract in reliance upon the other contracting party's innocent misrepresentation as to material facts?

	Compensatory damages	Punitive damages	Rescission
a.	No	No	No
b.	Yes	No	Yes
c.	No	No	Yes
d.	Yes	Yes	No

____ 4. Under the UCC Sales Article, a plaintiff who proves fraud in the formation of a contract may
   a. Elect to rescind the contract and need not return the consideration received from the other party.
   b. Be entitled to rescind the contract and sue for damages resulting from the fraud.
   c. Be entitled to punitive damages provided physical injuries resulted from the fraud.
   d. Rescind the contract even if there was no reliance on the fraudulent statement.

CHAPTER 18

___ 5. Kaye contracted to sell Hodges a building for $310,000. The contract required Hodges to pay the entire amount at closing. Kaye refused to close the sale of the building. Hodges sued Kaye. To what relief is Hodges entitled?
   a. Punitive damages and compensatory damages.
   b. Specific performance and compensatory damages.
   c. Consequential damages or punitive damages.
   d. Compensatory damages or specific performance.

___ 6. In general, a clause in a real estate contract entitling the seller to retain the purchaser's down payment as liquidated damages if the purchaser fails to close the transaction, is enforceable
   a. In all cases, when the parties have a signed contract.
   b. If the amount of the down payment bears a reasonable relationship to the probable loss.
   c. As a penalty, if the purchaser intentionally defaults.
   d. Only when the seller cannot compel specific performance.

___ 7. Master Mfg., Inc. contracted with Accur Computer Repair Corp. to maintain Master's computer system. Master's manufacturing process depends on its computer system operating properly at all times. A liquidated damages clause in the contract provided that Accur pay $1,000 to Master for each day that Accur was late responding to a service request. On January 12, Accur was notified that Master's computer system failed. Accur did not respond to Master's service request until January 15. If Master sues Accur under the liquidated damage provision of the contract, Master will
   a. Win, unless the liquidated damage provision is determined to be a penalty.
   b. Win, because under all circumstances liquidated damage provisions are enforceable.
   c. Lose, because Accur's breach was not material.
   d. Lose, because liquidated damage provisions violate public policy.

___ 8. Foster Co. and Rice executed a contract by which Foster was to sell a warehouse to Rice for $270,000. The contract required Rice to pay the entire $270,000 at the closing. Foster has refused to close the sale of the warehouse to Rice. If Rice commences a lawsuit against Foster, what relief would Rice likely be entitled to?
   a. Specific performance or compensatory damages.
   b. Specific performance and compensatory damages.
   c. Compensatory damages or punitive damages.
   d. Compensatory damages and punitive damages.

CHAPTER 19
ACCOUNTANTS' LIABILITY AND MALPRACTICE

CHAPTER OUTLINE

A. GENERAL PRINCIPLES

1. WHAT CONSTITUTES MALPRACTICE

Malpractice is a failure by an accountant or other professional to use the care and skill that other members of their profession in the community would use under similar circumstances.

2. CHOICE OF REMEDY

- ***Breach of contract or tort action***: ▸ Typically, malpractice is both the tort of negligence and a breach of a contract to render professional services. ▸ An injured patient or client has the right to decide whether to sue for the tort or for the breach of contract. For several reasons, plaintiffs in most cases elect to sue for the tort.
- ***Action by third person***: In general, a third party (i.e., a person who did not contract directly with the professional) can sue a professional for malpractice only on the basis of tort law; a breach of contract action is generally not available to a third party.

3. THE ENVIRONMENT OF ACCOUNTANTS' MALPRACTICE LIABILITY

Many factors have caused the scope of accountants' malpractice liability to expand in this century.

4. LIMITATION OF LIABILITY

GENERAL RULE. An accountant can disclaim liability for negligence malpractice if a disclaimer is: (1) clear and unambiguous; and (2) conspicuous (a reasonable person would notice the disclaimer).
LIMITATIONS. ▸ Disclaimers do not protect an accountant from liability: (1) if the accountant knows or has reason to know that statements are false; or (2) statements are intentionally misstated. ▸ In some states, disclaimers cannot be enforced against a third party who is suing for malpractice.
STUDY HINT. A disclaimer is valid if an accountant must rely on data supplied by others or the data cannot be verified, no opinion is expressed regarding the data, and these facts are disclosed.

5. CONTRIBUTORY NEGLIGENCE OF PLAINTIFF

▸ A client's negligence in relying on negligently prepared papers may reduce an accountant's malpractice liability. ▸ A third party who negligently relies on negligently prepared papers cannot sue an accountant for malpractice. ▸ It may be negligence to rely on preliminary (working) papers.

B. MALPRACTICE LIABILITY OF NONACCOUNTANTS

6. STANDARD OF CARE

GENERAL RULE. Doctors, lawyers, and other professionals, such as surveyors and safety inspectors, must use the care and skill used by others in the same profession in the same community.
LIMITATION. The standard of care that a professional must exercise may change over time. To some degree, the standard may also vary in different parts of the country.

7. PERSONS ENTITLED TO DAMAGES

(a) Other contracting party

A party who contracted with a professional who committed malpractice may sue the professional for damages caused by the breach of contract (or tort) resulting from the malpractice.

(b) Third persons

Courts disagree regarding a third party's right to sue for negligence malpractice that is committed by a nonaccountant with whom the party had not contracted. Three approaches are:

- *Privity of contract rule*: Some courts hold that a person cannot sue for malpractice if the person is not in privity of contract with the wrongdoer, i.e., the person did not contract directly with the wrongdoer. Some courts apply this rule only if the person is suing solely for an economic (monetary) loss, and not for personal injury or property damage.
- *Abandonment of privity of contract rule*: A number of courts now permit a person to sue for malpractice even if the person did not directly contract with the wrongdoer. In some states the privity of contract requirement has been abolished, and in other states a party may recover so long as there was a foreseeable risk of harm to anyone.
- *Relaxation of privity of contract rule*: Some courts still generally follow the privity of contract rule, but may allow a third party to recover for negligent malpractice if the third party has a particularly close relation to the wrongdoer or to the transaction in question.

C. ACCOUNTANTS' MALPRACTICE LIABILITY

8. STANDARDS OF CONDUCT FOR ACCOUNTANTS

Accountants have a duty to exercise the care, skill, and competence that reasonably competent members of the accounting profession would exercise under similar circumstances. Accountants are liable to their clients for damages resulting from a breach of this duty (i.e., for malpractice).

9. LIABILITY OF ACCOUNTANT FOR CLIENT'S LIABILITY

It is not settled whether a client can sue an accountant for malpractice as soon as the client becomes responsible for additional taxes because of the malpractice or whether the client must actually pay the additional taxes before suing.

10. NONLIABILITY TO THE INTERLOPER

An accountant is not liable to a person who is not related to the transaction in question and who unforeseeably relies on statements without being authorized to do so, i.e., an interloper.

11. NONLIABILITY TO PERSON AFFECTED BY THE DECISION OF ACCOUNTANT'S CLIENT

GENERAL RULE. According to at least one court, a person cannot sue an accountant for malpractice merely because the accountant's client made an unfavorable decision with regard to that person based on incorrect financial materials furnished by the accountant.

STUDY HINT. Example: client does not contract with a third party because of incorrect financial report. Third party cannot sue accountant because of the incorrect report.

12. ACCOUNTANTS' NEGLIGENCE MALPRACTICE LIABILITY TO THIRD PERSONS

There are a number of conflicting theories to determine whether a third party can sue an accountant for negligence due to malpractice. These theories are as follows:

- *The privity rule*: ▸ Only an accountant's client (who is in privity of contract with the accountant) can sue for malpractice. A third party cannot sue for malpractice based on negligence. ▸ Example: Third Party Bank cannot recover against Accountant if the bank suffered a loss when it loaned money to Client based on materials negligently prepared by Accountant for Client.
- *The contact rule*: ▸ An accountant is liable to a third party if: (1) the accountant met or communicated with the third party; and (2) the accountant knew the purpose for which the third party intended to use the accountant's work and foresaw the other party's reliance. ▸ Example: Accountant prepared statements for Client, and Accountant took the materials to Third Party Bank to negotiate a loan for Client.
- *The known-user rule*: ▸ An accountant is liable only if the accountant actually knew that a *specific* third party or a member of a specific, identified group would rely on the work. ▸ Example: Client tells Accountant that statements will be given to Third Party Bank in order to obtain a loan. (Note: The fact that it is foreseeable that someone may rely on the work is not sufficient.)
- *The foreseeable-user rule*: ▸ An accountant is liable to a third party who is a member of a class that the accountant should reasonably foresee may rely on the work. ▸ Example: Third Party Bank may sue Accountant for malpractice if Client tells Accountant that Client intends to use statements prepared by Accountant to obtain a loan from someone. (The *Restatement of Torts* adopts this approach.)
- *The intended user rule*: An accountant is liable only to third parties who were expected or intended to rely on the work. Example: Accountant gives financial statements to Third Party, or Accountant gives financial statements to Client knowing that Client will give them to Third Party.
- *The flexible rule*: Privity not required; no fixed test; courts decide each case on its own facts.

13. ACCOUNTANTS' FRAUD MALPRACTICE LIABILITY TO THIRD PERSONS

- *What constitutes fraud by accountants*: An accountant commits fraud by knowingly or recklessly making a false statement with the intent that another party rely on the statement, and the other party relies on the statement causing the party a loss.
- *Fraud liability of accountant to intended victims*: An accountant is liable to anyone: (1) who is intended by the accountant to rely on a fraudulent statement; or (2) who is a member of a group that is expected to rely on the statement. Privity of contract is not required for liability for fraud.

14. ACCOUNTANTS' MALPRACTICE LIABILITY UNDER STATUTES

- *Securities Act of 1933*: ▸ This Act regulates initial sales of securities, and it requires disclosure of information in a registration statement. ▸ An accountant may be liable if: (1) the accountant consents to being named in a registration statement and it contains false statements or omissions (Section 11); or (2) the accountant's conduct is a substantial factor in causing a fraudulent sale of securities (Section 12).
- *Securities Exchange Act of 1934*: ▸ This Act regulates the resale of securities. ▸ In connection with a resale of securities, Section 10(b) and Rule 10b-5 make an accountant liable for losses suffered by others due to the accountant's false or misleading statements or failure to disclose information *if* the accountant acted with scienter (i.e., guilty knowledge or intent to deceive).
- *Liability of accountants under antiracketeering statutes*: An accountant may be liable for treble damages under RICO if the accountant's malpractice aids or furthers a pattern of racketeering.

REVIEW OF TERMS AND PHRASES

Select the term or phrase that best matches a statement or definition stated below. Each term or phrase is the best match for only one statement or definition.

Terms and Phrases

a. Interloper
b. Malpractice
c. Privity of contract
d. RICO
e. Securities Act of 1933
f. Securities Exchange Act of 1934

Statements and Definitions

____ 1. Direct contractual relationship between two parties.

____ 2. Federal securities law that generally regulates the initial issuance and sale of securities in interstate commerce.

____ 3. Failure to use the care and skill used by other members of the same profession in the community.

____ 4. Federal securities law that generally regulates the secondary sale (resale) of securities in interstate commerce.

____ 5. Person who is unrelated to a matter involving an accountant's preparation of financial materials for a client and who unforeseeably relies on the materials without being authorized to do so.

____ 6. Federal law that entitles an injured party to bring an action for treble (triple) damages that were caused by a pattern of racketeering.

REVIEW OF CONCEPTS

Write **T** if the statement is true, write **F** if it is false.

____ 1. In general, a client may sue an accountant or other professional who has committed malpractice for either the tort or the breach of contract that results from the malpractice.

____ 2. In general, a third party can sue a professional for malpractice only on the basis of tort law.

____ 3. The scope of an accountant's malpractice liability has expanded significantly during this century.

____ 4. An accountant is liable for all losses suffered by a third party who relied on negligently prepared materials even if the third party was negligent in relying on such materials.

____ 5. There is disagreement among courts regarding whether, and under what circumstances, third parties can sue for malpractice that is committed by nonaccountant professionals.

____ 6. Under the *contact rule*, an accountant is not liable to a third party who relied on materials that the accountant negligently prepared unless the accountant met with or had contact with the third party.

____ 7. Under the *flexible rule*, an accountant's liability to third parties is determined on a case-by-case basis.

____ 8. Under the *privity rule*, a professional is not liable for malpractice to a third party with whom the professional did not directly contract.

____ 9. Accountants have a legal duty to exercise the same degree of care, skill, and competence that other accountants in the community exercise; violation of this duty constitutes malpractice.

____ 10. An interloper can sue an accountant for losses caused by the accountant's malpractice.

____ 11. According to some courts, if an accountant negligently prepared an incorrect profit and loss statement for a company and a manager for the company were denied a promotion because of this incorrect statement, the manager could not sue the accountant for malpractice.

____ 12. Under the *intended user rule*, a negligent accountant is liable to a third party who relies on the accountant's work even if the accountant did not expect or intend that this third party would rely on the work.

____ 13. An accountant who fraudulently prepared financial statements is generally liable to anyone who was intended or expected to rely on such statements.

____ 14. In connection with a resale of securities, the Securities Exchange Act of 1934 imposes liability on an accountant for losses suffered by others who rely on incorrect financial statements that were negligently prepared by the accountant even if the accountant did not act with scienter.

____ 15. If an accountant's malpractice aids or furthers a pattern of racketeering, the accountant may have criminal liability but the accountant cannot be held liable for damages under RICO.

REVIEW OF CHAPTER - APPLICATION OF CONCEPTS

MULTIPLE CHOICE QUESTIONS

____ 1. Carol is a CPA who agreed to prepare a financial statement for Q&R Inc. The contract contains a clear, unambiguous, and conspicuous disclaimer of liability for any incorrect matters stated in the financial statement. If the statement is partly incorrect, in most states the disclaimer would:
  a. Avoid liability for incorrect matters regarding facts relating to Q&R's foreign operations that Carol could not verify, if this limitation is clearly stated in the financial statement.
  b. Avoid liability for incorrectly stated matters that Carol intentionally misstated.
  c. Avoid liability for incorrectly stated matters that Carol had reason to know were inaccurate.
  d. Not avoid liability for any incorrect matters because accountants' disclaimers are prohibited.

____ 2. Carl is a CPA and, pursuant to a contract with Draco Inc., Carl prepared financial statements for Draco. Carl negligently prepared the statements. Carl knew Draco might use the statements to obtain a loan from an unnamed lender. In fact, Lucky Bank lent money to Draco on the basis of these statements. As a result of Carl's malpractice, both Draco and Lucky Bank suffered a loss. If the *privity of contract rule* is applied in this case, who can sue Carl for malpractice?
  a. Only Draco Inc.
  b. Only Lucky Bank.
  c. Draco Inc. and Lucky Bank.
  d. Neither Draco Inc. nor Lucky Bank.

CHAPTER 19

_____ 3. Stu is a CPA and, pursuant to a contract with Hit Co., Stu prepared financial statements for Hit Co. Stu negligently prepared the statements. Stu knew Hit Co. planned to use the statements in order to obtain a contract from the State of New York and he knew that the State would rely on the statements. Based on these statements, the State did contract with Hit Co., and the State suffered a loss as a result of Stu's malpractice. Select the correct answer if the *contact rule* is used in this case.
   a. The State of New York can sue Stu for malpractice even if Stu never met, communicated with, or had any contact with New York officials.
   b. The State of New York can sue Stu for malpractice if Stu met with New York officials regarding the financial statements of Hit Co.
   c. The State of New York cannot sue Stu for malpractice even if Stu had contact with New York officials regarding the financial statements of Hit Co.
   d. The State of New York could sue Stu for malpractice only if they were in privity of contract.

_____ 4. Kim is a CPA and, pursuant to a contract with ABC Inc., Kim prepared financial statements for ABC. Kim negligently prepared the statements. Kim knew ABC planned to use the statements to obtain a loan from Bucks Bank. Based on these statements, Bucks lent ABC money and Bucks suffered a loss as a result of Kim's malpractice. Select the correct answer if the *known user rule* is strictly applied in this case.
   a. Bucks cannot sue Kim for malpractice. Under this rule, third parties cannot sue an accountant for malpractice.
   b. Bucks can sue Kim for malpractice only if she actually met with officials of Bucks.
   c. Bucks can sue Kim for malpractice even if she never had any contact with officials of Bucks.
   d. Bucks could sue Kim for malpractice only if they were in privity of contract.

_____ 5. Dan is a CPA and, pursuant to a contract with A&A, Dan prepared financial statements for A&A. Dan negligently prepared the statements. Dan knew A&A planned to use the statements to buy inventory on credit. Based on these statements, Acme sold inventory to A&A and Acme suffered a loss due to Dan's malpractice. Select the right answer if the *foreseeable user rule* is applied.
   a. Acme cannot under any circumstance sue Dan for malpractice.
   b. Acme can sue Dan for malpractice even if Dan did not know A&A was buying from Acme.
   c. Acme can sue Dan for malpractice only if Dan knew that A&A intended to buy from Acme.
   d. Acme can sue Dan for malpractice only if Dan actually met with Acme officials.

CASE PROBLEM

Ben, a CPA, prepared financial statements for Lips Co. The statements were seriously inaccurate due to Ben's negligence and his failure to diligently verify matters presented in the statements. However, Ben did not know the statements were inaccurate. The statements were made as part of a registration statement for the initial sale of Lips Co. stock in interstate commerce. With his consent, Ben was stated in the registration statement as preparing the financial statements. (a) Does the Securities Act of 1933 apply to this offering? (b) Will Ben have liability under this Act if investors suffer a loss due to their reliance on the statements prepared by Ben?

CPA REVIEW

The following questions were given on CPA examinations. The answers for these questions are the unofficial answers prepared by the American Institute of Certified Public Accountants, Inc. (AICPA). All material is reproduced with permission of the AICPA.

____ 1. Under common law, which of the following statements most accurately reflects the liability of a CPA who fraudulently gives an opinion on an audit of a client's financial statements?
   a. The CPA is liable only to third parties in privity of contract with the CPA.
   b. The CPA is liable only to known users of the financial statements.
   c. The CPA probably is liable to any person who suffered a loss as a result of the fraud.
   d. The CPA probably is liable to the client even if the client was aware of the fraud and did not rely on the opinion.

____ 2. Beckler & Associates, CPAs, audited and gave an unqualified opinion on the financial statements of Queen Co. The financial statements contained misstatements that resulted in a material overstatement of Queen's net worth. Queen provided the audited financial statements to Mac Bank in connection with a loan made by Mac to Queen. Beckler knew that the financial statements would be provided to Mac. Queen defaulted on the loan. Mac sued Beckler to recover for its losses associated with Queen's default. Which of the following must Mac prove in order to recover?
   I. Beckler was negligent in conducting the audit.
   II. Mac relied on the financial statements.
   a. I only.
   b. II only.
   c. Both I and II.
   d. Neither I nor II.

____ 3. Which of the following statements best describes whether a CPA has met the required standard of care in conducting an audit of a client's financial statements?
   a. The client's expectations with regard to the accuracy of audited financial statements.
   b. The accuracy of the financial statements and whether the statements conform to generally accepted accounting principles.
   c. Whether the CPA conducted the audit with the same skill and care expected of an ordinarily prudent CPA under the circumstances.
   d. Whether the audit was conducted to investigate and discover all acts of fraud.

____ 4. Which of the following is the best defense a CPA firm can assert in defense to a suit for common law fraud based on their unqualified opinion on materially false financial statements?
   a. Lack of privity.
   b. Lack of scienter.
   c. Contributory negligence on the part of the client.
   d. A disclaimer contained in the engagement letter.

CHAPTER 19

5. Sun Corp. approved a merger plan with Cord Corp. One of the determining factors in approving the merger was the financial statements of Cord that were audited by Frank & Co., CPAs. Sun had engaged Frank to audit Cord's financial statements. While performing the audit, Frank failed to discover certain irregularities that later caused Sun to suffer substantial losses. For Frank to be liable under common law negligence, Sun at a minimum must prove that Frank
   a. Knew of the irregularities.
   b. Failed to exercise due care.
   c. Was grossly negligent.
   d. Acted with scienter.

6. Krim, President and CEO of United Co., engaged Smith, CPA, to audit United's financial statements so that United could secure a loan from First Bank. Smith issued an unqualified opinion on May 20, 1988, but the loan was delayed. On August 5, 1988, on inquiry to Smith by First Bank, Smith, relying on Krim's representation, made assurances that there was no material change in United's financial status. Krim's representation was untrue because of a material change which took place after May 20, 1988. First relied on Smith's assurances of no change. Shortly thereafter, United became insolvent. If First sues Smith for negligent misrepresentation, Smith will be found
   a. Not liable, because Krim misled Smith, and a CPA is not responsible for a client's untrue representations.
   b. Liable, because Smith should have undertaken sufficient auditing procedures to verify the status of United.
   c. Not liable, because Smith's opinion only covers the period up to May 20.
   d. Liable, because Smith should have contacted the chief financial officer rather than the chief executive officer.

7. If a stockholder sues a CPA for common law fraud based on false statements contained in the financial statements audited by the CPA, which of the following, if present, would be the CPA's best defense?
   a. The stockholder lacks privity to sue.
   b. The false statements were immaterial.
   c. The CPA did not financially benefit from the alleged fraud.
   d. The contributory negligence of the client.

8. When CPAs fail in their duty to carry out their contracts for services, liability to clients may be based on

	Breach of contract	Strict liability
a.	Yes	Yes
b.	Yes	No
c.	No	No
d.	No	Yes

CHAPTER 20
PERSONAL PROPERTY

CHAPTER OUTLINE

A. GENERAL PRINCIPLES

1. PERSONAL PROPERTY

GENERAL RULES. ▸ Personal property includes: (1) rights in tangible, movable property; (2) choses in action (legal claims and debts); and (3) intangible rights, such as copyrights, patents, and trademarks.
▸ Personal property does not include rights in real property (i.e., land, things embedded in land, such as gasoline tanks, and things attached to the land, such as buildings).
STUDY HINT. A person may own the entire interest or only a partial interest in property.

2. LIMITATIONS ON OWNERSHIP

A party who owns the entire interest in property has absolute ownership of the property. But this ownership is subject to the rights of creditors and to the government's power to tax and regulate.

B. ACQUISITION OF TITLE TO PERSONAL PROPERTY

3. GIFTS

A gift of property is a: (1) passing of title; (2) made with the intent to pass title; (3) without receiving money or value in consideration for the passing of title. Types of gifts include:

- ***Inter vivos gifts***: ▸ An inter vivos gift is made if a donor: (1) expresses the intent to convey all rights to property at the present time; and (2) delivers the property to the donee, or makes symbolic (constructive) delivery of the property by delivering the means to control the property or a symbol of ownership, such as keys or documents of title. ▸ Depositing money into a joint bank account with an adult donee with the intent to make a gift constitutes a gift of the money deposited.

- ***Gifts causa mortis***: ▸ A gift causa mortis is a conditional gift made by a donor who believes that he or she will soon die, and it is made with the intent that a donee will own the property if the donor dies.
▸ A gift causa mortis fails and the intended donee acquires no rights if: (1) the donor does not die; (2) the donee dies first; or (3) the donor takes back the gift before death.

- ***Gifts and transfers to minors***: ▸ Several Uniform Acts allow property to be given or transferred to a minor by delivering the property to a custodian. The custodian may use the property for the minor's benefit, education, maintenance, and support. ▸ Under these Uniform Acts, a minor is usually entitled to possession of the property at age 21. ▸ A gift cannot be revoked once it is made in accordance with these Uniform Acts.

- ***Conditional gifts***: ▸ A conditional gift transfers rights only when certain stated conditions are met. A gift may be subject to a condition precedent or a condition subsequent. ▸ Marriage engagement gifts are conditional gifts. Most states allow recovery of an engagement gift if the person seeking to recover the gift did not unreasonably terminate the engagement.

- ***Anatomical gifts***: ▸ Anatomical gifts are gifts of organs or body parts. ▸ The Uniform Anatomical Gift Act allows anatomical gifts to be made by persons who are 18 or older, or by certain members of a decedent's family.

4. FINDING OF LOST PROPERTY

GENERAL RULES. ▸ Lost property is property that an owner has misplaced without intending to give up ownership. ▸ A person who finds lost property does not acquire title to the property. At most, a finder of lost property is entitled to possession of the property until it is claimed by the owner.
LIMITATIONS. ▸ Lost property that is found in a public place must be turned over to the manager of the place if it appears that the property was intentionally placed there by its owner. ▸ In some states, a finder of lost property may sell or keep the property if the true owner does not claim it.

5. TRANSFER BY NONOWNER

GENERAL RULE. A person who does not own property cannot pass title to the property.
LIMITATION. In some cases, an owner's agent or another party to whom the owner has entrusted property may have the power to sell or transfer title to the property.
STUDY HINT. One cannot acquire title from a thief; the true owner may recover the property.

6. OCCUPATION OF PERSONAL PROPERTY

GENERAL RULE. Subject to possible statutory limitations, the first person to find and take possession of abandoned property (i.e., property voluntarily left behind or given up) or to take control of a wild animal becomes the owner of the abandoned property or wild animal.
LIMITATION. Property left behind due to an emergency is not abandoned property.

7. ESCHEAT

Escheat statutes typically provide that a state owns personal property that is not claimed by anyone.

C. MULTIPLE OWNERSHIP OF PERSONAL PROPERTY

8. TENANCY IN COMMON

GENERAL RULE. Tenants in common own undivided fractional interests in the same property. An owner may transfer an interest during life or upon death without terminating a tenancy in common.
LIMITATION. Partition (division) of tenancy in common property results in each owner's acquiring complete ownership of a specific portion of the property.

9. JOINT TENANCY

GENERAL RULE. Joint tenants jointly own property with a right of survivorship.
LIMITATION. To create a joint tenancy, many states require that an instrument state that the co-owners are acquiring title "with right of survivorship."
STUDY HINTS. ▸ If a joint tenant transfers his or her interest to a third party, the new owners become tenants in common. ▸ If a joint tenant dies, surviving owners acquire the deceased owner's interest.

10. TENANCY BY ENTIRETY

GENERAL RULES. ▸ At common law, transfer of property to a husband and wife created a tenancy by entirety. If a spouse died, the surviving spouse got the decedent's interest in the property. ▸ A creditor of *both* spouses can execute on (take and sell) property that is held by the entirety.
LIMITATIONS. ▸ A spouse cannot unilaterally transfer his or her interest. ▸ Creditors of only one spouse cannot claim property. ▸ Divorce converts tenancy by entirety into tenancy in common.

11. COMMUNITY PROPERTY

In certain states, most property acquired by either spouse during marriage is community property.

REVIEW OF TERMS AND PHRASES

Select the term or phrase that best matches a statement or definition below. Each term or phrase is the best match for only one statement or definition.

Terms and Phrases

a. Abandoned property
b. Community property
c. Conditional gift
d. Escheat
e. Gift causa mortis
f. Inter vivos gift
g. Joint tenancy
h. Lost property
i. Personal property
j. Tenancy in common

Statements and Definitions

____ 1. Gift that is made in contemplation of death and that is conditioned upon the death of the donor.

____ 2. Transfer of ownership of unclaimed property to the state.

____ 3. In some states, most property that is acquired by a husband or wife during marriage.

____ 4. Present gift of property.

____ 5. Property that an owner intends to give up.

____ 6. Type of co-ownership; persons own undivided interest in same property; no right of survivorship.

____ 7. Gift that is effective only if certain stated conditions are satisfied.

____ 8. Type of co-ownership; if a co-owner dies, the other co-owners acquire the decedent's interest.

____ 9. Property that an owner has misplaced without intending to give up ownership.

____ 10. Broad category of property that includes all property rights except rights in real property.

REVIEW OF CONCEPTS

Write **T** if the statement is true, write **F** if it is false.

____ 1. If a donor makes a gift causa mortis but the donor does not die, then the gift fails and the donee receives nothing.

____ 2. Real property, such as land and things attached to land, are one type of personal property.

____ 3. In many states, in order to create a joint tenancy, title must be taken by the parties specifically stating that they are taking title "with right of survivorship."

____ 4. When personal property held in tenancy in common is partitioned, the person who owns the largest share of the property is awarded title to all of it.

____ 5. If *X* and *Y* own property as tenants in common and *X* dies, then *X*'s interest in the property will pass to *X*'s heirs. In this event, *X*'s heirs and *Y* will own the property as tenants in common.

____ 6. If *A* and *B* own property by joint tenancy and *A* transfers her interest in the property to *C*, then *B* and *C* will own the property as joint tenants.

____ 7. A person cannot own a partial interest in an item of personal property; a person must own all or no portion of an item.

____ 8. Persons over the age of 18 may now legally make an anatomical gift.

____ 9. A third party who in good faith buys an item of personal property from a thief acquires good title to the property if the third party did not know that the property was stolen and paid value for it.

____ 10. Community property laws are now applied in all states.

REVIEW OF CHAPTER - APPLICATION OF CONCEPTS

MULTIPLE CHOICE QUESTIONS

____ 1. Grandma, who was in good health, intended to make a present gift of her car to Rob. Grandma wrote: "I give my Cadillac to Rob," and she gave Rob the keys to the car that was located 100 miles away. Prior to Rob's taking possession of the car, Grandma died. Under these facts:
   a. Grandmother did not make a valid inter vivos gift of the car to Rob.
   b. Grandmother made a valid inter vivos gift of the car to Rob.
   c. Grandmother made a valid gift causa mortis of the car to Rob.
   d. Grandmother made a valid conditional gift of the car to Rob.

____ 2. In accordance with an applicable Uniform Act, Jean made a completed gift of some corporate stock to her 17-year-old daughter. Jean was named as the custodian of the stock. Under these facts:
   a. Jean cannot spend income from the stock to pay for her daughter's college tuition.
   b. Jean can spend income from the stock to pay for Jean's personal credit card bills.
   c. In most cases, Jean's daughter would be entitled to receive the stock when she turns 21.
   d. Jean can revoke the gift of the stock whenever she wants, reclaiming the stock as her own.

___ 3. George found a "lost" diamond bracelet in the wall safe in his hotel room (a public place). Which answer best describes George's rights to the bracelet?
   a. George owns the bracelet. A person automatically owns lost property that he or she finds.
   b. Pursuant to the doctrine of escheat, George automatically owns the bracelet.
   c. George may keep the bracelet until the owner reclaims it.
   d. George must turn the bracelet over to the hotel manager for safekeeping for the bracelet's true owner.

___ 4. Thief stole Mary's VCR, and Thief sold the VCR to Gordon for $300. Gordon did not know that the VCR was stolen, and he paid the $300 purchase price to Thief. Under these facts:
   a. Gordon did not acquire title to the VCR even though he bought it for value and in good faith.
   b. Gordon acquired valid title to the VCR because he bought it for value and he was unaware that the VCR was stolen.
   c. Mary cannot recover the VCR from Gordon.
   d. The VCR is an example of abandoned property.

___ 5. John and Judy are husband and wife, and they own certain real property as tenants by the entirety. Under these facts:
   a. If Judy dies, her interest in the property will pass to the persons named in her will.
   b. John or Judy can individually transfer their respective interests in the property to anyone they choose.
   c. Foremost Finance, a creditor of both John and Judy, cannot execute on the property.
   d. Lonesome Loan Co., John's individual creditor, cannot execute on the property while John and Judy are both alive.

CASE PROBLEM

Answer the following problem, briefly explaining your answer.

Jethro was diagnosed as having advanced brain cancer and the doctors believed that he had only a few days to live. He told Sally May, his girlfriend, that he wanted her to have his car when he died. Sally May immediately took possession of the car. As it turns out, the doctors misdiagnosed Jethro's condition and he rapidly recovered. Several weeks later, Jethro was struck by a hit and run driver and he died shortly afterwards. Who is entitled to the car - Sally May or Jethro's estate?

CPA REVIEW

The following questions were given on CPA examinations. The answers for these questions are the unofficial answers prepared by the American Institute of Certified Public Accountants, Inc. (AICPA). All material is reproduced with permission of the AICPA.

____ 1. Which of the following would change if an asset is treated as personal property rather than as real property?

	Requirements for transfer	Creditor's rights
a.	Yes	No
b.	No	Yes
c.	Yes	Yes
d.	No	No

____ 2. Which of the following factors help determine whether an item of personal property has become a fixture?

	Manner of affixation	Value of the item	Intent of the annexor
a.	Yes	Yes	Yes
b.	Yes	Yes	No
c.	Yes	No	Yes
d.	No	Yes	Yes

____ 3. Which of the following items is tangible personal property?
    a. Share of stock.
    b. Trademark.
    c. Promissory note.
    d. Oil painting.

____ 4. Which of the following factors is **least** significant in determining whether an item of personal property has become a fixture?
    a. The extent of injury that would be caused to the real property by the removal of the item.
    b. The value of the item.
    c. The manner of attachment.
    d. The adaptability of the item to the real estate.

CHAPTER 21
INTELLECTUAL PROPERTY RIGHTS

CHAPTER OUTLINE

A. TRADEMARKS AND SERVICE MARKS

1. **INTRODUCTION**

    GENERAL RULES. ▸ A trademark is a word, name, symbol, or combination of these that identifies the manufacturer of a product. A service mark is the same thing, except it identifies the provider of a service. ▸ Registration of a mark on the federal Principal Register entitles a person to the exclusive use of a mark.
    LIMITATION. The validity of a trademark registration may be challenged at any time within five years after the a mark is registered.
    STUDY HINT. Subject to certain limits, an advance registration of a mark may be made for up to three years prior to actual use of the mark by filing an application certifying a bona fide "intent-to-use."

2. **REGISTRABLE MARKS**

    GENERAL RULES. ▸ A mark may be registered if it distinguishes a person's product or service from products or services of competitors. ▸ Arbitrary, fanciful, or suggestive marks are presumed to be distinctive and to merit protection. ▸ Generic terms that merely describe a class of products cannot be registered. Examples: "motor oil"; "airline." ▸ Descriptive or geographical terms, and surnames cannot be registered unless they acquire a secondary meaning. Examples: descriptive mark: "anti-knock gasoline"; geographic mark: "California wine"; surname: "Lucas' Pizza."
    LIMITATION. Descriptive or geographical terms, and surnames may be protected if they acquire a secondary meaning, that is, when through long usage the public identifies the mark with a particular product or service of a specific provider. Example: "Best Western" Motels.
    STUDY HINT. ▸ Arbitrary or fanciful names are names that have no other meaning. Example: "7-Up." ▸ Suggestive terms indirectly hint as to the nature of a product. Example: "Duracell" battery. ▸ In rare instances, the color of a product may be registered as the trademark for a product.

3. **TRADE DRESS PROTECTION**

    ▸ Trade dress is the total appearance of a product, including its packaging, label, shape, and size. Trade dress may also include physical structures associated with a particular product or service, such as the distinctive shape of a fast food chain sign. ▸ Trade dress may qualify as a protected trademark or service mark if it is distinctive and identifies the source of a specific product or service.

4. **INJUNCTION AGAINST IMPROPER USE OF MARK**

    The owner of a mark may obtain a court order (injunction) to prevent the improper use or duplication of a mark if such use may likely confuse the public regarding the source of a product.

5. **ABANDONMENT OF EXCLUSIVE RIGHT TO MARK**

    If the owner of a mark permits widespread use of the mark to describe a general class of products, the exclusive right to the mark may be lost. Examples: "cellophane"; "aspirin."

B. COPYRIGHTS

GENERAL RULE. A copyright is the exclusive right to use an original expression that is preserved in a tangible form.
LIMITATION. A person cannot copyright a mere idea.
STUDY HINT. Under an international treaty known as the Berne Convention, a work that is copyrighted under U.S. law is entitled to protection in all other countries who have approved this convention.

6. DURATION OF COPYRIGHT

GENERAL RULE. A copyright gives the creator of the work the exclusive right to use or reproduce a literary, artistic, dramatic, audiovisual, or musical work or computer program for the creator's life plus 50 years.
LIMITATION. If a work is a "work made for hire," meaning that a person was hired specifically to create the copyrighted work, then the business employing the creator may register the copyright and is entitled to protection for 100 years from creation or 75 years from publication, whichever is less.

7. COPYRIGHT NOTICE

▸ Prior to 1989, the author of an original work secured his or her copyright protection by (1) placing the word "copyright" or the symbol © on the work together with other information and (2) registering the copyright with the Copyright office. ▸ Under current law, placing notice of copyright on a work is strongly suggested, but is no longer required in order to be protected.

8. WHAT IS COPYRIGHTABLE

Many types of expressions can be copyrighted, including writings, books, musical compositions, architectural works, paintings, sculptures, photographs, audio and video recordings, compilations of facts and data, and computer programs.

9. RIGHTS OF COPYRIGHT HOLDERS

▸ A copyright owner is granted the exclusive right to: (1) reproduce or copy the work; (2) rent, sell, license, or otherwise dispose of the work; (3) perform or display the work publicly; and (4) prepare any further works based on the copyrighted work. ▸ Copyright law generally establishes statutory rates that must be paid when a person uses a copyrighted work, such as commercially singing a copyrighted song.

10. LIMITATION ON EXCLUSIVE CHARACTER OF COPYRIGHT

"Fair use" permits the limited use of copyrighted matters for purposes of criticism, parody, teaching, research, or news reporting.

C. PATENTS

A patent is the exclusive right to own and use an invention or design.

11. TYPES, DURATION, AND NOTICE

GENERAL RULE. Devices, processes, and inventions that embody new, useful, and nonobvious scientific principles, technologies, or processes can be patented. Three types of patents and the period for which they may be patented are:

- Utility patents: Utility patents include patents for most new products and processes and they are valid for 20 years.
- Plant patents: Patents for new varieties of asexually reproduced plants and they are also valid for 20 years.
- Design patents: Design patents may be obtained for new, original, ornamental designs for manufactured goods and they are valid for 14 years.

LIMITATION. The word "patent" and the patent number must be stated on a patented item in order to recover damages from an infringer.

12. PATENTABILITY AND EXCLUSIVE RIGHTS

To acquire patent protection, an invention must be novel, nonobvious, and useful.

D. SECRET BUSINESS INFORMATION

13. TRADE SECRETS

- A trade secret is secret business information that gives its owner a competitive advantage over others.
- Trade secrets may include a special formula, recipe, method of production or operation, or a compilation of data, such as market statistics or customer lists.

14. LOSS OF PROTECTION

GENERAL RULE. A trade secret is no longer protected if it is disclosed to the public, unless the secret is only disclosed in a restrictive manner to persons who know of its confidential nature.
STUDY HINT. Unpatented goods may be "reverse engineered" after unrestricted public sale.

15. DEFENSIVE MEASURES

Employers should allow employees access to trade secrets only on a "need-to-know" basis.

E. PROTECTION OF COMPUTER SOFTWARE AND MASK WORKS

16. COPYRIGHT PROTECTION OF COMPUTER PROGRAMS

- In general, computer programs may be copyrighted. - The Computer Software Copyright Act protects copyrighted programs from infringement. - Infringement is determined by examining the similarity of significant steps of programs, instead of just comparing the number of similar steps.

17. PATENT PROTECTION OF PROGRAMS

In appropriate cases, computer programs may be patented.

18. TRADE SECRETS

Trade secret laws are sometimes used to protect computer programs.

19. RESTRICTIVE LICENSING

Creators of software frequently impose restrictions in licensing agreements that provide greater protection than is available under copyright laws. Such restrictions may include: (1) limits on reverse engineering, which is used to learn the structure of a program; or (2) limits on renting or relicensing to third persons, which helps to prevent unauthorized copying.

20. SEMICONDUCTOR CHIP PROTECTION

The Semiconductor Chip Protection Act gives an owner of a mask work exclusive rights for ten years.

REVIEW OF TERMS AND PHRASES

Select the term or phrase that best matches a statement or definition below. Each term or phrase is the best match for only one statement or definition.

Terms and Phrases

a. Computer Software Copyright Act
b. Copyright
c. Hardware
d. Mask
e. Patent
f. Semiconductor chip
g. Semiconductor Chip Protection Act
h. Service mark
i. Software
j. Trade dress
k. Trademark
l. Trade secret

Statements and Definitions

____ 1. Private information that gives its owner a business advantage and which is protected by state law.

____ 2. Programs or instructions that control hardware.

____ 3. Equipment that is used in a computer system, such as a disk drive, monitor, or keyboard.

____ 4. Stencil that controls the etching process by which transistors are attached to semiconductor chips.

____ 5. A product's total image.

____ 6. Small square base with transistors that enables a computer to function according to a program.

____ 7. Exclusive right to use a mark that identifies a service.

____ 8. Exclusive right to use or reproduce a literary, artistic, musical, or audiovisual work.

____ 9. Federal law that may provide copyright protection for computer programs.

____ 10. Federal law that provides copyright protection for certain mask works.

____ 11. Exclusive right to use a mark that identifies a product.

____ 12. Exclusive right to make, use, and sell a device, process, or invention.

REVIEW OF CONCEPTS

Write **T** if the statement is true, write **F** if it is false.

____ 1. Patents are granted by state governments, not by the federal government.

____ 2. Trademarks may be protected for up to three years prior to the time that they are actually used.

____ 3. A descriptive mark may be registered as a trademark if it acquires a secondary meaning.

____ 4. In general, generic terms can be effectively registered as trademarks or service marks.

____ 5. A term acquires a secondary meaning when, through prolonged use, the public has come to associate that term with a particular product.

____ 6. In some cases, registration of a mark will not prevent its use by another party for a different, noncompetitive product or service that is sold in a different market.

____ 7. A copyright provides protection for the creator's life plus an additional 100 years.

____ 8. In general, mere ideas and concepts cannot be copyrighted or patented.

____ 9. A trade secret may be disclosed without losing its legal protection if it is restrictively disclosed to another person who is aware of its secret nature.

____ 10. An employment contract cannot require an employee to transfer to an employer the rights to employment-related inventions that the employee invented during the course of his or her employment.

____ 11. In general, a competitor is legally entitled to "reverse engineer" or copy a product if the product is sold to the public and the product has not been copyrighted or patented.

____ 12. A patent grants a patent owner the exclusive right to use and sell the patented item for 20 years.

____ 13. Confidential customer lists cannot be trade secrets that are protected from being wrongfully taken by competitors.

____ 14. Copyright infringement of programs is determined by focusing on the number of steps programs share in common and not by focusing on the similarity between significant program steps.

____ 15. Federal law expressly prohibits the patenting of any computer programs.

CHAPTER 21

REVIEW OF CHAPTER - APPLICATION OF CONCEPTS

MULTIPLE CHOICE QUESTIONS

_____ 1. Which of the following is NOT a requirement for obtaining a patent on a device?
   a. The device must be useful.
   b. The device must be new.
   c. The device must be nonobvious.
   d. The device must be capable of commercial exploitation.

_____ 2. Which of the following items CANNOT be copyrighted?
   a. A new book.
   b. A new idea for a movie.
   c. A new photograph.
   d. A new musical arrangement.

_____ 3. Ken invented a new type of mathematical calculator that he called "Wiser Guyser." Under these facts, the name "Wiser Guyser":
   a. Can be protected by registration for a patent.
   b. Can be protected by registration for a copyright.
   c. Can be protected by registration for a trademark.
   d. Cannot be protected.

_____ 4. Carl invented a new eating instrument for people who like to eat fast: a five-pronged fork. (Normal forks have only four prongs). Under these facts, can Carl patent his new fork?
   a. Yes, it is novel.
   b. Yes, it is useful.
   c. Yes, it is both novel and useful.
   d. No, it is an obvious derivative of an existing product, the four-pronged fork.

_____ 5. Which of the following names can be registered for trademark protection?
   a. "Motor oil," the name of a product that is used to lubricate engines.
   b. "Hot sauce," the name for a spicy food additive.
   c. "DuraBond," the name for a new type of glue.
   d. "Southern food," the name for food from the southern part of the United States.

_____ 6. Benders, a bar and grill, has been in business for many years, and it has an excellent reputation. John wanted his restaurant to be a success, so he remodeled his restaurant so the storefront looked the same as the unique design of Benders' establishment and he erected a sign over his restaurant reading "Benters." In this case, John is liable for:
   a. Patent infringement.
   b. Copyright infringement.
   c. Theft.
   d. Unfair competition.

_____ 7. Selma wrote a computer program and copyrighted it under U.S. copyright law. Selma allowed a German to review the program, but the German firm stated that they were not interested in the program. Unknown to Selma, the German firm duplicated the program and is selling it in Germany. Germany has signed the Berne convention. Under these facts:
   a. Selma cannot enforce her copyright against the German firm.
   b. Selma can enforce her copyright against the German firm only if it agrees to be sued.
   c. Selma can enforce her copyright against the German firm under the Berne convention.
   d. a and b.

_____ 8. For many years, Wowee Corp. has manufactured and sold high-quality toy slot cars known as "Wowee Toys." Wowee registered this trademark ten years ago. One year ago, Waui Enterprises, a travel agency, commenced business and started marketing cruise packages called "Waui Cruises." Has Waui Enterprises violated Wowee Corp.'s trademark?
   a. No, because the mark "Wowee Toys" was not properly registrable.
   b. No, because Waui Enterprises can challenge the validity of the registration of this mark.
   c. No, because the mark "Waui Cruises" is not the same or deceptively similar to the mark "Wowee Toys."
   d. Yes.

_____ 9. Jesse created a fictional tale about the life of a squirrel who became king of the animal world. He did not write it down, but instead told it neighborhood children. His tale was so popular with little children that he then wrote it down. Under these facts:
   a. Jesse cannot copyright the idea for his tale.
   b. Jesse can copyright the idea for his tale.
   c. Jesse can copyright the written version of his tale.
   d. a and c.

_____ 10. Over a five-year period, Jackson Corp. spent considerable time and money to develop a private list of 200,000 area homeowners. This list tracks home values, year of construction, and last home-repair project. This list has proven invaluable for marketing its home-improvement services. Under these facts, Jackson Corp. should protect this information as a:
   a. Patent
   b. Trade secret
   c. Trademark
   d. Service mark

_____ 11. In 1984, Hillary Thompson began selling enormous pieces of sour ball candy called "Thompson's Giant Sour Ball Candies." By the 1990s, Hillary's candies had become nationally known, and people thought only of her candy when they heard the words "Thompson's Giant Sour Ball Candies." Is the name for this candy entitled to trademark protection?
  a. No, the name is merely descriptive.
  b. No, the name is merely Hillary's surname.
  c. No, the name is merely generic.
  d. Yes, the name has acquired a secondary meaning.

_____ 12. Select the correct answer.
  a. Federal law does not provide any protection for software.
  b. Software may be copyrighted.
  c. Software may sometimes be patented.
  d. b and c.

_____ 13. Logic Co. has developed unique software for inventory control for plane manufacturers. Which action can Logic Co. take to try to protect its software?
  a. It may apply for copyright protection pursuant to the Computer Software Copyright Act.
  b. It may place anti-renting restrictions in licensing agreements for the software.
  c. It may place anti-reverse engineering restrictions in licensing agreements for the software.
  d. All of the above.

CASE PROBLEM

Answer the following problem, briefly explaining your answer.

Baxco Corp. makes and sells several products, and it wants to register the products' names on the Principal Register in order to obtain federal trademark protection. Baxco wants to register: (1) "Xeri-fun," the name of a new candy; (2) "Appalachian Whiskey," the name of an alcoholic product that Baxco has sold for many years and a name that the public associates only with Baxco's product; and (3) "soft-serve ice cream," the name of Baxco's machine-dispensed ice cream. (Soft-serve ice cream is a type of ice cream that includes any ice cream that is dispensed from a machine. Numerous companies throughout the U.S. sell their own "soft-serve ice cream.")

(a) Is Baxco entitled to register the foregoing marks? (b) If Baxco properly registers a mark, what can Baxco do if another party intentionally uses or infringes upon the registered mark?

CHAPTER 22
BAILMENTS

CHAPTER OUTLINE

A. GENERAL PRINCIPLES

1. **DEFINITION**

   A bailment is a relationship whereby personal property is delivered by a party (bailor) to another party (bailee), and the property must be returned or delivered in the manner agreed to by the parties.

2. **ELEMENTS OF BAILMENT**

   GENERAL RULES. ▸ Elements of a bailment are: (1) an agreement; and (2) delivery and acceptance of bailed property. ▸ A bailment agreement typically is a contract. The agreement may be express or implied, and it may be oral or written. ▸ A bailment is made when bailed property is delivered to the bailee, and the bailee accepts the property subject to the terms of the bailment agreement.
   LIMITATION. Acceptance requires knowledge that goods are in one's possession and control. Without this knowledge there is no bailment and a party is not responsible for goods of others.
   STUDY HINT. ▸ Delivery can be actual or constructive. ▸ Examples: actual: TV is delivered to a repair shop; constructive: keys to a car are given to a bailee who takes possession of the car.

3. **NATURE OF THE PARTIES' INTERESTS**

   ■ *Bailor's interest*: ▸ A bailor only needs to have a right to possession of bailed goods in order to have the rights of a bailor, including the right to return of bailed goods and the right to sue for damages for wrongful injury to bailed goods. ▸ A bailor does not need to actually own bailed goods in order to have the rights of a bailor.

   ■ *Bailee's interest*: ▸ A bailee has only the right to possess and use bailed goods to the extent that such rights are given by the bailment agreement. A bailee does not receive title to bailed goods. A bailee does not have the right to sell bailed goods unless the bailee is the bailor's authorized agent. ▸ In most cases, a bailee's wrongful sale of bailed goods does not transfer title to a third party purchaser, and the bailor can recover the goods from the third party buyer. But, a bailor cannot recover bailed goods from a third party buyer if: (1) the bailor misled the party into thinking that a bailee was the owner; or (2) the bailor entrusted goods to a bailee who deals in (buys and sells) that kind of goods, and the goods were sold in the ordinary course of business.

4. **CLASSIFICATION OF BAILMENTS**

   ▸ *Extraordinary bailment*: bailment that involves a public interest and imposes special duties and liabilities. Example: bailment by a common carrier. ▸ *Ordinary bailment*: any other bailment.
   ▸ *Contract bailment*: bailment agreed to in return for compensation or other value. ▸ *Gratuitous bailment*: bailment agreed to without expectation of compensation or other value.
   ▸ *Bailment for sole benefit of bailor*: bailee receives no benefits. Example: Denise asks a friend to hold her purse while she makes a phone call. ▸ *Bailment for sole benefit of bailee*: bailor receives no benefits. Example: Iris borrowed Li's hedge clippers. ▸ *Mutual benefit bailment*: both parties derive a benefit. Example: Pat left her car with Zeno's Garage for repairs.

5. CONSTRUCTIVE BAILMENTS

GENERAL RULE. If a party comes into possession of property without the owner's consent, the possessor is a bailee pursuant to a constructive bailment.
STUDY HINT. A constructive bailment arises when government officers impound one's property.

6. RENTING OF SPACE DISTINGUISHED

A bailment is not created if a person stores personal property in: (1) a locker or other space, and (2) the person keeps the exclusive right to use and control that locker or other space.

7. BAILMENT OF CONTENTS OF CONTAINER

GENERAL RULES. ▸ The parties' reasonable, objective intent determines whether a bailment of a container is also a bailment of the contents of the container. ▸ Unless otherwise agreed, a bailment of an article is also a bailment of items reasonably and normally found in the article.
STUDY HINT. ▸ Bailment of a car (possession and control given to attendant) includes contents in the trunk, but not unusual items in the car. ▸ Example: Bob received Pam's car. A box is in the trunk and, unknown to Bob, a gold ring is in the glove box. Bailment includes the car and box; not the ring.

B. RIGHTS AND DUTIES OF THE PARTIES

8. DUTIES OF THE BAILEE

- *Performance*: If there is a bailment contract, a bailee must perform all terms of the contract.
- *Care of property*: ▸ A bailee must use the care that a reasonable person would use to prevent foreseeable harm. ▸ Some courts state the standard of care as: (1) bailment for sole benefit of bailor: slight care; liable for gross negligence; (2) mutual benefit bailment: liable for ordinary negligence; (3) bailment for sole benefit of bailee: great care; liable for slight negligence.
- *Liability for damage*: ▸ A bailee is liable for damages resulting from: (1) a failure to properly care for bailed property; or (2) unauthorized use of bailed property. ▸ A bailee is not liable for damage caused by acts of third parties, accidents (if no one is at fault), or acts of God.
- *Contract modification of liability*: ▸ A bailee's liability may be expressly expanded by a bailment contract. ▸ A bailee can generally limit liability for negligence (not willful wrongs) if: (1) the bailment does not involve a public interest (i.e., a fundamental service or good needed by most persons is not involved); (2) statutes do not forbid disclaimers of liability; (3) the limitation is part of the contract; and (4) the bailor has notice of the limitation at the time of contracting.
- *Insurance*: ▸ A bailee need not insure bailed goods unless required to do so by statute or contract. ▸ Insurance terms regarding rented property that unreasonably limit coverage (such as no coverage for accidents resulting from intoxication) are often invalidated as being against public policy.
- *Maintenance of property*: In a bailment for hire a bailee must pay for ordinary maintenance unless a bailment is for a short term. The bailor, however, must usually pay for repairs if the bailee did not cause the damage.
- *Unauthorized use*: A bailee is liable for conversion (a tort) for unauthorized use of bailed goods.
- *Return of property*: ▸ A bailee must return or deliver the identical goods that were bailed. ▸ But in the case of fungible goods, only goods of the same quantity and quality need be returned. ▸ Return or delivery is to be made in accordance with the bailment contract.
- *Bailee's lien*: ▸ A bailee has a lien on goods entitling the bailee to keep possession of goods until all charges are paid. If not paid, some state statutes allow a bailee to give notice and sell bailed goods in order to obtain payment. ▸ A lien is lost if goods are voluntarily returned to a bailor.

9. BURDEN OF PROOF

In a suit by a bailor, the bailor must prove that bailed goods were not returned or were damaged due to the bailee's fault. This burden is initially met if a bailor proves that goods were delivered, but were not returned or were damaged. If this is proven, the bailor may recover damages unless a bailee proves that the loss or damage was not caused by the bailee's lack of care or unauthorized use of the goods.

10. RIGHTS OF THE BAILOR

▸ A bailor may sue a bailee for breach of contract if goods are not properly returned or rent is not paid. The bailor may sue for negligence, willful destruction, or conversion if the bailee wrongfully damages or destroys the goods. ▸ A bailor may sue a third party who wrongfully damages or takes bailed goods.

11. DUTIES OF THE BAILOR

(a) Condition of the property

GENERAL RULES. ▸ In a mutual benefit bailment, a bailor has a duty to provide a good that is reasonably fit for the purposes contemplated by the parties. ▸ If a bailor receives some benefit under the bailment, then the bailor must warn the bailee of known dangers and also reasonably investigate to discover defects. ▸ In a bailment for the sole benefit of bailee, a bailor has a duty to warn a bailee of known dangers.
LIMITATIONS. ▸ Typically, a bailor is not liable for injuries caused by an unknown defect that could not be discovered by a reasonable inspection. ▸ A bailee who is aware of a danger and voluntarily uses a defective good may be barred from recovering damages from a bailor.

(b) Implied warranty and strict liability

GENERAL RULES. ▸ Often, the duties described above regarding bailed goods are called implied warranties. ▸ In commercial leases of goods, it is implied that a bailed goods are fit for intended uses. Also, bailors may make express warranties regarding bailed goods. If goods fail a warranty, a bailor is liable even if the bailor was unaware of a defect and was not negligent.
STUDY HINT. In many states, strict liability also applies to bailments.

12. LIABILITY TO THIRD PERSONS

- *Liability of bailee*: A bailee who wrongfully injures a third party with a bailed good is liable to the same extent the bailee would be liable had the bailee owned the good.
- *Liability of bailor*: ▸ In general, a bailor is not liable for harm caused by a bailee while using bailed goods. ▸ However, a bailor may be liable for harm suffered by a third party if the harm occurs because: (1) goods were dangerous and this was unknown to the bailee; (2) dangerous goods were entrusted to a bailee who was known to be incompetent or reckless; (3) goods were defective and the bailor would have been liable had it been the bailee who was injured; or (4) the bailee is an employee of the bailor and the employee was acting within the scope of employment.
- *Test-drive situations*: When a customer takes a car on a test drive unaccompanied by the seller, a bailment exists, and a seller is typically not liable for harm caused by the customer. (Note: The customer is liable to the seller for any harm caused to a vehicle during the customer's test-drive.)
- *Family purpose doctrine*: Many (but not all) states hold a bailor liable for harm caused by the negligent operation of a car by a member of the bailor's family if the bailor furnished the car.

REVIEW OF TERMS AND PHRASES

Select the term or phrase that best matches a statement or definition stated below. Each term or phrase is the best match for only one statement or definition.

Terms and Phrases

a. Act of God
b. Bailee
c. Bailment
d. Bailor
e. Contract bailment (bailment for hire)
f. Extraordinary bailment
g. Family purpose doctrine
h. Fungible goods
i. Gratuitous bailment
j. Implied warranty
k. Lien
l. Ordinary bailment

Statements and Definitions

____ 1. Duty of certain bailors regarding the fitness of bailed goods.

____ 2. Bailment made in consideration for compensation or other value.

____ 3. Party to a bailment who transfers possession of personal property to the other party.

____ 4. Bailment that is not made in consideration for compensation or other value.

____ 5. Legal relationship by which possession of personal property is transferred to a person pursuant to an agreement that the identical property will be returned or disposed of as agreed.

____ 6. Legal right to retain personal property until another person performs a legal obligation.

____ 7. Party to a bailment who receives possession of personal property from the other party.

____ 8. Bailment that imposes unusual duties or liabilities upon a party.

____ 9. Goods that are interchangeable with one another; one good is equivalent to another good.

____ 10. Natural occurrence, such as a tornado, that is not reasonably foreseeable.

____ 11. Bailment that imposes the normal range of duties and liabilities upon the parties.

____ 12. Principle that imposes liability on a bailor for damages caused by a family member's negligent operation of a car if the bailor furnished the car to the family member.

REVIEW OF CONCEPTS

Write **T** if the statement is true, write **F** if it is false.

____ 1. A bailment cannot be implied from the conduct of parties; a bailment must be expressly made.

____ 2. Lessor leases a home to Lessee. This transaction is not a bailment.

____ 3. A bailor cannot recover damages from a bailee or a third party who wrongfully damaged bailed goods unless the bailor is the actual owner of the goods.

____ 4. A bailee has a right to use bailed goods for any purpose the bailee chooses.

____ 5. A bailee only receives possession of bailed goods; a bailee does not receive title to bailed goods.

____ 6. A bailment for the sole benefit of the bailor is created if a person gratuitously keeps and takes care of a friend's pet.

____ 7. If a party finds lost personal property that belongs to someone else, the finder possesses the property as a bailee pursuant to a constructive bailment.

____ 8. If a parking garage parks a car and the garage keeps the car keys and retains control over the car, then a bailment has been created.

____ 9. A bailment of a car is automatically a bailment of all property inside the car.

____ 10. A bailee is liable for the tort of conversion if the bailee makes unauthorized use of bailed goods.

____ 11. What constitutes reasonable care in a bailment is a fixed standard. The standard of care is not affected by the nature of the goods or by the bailee's experience in caring for this type of good.

____ 12. According to some courts, a bailee in a bailment for the sole benefit of the bailee owes a duty of great care, and the bailee will be liable for damages caused by the bailee's slight negligence.

____ 13. A bailee is generally liable for any damage to bailed goods even if the bailee is not at fault and damage is due to an act of a third party or an act of God.

____ 14. A bailor is commonly prohibited from limiting its liability for its negligence if the bailment involves a public interest.

____ 15. A limitation of liability stated on a receipt that is given to a bailee after a bailment contract is made is generally not effective to limit the bailor's liability.

REVIEW OF CHAPTER - APPLICATION OF CONCEPTS

MULTIPLE CHOICE QUESTIONS

____ 1. Select the correct answer.
   a. Rose rents a locker at Airport and she puts a bag in the locker. Rose keeps the locker key. In this case, the bag has been delivered to and accepted by Airport, and Airport is a bailee.
   b. Hill rents a boat to Dan. The boat is located at a lake 30 miles away. Hill gives Dan keys to the boat. Dan drives to the lake and takes possession of the boat. In this case, the boat has been delivered to and accepted by Dan, and Dan is a bailee.
   c. Unknown to Lon, Jake left a bike at Lon's house. In this case, the bike has been delivered to and accepted by Lon, and Lon is a bailee.
   d. b and c.

____ 2. Sis rented a stereo from Rent Co. Without Rent Co.'s authorization, Sis sold the stereo to Violet who did not know that the stereo belonged to Rent Co. Under these facts:
   a. Sis was legally entitled to sell the stereo. Violet received good title to the stereo.
   b. Sis was not legally entitled to sell the stereo. However, since Rent Co. rented the stereo to Sis, Sis had the power to transfer Rent Co.'s title and Violet received good title to the stereo.
   c. Sis was not legally entitled to sell the stereo. Violet did not receive good title to the stereo.
   d. None of the above.

____ 3. Quinn rented a paint spray gun from U-Rent-Um Rentals for $25 per day. This bailment is a:
   a. Bailment for the sole benefit of the bailor.
   b. Bailment for the sole benefit of the bailee.
   c. Mutual benefit bailment.
   d. Gratuitous bailment.

____ 4. Roxie agreed to repair Tom's TV for $100. Pursuant to their contract, Tom delivered the TV to Roxie and Roxie properly repaired the TV. Under these facts:
   a. Roxie has a duty to exercise ordinary care for the TV, and she will be liable for damage to the TV only if it results from her negligence.
   b. Roxie has a duty only to exercise slight care for the TV, and she will be liable for damage to the TV only if it results from her gross negligence.
   c. Roxie is obligated to insure the TV while it is in her possession.
   d. Roxie is entitled to personally use the TV.

____ 5. Select the correct answer.
   a. Ace Rentals rented a car to Nel for two weeks. While driving the car, Nel negligently injured a pedestrian. In this case Nel, but not Ace Rentals, is liable to the pedestrian.
   b. Dad allowed Son to drive the family car. Son negligently caused an accident. In many states, the family purpose doctrine would apply thereby imposing liability on Dad for Son's negligence.
   c. Rex wanted to buy a truck. Dealer let Rex take a truck home overnight to test drive. Rex negligently caused an accident. In this case Rex, but not Dealer, is liable for the accident.
   d. All of the above.

_____ 6. Which of the following is NOT a required element for a bailment?
   a. An agreement between the bailee and bailor.
   b. A written bailment agreement.
   c. Delivery of the bailed goods to the bailee.
   d. Acceptance of the bailed goods by the bailee.

_____ 7. Brighton parked his car in a public garage and walked away, keeping the keys to the car. Sarah gave her keys to a parking valet, who parked Sarah's car and kept the keys until she returned. Under these facts, who created a bailment?
   a. Only Brighton.
   b. Only Sarah.
   c. Both Brighton and Sarah.
   d. Neither Brighton nor Sarah.

_____ 8. Ursula checked her coat at a restaurant's cloak room. The coat had a $5,000 bracelet in the pocket. Under these facts, a bailment has been created for:
   a. Only the coat.
   b. Only the bracelet.
   c. Both the coat and the bracelet.
   d. Neither the coat nor the bracelet.

_____ 9. Kim asked Jake to hold her purse while she made a phone call. This bailment is a:
   a. Bailment for the sole benefit of the bailor.
   b. Bailment for the sole benefit of the bailee.
   c. Mutual benefit bailment.
   d. Consignment.

_____ 10. Mary brought her car to Fred's Garage for repairs and Fred charged Mary $500 for the repairs, a reasonable charge. Mary, however, thought the charges were too high and refused to pay. Fred told Mary that he would not give her the car until she paid. Under these facts:
   a. Fred acted properly, but he must return the car within 30 days to Mary.
   b. Fred acted properly and he may retain possession of the car until Mary pays.
   c. Fred acted properly, but he will lose his lien on the car if he returns it to Mary.
   d. b and c.

_____ 11. Ralph asked Judy to take his Ferrari to the garage for him. While driving to the garage, Judy could not help herself and drove the car at 100 mph when the posted speed limit was only 45 mph. Under state law, driving 30 miles above the speed limit is considered reckless (grossly negligent) driving. Judy wrecked the car. Is Judy liable to Ralph for the damage to his car?
   a. No, because this is a bailment for the sole benefit of the bailor and a bailee is not liable for damage to bailed goods.
   b. No, unless Ralph specifically instructed Judy not to exceed the posted speed limit.
   c. Yes, because this is a bailment for the sole benefit of the bailor and a bailee is liable for damage to bailed goods that results from the bailee's gross negligence.
   d. Yes, because this is a bailment for the sole benefit of the bailor and a bailee is strictly liable for damage to bailed goods, whether the bailee is negligent or not.

CASE PROBLEM

Roger wanted to go waterskiing, but he did not have any skis. Roger's friend, Manuel, loaned Roger a pair of skis. Manuel did not charge Roger a rental fee. While Roger was skiing, a defective foot support on one ski accidentally pulled loose, causing Roger to fall and break his leg. Manuel did not know that the foot support was defective. However, Manuel did not inspect the skis before lending them to Roger.

(a) What type of bailment is involved in this case? (b) Describe the duty that Manuel owed to Roger. (c) Is Manuel liable to Roger for Roger's injuries? (d) Is Roger liable to Manuel for the damage to the skis?

CPA REVIEW

The following questions were given on CPA examinations. The answers for these questions are the unofficial answers prepared by the American Institute of Certified Public Accountants, Inc. (AICPA). All material is reproduced with permission of the AICPA.

____ 1. Which of the following standards of liability best characterizes the obligation of a common carrier in a bailment relationship?
    a. Reasonable care.
    b. Gross negligence.
    c. Shared liability.
    d. Strict liability.

____ 2. Which of the following requirements must be met to create a bailment?
    I. Delivery of personal property to the intended bailee.
    II. Possession by the intended bailee.
    III. An absolute duty on the intended bailee to return or dispose of the property according to the bailor's directions.

    a. I and II only.
    b. I and III only.
    c. II and III only.
    d. I, II, and III.

CHAPTER 23
LEGAL ASPECTS OF WAREHOUSING, TRANSPORTATION, FACTORING, AND HOTEL KEEPING

CHAPTER OUTLINE

A. **WAREHOUSERS**

1. **DEFINITIONS**

   ▸ *Warehouser*: a party who engages in the business of storing goods for others for compensation. ▸ *Public warehouser*: a warehouser who stores goods for the public without discrimination.

2. **RIGHTS AND DUTIES OF WAREHOUSERS**

   GENERAL RULES. ▸ A warehouser is treated as a bailee in a mutual benefit bailment. Thus, a warehouser is liable only for negligent loss or damage to goods. ▸ A warehouser has a specific lien on goods in its possession for charges relating to those goods; goods may be sold to obtain payment.
   LIMITATIONS. ▸ Unless otherwise agreed, a lien attaches to only those goods for which charges are owed. ▸ Goods must be returned if charges and expenses are paid prior to sale of the goods.

3. **WAREHOUSE RECEIPTS**

   GENERAL RULE. A warehouse receipt is a writing issued by a warehouser (issuer) acknowledging receipt of goods for storage from a customer (depositor). A receipt states the terms of the contract.
   STUDY HINTS. ▸ Warehouse receipts do not need to be in any particular form. ▸ Warehouse receipts are one type of document of title, i.e., a document evidencing a person's right to goods.

4. **RIGHTS OF HOLDERS OF WAREHOUSE RECEIPTS**

   - *Nonnegotiable warehouse receipts*: ▸ A warehouse receipt is a nonnegotiable warehouse receipt if it requires delivery of goods to a named person, and the words "bearer" or "order" are not used. Example: "Deliver goods to Jim Hood." ▸ A transferee of a nonnegotiable warehouse receipt receives only the same right and title to goods as the transferor of the warehouse receipt had. ▸ The rights of a transferee of a nonnegotiable warehouse receipt may be defeated by a person who in good faith buys the goods from the transferor of the warehouse receipt.

   - *Negotiable warehouse receipts*: ▸ A receipt is a negotiable warehouse receipt if it requires delivery of goods to "bearer" or "to the order of" a named person. Example: "Deliver goods to the order of Jim Hood." ▸ A party receives good title to a negotiable receipt and the goods it represents if: (1) the party takes the receipt by negotiation; or (2) the receipt is duly negotiated to that person. The rights of a person to whom a receipt is duly negotiated are superior to those of almost everyone, except the original owner of goods if the goods were stolen from the owner. ▸ *Negotiation* means: (1) delivery of a receipt to the holder (buyer) if goods are to be delivered to "bearer"; or (2) proper indorsement of a receipt and delivery of the receipt if goods are to be delivered "to the order of" a person. ▸ *Duly negotiated* means: a holder takes a receipt: (1) in good faith; (2) in the ordinary course of business; (3) without notice of any defenses; and (4) the holder pays value for the receipt.

   - *Warranties*: A person who transfers any document of title for value impliedly guarantees to the transferee that: (1) the document is genuine; (2) its transfer is proper and effective; and (3) the transferor has no knowledge of any facts that would impair the value or validity of the document.

5. FIELD WAREHOUSING

Field warehousing: goods are stored on an owner's premises; a warehouser controls the storage area.

6. LIMITATION OF LIABILITY OF WAREHOUSER

GENERAL RULE. A warehouser can limit its liability if: (1) for a higher fee, a customer has the right to store goods without limited liability; and (2) a limit is stated for each item or unit of weight.

STUDY HINT. A limitation of liability is not effective if the customer is not informed of it at the time of contracting.

B. COMMON CARRIERS

7. DEFINITIONS

- *Basic definitions*: ▸ *Carrier*: party who agrees to transport goods, regardless of the method of shipment. ▸ *Consignor*: party who delivers goods to a carrier for shipment (i.e., a consignor is the shipper). ▸ *Consignee*: party to whom goods are shipped.
- *Types of carriers*: ▸ *Common carrier*: carrier willing to transport goods for compensation for any member of the public without discrimination. ▸ *Contract carrier*: carrier only transporting goods pursuant to individual contracts. ▸ *Private carrier*: carrier owned and operated by the shipper.
- *Controlling law*: ▸ Common carriers: common carrier law. ▸ Contract carriers: bailment law. ▸ Private carriers: employment law.

8. BILLS OF LADING

- *Definitions*: ▸ *Bill of lading*: document of title issued by a carrier for goods to be shipped by land. ▸ *Airbill*: document issued for goods to be shipped by air. ▸ *Nonnegotiable (straight) bill of lading*: goods are shipped to a named person; the words "bearer" or "order" are not used. ▸ *Negotiable bill of lading*: goods are shipped to "bearer" or "to the order of" a named person.
- *Law*: ▸ Intrastate shipment: UCC. ▸ Interstate shipment: Federal Bills of Lading Act.
- *Rules*: Rules regarding the transfer of bills of lading, rights of transferees of bills, and warranties are determined by the same rules previously discussed for warehouse receipts. (see Section 4 above)

9. RIGHTS OF COMMON CARRIER

GENERAL RULE. A common carrier can: (1) adopt reasonable business rules; (2) determine rates in order to earn a fair return (subject to government regulations); (3) charge a demurrage; and (4) have a specific lien on goods for shipment fees, demurrage charges, and expenses for preserving and selling goods.

LIMITATIONS. ▸ A lien only attaches to the goods that are shipped under the contract for which charges are owing. ▸ A lien is lost to the extent goods are delivered to the consignee.

10. DUTIES OF COMMON CARRIER

GENERAL RULES. ▸ A common carrier must: (1) accept and ship goods for all persons to the extent it can do so; (2) furnish proper storage and shipping facilities; (3) load and unload goods (unless otherwise agreed); and (4) ship and deliver goods in accordance with shipment contracts. ▸ Delivery under negotiable bill of lading: carrier must not deliver without first getting a properly indorsed bill of lading. ▸ Delivery under straight bill: carrier may deliver goods to consignee without getting bill.

LIMITATION. A common carrier is not obligated to carry goods if: (1) the goods are not appropriate for transportation; or (2) the carrier does not have the necessary facilities for shipment.

11. LIABILITIES OF COMMON CARRIER

- *Liability during shipment*: In general, a common carrier has absolute liability for any damage or loss to goods, but it does not have liability for losses that are caused by or result from: (1) act of God (natural phenomenon); (2) act of public enemy; (3) act of government official; (4) act of shipper (improper packaging); or (5) inherent nature of goods (such as perishable food).
- *Liability for delay*: A carrier is liable for damages caused by its failure to deliver in a reasonable time. But, a shipper bears the risk for losses caused by ordinary delays associated with shipping.
- *Liability C.O.D. (cash-on-delivery) shipment*: Common carrier must not deliver goods without first receiving payment and if it improperly does so, then it is liable to the shipper for damages.
- *Liability for rejected goods*: A carrier is liable only for its negligence once delivery is offered, but refused. But, absolute liability is reinstated once new shipping instructions are received.
- *Limitation of liability*: Subject to certain limits, a carrier can generally limit its liability.
- *Notice of claim:* Bill of lading or laws may require notice within a set time in order to claim damages.

C. FACTORS

12. DEFINITIONS

▸ *Factor*: special bailee (consignee) who sells bailed (consigned) goods. ▸ *Selling on consignment*: entrusting goods to another who is to sell the goods. ▸ *Consignor*: owner who consigns goods. ▸ *Consignee*: person to whom goods are consigned. ▸ *Commission:* compensation paid to a factor.

13. EFFECT OF FACTOR TRANSACTION

An authorized sale of consigned goods by a factor passes title to the goods to the buyer unless the consignor did not own the goods. In certain cases, a factor's creditors may take consigned goods.

D. HOTELKEEPERS

14. DEFINITIONS

▸ *Hotelkeeper*: operator of a hotel or motel, or other person who regularly offers temporary accommodations to guests. ▸ *Guest*: transient person who stays overnight. A guest is not a person visiting a guest or a person who stays overnight with a guest without a hotelkeeper's knowledge.

15. DURATION OF GUEST RELATIONSHIP

A hotelkeeper-guest relationship begins when a guest is received by a hotelkeeper, and it ends when the guest leaves (with baggage) or the guest arranges for permanent lodging with the hotelkeeper.

16. HOTELKEEPER'S LIABILITY FOR GUEST'S PROPERTY

▸ A hotelkeeper is a bailee regarding property actually given to the hotelkeeper. ▸ At common law, a hotelkeeper had absolute liability for loss of guest's property, subject to the same exceptions that apply to common carriers. ▸ By statute, most states now allow hotelkeepers to limit their liability.

17. HOTELKEEPER'S LIEN

A hotelkeeper has a lien on a guest's baggage for room charges. To obtain payment, baggage may be sold. A lien is lost if: (1) charges are paid; or (2) baggage is unconditionally returned to a guest.

18. BOARDERS OR LODGERS

A boarder takes lodging on a permanent basis. A hotelkeeper is liable for negligent damage to a boarder's property. A hotelkeeper has no lien unless given this right by contract or statute.

REVIEW OF TERMS AND PHRASES

Select the term or phrase that best matches a statement or definition stated below. Each term or phrase is the best match for only one statement or definition.

Terms and Phrases

a. Airbill
b. Boarder
c. Common carrier
d. Contract carrier
e. Demurrage
f. Factor
g. Field warehousing
h. Guest
i. Negotiable bill of lading
j. Negotiation
k. Nonnegotiable (straight) bill of lading
l. Private carrier
m. Public warehouser
n. Special bailments
o. Warehouse receipt

Statements and Definitions

____ 1. Warehousing arrangement whereby goods are stored in a separate area on an owner's premises, and a warehouser is given exclusive control of this area.

____ 2. Document of title issued by a carrier when it receives goods to be shipped by air transportation.

____ 3. Transient person who stays overnight at an establishment operated by a hotelkeeper.

____ 4. Party who stores goods for compensation for members of the public without discrimination.

____ 5. Carrier that holds itself out as being willing to provide transportation for compensation for any member of the public without discrimination.

____ 6. Broad category of bailments that involves a strong public interest.

____ 7. Process by which a negotiable document of title is properly transferred.

____ 8. Charge assessed by a carrier because of an unreasonable delay in loading or unloading goods due to the fault of the consignor (shipper) or the consignee.

____ 9. Bill of lading shipping goods to a person without using the words "bearer" or "to the order of."

____ 10. Carrier that transports goods for compensation under individual contracts, and the carrier does not hold itself out as being willing to provide transportation for all members of the public.

____ 11. Special bailee who sells consigned goods that belong to another party.

____ 12. Bill of lading shipping goods to the "bearer" or "to the order of" a named person.

____ 13. Carrier that is owned and operated by the party who is shipping the goods.

____ 14. Document of title that is issued by a party who accepts goods for storage.

____ 15. Person who stays on a permanent basis at an establishment operated by a hotelkeeper.

REVIEW OF CONCEPTS

Write **T** if the statement is true, write **F** if it is false.

_____ 1. In general, a warehouser is absolutely liable for any damage or loss to stored goods.

_____ 2. Unless otherwise expressly stated, a warehouser has a lien on stored goods to secure payment of only the storage charges and expenses that relate to the goods being stored.

_____ 3. A warehouse receipt typically is a receipt for stored goods, a memorandum of the storage contract, and a document of title.

_____ 4. To negotiate a negotiable warehouse receipt that requires delivery to the "bearer," the transferor of the receipt must first indorse the receipt and then deliver the receipt to the transferee.

_____ 5. Assume that a thief steals a stereo, the thief receives a negotiable warehouse receipt when he stores the stereo, and the receipt is negotiated to a third party who takes it by due negotiation. In this situation, the original owner of the stereo still has the superior right to the stereo.

_____ 6. A person who for value transfers a negotiable or nonnegotiable warehouse receipt does not impliedly warrant that the receipt is genuine and that the transfer is proper.

_____ 7. In general, a warehouser cannot limit its liability unless it first allows a customer the opportunity to pay a higher fee for storing the goods without a limitation of liability.

_____ 8. Bills of lading regarding shipment of goods in interstate commerce are generally governed by the Federal Bills of Lading Act.

_____ 9. In a dispute between a good faith transferee of a bill of lading and a carrier, statements in the bill of lading regarding contents, quantity, or weight are not binding on the carrier.

_____ 10. A common carrier is only required to ship goods for those parties that it may choose to serve.

_____ 11. In general, a common carrier has no duty to load or unload goods that are delivered to it for shipment.

_____ 12. If a carrier tenders delivery of goods but delivery is refused, the carrier is then treated as a warehouser and it is liable only for damage or loss to goods that is caused by its negligence.

_____ 13. If a factor sells stolen goods for a thief/consignor, the factor may be liable to the owner of the goods for damages due to conversion even if the factor did not know that the goods were stolen.

_____ 14. The hotelkeeper-guest relationship begins as soon as a person calls to make a room reservation.

_____ 15. At common law, a hotelkeeper did not have a lien on the baggage of a boarder.

REVIEW OF CHAPTER - APPLICATION OF CONCEPTS

MULTIPLE CHOICE QUESTIONS

____ 1. Charles owned tools that he stored with Ace Warehouser. Ace issued Charles a *nonnegotiable* warehouse receipt for the tools. Charles sold the tools to Zeke who bought them for value, and Zeke took possession of the tools in good faith. Later, Charles sold the warehouse receipt to Alice who bought it for value and in good faith. Who has the superior right to the tools?
   a. Charles
   b. Zeke
   c. Alice
   d. Zeke and Alice have equal rights to the tools.

____ 2. Irving stored furniture with We-Store-Um, a warehouser. We-Store-Um issued Irving a warehouse receipt that directs the furniture to be delivered to the "bearer." Irving negotiated the warehouse receipt to Steve who took it by due negotiation. The next day, We-Store-Um delivered the furniture to Irving without first receiving the warehouse receipt. Under these facts:
   a. The warehouse receipt is a nonnegotiable warehouse receipt.
   b. The warehouse receipt is a negotiable warehouse receipt.
   c. We-Store-Um was legally entitled to deliver the furniture to Irving. We-Store-Um is not liable to Steve for damages he may suffer because the furniture was delivered to Irving.
   d. a and c.

____ 3. Keep-On-Trucking, a common carrier, contracted to ship equipment for Judd Fabricators. The equipment was damaged during shipment. Subject to certain exceptions, Keep-On-Trucking is:
   a. Liable for the damage only if the damage was due to its intentional wrongdoing.
   b. Liable for the damage only if the damage was due to its negligence.
   c. Absolutely liable for the damage even if the damage was not due to Keep-On-Trucking's fault.
   d. Not liable for the damage; the risk of loss or damage is always borne by the shipper.

____ 4. In which case is Conn Carrier, a common carrier, liable for the damage or loss in question?
   a. Goods being transported by Conn were stolen by a thief.
   b. Goods being transported by Conn were destroyed by an unforeseeable earthquake.
   c. Goods being transported by Conn were damaged due to improper packaging by the shipper.
   d. Goods being transported by Conn were confiscated by government health officials.

____ 5. Daisy checked into the Palms Motel for an overnight stay. Daisy left a cashmere coat in her room. While Daisy was having dinner, her coat was taken from her room. Under these facts:
   a. At common law, the Palms has absolute liability for the loss of the coat.
   b. At common law, the Palms is liable for the lost coat only if the loss was due to its negligence.
   c. In most states today, statutes would prohibit the Palms from limiting its liability for the coat.
   d. a and c.

_____ 6. What is a warehouser's standard of care for stored goods?
   a. A warehouser is strictly liable for any loss or damage to stored goods.
   b. A warehouser is liable for loss or damage that results from the slightest negligence on the part of the warehouser.
   c. A warehouser is liable for loss or damage that results from ordinary negligence on the part of the warehouser.
   d. A warehouser is liable for loss or damage only if it results from gross negligence on the part of the warehouser.

_____ 7. Which of the following is NOT a document of title?
   a. A nonnegotiable bill of lading.
   b. A negotiable bill of lading.
   c. A negotiable warehouse receipt.
   d. A negotiable promissory note.

_____ 8. A person who for value negotiates a warehouse receipt for stored goods does NOT warrant that:
   a. The goods are fit for the ordinary purposes for which they are intended.
   b. The person owns the goods.
   c. The warehouse receipt is genuine.
   d. a and b.

_____ 9. AirOne Airlines issued Carla a negotiable bill of lading "to the order of Carla Rodriguez" for goods that she was shipping. What must Carla do in order to negotiate this bill of lading to Harold, a customer?
   a. Carla must only deliver the bill of lading to Harold.
   b. Carla must indorse the bill of lading and deliver it to Harold.
   c. Carla must deliver the bill of lading to AirOne Airlines who must then cancel the bill of lading and issue a new one to Harold.
   d. Carla cannot negotiate the bill of lading to Harold. She must take delivery of the goods.

CASE PROBLEM

Answer the following problem, briefly explaining your answer.

Bob, Joe, and Sam separately registered as guests at the Essex Motel. All three guests wrongfully failed to pay their respective room charges, and the Essex refused to return their baggage. Bob then paid the charge for his room. At Joe's request, the Essex returned Joe's baggage even though he had not paid.

(a) What rights does the Essex have with regard to Sam's baggage? (b) What rights does the Essex have with regard to Joe's baggage? (c) Must the Essex return Bob's baggage to him?

CHAPTER 23

CPA REVIEW

The following questions were given on CPA examinations. The answers for these questions are the unofficial answers prepared by the American Institute of Certified Public Accountants, Inc. (AICPA). All material is reproduced with permission of the AICPA.

_____ 1. Bond Corp. issued a negotiable warehouse receipt to Grey for goods stored in Bond's warehouse. Grey's goods were lost due to Bond's failure to exercise such care as a reasonably careful person would under like circumstances. The state in which this transaction occurred follows the UCC rule with respect to a warehouseman's liability for lost goods. The warehouse receipt is silent on this point. Under the circumstances, Bond is
    a. Liable because it was negligent.
    b. Liable because it is strictly liable for any loss.
    c. Not liable unless Grey can establish that Bond was grossly negligent.
    d. Not liable because the warehouse receipt was negotiable.

_____ 2. Klep burglarized the premises of Apple Sales Co. He stole several negotiable warehouse receipts which were deliverable to the order of Apple. Klep indorsed Apple's name on the instruments and transferred them to Margo Wholesalers, a bona fide purchaser for value. As between Apple and Margo,
    a. Apple will prevail since the warehouseman must be notified before any negotiation is effective.
    b. Apple will prevail since the thief's indorsement prevents a due negotiation.
    c. Margo will prevail since it has taken a negotiable warehouse receipt as a bona fide purchaser for value.
    d. Margo will prevail since the warehouse receipt was converted to a bearer instrument by Klep's indorsement.

_____ 3. Unless otherwise agreed, which of the following warranties will not be conferred by a person negotiating a negotiable warehouse receipt for value to his immediate purchaser?
    a. The document is genuine.
    b. The transferor is without knowledge of any fact which would impair its validity or worth.
    c. The goods represented by the warehouse receipt are of merchantable quality.
    d. Negotiation by the transferor is rightful and fully effective with respect to the title to the document.

_____ 4. The procedure necessary to negotiate a document of title depends principally on whether the document is
    a. An order document or a bearer document.
    b. Issued by a bailee or a consignee.
    c. A receipt for goods stored or goods already shipped.
    d. A bill of lading or a warehouse receipt.

CHAPTER 24
NATURE AND FORM OF SALES

CHAPTER OUTLINE

A. NATURE AND LEGALITY

A sale of goods is a (1) present transfer of title (2) to movable personable property (3) that is made for a price. The price paid for goods may be money, property, or performance of a service by a buyer.

1. **SUBJECT MATTER OF SALES**

    GENERAL RULES. ▸ "Goods" include any tangible property that is movable at the time it is identified to a contract. ▸ Goods include new and used goods. ▸ Goods do not include: (1) investment securities (stocks or bonds); (2) choses in action (promissory notes); or (3) real estate (land and permanent buildings).
    STUDY HINTS. ▸ A party can contract to sell existing goods (goods existing and owned by a seller at time of contracting) or future goods (any other goods). ▸ A contract to sell goods at a future date or a contract to sell future goods is not a "sale"; it is a "contract to sell."

2. **SALE DISTINGUISHED FROM OTHER TRANSACTIONS**

    GENERAL RULE. A "sale" requires a present transfer of title. A sale does not include a: (1) bailment or lease of goods; (2) gift; (3) contract to sell (contract to make a future transfer of title); (4) option to purchase (power to make a contract to sell); (5) conditional sale; or (6) contract for services.
    STUDY HINT. ▸ If a contract is a "mixed" contract that requires a party to both sell goods and render a service, the contract is classified by its dominant element. Therefore, if the sale of goods is the dominant aspect of the contract and the service is merely incidental, it is a sales contract. ▸ Example: A&A Appliances contracts to sell a stove to Joan for $500. The price includes $450 for the stove, and $50 for delivery and installation of the stove. This contract is a sales contract.

3. **LAW OF CONTRACTS APPLICABLE**

    Article 2 of the UCC establishes numerous special rules for sales contracts. These rules include:

    - *Definiteness of contract*: A sales contract may be formed even if one or more terms is not stated.
    - *Offer*: ▸ A merchant cannot revoke a "firm offer" if: (1) in a signed writing; (2) the merchant promised not to revoke the offer to buy or sell goods. ▸ A firm offer is irrevocable for the time stated, not to exceed three months. If no time is stated, it is irrevocable for a reasonable time. ▸ A firm offer is irrevocable even if consideration is not given for the promise not to revoke.
    - *Manner of acceptance*: Unless otherwise clearly stated by an offeror, an offer may be accepted in any manner and using any means of communication that is reasonable under the circumstances.
    - *Acceptance with additional terms (in general)*: A definite, unconditional statement of acceptance is generally a valid acceptance and forms a contract even though the acceptance states a new term that is in addition to the terms stated in the offer. An additional term in an acceptance does not necessarily create a rejection or counteroffer.

- *Acceptance with additional terms (nonmerchants)*: If a valid acceptance has an additional term and either party is not a merchant, a contract is formed and it is comprised solely of the terms stated in the offer. The additional term is not part of the contract unless the offeror agrees to it.
- *Acceptance with additional terms (merchants)*: ▸ If a valid acceptance has an additional term and both parties are merchants, then: (1) a contract is formed and (2) the new term is part of the contract unless: (a) the offer limits acceptance to the offer's terms; (b) the term materially alters the contract; or (c) the offeror objects to the term within a reasonable time. ▸ A term is not a material change if it is a common business term and it does not significantly alter the parties' duties. Example: typical contract term that charges interest on late payments.
- *Acceptance with conflicting terms*: If an acceptance contains terms that conflict with terms of an offer but the parties nonetheless intend to contract (e.g., the parties perform the intended contract), then Article 2 recognizes that a contract is formed. In this case, the contract consists of terms upon which the offer and acceptance agree, coupled with other terms implied by law.
- *Price*: The contract price is: (1) the price expressly agreed upon; or (2) if no price is stated, the price is a reasonable price (which is often determined by industry custom or market price).
- *Output and requirement contracts*: ▸ Parties can contract to buy and sell a quantity of goods measured by a seller's production (an output contract), or by a buyer's needs (a requirements contract). ▸ Limits: (1) parties must act in good faith; and (2) the amount offered or requested cannot be unreasonably different from contract estimates or from prior output or requirements.
- *Indefinite duration contract*: If a contract requires periodic deliveries of goods but a fixed term is not stated, the contract continues for a reasonable time. Either party may terminate such a contract by giving written notice of termination.
- *Modification of contract*: A good faith contract modification is valid even without consideration.
- *Parol evidence rule*: ▸ A final and exclusive written contract can be explained using parol evidence (prior oral statements), but parol evidence cannot be used to add to or contradict the terms of the written contract. ▸ If a writing is a final statement of only part of a contract, parol evidence may also be used to prove consistent, additional terms.
- *Usage of trade and course of dealing*: Evidence of usage of trade (practice of doing business regularly followed in a trade) and course of dealing (series of prior dealings between the same parties) may be used to: (1) explain the meaning of contract terms; and (2) supply missing terms.
- *Fraud and other defenses*: A defrauded party may cancel a sales contract *and* sue for damages.

4. **ILLEGAL SALES**

   GENERAL RULES. ▸ A sale is illegal if the subject matter is illegal, the contract states that the subject matter is to be used in an illegal manner, or a seller helps a buyer to make illegal use of purchased goods. ▸ In general, no remedies are available for breach of an illegal contract.

   LIMITATION. A seller may be liable for harm caused by a product even if the sale was illegal.

5. **BULK TRANSFERS**

   GENERAL RULES. ▸ A bulk transfer is a: (1) transfer of a major part of materials, supplies, merchandise, or other inventory; (2) made not in the ordinary course of business; (3) by a merchant whose principal business is selling inventory. ▸ In some states, Article 6 of the UCC requires that the seller's creditors be given prior notice of a bulk transfer. If notice is not given, a seller's creditors may have the right to reclaim the sold property.

   LIMITATION. In 1989, the National Conference of Commissioners of Uniform State Laws recommended that Article 6 be repealed. A number of states have followed this recommendation and have repealed this portion of the UCC.

B. FORM OF SALES CONTRACT

6. AMOUNT

Sales contracts for $500 or more are required by the statute of frauds to be evidenced by a writing.

7. NATURE OF THE WRITING REQUIRED

GENERAL RULES. ▸ The statute of frauds requires that a writing: (1) indicate that parties have made a contract; (2) state the quantity of goods; and (3) be signed by the party who is using the statute of frauds as a defense (the defendant) or by that party's agent. ▸ If both parties are merchants, the writing requirement is met if: (1) one merchant signs a sufficient written confirmation; (2) the confirmation is sent to the other merchant; and (3) the other merchant does not object in writing within ten days.
STUDY HINTS. ▸ A writing can satisfy the statute of frauds even if it is not made for that purpose and it is not a formal written contract. ▸ Two or more writings may comprise the necessary writing.

8. EFFECT OF NONCOMPLIANCE (WITH THE STATUTE OF FRAUDS)

Noncompliance renders a contract unenforceable, but parties can voluntarily perform the contract.

9. EXCEPTIONS TO REQUIREMENT OF A WRITING

- ***Nonresellable goods***: An oral contract for specially made goods is enforceable if: (1) goods are not suitable for resale; and (2) before the buyer disavows the contract, the seller has made a substantial beginning either in making the goods or in committing to obtain the goods.
- ***Other exceptions***: ▸ An oral contract is enforceable *to the extent that*: (1) goods are delivered to and received and accepted by a buyer; (2) the price is paid and accepted by a seller; or (3) the party who refuses to perform admits in judicial proceedings or pleadings that a contract was made. ▸ Part payment for a single item makes the contract enforceable. ▸ Payment for less than all items purchased makes the contract enforceable for only the items for which payment is made.

10. NON-CODE REQUIREMENTS

Federal and state laws may impose additional requirements regarding consumer sales contracts.

11. BILL OF SALE

A bill of sale is a writing evidencing a sale or transfer of title; it is not a contract.

C. UNIFORM LAW FOR INTERNATIONAL SALES

United Nations Convention on Contracts for the International Sale of Goods (CISG) governs sales contracts made between a party in the U.S. and a party in a country that has adopted this convention.

12. SCOPE OF THE CISG

▸ CISG does not apply to: (1) sales contracts that exclude its application; (2) contracts for goods purchased for personal, family, or household use; (3) service contracts; or (4) liability for death or personal injury caused by goods. ▸ The CISG is similar in many respects to Article 2 of the UCC.

13. IRREVOCABLE OFFERS

▸ Under the CISG, an offer is irrevocable if: (1) it states that it is irrevocable or (2) the offeree reasonably relies on it as being irrevocable. An irrevocable offer under the CISG may be made orally or in writing, and an irrevocable offer is valid even if consideration is not given for it.

14. STATUTE OF FRAUDS

The CISG eliminates the writing requirement of the statute of frauds.

D. LEASES OF GOODS

Article 2A of the UCC governs leases of tangible movable goods. A lease is "a transfer of the right to possession and use of goods for a term in return for consideration."

15. TYPES OF LEASES

Article 2A governs all leases and subleases of goods including the following types of lease:

- *Consumer lease*: (1) lease of goods (2) made by a merchant lessor (lessor is regularly engaged in the business of selling or leasing goods of that kind) (3) to a natural person (not a corporation) (4) for personal, family, or household use (5) and total payments under the lease are $25,000 or less.
- *Commercial (nonconsumer) lease*: any lease of goods that is not a consumer lease.
- *Finance lease*: lease of goods whereby (1) lessee (not the lessor) selects the goods, (2) lessor then acquires or leases the goods from a supplier on terms that are acceptable to the lessee, and (3) the lessee then leases or subleases the goods from the lessor.

16. FORM OF THE LEASE CONTRACT

▸ A lease of goods must be evidenced by a writing to be enforceable if the total lease payments are $1,000 or more. A writing must (1) describe the goods, (2) state the term of the lease, (3) indicate that a lease has been made, and (4) be signed by the party against whom the lease is being enforced.

17. WARRANTIES

GENERAL RULE. With one limitation (under a finance lease), a lessor of goods makes the same express or implied warranties to a lessee as a seller of goods makes to a buyer (unless warranties are properly disclaimed or modified).

LIMITATION. Under a finance lease, warranties made by a supplier to a lessor are passed through to the lessee who enforces them directly against the supplier. The lessor under a finance lease makes no implied warranties and is liable for only express warranties (if any) made by the lessor to the lessee.

18. IRREVOCABLE PROMISES: COMMERCIAL FINANCE LEASES

GENERAL RULE. Under a commercial finance lease, a lessee's obligations to a lessor become irrevocable upon the lessee's acceptance of the goods, and the lessee must perform all of his or her lease obligations even if the goods are defective ("hell or high water clause"). The lessee's sole remedy is to sue the supplier, or to sue the lessor for breach of express warranty if the lessor made such a warranty.

LIMITATION. The foregoing rules do not apply to consumer leases or other forms of leases.

19. DEFAULT

▸ The lease agreement and Article 2A determine whether a party is in default. If a lessee defaults, the lessor can recover any rent due, future rent, and incidental damages.

REVIEW OF TERMS AND PHRASES

MATCHING EXERCISE

Select the term or phrase that best matches a statement or definition stated below. Each term or phrase is the best match for only one statement or definition.

Terms and Phrases

a. Bill of sale
b. CISG
c. Commercial lease
d. Conditional sale
e. Consumer lease
f. Contract to sell
g. Existing goods
h. Finance lease
i. Firm offer
j. Future goods
k. Gift
l. Goods
m. Lease
n. Option to purchase
o. Sale of goods

Statements and Definitions

____ 1. Present transfer of title to movable personal property in consideration for a price.

____ 2. Goods that are physically existing and owned by a seller at the time a sales contract is made.

____ 3. Goods that do not exist, or are not owned by a seller, at the time a sales contract is made.

____ 4. Contract whereby title to goods will be transferred at a future time.

____ 5. Contract whereby title to goods does not pass to a buyer until payment in full is made.

____ 6. Merchant's signed, written offer to buy or sell goods which promises that the offer will not be revoked for a certain period of time, not to exceed three months.

____ 7. Contract that gives one party the power to accept the other party's offer to make a sales contract.

____ 8. Transfer of the right to possession or use of goods for a term in return for consideration.

____ 9. Property that is movable at the time that it is identified to a contract.

____ 10. Lease of goods by which a lessee selects the goods and a lessor then obtains the goods from a supplier.

____ 11. Writing that merely evidences the making of a sale or a transfer of title to a buyer.

____ 12. Gratuitous (free) transfer of title to property.

____ 13. International convention that governs many international sales of goods.

____ 14. Lease of goods by a natural person primarily for personal, family, or household use.

____ 15. All leases of goods that do not meet the requirements for being a consumer lease.

COMPLETION EXERCISE

Fill in the blanks with the words that most accurately complete each statement. Answers may or may not include terms used in the matching exercise. A term cannot be used to complete more than one statement.

1. Contracts for the sale of goods between parties in the United States are generally governed by _____ ____ of the _____ _____ _____.

2. Many international contracts for the sale of goods are governed by an international convention (agreement) commonly known as the _____.

3. Under a "_____ _____" formula, a buyer agrees to pay a price that is equal to the seller's cost of acquiring the goods plus an additional percent of the cost as a profit for the seller.

4. Baxter Farms contracted to sell its entire 1999 wheat crop to the Delta Grain Co-op. This contract is an example of a(n) _____ contract.

5. Star Aerospace Co. contracts to buy from Seller all of the jet engines that Star needs in order to manufacture its new LXT-1000 aircraft. This contract is an example of a(n) _____ contract.

6. _____ ____ _____ is a common practice that is regularly followed in an industry or trade that may be used to interpret a sales contract or to furnish missing terms.

7. _____ ____ _____ is a pattern of prior dealings between the parties to a sales contract that may be used to interpret the contract or to furnish missing terms.

8. The section of Article 2 known as the _____ ____ _____ requires that contracts for the sale of goods for a price of $500 or more must be evidenced by a writing to be enforceable.

9. The _____ _____ _____ generally prohibits using evidence of prior oral statements to add to or contradict the terms of a final written sales contract.

10. _____ ____ of the UCC governs leases of goods.

REVIEW OF CONCEPTS

Write **T** if the statement is true, write **F** if it is false.

____ 1. A sale of goods is made if a seller transfers title to goods in exchange for a buyer's service.

____ 2. A contract to sell a promissory note is not a sale of goods.

____ 3. Article 2 of the UCC only applies to sales of new goods; it does not apply to sales of used goods.

____ 4. One cannot make a present sale of future goods; such an agreement is only a contract to sell.

____ 5. Article 2 of the UCC only applies to sales of goods made between merchants.

____ 6. If a contract requires a seller to convey title to a good and to perform a service, then the contract is always viewed as being a sale of goods that is governed by Article 2 of the UCC.

_____ 7. A sales contract cannot be formed if one or more terms is not stated.

_____ 8. A merchant can revoke a firm offer unless the party to whom the offer is made gives the merchant consideration for the firm offer.

_____ 9. If a seller clearly states an exclusive manner of acceptance, then the offer can be accepted in only that manner.

_____ 10. If an acceptance states a term that conflicts with a term in the offer for the sale of goods but the buyer and seller perform the intended contract, Article 2 will recognize the creation of a contract.

_____ 11. If both parties to a contract are merchants, an additional term that is stated in an acceptance does not become part of the contract if it would materially change the contract or the offeror objects to the term within a reasonable time.

_____ 12. If a sales contract requires a seller to periodically deliver goods but the contract does not state a fixed duration, then the contract continues for a reasonable time.

_____ 13. A sales contract can validly provide that one party may determine the price to be paid.

_____ 14. Under a requirements contract, a seller must meet all of the buyer's requirements even if the quantity demanded is unreasonably different from the buyer's prior requirements.

_____ 15. A good faith modification of a sales contract is invalid unless it is supported by consideration.

_____ 16. Parol evidence cannot be used to explain the meaning of terms in a final, exclusive written sales contract.

_____ 17. If a buyer of goods is defrauded, the buyer can rescind the sales contract and recover any money paid, but the buyer cannot sue the seller for any damages caused by the seller's fraud.

_____ 18. An illegal sales contract cannot be enforced and parties are generally denied any remedies.

_____ 19. The bulk transfer rules of Article 6 of the UCC do not apply to a sale by a party who does not primarily engage in the sale of inventory.

_____ 20. The writing requirement of the statute of frauds regarding sales contracts is satisfied only if there is a formal written contract that is signed by both the seller and the buyer.

_____ 21. A lease of goods is not classified as a consumer lease if the total lease payments exceed $25,000.

_____ 22. Leases of goods must be evidenced by a sufficient writing if total lease payments are $250 or more.

_____ 23. A writing evidencing a lease of goods must state the monthly and total lease payments to be paid.

_____ 24. A lessor under a finance lease does not make the implied warranties that a seller of goods makes in connection with a sale of goods under Article 2.

_____ 25. If a lessee defaults under a lease of goods, the lessor can sue only to recover the leased goods. The lessor cannot sue for any damages.

CHAPTER 24

REVIEW OF CHAPTER - APPLICATION OF CONCEPTS

MULTIPLE CHOICE QUESTIONS

____ 1. Which contract is a sales contract that is governed by Article 2 of the UCC?
 a. Floors Inc., a carpet manufacturer, contracts to sell a shipment of carpeting to Retailer.
 b. Earl contracts to sell his farm to Mindy.
 c. Wayne contracts to sell 500 shares of Acme Inc. stock to Claire.
 d. Bob contracts to sell a promissory note to Amanda.

____ 2. Which agreement is a sales contract that is governed by Article 2 of the UCC?
 a. Dr. Hanson agrees to donate some Walt Whitman books to the college library.
 b. Terri contracts to buy a portable, pre-made storage shed. The total price is $10,000, which includes $500 for the seller's labor that is required to assemble the shed.
 c. Vicky contracts to pay Ted $3,000 to paint Vicky's house. The price includes $2,500 for labor and $500 for paint and other supplies.
 d. Zodiac Rentals rents a saw to Carl.

____ 3. Braxon Co., a merchant, offered to buy a tool from S&S Inc., a merchant. The offer was silent regarding the time for delivery of the tool. S&S sent Braxon a definite, unconditional acceptance that stated that S&S would deliver the tool within 14 days after the date of acceptance. This additional delivery term was common in the industry, and it would not surprise or cause hardship to Braxon. Braxon did not object to this additional term. Under these facts:
 a. A contract was not formed because the acceptance stated a term that was not in the offer.
 b. A contract would be formed only if Braxon agreed to the delivery term in the acceptance.
 c. A contract was formed, and the additional delivery term is part of the contract.
 d. A contract was formed, but the additional delivery term is not part of the contract.

____ 4. Gold Producer agreed to sell 50 ounces of gold to Gold Wholesaler. Both parties are merchants who regularly engage in the gold industry. The parties definitely intended to contract, but the parties intentionally did not state the price to be paid. Under these facts:
 a. The agreement is invalid because it fails to state the price to be paid.
 b. The agreement is a valid contract; Wholesaler must pay a reasonable price.
 c. The agreement is a valid contract; Wholesaler can pay whatever price it chooses to pay.
 d. The agreement is a valid contract; Wholesaler must pay the price Producer requests.

____ 5. Wren Equipment Sales Co. bought a crane from Equipment Manufacturer pursuant to a final written contract. The contract ambiguously states that Manufacturer will "reasonably train" Wren's employees to use the crane. The contract also states that Manufacturer will store the crane with a public storage company for 30 days, but it does not state who will pay the storage costs. Prior to signing the contract, Manufacturer had orally promised to store the crane for 60 days. (Mistake is not involved in this question.) Under these facts:
 a. Parol evidence can be used to prove the meaning of the ambiguous term "reasonably train."
 b. Parol evidence can be used to change the terms of the contract by proving Manufacturer's promise to store the crane for 60 days.
 c. A usage of trade can be used to prove who must pay the storage fees.
 d. a and c.

_____ 6. Which contract is *unenforceable* because it violates the statute of frauds?
   a. A&M orally contracted to buy a shipment of sugar from Refinery for $2,000. A&M immediately sent Refinery a signed, written confirmation that stated all of the contract terms. Refinery received the confirmation, and Refinery never objected to the confirmation.
   b. Seller sold Buyer a truck for $5,000. Both parties signed a writing confirming their agreement and the contract terms. The writing, however, does not state the contract price.
   c. Judy made an oral contract to buy cosmetics for $800.
   d. Rod made an oral contract to buy a stereo for $300.

_____ 7. Which contract is enforceable?
   a. Peter orally contracted to sell a shipment of nuts to Bill for $1,000. Peter delivered the nuts to Bill, who received and accepted the nuts.
   b. Jarvis orally contracted to sell a car to Buyer for $5,000. Buyer paid Jarvis $3,500 of the purchase price. Jarvis accepted this payment.
   c. Cy orally contracted to sell a horse to Buyer for $1,000. Cy now refuses to perform the contract because it is oral. At trial, Cy admitted making the contract.
   d. All of the above.

_____ 8. Which agreement is a commercial finance lease that is governed by Article 2A of the UCC?
   a. Cindy agreed to buy a TV for her bar and grill restaurant.
   b. Tom agreed to lease an office building for his business.
   c. Pat agreed to lease an automobile for his personal use. Pat selected the automobile from Lessor's existing fleet of lease automobiles.
   d. JD agreed to lease portable carpet cleaning equipment from Lessor. JD selected the equipment and Lessor then purchased the equipment from Supplier on terms that were satisfactory to JD.

_____ 9. Which lease is *unenforceable?*
   a. James orally agreed to lease a computer for total lease payments of $500.
   b. Katherine orally agreed to lease a truck for total lease payments of $4,000.
   c. Jack orally agreed to lease a plane for total lease payments of $15,000. Jack sent the lessor a signed letter confirming the lease, describing the plane, and stating the lease term. Jack now refuses to perform the lease.
   d. All of the above.

_____ 10. Jackson Co. leased a crane from R&R Rental Co. for two years. After 18 months, Jackson Co. defaulted on the lease. Jackson Co. failed to pay $900 past rent, and it also failed to pay the remaining $1,800 future rent under the lease. R&R retook the crane, but it was unable to rent the crane to any one else. R&R incurred a $200 shipping expense and a $300 storage expense due to Jackson Co.'s default. In this case, what damages can R&R recover from Jackson Co.?
   a. $ 0
   b. $ 900
   c. $ 2,700
   d. $ 3,200

CASE PROBLEMS

Answer the following problems, briefly explaining your answers.

1. Barney, a consumer, sent a purchase order for a table saw to Tonko Manufacturers. The order was silent regarding how disputes between the parties would be settled. Tonko sent back a definite, unconditional acceptance that contained an additional term which stated that disputes must be submitted to arbitration. Barney received the acceptance, but he never agreed or objected to the additional term.

   (a) Did Tonko's acceptance form a sales contract between Barney and Tonko? (b) If a sales contract was formed, was the additional term in the acceptance part of the contract? (c) What would have been the effect if Barney had agreed to the additional term?

   _____
   _____
   _____
   _____

2. Allied Stores, a retail furniture merchant, decided to liquidate its business. Allied made an extraordinary sale of its entire furniture inventory to Bosco Inc. Allied's creditors were not given notice of the sale. Bosco paid the agreed-upon $40,000 purchase price to Allied, which failed to pay its creditors.

   (a) Was the sale of inventory to Bosco a bulk transfer that was subject to Article 6 of the UCC? (b) What should Bosco have done in this case? (c) Can Allied's creditors reach (retake) the inventory from Bosco? (d) Is Bosco liable for Allied's debts?

   _____
   _____
   _____
   _____

3. Ameri Inc., a U.S. firm, exports tennis racquets. Ameri Inc. contracted to sell a shipment of racquets to Dover Co., a wholesaler located in a foreign country that has adopted the CISG. Ameri Inc. also contracted to sell a racquet to Felipe for his personal use. Felipe is a foreign citizen residing in a country that has adopted the CISG. In addition, Ameri Inc. sold a shipment of racquets to Kiev Inc., a company doing business in a foreign country that has not adopted the CISG.

   (a) What is the CISG? (b) Does the CISG govern the contracts between Ameri Inc. and Dover Co., Felipe, or Kiev Inc.? (c) Under the CISG, must contracts be evidenced by a writing to be enforceable?

   _____
   _____
   _____
   _____

CPA REVIEW

The following questions were given on CPA examinations. The answers for these questions are the unofficial answers prepared by the American Institute of Certified Public Accountants, Inc. (AICPA). All material is reproduced with permission of the AICPA.

_____ 1. Under the Sales Article of the UCC, which of the following statements is correct?
   a. The obligations of the parties to the contract must be performed in good faith.
   b. Merchants and nonmerchants are treated alike.
   c. The contract must involve the sale of goods for a price of more than $500.
   d. None of the provisions of the UCC may be disclaimed by agreement.

_____ 2. Bean ordered 40 beige refrigerators at list price from Tish Co. Immediately upon receipt of Bean's order, Tish sent Bean an acceptance which was received by Bean. The acceptance indicated that shipment would be made within ten days. On the tenth day Tish discovered that all of its supply of beige refrigerators had been sold. Instead it shipped 40 white refrigerators, stating clearly on the invoice that the shipment was sent only as an accommodation. Which of the following is correct?
   a. Bean's order is a unilateral offer, and can only be accepted by Tish's shipment of the goods ordered.
   b. Tish's shipment of white refrigerators is a counteroffer, thus no contract exists between Bean and Tish.
   c. Tish's note of accommodation cancels the contract between Tish and Bean.
   d. Tish's shipment of white refrigerators constitutes a breach of contract.

_____ 3. An oral agreement concerning the sale of goods entered into without consideration is binding if the agreement
   a. Is a firm offer made by a merchant who promises to hold the offer open for 30 days.
   b. Is a waiver of the non-breaching party's rights arising out of a breach of the contract.
   c. Contradicts the terms of a subsequent written contract that is intended as the complete and exclusive agreement of the parties.
   d. Modifies the price in an existing, enforceable contract from $525 to $475.

_____ 4. Baker and Able signed a contract which required Able to purchase 600 books from Baker at 90¢ per book. Subsequently, Able, in good faith, requested that the price of the books be reduced to 80¢ per book. Baker orally agreed to reduce the price to 80¢. Under the circumstances, the oral agreement is
   a. Unenforceable, because Able failed to give consideration, but proof of it will be otherwise admissible into evidence.
   b. Unenforceable, due to the statute of frauds, and proof of it will be inadmissible into evidence.
   c. Enforceable, but proof of it will be inadmissible into evidence.
   d. Enforceable, and proof of it will be admissible into evidence.

_____ 5. To satisfy the UCC Statute of Frauds, a written agreement for the sale of goods must
   a. Contain payment terms.
   b. Be signed by both buyer and seller.
   c. Indicate that a contract for sale has been made.
   d. Refer to the time and place of delivery.

_____ 6. Webstar Corp. orally agreed to sell Northco, Inc. a computer for $20,000. Northco sent a signed purchase order to Webstar confirming the agreement. Webstar received the purchase order and did not respond. Webstar refused to deliver the computer to Northco, claiming that the purchase order did not satisfy the UCC Statute of Frauds because it was not signed by Webstar. Northco sells computers to the general public and Webstar is a computer wholesaler. Under the UCC Sales Article, Webstar's position is
   a. Incorrect because it failed to object to Northco's purchaser order.
   b. Incorrect because only the buyer in a sale-of-goods transaction must sign the contract.
   c. Correct because it was the party against whom enforcement of the contract is being sought.
   d. Correct because the purchase price of the computer exceeded $500.

_____ 7. Jefferson Hardware ordered three hundred Ram hammers from Ajax Hardware. Ajax accepted the order in writing. On the final date allowed for delivery, Ajax discovered it did not have enough Ram hammers to fill the order. Instead, Ajax sent three hundred Strong hammers. Ajax stated on the invoice that the shipment was sent only as an accommodation. Which of the following statements is correct?
   a. Ajax's note of accommodation cancels the contract between Jefferson and Ajax.
   b. Jefferson's order can only be accepted by Ajax's shipment of the goods ordered.
   c. Ajax's shipment of Strong hammers is a breach of contract.
   d. Ajax' s shipment of Strong hammers is a counteroffer and no contract exists between Jefferson and Ajax.

_____ 8. Cookie Co. offered to sell Distrib Markets 20,000 pounds of cookies at $1.00 per pound, subject to certain specified terms for delivery. Distrib replied in writing as follows: "We accept your offer for 20,000 pounds of cookies at $1.00 per pound, weighing scale to have valid city certificate." Under the UCC
   a. A contract was formed between the parties.
   b. A contract will be formed only if Cookie agrees to the weighing scale requirement.
   c. No contract was formed because Distrib included the weighing scale requirement in its reply.
   d. No contract was formed because Distrib' s reply was a counteroffer.

CHAPTER 25
RISK AND PROPERTY RIGHTS

CHAPTER OUTLINE

A. TYPES OF POTENTIAL PROBLEMS AND TRANSACTIONS

1. TYPES OF PROBLEMS

- Insurable interest rules determine whether an insurer must pay for a loss to goods.
- Rules regarding title to goods often determine the rights of creditors to goods.
- Risk of loss rules determine whether a seller or buyer bears a loss caused by a casualty to goods.

2. NATURE OF THE TRANSACTION

- ■ *Nature of goods*: ▸ Rights regarding insurable interest, title, and risk of loss often depend on the type of goods sold. Goods may be: (1) *existing goods* (goods existing and owned by a seller at time of contracting); (2) *future goods* (goods not existing, or not owned by the seller, at time of contracting); (3) *identified goods* (specific goods that are designated as being for a buyer); or (4) *unidentified goods* (goods not specifically designated as being for a buyer). ▸ Goods are identified if: (1) specific, existing goods are described in a contract as being for a buyer; or (2) specific goods are identified as being for a particular buyer by being marked, shipped, or segregated.
- ■ *Nature of delivery obligations*: ▸ Rights may be affected by a seller's delivery obligations. A seller may be required to: (1) deliver goods at the seller's business; (2) deliver goods to a carrier for shipment to a buyer (a contract for shipment to buyer); (3) deliver goods to a buyer at the destination (a contract for delivery at destination); or (4) deliver documents of title to the buyer.

3. EXISTING GOODS IDENTIFIED AT TIME OF CONTRACTING

GENERAL RULE. Unless otherwise agreed, (1) if goods are existing and identified at the time of contracting and (2) no documents of title are involved, then the following rules apply:

- ■ *Insurable interest*: ▸ A seller has an insurable interest in goods if the seller has title to or a security interest in the goods. ▸ A buyer has an insurable interest at the time of contracting.
- ■ *Title*: Title to goods passes to the buyer at the time of contracting.
- ■ *Risk of loss*: ▸ If a seller is a merchant, risk passes when a buyer takes physical possession of goods. ▸ If a seller is a nonmerchant, risk passes when delivery to a buyer is offered (tendered).

STUDY HINT. A seller and buyer may both have an insurable interest in goods at the same time.

4. GOODS REPRESENTED BY NEGOTIABLE DOCUMENT OF TITLE

Unless otherwise agreed, (1) if goods are existing and identified at the time of contracting, but (2) a seller is required to deliver a document of title to the buyer, then these rules apply:

- ■ *Insurable interest*: ▸ A seller has an insurable interest in goods if the seller has title to, or a security interest in, the goods. ▸ A buyer has an insurable interest at the time of contracting.
- ■ *Title*: Title to goods passes when the seller delivers the document of title to the buyer.
- ■ *Risk of loss*: Risk of loss generally passes to a buyer when a seller delivers the document of title.

5. **FUTURE AND UNIDENTIFIED GOODS**

   If goods are future goods or goods are unidentified at the time of contracting, then these rules apply:

   - *Insurable interest*: ▸ A seller has an insurable interest if the seller has title to or a security interest in goods. ▸ A buyer has an insurable interest when goods are identified to the contract.
   - *Title and risk of loss*: ▸ *Contract for shipment to buyer*: title and risk of loss pass to a buyer when goods are delivered to a carrier for shipment. ▸ *Contract for delivery at destination*: title and risk of loss pass when goods are tendered or made available to the buyer at the destination.

6. **DAMAGE TO OR DESTRUCTION OF GOODS**

   - *Damage to identified goods before risk of loss passes*: ▸ A contract for the sale of goods is avoided (terminated) if: (1) goods essential to the contract are identified at time of contracting; (2) the risk of loss has not passed to the buyer; and (3) the goods are destroyed without fault of either party. ▸ If a partial loss occurs, a buyer may inspect the goods and either: (1) cancel the contract; or (2) accept the goods with an appropriate reduction in price.
   - *Damage to identified goods after risk of loss passes*: If a casualty occurs and a buyer has the risk of loss, the contract is not avoided; the buyer must pay the contract price for the goods, and the buyer must bear any financial loss resulting from the casualty.
   - *Damage to unidentified goods*: In general, casualty to unidentified goods does not affect a sales contract, and both parties must still perform. The seller bears the loss to unidentified goods.

7. **EFFECT OF SELLER'S BREACH**

   A seller generally bears the risk of loss if the seller breaches, giving a buyer a right to reject goods.

8. **RETURNABLE GOODS TRANSACTIONS**

   GENERAL RULE. Parties may enter into transactions whereby they agree that goods can be returned even though the goods meet all contract specifications. These transactions may be a:

   - *Sale on approval*: ▸ In a sale on approval, a sale does not occur until a buyer approves (accepts) goods, i.e., a buyer clearly indicates that the buyer regards the goods as his or her own property. Approval of goods may be by (1) express words, (2) conduct, or (3) lapse of time. ▸ Testing or trying out goods in a permitted manner is not an approval. Failure to return goods within the time agreed or within a reasonable time is an approval. ▸ Title and risk of loss do not pass to a buyer until the buyer approves goods. ▸ A seller bears the risk of loss and expense for return of goods. ▸ A buyer's creditors cannot reach goods prior to a buyer's approval of goods.
   - *Sale or return*: ▸ A sale or return is a sale with an option for a buyer to return goods. ▸ Goods may be returned when agreed, or within a reasonable time if no time is stated. Goods must be returned in their original condition. ▸ The general rules regarding insurable interest, title, and risk of loss apply to a sale or return contract. ▸ A buyer bears the expense and risk of loss in returning goods. ▸ In general, a buyer's creditors can claim goods held by a buyer pursuant to a sale or return contract.
   - *Consignment sale*: ▸ A consignment is a transaction whereby an owner of goods (the consignor) delivers them to a seller (the consignee) to be sold for the benefit of the owner. ▸ Title is not transferred by the owner to the consignee. ▸ A consignment is treated as a sale or return. Consequently, a consignee's creditors usually *can* take possession of consigned goods if necessary to satisfy a claim against the consignee unless the consignor files an appropriate notice in accordance with Article 9 of the UCC.

   STUDY HINT. If the nature of a transaction is unclear, it is a sale on approval if goods are intended for a consumer's personal use; it is a sale or return if intended for resale by a merchant.

9. RESERVATION OF A SECURITY INTEREST

▸ In a C.O.D. shipment, a buyer must pay for goods before taking delivery. ▸ A seller's retention of a security interest or shipping goods C.O.D. does not affect the passing of title or risk of loss.

10. EFFECT OF SALE ON TITLE

GENERAL RULE. In general, a buyer of goods receives only the title (if any) held by the seller.
LIMITATIONS. Exceptions and qualifications to the foregoing general rule include:

- *Estoppel*: Wrongful or misleading conduct by an owner of goods that would unfairly cause a buyer a loss may estop (prevent) the owner from asserting ownership to goods.

- *Powers*: A lienholder or pledgee may have a right to sell another's property to enforce a claim.

- *Negotiable documents of title*: A good faith buyer of a negotiable document of title (e.g., a warehouse receipt) may get better title to goods than was possessed by the transferor of the document.

- *Voidable title*: ▸ A seller has voidable title to goods if the seller: (1) bought goods and paid with a "bad" check; (2) bought goods in a cash sale, but failed to pay; or (3) acquired title by fraud. ▸ A good faith buyer for value acquires good title to goods if the seller had voidable title.

- *Sale by entrustee*: ▸ A merchant who regularly buys and sells goods of the kind in question, and to whom a good is entrusted, has the power to transfer the owner's title to a buyer in the ordinary course of business (i.e., a buyer who in good faith purchases an item of inventory from a merchant who regularly buys and sells goods of that kind). Example: Carla left her CD player to be repaired with Acme Electronics, a merchant that regularly buys and sells used CD players. Acme could transfer Carla's title to a good faith buyer. ▸ The foregoing rule does not apply if an owner leaves a good with a party who does not regularly buy and sell goods of that kind. Example: Tony lent his car to Roger, a teenage friend. Roger does not have the power to transfer Tony's title to the car.

STUDY HINTS. ▸ A buyer who receives good or valid title is the legal owner of the goods, and the original owner cannot recover the goods from the buyer. ▸ If a buyer receives only voidable or void (no) title, the original owner can recover the goods even if the buyer acted in good faith and paid value for the goods.

B. SPECIAL SITUATIONS

11. SELF-SERVICE STORES

Regarding self-service stores, courts disagree when a contract for sale is made. Approaches include:

- *Majority rule*: A contract is not made, and title does not pass until a buyer pays for goods.
- *Minority rule*: A "contract to sell" is formed when a customer takes an item from a shelf.
- *Minority rule*: A completed sale occurs, and title passes, when a buyer takes an item from a shelf.

12. AUCTION SALES

Title to a good passes when an auctioneer's hammer signifies that a good or lot is sold to a bidder.

REVIEW OF TERMS AND PHRASES

Select the term or phrase that best matches a statement or definition stated below. Each term or phrase is the best match for only one statement or definition.

Terms and Phrases

a. C.O.D.
b. Consignment
c. Existing goods
d. Future goods
e. Identified goods
f. Sale on approval
g. Sale or return
h. Unidentified goods
i. Voidable title

Statements and Definitions

____ 1. Transaction that permits a party to return goods if the party does not approve of the goods.

____ 2. Goods that have not been designated as being for a particular buyer.

____ 3. Transaction whereby a buyer must pay for goods before taking delivery.

____ 4. Specific goods designated as being for a particular buyer.

____ 5. Transaction that permits a merchant to return goods that it has purchased.

____ 6. Goods that do not exist, or are not owned by a seller, at the time of contracting.

____ 7. Defective title to goods that is acquired by a person who pays for the goods with a "bad" check, who fails to pay the cash purchase price for the goods, or who obtains the goods by fraud.

____ 8. Transfer of possession of property to a party coupled with an authorization to sell the property.

____ 9. Goods that exist and are owned by a seller at the time of contracting.

REVIEW OF CONCEPTS

Write **T** if the statement is true, write **F** if it is false.

____ 1. Seller owns an existing inventory of shovels, and Seller contracts to sell one unspecified shovel from this inventory. In this situation, the shovel sold is an existing and identified good.

____ 2. A buyer has an insurable interest in goods only if the buyer has title to the goods.

____ 3. If a sales contract involves goods that are existing and identified at the time of contracting but a document of title is required to be delivered to the buyer, title and risk of loss do not generally pass to the buyer until the document of title is delivered to the buyer.

____ 4. In a sales contract involving either future goods or goods not identified at the time of contracting, goods are not identified until they are actually delivered to a buyer.

____ 5. A contractual term requiring a seller to "ship to" a buyer is a contract for shipment to the buyer, not a contract for delivery at a destination.

_____ 6. Seller sold existing, identified furniture to Buyer. If Seller must deliver a document of title to Buyer, then title and risk of loss do not pass to Buyer until the document of title is delivered.

_____ 7. In general, a seller's breach of contract has no effect on who bears the risk of loss.

_____ 8. If an agreement is unclear on the point, a transaction that allows a buyer to return conforming goods is interpreted as being a sale on approval if the goods are intended for personal use by a consumer, but it is a sale or return if the goods are intended to be resold by a merchant.

_____ 9. In a sale or return contract, the expense and risk of loss of returning goods is borne by the seller.

_____ 10. A buyer's creditors do not have any rights to goods received by the buyer pursuant to a sale on approval before the buyer approves of the goods.

_____ 11. The fact that goods are shipped C.O.D. or that a seller retains a security interest in goods does not affect when title or risk of loss will pass to a buyer.

_____ 12. If a buyer purchases goods from a thief, then the buyer receives only void (no) title, and the owner of the goods may recover the goods from the buyer.

_____ 13. Creditors of a consignee can never reach and execute on consigned goods because title to the consigned goods belongs to the consignor (the owner).

_____ 14. According to the majority rule, a sale occurs and title to goods passes to a buyer the moment the buyer takes an item from a shelf at a self-service store.

_____ 15. In an auction sale, title does not pass to a buyer until the buyer has in fact paid the price.

REVIEW OF CHAPTER - APPLICATION OF CONCEPTS

MULTIPLE CHOICE QUESTIONS

_____ 1. On May 1, John contracted to buy an existing, identified filing cabinet from Seller, a merchant. Documents of title were not involved. Delivery was required to be made at Seller's business. On June 1, Seller tendered delivery of the filing cabinet to John, but John did not take the filing cabinet. On July 1, John took physical possession of the filing cabinet. Under these facts:
   a. John had an insurable interest in the filing cabinet on May 1.
   b. Title to the filing cabinet passed to John on June 1.
   c. Risk of loss passed to John on July 1.
   d. a and c.

_____ 2. On March 15, Seller contracted to sell a shipment of eyeglasses to SEE Co. The eyeglasses were future goods, not yet identified. As required by the contract, Seller duly delivered the eyeglasses to a carrier for shipment to buyer on April 15. (Seller was *not* required to deliver the eyeglasses at the destination.) On May 15, the shipment was delivered to SEE Co. at the destination. Under these facts, when did title and risk of loss pass to SEE Co.?
   a. March 15.
   b. April 15.
   c. May 15.
   d. Title and risk of loss never passed to SEE Co.

_____ 3. Select the right answer. (The damage to the goods in question was not the fault of either party.)
   a. Walt contracted to buy a one-of-a-kind statue from Seller. The statue was identified and existing at time of contracting. Before risk of loss passed to Walt, the statue was destroyed. In this case, the contract is not avoided, and Seller is in breach if Seller fails to perform.
   b. Seller contracted to sell a desk to Bill. After risk of loss had passed to Bill, the desk was destroyed. In this case, the contract is avoided, and Bill is not required to pay for the desk.
   c. Seller contracted to sell an unidentified G.E. oven to Lisa. Before risk of loss passed, Seller's inventory of ovens was destroyed. In this case, the contract is not avoided, Seller bears the loss, and Seller is liable for breach if an appropriate oven is not delivered to Lisa.
   d. b and c.

_____ 4. Fran received a hair dryer from Seller pursuant to a sale on approval agreement. The agreement allows Fran to test the dryer for 14 days, and Fran may return the dryer at any time during this period if she is not satisfied. Fran received the dryer on June 1. Fran tested the dryer for seven days, and she shipped it back to Seller on June 9. During return shipment, the dryer was damaged. Under these facts:
   a. Title and risk of loss passed to Fran on June 1.
   b. Title and risk of loss never passed to Fran.
   c. Fran must pay for the return shipment of the dryer.
   d. Fran was not entitled to return the dryer because she used it; Fran must pay for the dryer.

_____ 5. Nicole sold a fax machine to Jasper. Jasper paid Nicole with a "bad" check, and Jasper's bank refused to pay the check due to insufficient funds. Prior to Nicole's rescinding the sale, Jasper took the fax and sold it to Gary for value. Gary was unaware of the transaction between Nicole and Jasper. Under these facts:
   a. Gary received only voidable title to the fax.
   b. Gary received valid or good title to the fax.
   c. Nicole cannot recover the fax from Gary.
   d. b and c.

CASE PROBLEM

Did Buyer receive Owner's title to the goods in question? Briefly explain your answer.

(a) Owner delivered her lawn mower to AAA Lawn Mowers, a merchant who regularly bought and sold used mowers. AAA was supposed to repair the mower. Instead, AAA sold the mower to Buyer in the ordinary course of business. Buyer paid for the mower, and Buyer did not know that the mower belonged to Owner.

(b) Owner delivered her car to Wet N' Wild, a retail car wash. Wet N' Wild did not normally buy or sell cars. Without Owner's permission, Wet N' Wild sold Owner's car to Buyer for $8,000, a fair price. Buyer did not know that the car belonged to Owner, or that the sale was improper.

_____

_____

_____

_____

_____

CPA REVIEW

The following questions were given on CPA examinations. The answers for these questions are the unofficial answers prepared by the American Institute of Certified Public Accountants, Inc. (AICPA). All material is reproduced with permission of the AICPA.

____ 1. Quick Corp. agreed to purchase 200 typewriters from Union Suppliers, Inc. Union is a wholesaler of appliances and Quick is an appliance retailer. The contract required Union to ship the typewriters to Quick by common carrier, "F.O.B. Union Suppliers, Inc. Loading Dock." Which of the parties bears the risk of loss during shipment?
   a. Union, because the risk of loss passes only when Quick receives the typewriters.
   b. Union, because both parties are merchants.
   c. Quick, because title to the typewriters passed to Quick at the time of shipment.
   d. Quick, because the risk of loss passes when the typewriters are delivered to the carrier.

____ 2. Bond purchased a painting from Wool, who is not in the business of selling art. Wool tendered delivery of the painting after receiving payment in full from Bond. Bond informed Wool that Bond would be unable to take possession of the painting until later that day. Thieves stole the painting before Bond returned. The risk of loss
   a. Passed to Bond at Wool's tender of delivery.
   b. Passed to Bond at the time the contract was formed and payment was made.
   c. Remained with Wool, because the parties agreed on a later time of delivery.
   d. Remained with Wool, because Bond had not yet received the painting.

Questions 3 and 4 are based on the following:

On May 2, Lace Corp., an appliance wholesaler, offered to sell appliances worth $3,000 to Parco, Inc., a household appliances retailer. The offer was signed by Lace's president, and provided that it would not be withdrawn before June 1. It also included the shipping terms: "FOB- Parco's warehouse." On May 29, Parco mailed an acceptance of Lace's offer. Lace received the acceptance June 2.

____ 3. Risk of loss for the appliances will pass to Parco when they are
   a. Identified to the contract.
   b. Shipped by Lace.
   c. Tendered at Parco's warehouse.
   d. Accepted by Parco.

____ 4. If Lace inadvertently ships the wrong appliances to Parco and Parco rejects them two days after receipt, title to the goods will
   a. Pass to Parco when they are identified to the contract.
   b. Pass to Parco when they are shipped.
   c. Remain with Parco until the goods are returned to Lace.
   d. Revert to Lace when they are rejected by Parco.

_____ 5. Lazur Corp. agreed to purchase 100 radios from Wizard Suppliers, Inc. Wizard is a wholesaler of small home appliances and Lazur is an appliance retailer. The contract required Wizard to ship the radios to Lazur by common carrier, "F.O.B. Wizard Suppliers, Inc. Loading Dock." Risk of loss for the radios during shipment to Lazur would be on
   a. Lazur, because the risk of loss passes when the radios are delivered to the carrier.
   b. Wizard, because the risk of loss passes only when Lazur receives the radios.
   c. Wizard, because it is a shipment contract.
   d. Lazur, because title to the radios passes to Lazur at the time of shipment.

_____ 6. Which of the following factors is most important in deciding who bears the risk of loss between merchants when goods are destroyed during shipment?
   a. The agreement of the parties.
   b. Whether the goods are perishable.
   c. Who has title at the time of the loss.
   d. The terms of applicable insurance policies.

_____ 7. On Monday, Wolfe paid Aston Co., a furniture retailer, $500 for a table. On Thursday, Aston notified Wolfe that the table was ready to be picked up. On Saturday, while Aston was still in possession of the table, it was destroyed in a fire. Who bears the loss of the table?
   a. Wolfe, because Wolfe had title to the table at the time of loss.
   b. Aston, unless Wolfe is a merchant.
   c. Wolfe, unless Aston breached the contract.
   d. Aston, because Wolfe had not yet taken possession of the table.

_____ 8. Lazur Corp. entered into a contract with Baker Suppliers, Inc. to purchase a used word processor from Baker. Lazur is engaged in the business of selling new and used word processors to the general public. The contract required Baker to ship the goods to Lazur by common carrier pursuant to the following provision in the contract: "F.O.B.-Baker Suppliers, Inc. loading dock." Baker also represented in the contract that the word processor had been used for only 10 hours by its previous owner. The contract included the provision that the word processor was being sold "as is" and this provision was in a larger and different type style than the remainder of the contract.

(A)ssume that during shipment to Lazur the word processor was seriously damaged when the carrier's truck was involved in an accident. When the carrier attempted to deliver the word processor, Lazur rejected it and has refused to pay Baker the purchase price. Under the UCC Sales Article,
   a. Lazur rightfully rejected the damaged computer.
   b. The risk of loss for the computer was on Lazur during shipment.
   c. At the time of the accident, risk of loss for the computer was on Baker because title to the computer had not yet passed to Lazur.
   d. Lazur will not be liable to Baker for the purchase price of the computer because of the F.O.B. provision in the contract.

CHAPTER 26
OBLIGATIONS AND PERFORMANCE

CHAPTER OUTLINE

A. GENERAL PRINCIPLES

1. **OBLIGATION OF GOOD FAITH**

   ▸ Every party has an implied duty to act in good faith in performing and enforcing a sales contract.
   ▸ Good faith requires nonmerchants to act honestly. Good faith requires merchants to act honestly and to also observe reasonable business standards of fair dealing.

2. **TIME REQUIREMENTS OF OBLIGATIONS**

   GENERAL RULE. ▸ Unless otherwise agreed, if a sale is for cash and it does not involve movement of goods, a buyer and seller must perform at the same time; i.e., a buyer must pay at the time goods are delivered. ▸ Example: Ferris contracted to buy a TV for $400 cash, and delivery is to be made at Seller's place of business. In this case, Ferris must pay the $400 when he takes the TV.
   STUDY HINT. If a seller and buyer are obligated to perform at the same time but one fails to perform, then the other party may withhold performance without breaching the contract.

3. **REPUDIATION OF THE CONTRACT**

   GENERAL RULES. ▸ A repudiation occurs if a seller or buyer clearly expresses an intent not to perform a contract at the time of performance. ▸ An anticipatory repudiation occurs if, prior to the time performance is required, a party's words or actions clearly indicate that the party is unwilling to perform a contract. Example: Roger contracted to sell his car to Molly on June 1. On May 1, Roger told Molly that he refused to sell his car to her and that he had instead sold the car to Tom. This is an anticipatory repudiation.
   STUDY HINT. If a party fails to perform because the party incorrectly believes that the other party has committed a repudiation or anticipatory repudiation, then the nonperforming party is in breach of contract.

4. **ADEQUATE ASSURANCE OF PERFORMANCE**

   ■ *Right to demand adequate assurance of performance*: If a contracting party is reasonably insecure regarding whether the other party will perform, the insecure party may make written demand on the other party for an adequate assurance of proper performance.

   ■ *Form of assurance*: ▸ The party on whom a demand for assurance is made must give "such assurance of due performance as is adequate under the circumstances of the particular case." ▸ The UCC does not specify a particular form for assurances of performance. Therefore, what constitutes an adequate assurance depends on the facts of each case. Example: A statement by a large, international oil company that it will perform a $50,000 contract may be an adequate assurance, whereas such a statement by a financially troubled small company may be insufficient.

   ■ *Failure to give assurance*: ▸ If a contracting party wrongfully fails to give an adequate assurance of performance within 30 days, then the other party may: (1) treat such failure as a repudiation of the contract; (2) sue for damages for breach of contract; and (3) buy alternative goods from a third party.

B. DUTIES OF THE PARTIES

5. SELLER'S DUTY TO DELIVER

A seller has a duty to deliver goods (i.e., transfer possession of goods) to the buyer in accordance with the terms of the sales contract. *Unless otherwise agreed*, specific duties include the following:

(a) Place, time, and manner of delivery

GENERAL RULE. ▸ Delivery is required (1) within a reasonable time after contracting (2) at the seller's place of business or, if there is no business, at the seller's residence.

LIMITATIONS. ▸ If a contract is for the sale of identified goods and, at the time of contracting, the parties know the goods are in a particular place, then that place is the place of delivery. ▸ If an agreed method of delivery is unavailable or commercially impracticable, the seller must utilize and the buyer must accept a reasonable, alternative method of delivery if one is available.

STUDY HINT. The obligation of parties to use a reasonable, alternative method of delivery is most often incurred in connection with transportation strikes, embargoes, or boycotts.

(b) Quantity delivered

In general, a buyer can demand that all goods be delivered at the same time, and a buyer can refuse an improper partial delivery of goods.

(c) Cure of defective tender or delivery

GENERAL RULE. Broadly speaking, a buyer may reject (i.e., refuse to take or accept) goods that do not perfectly conform to contract requirements.

LIMITATION. A buyer cannot reject goods if a seller exercises its "right to cure" by tending conforming goods (i.e., a seller properly offers to deliver conforming goods in place of nonconforming goods). A seller has the following right to cure an improper (nonconforming) performance:

- *Contract time not expired*: A seller can cure if: (1) the seller gives the buyer seasonable (timely) notice of an intent to cure; and (2) the seller tenders conforming goods within the original time for performance.

- *Contract time expired*: After the original time to perform has expired, a seller has an additional reasonable time within which to cure if: (1) the seller reasonably believed that the goods delivered were acceptable; and (2) the seller gives timely notice of an intent to cure.

STUDY HINT. In order to properly cure a defective performance, a seller must tender goods that conform to all contract requirements.

6. BUYER'S DUTY TO ACCEPT GOODS

A buyer must accept and pay for goods that conform to the contract.

(a) Right to examine goods

▸ In general, a buyer may inspect goods prior to paying the contract price. ▸ But, if goods are shipped C.O.D., a buyer must pay for the goods before inspecting them.

(b) What constitutes acceptance of goods

GENERAL RULES. ▸ A buyer must accept conforming goods, and a failure to do so is a breach of contract. ▸ A buyer accepts goods if: (1) the buyer expressly states that goods conform to contract requirements, or that the buyer will keep goods even though they do not conform; (2) the buyer fails to effectively reject goods; for example, the buyer waits too long to reject after inspecting the goods; or (3) the buyer does any act that is inconsistent with a rejection (or that is inconsistent with a seller's ownership of the goods).

STUDY HINTS. ▸ Examples of acceptance: (1) buyer resells all or a portion of the purchased goods; (2) buyer continues to use purchased goods for a substantial time without attempting to reject them; or (3) buyer significantly alters purchased goods. ▸ If a buyer accepts goods, the buyer must generally pay the contract price for the goods. However, the buyer may still recover damages if the goods do not conform to contract requirements (see Chapter 28).

7. BUYER'S DUTY TO PAY

- *Duty to pay*: In general, a buyer must pay the contract price for goods that the buyer accepts.

- *Time of payment*: ▸ Payment is generally due when goods are properly delivered to a buyer. ▸ However, a sales contract may require payment in advance, or a contract may allow a buyer to purchase on credit, thereby postponing the time for payment.

- *Form of payment*: ▸ A buyer may offer payment by check (or by a promissory note) if this is a generally accepted manner of payment. But, a buyer must pay in cash if this is demanded by the seller. If a seller demands cash, then the seller must give the buyer a reasonable extension of time within which to obtain the required cash. ▸ If payment is made by check and the check is not paid by the buyer's bank, the purchase price remains unpaid.

8. DUTIES UNDER PARTICULAR (SHIPPING) TERMS

A sales contract may use special shipping terms to identify the rights and duties of parties. These terms include:

- *C.I.F., C. & F.*: C.I.F. means that the contract price includes (1) the selling price (cost) for the goods and (2) the cost of insurance and shipping (freight) to a named destination. ▸ C. & F. means that the contract price includes (1) the price for the goods and (2) the cost of shipping to a named destination. ▸ Under a C.I.F. or C. & F. contract, title and risk of loss (including any loss caused by delays during shipment) pass to a buyer when the seller delivers goods to the carrier.

- *F.O.B.*: ▸ F.O.B. (free on board) stated with the place of shipment means: (1) a seller must deliver goods to a carrier at that place; and (2) the seller bears the expense and risk of delivering goods to the carrier. The expense of shipping and the risk of loss during shipment is the buyer's responsibility. ▸ F.O.B. stated with a destination point means: (1) a seller must properly tender delivery of goods to the buyer at the destination; and (2) the seller bears the expense and risk of loss of shipping goods to the named destination. ▸ Example: Seller, in Miami, shipped goods to Acme Inc. in Seattle. The goods were sold "F.O.B. Seattle." In this situation, Seller must pay the expense of shipping the goods to Seattle, and Seller bears the risk of loss during shipment.

- *F.A.S., Ex-ship*: ▸ F.A.S. (free alongside) means that a seller bears the expense and risk of loss for delivering goods alongside a named vessel. Title and risk of loss pass to a buyer at that point. ▸ Ex-ship obligates a seller to deliver and unload goods from a ship at a named destination port. Title and risk of loss pass to a buyer when the goods are properly unloaded.

REVIEW OF TERMS AND PHRASES

Select the term or phrase that best matches a statement or definition stated below. Each term or phrase is the best match for only one statement or definition.

Terms and Phrases

a. Acceptance (of goods)
b. Anticipatory repudiation
c. C. & F. contract
d. C.I.F. contract
e. Cure
f. Ex-ship contract
g. F.A.S. contract
h. F.O.B. contract
i. Good faith
j. Rejection (of goods)
k. Repudiation
l. Seasonable

Statements and Definitions

____ 1. Clear declaration made prior to time for performance that a party will not perform a contract.

____ 2. Wrongful failure to perform a contract at the time performance is required.

____ 3. Buyer agrees to take goods as his or her own.

____ 4. Contract obligating a seller to deliver and unload goods from a ship at a named port.

____ 5. Timely.

____ 6. Contract for which the contract price includes the price for the goods and the cost of shipping and insurance to the destination; title and risk pass when goods are delivered to the carrier.

____ 7. Contract requiring a seller to bear expense and risk of delivering goods alongside a named vessel.

____ 8. Contract for which the contract price includes the price for the goods and the cost of shipping to a named destination; title and risk of loss pass when goods are delivered to the carrier.

____ 9. Contract that requires a seller to either deliver goods to a carrier for shipment to a buyer, or to tender delivery of goods to the buyer at a named destination.

____10. Seller corrects an improper performance by delivering conforming goods to a buyer.

____11. Buyer's refusal to accept goods as his or her own.

____12. Duty to act honestly and, for merchants, to also follow business standards of fair dealing.

REVIEW OF CONCEPTS

Write **T** if the statement is true, write **F** if it is false.

____ 1. Good faith requires a nonmerchant to act honestly.

____ 2. In a cash sale not involving movement of goods, a buyer's duty to pay and a seller's duty to deliver goods are concurrent, i.e., payment and delivery must be performed at the same time.

____ 3. Ken and Renee made a contract. Ken mistakenly believed that Renee had breached the contract and, therefore, he refused to perform his obligations under the contract. In this case, Ken has not committed a repudiation and he has not breached the contract.

____ 4. If a contracting party repudiates a contract, the other party is excused from having to perform the contract but the other party is not entitled to sue the repudiating party for damages.

____ 5. If a contracting party anticipatorily repudiates a contract, the other party can treat the anticipatory repudiation as a repudiation of the contract and may sue for breach of contract.

____ 6. If a contracting party reasonably feels insecure about the likelihood that the other party will perform, the insecure party can make written demand for an adequate assurance of performance.

____ 7. If a contracting party fails to give an adequate assurance of performance when properly requested to do so, the other party may treat such failure as a repudiation of the contract.

____ 8. If a contract requires shipment by railroad but this transportation is unavailable due to a strike, the contract is automatically canceled even if reasonable, alternative transportation is available.

____ 9. A seller may make a curative tender by tendering goods that meet contract requirements, or by tendering substitute goods that the seller believes are an acceptable alternative.

____ 10. A buyer is generally entitled to examine goods prior to payment unless goods are shipped C.O.D.

____ 11. In a C.I.F. contract, title and risk of loss do not pass until goods are delivered at the destination.

____ 12. In a C. & F. contract, the contract price includes the price of the goods, the cost of insurance, and freight expenses.

____ 13. In an F.A.S. contract, a seller bears the expense of delivering goods alongside a named vessel.

____ 14. In an F.A.S. contract, title and risk of loss pass to a buyer at the time the contract is made.

____ 15. In an ex-ship contract, a seller must deliver and unload goods from the ship at the destination point; title and risk of loss do not pass to the buyer until the goods are properly unloaded.

REVIEW OF CHAPTER - APPLICATION OF CONCEPTS

MULTIPLE CHOICE QUESTIONS

____ 1. Foodco, a merchant, and Jan made a contract whereby Foodco granted Jan the right to sell Foodco's products in a certain region. However, the contract states that Foodco may allow others to also sell in this region if Foodco determines that additional sales representatives are needed. The contract is silent regarding good faith. Under these facts:
   a. Foodco must act in good faith since the UCC implies this duty. Good faith requires Foodco to act honestly, and to also observe reasonable business standards of fair dealing.
   b. Foodco must act in good faith since the UCC implies this duty. Good faith only requires Foodco to act honestly.
   c. Foodco must act in good faith since the UCC implies this duty. Good faith prohibits Foodco from exercising any contract right that may be detrimental to Jan.
   d. Foodco is under no duty to act in good faith since the contract is silent on this matter.

____ 2. Decor Inc. contracted to sell wallpaper to Karen. The wallpaper is located at Decor's place of business. The contract is silent regarding time and place of delivery. Under these facts:
   a. Decor is obligated to deliver the wallpaper to Karen at her home.
   b. Decor is obligated to deliver the wallpaper to Karen at Decor's place of business.
   c. Decor is obligated to have the wallpaper ready for delivery only at such time Decor chooses.
   d. Decor is obligated to have the wallpaper ready for delivery whenever Karen demands delivery.

____ 3. On May 1 (the required delivery date), Seller delivered goods that Seller reasonably believed were acceptable. The next day, Seller was told that the goods were nonconforming. Seller immediately gave notice that the improper performance would be cured. Under these facts:
   a. Seller cannot cure. A seller cannot cure an improper performance.
   b. Seller cannot cure. A seller can cure only if a cure is done within the original contract time.
   c. Seller can cure if Seller tenders conforming goods to the buyer within a reasonable time.
   d. Seller can cure whenever Seller chooses to do so.

____ 4. In which case did Buyer accept the goods in question?
   a. Buyer bought a tractor. During inspection Buyer learned that the tractor was nonconforming. After using the tractor for nine months, Buyer told Seller that the tractor was unacceptable.
   b. Buyer bought an electric barbecue. When Buyer first attempted to use the barbecue, it did not work properly. Buyer immediately told Seller that the barbecue was unacceptable.
   c. Buyer bought a computer. When the computer was delivered, Buyer discovered that the computer was nonconforming. Nonetheless, Buyer modified numerous significant internal components of the computer. Later, Buyer told Seller that the computer was unacceptable.
   d. a and c.

____ 5. Art contracted to buy a sofa for $500 cash. Art is to take delivery at Seller's place of business where the sofa is located. Art has inspected and accepted the sofa. Under these facts:
   a. Art has the right to pay at any time within 30 days after he takes delivery of the sofa.
   b. Art has the right to pay for the sofa by check, and Seller cannot demand payment in cash.
   c. Art may offer to pay by check if this is a normal method of payment. But, Seller can demand cash if Art is given a reasonable extension of time within which to obtain the cash.
   d. Art must pay for the sofa in cash. Art cannot offer to pay by check even if this is a normal method of payment.

CASE PROBLEM

Seller, in Jacksonville, contracted to sell a shipment of oranges to Buyer in Omaha. The contract states that the oranges are sold "F.O.B. Jacksonville."

(a) Who bears the expense and risk of loss of delivering the oranges to the carrier for shipment? (b) Who bears the expense of shipping the oranges to Buyer in Omaha? (c) If the oranges are damaged during shipment, who bears the risk of loss?

CPA REVIEW

The following questions were given on CPA examinations. The answers for these questions are the unofficial answers prepared by the American Institute of Certified Public Accountants, Inc. (AICPA). All material is reproduced with permission of the AICPA.

____ 1. Smith contracted in writing to sell Peters a used personal computer for $600. The contract did not specifically address the time for payment, place of delivery, or Peters' right to inspect the computer. Which of the following statements is correct?
   a. Smith is obligated to deliver the computer to Peters' home.
   b. Peters is entitled to inspect the computer before paying for it.
   c. Peters may not pay for the computer using a personal check unless Smith agrees.
   d. Smith is not entitled to payment until 30 days after Peters receives the computer.

____ 2. Under the Sales Article of the UCC, which of the following events will release the buyer from all its obligations under a sales contract?
   a. Destruction of the goods after risk of loss passed to the buyer.
   b. Impracticability of delivery under the terms of the contract.
   c. Anticipatory repudiation by the buyer that is retracted before the seller cancels the contract.
   d. Refusal of the seller to give written assurance of performance when reasonably demanded by the buyer.

____ 3. Rowe Corp. purchased goods from Stair Co. that were shipped C.O.D. Under the Sales Article of the UCC, which of the following rights does Rowe have?
   a. The right to inspect the goods before paying.
   b. The right to possession of the goods before paying.
   c. The right to reject nonconforming goods.
   d. The right to delay payment for a reasonable period of time.

____ 4. Lazur Corp. agreed to purchase 100 radios from Wizard Suppliers, Inc. Wizard is a wholesaler of small home appliances and Lazur is an appliance retailer. The contract required Wizard to ship the radios to Lazur by common carrier, "F.O.B. Wizard Suppliers, Inc. Loading Dock." Under the UCC Sales Article
   a. Title to the radios passes to Lazur at the time they are delivered to the carrier, even if the goods are nonconforming.
   b. Lazur must inspect the radios at the time of delivery or waive any defects and the right to sue for breach of contract.
   c. Wizard must pay the freight expense associated with the shipment of the radios to Lazur.
   d. Lazur would have the right to reject any shipment if Wizard fails to notify Lazur that the goods have been shipped.

CHAPTER 26   225

___ 5. Lazur Corp. entered into a contract with Baker Suppliers, Inc. to purchase a used word processor from Baker. Lazur is engaged in the business of selling new and used word processors to the general public. The contract required Baker to ship the goods to Lazur by common carrier pursuant to the following provision in the contract: "F.O.B.-Baker Suppliers, Inc. loading dock." Baker also represented in the contract that the word processor had been used for only 10 hours by its previous owner. The contract included the provision that the word processor was being sold "as is" and this provision was in a larger and different type style than the remainder of the contract.

(A)ssume that the contract between Lazur and Baker is otherwise silent. Under the UCC Sales Article,
   a. Lazur must pay Baker the purchase price before Baker is required to ship the word processor to Lazur.
   b. Baker does not warrant that it owns the word processor.
   c. Lazur will be entitled to inspect the word processor before it accepts or pays for it.
   d. Title to the word processor passes to Lazur when it takes physical possession.

___ 6. Yost Corp., a computer manufacturer, contracted to sell IS computers to Ivor Corp., a computer retailer. The contract specified that delivery was to be made by truck to Ivor's warehouse. Instead, Yost shipped the computers by rail. When Ivor claimed that Yost did not comply with the contract, Yost told Ivor that there had been a trucker's strike when the goods were shipped. Ivor refused to pay for the computers. Under these circumstances, Ivor
   a. Is obligated to pay for the computers because Yost made a valid substituted performance.
   b. Is obligated to pay for the computers because title to them passed to Ivor when Ivor received them.
   c. May return the computers and avoid paying for them because of the way Yost delivered them.
   d. May return the computers and avoid paying for them because the contract was void under the theory of commercial impracticability.

___ 7. On March 7, 1988, Wax Corp. contracted with Noll Wholesalers to supply Noll with specific electrical parts. Delivery was called for on June 3, 1988. On May 2, 1988, Wax notified Noll that it would not perform and that Noll should look elsewhere. Wax had received a larger and more lucrative contract on April 21, 1988, and its capacity was such that it could not fulfill both orders. The facts
   a. Will prevent Wax from retracting its repudiation of the Noll contract.
   b. Are not sufficient to clearly establish an anticipatory repudiation.
   c. Will permit Noll to sue only after June 3, 1988, the latest performance date.
   d. Will permit Noll to sue immediately after May 2, 1988, even though the performance called for under the contract was not due until June 3, 1988.

___ 8. If a contract for the sale of goods includes a C. & F. shipping term and the seller has fulfilled all of its obligations, the
   a. Title to the goods will pass to the buyer when the goods are received by the buyer at the place of destination.
   b. Risk of loss will pass to the buyer upon delivery of the goods to the carrier.
   c. Buyer retains the right to inspect the goods prior to making payment.
   d. Seller must obtain an insurance policy at its own expense for the buyer's benefit.

CHAPTER 27
WARRANTIES AND OTHER PRODUCT LIABILITY THEORIES

CHAPTER OUTLINE

A. GENERAL PRINCIPLES

1. THEORIES OF LIABILITY

Potential theories of products liability include: (1) express warranty; (2) implied warranty; (3) negligence; (4) fraud; and (5) strict tort liability.

2. NATURE OF HARM

GENERAL RULES. ▸ Types of harm: (1) personal injuries; (2) property damage; and (3) economic or commercial loss. One can usually sue for any type of harm that is caused. For example, under the modern view, courts permit a consumer to sue for purely economic losses even if the consumer was not in privity of contract with the defendant.
STUDY HINT. Economic losses include lost profits and damage to the purchased good itself.

3. WHO MAY SUE AND BE SUED

- *The plaintiff (who may sue)*: ▸ In most states, a buyer, a member of a buyer's family or household, or a buyer's guest may sue for personal injuries that are suffered due to a breach of warranty. ▸ Under the modern view, other third parties (including bystanders, customers, and employees) who suffers foreseeable physical harm can sue for product liability. Some states will not allow parties to sue only for economic losses unless there is privity of contract.
- *The defendant (who may be sued)*: ▸ A seller, wholesaler, or manufacturer of a good or component part can generally be sued for product liability. ▸ If privity of contract is required to sue, many courts find this requirement met if a plaintiff had direct dealings with a defendant.

B. EXPRESS WARRANTIES

4. DEFINITION OF EXPRESS WARRANTY

An express warranty is a (1) statement of fact or promise regarding the quality or performance of a good (2) that is a basis of the sale (i.e., it is presumed to be part of the contract).

5. FORM OF EXPRESS WARRANTY

No special words are needed; an express warranty may be written, oral, or arise due to a seller's conduct. Express warranties may arise from statements made in negotiations, ads, labels, etc.

6. TIME OF MAKING EXPRESS WARRANTY

GENERAL RULE. An express warranty may be made before or after a contract is made.
STUDY HINT. A warranty made following a sale is valid even if consideration is not given.

7. SELLER'S OPINION OR STATEMENT OF VALUE

GENERAL RULE. Statements of value, opinions, and sales talk do not create express warranties.
LIMITATION. An expert seller's opinion that is relied upon by a buyer may create a warranty.

8. **WARRANTY OF CONFORMITY TO DESCRIPTION, SAMPLE, OR MODEL**

   An express warranty may be created by a description of goods (labels), or by showing a buyer a sample (specimen of actual goods to be furnished) or a model (example of what goods will be like).

9. **FEDERAL REGULATION OF EXPRESS WARRANTIES**

   Federal law regulates express warranties made in sales of consumer goods for $15 or more. This law requires that express warranties be labeled as either full or limited, and meet these requirements:

   - *Full warranties*: ▸ Seller must fix or replace a defective good within a reasonable time, without cost to a buyer. If this cannot be done, a buyer has the choice to request a refund or a free replacement. ▸ A full warranty is valid for its stated period regardless of a change of ownership. ▸ Implied warranties cannot be limited to a duration shorter than the term of a full warranty.
   - *Limited warranties*: Any express warranty that gives less protection than is given by a full warranty.

10. **EFFECT OF BREACH OF EXPRESS WARRANTY**

    A seller is liable for all harm caused by a breach of an express warranty even if the seller was not negligent and the seller did not know that a good failed to satisfy the express warranty.

C. **IMPLIED WARRANTIES**

11. **DEFINITION OF IMPLIED WARRANTY**

    An implied warranty is one implied by law that automatically arises when a sales contract is made.

12. **IMPLIED WARRANTIES OF ALL SELLERS**

    - *Warranty of title*: ▸ Most sellers warrant: (1) a buyer will receive good title; and (2) the seller has the right to transfer title. ▸ Title is not warranted if: (1) a contract disclaims this warranty; or (2) goods are sold by a sheriff, a creditor enforcing a lien, or an administrator of an estate.
    - *Warranty against encumbrances*: Every seller warrants that, when delivered, goods will not be subject to a security interest that the buyer did not know about when the contract was made.
    - *Warranty of fitness for a particular purpose*: This warranty arises if: (1) a seller has reason to know a buyer has an unusual purpose for a good, and that the buyer is relying on the seller to select an appropriate good; and (2) the buyer actually relies on the seller to select the good.

13. **ADDITIONAL IMPLIED WARRANTIES OF MERCHANT SELLER**

    - *Warranty against infringement*: Merchant sellers warrant against patent/trademark infringement.
    - *Warranty of merchantability or fitness for normal use*: ▸ Merchant sellers impliedly warrant that goods are merchantable, i.e., goods will perform ordinary tasks in a safe manner. ▸ This warranty requires goods to be fit for the ordinary purposes for which they are sold, but goods do not have to be the best or perfect. ▸ Sellers may breach this warranty without being negligent.

14. **WARRANTIES IN PARTICULAR SALES**

    - *Sale on buyer's specifications*: Ordinary warranties apply except: (1) no warranty of fitness for a particular purpose can arise; and (2) a seller is not liable for a loss caused by a design defect.
    - *Sale of secondhand (used) goods*: Most (not all) courts hold that the warranty of merchantability applies to used goods, although the fitness required for used goods is less than for new goods.
    - *Sale of food or drink*: The fitness (merchantability) of food is determined by one of two tests: (1) *reasonable expectations test*: an unintended substance in food, whether natural or foreign, renders food unfit if an ordinary person would not expect to find the substance in the food; or (2) *foreign substance-natural substance test*: food is fit if an unintended substance is natural, such as a pit in a prune; it is unfit if the substance is foreign, such as a stone in pea soup.

15. NECESSITY OF DEFECT

▸ Traditionally, a claim for breach of the warranty of merchantability required proof that a good was defective. Many courts have now eliminated this requirement, and liability results if goods are unfit for intended purposes. ▸ Proof of a defect is not needed to prove a breach of express warranty.

16. WARRANTIES IN THE INTERNATIONAL SALE OF GOODS

Warranties of merchantability and fitness for particular purpose may apply, but can be disclaimed.

D. DISCLAIMER OF WARRANTIES

17. VALIDITY OF DISCLAIMER

- ■ *Disclaimers*: ▸ A seller and buyer may agree to disclaim (eliminate) any or all express or implied warranties. ▸ Disclaimers of the warranty of merchantability: (1) may be oral or written; (2) must use the word "merchantability"; and (3) must be conspicuous, if written. ▸ Disclaimers of the warranty of fitness for a particular purpose must be (1) written and (2) conspicuous.
- ■ *Unconscionability*: ▸ In general, disclaimers permitted by Article 2 are not unconscionable. ▸ In some states, however, disclaimers may be invalid due to public policy or consumer laws.

18. PARTICULAR LANGUAGE FOR DISCLAIMERS

▸ The implied warranties of merchantability and fitness for a particular purpose may be excluded by a general disclaimer such as "as is" or "with all faults," but an oral disclaimer must be brought to the buyer's attention. ▸ Disclaimers do not prohibit suits for fraud, negligence, or strict tort liability.

19. EXCLUSION OF WARRANTIES BY EXAMINATION OF GOODS

If a buyer examines (or refuses to examine) a good, sample, or model before contracting, *no implied warranties* are made regarding matters the buyer should have discovered by examining the good.

20. POST-SALE DISCLAIMER

A disclaimer is invalid if it is not communicated to a buyer until after a sales contract is made.

E. OTHER THEORIES OF PRODUCT LIABILITY

21. NEGLIGENCE

A negligent seller or manufacturer may be sued by a person who is injured by a defective product, and privity of contract is not required.

22. FRAUD

A party defrauded in connection with the purchase of a product may sue for the tort of fraud.

23. STRICT TORT LIABILITY

▸ A manufacturer of a good or component part, a distributor, or a retailer has strict tort liability for injuries suffered by anyone due to a defective, unreasonably dangerous product; privity of contract is not required. ▸ Strict tort liability is not absolute liability; this liability is imposed only if a product is defective. ▸ Assumption of risk by an injured party is a defense; contributory negligence is not.

24. CUMULATIVE THEORIES OF LIABILITY

In some cases, a plaintiff may be able to sue on two or more theories of product liability.

REVIEW OF TERMS AND PHRASES

MATCHING EXERCISE

Select the term or phrase that best matches a statement or definition stated below. Each term or phrase is the best match for only one statement or definition.

Terms and Phrases

a. Conspicuous
b. Disclaimer
c. Economic loss
d. Express warranties
e. Full warranty
f. Implied warranties
g. Limited warranty
h. Warranty against encumbrances
i. Warranty against infringement
j. Warranty of fitness for a particular purpose
k. Warranty of merchantability
l. Warranty of title

Statements and Definitions

____ 1. Broad category of warranties that automatically arise when a sales contract is made.

____ 2. Noticeable to a reasonable person.

____ 3. Broad category of warranties that arise due to the words or conduct of a seller.

____ 4. Disavowal or elimination of a warranty.

____ 5. Under federal law, a classification of express warranty in a sale of consumer goods that, among other things, obligates a seller to fix or replace a defective product within a reasonable period of time without cost to a buyer.

____ 6. Warranty that a buyer will receive good title and that the seller has the right to transfer title.

____ 7. Damage that a product causes to itself, or other purely monetary loss, such as lost profits.

____ 8. Warranty that a good is not subject to a lien that the buyer is unaware of at the time of contracting.

____ 9. Implied warranty that a good can perform an unusual use that is intended by a buyer.

____ 10. Under federal law, a classification of express warranty in a sale of consumer goods that provides less protection than would be provided by a full warranty.

____ 11. Implied warranty that a good is fit for the ordinary purposes for which the good is sold.

____ 12. Warranty that a good does not violate the patent or trademark rights of others.

COMPLETION EXERCISE

Fill in the blanks with the words that most accurately complete each statement. Answers may or may not include terms used in the matching exercise. A term cannot be used to complete more than one statement.

1. A party who regularly deals in goods of the kind that are being sold is called a _____.

2. A seller's statement of fact or promise regarding a good does not create an express warranty unless the statement or promise is part of the _____ ____ ____ _____.

3. A _____ is a specimen or portion of the actual goods to be furnished to a buyer.

4. A replica or example of what purchased goods will be like is called a _____.

5. Federal law regulates express warranties made in connection with the sale of _____ _____ for _____ dollars or more.

6. Three implied warranties that may be made by any seller are the _____ ____ _____, _____ _____ _____, and _____ ____ _____ ____ ____ _____ _____.

7. Two implied warranties that are generally made by merchant sellers are the _____ _____ _____ and _____ ____ _____.

8. The theory of product liability that holds a manufacturer liable for personal injuries caused by a defective and unreasonably dangerous product is known as _____ _____ _____.

REVIEW OF CONCEPTS

Write **T** if the statement is true, write **F** if it is false.

____ 1. Under the modern view, courts may permit a consumer to sue for purely economic losses even if the consumer was not in privity of contract with a defendant.

____ 2. In most states, only a buyer can sue for personal injuries caused by a breach of warranty.

____ 3. A buyer who is injured by a defective and unreasonably dangerous good may be able to sue the seller and/or the manufacturer of the good.

____ 4. Statements of fact made by a seller in advertisements or catalogs cannot create an express warranty.

____ 5. Statements of value and opinions do not ordinarily create express warranties.

____ 6. A warranty made after a sale is not binding unless the buyer paid consideration for the warranty.

____ 7. Federal law requires a seller to expressly warrant consumer goods that are sold.

____ 8. In general, a warranty cannot be called a "full warranty" if a consumer buyer is required to pay for the cost of shipping a defective good back to the seller.

____ 9. A description of goods does not create an express warranty unless it is stated in the contract.

____10. Seller showed Buyer a sample of wheat that Seller offered to sell to Buyer. In this case, Seller's conduct created an express warranty that Buyer's wheat would be the same as the sample.

____11. A seller cannot be held liable for breach of an express warranty unless the seller was negligent in making the good or the seller knew the warranty was false.

____12. If an express warranty conflicts with a warranty of merchantability, the express warranty prevails.

____13. If a seller manufactures a good in accordance with specifications furnished by a buyer, then the seller cannot be liable for breach of any express or implied warranties.

____14. Most courts hold that a merchant's sale of used goods may give rise to a warranty of merchantability.

____15. A product is defective if it is improperly designed or manufactured, or if a buyer is given inadequate instructions for using the good or inadequate warnings of potential dangers.

____16. Under the CISG, warranties of merchantability cannot be disclaimed.

____17. A buyer's examination of goods does not affect the existence or extent of implied warranties.

____18. A disclaimer of warranty is invalid if it is not communicated to a buyer until after a sale is made.

____19. In general, a disclaimer does not eliminate liability for fraud, negligence, or strict tort liability.

____20. Assumption of risk is a defense to a claim for strict liability.

REVIEW OF CHAPTER - APPLICATION OF CONCEPTS

MULTIPLE CHOICE QUESTIONS

____ 1. In which situation does Seller make an express warranty?
   a. During negotiations, Seller gave Byron a brochure regarding a ring that Byron was considering purchasing. The brochure stated that the ring was sterling silver.
   b. During negotiations for the sale of a drill, Seller stated to Buyer: "This drill is the best little drill on the market today." Seller did not say or do anything else.
   c. During negotiations for the sale of a chair to be specially manufactured, Seller showed Buyer a model of what the chair would be like. Seller did not say or do anything else.
   d. a and c.

____ 2. Carson Co. sold Tami a watch for $25 for her personal use. In connection with the sale, Carson made a "Full Warranty," guaranteeing the watch against any defects for one year. In this case:
   a. If during the warranty period the watch fails due to a defect, then Carson must repair the watch. However, Carson can charge Tami a reasonable fee for repairing the watch.
   b. If during the warranty period the watch fails due to a defect and Carson fails to fix or replace the watch within a reasonable time, then Tami can demand a refund or a new watch.
   c. If Tami sells the watch to Gina, Gina will not have any right to enforce the warranty.
   d. Carson is entitled to disclaim all implied warranties.

_____ 3. Select the correct statement.
   a. K&L foreclosed a lien on a debtor's goods. K&L held a sale of the goods. Prior to sale, buyers were told that only the debtor's interest, if any, was being sold. As it turns out, the debtor had defective title to the goods. In this case, K&L breached the warranty of title.
   b. Kit sold an engine to Buyer. Unknown to the parties, Kit did not have title to the engine. In this case, Kit breached the warranty of title.
   c. John sold a car to Sam. Unknown to Sam, the car was subject to a lien. Prior to delivery, John had the lien removed. In this case, John breached the warranty against encumbrances.
   d. All of the above are correct.

_____ 4. In which case is the implied warranty of fitness for a particular purpose breached?
   a. Manufacturer sold an egg incubator to a zoo. At time of contracting, Manufacturer knew the zoo needed an incubator for hatching ostrich eggs (an unusual purpose), and that the zoo was relying on Manufacturer to select an appropriate incubator. (The zoo did in fact rely on Manufacturer.) The incubator delivered did not hatch ostrich eggs; it baked them.
   b. Buyer needed a paint that could withstand unusual, prolonged heat. Buyer developed a paint formula and furnished Manufacturer with specifications for the paint. The paint was made in accordance with the specifications, but it failed to perform the unusual task.
   c. Seller sold Buyer a lawn mower. Unknown to Seller, Buyer intended to use the mower to cut three-foot-tall salt marsh grass, an unusual purpose. The mower failed to cut this grass.
   d. a and b.

_____ 5. The implied warranty of merchantability is breached in which case?
   a. Juanita (a nonmerchant) sold Buyer a new toaster that Juanita had received as a gift. The toaster cannot toast bread.
   b. Seller (a merchant) sold an ordinary private airplane to Buyer. The airplane operates safely and it is fit for ordinary private use. However, the plane cannot perform acrobatic stunts.
   c. Manufacturer, a merchant, sold a portable plastic pool to Buyer. The pool leaks badly, and it cannot be repaired. However, Manufacturer was not negligent in making the pool.
   d. All of the above.

_____ 6. M&M Cafe sold JoJo a guacamole taco. The taco had a piece of avocado pit in it. Although guacamole is made from avocados which have pits, an ordinary person would not reasonably expect to find a piece of an avocado pit in a guacamole taco. Under these facts:
   a. M&M did not breach the warranty of merchantability; the UCC does not apply to food sales.
   b. Under the natural substance-foreign substance test, the taco is fit (merchantable).
   c. Under the reasonable expectations test, the taco is fit (merchantable).
   d. b and c.

_____ 7. Seller (a used car dealer) sold Buyer a 1991 truck. Seller expressly warranted that the truck was a 1992 truck. Prior to contracting, Seller demanded that Buyer inspect the truck, but Buyer refused. An inspection would have revealed that the engine hoses were cracked, rendering the truck unfit to drive. An inspection would not have revealed the true model year of the truck. *After* the contract was made, Seller disclaimed all warranties. Under these facts:
   a. Buyer can sue for breach of the express warranty regarding the model year of the truck.
   b. Buyer can sue for breach of the warranty of merchantability due to the cracked hoses.
   c. Buyer cannot sue Seller for breach of any express or implied warranties because Seller disclaimed all warranties.
   d. a and b.

CHAPTER 27

CASE PROBLEMS

Answer the following problems, briefly explaining your answers.

1. Aqua Boats manufactured a boat, and it sold the boat to Crest Sales Co. Aqua disclaimed all warranties. Crest sold the boat to Gary for family use. Crest expressly warranted to Gary that the boat's hull was shatterproof. While Gary and his wife were boating one day, the boat struck a small rock. The rock shattered the boat's hull, causing the boat to sink. Not only did the boat not satisfy the warranties made by Crest, but the boat was also defective and unreasonably dangerous. Gary and his wife suffered personal injuries, they lost personal property on the boat, and the boat itself was lost.

    (a) Who can sue Crest for breach of warranty? (b) Can Gary and his wife both sue for strict tort liability? (c) Do Aqua and Crest both have strict tort liability? (d) For what harm can Gary and his wife recover?

2. Vision Inc., a maker of commercial microscopes, plans to sell a new microscope. Vision is concerned about potential liability for implied warranties. Vision asks you: (a) Can Vision disclaim the warranties of merchantability and fitness for a particular purpose, or are disclaimers unconscionable? (b) Can Vision disclaim the warranty of merchantability by burying a disclaimer in the contract, using the same size, type, and color of print that is used for other terms? (c) If Vision's contracts conspicuously state that microscopes are sold "AS IS," what effect would this term have on implied warranties?

3. Yampa Co. manufactures mountain climbing boots. Yampa disclaims all warranties regarding its boots. However, Yampa falsely misrepresents that its boots are waterproof. Also, Yampa uses a type of glue to assemble its boots that disintegrates when boots get wet. (A reasonably prudent manufacturer would not use this glue.) In addition, the tread design of Yampa's boots is defective and unreasonably dangerous. Numerous climbers have been injured due to the foregoing types of misconduct by Yampa.

    (a) On what theories of products liability can Yampa be held liable? (b) Is privity of contract necessary to hold Yampa liable? (c) Could a buyer hold Yampa liable on the basis of several theories of liability?

CPA REVIEW

The following questions were given on CPA examinations. The answers for these questions are the unofficial answers prepared by the American Institute of Certified Public Accountants, Inc. (AICPA). All material is reproduced with permission of the AICPA.

____ 1. Under the Sales Article of the UCC, which of the following statements is correct regarding the warranty of merchantability arising when there has been a sale of goods by a merchant seller?
   a. The warranty must be in writing.
   b. The warranty arises when the buyer relies on the seller's skill in selecting the goods purchased.
   c. The warranty cannot be disclaimed.
   d. The warranty arises as a matter of law when the seller ordinarily sells the goods purchased.

____ 2. High sues the manufacturer, wholesaler, and retailer for bodily injuries caused by a power saw High purchased. Which of the following statements is correct under strict liability theory?
   a. Contributory negligence on High's part will always be a bar to recovery.
   b. The manufacturer will avoid liability if it can show it followed the custom of the industry.
   c. Privity will be a bar to recovery insofar as the wholesaler is concerned if the wholesaler did not have a reasonable opportunity to inspect.
   d. High may recover even if he cannot show any negligence was involved.

____ 3. Vick bought a used boat from Ocean Marina that disclaimed "any and all warranties" in connection with the sale. Ocean was unaware the boat had been stolen from Kidd. Vick surrendered it to Kidd when confronted with proof of the theft. Vick sued Ocean. Who is likely to prevail and why?
   a. Vick, because the implied warranty of title has been breached.
   b. Vick, because a merchant cannot disclaim implied warranties.
   c. Ocean, because of the disclaimer of warranties.
   d. Ocean, because Vick surrendered the boat to Kidd.

____ 4. With respect to the sale of goods, the warranty of title
   a. Applies only if the seller is a merchant.
   b. Applies only if it is in writing and signed by the seller.
   c. Provides that the seller deliver the goods free from any lien of which the buyer lacked knowledge when the contract was made.
   d. Provides that the seller cannot disclaim the warranty if the sale is made to a bona fide purchaser for value.

CHAPTER 27

5. Under the UCC Sales Article, an action for breach of the implied warranty of merchantability by a party who sustains personal injuries may be successful against the seller of the product only when
   a. The seller is a merchant of the product involved.
   b. An action based on negligence can also be successfully maintained.
   c. The injured party is in privity of contract with the seller.
   d. An action based on strict liability in tort can also be successfully maintained.

6. Lazur Corp. entered into a contract with Baker Suppliers, Inc. to purchase a used word processor from Baker. Lazur is engaged in the business of selling new and used word processors to the general public. The contract required Baker to ship the goods to Lazur by common carrier pursuant to the following provision in the contract: "F.O.B.-Baker Suppliers, Inc. loading dock." Baker also represented in the contract that the word processor had been used for only 10 hours by its previous owner. The contract included the provision that the word processor was being sold "as is" and this provision was in a larger and different type style than the remainder of the contract.
   With regard to the contract between Lazur and Baker,
   a. An implied warranty of merchantability does not arise unless both Lazur and Baker are merchants.
   b. The "as is" provision effectively disclaims the implied warranty of title.
   c. No express warranties are created by the contract.
   d. The "as is" provision would not prevent Baker from being liable for a breach of any express warranties created by the contract.

7. Morgan is suing the manufacturer, wholesaler, and retailer for bodily injuries caused by a power saw Morgan purchased. Which of the following statements is correct under the theory of strict liability?
   a. The manufacturer will avoid liability if it can show it followed the custom of the industry.
   b. Morgan may recover even if he cannot show any negligence was involved.
   c. Contributory negligence on Morgan's part will always be a bar to recovery.
   d. Privity will be a bar to recovery insofar as the wholesaler is concerned if the wholesaler did not have a reasonable opportunity to inspect.

8. On May 2, Handy Hardware sent Ram Industries a signed purchase order that stated, in part, as follows: "Ship for May 8 delivery 300 Model A-X socket sets at current dealer price. Terms 2/10/net 30."
   Ram received Handy's purchase order on May 4. On May 5, Ram discovered that it had only 200 Model A-X socket sets and 100 Model W-Z socket sets in stock. Ram shipped the Model A-X and Model W-Z sets to Handy without any explanation concerning the shipment. The socket sets were received by Handy on May 8.
   Assuming a contract exists between Handy and Ram, which of the following implied warranties would result?
   I. Implied warranty of merchantability.
   II. Implied warranty of fitness for a particular purpose.
   III. Implied warranty of title.
   a. I only.
   b. III only.
   c. I and III only.
   d. I, II and III.

CHAPTER 28
REMEDIES FOR BREACH OF SALES CONTRACTS

CHAPTER OUTLINE

A. STATUTE OF LIMITATIONS

1. TIME LIMITS FOR SUITS UNDER THE UCC

An action for breach of contract must be filed within four years after a cause of action arises. A cause of action arises: (1) for a breach of warranty for *future performance* when the performance begins; and (2) for a breach for nonpayment by a buyer at the time the buyer fails to pay.

2. TIME LIMITS FOR OTHER SUITS

Actions for strict tort liability, fraud, or negligence are subject to tort statute of limitations.

B. REMEDIES OF THE SELLER

Seller's remedies include: (1) stopping or withholding delivery; (2) canceling the contract; (3) suing for incidental damages; and (4) suing for the purchase price or for damages caused by a breach.

3. SELLER'S LIEN

GENERAL RULE. A seller has a lien on goods that entitles the seller to retain possession of the goods until the buyer pays for them.
LIMITATION. A seller's lien may be lost by: (1) waiver; (2) delivery of goods to a carrier for delivery to a buyer; (3) delivery of goods to a buyer; or (4) the buyer's payment or tender of payment.

4. RESALE BY SELLER

GENERAL RULES. ▸ If a buyer breaches, a seller may resell goods by public or private sale. ▸ If goods are resold, damages are: (1) contract price minus resale price; plus (2) incidental damages.
LIMITATION. A buyer must be notified of a private sale and, in most cases, of a public sale.
STUDY HINTS. ▸ If a seller resells goods, the seller may not sue for the contract price. ▸ If a seller makes a profit on the resale of goods, the seller is entitled to retain the profit.

5. CANCELLATION BY SELLER

GENERAL RULES. ▸ If a buyer commits a material breach of contract, the seller may cancel the contract unless the seller sues for the purchase price. ▸ Cancellation of a contract terminates unperformed duties of both parities, but it does not affect a seller's right to recover damages.
STUDY HINT. The right to cancel a contract is in addition to a seller's other remedies.

6. SELLER'S ACTION FOR PURCHASE PRICE OR DAMAGES (IF GOODS NOT RESOLD)

- *Purchase price*: If a buyer fails to pay for accepted goods or for specially manufactured goods that cannot be resold, a seller can recover (1) the purchase price and (2) incidental damages.
- *Damages*: If a buyer commits any other breach and the seller does not resell the goods, then the seller recovers: (1) contract price minus market price, or if these damages do not adequately compensate for a loss, lost profits and an allowance for overhead; plus (2) incidental damages.

7. SELLER'S NONSALE REMEDIES (IN ADDITION TO ARTICLE 2 REMEDIES)

When a buyer breaks a seller may have additional, non-code remedies. ▸ Example: seller and buyer may have entered into a *secured transaction*, whereby the seller can retake goods if a buyer fails to pay.

C. REMEDIES OF THE BUYER

8. REJECTION OF IMPROPER TENDER

GENERAL RULE.   In general, if a seller fails to perfectly perform, a buyer may: (1) reject all goods; (2) accept all goods; or (3) accept any commercial unit of goods and reject the remainder.
LIMITATIONS.   ▸ Rejection must be within a reasonable time after delivery, and a buyer must give timely notice of rejection. ▸ After rejection, a buyer cannot use goods as his or her own.
STUDY HINT.   A rightful rejection means the buyer: (1) does not have to pay the contract price; (2) does not own the goods; and (3) may sue for damages caused by the seller's breach.

9. REVOCATION OF ACCEPTANCE

GENERAL RULE.   A buyer can revoke an acceptance of goods if a nonconformity substantially impairs the value of the goods to the buyer.
STUDY HINTS.   ▸ Substantial impairment means a significant injury to the value of goods; minor defects are not sufficient. ▸ Revocation of acceptance, by itself, does not cancel the contract.

10. PROCEDURE FOR REVOKING ACCEPTANCE

- *Notice of revocation*: A buyer must give a seller notice that the buyer is revoking an acceptance.
- *Time for revocation*: A buyer must give notice within a reasonable time after the buyer discovers or should discover that goods do not conform. ▸ Time is extended while a seller tries to cure.
- *Disposition of goods after revocation*: ▸ After revocation of acceptance (or rejection), a buyer must hold goods awaiting a seller's directions; failure to do so makes a buyer liable for damages. ▸ A buyer may retain goods after revocation as security for repayment of the purchase price.

11. BUYER'S ACTION FOR DAMAGES FOR NONDELIVERY (NO ACCEPTANCE OF GOODS)

GENERAL RULE.   If goods are not delivered (or a buyer refuses nonconforming goods), a buyer can: (1) "cover" and sue for damages equal to cover price less contract price, or not cover and sue for damages equal to market price less contract price; and (2) sue for incidental damages.
STUDY HINT.   A buyer is not required to cover (i.e., to buy comparable replacement goods).

12. ACTION FOR BREACH OF WARRANTY (BUYER ACCEPTS GOODS)

GENERAL RULE.   If a seller breaches but the buyer accepts the goods, damages are: (1) *breach of warranty*: value of goods had they conformed to warranties minus actual value; or *other breaches*: actual damages (typically, contract price less actual value); plus (2) incidental damages.
LIMITATION.   A buyer must give due notice of any breach or a buyer cannot sue for the breach.
STUDY HINT.   A buyer may deduct damages from the unpaid portion of the purchase price.

13. CANCELLATION (OF THE SALES CONTRACT) BY BUYER

▸ A buyer may cancel if a seller breaches, unless the buyer accepts and keeps the goods. ▸ Cancellation ends a buyer's duty to take and pay for goods; it does not affect a buyer's rights to remedies. ▸ A buyer who cancels can recover damages, any money paid, and the value of property traded in.

14. BUYER'S RESALE OF GOODS

On rejection or revocation of acceptance, a buyer has a security interest in goods held by the buyer to secure repayment of money paid and expenses incurred; a buyer may resell goods if necessary.

15. ACTION FOR CONVERSION OR RECOVERY OF GOODS (SPECIFIC PERFORMANCE)

▸ A buyer may obtain specific performance of a contract if: (1) unique goods are not delivered; or (2) in other proper cases, such as when essential, irreplaceable goods are not delivered. ▸ A rise in the market price for goods, standing alone, will not justify awarding specific performance.

16. NONSALE REMEDIES OF THE BUYER (IN ADDITION TO ARTICLE 2 REMEDIES)

▸ A buyer may sue under tort law for fraud, negligence, or strict tort liability. ▸ A defrauded buyer can cancel the sales contract *and* sue the seller for damages.

D. CONTRACT PROVISIONS ON REMEDIES

17. LIMITATION OF DAMAGES

- ■ *Liquidation of damages*: Liquidated damages (fixed damages) are valid if reasonable in light of: (1) actual damages; (2) difficulty in estimating damages; and (3) impracticality of other remedies.
- ■ *Exclusion of damages*: ▸ A contract can limit damages if a limit is conscionable. ▸ It is prima facie unconscionable to limit damages for personal injuries caused by defective consumer goods.

18. DOWN PAYMENTS AND DEPOSITS

A buyer's deposit must be returned *to the extent it exceeds* (1) liquidated damages or (2) if liquidated damages are not stated, the lesser of 20 percent of the price or $500 (unless actual losses are more).

19. LIMITATION OF REMEDIES

▸ Parties may limit remedies that are available for a breach. ▸ Example: A buyer's remedies for a nonconforming product may be limited to requesting the seller to repair or replace the product.

20. WAIVER OF DEFENSES

A buyer cannot use a breach of contract defense against a seller (or assignee) if (1) a contract has a waiver of defense clause stating that defenses are waived or (2) a buyer impliedly waives defenses.

21. PRESERVATION OF DEFENSES

In certain consumer transactions, FTC rules require contracts to have a notice preserving the right of consumers to assert defenses against a party acquiring the contract; many states have similar laws.

E. REMEDIES IN THE INTERNATIONAL SALE OF GOODS

22. REMEDIES OF THE SELLER

A seller's remedies include requiring a buyer to pay the price or declaring the sales contract void.

23. REMEDIES OF THE BUYER

A buyer may reject goods only if a seller commits a fundamental (material) breach of the contract.

CHAPTER 28

REVIEW OF TERMS AND PHRASES

Select the term or phrase that best matches a statement or definition stated below. Each term or phrase is the best match for only one statement or definition.

Terms and Phrases

a. Cancellation
b. Cover
c. Incidental damages
d. Liquidated damages clause
e. Rejection
f. Revocation of acceptance
g. Secured transaction
h. Specific performance
i. Substantial impairment
j. Waiver of defense clause

Statements and Definitions

____ 1. Buyer's retraction of an acceptance of goods.

____ 2. Contract term that states the amount of damages to be paid if a party breaches a contract.

____ 3. Contract term that prevents a buyer from asserting a breach of contract defense against a seller or a third party who acquired the seller's rights under the contract.

____ 4. Transaction that allows a seller to retake goods (collateral) if a buyer fails to pay a debt.

____ 5. Remedy that requires a party to perform a contract.

____ 6. Significant or material injury to the value of goods to a buyer.

____ 7. Good faith purchase of comparable replacement goods following a seller's breach of contract.

____ 8. Termination of a sales contract that does not affect a nonbreaching party's right to remedies.

____ 9. Out-of-pocket expenses incurred by a party due to the other party's breach of contract.

____ 10. Refusal by a buyer to accept a seller's nonconforming tender or to accept nonconforming goods.

REVIEW OF CONCEPTS

Write **T** if the statement is true, write **F** if it is false.

____ 1. A breach of contract suit must be commenced within two years after the cause of action arises.

____ 2. A nonbreaching party's cancellation of a contract terminates the party's right to sue for damages.

____ 3. A buyer cannot reject goods unless a nonconformity substantially impairs the value of the goods to the buyer.

____ 4. After a rejection of goods, a buyer cannot use the rejected goods as his or her own property.

____ 5. In general, a revocation of acceptance and a rejection have the same legal effect.

_____ 6. If a seller breaches a contract, the buyer can sell goods in the buyer's possession if this is necessary in order for the buyer to recover payments that the buyer has made to the seller.

_____ 7. If a seller refuses to deliver goods, a buyer is always entitled to specific performance.

_____ 8. The UCC forbids liquidation of damage clauses in sales contracts.

_____ 9. A contract term that excludes recovery of damages is generally valid if the clause is not unconscionable and the contract does not involve consumers.

_____ 10. It is prima facie unconscionable for a sales contract to limit damages for personal injuries that are caused by nonconforming consumer goods.

_____ 11. A seller is legally entitled to keep a buyer's entire down payment or deposit if a buyer breaches.

_____ 12. A sales contract can limit the remedies that will be available if a party breaches the contract.

_____ 13. In general, a buyer cannot assert a breach of contract defense against a third party (assignee) who acquired the seller's rights under a contract if the contract includes a waiver of defense clause.

_____ 14. FTC regulations require certain consumer contracts to contain a notice that reserves the right of a consumer to assert defenses against an assignee of the contract.

_____ 15. CISG allows a buyer to reject any goods that do not perfectly conform to contract specifications.

REVIEW OF CHAPTER - APPLICATION OF CONCEPTS

MULTIPLE CHOICE QUESTIONS

_____ 1. Seller sold his personal motorcycle to Buyer for $5,000. Prior to delivery or payment, Buyer breached the contract and refused to take the cycle. After the breach, Seller properly held a public sale and sold the cycle for $4,500. Seller had to pay a $500 commission to the auctioneer who conducted the sale. Under these facts, Seller can recover how much in damages?
   a. $ 0
   b. $ 500
   c. $ 1,000
   d. $ 5,000

_____ 2. Select the correct answer.
   a. AAA Appliances sold an oven to Beth for $600. Beth refused the oven and breached the contract. AAA would have made a profit of $300 on the sale. At the time the oven was tendered to Beth, the oven's market price was $500. In this case, AAA can recover $300 in damages.
   b. Ike sold his personal record collection to Brie for $500. Brie refused the records and breached the contract. The market price of the records was $200 at the time they were tendered to Brie. Ike did not resell the records. In this case, Ike can recover $300 in damages.
   c. Seller sold a set of encyclopedias to Buyer for $1,000. Buyer accepted the encyclopedias, but Buyer refuses to pay. In this case, Seller can recover the $1,000 purchase price.
   d. All of the above.

_____ 3. Grace purchased an organ from Mistro Music Store. Mistro warranted that the organ was solid oak. When the organ was delivered, Grace discovered that the organ was pine, stained with an oak finish. Mistro refuses to replace the organ with a conforming organ. Under these facts:
   a. Grace can reject the organ if she gives notice within a reasonable time after delivery.
   b. Grace can reject the organ, and she can continue to use the organ after rejection.
   c. Grace can reject the organ, but if she does so, she cannot sue Mistro for damages.
   d. Grace can reject the organ only if the nonconformity substantially impairs the value of the organ to Grace.

_____ 4. Mary bought and paid for a sewing machine. Mary accepted the machine, unaware that the machine was nonconforming. Soon afterwards, the machine broke down due to the nonconformity. Seller failed to cure the nonconformity. Under these facts:
   a. Mary cannot revoke her acceptance because she accepted the sewing machine.
   b. Mary can revoke her acceptance only if the nonconformity substantially impairs the value of the sewing machine to Mary.
   c. Mary is not required to give Seller notice that she is revoking her acceptance.
   d. If Mary revokes her acceptance, she must immediately return the sewing machine to Seller. Mary cannot retain the sewing machine as security for repayment of the purchase price.

_____ 5. Ralph bought a power sander from Seller for $500. *Prior to paying*, Ralph properly rejected the sander due to Seller's breach. An identical sander can be purchased elsewhere for $550. The market price of the sander at the time Ralph learned of the breach was $600. Under these facts:
   a. If Ralph buys the replacement sander, Ralph can recover $50 in damages.
   b. If Ralph buys the replacement sander, Ralph cannot recover any damages.
   c. If Ralph does not buy the replacement sander, Ralph can recover $600 in damages.
   d. If Ralph does not buy the replacement sander, Ralph cannot recover any damages.

CASE PROBLEM

Answer the following problem, briefly explaining your answer.

During a promotional sale, Alicia bought a used car from Seller for $10,000. Seller warranted that the car had no defects. The car would have been worth $11,000 had it complied with Seller's warranty. In fact, the car's transmission was defective, a breach of warranty. As a result, the actual value of the car was only $9,000. Alicia spent $200 for a rental car when the transmission of the car she purchased failed and she could not drive the car. Alicia has accepted the car, and she intends to keep the car.

(a) Is Alicia required to give Seller notice of the breach? (b) What are the consequences if Alicia does not give notice of the breach? (c) If Seller refuses to cure the breach (i.e., Seller refuses to replace or repair the transmission), how much in damages can Alicia recover? (d) Is Alicia entitled to cancel the contract?

CPA REVIEW

The following questions were given on past CPA examinations. The answers for these questions are the unofficial answers prepared by the American Institute of Certified Public Accountants, Inc. (AICPA). All material is reproduced with permission of the AICPA.

_____ 1. Under the UCC Sales Article, which of the following legal remedies would a buyer not have when a seller fails to transfer and deliver goods identified to the contract?
   a. Suit for specific performance.
   b. Suit for punitive damages.
   c. Purchase substitute goods (cover).
   d. Recover the identified goods (capture).

_____ 2. Cara Fabricating Co. and Taso Corp. agreed orally that Taso would custom manufacture a compressor for Cara at a price of $120,000. After Taso completed the work at a cost of $90,000, Cara notified Taso that the compressor was no longer needed. Taso is holding the compressor and has requested payment from Cara. Taso has been unable to resell the compressor for any price. Taso incurred storage fees of $2,000. If Cara refuses to pay Taso and Taso sues Cara, the most Taso will be entitled to recover is
   a. $ 92,000
   b. $105,000
   c. $120,000
   d. $122,000

Questions 3 and 4 are based on the following information:

On April 5, 1987, Anker, Inc., furnished Bold Corp. with Anker's financial statements dated March 31, 1987. The financial statements contained misrepresentations which indicated that Anker was solvent when in fact it was insolvent. Based on Anker's financial statements, Bold agreed to sell Anker 90 computers, "F.O.B.-Bold's loading dock." On April 14, Anker received 60 of the computers. The remaining 30 computers are in the possession of the common carrier and in transit to Anker.

_____ 3. If on April 28, Bold discovered that Anker was insolvent, then with respect to the computers delivered to Anker on April 14, Bold may
   a. Reclaim the computers upon making a demand.
   b. Reclaim the computers irrespective of the rights of any subsequent third party.
   c. Not reclaim the computers since ten days have elapsed from its delivery.
   d. Not reclaim the computers since it is entitled to recover the price of the computers.

_____ 4. With respect to the remaining 30 computers in transit, which of the following statements is correct if Anker refuses to pay Bold in cash and Anker is not in possession of a negotiable document of title covering the computers?
   a. Bold may stop delivery of the computers to Anker since their contract is void due to Anker's furnishing of the false financial statements.
   b. Bold may stop delivery of the computers to Anker despite the fact that title had passed to Anker.
   c. Bold must deliver the computers to Anker on credit since Anker has not breached the contract.
   d. Bold must deliver the computers to Anker since the risk of loss had passed to Anker.

_____ 5. On February 15, Mazur Corp. contracted to sell 1,000 bushels of wheat to Good Bread, Inc. at $6.00 per bushel with delivery to be made on June 23. On June 1, Good advised Mazur that it would not accept or pay for the wheat. On June 2, Mazur sold the wheat to another customer at the market price of $5.00 per bushel. Mazur had advised Good that it intended to resell the wheat. Which of the following statements is correct?
   a. Mazur can successfully sue Good for the difference between the resale price and the contract price.
   b. Mazur can resell the wheat only after June 23.
   c. Good can retract its anticipatory breach at any time before June 23.
   d. Good can successfully sue Mazur for specific performance.

_____ 6. Lazur Corp. entered into a contract with Baker Suppliers, Inc. to purchase a used word processor from Baker. Lazur is engaged in the business of selling new and used word processors to the general public. The contract required Baker to ship the goods to Lazur by common carrier pursuant to the following provision in the contract: "F.O.B.-Baker Suppliers, Inc. loading dock." Baker also represented in the contract that the word processor had been used for only 10 hours by its previous owner. The contract included the provision that the word processor was being sold "as is" and this provision was in a larger and different type style than the remainder of the contract. For this item only, assume that Lazur refused to accept the word processor even though it was in all respects conforming to the contract and that the contract is otherwise silent. Under the UCC Sales Article,
   a. Baker can successfully sue for specific performance and make Lazur accept and pay for the word processor.
   b. Baker may resell the word processor to another buyer.
   c. Baker must sue for the difference between the market value of the word processor and the contract price plus its incidental damages.
   d. Baker cannot successfully sue for consequential damages unless it attempts to resell the word processor.

_____ 7. Larch Corp. manufactured and sold Oak a stove. The sale documents included a disclaimer of warranty for personal injury. The stove was defective. It exploded causing serious injuries to Oak's spouse. Larch was notified one week after the explosion. Under the UCC Sales Article, which of the following statements concerning Larch's liability for personal injury to Oak's spouse would be correct?
   a. Larch cannot be liable because of a lack of privity with Oak's spouse.
   b. Larch will not be liable because of a failure to give proper notice.
   c. Larch will be liable because the disclaimer was not a disclaimer of all liability.
   d. Larch will be liable because liability for personal injury cannot be disclaimed.

_____ 8. Cain and Zen Corp. orally agreed that Zen would specially manufacture a machine for Cain at a price of $40,000. After Zen completed the work at a cost of $30,000, Cain notified Zen that it no longer needed the machine. Zen is holding the machine for Cain and has requested payment from Cain. Despite making reasonable efforts, Zen has been unable to resell the machine for any price. Zen has incurred warehouse fees of $500 for storing the machine. If Cain refuses to pay Zen and Zen sues Cain, the most Zen will be entitled to recover is
   a. $0
   b. $30,500
   c. $40,000
   d. $40,500

CHAPTER 29
CONSUMER PROTECTION

CHAPTER OUTLINE

A. GENERAL PRINCIPLES

1. EXPANSION OF PROTECTION

GENERAL RULE. Consumer protection laws (deceptive trade practices laws) protect "consumers," which in many states includes any person, business, or governmental body that uses goods or services.
STUDY HINT. A single, unintentional violation of a consumer protection law may cause liability.

2. PROOF OF CONSUMER STATUS

In a consumer protection action, a consumer must prove that he or she is a "consumer."

3. WHO IS A DEFENDANT IN A CONSUMER PROTECTION SUIT?

In general, defendants in a consumer protection lawsuit are (1) persons or businesses (2) who regularly engage in (3) the type of transaction that resulted in the injury to the consumer.

4. FAULT OF DEFENDANT

Consumer protection laws typically require some fault, i.e., commission of a prohibited act or omission.

5. CONSUMER NEGLIGENCE

‣ Consumer laws may not protect consumers from their negligence, e.g., failure to read contracts. ‣ In general, a consumer cannot use prior oral statements in order to contradict a final written contract.

6. CONSUMER REMEDIES

GENERAL RULES. ‣ Depending on the state, consumer laws may be enforced by: (1) an administrator who monitors compliance with the Uniform Consumer Credit Code (UCCC); (2) a state attorney general who may file an action on behalf of consumers; or (3) individual consumers. ‣ Some statutes require a refund for or replacement of defective goods that cannot be repaired in a reasonable time. Other statutes void a consumer contract that violates the statute.
LIMITATION. Defendants are liable only if their actions are specifically covered by statutes.

7. CIVIL AND CRIMINAL PENALTIES

GENERAL RULE. General laws, consumer protection statutes, and deceptive trade practices laws may subject a seller or lender to civil and/or criminal penalties for wrongful consumer practices.
STUDY HINT. Consumer protection laws generally provide that creditors who fail to disclose required information to a consumer cannot enforce the consumer's obligation.

B. AREAS OF CONSUMER PROTECTION

8. ADVERTISING

GENERAL RULES. ‣ Laws commonly forbid deceptive advertising, and these laws are liberally (broadly) interpreted. ‣ The Federal Trade Commission (FTC) can issue orders forbidding deceptive ads, and it may require retractive advertising to correct false or deceptive statements.
STUDY HINT. False advertising laws are intended to prevent misleading (deceptive) ads even if an advertiser is not acting fraudulently. Thus, good faith and lack of intent to deceive are not defenses.

9. **SEALS OF APPROVAL**

    Falsely stating that a product is "approved" renders a seller liable for breach of guarantee and fraud.

10. **LABELING**

    Exaggerated terms and misleading labels are prohibited by consumer protection regulations.

11. **SELLING METHODS**

    - *Deceptive practices*: Deceptive statements and business methods are prohibited by consumer laws; it is not necessary to prove that a seller committed fraud or intentionally deceived a consumer.

    - *Disclosure of transaction terms*: ▸ Federal law requires a lender to disclose all (1) interest charges and (2) points or fees for making a loan. ▸ If a seller advertises that he or she will sell or lease on credit, a seller must disclose: (1) total cash price; (2) down payment required; (3) number, amount, and due dates of payments; and (4) annual percentage rate of credit costs (APR).

    - *More-than-four-installments rule*: ▸ The Truth in Lending Act applies to any consumer contract that is payable in more than four installments, whether a finance charge is expressly stated or not. ▸ If such a consumer contract does not expressly impose a finance charge, this Act requires that the contract "clearly and conspicuously" state that "the cost of credit is included in the price."

    - *Contract on two sides*: If a consumer contract is printed on both sides of a page, each side must warn a consumer to read the opposite side, and the consumer must sign at the end of the second page.

    - *Motor Vehicle Information and Cost Savings Act*: ▸ A car buyer who is harmed when a dealer fails to disclose that an odometer has been reset can recover the greater of three times the actual loss, or $1,500. ▸ A seller is liable if he or she knew or should have known an odometer is wrong.

    - *Consumer Leasing Act of 1976*: Lessors of cars and durable goods must fully disclose all details.

    - *Home-solicited sales*: ▸ A sale of goods or services for $25 or more that is made at a buyer's home can be set aside within three business days after the sale. ▸ There is no requirement that goods be defective or that a seller acted improperly in order to set aside a contract.

    - *Referral sales*: UCCC forbids reducing a price because a buyer referred customers to the seller.

    - *Telemarketing fraud*: FTC regulations limit the time of telemarketing calls, require a statement of what telemarketers are selling, and prohibit access to bank accounts without authorization.

12. **THE CONSUMER CONTRACT**

    - *Form of contract*: Contracts must: (1) itemize payments; (2) allocate payments among principal, interest, and insurance; (3) be printed in a certain type size; and (4) be given to the buyer.

    - *Contract terms*: ▸ The UCCC forbids terms that allow a judgment to be entered against a debtor without giving the debtor a chance to make a defense. ▸ Some states forbid acceleration clauses that make an entire debt due if a debtor fails to make a payment. ▸ The federal Warranty Disclosure Act establishes disclosure standards for warranties for consumer goods.

    - *Limitation of credit*: Laws commonly forbid open-end home mortgages that secure a present debt plus future debts, and terms granting a security interest in all household goods of a debtor.

    - *Unconscionability*: Charging excessive prices for goods sold on credit, and price gouging in abnormal market situations (i.e., high demand-low supply situations) may be unconscionable.

13. **CREDIT CARDS**

    GENERAL RULE.   The holder of a credit card may be liable for up to $50 of unauthorized use.
    LIMITATION.   Unauthorized purchases by an authorized user (i.e., by someone who is permitted to use a credit card) are deemed authorized use, and the cardholder is liable for all such charges.
    STUDY HINT.   It is unlawful to issue credit cards to persons who have not applied for them.

14. PAYMENTS

Generally, payments on an open charge account must be applied to the earliest (oldest) charges.

15. PRESERVATION OF CONSUMER DEFENSES

FTC regulations require consumer contracts to include a clause that allows a consumer to assert against a third party (an assignee) any defenses that would have been available against the seller.

16. PRODUCT SAFETY

GENERAL RULE. The Consumer Product Safety Act: (1) sets product safety standards; (2) establishes civil and criminal penalties; and (3) authorizes suits for damages and injunctions against violators.
STUDY HINT. Tampering with consumer products is a federal crime.

17. CREDIT, COLLECTION, AND BILLING METHODS

- *Credit discrimination*: ▸ Under the Consumer Credit Protection Act (CCPA), it is illegal to discriminate against an applicant for credit because of race, color, religion, national origin, marital status, sex, age, or because all or a part of the applicant's income is derived from public assistance.
- *Correction of errors*: A creditor or credit card issuer must investigate and respond in writing to written complaints by consumers regarding alleged credit card errors.
- *Improper collection methods*: ▸ The Fair Debt Collection Practices Act generally forbids unreasonable debt collection practices. This Act only applies to parties who engage in the business of collecting debts for others, such as collection agencies. ▸ Prohibited acts may include: (1) notifying an employer that an employee is delinquent on a debt; (2) sending bills that appear to be legal process; and (3) sending delinquency notices in a manner easily seen by others.
- *Consumer leases*: Some states give consumer leases the same protection as consumer credit sales.

18. PROTECTION OF CREDIT STANDING AND REPUTATION

- *Scope of law*: ▸ The Fair Credit Reporting Act (FCRA) regulates "consumer credit" transactions. ▸ The FCRA does not apply to credit given for business purposes. ▸ It is a crime to obtain or furnish a report for an improper purpose.
- *Privacy*: ▸ Credit bureaus must: (1) inform a person who is being investigated of the right to learn the results of the investigation; and (2) on request, state to whom credit reports were given.
- *Protection from false information*: ▸ On request, a credit bureau must disclose to a party certain data in the party's file. ▸ Disputed information must be verified within a reasonable time. ▸ Adverse material discovered in an investigation which is more than three months old must be verified before it is given to a client. ▸ Most legal actions cannot be reported after seven years, and bankruptcies cannot be reported after ten years.

19. PROTECTION FROM DISCRIMINATION

Consumers are protected from discrimination by federal and state laws and agency policy statements.

20. PHYSICAL PROTECTION OF CONSUMERS

Consumers are protected from physical harm by product liability theories and warranties.

21. EXPANSION OF CONSUMER PROTECTION

- *Sale of securities*: States have enacted blue sky laws to prevent fraudulent sales of stock.
- *Real estate development sales*: Sellers of subdivided land may have to file a development statement with HUD and provide a property report to prospective buyers or tenants.
- *Service contracts*: A consumer service contract is subject to UCCC regulations if it is (1) for $25,000 or less and (2) a credit charge is imposed or the contract is paid in installments.
- *Franchises*: Prospective buyers of franchises must be given a detailed disclosure statement.
- *Automobile lemon laws*: All states have lemon laws to protect consumers who buy defective cars.

REVIEW OF TERMS AND PHRASES

Select the term or phrase that best matches a statement or definition stated below. Each term or phrase is the best match for only one statement or definition.

Terms and Phrases

a. Acceleration clause
b. Blue sky laws
c. Consumer credit
d. Fair Credit Reporting Act
e. Fair Debt Collection Practices Act
f. Federal Warranty Disclosure Act
g. FTC
h. Investigative consumer report
i. Lemon laws
j. Open-end mortgage
k. Retractive advertising
l. Truth in Lending Act

Statements and Definitions

____ 1. Action required by the FTC to correct false or deceptive advertisements.

____ 2. State laws enacted to prevent fraudulent sales of corporate stock.

____ 3. Security interest in a home that secures payment of a specific debt as well as payment of future loans that may be made to a consumer.

____ 4. State laws that provide special protection for consumers who are sold defective cars for their personal, family, or household use.

____ 5. Federal law that prohibits unreasonable methods of debt collection.

____ 6. Federal law that establishes disclosure standards for stating warranties for consumer goods.

____ 7. Federal agency that enforces federal advertising regulations.

____ 8. Contract term that allows a creditor to require payment of an entire debt if a debtor defaults.

____ 9. Credit that is extended to a person for his or her personal, family, or household use.

____ 10. Credit report on a person that is based upon personal investigations and interviews.

____ 11. Federal law that protects consumers from abuses in the gathering and disclosure of credit-related information.

____ 12. Federal law that regulates disclosure of finance charges in consumer contracts that are payable in more than four installments.

REVIEW OF CONCEPTS

Write **T** if the statement is true, write **F** if it is false.

____ 1. In many states, consumer protection laws protect individual consumers and also certain businesses or governments that purchase goods or services.

____ 2. The defendant in a consumer protection lawsuit is usually a party who regularly sells goods or services of the kind involved in the lawsuit.

____ 3. Consumer laws do not typically allow a consumer to rescind a contract merely because the consumer misunderstood the contract due to the consumer's negligent failure to read the contract.

____ 4. In general, a seller cannot enforce a consumer's obligation if the seller failed to disclose information that was required to be disclosed by consumer protection laws.

____ 5. In general, a seller violates deceptive advertising laws only if the seller acts in bad faith or with the intent to deceive consumers.

____ 6. A merchant who sells a product with a "seal of approval" may be liable for breach of a guarantee if the product has not in fact been approved by the indicated party.

____ 7. A car dealer who sells a car without disclosing that the odometer has been reset violates the Motor Vehicle Information and Cost Savings Act if the seller knows or should know that the odometer was reset.

____ 8. Federal law does not regulate the disclosure of finance charges in consumer contracts.

____ 9. It is unlawful to send credit cards to persons who have not applied for them.

____ 10. Consumer protection laws generally require a creditor to apply payments on open charge accounts to the most recent charges.

____ 11. A person who violates the Consumer Product Safety Act may be prohibited (enjoined) from selling unsafe products, and the person may also be sued for damages.

____ 12. A credit card issuer must investigate and respond in writing to written complaints by consumers regarding alleged credit card errors.

____ 13. Under federal law, it is permissible to disqualify an applicant for credit because the person's income is derived in whole or in part from public assistance.

____ 14. Franchisors are not subject to FTC regulations.

____ 15. A $24,000 consumer service contract that is payable in installments is subject to the UCCC.

REVIEW OF CHAPTER - APPLICATION OF CONCEPTS

MULTIPLE CHOICE PROBLEMS

____ 1. Under many consumer protection statutes, a consumer would include:
   a. A woman who had her hair colored at a beauty shop.
   b. A multi-national corporation that contracted for the purchase of shipping crates.
   c. A city that contracted for garbage collection for its residents.
   d. All of the above.

____ 2. Nutri-Shop, a health-food store, purchased and offered for sale multi-grain muffins from a new supplier. Nutri-Shop believed that the muffins contained no fat, and it added a "Fat-Free" label to the muffins. It was later determined that each muffin contained 16 grams of fat, and a customer brought suit against Nutri-Shop for misleading labeling. This was the only time Nutri-Shop had been charged with misleading labeling. Under these facts:
   a. Nutri-Shop will probably be held liable for misleading labeling.
   b. Nutri-Shop cannot be held liable because this was a one-time violation, not a pattern of illegal conduct.
   c. Nutri-Shop cannot be held liable because it did not intend to violate the law.
   d. Nutri-Shop has the burden of proving that the person who brought suit is not a consumer under the consumer protection statute under which the charges were brought.

____ 3. Which of the following is *not* a remedy under consumer protection legislation?
   a. Refund of the purchase price if defective goods cannot be repaired within a reasonable time.
   b. Voiding a contract so that the consumer can keep the goods without making further payment after the seller violates the statute.
   c. A lawsuit brought by the state attorney general on behalf of injured consumers.
   d. All of the above may be remedies under consumer protection laws.

____ 4. Hope's Department Store planned its 4th of July advertising brochure and sent it to the printer the second week of June. The brochure was sent to customers the third week of June, and the prices in the ad were to be good July 2-5. One of the featured items was a 3-speed oscillating fan that came in a variety of colors. The regular price of the fan was $29.95 and the sale price was $24.95. On June 10, the inventory of this particular fan was fifty units, but because of unusually hot weather during June, all of Hope's inventory of this 3-speed oscillating fan was sold by July 1. Under these facts:
   a. Hope could not be liable for false advertising because at the time the advertising brochure was planned and printed, Hope had the 3-speed oscillating fans in stock.
   b. Hope could not be liable for false advertising because the demand for the fan prior to the sale was unusually high and Hope could not have predicted its inventory would be depleted prior to the sale date.
   c. Hope is liable for false advertising because the 3-speed fan it advertised at a reduced price was out of stock at the time the sale was to begin.
   d. Hope could not be liable for false advertising because statutes prohibiting false advertising are strictly interpreted.

____ 5. Under consumer protection statutes:
   a. Fraud is the most significant element.
   b. A breach can occur without proof that the wrongdoer intended to deceive anyone.
   c. Fault of the actor is the usual basis for liability.
   d. The motives of those dealing with consumers are typically examined.

____ 6. Swift's advertised a Model 3446 Sony television for six monthly payments of $100 each. No finance charges were expressly stated. Under these facts:
   a. The Truth in Lending Act will govern this consumer sale.
   b. The Truth in Lending Act will not govern this sale because payment is to be made in more than four installments.
   c. The Truth in Lending Act will not govern this sale because there is no finance charge expressly imposed.
   d. There are no statutory requirements as to what statements must be made in the advertisement.

_____ 7. Sonya contracted to buy storm windows for her home for $2,000. The contract was negotiated and signed at her home. The next day, Sonya decided she could not afford the windows. What are Sonya's options under federal law?
   a. Sonya can rescind (set aside) the sale within three days after signing the contract.
   b. Sonya can rescind the sale only if the seller was guilty of misconduct.
   c. Sonya can rescind the sale only if she can prove the windows are defective.
   d. Sonya cannot rescind the sale once the contract is signed.

_____ 8. A Federal Trade Commission regulation designed to stop telemarketing fraud:
   a. Allows access to consumers' bank accounts as long as the telemarketer states truthfully what he or she is selling.
   b. Subjects telemarketers to fines if they continue to call persons who have asked not to be called.
   c. Subjects telemarketers to fines if they call consumers before 9 a.m. or after 8 p.m.
   d. Subjects telemarketers to fines if they do not identify themselves, the company they represent, and the type and price of product or service they are selling.

_____ 9. Ace Siding Company is preparing a contract to sell Anita new siding for her home. Ace is selling the siding to Anita on credit for $10,000. Under these facts:
   a. Under FTC rules, the contract must contain a clause stating that an assignee of the contract will be subject to any defenses that Anita could have asserted against Ace.
   b. In many states, Ace cannot take an open-end mortgage that will secure payment of the contract price for the siding and payment of any future debts that Anita may owe Ace.
   c. In some states, the contract cannot contain an acceleration clause that would make the entire debt due if Anita fails to make a monthly payment.
   d. All of the above.

_____ 10. Jake authorized his girlfriend Jolene to use his credit card in order to buy a birthday gift for Jake's mother. Without his permission, Jolene also used the card to buy an $800 leather coat for herself. Jake refused to pay the credit charge for the coat since Jolene was not authorized to use his card for that purpose. Under these facts:
   a. Jake is required to pay for only $50 of the unauthorized charge for the coat.
   b. Jake is required to pay for only $500 of the unauthorized charge for the coat.
   c. Jake must pay the entire $800 charge for the coat.
   d. Jake is not required to pay for any portion of the charge for the coat.

_____ 11. Mark was delinquent in repaying a loan. The loan was turned over to Assured Collections. Assured sent letters to Mark that appeared to be court orders to pay. It also sent collection letters to Mark's work in envelopes marked "Final Demand for Delinquent Payment," and Assured told Mark's employer of the delinquent loan. Mark's employer concluded Mark was untrustworthy and fired him. In all likelihood, did Assured violate the Fair Debt Collection Practices Act?
   a. No. The Act does not apply to parties who engage in the business of collecting debts for others.
   b. No. The Act does not apply if a debtor is in fact delinquent on an obligation.
   c. No. The Act only applies to collection of business obligations.
   d. Yes.

____ 12. Kay applied for a personal loan from Last Bank. Last Bank requested a credit report from R&R Credit Bureau. R&R conducted an investigation of Kay in order to prepare an investigative consumer report. R&R discovered that Kay had received a discharge in bankruptcy seven years previously, and that six months ago a neighbor stated that Kay was unemployed. In this case:
   a. R&R cannot report the bankruptcy to Last Bank.
   b. R&R cannot report the neighbor's statement to Last Bank without verifying its accuracy.
   c. R&R does not have to inform Kay that she is entitled to discover the results of R&R's investigation of her.
   d. R&R does not have to disclose any information to Kay regarding anything in its files on her.

____ 13. Maxine bought a new convertible, but had continuing problems with the transmission and with the braking system. She returned the car to the dealer numerous times for repair, but the problems were not satisfactorily resolved. Under these facts:
   a. It is unlikely Maxine lives in a state with an automobile lemon law, since this type of law is relatively new and is not yet widespread.
   b. If Maxine lives in a state with an automobile lemon law, it would be unlikely to apply unless her car is used primarily for business rather than personal driving.
   c. If Maxine lives in a state with an automobile lemon law, it would probably give her greater protection than would be given under the Uniform Commercial Code to buyers of other types of goods.
   d. If Maxine lives in a state with an automobile lemon law, her only possible remedy would be damages for the loss of use and value of her car.

CASE PROBLEM

Answer the following problem, briefly explaining your answer.

Farr RV Sales Co. plans to advertise for sale and sell a consumer recreational vehicle. The vehicle will be sold on credit for $24,000, payable in 48 monthly installments. The buyer will be required to pay a down payment and to pay interest on the unpaid portion of the purchase price. Farr intends to use a form of contract that is printed on both sides of a sheet of paper.

(a) What federal law will generally regulate the disclosure of finance terms in this case? (b) What financial terms must Farr disclose to a buyer? (c) What specific requirements must be satisfied due to the fact that the contract will be printed on both sides of a sheet of paper?

CHAPTER 30
KINDS OF INSTRUMENTS, PARTIES, AND NEGOTIABILITY

CHAPTER OUTLINE

A. TYPES OF NEGOTIABLE INSTRUMENTS AND PARTIES

GENERAL RULE. Negotiable instruments, also known as commercial paper (sometimes referred to as "paper" in this study guide) are important because a transferee of a negotiable instrument may acquire a greater right to demand payment from a debtor than would an assignee of a contract.

STUDY HINT: ► *Negotiable instrument example*: Beth signed a negotiable promissory note to pay for goods, and Seller failed to deliver the goods. If Seller transferred the note to Rod (a holder in due course), Beth must pay Rod. ► *Contract example*: Bill signed a contract promising to pay for goods, and Seller failed to deliver the goods to Bill. Bill is not obligated to pay even if Seller assigned the contract to a third party.

1. **DEFINITION**

    ► A negotiable instrument (commercial paper) is a transferable signed, written promise or order to pay a specific sum of money. ► Instruments are negotiable when they contain the terms required by the UCC.

2. **KINDS OF INSTRUMENTS**

    - ***Promissory note***: ► Unconditional written, signed promise to pay a sum certain in money on demand or at a definite time to order or bearer. ► Parties: maker and payee.
    - ***Draft***: ► Unconditional written order by one party directing another to pay a sum certain in money on demand or at a definite time to order or bearer. ► Parties: drawer, drawee, and payee.
    - ***Check***: ► Special type of draft whereby a depositor (drawer) orders a bank or credit union (drawee) to pay the amount of the check to a payee on demand. ► A check's distinguishing features are that it (1) is drawn on a bank or credit union as drawee and (2) is payable on demand. ► Four special types of checks are cashier's checks, teller's checks, traveler's checks, and bank money orders.
    - ***Certificate of deposit***: ► Promissory note issued by a bank, which acknowledges receipt of money and states a promise to pay the certificate when it becomes due. ► Parties: maker (bank), payee.

3. **PARTIES TO INSTRUMENTS**

    - ***Maker***: Party who creates and originally signs a promissory note. Example: Mary signs and issues a negotiable promissory note promising to pay $100 to Ellie. Mary is a maker.
    - ***Drawer***: Party who creates and originally signs a draft or check. Example: Dave signs his check ordering his bank to pay $100 to Paul. Dave is a drawer.
    - ***Drawee***: Party ordered by a drawer to pay a draft or check. Example: Dave issues his check ordering his bank, ABC Bank, to pay $100 to Paul. ABC Bank is a drawee.
    - ***Payee***: Party originally named on the face of an instrument as the party to receive payment. Example: Dave issues his check ordering ABC Bank to pay $100 to Paul. Paul is a payee.
    - ***Acceptor***: Drawee who, in writing on a draft, agrees to pay the draft. Example: Dave issues a check ordering ABC Bank to pay $100 to Paul, and ABC Bank in writing on the check agrees to pay. ABC Bank is an acceptor.
    - ***Indorser***: Holder who signs the back of a negotiable instrument. Example: Dave issues his check payable to the order of Paul, and Paul signs the back of the check. Paul is an indorser.

- *Indorsee*: Party to whom an indorsed instrument is made payable. Example: Paul indorses a check stating "Pay to Irene." Irene is an indorsee.
- *Bearer*: Party in physical possession of an instrument that is payable to bearer or cash.
- *Holder*: Party to whom paper is issued, or to whom paper is subsequently negotiated.
- *Holder in due course*: Holder who takes an instrument for value, in good faith, and without notice that it is overdue or dishonored, or that there are defenses against or claims to it.
- *Holder through a holder in due course*: Party who becomes a holder of an instrument at any time after it has been held by a holder in due course.
- *Accommodation party*: Party who voluntarily signs an instrument to strengthen its collectability. Accommodation indorsement by one not owning an instrument is an "anomalous indorsement."
- *Guarantor*: Party who guarantees payment or collection of paper. ▸ *Payment guaranteed*: guarantor agrees to pay when paper is due without requiring a holder to first seek payment from others.
▸ *Collection guaranteed*: guarantor agrees to pay if a holder first tries and fails to collect from a maker or acceptor. ▸ If the nature of a guarantee is unclear, it is presumed to be a guarantee of payment.

4. **LIABILITY OF PARTIES (TO PAY AN INSTRUMENT)**

   GENERAL RULES. ▸ *Primary liability*: maker of a promissory note; acceptor of a draft; guarantor of payment. ▸ *Secondary (conditional) liability*: unqualified indorser. ▸ *No primary or secondary liability*: qualified indorser; party transferring an instrument without signing it; drawee prior to accepting a draft; guarantor of collection prior to a holder's unsuccessfully trying to collect payment.
   STUDY HINT. An accommodation party may be held liable to pay paper even if no consideration is received. An accommodation party may recover any sums paid from the party accommodated.

B. **NEGOTIABILITY**

5. **DEFINITION OF NEGOTIABILITY**

   GENERAL RULE. If commercial paper meets the definition of negotiability, it is a negotiable instrument and a transferee can be a holder in due course, taking it free of many defenses that can avoid a right to be paid. If paper is nonnegotiable, a transferee has only rights of an assignee of a contract.
   STUDY HINTS. ▸ Negotiability is determined when an instrument is issued or completed. ▸ The instrument itself must satisfy all negotiability requirements. ▸ Negotiability is the characteristic that distinguishes commercial paper or negotiable instruments from ordinary contracts.

6. **REQUIREMENTS OF NEGOTIABILITY**

   ▸ In general, a negotiable instrument must: (1) be in writing; (2) be signed by a maker or drawer; (3) contain a promise or order; (4) of an unconditional nature; (5) to pay in money; (6) a sum certain; (7) on demand or at a definite time; (8) to order or bearer. ▸ Important negotiability rules include:
   - *Writing*: ▸ Writing includes any permanent writing, including handwriting. ▸ Parol evidence rule forbids proving a prior oral agreement in order to change a final, complete, written instrument.
   - *Signature*: ▸ Paper must be signed by a maker or drawer. ▸ An agent can sign for a principal, and the agent is generally not liable on the paper. ▸ If an agent signs paper without disclosing a principal's identity and the agent's representative capacity, the agent may be liable. ▸ An agent is not liable on a check drawn on a principal's bank account, even if the agent's representative capacity is not stated. ▸ If the instrument does not show the representative capacity of the signer or it fails to identify the represented person, the representative is liable to any holder or transferee of the instrument unless the representative proves that the original parties did not intend the representative to be bound.
   - *Promise or order to pay*: ▸ A promissory note must contain a promise to pay money; a draft or check must contain an order to pay money. ▸ An IOU is not a negotiable instrument.

- ***Unconditional promise or order***: ▸ A promise or order to pay must be unconditional; it cannot depend on an event not certain to occur. Examples of conditional promises: promise to pay if party performs a contract; promise to pay is subject to terms of another contract. ▸ A drawer's personal indication to charge an instrument to a certain account is allowed. Example: check states "charge petty cash." ▸ The issuer of a negotiable instrument is not required to be personally obligated to pay; that is, the paper may be payable out of a trust, estate, partnership, or unincorporated association.
- ***Payment in money***: Paper must be payable in money. Money is defined broadly.
- ***Sum certain***: ▸ Negotiable instruments must state the precise amount to be paid. ▸ Instruments can state a separate interest rate to be charged after maturity, and they can require payment of collection costs and attorney fees. ▸ In most states, the sum payable under a negotiable instrument is certain even if it calls for the payment of a floating or a variable interest rate.
- ***Time of payment***: ▸ A negotiable instrument must be payable on demand or at a definite time.
  ▸ *Payable on demand*: payable "on demand," "at sight," "upon presentation," or if no time for payment is stated. ▸ *Payable at definite time*: payable on or before a stated or readily ascertainable date. ▸ A negotiable instrument can properly include these terms: (1) acceleration clause; (2) holder may extend time for payment; (3) maker or acceptor may extend time for payment to a later, definite date; and (4) payment may be extended to a later, definite date automatically after a specified event. ▸ Undated instruments are valid. ▸ The date on demand paper controls the time for payment, and paper is not due before the date stated.
- ***Order or bearer***: ▸ Negotiable instruments other than checks must be payable to order or bearer.
  ▸ *Order paper*: drawn "to the order of *X*" or "to *X* or order"; after indorsement if indorsement states the next party to be paid. ▸ *Bearer paper*: drawn "pay to bearer," "pay to the order of *X* or bearer," or "pay to cash"; after indorsement if last indorsement is a blank indorsement; no payee is identified.

7. **FACTORS NOT AFFECTING NEGOTIABILITY**

    An instrument may be negotiable even if: (1) the date of execution is omitted, (2) the instrument is antedated or postdated, or (3) a debtor is required to give or maintain collateral.

8. **AMBIGUOUS LANGUAGE**

    ▸ Words control over conflicting numbers. ▸ Handwriting prevails over conflicting typewritten or printed terms. ▸ Typewritten terms prevail over conflicting preprinted terms.

9. **STATUTE OF LIMITATIONS**

    ▸ There is a three-year period for most suits on negotiable instruments, and a six-year period for actions on certificates of deposit and accepted drafts.

10. **DISCHARGE OF PARTIES**

    - ***Primary parties***: maker of note, drawee-acceptor of draft, and guarantor of payment. ▸ Primary parties are required to pay the instruments when they are due. Liability continues for the period of the statute of limitations.
    - ***Secondary parties***: drawer of draft and unqualified indorser. ▸ Liability arises after: (1) presentment of the paper for payment or acceptance, (2) dishonor, and (3) notice of dishonor. Secondary parties have conditional liability that may be enforced only if the primary party fails to pay.
    - ***Parties with no liability for payment***: drawee, qualified indorser, nonsigning party, and nonsigning bearer. ▸ The holder of an instrument cannot obtain payment from these persons regardless of whether payment is demanded or suit is brought.

REVIEW OF TERMS AND PHRASES

Select the term or phrase that best matches a statement or definition stated below. Each term or phrase is the best match for only one statement or definition.

Terms and Phrases

a. Acceptor
b. Accommodation party
c. Bearer paper
d. Certificate of deposit
e. Check
f. Drawee
g. Drawer
h. Guarantor
i. Holder
j. Holder in due course
k. Holder through a holder in due course
l. Indorsee
m. Indorser
n. Maker
o. Negotiable draft
p. Negotiable promissory note
q. Order paper
r. Payee

Statements and Definitions

____ 1. Party to whom an instrument is originally made payable (party stated on face of instrument).

____ 2. Special type of draft that orders a drawee bank to pay the draft on demand.

____ 3. Owner of a negotiable instrument who signs on the back of the instrument.

____ 4. Drawee who agrees to pay a draft by writing such agreement on the draft.

____ 5. Party to whom an indorsement directs payment to be made.

____ 6. Party whom a drawer orders to pay a draft or check.

____ 7. Party who voluntarily signs a draft in order to strengthen the likelihood of payment.

____ 8. Holder of a negotiable instrument if any prior holder was a holder in due course.

____ 9. Party who originally signs and issues a draft or check.

____ 10. Instrument issued to bearer or to cash, or one that is indorsed in blank.

____ 11. Holder who takes an instrument for value, in good faith, and without notice of certain matters.

____ 12. Party who guarantees payment or collection of an instrument.

____ 13. Instrument issued by a bank, which acknowledges receipt of funds and contains a promise by the bank to repay this sum when the instrument becomes due.

____ 14. Party who originally signs and issues a promissory note.

____ 15. Unconditional signed, written order by one person ordering another party to pay on demand or at a definite time a sum certain in money to order or to bearer.

____ 16. Party to whom a negotiable instrument has been negotiated.

____ 17. Instrument originally made payable to the order of a named person, or an instrument that is specially indorsed to a named indorsee.

____ 18. Unconditional signed, written promise to pay on demand or at a definite time a sum certain in money to order or to bearer.

REVIEW OF CONCEPTS

Write **T** if the statement is true, write **F** if it is false.

____ 1. Subject to certain limits, a transferee of commercial paper (a negotiable instrument) may acquire a greater right to payment than an assignee of a contract right would acquire.

____ 2. A draft or check has two original parties: a maker and a payee.

____ 3. "Payment guaranteed" means a guarantor agrees to pay an instrument only if a holder first attempts and fails to collect payment from the maker or acceptor of the instrument.

____ 4. "Collection guaranteed" means a guarantor agrees to pay an instrument only if a holder first attempts and fails to collect payment from the maker or acceptor of the instrument.

____ 5. If an accommodation party must pay an instrument, the accommodation party does not have a right to recover the amount paid from the person accommodated.

____ 6. The rights of parties to a nonnegotiable instrument are governed by general rules of contract law.

____ 7. If an agent signs an instrument for a principal, disclosing the identity of the principal and the fact that the agent is signing only as an agent, the agent is not personally liable to pay the instrument.

____ 8. If an agent signs a check drawn on the principal's bank account without stating the agent's representative capacity, then the agent may be personally liable to pay the check.

____ 9. A term in a note requiring a maker to provide collateral renders the note nonnegotiable.

____ 10. A term in a note authorizing a holder to accelerate the due date if the maker defaults renders the note nonnegotiable.

____ 11. Numbers written as words in an instrument prevail over conflicting numbers written as figures.

____ 12. The UCC does not state a statute of limitations within which a lawsuit must be filed in order to enforce commercial paper (a negotiable instrument).

REVIEW OF CHAPTER - APPLICATION OF CONCEPTS

MULTIPLE CHOICE QUESTIONS

____ 1. Pat (as drawer) signed and issued a negotiable instrument ordering Charles (as drawee) to pay $100 on demand to Mike (as payee). Under these facts, this instrument is a:
   a. Negotiable promissory note.
   b. Negotiable draft.
   c. Check.
   d. Certificate of deposit.

____ 2. Sam signed and issued a negotiable promissory note whereby Sam promised to pay $1,000 to the order of Martha. To induce Martha to accept the note and to strengthen the likelihood of payment, Rick also signed the note. The note was then delivered to Martha. Under these facts:
   a. Martha is an indorser.
   b. Sam is a drawee.
   c. Sam is a drawer.
   d. Rick is an accommodation party.

___ 3. B&K Inc. wanted to borrow $5,000 from Myra. A promissory note was written out in longhand. The note stated that B&K Inc. promised to pay $5,000 on demand to the order of Myra. Tim Blue, President of B&K Inc., was authorized to sign the note and he signed it:

> B&K Inc.
>
> By _____ *Tim Blue* _____
>
> Tim Blue, President of B&K Inc.

   a. The note is nonnegotiable because it is handwritten.
   b. The note is nonnegotiable because it is only signed by an agent of B&K Inc.
   c. The note satisfies the writing and signature requirements and it may be negotiable.
   d. Tim Blue is personally liable to pay the note if B&K Inc. fails to pay the note.

___ 4. Which of the following terms in a promissory note would render the note nonnegotiable?
   a. Maria signed a note promising to pay $1,000 to the order of Jasmine. The duty to pay is subject to the terms of a separate loan contract made between Maria and Jasmine.
   b. Kyle signed a note promising to pay $1,000 and 100 bushels of wheat to the order of Kristen.
   c. Pete signed a note promising to pay $1,000 to the order of Yvette. In the note, Pete also promised to pay reasonable collection costs and attorney's fees if he failed to pay the note.
   d. a and b.

___ 5. Which of the following facts or terms would render a promissory note nonnegotiable?
   a. Carrie issued a promissory note that would ordinarily be negotiable. However, the note is silent regarding when Carrie is to pay the note.
   b. Lou issued a promissory note that would ordinarily be negotiable. However, the note states that the holder of the note may extend time for payment if the holder chooses to do so.
   c. April, a student, issued a promissory note that would ordinarily be negotiable. However, payment of the note is required only if April graduates from college.
   d. Hin issued a promissory note that would ordinarily be negotiable. However, the note was stated to be "payable to bearer."

CASE PROBLEM

Answer the following problem, briefly explaining your answer.

On June 1, 1997, Rex executed a promissory note and he delivered the note to Sam West. The note stated "On June 1, 2002, I promise to pay to the order of Sam West One Thousand Dollars ($1,000), together with annual interest at the rate of ten percent (10%) per year."

(a) Classify the parties to the promissory note. (b) Is the note negotiable or nonnegotiable? (c) Is the note order paper or bearer paper? (d) Would the note be negotiable if it instead required Rex to pay interest at the rate of 2 percent over the prime rate charged by Citicorp Bank from time to time?

CPA REVIEW

The following questions were given on CPA examinations. The answers for these questions are the unofficial answers prepared by the American Institute of Certified Public Accountants, Inc. (AICPA). All material is reproduced with permission of the AICPA.

____ 1. For which of the following negotiable instruments is a bank not an acceptor?
   a. Cashier's check.
   b. Certified check.
   c. Certificate of deposit.
   d. Bank acceptance.

____ 2. Under the Commercial Paper Article of the UCC, which of the following documents would be considered an order to pay?
   I. Draft
   II. Certificate of deposit
   a. I only.
   b. II only.
   c. Both I and II.
   d. Neither I nor II.

____ 3. Under the Commercial Paper Article of the UCC, for an instrument to be negotiable it must
   a. Be payable to order or to bearer.
   b. Be signed by the payee.
   c. Contain references to all agreements between the parties.
   d. Contain necessary conditions of payment.

____ 4. Under the Commercial Paper Article of the UCC, which of the following circumstances would prevent a promissory note from being negotiable?
   a. An extension clause that allows the maker to elect to extend the time for payment to a date specified in the note.
   b. An acceleration clause that allows the holder to move up the maturity date of the note in the event of default.
   c. A person having a power of attorney signs the note on behalf of the maker.
   d. A clause that allows the maker to satisfy the note by the performance of services or the payment of money.

____ 5. Which of the following negotiable instruments is subject to the UCC Commercial Paper Article?
   a. Corporate bearer bond with a maturity date of January 1, 2001.
   b. Installment note payable on the first day of each month.
   c. Warehouse receipt.
   d. Bill of lading payable to order.

Question 6 is based on the following instrument. An instrument reads as follows:

$10,000 Ludlow, Vermont February 1, 1993

I promise to pay to the order of Custer Corp. $10,000 within 10 days after the sale of my two-carat diamond ring. I pledge the sale proceeds to secure my obligation hereunder.

_____R. Harris_____
R. Harris

____ 6. Which of the following statements correctly describes the above instrument?
  a. The instrument is nonnegotiable because it is not payable at a definite time.
  b. The instrument is nonnegotiable because it is secured by the proceeds of the sale of the ring.
  c. The instrument is a negotiable promissory note.
  d. The instrument is a negotiable sight draft payable on demand.

____ 7. Which of the following conditions, if present on an otherwise negotiable instrument, would affect the instrument's negotiability?
  a. The instrument is payable six months after the death of the maker.
  b. The instrument is payable at a definite time subject to an accelerated clause in the event of a default.
  c. The instrument is postdated.
  d. The instrument contains a promise to provide additional collateral if there is a decrease in value of the existing collateral.

Question 8 relates to the following instrument:

May 19, 1991

I promise to pay to the order of A.B. Shark $1,000 (One thousand and one hundred dollars) with interest thereon at the rate of 12% per annum.

_____T.T. Tile_____
T.T. Tile

Guaranty

I personally guaranty payment by T. T. Tile.

_____N.A. Abner_____
N. A. Abner

____ 8. The instrument is
  a. Nonnegotiable even though it is payable on demand.
  b. Nonnegotiable because the numeric amount differs from the written amount.
  c. Negotiable even though a payment date is not specified.
  d. Negotiable because of Abner's guaranty.

CHAPTER 31
TRANSFER OF COMMERCIAL PAPER

CHAPTER OUTLINE

A. TRANSFER OF NEGOTIABLE INSTRUMENTS

1. EFFECT OF TRANSFER

GENERAL RULES. ▸ Negotiable instruments are transferred by negotiation or assignment. ▸ Effect of negotiation: (1) transferee is a holder and may be a holder in due course; (2) transferee may have a greater right to payment than the transferor; (3) transferee may take paper free from some defenses. ▸ Effect of assignment: (1) transferee is an assignee and cannot be a holder or holder in due course; (2) transferee has the same right to payment as the transferor; (3) transferee is subject to all defenses.
STUDY HINT. Negotiation means paper is transferred in such a way that a transferee is a holder.

2. TIME FOR DETERMINING ORDER OR BEARER CHARACTER OF AN INSTRUMENT

GENERAL RULES. ▸ Requirements for negotiation are dictated by whether paper is order or bearer paper. ▸ Whether paper is order or bearer paper is determined when it is about to be transferred.
STUDY HINT. Instruments may change back and forth between being order and bearer paper.

3. NEGOTIATION OF INSTRUMENTS

- *In general*: ▸ Negotiation of order paper requires: (1) a proper indorsement; and (2) authorized delivery of the paper to a transferee. ▸ Indorsement and delivery may be made by the party to whom paper is then payable, or by that person's authorized agent.
- *Multiple payees and indorsees*: ▸ Paper payable to joint payees (indorsees) ("pay to the order of Tom *and* Mae") requires indorsement by both parties. ▸ Paper payable to alternate payees ("pay to order of Tom *or* Mae") may be indorsed and delivered by either party. ▸ If multiple payees are named but it is not clear whether they are joint or alternate, they are considered to be alternate.
- *Agent or officer as payee*: Paper payable to a government official or corporate officer can be indorsed and negotiated by either the agent or the government body or corporation they represent.
- *Missing indorsement*: A transfer of order paper without an indorsement is only an assignment. A transferee who gives value for the paper can require the transferor to indorse the paper.

4. NEGOTIATION OF BEARER INSTRUMENTS

Negotiation of bearer paper requires only a transfer of possession; indorsement is only required if the transferee insists. A transferor who indorses bearer paper incurs the liability of an indorser.

5. FORGED AND UNAUTHORIZED INDORSEMENTS

GENERAL RULES. ▸ A forged or unauthorized indorsement is legally not the indorsement of the person whose name is signed. Therefore, order paper is not negotiated if an indorsement required for negotiation is forged or unauthorized. ▸ A bank that negotiates a check bearing a forged or unauthorized indorsement is liable for the amount of the check to the check's true owner.
LIMITATION. A forged (unauthorized) indorsement is an effective indorsement if it is ratified.
STUDY HINT. In general, there cannot be a holder, holder in due course, or holder through a holder in due course after order paper has been transferred under a forged, required indorsement.

6. **IMPOSTOR RULE (EXCEPTION TO RULE REGARDING FORGED INDORSEMENTS)**
    - *When impostor rule applicable*: A forged indorsement may effectively negotiate order paper if:
        ▸ *Impersonating payee*: Party pretending to be a payee convinces a drawer (maker) to issue paper owed to the payee. Example: Jim, using a forged license, is issued a check that was owed to Pat.
        ▸ *Dummy payee*: Drawer (maker) issues an instrument payable to a payee, but does not intend the payee to have any interest in the instrument. Example: To defraud creditors, Drawer issues a check payable to a payee; Drawer then forges the payee's signature and cashes the check.
        ▸ *Dummy payee supplied by employee*: Employee causes employer to issue paper payable to a payee, and the employee keeps the paper and forges the indorsement. Example: Ty (bookkeeper) issued a check on behalf of his employer payable to Hank, and Ty kept and cashed the check.
    - *Effect of impostor rule*: A forged indorsement is treated as a genuine indorsement.
    - *Limitations on impostor rule*: ▸ This rule does not apply if an instrument is issued to an actual creditor for the correct amount of a debt and someone (even an employee) steals it and forges the indorsement. ▸ Also, party must take paper in good faith and for payment/collection.
    - *Negligence*: The impostor rule applies even if a drawee bank negligently pays an instrument.

7. **EFFECT OF INCAPACITY OR MISCONDUCT ON NEGOTIATION**
    ▸ Negotiation is valid even if: (1) by a minor or party who lacks capacity; (2) obtained by fraud or mistake; or (3) done in breach of duty not to transfer. ▸ But, transferor can set aside negotiation unless the paper is held by party with rights of a holder in due course or by one who gave value, without notice of the defense.

8. **LOST PAPER**
    - *Lost order paper*: A finder of lost order paper is not a holder and cannot enforce payment. The original owner of a lost instrument can still enforce it against any party who is liable on it.
    - *Lost bearer paper*: A finder of lost bearer paper is a holder and may enforce payment.

B. **KINDS OF INDORSEMENTS**

9. **BLANK INDORSEMENT**
    - *Description*: Indorser signs an instrument without indicating to whom it is to be paid.
    - *Example*: Sara Thompson (payee) indorsed a check "Sara Thompson."
    - *Effect of blank indorsement*: (1) passes ownership; (2) creates bearer paper; (3) creates implied warranties by indorser; and (4) imposes secondary liability on indorser to pay the instrument.
    - *Converting a blank indorsement*: The holder after a blank indorsement may write above the indorsement a name of a person to whom it is payable; doing so converts paper into order paper.

10. **SPECIAL INDORSEMENT**
    - *Description*: Signature of indorser coupled with words specifying the person (or bank account) to whom the instrument is payable. (Note: Stating a debt to be paid is not a special indorsement.)
    - *Example*: Sara Thompson (payee) indorsed a check "Pay to Karen Kay (signed) Sara Thompson."
    - *Effect of special indorsement*: (1) passes ownership; (2) creates order paper; (3) creates implied warranties by indorser; and (4) imposes secondary liability on indorser to pay the instrument.

11. **QUALIFIED INDORSEMENT**
    - *Description*: Blank or special indorsement coupled with "without recourse" or similar words.
    - *Example*: Sara Thompson (payee) indorsed a check "Without recourse, Sara Thompson."
    - *Effect of qualified indorsement*: (1) passes ownership; (2) creates certain implied warranties by indorser; and (3) does not impose secondary liability on indorser to pay the instrument.

12. RESTRICTIVE INDORSEMENT

Restrictive indorsements condition an indorsee's right to receive payment or restrict disposition of funds. Example: Ina indorsed a check "For deposit, Ina Lee." Such a check may still be negotiated.

13. ANOMALOUS INDORSEMENT

Defined: indorsement by a party who is not a holder or a holder's agent. The indorser has the liability of an ordinary indorser. This indorsement does not affect the character of the instrument.

14. CORRECTION OF NAME BY INDORSEMENT

▸ A payee (indorsee) whose name is misspelled can indorse the misspelled name, the correct name, or both. ▸ A person giving value or taking the instrument for collection may require indorsement of both names. ▸ Fictitious or trade names are treated the same as misspelled names and the same procedures for correction apply.

15. BANK INDORSEMENT

If a customer does not indorse a check when it is deposited, the bank can supply the indorsement.

C. NEGOTIATION WARRANTIES

16. WARRANTIES OF UNQUALIFIED INDORSER

- *Scope of warranties*: An indorser making an unqualified indorsement for consideration warrants:

  (1) indorser is entitled to enforce the instrument; (2) all signatures are genuine and authorized; (3) the instrument has not been altered; (4) the instrument is not subject to any defense or claim of any party that can be asserted against the indorser; and (5) the indorser has no knowledge of an insolvency proceeding against a maker, an acceptor, or the drawer of an unaccepted draft. No distinction is made between the warranties of an unqualified blank indorsement and an unqualified special indorsement.

- *What is not warranted*: An indorser does not warrant that a maker or drawee will actually pay. A holder's indorsement of a check does not warrant that the drawer's account has sufficient funds to pay the check.

- *Beneficiary of implied warranties*: ▸ Warranties of an unqualified indorser pass to the transferee and any subsequent transferee. There is no requirement that a subsequent transferee act in good faith or be a holder.

- *Disclaimer of warranties*: Warranties can be disclaimed for all instruments except checks.

- *Notice of breach of warranty*: Notice must be given within 30 days after learning of or having reason to know of the breach and the identity of the indorser to protect rights.

17. WARRANTIES OF OTHER PARTIES

- *Qualified indorser*: Qualified indorsers make the same warranties as unqualified indorsers.
- *Transfer by delivery (no indorsement)*: The transferor makes the same warranties as an unqualified indorser, but they can be enforced only by the immediate transferee.

D. ASSIGNMENT OF INSTRUMENTS

18. ASSIGNMENT BY ACT OF THE PARTIES

A negotiable instrument can be assigned. If a necessary indorsement is missing, the transferee has only the rights of an assignee. A transferee who gives value can require the transferor to indorse the paper.

19. ASSIGNMENT BY OPERATION OF LAW

An assignment by operation of law occurs when because of the law one person's title to an instrument vests in another person. Ownership passes automatically to a trustee in bankruptcy or to a decedent's personal representative.

REVIEW OF TERMS AND PHRASES

Select the term or phrase that best matches a statement or definition stated below. Each term or phrase is the best match for only one statement or definition.

Terms and Phrases

a. Alternate payees
b. Assignment
c. Beneficiaries of warranties
d. Blank indorsement
e. Converting a blank indorsement
f. Impostor rule
g. Joint payees
h. Negotiation
i. Qualified indorsement
j. Restrictive indorsement
k. Special indorsement
l. Unauthorized indorsement
m. Unqualified indorsement
n. Warranties

Statements and Definitions

_____ 1. Indorsement that states the person to whom the instrument is to be paid.

_____ 2. Indorsement signed "without recourse," thereby negating the indorser's secondary liability.

_____ 3. Indorsement that is made by an agent who has no authority to make the indorsement.

_____ 4. Indorsement that is not stated to be "without recourse" and that does not purport to eliminate the indorser's secondary liability to pay the instrument.

_____ 5. Two or more payees, all of whom must indorse an instrument in order to negotiate it.

_____ 6. Indorsement that conditions the right of an indorsee to be paid an instrument or that restricts disposition of funds paid in satisfaction of an instrument.

_____ 7. Indorsement that consists only of the signature of the indorser.

_____ 8. Exception to the general rule that order paper cannot be negotiated by a forged indorsement.

_____ 9. Parties who are protected by a warranty and who may bring an action for damages caused by a breach of warranty.

_____ 10. Transfer of commercial paper in the manner required for a transferee to be a holder.

_____ 11. Transfer of commercial paper in a manner not satisfying the requirements for negotiation.

_____ 12. Holder writing above a blank indorsement a statement designating a special indorsee to be paid.

_____ 13. Guarantees regarding certain matters that are impliedly made by an indorser who makes an unqualified indorsement for consideration.

_____ 14. Two or more payees, any one of whom can indorse and negotiate an instrument.

REVIEW OF CONCEPTS

Write **T** if the statement is true, write **F** if it is false.

_____ 1. The requirements for negotiating commercial paper depend on whether the paper is order or bearer paper at the time of transfer.

_____ 2. Order paper can be negotiated by merely delivering the paper to the transferee; the indorsement of the transferor is not needed to negotiate order paper.

____ 3. A transferee who takes an instrument by assignment has only the same right to enforce payment as the transferor (assignor) had, and the transferee takes it subject to all defenses.

____ 4. If a negotiable promissory note is payable to "Alice Jones or Dick Roberts," the indorsements of both Alice and Dick are needed to negotiate the note.

____ 5. A check payable to "Ed Fry, President of Bay Co.," can be indorsed and negotiated by only Ed.

____ 6. If a drawee bank pays a check following a forged, required indorsement, the drawee bank may be liable for the amount of the check to the check's true owner.

____ 7. Employer issued a check to a creditor in payment of an actual debt. Employer's agent then stole the check. In this case, the agent can negotiate the check by forging the creditor's indorsement.

____ 8. Employer is fraudulently induced by Employer's agent to issue a check to a fictitious (nonexistent) creditor, and Employer gives the check to the agent. In this case, the agent can negotiate the check by indorsing the fictitious creditor's name.

____ 9. Sue impersonated Ida. Sue convinced Drawer to issue a check payable to Ida, and to give the check to Sue. In this case, Sue cannot negotiate the check by forging Ida's indorsement.

____ 10. An instrument cannot be negotiated if a required indorsement is made by a minor.

____ 11. A person who finds lost bearer paper may be entitled to enforce payment of the paper.

____ 12. Payee indorsed a check "Without recourse, Payee." In this case, the qualified indorsement destroys the negotiable character of the paper.

____ 13. A bank can supply a customer's indorsement if the customer fails to indorse a deposited check.

____ 14. A person negotiating a note by delivery only (no indorsement) makes no implied warranties.

____ 15. If an owner of an instrument dies, title passes automatically to the decedent's representative.

REVIEW OF CHAPTER - APPLICATION OF CONCEPTS

MULTIPLE CHOICE QUESTIONS

____ 1. Tom (as maker) issued and delivered to Sid a note payable to the order of Sid. In this case:
   a. To negotiate the note, Sid must indorse the note and deliver it to the transferee.
   b. Sid can assign the note to Bev merely by delivering it to Bev; Sid's indorsement is not necessary to assign the note to Bev.
   c. If a thief steals the note from Sid, forges Sid's indorsement, and delivers it to a good faith transferee for value, then the note has been negotiated to the transferee.
   d. a and b.

____ 2. Greg (as drawer) issued and delivered a check to Rose payable to the order of cash. In this case:
   a. To negotiate the check, Rose must indorse the check and deliver it to a transferee.
   b. To negotiate the check, Rose is only required to deliver the check to a transferee.
   c. If a thief steals the check from Rose and transfers it to an innocent transferee, the thief has not negotiated the check to the transferee, and the transferee cannot be a holder.
   d. a and c.

3. Drawer issued a check payable to the order of Penny Thorpe. Penny indorsed the check "Penny Thorpe" and delivered it to Terry who took it in good faith and for value. Under these facts:
   a. Penny's indorsement is a special indorsement.
   b. The check was order paper both prior to and after its negotiation by Penny to Terry.
   c. Penny may have secondary liability to pay the check if it is not paid by the drawee.
   d. Penny did not make any implied warranties to Terry.

4. Drawer issued a check payable to the order of cash and delivered it to Peter Bryan. Peter indorsed the check "Pay to Carla Wilson, (signed) Peter Bryan" and delivered it to Carla who took it in good faith and for value. Under these facts:
   a. Peter's indorsement is a special indorsement. To further negotiate this check, Carla must indorse the check and deliver it to a subsequent transferee.
   b. The check was bearer paper both prior to and after its negotiation by Peter to Carla.
   c. Peter has no secondary liability to pay the check if it is not paid by the drawer or drawee.
   d. Peter did not make any implied warranties to Carla.

5. Maker issued and delivered her negotiable promissory note to Perry Mills. Perry negotiated the note to Hans who took it in good faith and for value. Perry indorsed the note "Without recourse, Perry Mills." Under these facts:
   a. Perry's indorsement is an unqualified indorsement.
   b. Perry's indorsement is a qualified indorsement that destroys the negotiable nature of the note.
   c. If Maker fails to pay the note, Perry does not have secondary liability to pay it.
   d. Perry did not make any implied warranties to Hans.

CASE PROBLEM

Answer the following problem, briefly explaining your answer.

Drawer issued a check for $100 payable to the order of Leslie Fay. Leslie indorsed the check "Leslie Fay," and she delivered it to Bella who paid $100 to Leslie. Bella transferred the check to Henry without indorsing the check, and Henry paid Bella $100 for the check. The drawee bank refused to pay the check when it was presented for payment by Henry because there were insufficient funds in Drawer's account.

(a) Was Leslie's indorsement a qualified or unqualified indorsement? (b) Did Leslie negotiate the check to Bella? (c) Did Bella negotiate the check to Henry? (d) What warranties did Leslie and Bella make? (e) Did the drawee bank's refusal to pay the check constitute a breach of any warranty by Leslie or Bella?

CPA REVIEW

The following questions were given on CPA examinations. The answers for these questions are the unofficial answers prepared by the American Institute of Certified Public Accountants, Inc. (AICPA). All material is reproduced with permission of the AICPA.

____ 1. One of the requirements to qualify as a holder of a negotiable bearer check is that the transferee must
   a. Receive the check that was originally made payable to bearer.
   b. Take the check in good faith.
   c. Give value for the check.
   d. Have possession of the check.

____ 2. Under the Commercial Paper Article of the UCC, which of the following statements best describes the effect of a person endorsing a check "without recourse"?
   a. The person has no liability to prior endorsers.
   b. The person makes no promise or guarantee of payment on dishonor.
   c. The person gives no warranty protection to later transferees.
   d. The person converts the check into order paper.

Question 3 relates to the instrument below. The following endorsements appear on the back of a negotiable promissory note payable to Lake Corp.

Pay to John Smith only
Frank Parker, President of Lake Corp.

John Smith

Pay to the order of Sharp, Inc., without recourse, but only if Sharp delivers computers purchased by Mary Harris by March 15, 1993
Mary Harris

Sarah Sharp, President of Sharp, Inc.

____ 3. Which of the following statements is correct?
   a. The note became nonnegotiable as a result of Parker's endorsement.
   b. Harris' endorsement was a conditional promise to pay and caused the note to be nonnegotiable.
   c. Smith's endorsement effectively prevented further negotiation of the note.
   d. Harris' signature was not required to effectively negotiate the note to Sharp.

____ 4. West Corp. received a check that was originally made payable to the order of one of its customers, Ted Burns. The following endorsement was written on the back of the check: Ted Burns, without recourse, for collection only. Which of the following describes the endorsement?

	Special	Restrictive
a.	Yes	Yes
b.	No	No
c.	No	Yes
d.	Yes	No

CHAPTER 31

____ 5. In order to negotiate bearer paper, one must
   a. Endorse the paper.
   b. Endorse and deliver the paper with consideration.
   c. Deliver the paper.
   d. Deliver and endorse the paper.

Question 6 relates to the instrument below. The following endorsements appear on the back of a negotiable promissory note made payable "to bearer." Clark has possession of the note.

Pay to Sam North
Alice Fox
Sam North
(without recourse)

____ 6. Which of the following statements is correct?
   a. Clark's unqualified endorsement is required to further negotiate the note.
   b. To negotiate the note, Clark must have given value for it.
   c. Clark is not a holder because North's qualified endorsement makes the note nonnegotiable.
   d. Clark can negotiate the note by delivery alone.

____ 7. Under the Commercial Paper Article of the UCC, which of the following requirements must be met for a transferee of order paper to become a holder?
   I. Possession
   II. Endorsement of transferor
   a. I only.
   b. II only.
   c. Both I and II.
   d. Neither I nor II.

Question 8 relates to the instrument below.

Pay to John Jacobs
Mary Noah
John Jacobs
(without recourse)

____ 8. The following indorsements appear on the back of a negotiable promissory note made payable "to bearer." The note is in the possession of James Mix.
   Which one of the following statements is correct?
   a. Mix is not a holder because Jacobs' qualified indorsement makes the note non-negotiable.
   b. Mix can negotiate the note by delivery alone.
   c. The unqualified indorsement of Mix is required in order to further negotiate the note.
   d. In order for Mix to negotiate the note Mix must have given value for it.

CHAPTER 32
RIGHTS OF HOLDERS AND DEFENSES

CHAPTER OUTLINE

A. KINDS OF CLAIMANTS

1. TYPES OF PARTIES

One claiming a right to be paid paper may be an assignee or a holder. A holder is (1) an ordinary holder or (2) a favored holder (i.e., holder in due course or holder through a holder in due course).

2. ORDINARY HOLDERS AND ASSIGNEES

GENERAL RULES. ▸ An ordinary holder is a party to whom is transferred (1) a negotiable instrument (2) by negotiation, but (3) who fails for any reason to qualify as a holder in due course. ▸ In general, an ordinary holder can: (1) enforce payment of an instrument; and (2) cancel another's liability on an instrument. ▸ An assignee has the same rights as an ordinary holder.

STUDY HINTS. ▸ The fact that a person is only an ordinary holder is irrelevant unless the party from whom payment is demanded has a limited defense that can avoid liability for payment. ▸ A holder can sue anyone who is liable on paper regardless of the order in which they signed the paper.

3. FAVORED HOLDERS

(a) Holder in due course

A holder in due course is a party to whom is transferred: (1) a negotiable instrument; (2) by negotiation; (3) for value; (4) in good faith; (5) without notice that the instrument is overdue or has been dishonored; and (6) without notice of any defense or adverse claim. ▸ Important rules:

- ***Value***: ▸ Value is (1) *actually* performing an act for which paper is given, or (2) taking paper as security for, or in payment of, an existing debt. ▸ A bank gives value for a check only when it pays cash for a check or when a customer deposits a check into an account and the customer withdraws the money from the account. ▸ An unperformed promise is not value. ▸ The UCC has additional rules regarding value that apply in certain cases.

- ***Good faith***: ▸ Good faith: honesty in fact and observance of reasonable standards of fair dealing. ▸ Bad faith is a transferee's knowledge of facts that indicate a transfer may be improper. Ignorance of facts due to negligence is not bad faith.

- ***Ignorance of instrument's being overdue or dishonored***: ▸ *Overdue*: (1) a time instrument is overdue the day after payment is due (or after a due date has been accelerated); (2) a demand instrument is overdue when a reasonable time has elapsed after its issuance. ▸ *Dishonored*: a maker or drawee has refused to pay an instrument. ▸ It is not improper to negotiate an instrument that is overdue or that has been dishonored; it simply means that a subsequent party who takes an instrument with notice of such matters cannot be a holder in due course.

- ***Ignorance of defenses and adverse claims***: ▸ A transferee is not a holder in due course if, at time of acquisition, he or she had notice that (1) a party who is liable on the paper had a defense to paying, or (2) someone else claimed to own the paper. However, holder in due course status is not affected if notice is received after a transferee acquires the paper. ▸ Knowing a party has been discharged does not bar a transferee from being a holder in due course, and recorded documents do not give notice of any defenses or conflicting claims.

(b) Holder through a holder in due course ("shelter rule")

- *Defined*: (1) Party to whom a negotiable instrument is negotiated (i.e., a holder) (2) at any time after the instrument was held by anyone who was a holder in due course.
- *Example*: Drawer issued a check to Paul. Paul negotiated it to a holder in due course who then negotiated it to Ann. Ann did not pay value, and she had notice that the check was overdue and that Drawer claimed a defense. Ann is a holder through a holder in due course.
- *Rights*: Holder through a holder in due course has the same rights as holder in due course.
- In an action to collect a negotiable instrument, a plaintiff must prove that he or she is a favored holder only if the defendant asserts a universal defense.

B. DEFENSES

4. CLASSIFICATION OF DEFENSES

Parties with primary or secondary liability may have a defense that partially or completely avoids their liability to pay an instrument. Defenses are either limited defenses or universal defenses.

5. DEFENSES AGAINST ASSIGNEE OR ORDINARY HOLDER

An assignee or ordinary holder takes an instrument subject to all limited and universal defenses.

6. LIMITED DEFENSES NOT AVAILABLE AGAINST A HOLDER IN DUE COURSE

- *Ordinary contract defenses*: Breach of warranty and failure of consideration are limited defenses.
- *Incapacity of defendant*: Lack of capacity (other than that of minority) is a limited defense if it renders a contract voidable. Incapacity that renders a contract void is a universal defense.
- *Fraud in the inducement*: ▸ This type of fraud occurs when a party knowingly executes an instrument, but the party has been fraudulently induced into signing it. ▸ Example: Buyer issued Seller a check in payment for land that Seller misrepresented to Buyer. Seller negotiated the check to Vick, a holder in due course. Seller's fraud is a limited defense, and Buyer must pay Vick the amount of the check.
- *Prior payment or cancellation:* ▸ The fact that a party has paid an instrument or that it has been canceled are limited defenses. ▸ Example: Mel issued a note payable June 1. On March 1, Mel paid the note, but he failed to take it back. On May 1, the note was negotiated to Ray, a holder in due course. Mel's prior payment is a limited defense, and he cannot assert it against Ray.
- *Nondelivery of an instrument*: ▸ The fact that paper is stolen, and then delivered without the original owner's authority is a limited defense. ▸ Example: Dave issued a check payable to cash, and he delivered it to Paul. Thief stole the check and negotiated it to Hal, a holder in due course. The unauthorized delivery to Thief is a limited defense; Paul cannot assert it against Hal.
- *Conditional or specified purpose delivery*: ▸ The fact that an unconditional instrument is actually subject to secret, unfulfilled conditions is a limited defense. ▸ Example: Molly issued a note to Patti, subject to an oral condition that it was not payable until Patti transferred property to Molly. Patti negotiated the note to Hazel, a holder in due course who was unaware of the condition. Molly cannot assert the conditional delivery to Patti as a defense to paying Hazel.
- *Duress (threats)*: Duress is a limited defense if it renders a contract voidable under state law.
- *Unauthorized completion*: ▸ Unauthorized completion of paper is a limited defense. ▸ Example: Dora issued a check, leaving the amount blank. Dora gave the check to Son and told him not to complete it for more than $20. Son filled in $200, and negotiated it to Hugh, a holder in due course. Dora cannot assert the unauthorized completion against Hugh; Dora must pay $200.
- *Theft*: The fact that an instrument has been stolen from an owner is a limited defense.

7. UNIVERSAL DEFENSES AVAILABLE AGAINST ALL HOLDERS

- *Fraud as to the nature or terms of the paper*: ▸ This type of fraud occurs when a maker, drawer, or indorser is defrauded regarding the legal nature or essential terms of an instrument. ▸ Example: Lois, an elderly person, signs a note because she is defrauded into believing that it is only a request for credit. ▸ This defense cannot be raised if the fraud results from the party's own negligence.

- *Forgery or lack of authority*: ▸ A maker, drawer, or indorser can use against anyone the defense that his or her signature was forged or was made without authority. ▸ Example: Thief stole Dee's checkbook and forged her signature on a check. Dee can assert this defense against anyone.

- *Duress depriving control*: Duress that renders a contract void is a universal defense.

- *Incapacity*: Lack of contractual capacity due to minority is a universal defense. Lack of capacity due to other reasons is a universal defense only if it renders an obligation void under state law.

- *Illegality*: ▸ Illegality is a universal defense if it renders a contract void under state law. ▸ Example: A note is issued in payment for stolen goods. ▸ But, if paper is issued in an illegal transaction that is not void under state law, the defense is merely a limited defense.

- *Alteration*: ▸ An alteration occurs if a party to a paper fraudulently alters terms of the paper changing the obligation of another party to the paper. ▸ A holder in due course and a paying bank or drawee can enforce an altered instrument according to its original terms. ▸ Example: Dan issued a check for $10 to Pete, and Pete changed the amount to $100. Pete negotiated the check to Holly, a holder in due course. Holly can enforce the check for $10.

8. ADVERSE CLAIMS TO THE INSTRUMENT

GENERAL RULES. ▸ An adverse claim of ownership to paper may arise if: (1) a party is defrauded into transferring paper to another party; or (2) paper is wrongfully taken from a party. ▸ An adverse claim can be asserted against an assignee or ordinary holder, enabling the adverse claimant to recover the instrument. ▸ An adverse claim cannot be asserted against a party with rights of a holder in due course. ▸ Example: Drew issued a check to Pam. Ted fraudulently induced Pam to indorse the check to Ted. Ted then negotiated the check to Harry, a holder in due course. Pam's adverse claim to the check cannot be asserted against Harry, and Pam cannot recover the check.

STUDY HINT. Adverse claims are asserted when a prior owner tries to reclaim ownership of paper, whereas defenses are asserted when a person tries to avoid his or her liability to pay an instrument.

9. AVOIDANCE OF HOLDER IN DUE COURSE PROTECTION

- *Participating transferee*: If a transferee of a negotiable instrument is closely connected or related to either (1) the transaction that gave rise to the instrument or (2) to the transferor of the instrument, then a court may hold that the knowledge of the transferor is imputed to the transferee. This imputed knowledge may negate the transferee's holder in due course status.

- *The Federal Trade Commission (FTC) rule*: ▸ An FTC rule requires that a contract in a consumer credit transaction contain a notice that a buyer may assert all defenses against any person enforcing a negotiable promissory note given in connection with the transaction. ▸ A consumer credit transaction is one for the sale of goods or services for personal, family, or household use. This rule does not apply to commercial transactions. ▸ Example: Kim issued a negotiable note to May Co. to pay for a bed for her home. FTC rules would require this note to contain the foregoing notice and, if this notice was stated, then Kim could use any defense against a subsequent holder in due course who acquired the note. ▸ If a notice preserving consumer defenses is stated in a negotiable instrument, no subsequent person can be a holder in due course.

REVIEW OF TERMS AND PHRASES

Select the term or phrase that best matches a statement or definition stated below. Each term or phrase is the best match for only one statement or definition.

Terms and Phrases

a. Adverse claim
b. Bad faith
c. Consumer credit transaction
d. Dishonor
e. Favored holder
f. Fraud in the inducement
g. Good faith
h. Limited defenses
i. Ordinary holder
j. Overdue
k. Universal defenses
l. Value

Statements and Definitions

_____ 1. Credit purchase of goods or services for personal, family, or household use.

_____ 2. Honesty in fact and observation of reasonable standards of fair dealing.

_____ 3. Defenses to payment that can be asserted against any party, including a holder in due course.

_____ 4. Misrepresentation that induces a party to knowingly sign a negotiable instrument.

_____ 5. Conflicting claim of ownership to a negotiable instrument.

_____ 6. Defenses to payment that can be asserted against an assignee or ordinary holder, but cannot be asserted against a holder in due course or a holder through a holder in due course.

_____ 7. Holder in due course or holder through a holder in due course.

_____ 8. Actual performance of an act in exchange for an instrument, or taking an instrument as security or payment for an existing obligation.

_____ 9. Holder of paper who is not a favored holder.

_____ 10. Instrument is not paid when due, or an instrument that is payable on demand is not paid within a reasonable time after it was issued.

_____ 11. Knowledge of facts by a transferee of paper which indicates that the transfer may be improper.

_____ 12. Refusal by a maker or drawee to accept or pay an instrument.

REVIEW OF CONCEPTS

Write **T** if the statement is true, write **F** if it is false.

_____ 1. An ordinary holder does not have any right to demand or enforce payment of an instrument.

_____ 2. In general, a person entitled to payment may sue any one or more of the parties liable to pay the instrument, regardless of the order in which the parties signed the instrument.

_____ 3. A holder through a holder in due course has the same right to collect and enforce payment of a negotiable instrument as does a holder in due course.

_____ 4. Evidence that a person paid an extremely small price for an instrument may indicate bad faith.

_____ 5. It is illegal to negotiate an instrument that is overdue.

_____ 6. A person has notice of a fact only when the person has actual knowledge of the fact.

_____ 7. Limited defenses can be asserted against anyone, including a holder in due course.

_____ 8. Duress is a universal defense if, under state law, duress would render a contract void.

_____ 9. Ordinary contract defenses are limited defenses that cannot be used against holders in due course.

_____ 10. Maker issued a note due May 1. Maker prepaid the note on March 1, but Maker did not retake the note. On April 1, the payee negotiated the note to Hal, a holder in due course. In this case, Maker's prior payment is a limited defense, and it cannot be asserted against Hal.

_____ 11. Drawer issued an incomplete check. Drawer gave the check to Ginger, telling Ginger to complete it for $100. Ginger completed the check for $500, and she negotiated it to Hank, a holder in due course. In this case, Drawer is liable to Hank for only $100.

_____ 12. Maker issued a note for $500. Payee raised the amount to $5,000. The note was negotiated to Fay, a holder in due course. In this case, the alteration is a universal defense and Maker must pay Fay $500.

_____ 13. Dan issued a bearer check to Payee. Thief stole the check from Payee and negotiated it to Ike, a holder in due course. In this case, Payee can assert an adverse claim and recover the check from Ike.

_____ 14. If a transferor and transferee of a negotiable instrument are very closely related to one another, a court may charge the transferee with knowledge of facts known to the transferor.

_____ 15. In a consumer credit transaction, FTC rules require a contract to state a notice allowing a consumer to use all defenses arising out of the transaction against any holder of a note.

REVIEW OF CHAPTER - APPLICATION OF CONCEPTS

MULTIPLE CHOICE QUESTIONS

_____ 1. In which case did Holder give value sufficient to be a holder in due course?
   a. Drawer issued a check to Paul. Paul indorsed the check, and delivered it to Holder as a gift.
   b. Maker issued a check to Rod. Rod indorsed the check and delivered it to Holder in payment for services Holder promised to perform for Rod. Holder did not perform the services.
   c. Maker issued a negotiable note payable to Priscilla. Priscilla indorsed the note and negotiated it to Holder in payment of an existing debt that she owed Holder.
   d. b and c.

_____ 2. Mac issued a negotiable note to Peg to pay for goods. Peg negotiated the note to Chris, who negotiated the note to Herb. Herb paid value for the note, and he took it in good faith. Which additional fact would *not* prevent Herb from being a holder in due course?
   a. The note was due June 1, and Chris negotiated the note to Herb on July 1.
   b. At the time the note was negotiated to Herb, Herb knew that the note had become due and that Mac had refused to pay it.
   c. At the time the note was negotiated to Herb, Herb knew that Peg claimed ownership of the note because she had been defrauded into transferring it to Chris.
   d. One day after the note was negotiated to Herb, Mac informed Herb that the goods delivered to Mac were defective, and he had a breach of contract defense.

____ 3. In which case does Denise have a limited defense that cannot be used against a favored holder?
   a. Denise issued a check to Contractor in payment for certain remodeling work. Contractor performed the work improperly, a breach of contract.
   b. Denise issued a check to Payton. Denise issued the check due to wrongful physical abuse by Payton. Under state law, the duress exerted by Payton would render the obligation void.
   c. Denise's checkbook was stolen by Thief. Thief forged Denise's signature to a check.
   d. When Denise was a minor, she issued a check in payment for a magazine subscription.

____ 4. In which case does Dana have a universal defense that can be asserted against all holders?
   a. While intoxicated, Dana bought a painting and she issued a check in payment. Under state law, Dana's lack of capacity due to intoxication would render the obligation voidable.
   b. Dana issued a check in payment for illegal drugs. Under state law, negotiable instruments issued for illegal drugs are void.
   c. Dana issued a check to Perry as payment for landscaping services that Perry agreed to perform. Perry wrongfully failed to perform the services.
   d. Dana issued a check to Stockbroker. Delivery of the check was conditioned on Stockbroker's delivery of certain stock to Dana. Stockbroker failed to deliver the stock to Dana.

____ 5. Select the correct answer.
   a. Dexter issued a check to the order of Paula. Paula indorsed the check in blank. Thief stole the check and negotiated it to Hall, a holder in due course. In this case, Paula can assert her adverse claim to the check against Hall, and she may reclaim the check from Hall.
   b. Max issued a negotiable note to Paul due to Paul's wrongful threats. Under state law, Paul's threats would render an obligation voidable. Paul negotiated the note to Haxley, a holder in due course. In this case, Max has a universal defense, and he is not obligated to pay Haxley.
   c. Mindy issued a negotiable note to P&P Co. to pay for a stove for her home. The note contained all notices required by FTC rules. The stove breached various warranties. P&P negotiated the note to Harry, who took it for value, in good faith, and with no notice of the breach. In this case, Mindy can assert the breach of warranty defense against Harry.
   d. All of the above are correct.

CASE PROBLEM

Answer the following problem, briefly explaining your answer.

Manley issued a $20,000 negotiable note to Preston to pay for a parcel of land. Preston misrepresented to Manley that the parcel contained fifty acres, when in fact it contained only forty acres. Preston negotiated the note to Carl. Carl paid Preston $20,000 for the note, and he took it without notice of Preston's fraud. Later, Carl negotiated the note to Ned who knew that Manley claimed that he had been defrauded.

(a) Is Carl a holder in due course? (b) Is Ned a favored holder? If so, what kind of holder is Ned? (c) Manley's defense of fraud is what type of defense? (d) Can Manley assert this defense against Ned?

_____
_____
_____
_____
_____

CPA REVIEW

The following questions were given on CPA examinations. The answers for these questions are the unofficial answers prepared by the American Institute of Certified Public Accountants, Inc. (AICPA). All material is reproduced with permission of the AICPA.

____ 1. Jim Bass is in possession of a negotiable promissory note made payable "to bearer." Bass acquired the note from Mary Frank for value. The maker of the note was Fred Jackson. The following indorsements appear on the back of the note:

> *Sam Peters*
>
> Pay to Jim Bass
>
> *Mary Frank*
>
> *Jim Bass*
>
> (without recourse)

Bass presented the note to Jackson, who refused to pay it because he was financially unable to do so. Which of the following statements is correct?
  a. Peters is not secondarily liable on the note because his indorsement was unnecessary for negotiation.
  b. Peters is not secondarily liable to Bass.
  c. Frank will probably not be liable to Bass unless Bass gives notice to Frank of Jackson's refusal to pay within a reasonable time.
  d. Bass would have had secondary liability to Peters and Frank if he had not qualified his indorsement.

____ 2. Hunt has in his possession a negotiable instrument which was originally payable to the order of Carr. It was transferred to Hunt by a mere delivery by Drake, who took it from Carr in good faith in satisfaction of an antecedent debt. The back of the instrument read as follows, "Pay to the order of Drake in satisfaction of my prior purchase of a new video calculator, signed Carr." Which of the following is correct?
  a. Hunt has the right to assert Drake's rights, including his standing as a holder in due course and also has the right to obtain Drake's signature.
  b. Drake's taking the instrument for an antecedent debt prevents him from qualifying as a holder in due course.
  c. Carr's endorsement was a special endorsement; thus Drake's signature was not required in order to negotiate it.
  d. Hunt is a holder in due course.

____ 3. A person who endorsed a check "without recourse"
  a. Has the same liability as an accommodation endorser.
  b. Only negates his liability insofar as prior parties are concerned.
  c. Gives the same warranty protection to his transferee as does a special or blank endorser.
  d. Does not promise or guarantee payment of the instrument upon dishonor even if there has been a proper presentment and proper notice has been given.

CHAPTER 32

____ 4. Silver Corp. sold 20 tons of steel to River Corp. with payment to be by River's check. The price of steel was fluctuating daily. Silver requested that the amount of River's check be left blank and Silver would fill in the current market price. River complied with Silver's request. Within two days, Silver received River's check. Although the market price of 20 tons of steel at the time Silver received River's check was $80,000, Silver filled in the check for $100,000 and negotiated it to Hatch Corp. Hatch took the check in good faith, without notice of Silver's act or any other defense, and in payment of an antecedent debt. River will
   a. Not be liable to Hatch, because the check was materially altered by Silver.
   b. Not be liable to Hatch, because Hatch failed to give value when it acquired the check from Silver.
   c. Be liable to Hatch for $100,000.
   d. Be liable to Hatch, but only for $80,000.

____ 5. Frey paid Holt $2,500 by check pursuant to an agreement between them whereby Holt promised to perform in Frey's theater within the next year. Holt endorsed the check, making it payable to Len Able. Holt's status with regard to the check was one of a(an)
   a. Assignee since a payee may not also be a holder in due course.
   b. Holder since Holt's promise failed to satisfy the value requirement necessary to become a holder in due course.
   c. Holder in due course under the shelter rule since Able's rights as a holder in due course revert to Holt.
   d. Holder in due course since all the requirements have been satisfied.

____ 6. Under the Commercial Paper Article of the UCC, which of the following requirements must be met for a person to be a holder in due course of a promissory note?
   a. The note must be payable to bearer.
   b. The note must be negotiable.
   c. All prior holders must have been holders in due course.
   d. The holder must be the payee of the note.

____ 7. Under the Commercial Paper Article of the UCC, which of the following circumstances would prevent a person from becoming a holder in due course of an instrument?
   a. The person was notified that payment was refused.
   b. The person was notified that one of the prior endorsers was discharged.
   c. The note was collateral for a loan.
   d. The note was purchased at a discount.

____ 8. Under the Commercial Paper Article of the UCC, in a nonconsumer transaction, which of the following are real defenses available against a holder in due course?

	Material alteration	Discharge in bankruptcy	Breach of contract
a.	No	Yes	Yes
b.	Yes	Yes	No
c.	No	No	Yes
d.	Yes	No	No

CHAPTER 33
CHECKS AND FUNDS TRANSFERS

CHAPTER OUTLINE

A. CHECKS

1. NATURE OF A CHECK

GENERAL RULES. ▸ A check is a special type of draft. ▸ Unique features: (1) drawee is always a bank; (2) a check assumes there are funds on deposit to pay it; and (3) a check is demand paper.
LIMITATION. A postdated check (a check that is dated later than the date that it is actually issued) is not payable until the date shown. Thus, a postdated check is, in effect, a time instrument.
STUDY HINTS. ▸ A drawer has conditional liability to pay a dishonored check. ▸ It may be a crime if a check is not paid due to insufficient funds and it was issued with the intent to defraud. ▸ A check may be an ordinary check, a cashier's check (check drawn by a bank on itself), or a teller's check (check drawn by a bank on another bank in which it has funds deposited).

2. CERTIFIED CHECKS

GENERAL RULES. ▸ A certified check is a check that has been accepted by the drawee bank, whereby the bank agrees to pay it regardless of the balance in the drawer's account at the time payment is demanded. ▸ Certification may be obtained by: (1) a holder (discharges all prior indorsers and drawer from conditional liability); or (2) by a drawer (does not discharge any parties).
LIMITATION. A certification must be written on the check and duly signed by a bank officer.
STUDY HINT. By certifying a check, a drawee bank incurs primary liability to pay it.

3. LIABILITY OF DRAWER

GENERAL RULES. ▸ A drawer has conditional liability to pay a check if a drawee bank does not accept (dishonors) a check. ▸ If a bank pays a check but the drawer's account has insufficient funds to cover it, the payment is treated as a loan from the bank to the drawer, and it must be repaid.
LIMITATION. If an account has two parties and one signs a check creating an overdraft, the nonsigning party has no duty to repay the check if he or she received no benefit from the proceeds.

4. THE DEPOSITOR-BANK RELATIONSHIP (DEPOSITARY BANK'S DUTY TO CUSTOMER)

- **Privacy**: A bank must maintain the confidentiality of customer information.
- **Payment**: A depositary bank has a duty to pay checks to the extent there are sufficient funds.
- **Stale checks**: A bank may pay a stale check (i.e., one presented for payment more than six months after the date issued), but it is not required to do so unless the check is certified.
- **Payment after depositor's death**: A bank may pay a check for ten days after a depositor's death or for ten days after being notified of death unless told not to do so by an interested party.

5. STOPPING PAYMENT OF A CHECK

GENERAL RULES. ▸ A drawer can stop payment by notifying the drawee bank. ▸ An order may be oral or written; if oral, it is binding for fourteen days; if written, it is effective for six months.
LIMITATION. A drawer cannot stop payment of a certified check or a cashier's check.
STUDY HINT. A drawer may be liable on a check even if payment is stopped.

6. TIME OF PRESENTMENT OF A CHECK FOR PAYMENT

▸ A check can ordinarily be presented for payment immediately after it is issued. But, if a check is postdated, it cannot be presented until the date stated on the check. ▸ A check is overdue the day after demand for payment is made or ninety days after the date of the check, whichever is earlier. ▸ In order to charge a secondary party on a check, presentment for payment must be made on the primary party within a "reasonable time" after the secondary party signs the paper. To hold a drawer liable, the "reasonable time" for presentment is presumed to be thirty days from the date of the check or the date it was issued. To hold an indorser liable, the check should be presented within seven days after it is indorsed.

7. DISHONOR OF A CHECK

GENERAL RULES. ▸ Dishonor occurs if a drawee bank refuses to accept or pay a check drawn on it by a depositor. ▸ A bank is liable to the drawer for any damages caused by a wrongful dishonor. ▸ A dishonor is wrongful if: (1) a check is properly payable and (2) the account has funds to pay it. A dishonor for lack of funds is also wrongful if a bank has agreed to pay a drawer's overdrafts.
LIMITATION. Drawee is not liable to *a holder* for wrongfully dishonoring an uncertified check.
STUDY HINT. Improper notice of dishonor may discharge the drawer or indorsers.

8. AGENCY STATUS OF COLLECTING BANK

A collecting bank is typically only a depositor's agent for purposes of collecting a check. Until final settlement, the depositor owns the check and bears the risk of nonpayment.

9. DUTY OF A BANK

▸ Banks must use ordinary care in handling checks. Parties in the bank collection process may alter their rights, but liability for bad faith or failure to exercise ordinary care cannot be disclaimed. ▸ Ordinarily, banks need not physically inspect checks that are automatically processed. ▸ Anyone encoding data on an item or transmitting the information electronically warrants that the information is correct.

B. LIABILITY OF A BANK

10. PREMATURE PAYMENT OF A POSTDATED CHECK

A bank is not liable to a drawer for paying a postdated check prior to the date stated unless the drawer gave the bank prior notice that the check was being issued and should not be paid until the stated date.

11. PAYMENT OVER A STOP PAYMENT ORDER

A bank that pays a depositor's check contrary to a valid stop payment order is liable to the depositor for any damages caused unless there was a valid limitation of liability. But, a bank must be given a reasonable time within which to act on an order (usually a few hours is sufficient).

12. PAYMENT ON FORGED SIGNATURE OF DRAWER

GENERAL RULE. A drawee is liable to a drawer if it pays a check with a forged (i.e., unauthorized and fraudulent) drawer's signature, even if the drawee could not detect the forgery.
LIMITATIONS. ▸ Preclusion rule: Depositor whose negligence substantially contributed to a forgery cannot assert the forgery and cannot make a drawee bank recredit its account if the bank paid the item. ▸ Preclusion rule also applies if a drawer's negligence contributes to alteration of a check.
STUDY HINT. Ordinarily, a drawee bank bears any loss caused by its payment over a forged drawer's signature. The drawee cannot recover from an innocent drawer or indorser on any theory.

13. PAYMENT ON A FORGED OR MISSING INDORSEMENT

If a bank pays a depositor's check that has a forged required indorsement or a required indorsement is missing, the bank must recredit the depositor's account and the depositor will not bear the loss.

14. ALTERATION OF A CHECK

A drawee bank that pays an altered check can charge a drawer's account for only the original amount of the check, unless the alteration is due to the drawer's negligence.

15. UNAUTHORIZED COLLECTION OF A CHECK

- A bank that improperly collects payment of a check for a customer is liable to the true check owner.
- A collecting bank is not liable if it is obeying its customer's instructions.

16. TIME LIMITATIONS

- ***Non-Code statute of limitations***: Non-UCC statutes of limitations determine the time within which to bring actions for violation of the customer-bank contract or for conversion of a check.
- ***Statute of limitations for liability under Article 4***: three years.
- ***Statute of limitations for single forgery or alteration***: Drawee bank that uses ordinary care is not liable to a drawer for a forged or altered check if: (1) the drawer did not use reasonable care to inspect the checks and notify the bank of unauthorized signatures or alterations; (2) drawer did not give the bank notice of a forged drawer's signature or alteration within one year after receipt of the bank statement; or (3) drawer did not give the bank notice of a forged indorsement within 3 years after receipt of a statement.
- ***Statute of limitations for series of unauthorized signatures/alterations by same person:*** Failure to notify the bank of first wrong within thirty days may cause liability for future wrongs.

C. CONSUMER FUNDS TRANSFERS

17. ELECTRONIC FUND TRANSFERS ACT (EFTA)

Electronic fund transfer is a transfer of funds (not using check, draft, or other paper instrument) that electronically authorizes institutions to credit or debit funds to or from an account. EFTA governs such transfers made by consumers.

18. KINDS OF ELECTRONIC FUND TRANSFER SYSTEMS

- EFT systems include: automated teller machine (ATM); pay-by-phone system; direct deposit and withdrawal; and point-of-sale terminal. - Consumers must be informed in advance of all terms for EFT services and must be given periodic statements of account activity. With certain exceptions, financial institutions are liable to consumers for violation of EFT account terms.

19. CONSUMER LIABILITY

- Consumer's maximum liability for unauthorized use of EFT card: (1) $50 if issuer is notified within two days after consumer learns of loss of card; or (2) $500 if no notice is given within two days. - A consumer bears a loss caused by a failure to report an improper transfer within sixty days after a statement was sent.

D. FUNDS TRANSFERS

20. WHAT LAW GOVERNS

UCC Art. 4A governs funds transfers if a state adopted 4A or if a Federal Reserve Bank is involved.

21. CHARACTERISTICS OF FUNDS TRANSFERS

Article 4A transfers typically involve large sums of money between sophisticated nonconsumers.

22. PATTERN OF FUNDS TRANSFERS

▸ Funds transfers may involve two or more parties. ▸ Example: A&A buys land for $500,000 and A&A tells its bank to debit its account for $500,000 and to credit the seller's account for this sum.

23. SCOPE OF UCC ARTICLE 4A

Article 4A governs most funds transfers, but does not govern: transfers by consumers regulated by the EFTA, debit transfers, nonbank transfers of money (e.g., Western Union), or payments made by check.

24. DEFINITIONS

▸ *Funds transfer*: request to pay money to an account or party. ▸ *Originator*: party starting funds transfer. ▸ *Beneficiary*: party (account) for whose benefit funds are transferred. ▸ *Beneficiary's bank*: final bank in transfer--pays beneficiary. ▸ *Payment order*: request that bank make a funds transfer. ▸ *Acceptance*: beneficiary bank applies or agrees to apply funds for the benefit of a beneficiary.

25. FORM OF PAYMENT ORDER

Article 4A does not regulate the form of payment orders. Payment orders may be oral or written.

26. MANNER OF TRANSMITTING PAYMENT ORDER

Article 4A does not regulate the manner of carrying out funds transfers; computers are often used.

27. SECURITY PROCEDURE

Banks should adopt reasonable security procedures for verifying the accuracy of payment orders.

28. REGULATION BY AGREEMENT AND FUNDS TRANSFER SYSTEM RULE

Parties' agreement or clearinghouse rules may designate controlling law or change Article 4A rules.

29. ACCEPTANCE OF PAYMENT ORDER

A bank accepts an order when it complies with the order. When a beneficiary bank accepts a payment order, the beneficiary bank takes the place of the originator as the debtor, and the debt to the beneficiary is paid or reduced by the amount of the payment order.

30. REIMBURSEMENT OF THE BANK

Ultimately, an originator is responsible for the cost of funds the originator ordered to be transferred.

31. REFUND ON NONCOMPLETION OF TRANSFER

If a funds transfer is not completed, an originator is entitled to be repaid any advance payments.

32. ERROR IN FUNDS TRANSFER

A bank that prepares an incorrect payment order is liable for any overpayment, duplicate payment, or a payment to the wrong person or account because of an error in the designation.

33. LIABILITY FOR LOSS

Bank is not liable for executing an unauthorized order if a commercially reasonable security procedure is used unless someone unrelated to the originator made the order.

REVIEW OF TERMS AND PHRASES

MATCHING EXERCISE

Select the term or phrase that best matches a statement or definition stated below. Each term or phrase is the best match for only one statement or definition.

Terms and Phrases

a. Article 4A
b. Beneficiary
c. Beneficiary's bank
d. Cashier's check
e. Certified check
f. Electronic Fund Transfers Act (EFTA)
g. Funds transfer
h. Originator
i. Payment order
j. Postdated check
k. Stale check
l. Stop payment order

Statements and Definitions

____ 1. Instruction by a drawer to a drawee bank not to pay a check.

____ 2. Check that is dated later than the date on which it is actually issued.

____ 3. Request to pay money to or for the credit of a party without physically transferring money.

____ 4. Check that is drawn by a bank upon itself and that is payable to another party.

____ 5. Party who initiates a funds transfer request.

____ 6. Check that is accepted by a drawee bank at the request of the drawer or a holder.

____ 7. Law that generally regulates electronic funds transfers that are made by nonconsumers.

____ 8. Direction or request made by an originator or subsequent bank to make a funds transfer.

____ 9. Final bank that makes payment or gives credit to a beneficiary in accordance with payment order.

____10. Party who ultimately receives funds pursuant to a funds transfer.

____11. Law that governs electronic fund transfers by consumers.

____12. Check presented more than six months after the date on which it was issued.

COMPLETION EXERCISE

Fill in the blanks with the words that most accurately complete each statement. Answers may or may not include terms used in the matching exercise. A term cannot be used to complete more than one statement.

1. A check is a special type of _____.

2. An oral stop payment order is effective for _____ _____ and a written stop payment order is effective for _____ _____.

3. _____ is a drawee bank's agreement that it will pay a check when it is presented for payment, regardless of the balance in the drawer's account at the time the check is presented.

4. A drawer cannot require a drawee bank to recredit its account due to a forged drawer's signature or alteration of a check unless the drawer gave the bank notice of such matters within _____ _____ after the drawer received his or her bank statement.

5. In the bank collection process, a bank must exercise _____ _____ in handling checks.

6. The EFTA regulates electronic fund transfers made by _____.

7. Two examples of electronic fund transfer systems are _____ and _____.

REVIEW OF CONCEPTS

Write **T** if the statement is true, write **F** if it is false.

_____ 1. A drawer may be criminally prosecuted for issuing a bad check if the drawer's account has insufficient funds to pay the check and the check was issued with the intent to defraud a payee.

_____ 2. A postdated check is payable immediately after issuance even though it is dated with a later date.

_____ 3. In general, a drawer can stop payment of a certified or cashier's check.

_____ 4. Certification of a check must be written on the check and must be signed by an agent of the bank.

_____ 5. An indorser's conditional liability is discharged if a check is not presented for payment within three days after the date the indorser signed the check.

_____ 6. A bank cannot be held liable by a drawer for damages caused by a wrongful dishonor of a check.

_____ 7. A drawee bank is liable for a drawer's damages that are caused by the bank's payment of a check in violation of a valid stop payment order unless there was a valid limitation of liability.

_____ 8. Drawer issued a postdated check and informed Drawee Bank of this fact. Nonetheless, Drawee Bank paid the check before the date of the check. In this case, Drawee Bank cannot be held liable for damages that Drawer may suffer due to the early payment the check.

_____ 9. If a drawee bank charges a drawer's account for a check that has a forged required indorsement, the drawee bank must recredit the drawer's account for the amount of the check.

_____ 10. A drawer may lose the right to assert against a drawee bank a claim that a check had been altered if the drawer's negligence substantially contributed to the alteration.

_____ 11. A drawer may be barred from asserting a forged or unauthorized signature or alteration against a drawee bank if the drawer failed to exercise proper care in examining a bank statement or canceled checks and in notifying the drawee bank of any improper payment.

_____ 12. The EFTA governs consumers' funds transfers that are accomplished by issuance of checks.

_____ 13. A consumer's liability for unauthorized use of his or her EFT card is limited to $500 if notice is given to the issuer within two days after the consumer learned of the loss or theft of the card.

_____ 14. Under Article 4A, payment orders that direct funds transfers must be in writing.

_____ 15. Under Article 4A, as a general rule a bank is not liable for a loss caused by its execution of an unauthorized payment order if the order was verified by a reasonable security procedure.

REVIEW OF CHAPTER - APPLICATION OF CONCEPTS

MULTIPLE CHOICE QUESTIONS

_____ 1. Drawer issued a check to Patty. Patty indorsed the check in blank and negotiated it to Harold. At Harold's request, Bank of Fruita, the drawee bank, certified the check. In this case:
   a. Certification discharged Drawer from its conditional liability to pay the check.
   b. Certification discharged Patty from her conditional liability to pay the check.
   c. When the check is presented for payment, Bank of Fruita must pay the check even if there are insufficient funds in Drawer's account to pay the check.
   d. All the above are correct.

_____ 2. Select the correct answer.
   a. Kunio has a checking account at City Bank. Kunio is under FBI investigation. In this case, the FBI cannot obtain Kunio's bank records without his consent or a valid search warrant.
   b. On January 1, Anna issued a check to Lee. On August 1, Lee presented the check to Anna's bank and the bank refused to cash it. In this case, Anna's bank breached a duty to Anna.
   c. Al died on May 1. Al's bank was informed of his death on May 4. A check issued by Al was presented for payment on May 12. In this case, the bank cannot properly pay the check.
   d. All of the above are correct.

_____ 3. Oscar issued a check to Juan. Juan negotiated the check to Laura, a holder in due course. On April 2, Oscar gave his bank an oral stop payment order on the check because the check had been issued as payment for goods that breached certain warranties (a limited defense). On April 4, Laura presented the check for payment, and Oscar's bank paid the check. In this case:
   a. The stop payment order was not binding. Stop payment orders must be made in writing.
   b. The stop payment order was not binding. A bank has three days before it must act in accordance with a stop payment order.
   c. The stop payment order was binding, but Oscar is still liable to pay the check to Laura.
   d. The stop payment order was binding, and it terminated Oscar's liability to pay the check.

_____ 4. Cody has a checking account with State Bank. Cody has $10,000 in his checking account. Cody issued a check to Paul for $5,000. Paul properly presented the check for payment to State Bank, but the bank dishonored the check. As a result, Cody incurred $100 damages and Paul incurred $50 damages. In this case:
   a. State Bank is not liable to Cody or Paul.
   b. State Bank is liable to Paul for $50 in damages, but it is not liable to Cody.
   c. State Bank is liable to Cody for $100 in damages, but it is not liable to Paul.
   d. State Bank is liable to Cody for $100 in damages, and it is liable to Paul for $50 in damages.

_____ 5. Dan's checkbook was stolen by Thief. Thief forged Dan's signature on a check and issued it to Penny, who was unaware of the forgery. Penny presented the check for payment to First Bank, the drawee bank. First Bank paid the check and charged Dan's account for the amount of the check. In this case:
   a. First Bank was entitled to charge Dan's account for the check, and it has no obligation to recredit his account.
   b. First Bank must recredit Dan's account for the amount of the check.
   c. Between First Bank and Dan, First Bank must bear any loss that may occur due to its payment of the check.
   d. b and c.

CHAPTER 33

CASE PROBLEMS

Answer the following problems, briefly explaining your answers.

1. Jeff duly issued a check to Ernie for $100. Ernie wrongfully raised the amount to $1,000, and he presented the check to Last Bank, the drawee. Last Bank paid Ernie $1,000 out of Jeff's account. Last Bank exercised reasonable care at all times. One week after receiving his bank statement, Jeff noticed the improper payment, and he informed Last Bank of the alteration.

    (a) Describe Jeff's duty to examine his bank statement and to report alterations to Last Bank. (b) Did Jeff give timely notice of the alteration? (c) For how much, if any, can Last Bank charge Jeff's account?

2. Greg has a bank account with First Federal Bank. First Federal issued Greg an ATM card that allowed him to withdraw funds from his personal bank account through the use of automated teller machines. On Monday Greg's ATM card was stolen by a thief who used it to withdraw $750 from Greg's account. Greg discovered the theft on Thursday, and he immediately informed First Federal of the theft.

    (a) What law governs Greg's rights in this case? (b) Describe a consumer's liability for the unauthorized use of a lost or stolen EFT card. (c) For how much of the unauthorized transfer is Greg liable?

3. Agrico purchased equipment from Bristol Inc. Agrico issued a payment order directing its bank, Ventura Bank, to transfer $1 million from its account to Bristol's account in Bank of Taos. Through a Federal Reserve bank, Ventura Bank erroneously issued an order directing Bank of Taos to credit Bristol's account with $2 million. Bank of Taos accepted the payment order after complying with reasonable security procedures, and it credited Bristol's account with $2 million.

    (a) What law governs this funds transfer? (b) In this case, who is the originator, the beneficiary, and the beneficiary's bank? (c) For how much can Ventura Bank charge Agrico's account? (d) Who will bear any loss caused by the improper payment?

CPA REVIEW

The following questions were given on CPA examinations. The answers for these questions are the unofficial answers prepared by the American Institute of Certified Public Accountants, Inc. (AICPA). All material is reproduced with permission of the AICPA.

___ 1. West Corp. received a check that was originally made payable to the order of one of its customers, Ted Burns. The following endorsement was written on the back of the check: Ted Burns, without recourse, for collection only. Which of the following describes the endorsement?

	Special	Restrictive
a.	Yes	Yes
b.	No	No
c.	No	Yes
d.	Yes	No

___ 2. One of the requirements to qualify as a holder of a negotiable bearer check is that the transferee must
   a. Receive the check that was originally made payable to bearer.
   b. Take the check in good faith.
   c. Give value for the check.
   d. Have possession of the check.

___ 3. In general, which of the following statements is correct concerning the priority among checks drawn on a particular account and presented to the drawee bank on a particular day?
   a. The checks may be charged to the account in any order convenient to the bank.
   b. The checks may be charged to the account in any order provided no charge creates an overdraft.
   c. The checks must be charged to the account in the order in which the checks were dated.
   d. The checks must be charged to the account in the order of lowest amount to highest amount to minimize the number of dishonored checks.

A check has the following endorsements on the back:

Paul Folk, without recourse
George Hopkins, payment guaranteed
Ann Quarry, collection guaranteed
Rachel Ott

___ 4. Which of the following conditions occurring subsequent to the endorsements would discharge all of the endorsers?
   a. Lack of notice of dishonor.
   b. Late presentment.
   c. Insolvency of the maker.
   d. Certification of the check.

5. Cobb gave Garson a signed check with the amount payable left blank. Garson was to fill in, as the amount, the price of fuel oil Garson was to deliver to Cobb at a later date. Garson estimated the amount at $700, but told Cobb it would be no more than $900. Garson did not deliver the fuel oil, but filled in the amount of $1,000 on the check. Garson then negotiated the check to Josephs in satisfaction of a $500 debt with the $500 balance paid to Garson in cash. Cobb stopped payment and Josephs is seeking to collect $1,000 from Cobb. Cobb's maximum liability to Josephs will be
   a. $0
   b. $ 500
   c. $ 900
   d. $1,000

Question 6 relates to the instrument below. Fred Anchor is the holder of the following check

```
Peter Mason          Champaign, Illinois     4/30 1990
Pay to the order of Mary Nix or bearer $93.00
Ninety-Three ------------------------------------Dollars
Second Bank 0453-0978
Peter Mason
```

The check is endorsed on the back as follows:
Mary Nix, Pay to John Jacobs
Mark Harris
John Jacobs, (without recourse)

6. Jacobs gave the check to his son as a gift, who transferred it to Anchor for $78.00. Which of the following statements is correct?
   a. The unqualified endorsement of Jacobs was necessary in order to negotiate the check to his son.
   b. Nix's endorsement was required to negotiate the check to any subsequent holder.
   c. Anchor does not qualify as a holder because less than full consideration was given for the check.
   d. The check is bearer paper in Jacobs' son's hands.

7. For which of the following negotiable instruments is a bank not an acceptor?
   a. Cashier's check.
   b. Certified check.
   c. Certificate of deposit.
   d. Bank acceptance.

8. Blare bought a house and provided the required funds in the form of a certified check from a bank. Which of the following statements correctly describes the legal liability of Blare and the bank?
   a. The bank has accepted; therefore, Blare is without liability.
   b. The bank has not accepted; therefore, Blare has primary liability.
   c. The bank has accepted, but Blare has secondary liability.
   d. The bank has not accepted, but Blare has secondary liability.

CHAPTER 34
SECURED TRANSACTIONS IN PERSONAL PROPERTY
CHAPTER OUTLINE

A. **GENERAL PRINCIPLES**

1. **DEFINITIONS**

   ▸ A secured transaction is created when a buyer or borrower (debtor) grants a seller or lender (creditor or secured party) a security interest in personal property (collateral). ▸ A security interest allows a creditor to repossess and sell collateral if a debtor fails to pay a secured debt. ▸ A purchase money security interest secures the unpaid price for collateral or a loan used to buy the collateral.

2. **CREATION OF A SECURITY INTEREST (ATTACHMENT)**

   A security interest is created and enforceable ("attaches") when the following requirements are met: (1) there is a security agreement; (2) creditor gives value (lends money to debtor or sells goods to debtor on credit); and (3) debtor has rights in the collateral (debtor owns or leases the collateral).

3. **THE SECURITY AGREEMENT**

   ▸ A security agreement grants a security interest to a creditor. The agreement must identify the parties, describe the collateral and the debt that is secured, and express an intent to create a security interest. ▸ A security agreement must be written and signed by the debtor if the creditor does not have possession of collateral. An oral agreement will suffice if the creditor has possession of collateral.

4. **FUTURE TRANSACTIONS**

   ▸ A debtor may: (1) grant a security interest to secure future loans; and (2) grant a security interest in property a debtor may later acquire, thereby creating a "floating lien." The security interest attaches when the future credit is given or when a debtor gets the property. ▸ A security interest automatically attaches to proceeds from a sale of collateral. ▸ Liens in after-acquired consumer goods are restricted.

5. **CLASSIFICATION OF TANGIBLE COLLATERAL (GOODS)**

   ▸ *Consumer goods*: goods bought for personal, household, or family use. ▸ *Equipment*: goods bought for use in business. ▸ *Inventory*: goods bought for sale or lease; raw materials; work in process; and supplies used in a business. ▸ *Farm products*: crops, livestock, and supplies produced or used in a farming operation. ▸ A buyer's primary intended use determines how to classify collateral.

6. **PERFECTION OF SECURITY INTEREST (EFFECT OF ATTACHMENT & PERFECTION)**

   - *Attachment*: Once a security interest attaches, a secured party has the right *as against the debtor* to repossess and sell the collateral if the debtor defaults, even if the security interest is not perfected.
   - *Perfection*: A perfected security interest has a superior right to collateral as against the debtor, most subsequent creditors with security interests in collateral, and most buyers of the collateral.

7. **HOW PERFECTION IS OBTAINED (IN ADDITION TO FILING A FINANCING STATEMENT)**

   - *Creditor's possession*: Creditor takes possession of any tangible collateral (such as inventory).
   - *Consumer goods*: A purchase money security interest in consumer goods is automatically perfected.
   - *Motor vehicles*: In most states, a security interest in noninventory collateral for which a title is issued (such as a car) can be perfected *only* by having the lien stated on the certificate of title.

8. **THE FINANCING STATEMENT (PERFECTION BY FILING FINANCING STATEMENT)**

    GENERAL RULE.   Appropriate filing of a financing statement signed by a debtor perfects a security interest in any collateral except noninventory motor vehicles and certain documents (such as stock).
    LIMITATION.   A statement that does not adequately describe collateral (does not put third party on notice that there may be a lien) or that is filed in the wrong office does not perfect an interest.

9. **LOSS OF PERFECTION**

    - *Possessed collateral*: Perfection by possession is lost if a creditor returns collateral to the debtor.
    - *Consumer goods*: Perfection may be lost by resale of goods to a consumer. (See Section 10)
    - *Lapse of time*: Perfection obtained by filing a financing statement expires after five years unless a continuation statement is filed within six months prior to the expiration of a current statement.
    - *Removal from state*: In most cases, perfection is lost if collateral is removed to another state unless a creditor files a financing statement in the new state within four months after removal.
    - *Motor vehicles*: Perfection is lost if a new title is issued and the lien is not stated on the title.

B. **SECURED CREDIT SALES**

10. **CREDIT SALE OF CONSUMER GOODS**

    - *Attachment*: Security agreement must usually be written. For other rules see Sections 2-4.
    - *Perfection*: A security interest in consumer goods may be perfected: (1) by filing a financing statement; or (2) automatically (doing nothing) for a purchase money security interest.
    - *Priorities*: ▸ A creditor with a perfected interest has a superior right to collateral over a debtor and most third parties. ▸ But, a security interest in consumer goods that is perfected *without filing a financing statement* is inferior to rights of a subsequent buyer of the collateral who bought it: (1) without knowledge of the interest; (2) for value; and (3) for personal, family, or household use.

11. **CREDIT SALE OF INVENTORY**

    - *Attachment*: Security interest in inventory is created in the manner discussed in Sections 2-4.
    - *Perfection*: Security interest in inventory is perfected by either (1) filing a financing statement with an appropriate governmental office; or (2) possession of collateral by the secured party.
    - *Priorities*: See the general rules and exceptions discussed in Sections 19-22.
    - *Use of goods*: Debtor can sell or commingle collateral and need not replace inventory that is sold.

12. **CREDIT SALE OF EQUIPMENT**

    Most rules regarding security interests in inventory apply to security interests in equipment.

C. **SECURED LOANS**

13. **POSSESSORY TRANSACTION**

    ▸ Loans may be secured by a pledge, i.e., creditor (pledgee) takes possession of collateral (tangible goods or documents such as stock) of debtor (pledgor). ▸ Possession of collateral perfects interest.

14. **NONPOSSESSORY TRANSACTION**

    Loans may be secured by a security interest in most types of collateral without a creditor's taking possession of collateral. The general rules for attachment and perfection apply. (See Sections 2-9)

D. **RIGHTS OF PARTIES BEFORE DEFAULT**

15. **STATUS OF CREDITOR BEFORE (DEBTOR'S) DEFAULT**

    Prior to default, a creditor has rights determined by laws relating to the underlying transaction.

16. **STATUS OF DEBTOR BEFORE (DEBTOR'S) DEFAULT**

    Prior to default, a debtor has rights determined by laws relating to the underlying transaction.

17. **STATEMENT OF ACCOUNT**

    A debtor may request a creditor to approve (or correct) a written statement of the debtor's account.

18. **TERMINATION STATEMENT**

    When the debt is paid, a debtor can request a creditor to furnish a termination statement.

E. **PRIORITIES**

   19. **CONFLICTING INTERESTS (GENERAL PRIORITY RULES)**
       - *Two unperfected security interests*: First security interest to attach wins.
       - *One perfected and one unperfected security interest*: Perfected security interest wins.
       - *Two perfected security interests*: First security interest to attach, file, or be perfected wins.

   20. **PURCHASE MONEY SECURITY INTEREST (EXCEPTION TO GENERAL RULES)**

       ▸ *Inventory*: A perfected purchase money security interest in inventory wins over other creditors (even prior perfected liens) if (1) the purchase money security is perfected before a debtor receives collateral and (2) notice is given to prior secured parties. ▸ *Other collateral*: Same exception, except purchase money security only needs to be perfected within ten days after debtor receives collateral.

   21. **STATUS OF REPAIR OR STORAGE LIEN (POSSIBLE EXCEPTION TO GENERAL RULE)**

       One who repairs or stores goods has a lien on the goods to secure payment. This lien wins over a perfected security interest in the goods unless the lien is created by a statute that states otherwise.

   22. **STATUS OF BUYER OF COLLATERAL FROM DEBTOR**
       - *Unperfected security interest*: Buyer of collateral takes it subject to a prior unperfected security interest unless the buyer (1) paid value and (2) the buyer did not know of the security interest.
       - *Perfected security interest*: Buyer of collateral takes it subject to prior perfected interest unless a creditor consents to sale or buyer bought inventory from debtor in ordinary course of business.
       - *Resale of consumer goods*: See Section 10.

F. **RIGHTS OF PARTIES AFTER DEFAULT**

   23. **CREDITOR'S POSSESSION AND DISPOSITION OF COLLATERAL**
       - *Repossession*: On a debtor's default a creditor can use self-help to repossess collateral. A court order is not needed unless repossession cannot be done without committing a breach of the peace.
       - *Disposition of collateral*: ▸ Creditor may sell or lease collateral to obtain payment. ▸ Collateral may be sold at private or public sale; time and terms of sale must be commercially reasonable.

   24. **CREDITOR'S RETENTION OF COLLATERAL**

       With two exceptions, a creditor can keep collateral as payment in full of a secured debt.

   25. **DEBTOR'S RIGHT OF REDEMPTION**

       Debtor may redeem (recover) collateral at any time before a creditor has disposed of or contracted to sell the collateral. To redeem, debtor must pay the entire debt, plus any legal costs or expenses.

   26. **DISPOSITION OF COLLATERAL**

       With a few exceptions, reasonable notice of sale (which may be oral) must be given to a debtor.

   27. **POSTDISPOSITION ACCOUNTING**

       ▸ Proceeds from disposition of collateral are applied in this order: (1) expenses of disposing of collateral; (2) payment of the secured debt owed to the creditor; and (3) payment of debts owed to other parties with security interests in the collateral. ▸ A debtor is liable for any unpaid deficiency.

REVIEW OF TERMS AND PHRASES

Select the term or phrase that best matches a statement or definition stated below. Each term or phrase is the best match for only one statement or definition.

Terms and Phrases

a. Attachment
b. Collateral
c. Consumer goods
d. Continuation statement
e. Equipment
f. Farm products
g. Financing statement
h. Floating lien
i. Inventory
j. Perfected security interest
k. Pledge
l. Proceeds
m. Purchase money security interest
n. Security agreement
o. Termination statement

Statements and Definitions

__h__ 1. Security interest that attaches to after-acquired goods of a debtor.

__f__ 2. Crops, livestock, and supplies used or produced in farming operations.

__c__ 3. Goods used or bought primarily for personal, family, or household purposes.

__b__ 4. Property that is subject to a security interest.

__g__ 5. Document that is filed with an appropriate government office, thereby giving third parties notice of a security interest and perfecting a security interest in many kinds of collateral.

__d__ 6. Document that is filed to continue perfection of a security interest for an additional five years.

__e__ 7. Goods used or bought primarily for use in a business.

__o__ 8. Statement filed to give notice of payment of a secured debt and termination of a security interest.

__i__ 9. Goods held primarily for sale or lease by a debtor.

__n__ 10. Agreement signed by debtor that grants a secured party a security interest in described collateral.

__m__ 11. Security interest that secures repayment of either the unpaid purchase price for collateral or a loan that was used to purchase the collateral.

__j__ 12. Security interest that gives a creditor priority to collateral over most creditors who subsequently acquire a security interest in the collateral or buyers who subsequently purchase the collateral.

__a__ 13. Creation of an enforceable security interest in collateral.

__k__ 14. Secured transaction pursuant to which a creditor takes possession of the collateral.

__l__ 15. Cash, property, and other value received from a debtor's sale or other disposition of collateral.

REVIEW OF CONCEPTS

Write **T** if the statement is true, write **F** if it is false.

__T__ 1. Article 9 of the UCC governs secured transactions in personal property.

__T__ 2. A security agreement may be oral if the secured party retains possession of the collateral.

__T__ 3. Collateral is classified according to the debtor's primary intended use of the collateral.

__F__ 4. Only creditors with a perfected security interest can repossess collateral upon a debtor's default.

__T__ 5. In general, a perfected security interest gives a secured party a superior right to collateral over most subsequent security interests in the collateral and most buyers of the collateral.

__F__ 6. If a security interest is perfected in one state and the collateral is then moved to another state, nothing is required to be filed in the second state to continue perfection of the security interest.

__F__ 7. In most states, if a title is issued for a motor vehicle, a creditor can perfect a security interest in a noninventory motor vehicle only by filing a financing statement.

__F__ 8. Article 9 prohibits a creditor from taking a floating lien in after-acquired inventory.

__F__ 9. A financing statement must be signed by a debtor, but it need not describe the collateral.

__T__ 10. If a financing statement is filed in the wrong office, it does not perfect a security interest.

__F__ 11. Filing a financing statement perfects a security interest for ten years. [5]

__F__ 12. If two creditors each have an unperfected security interest in the same collateral, then each creditor has priority to one-half of the collateral.

__T__ 13. A perfected a security interest in Debtor's after-acquired equipment. B later sold new equipment to Debtor on credit. B took a purchase money security interest in the equipment, B perfected this interest two days after Debtor received the equipment, and B gave A proper notice of its interest. In this case, B's security interest in the new equipment has priority over A's security interest.

__F__ 14. Al sold equipment to Dan on credit. Dan properly granted Al a security interest in the equipment to secure the unpaid price. Al filed a financing statement, perfecting the security interest. Dan sold the equipment to Jim. In this case, Jim takes the equipment free from Al's security interest.

__F__ 15. Unless otherwise agreed, a secured party must always resell or otherwise dispose of collateral.

REVIEW OF CHAPTER - APPLICATION OF CONCEPTS

MULTIPLE CHOICE QUESTIONS

__a__ 1. IKR Finance loaned $1,000 to Debtor. Debtor agreed to repay the $1,000 in one year, and Debtor signed a written security agreement granting IKR a security interest in an item of equipment owned by Debtor to secure this debt. IKR did not perfect the security interest. In this case:
   a. The security interest is attached. If Debtor defaults, IKR can repossess and sell the collateral.
   b. The security interest has not attached because IKR does not have possession of the collateral.
   c. The security interest has not attached because IKR did not give value.
   d. The security interest has not attached because IKR failed to perfect the security interest.

__c__ 2. Select the collateral that is consumer goods:
   a. Debtor grants a security interest in an oven Debtor intends to use in Debtor's restaurant.
   b. Debtor grants a security interest in a stereo that Debtor intends to sell in Debtor's store.
   c. Debtor grants a security interest in a table saw that Debtor intends to use at home.
   d. Debtor grants a security interest in Debtor's corn crop that is growing on Debtor's farm.

___d___ 3. Spokes Inc. sold a bike to Dee on credit for Dee's personal use. Dee granted Spokes a security interest in the bike to secure payment of the unpaid purchase price. Spokes did not file a financing statement. Under these facts:
   a. Spokes' security interest in the bike is perfected.
   b. If Dee sells the bike to Phil for his personal use, Phil pays value, and Phil does not know of the security interest, then Phil will take the bike free from Spokes' security interest.
   c. If a repair shop obtains a *common law* lien on the bike for unpaid repair charges, Spokes' security interest will have priority over the common law lien.
   d. a and b.

___c___ 4. Leo lent $10,000 to B&B, a tire dealer. B&B signed a security agreement granting Leo a security interest in B&B's existing tire inventory. Leo did nothing to perfect this security interest, and B&B kept possession of the inventory. Under these facts:
   a. Leo's security interest is perfected; a security interest in inventory is automatically perfected.
   b. Leo's security interest is unperfected; Leo cannot repossess the inventory if B&B defaults.
   c. Leo's security interest is unperfected; Leo's security interest has priority over a subsequent unperfected security interest that another creditor may take in the inventory.
   d. Leo's security interest is unperfected; Leo's security interest has priority over a subsequent perfected security interest that another creditor may take in the inventory.

___d___ 5. On May 1, First Bank perfected a security interest in Debtor's inventory. On June 1, Bob bought an item of the secured inventory from Debtor for cash in the ordinary course of business. On July 1, Second Bank acquired a perfected security interest in Debtor's same inventory. In this case:
   a. Bob took the item of inventory subject to First Bank's security interest.
   b. First Bank has a security interest in the proceeds received from the sale of inventory to Bob.
   c. First Bank's security interest has priority over Second Bank's security interest.
   d. b and c.

CASE PROBLEM

Answer the following problem, briefly explaining your answer.

Acme Loans has a perfected security interest in Debtor's inventory to secure repayment of a $50,000 loan. Debtor has defaulted on three $1,000 monthly payments, and Acme has accelerated the entire debt.

(a) Can Acme repossess the inventory without obtaining a court order to do so?
(b) Can Acme commit a breach of the peace if necessary to repossess the inventory?
(c) If Acme repossesses the inventory, briefly describe the procedure for selling the collateral.
(d) Can Debtor redeem the collateral?
(e) How are proceeds from the sale to be applied? Would Debtor be liable for any deficiency?

CPA REVIEW

The following questions were given on CPA examinations. The answers for these questions are the unofficial answers prepared by the American Institute of Certified Public Accountants, Inc. (AICPA). All material is reproduced with permission of the AICPA.

____ 1. Under the Secured Transactions Article of the UCC, which of the following requirements is necessary to have a security interest attach?

	Debtor has rights in the collateral	Proper filing of a security agreement	Value given by the creditor
a.	Yes	Yes	Yes
b.	Yes	Yes	No
c.	Yes	No	Yes
d.	No	Yes	Yes

____ 2. Under the Secured Transactions Article of the UCC, which of the following purchasers will own consumer goods free of a perfected security interest in the goods?
   a. A merchant who purchases the goods for resale.
   b. A merchant who purchases the goods for use in its business.
   c. A consumer who purchases the goods from a consumer purchaser who gave the security interest.
   d. A consumer who purchases the goods in the ordinary course of business.

____ 3. Under the Secured Transactions Article of the UCC, what would be the order of priority for the following security interests in consumer goods?
   I. Financing agreement filed on April 1.
   II. Possession of the collateral by a creditor on April 10.
   III. Financing agreement perfected on April 15.
   a. I, II, III.
   b. II, I, III.
   c. II, III, I.
   d. III, II, I.

____ 4. Under the Secured Transactions Article of the UCC, which of the following remedies is available to a secured creditor when a debtor fails to make a payment when due?

	Proceed against the collateral	Obtain a general judgment against the debtor
a.	Yes	Yes
b.	Yes	No
c.	No	Yes
d.	No	No

CHAPTER 34

____ 5. Roth and Dixon both claim a security interest in the same collateral. Roth's security interest attached on January 1, 1989, and was perfected by filing on March 1, 1989. Dixon's security interest attached on February 1, 1989, and was perfected on April 1, 1989, by taking possession of the collateral. Which statement is correct?
   a. Roth's security interest has priority because Roth perfected before Dixon perfected.
   b. Dixon's security interest has priority because Dixon's interest attached before Roth's interest was perfected.
   c. Roth's security interest has priority because Roth's security interest attached before Dixon's security interest attached.
   d. Dixon's security interest has priority because Dixon is in possession of the collateral.

____ 6. Winslow Co., which is in the business of selling furniture, borrowed $60,000 from Pine Bank. Winslow executed a promissory note for that amount and used all of its accounts receivable as collateral for the loan. Winslow executed a security agreement that described the collateral. Winslow did not file a financing statement. Which of the following statements best describes this transaction?
   a. Perfection of the security interest occurred even though Winslow did not file a financing statement.
   b. Perfection of the security interest occurred by Pine having an interest in accounts receivable.
   c. Attachment of the security interest did not occur because Winslow failed to file a financing statement.
   d. Attachment of the security interest occurred when the loan was made and Winslow executed the security agreement.

____ 7. On July 8, Ace, a refrigerator wholesaler, purchased 50 refrigerators. This comprised Ace's entire inventory and was financed under an agreement with Rome Bank that gave Rome a security interest in all refrigerators on Ace's premises, all future acquired refrigerators, and the proceeds of sales. On July 12, Rome filed a financing statement that adequately identified the collateral. On August 15, Ace sold one refrigerator to Cray for personal use and four refrigerators to Zone Co. for its business. Which of the following statements is correct?
   a. The refrigerators sold to Zone will be subject to Rome's security interest.
   b. The refrigerator sold to Cray will not be subject to Rome's security interest.
   c. The security interest does not include the proceeds from the sale of the refrigerators to Zone.
   d. The security interest may not cover after-acquired property even if the parties agree.

____ 8. Drew bought a computer for personal use from Hale Corp. for $3,000. Drew paid $2,000 in cash and signed a security agreement for the balance. Hale properly filed the security agreement. Drew defaulted in paying the balance of the purchase price. Hale asked Drew to pay the balance. When Drew refused, Hale peacefully repossessed the computer. Under the UCC Secured Transactions Article, which of the following remedies will Hale have?
   a. Obtain a deficiency judgment against Drew for the amount owed.
   b. Sell the computer and retain any surplus over the amount owed.
   c. Retain the computer over Drew's objection.
   d. Sell the computer without notifying Drew.

CHAPTER 35
OTHER SECURITY DEVICES

CHAPTER OUTLINE

A. SURETYSHIP AND GUARANTY

1. DEFINITIONS

GENERAL RULE. A person may contractually agree to be responsible for the debt or obligation of another person. These agreements may take several forms including:

- *Suretyship*: ▸ A suretyship is a three-way contract by which a third party (surety) agrees to be *primarily liable* to a creditor (obligee) for the debt of another (principal debtor; principal; debtor). ▸ If the debtor fails to pay, the creditor can demand performance immediately from the surety without first trying to collect from the debtor. ▸ Example: Pam (principal) borrowed $20,000 from Creditor, and Stuart (surety) agreed to be surety. Payment is due May 1. On May 1, Creditor can demand payment from Pam or Stuart.
- *Guaranty*: ▸ A guaranty is a contract whereby a third party (guarantor) agrees to be *secondarily liable* for an obligation of a principal debtor if the debtor defaults. ▸ A creditor must first try to collect from a debtor before proceeding against a guarantor. ▸ Example: Paul (principal) bought a plane from Seller on credit, and Gary (guarantor) guaranteed the debt. When payment is due, Seller must try to collect from Paul. If Paul fails to pay, Seller can demand payment from Gary.
- *Absolute guaranty*: ▸ An absolute guaranty is a special type of guaranty by which a guarantor becomes *primarily liable* for an obligation of the debtor. ▸ An absolute guaranty generally creates the same obligations as a suretyship. ▸ A guaranty of payment is an absolute guaranty.

STUDY HINT. A suretyship is indicated if a third party co-signs a contract between a debtor and a creditor without indicating that the third party intends to only guarantee the debtor's performance.

2. INDEMNITY CONTRACT DISTINGUISHED

▸ An indemnity contract is an agreement, supported by consideration, whereby a party agrees to pay for a specified loss of another. ▸ Example: insurance contract. ▸ An indemnity contract is not a suretyship or a guaranty.

3. CREATION OF THE RELATION

Contract principles apply to suretyship, guaranty, and indemnity contracts. Rules include:

- *Offer and acceptance*: In creating a contract, there generally must be a definite offer and a definite acceptance. A creditor usually must notify a guarantor of the creditor's acceptance.
- *Statute of frauds*: ▸ In most states guaranty contracts must be in writing to be enforceable unless a guaranty is intended to primarily benefit the guarantor and not the debtor. ▸ Ordinarily, surety or indemnity contracts do not have to be written unless this is specifically required by statute.
- *Consideration*: ▸ When the original contract and the guaranty contract are made at the same time, the consideration under the original contract supports both contracts. ▸ If a guaranty contract is made after the original contract, a creditor must give the guarantor new consideration.

4. RIGHTS OF SURETIES

Sureties enjoy rights that help them to avoid losses in certain situations. These rights include:

- **Exoneration**: ▸ A surety may be released from liability that arises due to the creditor's improper action. ▸ Example: A surety may be released from liability if a creditor cannot collect from a debtor because the creditor inexcusably failed to take timely action to collect from the debtor.
- **Subrogation**: ▸ A surety that makes payment to a creditor acquires the creditor's claim and legal rights against the principal debtor. The surety may then collect the debt from the debtor. ▸ Example: Dan failed to pay a $5,000 debt to Chris, and Surety paid the debt. Surety is now subrogated to Chris' $5,000 claim, and Surety can sue Dan to collect this sum.
- **Indemnity**: ▸ A surety that has paid a creditor is entitled to reimbursement from the principal debtor for the amount paid. ▸ Example: Carlos defaulted on a debt and Surety paid the debt. Surety is entitled to be repaid by Carlos.
- **Contribution**: ▸ If more than one surety agrees to be liable for a debt, each surety is liable to the creditor for the entire debt until it has been paid in full. ▸ But, unless otherwise agreed, cosureties must pay an equal share of a debt. Consequently, a cosurety who pays a debt may seek contribution (reimbursement) from the other sureties to the extent that they failed to pay their share of the debt. ▸ Example: Bob and Mary are cosureties of a $1,000 debt owed by Dick. When Dick failed to pay, Bob paid the entire debt. Bob can recover $500 from Mary.

5. DEFENSES OF SURETIES

In certain situations, a surety may be able to avoid liability to a creditor by asserting either ordinary contract defenses or special defenses available to sureties.

(a) Ordinary contract defenses

GENERAL RULE. ▸ A surety may assert against a creditor any contract defense that a contracting party could ordinarily raise. Potential contract defenses include: (1) lack of contractual capacity; (2) failure of consideration; and (3) fraud or concealment of material facts by a creditor. ▸ Example: Jacqueline bought a TV on credit and Sara, a minor, agreed to be a surety for the debt. Sara can assert her minority in order to avoid paying this debt.

LIMITATION. Fraud that is committed by a debtor without the knowledge or participation of the creditor does not ordinarily release a surety.

STUDY HINT. At common law, a creditor did not have to voluntarily disclose important information to a surety. But, a growing modern view now requires disclosure in certain situations.

(b) Suretyship defenses

GENERAL RULE. A surety may avoid liability by raising special defenses that are available to sureties. These defenses include: (1) the original obligation is invalid (for example, the original contract is illegal and void); (2) the debtor has been discharged (for example, the debt has been paid); and (3) the original contract was materially modified without the surety's consent.

STUDY HINT. If an original obligation is materially modified to a surety's or guarantor's detriment and without their consent, the surety or guarantor is typically released from liability.

B. LETTERS OF CREDIT

A letter of credit is an agreement by which one party agrees, in advance, to pay drafts drawn by the beneficiary of the letter. A letter of credit is a (1) financing arrangement that enables a debtor to know how much money will be provided by the issuer of the letter of credit, and (2) a security device that assures a creditor regarding the sum of money it can legally demand from the letter of credit issuer.

6. DEFINITION

GENERAL RULES. ▸ A letter of credit is a legal commitment by the issuer of the letter to pay a stated sum of money to a beneficiary when specific conditions are met. ▸ A letter-of-credit transaction generally involves three contracts: (1) an agreement between the issuer and the issuer's customer to issue the letter of credit; (2) the letter of credit that obligates the issuer to pay a beneficiary; and (3) the underlying agreement between the issuer's customer and the beneficiary that typically gives rise to the obligation that is to be satisfied by payments made by the issuer.

LIMITATION. Consideration is not required to make or modify a letter of credit.

STUDY HINTS. ▸ A letter-of-credit issuer is the principal debtor on the letter of credit, and the letter of credit and its duties are independent of other agreements. Thus, a surety cannot refuse to pay a creditor because the debtor defrauded the surety. ▸ A beneficiary can enforce a letter of credit even if a beneficiary did not rely upon the letter of credit or give the issuer consideration for the letter of credit.

7. PARTIES

Parties to a letter-of-credit transaction include: (1) an issuer (commonly a bank) that is obligated to pay the letter of credit; (2) the issuer's customer who obtained issuance of the letter of credit; (3) a beneficiary who is entitled to receive payment; and (4) an advising bank.

8. DURATION

GENERAL RULE. A letter of credit continues for the time specified in the agreement or until the maximum amount of money to be paid pursuant to the letter of credit is paid by the issuer.

LIMITATION. Unless otherwise stated in a letter of credit, the letter of credit cannot be revoked or modified by the issuer or the issuer's customer without the consent of the beneficiary.

9. FORM

GENERAL RULES. ▸ A letter of credit must (1) be in writing and (2) be signed by the issuer. ▸ An instrument is presumed to be a letter of credit if it is credit issued by: (1) a bank that requires a documentary draft or documentary demand for payment as a condition for payment; or (2) someone other than a bank who requires that documents of title be furnished with a demand for payment.

LIMITATION. If an instrument does not require the foregoing documentary evidence, it is not a letter of credit unless the instrument is conspicuously stated to be a letter of credit.

10. DUTY OF ISSUER

GENERAL RULE. Provided the conditions specified in a letter of credit are met, an issuer must honor drafts properly drawn on the letter or be liable for breaching the contract with its customer.

LIMITATION. An issuer is responsible for assuring that a beneficiary has given the issuer all required documents before paying on the letter of credit, and an issuer cannot obtain reimbursement if it fails to do so. But, an issuer is not required to verify other matters relating to the transaction.

11. REIMBURSEMENT OF ISSUER

GENERAL RULE. An issuer of a letter of credit may obtain reimbursement from its customer for any proper payments made by the issuer pursuant to the letter of credit.

LIMITATION. An issuer cannot obtain reimbursement for: (1) improper payments; (2) payments that exceed the amount of the letter of credit; or (3) payments made after the letter of credit expired.

REVIEW OF TERMS AND PHRASES

Select the term or phrase that best matches a statement or definition stated below. Each term or phrase is the best match for only one statement or definition.

Terms and Phrases

a. Absolute guaranty
b. Beneficiary
c. Contribution
d. Creditor (obligee)
e. Exoneration
f. Guarantor
g. Guaranty contract
h. Indemnity contract
i. Letter of credit
j. Principal debtor
k. Subrogation
l. Suretyship contract

Statements and Definitions

__b__ 1. Person entitled to demand payment from an issuer of a letter of credit.

__a__ 2. Type of guaranty similar to a suretyship by which a guarantor incurs primary liability for a debt.

__i__ 3. Contract by which an issuer agrees to pay drafts issued by a beneficiary if certain specified conditions are met.

__c__ 4. Right of a cosurety to seek reimbursement from other sureties for their proportionate share of a debt that was paid by the cosurety.

__k__ 5. Right of a surety to acquire and enforce a creditor's claim and legal rights against a debtor.

__l__ 6. Three-way contract by which a party agrees to be primarily liable to a creditor for another's debt.

__h__ 7. Agreement supported by consideration by which a party agrees to pay for a specified loss.

__j__ 8. Person who incurs the original liability to pay a debt or to perform an obligation.

__e__ 9. Right of a surety to be released from liability for a loss that is caused by a creditor's wrongful failure to take timely action against the principal debtor.

__g__ 10. Contract by which a third party agrees to be secondarily liable for a debt or obligation of another.

__d__ 11. Person who is owed a debt that is subject to a guaranty or suretyship contract.

__f__ 12. Person who agrees to be secondarily liable for the debt or obligation of another.

REVIEW OF CONCEPTS

Write **T** if the statement is true, write **F** if it is false.

__T__ 1. A surety has primary liability for the obligation of the principal debtor.

__T__ 2. On a debtor's default, a creditor can collect immediately from the debtor or the debtor's surety.

__T__ 3. Under a typical (limited) guaranty contract, a creditor must attempt to collect payment from the principal debtor before the creditor can require payment by the guarantor.

__F__ 4. The general rules of contract law do not apply to suretyship contracts.

T 5. Suretyship contracts do not need to be in writing unless this is required by a special statute.

T 6. If a guaranty is made after and independent from the original contract, new consideration must be given for the guaranty in order to make the guaranty legally enforceable.

T 7. A surety who pays a debtor's obligation has a right to be indemnified (reimbursed) by the debtor.

F 8. Sureties can only assert special suretyship defenses; sureties are not entitled to assert ordinary contract defenses that the surety may have against the creditor.

T 9. In general, a guarantor's liability for an obligation may be terminated if the obligation is materially modified without the guarantor's consent.

F 10. A surety can be held liable for an obligation even if it arises out of an invalid, illegal contract.

F 11. A letter of credit involves only a single transaction, a contract between an issuer and its customer.

F 12. A beneficiary cannot enforce a letter of credit unless the beneficiary paid consideration to the issuer of the letter of credit.

T 13. A letter of credit must be in writing and it must be signed by the issuer.

F 14. An issuer of a letter of credit is obligated to verify the accuracy of statements made in documents that are submitted by a beneficiary for the purpose of obtaining payment of the letter of credit.

15. An issuer of a letter of credit is not entitled to reimbursement by the issuer's customer for payments that exceed the amount of the letter of credit.

REVIEW OF CHAPTER - APPLICATION OF CONCEPTS

MULTIPLE CHOICE QUESTIONS

a 1. Tasha wanted to buy a VCR on credit from Seller. In exchange for Seller's agreement to sell the VCR to Tasha, Annette agreed to guarantee Tasha's obligation for the purchase price. Under these facts:
   a. A suretyship contract is created.
   b. An indemnity contract is created.
   c. Annette's agreement to guarantee Tasha's obligation is not enforceable because Seller did not give any consideration to Annette.
   d. Annette's agreement to guarantee Tasha's obligation is not enforceable unless it is in writing.

c 2. Dina bought a car on credit from Creditor for $5,000. This debt is secured by a lien on the car. Samuel is the surety for this debt. Dina stopped paying and she was preparing to sell the car and abscond with the proceeds. Samuel notified Creditor of these facts, but Creditor failed to act for nine months enabling Dina to sell the car. Had Creditor acted, Samuel would have incurred no liability. Creditor sued Samuel as surety. What defense does Samuel have against Creditor?
   a. Defense of contribution.
   b. Defense of subrogation.
   c. Defense of exoneration.
   d. Samuel does not have any defense against Creditor.

CHAPTER 35   299

~~b~~ d 3. Lender agreed to loan $25,000 to Art, and Art's warehouse was collateral for the loan. To induce Jesse to be a surety for this loan, Lender altered documents given to Jesse to hide the fact that the warehouse had been condemned and was to be demolished. Jesse relied on these fraudulent documents and agreed to be surety. Unknown to Lender, Art also misrepresented his financial condition to Jesse. Art failed to repay the loan, the warehouse was demolished, and Lender sued Jesse as surety. What defense does Jesse have *against Lender*?
   a. Suretyships are illegal and unenforceable.
   b. Lender defrauded Jesse.
   c. Art defrauded Jesse.
   d. Jesse does not have any defense against Lender.

c 4. Glaxco contracted to buy $1 million of china from Seller on credit. Key S&L issued a letter of credit agreeing to pay Seller $250,000 upon receipt of documents evidencing delivery of the china to Glaxco. Glaxco failed to pay for the china, and Seller demanded payment of the entire price from Key S&L. Under these facts:
   a. Key S&L must pay $1 million to Seller.
   b. Key S&L must pay $250,000 immediately upon demand by Seller.
   c. Key S&L must pay $250,000 to Seller after it receives the required documents.
   d. Key S&L must not pay anything to Seller until Key S&L receives the required documents and Key S&L inspects the china to assure that Seller properly performed the contract.

a 5. Lex contracted to build a car wash for Owner. Bank issued a letter of credit authorizing Owner to issue drafts against the letter for up to $50,000 if Lex defaulted and Owner had to pay others to complete the contract. The letter was silent regarding revocation or modification. Without Owner's consent, Bank later unilaterally modified the letter to exclude any duty to pay due to a default resulting from a labor dispute. Subsequently, a labor dispute caused Lex to default, Owner paid another builder $50,000 to complete the contract, and Owner issued a $50,000 draft against the letter. In this case:
   a. Bank must pay $50,000 to Owner, and Bank can obtain reimbursement of this sum from Lex.
   b. Bank must pay $50,000 to Owner, and Bank cannot obtain reimbursement from Lex.
   c. Bank is not liable to Owner because it modified the letter of credit eliminating its liability.
   d. Bank can unilaterally revoke the letter of credit avoiding any liability to Owner.

CASE PROBLEM

David, Tom, and Janet formed a corporation. Last Bank loaned $75,000 to the corporation. David, Tom, and Janet agreed to be cosureties for the loan. The corporation has defaulted on the loan, and Last Bank plans to sue Janet for payment of the loan.

(a) Must Last Bank attempt to collect payment from the corporation before it can demand payment from the co-sureties? (b) Can Last Bank collect the full amount of the loan from Janet? (c) If Janet pays the loan, does she have a right to contribution from David and Tom? If so, how much can Janet recover from David and Tom? (d) Does Janet have a legal right against the corporation if she pays the loan?

CPA REVIEW

The following questions were given on past CPA examinations. The answers for these questions are the unofficial answers prepared by the American Institute of Certified Public Accountants, Inc. (AICPA). All material is reproduced with permission of the AICPA.

____ 1. Green was unable to repay a loan from State Bank when due. State refused to renew the loan unless Green provided an acceptable surety. Green asked Royal, a friend, to act as surety on the loan. To induce Royal to agree to become a surety, Green fraudulently represented Green's financial condition and promised Royal discounts on merchandise sold at Green's store. Royal agreed to act as surety and the loan was renewed. Later, Green's obligation to State was discharged in Green's bankruptcy. State wants to hold Royal liable. Royal may avoid liability
   a. If Royal can show that State was aware of the fraudulent representations.
   b. If Royal was an uncompensated surety.
   c. Because the discharge in bankruptcy will prevent Royal from having a right of reimbursement.
   d. Because the arrangement was void at the inception.

____ 2. Wright cosigned King's loan from Ace Bank. Which of the following events would release Wright from the obligation to pay the loan?
   a. Ace seeking payment of the loan only from Wright.
   b. King is granted a discharge in bankruptcy.
   c. Ace is paid in full by King's spouse.
   d. King is adjudicated mentally incompetent.

____ 3. Which of the following defenses would a surety be able to assert successfully to limit the surety's liability to a creditor?
   a. A discharge in bankruptcy of the principal debtor.
   b. A personal defense the principal debtor has against the creditor.
   c. The incapacity of the surety.
   d. The incapacity of the principal debtor.

____ 4. Which of the following rights does a surety have?

	Right to compel the creditor to proceed against principal debtor	Right to compel the creditor to collect from the principal debtor's collateral
a.	Yes	Yes
b.	Yes	No
c.	No	Yes
d.	No	No

5. Ingot Corp. lent Flange $50,000. At Ingot's request, Flange entered into an agreement with Quill and West for them to act as compensated co-sureties on the loan in the amount of $100,000 each. Ingot released West without Quill's or Flange's consent, and Flange later defaulted on the loan. Which of the following statements is correct?
   a. Quill will be liable for 50% of the loan balance.
   b. Quill will be liable for the entire loan balance.
   c. Ingot's release of West will have no effect on Flange's and Quill's liability to Ingot.
   d. Flange will be released for 50% of the loan balance.

6. A party contracts to guaranty the collection of the debts of another. As a result of the guaranty, which of the following statements is correct?
   a. The creditor may proceed against the guarantor without attempting to collect from the debtor.
   b. The guaranty must be in writing.
   c. The guarantor may use any defenses available to the debtor.
   d. The creditor must be notified of the debtor's default by the guarantor.

7. Which of the following events will release a noncompensated surety from liability?
   a. Release of the principal debtor's obligation by the creditor but with the reservation of the creditor's rights against the surety.
   b. Modification by the principal debtor and creditor of their contract that materially increases the surety's risk of loss.
   c. Filing of an involuntary petition in bankruptcy against the principal debtor.
   d. Insanity of the principal debtor at the time the contract was entered into with the creditor.

8. Nash, Owen, and Polk are co-sureties with maximum liabilities of $40,000, $60,000 and $80,000, respectively. The amount of the loan on which they have agreed to act as co-sureties is $180,000. The debtor defaulted at a time when the loan balance was $180,000. Nash paid the lender $36,000 in full settlement of all claims against Nash, Owen, and Polk. The total amount that Nash may recover from Owen and Polk is
   a. $0
   b. $24,000
   c. $28,000
   d. $140,000

CHAPTER 36
BANKRUPTCY

CHAPTER OUTLINE

A. BANKRUPTCY LAW

1. THE FEDERAL LAW

▸ Bankruptcy law is based upon the Bankruptcy Reform Act. ▸ Jurisdiction over bankruptcy matters is vested in the U.S. district courts, which refer bankruptcy matters to U.S. bankruptcy courts.

2. KINDS OF BANKRUPTCY PROCEEDINGS

Relief for individuals and businesses under the Bankruptcy Act includes: (1) liquidations under Chapter 7; (2) reorganizations under Chapter 11; and (3) extended payment plans under Chapter 13.

B. LIQUIDATION UNDER CHAPTER 7

3. COMMENCEMENT OF THE CASE

GENERAL RULES. ▸ A Chapter 7 bankruptcy case is commenced by the filing of a petition in the bankruptcy court. ▸ A case may be: (1) voluntary (petition is filed by a debtor); or (2) involuntary (petition is filed by a debtor's creditors). ▸ Individuals and most partnerships or corporations can voluntarily file for Chapter 7 bankruptcy. ▸ A husband and wife may file jointly for bankruptcy.
LIMITATION. Voluntary and involuntary petitions for Chapter 7 bankruptcy cannot be filed by or against railroads, banks, insurance companies, savings and loans, or credit unions. Involuntary petitions cannot be filed against farmers or nonprofit corporations.

4. NUMBER AND CLAIMS OF PETITIONING CREDITORS (INVOLUNTARY CASE)

If a debtor has twelve or more creditors, at least three creditors with unsecured claims totaling $10,000 or more must sign an involuntary bankruptcy petition. If there are fewer than twelve creditors (excluding employees and insiders), any creditor with an unsecured claim of $10,000 or more may sign.

5. GROUNDS FOR RELIEF FOR INVOLUNTARY CASE

GENERAL RULE. If a debtor does not contest an involuntary petition, a court may enter an order for relief if: (1) a debtor is not paying debts as they become due; or (2) within 120 days prior to filing a petition, a custodian was appointed for the debtor's property.
LIMITATIONS. ▸ Failure to pay a single creditor does not justify an order for relief unless: (1) the creditor has no adequate remedy outside of bankruptcy; or (2) the creditor can show fraudulent conduct by a debtor. ▸ An order for relief will not be granted if a debtor has no assets.

6. AUTOMATIC STAY

The filing of a voluntary or involuntary petition for bankruptcy gives rise to an automatic stay that prevents creditors from beginning or continuing any lawsuits or other legal action to collect debts. The stay continues until either: (1) the case is closed or dismissed; or (2) the debtor is discharged.

7. RIGHTS OF DEBTOR IN INVOLUNTARY CASE

A debtor may get damages, costs, and attorney fees if: (1) an involuntary case is dismissed other than by consent of the debtor and petitioning creditors; or (2) a creditor files a petition in bad faith.

8. TRUSTEE IN BANKRUPTCY

- Creditors can elect the trustee. If creditors do not elect a trustee, an interim trustee will be appointed.
- A trustee automatically assumes ownership of: (1) a debtor's nonexempt property owned at the time of filing of the petition; and (2) property inherited by a debtor within six months after filing.
- A trustee is given the rights and power of the most favored creditor (i.e., a creditor who has a security interest in a debtor's property). This permits a trustee to set aside: (1) voidable transfers of property; (2) preferences (i.e., voidable preferential payments that allow a creditor to receive a greater amount than would be received in a bankruptcy liquidation); and (3) statutory liens that became effective only on the filing of a petition in bankruptcy. See Section 9 for related rules.

9. VOIDABLE TRANSFERS (AND VOIDABLE PREFERENTIAL PAYMENTS)

GENERAL RULE. A trustee can set aside: (1) a debtor's transfer of property made within one year of filing that is done with an intent to defraud creditors, or that renders a debtor insolvent or unreasonably reduces a debtor's assets; (2) preferential payment of any past debt that is made by an insolvent debtor within ninety days prior to filing; and (3) preferential payment to an insider (relative, partner, director, or controlling person) that is made by an insolvent debtor within twelve months of filing.

LIMITATION. *Permitted transfers*: (1) transfers for present consideration (cash sales or purchases); (2) payments in the ordinary course of business (e.g., payment of current phone bill); (3) payments totaling less than $600 made by a person with primarily consumer debts; and (4) child support.

STUDY HINTS. ▸ If a transfer (payment) can be set aside, a trustee can recover property (money) from the transferee. ▸ A debtor is presumed to be insolvent within ninety days prior to filing for bankruptcy. ▸ Balance sheet test: insolvency means fair value of assets is less than liabilities.

C. ADMINISTRATION OF DEBTOR'S ESTATE

10. PROOF OF CLAIM

▸ Debtors must file a list of creditors, and the creditors are then notified of an action. ▸ A creditor must ordinarily file a proof of claim within ninety days after the creditors' first meeting.

11. PRIORITY OF CLAIMS

- *First*: Even though a debtor has filed for bankruptcy, secured creditors are eventually allowed to enforce their security interests in the debtor's property prior to payment of other creditors.
- *Second*: The remaining assets of the debtor are used to pay unsecured creditors according to the following priority: (1) costs and expenses of administration of the bankruptcy action; (2) ordinary business claims incurred after the case is begun and before a trustee is appointed; (3) a maximum of $4,000 per claim for wages or commissions owed to an employee and earned within ninety days of the bankruptcy filing or cessation of the debtor's business; (4) certain contributions to employee benefit plans for services rendered within 180 days prior to filing for bankruptcy or cessation of business; (5) a maximum of $1,800 per claim for undelivered consumer goods or services; (6) allowed alimony and child support claims; and (7) certain federal and state income taxes and property taxes.
- *Third*: All claims that are not completely satisfied by the foregoing payments share pro rata in the remaining assets, if any, of the debtor.

D. DEBTOR'S DUTIES AND EXEMPTIONS

12. DEBTOR'S DUTIES

Debtors must file: (1) a list of creditors; (2) a schedule of assets and liabilities; and (3) a statement of financial affairs. Debtors must submit to examination under oath at the first meeting of creditors.

13. DEBTOR'S EXEMPTIONS

- In general, debtors can choose to keep that property which is exempted from creditors' claims by federal law or that property which is exempted by state law. Federal exemptions include: residence up to $15,000; auto up to $2,400; household goods worth $8,000; alimony and child support.

E. DISCHARGE IN BANKRUPTCY

14. DENIAL OF DISCHARGE

A discharge will be denied if a debtor: (1) fraudulently transferred or concealed property; (2) failed to keep financial records; (3) made a false oath or account; (4) failed to explain a loss of assets; (5) refused to obey a court order or to testify after receiving immunity; (6) obtained a discharge within the past six years; or (7) waived a discharge in a writing filed with, and approved by, the bankruptcy court.

15. EFFECT OF DISCHARGE

GENERAL RULE. A discharge is a court decree that releases a debtor from most debts that are not paid in a bankruptcy proceeding.
LIMITATION. A debtor is not discharged from liability for: (1) certain taxes; (2) certain student loans (unless payment causes undue hardship); (3) loans dishonestly obtained; (4) unscheduled debts; (5) fraud, embezzlement, or larceny; (6) alimony or child support; (7) willful or malicious injury to property; (8) judgment for drunk driving; (9) certain luxury debts; and (10) certain cash advances.

F. REORGANIZATIONS AND PAYMENT PLANS UNDER CHAPTERS 11 AND 13

16. BUSINESS REORGANIZATIONS UNDER CHAPTER 11

GENERAL RULES. - Individuals, partnerships, and corporations in business may reorganize under Chapter 11. - A debtor submits a plan which specifies how creditors will be repaid. If confirmed by the court, the plan binds the debtor and all creditors.
LIMITATION. A plan must treat all creditors within the same class in the same manner.
STUDY HINTS. - A plan may provide for assumption, rejection, or assignment of executory contracts. - Typically, a plan will be confirmed if it is proposed in good faith and it is reasonable.

17. EXTENDED-TIME PAYMENT PLANS UNDER CHAPTER 13

- An individual who has regular income, unsecured debts less than $250,000, and secured debts less than $750,000 may propose a plan for installment payment of debts. - A plan must: (1) provide for payment in full of all priority claims; (2) treat creditors in the same class in the same manner; and (3) be approved by the court. - When payments under a confirmed plan are completed, a debtor is discharged from most unpaid debts that are dischargeable in a Chapter 7 liquidation proceeding.

18. PROTECTION AGAINST DISCRIMINATION

Laws cannot discriminate against persons because they have received a discharge in bankruptcy.

REVIEW OF TERMS AND PHRASES

MATCHING EXERCISE

Select the term or phrase that best matches a statement or definition stated below. Each term or phrase is the best match for only one statement or definition.

Terms and Phrases

a. Automatic stay
b. Balance sheet test
c. Confirmation of plan
d. Discharge
e. Exempt assets
f. Insider
g. Involuntary case
h. Liquidation proceeding
i. Preference
j. Priority
k. Proof of claim
l. Voluntary case

Statements and Definitions

__k__ 1. Creditor's written statement that alleges a claim against a debtor and the basis for the claim.

__h__ 2. Chapter 7 bankruptcy proceeding.

__f__ 3. Relative, business partner, director, or controlling person of an insolvent debtor.

__d__ 4. Court decree that releases a debtor from unpaid debts upon conclusion of a bankruptcy action.

__l__ 5. Bankruptcy proceeding that is commenced by the filing of a petition by a debtor.

__c__ 6. Approval of a Chapter 11 or Chapter 13 rehabilitation plan.

__a__ 7. Automatic prohibition that prevents a creditor from starting or continuing any legal action to collect a debt after a petition for bankruptcy has been filed.

__e__ 8. Assets that may be retained by a debtor despite the debtor's filing for Chapter 7 bankruptcy.

__j__ 9. The order in which payment is to be made under the Bankruptcy Act for certain unsecured claims.

__g__ 10. Bankruptcy proceeding that is commenced by the filing of a petition by creditors against a debtor.

__b__ 11. Method to determine whether a debtor is solvent by comparing the fair value of a debtor's assets to the debtor's liabilities.

__i__ 12. Improper transfer of property by a debtor to a creditor that allows the creditor to recover more than would be paid to the creditor pursuant to a bankruptcy liquidation.

COMPLETION EXERCISE

Fill in the blanks with the words that most accurately complete each statement. Answers may or may not include terms used in the matching exercise. A term cannot be used to complete more than one statement.

1. Jurisdiction of bankruptcy matters is vested in the federal __district__ __courts__.

2. In a Chapter 7 bankruptcy, the bankruptcy estate is administered by a __trustee in bankruptcy__ _____.

3. Individuals, partnerships, and corporations in business can reorganize their businesses pursuant to a __Chapter 11__ bankruptcy.

4. A __Chapter 13__ bankruptcy may be used by individuals with regular income to extend the time for payment of their debts.

5. If a debtor has more than twelve creditors, then at least __3__ unsecured creditors, with total unsecured claims of at least __10,000__ must sign an involuntary bankruptcy petition.

6. In general, a creditor must file a proof of claim within __ninety__ days after the first meeting of creditors.

7. A __claim__ is a creditor's asserted right to payment, whether the right is liquidated, unliquidated, contingent, or disputed.

8. A discharge may be denied if a debtor received a discharge in bankruptcy within the past __6__ years.

REVIEW OF CONCEPTS

Write **T** if the statement is true, write **F** if it is false.

__F__ 1. Bankruptcy courts are state courts.

__F__ 2. A creditor whose unsecured claim is $5,000 or more can file an involuntary petition for a Chapter 7 bankruptcy against a debtor if the debtor has fewer than twelve creditors.

__F__ 3. A debtor cannot contest an involuntary bankruptcy petition that is filed by the debtor's creditors.

__T__ 4. A debtor may sue a creditor for damages that are caused by the creditor's bad faith filing of an involuntary bankruptcy petition.

__T__ 5. In a Chapter 7 bankruptcy, a trustee generally assumes ownership of all nonexempt property belonging to the debtor at the time of filing of the petition for bankruptcy.

__T__ 6. A preferential transfer of property made to an insider by an insolvent debtor may be set aside by a trustee if the transfer was made within one year prior to the filing of a bankruptcy petition.

__T__ 7. A payment of any past debt may be set aside if payment was made by an insolvent debtor within ninety days prior to the filing of a petition for bankruptcy and the payment enables the creditor to receive more than would be received in a Chapter 7 liquidation.

__T__ 8. A debtor has the duty to file a list of creditors and a list of the debtor's assets and liabilities.

__F__ 9. Employees have priority to payment for all unpaid wages, regardless of amount.

__F__ 10. In general, a debtor can claim only the exempt property that is permitted by the Bankruptcy Act. States do not have the power to specify property that may be exempt in a bankruptcy action.

__T__ 11. A discharge does not release a debtor from liability for unpaid student loans that came due within seven years prior to filing for bankruptcy unless payment would cause an undue hardship to the debtor.

__F__ 12. A discharge releases a debtor from liability for unpaid alimony.

__T__ 13. A debtor may waive the right to have a debt discharged.

__F__ 14. In a Chapter 11 bankruptcy, the business of a debtor is discontinued and the assets of the debtor are liquidated in order to pay the creditors.

__T__ 15. A debtor is not discharged from any debt that arises from a judgment based on liability that was incurred as a result of the debtor's driving while legally intoxicated.

__T__ 16. A debtor's Chapter 11 rehabilitation plan will ordinarily be confirmed if it is proposed in good faith and it is reasonable.

__T__ 17. In general, a Chapter 11 plan that has been confirmed by the court is binding on all creditors and the creditors have only the rights stated in the plan.

__T__ 18. An individual whose unsecured or secured debts exceed certain limits may not be entitled to file a petition for Chapter 13 bankruptcy.

__T__ 19. A Chapter 13 debtor cannot be discharged unless all claims entitled to priority are paid in full.

__T__ 20. State and local laws cannot discriminate against a person due to the fact that the person has previously received a discharge in bankruptcy.

REVIEW OF CHAPTER - APPLICATION OF CONCEPTS

MULTIPLE CHOICE QUESTIONS

__a__ 1. Dollar Bank holds numerous delinquent unsecured loans. Dollar Bank wants to force its delinquent debtors into Chapter 7 liquidation proceedings in order to limit its losses. Against which creditors can Dollar Bank file an involuntary petition for Chapter 7 bankruptcy?
   a. McDonald & McDonald, a law firm doing business as a partnership.
   b. Running Rails Railroad Company.
   c. Farwell Credit Union.
   d. The Rock Insurance Company.

__c__ 2. B&B Bakery just filed for Chapter 7 bankruptcy. B&B is in default on a loan from Arco Finance. Arco has a perfected security interest in B&B's equipment to secure payment of this debt. Under these facts:
   a. Arco can file a lawsuit against B&B in state court to collect the loan.
   b. Arco can immediately repossess and sell B&B's equipment pursuant to its security interest.
   c. Arco cannot sue B&B in state court and it cannot immediately repossess the equipment due to an automatic stay, but Arco will have priority to the equipment in the bankruptcy action.
   d. Arco no longer has a right to be paid; this right was terminated by the bankruptcy filing.

_d_ 3. Barbara was unemployed and insolvent. On June 10, Barbara sold her gold watch to a jeweler for $1,500, a fair value. On June 11, Barbara paid: $300 to her landlord for the current month's rent; $1,100 to her grandmother in payment of an old loan that would not have been paid in a Chapter 7 liquidation; and $100 in payment of the minimum monthly amount due on her personal credit card. On August 1, Barbara filed a petition for Chapter 7 bankruptcy. Which transfer or payment can be set aside by the bankruptcy trustee?
   a. Sale of the watch.
   b. Rent payment.
   c. Credit card payment.
   d. Loan payment that was made to Barbara's grandmother.

_d_ 4. Joyce filed a voluntary petition for Chapter 7 bankruptcy. Which of the following facts would *not* be a sufficient ground to deny Joyce a discharge in bankruptcy?
   a. Joyce was discharged in bankruptcy five years prior to filing the present bankruptcy petition.
   b. One month prior to filing for bankruptcy, Joyce transferred a rare coin collection to her brother with the intent to conceal the coin collection from her creditors.
   c. At the meeting of her creditors, Joyce lied under oath regarding her assets.
   d. Two months prior to filing for bankruptcy, Joyce sold her condo for a fair price.

_b_ 5. Ramon filed for Chapter 7 bankruptcy, and he received a discharge. Certain debts were not paid in Ramon's bankruptcy. Which of the following unpaid debts was discharged?
   a. $2,000 in child support owed for the support of Ramon's minor children.
   b. $1,500 owed to MasterCard.
   c. $1,000 in federal income taxes owed for the prior year.
   d. $5,000 judgment resulting from Ramon's embezzlement of money from a former employer.

_b_ 6. ARK Co. has filed a petition for Chapter 11 bankruptcy. ARK is a lessee under a long-term, executory real estate lease. ARK is also indebted to ten unsecured creditors who are included in the same class of creditors. ARK's rehabilitation plan:
   a. Can provide for payment in full of some unsecured creditors and for only partial payment of other unsecured creditors.
   b. Must provide for equal treatment of all of the unsecured creditors.
   c. Cannot reject the lease.
   d. Is not binding on ARK's creditors even if the plan is confirmed by the bankruptcy court.

_c_ 7. Jason submitted a proposed Chapter 13 extended payment plan for confirmation. Under the plan, the trustee in bankruptcy will be paid only 90 percent of the trustee's fees. Unsecured, nonpriority creditors, including Lakewood City which is owed $500 for unpaid water bills, will be paid only 80 percent of their respective claims. Under these facts:
   a. The plan can provide for payment of only 90 percent of the bankruptcy trustee's fees.
   b. Jason will remain liable for all debts that are not paid in full.
   c. Jason generally will be discharged from unsecured, nonpriority debts that are not paid in full.
   d. Lakewood City can refuse to register Jason's car if he fails to pay the water bills in full.

CASE PROBLEMS

Answer the following problems, briefly explaining your answers.

1. Green Oaks Health Club Inc. cannot pay its debts as they become due, and it is has defaulted on all of its obligations. Green Oaks has ten creditors. Green Oaks' unsecured creditors are Apple Linen Co. which is owed $15,000, and Baker Co. which is owed $4,000.

    (a) Can Green Oaks file a voluntary petition for Chapter 7 bankruptcy? (b) Who can file an involuntary petition for Chapter 7 bankruptcy against Green Oaks? (c) If an involuntary petition is properly filed, would a court enter an order for relief against Green Oaks?

    ___
    ___
    ___
    ___

2. On March 1, Shane filed a petition for Chapter 7 bankruptcy. On March 1, Shane owned: investment land, a car worth $1,000, household furnishings worth $2,000, and $500 in a bank account. After filing for bankruptcy, Shane earned and was paid $1,000 in wages. On June 1, Shane's uncle died and Shane inherited $10,000. Shane duly elected to use the federal exemptions provided by the Bankruptcy Act.

    (a) In general, what are the powers and functions of a bankruptcy trustee? (b) Who selects the trustee? (c) In this case, to what property does the trustee acquire rights, and what property belongs to Shane?

    ___
    ___
    ___
    ___

3. Tarco Inc. filed for Chapter 7 bankruptcy. Tarco's assets are a building and $10,000 cash. Tarco has these creditors: (1) First Bank is owed $50,000. This debt is fully secured by the building. (2) Bud is owed $500 for a deposit he paid Tarco for consumer goods he never received. (3) Mr. Atkins, the bankruptcy trustee, is owed a $6,000 fee. (4) Tina is owed $1,000 for wages she earned thirty days prior to Tarco's filing for bankruptcy. (5) Fuller Co. has a $5,000 unsecured claim for goods it sold to Tarco.

    Discuss the rights of Tarco Inc.'s creditors to be paid.

    ___
    ___
    ___
    ___

CPA REVIEW

The following questions were given on past CPA examinations. The answers for these questions are the unofficial answers prepared by the American Institute of Certified Public Accountants, Inc. (AICPA). All material is reproduced with permission of the AICPA.

____ 1. Deft, CPA, is an unsecured creditor of Golf Co. for $6,000. Golf has a total of 10 creditors, all of whom are unsecured. Golf has not paid any of the creditors for three months. Under Chapter 11 of the Federal Bankruptcy Code. which of the following statements is correct?
   a. Golf may not be petitioned involuntarily into bankruptcy because there are less than 12 unsecured creditors.
   b. Golf may not be petitioned involuntarily into bankruptcy under the provisions of Chapter 11.
   c. Three unsecured creditors must join in the involuntary petition in bankruptcy.
   d. Deft may file an involuntary petition in bankruptcy against Golf.

____ 2. Which of the following transfers by a debtor, within ninety days of filing for bankruptcy, could be set aside as a preferential payment?
   a. Making a gift to charity.
   b. Paying a business utility bill.
   c. Borrowing money from a bank secured by giving a mortgage on business property.
   d. Prepaying an installment loan on inventory.

____ 3. By signing a reaffirmation agreement on April 15, 1991, a debtor agreed to pay certain debts that would be discharged in bankruptcy. On June 20, 1991, the debtor's attorney filed the reaffirmation agreement and an affidavit with the court indicating that the debtor understood the consequences of the reaffirmation agreement. The debtor obtained a discharge on August 25, 1991. The reaffirmation agreement would be enforceable only if it was
   a. Made after discharge.
   b. Approved by the bankruptcy court.
   c. Not for a household purpose debt.
   d. Not rescinded before discharge.

____ 4. Larson, an unemployed carpenter, filed for voluntary bankruptcy on August 14, 1990. Larson's liabilities are listed below.

   Credit card charges due May 2, 1989 $3,000
   Bank loan incurred June 1990   5,000
   Medical expenses incurred June 1983   7,000
   Alimony due during 1988   1,000

   Under the provisions of Chapter 7 of the Federal Bankruptcy Code, Larson's discharge will not apply to the unpaid
   a. Credit card charges.
   b. Bank loan.
   c. Medical expenses.
   d. Alimony.

CHAPTER 36

5. Which of the following claims will not be discharged in bankruptcy?
   a. A claim that arises from alimony or maintenance.
   b. A claim that arises out of the debtor's breach of a contract.
   c. A claim brought by a secured creditor that remains unsatisfied after the sale of the collateral.
   d. A claim brought by a judgment creditor whose judgment resulted from the debtor's negligent operation of a motor vehicle.

Questions 6 through 8 are based on the following:

Dart Inc., a closely held corporation, was petitioned involuntarily into bankruptcy under the liquidation provisions of Chapter 7 of the Federal Bankruptcy Code. Dart contested the petition.

Dart has not been paying its business debts as they became due, has defaulted on its mortgage loan payments, and owes back taxes to the IRS. The total cash value of Dart's bankruptcy estate after the sale of all assets and payment of administration expenses is $100,000.

Dart has the following creditors:

- Fracon Bank is owed $75,000 principal and accrued interest on a mortgage loan secured by Dart's real property. The property was valued at and sold, in bankruptcy, for $70,000.
- The IRS has a $12,000 recorded judgment for unpaid corporate income tax.
- JOG Office Supplies has an unsecured claim of $3,000 that was timely filed.
- Nanstar Electric Co. has an unsecured claim of $1,200 that was not timely filed.
- Decoy Publications has a claim of $14,000, of which $2,000 is secured by Dart's inventory that was valued and sold, in bankruptcy, for $2,000. The claim was timely filed.

6. What dollar amount would Nanstar Electric Co. receive?
   a. $0
   b. $800
   c. $1,000
   d. $1,200

7. What total dollar amount would Fracon Bank receive on its secured and unsecured claims?
   e. $70,000
   f. $72,000
   g. $74,000
   h. $75,000

8. What dollar amount would the IRS receive?
   a. $0
   b. $8,000
   c. $10,000
   d. $12,000

CHAPTER 37
INSURANCE

CHAPTER OUTLINE

A. THE INSURANCE CONTRACT

Insurance is a contract by which an insurer, for consideration, promises (1) to pay a party a sum of money if a specified casualty or loss occurs to property or a person in which the party has an insurable interest, or (2) to indemnify a party for a loss or liability to which that party is subjected.

1. THE PARTIES

- *Insurer (underwriter)*: Insurance firm or other party who promises to pay for a specified loss.
- *Insured (assured; policyholder)*: Person to whom a promise to insure is made.
- *Policy*: Written contract stating the terms of the insurer's agreement to pay for a loss.
- *Insurance agent*: Agent representing one insurance company in making an insurance contract.
- *Insurance broker*: Independent contractor who represents many insurers. Brokers are: (1) agents for insureds regarding obtaining policies; (2) agents for insurers regarding transmitting payments.

2. INSURABLE INTEREST

GENERAL RULES. ▸ An insurance contract cannot be enforced unless *the party obtaining insurance* has an insurable interest which means: (1) an insured who obtains property insurance will suffer a direct monetary loss if the property is destroyed; or (2) the beneficiary who insures another person's life must expect a monetary gain from the continued life of the person insured. ▸ The insurable interest must exist: (1) when loss to insured property occurs; or (2) when life insurance on another person was obtained.
LIMITATION. A person obtaining insurance on his or her own life may name anyone as a beneficiary, and the beneficiary need not have an insurable interest to enforce the insurance contract.
STUDY HINT. A business has an insurable interest in the life of partners or key employees.

3. THE CONTRACT

- ▸ General contract law governs insurance contracts, and insurance contracts must usually be written.
- ▸ Information stated on an insurance application is part of the contract and binds the applicant.
- ▸ Rules of interpretation: (1) policy terms that conflict with statutes are void; (2) terms required by law to be in a policy are implied into a policy if not expressly stated; and (3) if laws require a contract to state all terms, then a term not stated in a contract cannot be used to defeat a claim.

4. ANTILAPSE AND CANCELLATION STATUTES AND PROVISIONS

GENERAL RULE. If premiums for *life insurance* are not paid on time, laws or policies usually allow a thirty or thirty-one-day grace period within which to pay. If an insured fails to pay life insurance premiums on time, laws may make an insurer to: (1) issue a paid-up policy for a lesser amount; (2) issue extended insurance for a stated period; or (3) pay the policy's cash surrender value to the insured.
LIMITATIONS. ▸ An insurance contract may either permit or prohibit a unilateral cancellation by the insurer. ▸ An insurer is often required to give prior written notice of cancellation of a policy.

5. MODIFICATION OF CONTRACT

▸ Typically, both parties must consent to a modification. ▸ Changes are made by (1) endorsement or (2) attaching a rider. ▸ If a policy term and an endorsement conflict, the endorsement controls.

6. INTERPRETATION OF CONTRACT

▸ In general, insurance contracts are interpreted according to ordinary rules of contract interpretation. ▸ Contract terms are given the ordinary meaning that would be understood by the average person. ▸ If a policy term is ambiguous, it is interpreted in favor of the insured.

7. BURDEN OF PROOF

▸ If a claim is disputed, an insured must prove (1) a loss occurred (2) while a policy was in force and (3) the loss was covered by the policy. ▸ An insurer claiming a policy exception that avoids coverage of a loss must prove that the exception applies. ▸ Exceptions to coverage are interpreted against the insurer.

8. INSURER BAD FAITH

GENERAL RULES. ▸ An insurer has a duty to act in good faith in processing and paying claims. ▸ An insurer's negligent or bad faith refusal to defend an insured or to settle a case against an insured within policy limits may render the insurer liable for: (1) resultant damages; and (2) in some states, the excess judgment entered against the insured. ▸ In some states, an insurer's bad faith failure to pay an insured's claim renders the insurer liable for a statutory penalty or exemplary damages, and attorney fees.

LIMITATION. An insurer is not liable for damages or penalties if there are reasonable grounds for contesting an insured's claim.

STUDY HINT. Bad faith is an unfounded or frivolous refusal to honor the terms of a policy.

9. TIME LIMITATIONS ON INSURED

To recover, an insured must: (1) promptly notify an insurer of a claim; (2) submit proof of loss in the time required by the policy; and (3) start a legal action based on the policy in the time specified.

10. SUBROGATION OF INSURER

An insurer who pays an insured's claim acquires any claim the insured had against a third party who caused the loss. The insurer may sue the wrongdoer to recover any amounts paid by the insurer.

B. KINDS OF INSURANCE

11. BUSINESS LIABILITY INSURANCE

▸ A business may buy a comprehensive general liability (CGL) policy that insures it against liability for damages for bodily injury or property damage due to any occurrence. It covers such things as product liability and liability for cleanup of pollution. ▸ Other types of business insurance: liability insurance for directors and officers; product liability insurance; professional malpractice insurance.

12. MARINE INSURANCE (COVERS LOSSES RELATED TO TRANSPORTATION OF GOODS)

- *Ocean marine insurance*: This insurance insures goods being transported in international and coastal waters. ▸ Kinds of policies: (1) hull insurance covers physical damage to vessel; (2) cargo insurance insures cargo owner for loss to shipped goods; (3) liability insurance insures shipowner against liability for damage the owner's ship causes to other ships or their cargo; (4) freight insurance insures that a shipowner will be paid for transportation costs. ▸ An insurer may be required to reimburse an insured for expenses the insured incurred in order to avoid a covered loss.

- *Inland marine insurance*: Insures goods shipped by air and on land, rivers, lakes, or coastal waters.

13. FIRE AND HOMEOWNERS INSURANCE

- **Fire insurance**: Fire insurance covers property loss that is caused by an actual, hostile fire (a fire that is uncontrollable, burns with excessive heat, or escapes from where it is supposed to be).
- **Coinsurance**: ▸ An insurer is generally liable for the actual amount of loss up to the amount of the policy. This obligation may be limited by coinsurance which requires a policyholder to maintain a minimum amount of insurance, typically 80 percent of the insured property's value. If this required minimum amount of insurance is not carried, a policyholder's recovery is computed: (1) amount of loss multiplied by (2) amount of insurance actually carried divided by required minimum amount of insurance. ▸ Some states do not permit coinsurance clauses.
- **Assignment**: Unless otherwise agreed, fire insurance cannot be assigned without insurer's consent.
- **Occupancy**: Fire policy limits on permitted use and occupancy of property are strictly enforced.
- **Homeowners insurance**: Homeowners insurance covers: (1) fire losses; (2) liability for injuries suffered by others while on the insured's property; (3) liability for injuries unintentionally caused to others off the insured premises (no coverage for injuries caused by operation of motor vehicles); and (4) losses from theft. ▸ Policy protects all family members living with the insured.

14. AUTOMOBILE INSURANCE

Most auto insurers use the Personal Auto Policy (PAP) standard form. Important clauses of PAP:

- **Perils covered**: PAP covers: injuries to person or property of others; medical expenses of covered persons; damages insured is entitled to recover from uninsured motorists; damage to insured auto.
- **Covered persons**: Named insured; family members; others persons permitted to drive the car.
- **Use and operation**: The PAP policy covers the "use and operation" of a vehicle, which includes loading and unloading a vehicle as well driving the vehicle.
- **Notice and cooperation**: Insurer's duty is conditioned on insured's giving notice and cooperating.
- **No-fault insurance**: No-fault insurance laws: (1) require an insurer to pay for an insured's loss regardless of who was at fault; and (2) prevent an insured from suing the party at fault unless the insured dies or suffers certain permanent serious injuries, or damages exceed a certain amount.

15. LIFE INSURANCE

- **Types of life insurance**: The three major types of life insurance are:
  - ▸ *Term insurance*: Coverage terminates at the end of a specified period. The face amount of the policy is paid to a beneficiary if the insured dies during the policy period. If the insured lives beyond the policy period, the policy expires. The policy has little or no cash surrender value.
  - ▸ *Whole life insurance (ordinary life insurance)*: Coverage lasts throughout insured's lifetime, and a portion of each premium is an investment that accumulates as a cash surrender value.
  - ▸ *Endowment insurance*: Face amount of policy is paid if insured dies within the policy period. Otherwise, the policy amount is paid to the insured at the end of the policy period.
- **Additional coverage**: For an extra premium, life insurance may provide: (1) double indemnity that pays double the policy amount if death is caused by an accident; or (2) disability insurance that insures against a person's being unable to engage in any occupation due to injury or disease.
- **Exclusions**: Life insurance does not usually insure against death caused by: (1) suicide; (2) drugs; (3) another's intentional act; (4) execution for a crime; (5) war activities; or (6) operation of aircraft.
- **Beneficiary**: Most policies provide that a beneficiary may be changed without the beneficiary's consent.
- **Incontestability clause**: Laws often require life insurance to include an incontestability clause. If two years have passed since a policy was issued, this clause makes an insurer pay and prevents it from contesting a policy due to an insured's fraud or other misconduct in obtaining the policy.

REVIEW OF TERMS AND PHRASES

Select the term or phrase that best matches a statement or definition stated below. Each term or phrase is the best match for only one statement or definition.

Terms and Phrases

a. Bad faith
b. Beneficiary
c. Cash surrender value
d. Coinsurance clause
e. Comprehensive general liability insurance
f. Double indemnity clause
g. Endowment insurance
h. Incontestability clause
i. Insurable interest
j. Insurance agent
k. Insurance broker
l. Marine insurance
m. No-fault insurance law
n. Term life insurance
o. Whole life insurance

Statements and Definitions

__j__ 1. Party who represents one insurance company in making insurance contracts.

__b__ 2. Party who is legally entitled to receive insurance benefits upon the death of an insured.

__g__ 3. Life insurance that pays a policy's face amount to a beneficiary if an insured dies within the policy period, or it pays this sum to the insured if the insured is alive at the end of this period.

__l__ 4. Insurance that generally covers losses to goods occurring during transportation.

__a__ 5. Insurer's unreasonable refusal or delay in processing or paying a claim for a covered loss.

__i__ 6. Interest in insured property or person that is generally required to enforce an insurance policy.

__f__ 7. Contract term that entitles a beneficiary to recover twice the face amount of life insurance if the insured is killed in an accident.

__n__ 8. Life insurance written for a specified number of years; policy has little or no cash surrender value.

__k__ 9. Party who is an independent contractor representing numerous insurance companies.

__o__ 10. Life insurance for the entire life of an insured that has a cash surrender value.

__c__ 11. Investment component of a whole life insurance policy that increases in value over time.

__h__ 12. Contract term that, after a specified time, prevents an insurer from contesting a life insurance contract due to the insured's fraud or misconduct in obtaining the policy.

__m__ 13. Law that prohibits an injured party from suing the party at fault except in certain situations.

__e__ 14. Insurance that insures a business against liability for bodily injuries or property damage due to any occurrence.

__d__ 15. Contract term in fire insurance that requires an insured to carry a minimum amount of insurance.

REVIEW OF CONCEPTS

Write **T** if the statement is true, write **F** if it is false.

__T__ 1. In general, an insurance contract is governed by general rules of contract law, and it is interpreted according to ordinary rules of contract interpretation.

__T__ 2. Information on an insurance application may become part of the contract and bind an insured.

__F__ 3. Beneficiaries named by a person who is insuring his or her own life must have an insurable interest in order to recover under the policy.

__F__ 4. If a term of an insurance contract is unclear, it is interpreted in favor of the insurer.

__T__ 5. If statutes require that all terms be stated in a policy, then a term that is not stated in the insurance contract cannot be used by an insurance company to defeat an insured's claim.

__T__ 6. In order to recover, an insured must prove that a covered loss occurred within the policy period.

__T__ 7. An insurer is not in bad faith if it has reasonable grounds to believe that a claim is not valid.

__F__ 8. If an insurer pays an insured's claim, the insurer does not have subrogation rights that entitle the insurer to enforce the insured's right to recover from a third party who caused a loss.

__T__ 9. Inland marine insurance insures goods during domestic transportation by air; over land; or on rivers, lakes, or coastal waters.

__F__ 10. Coinsurance clauses in fire or homeowners insurance are permitted in all states.

__F__ 11. Homeowners insurance covers liability resulting from an insured's operation of a motor vehicle.

__T__ 12. Under no-fault insurance laws, a person wrongfully injured by another person in an automobile accident cannot sue the wrongdoer unless certain exceptions are applicable.

__T__ 13. A term life insurance policy generally has little or no cash surrender value.

__T__ 14. Incontestability clauses generally prohibit an insurer from contesting an insurance policy more than two years after a life insurance policy was issued.

__T__ 15. In 1988, Gil bought life insurance that included a typical incontestability clause. Gil did not disclose an existing heart ailment, and the insurer would not have issued the policy had it known of this condition. If Gil dies in 1997 of a heart attack, the insurer cannot contest the policy on the basis of Gil's nondisclosure.

REVIEW OF CHAPTER - APPLICATION OF CONCEPTS

MULTIPLE CHOICE QUESTIONS

__b__ 1. Jocelyn worked exclusively for SafetyFirst Insurance Company. She wrote a general liability policy for Luke, who wanted coverage for his business. Under these facts:
   a. Jocelyn is an insurance broker for SafetyFirst.
   (b.) Jocelyn is an insurance agent for SafetyFirst.
   c. Jocelyn is the underwriter for the general liability policy.
   d. SafetyFirst is the assured.

__a__ 2. Wayne is an independent contractor who writes insurance policies for several different insurance companies. He wrote an endowment life insurance policy for Jonathan with GrandLife Insurance Company. Under these facts:
   (a.) Wayne is an insurance broker, and he acted as an agent for Jonathan when obtaining the policy for him with GrandLife.
   b. Wayne is an insurance broker, and he acted solely as an agent for GrandLife when writing the policy for Jonathan.
   c. Wayne is an insurance agent, and he acted solely as an agent for GrandLife when writing the policy for Jonathan.
   d. Wayne is an insurance agent. He is acting as the agent of Jonathan for the purpose of obtaining his policy and Wayne is also acting as the agent of GrandLife with respect to transmitting Jonathan's payments to GrandLife.

___C___ 3. Which of the following is incorrect?
   a. A person has an insurable interest in property whenever the destruction of the property will cause a direct monetary loss to that person.
   b. To collect on property insurance, the insured must have an insurable interest at the time the loss occurs.
   c. To collect on life insurance, the beneficiary who obtained the policy must have had an insurable interest at the time of the insured's death.
   d. To collect on life insurance, the beneficiary who obtained the policy must have had an insurable interest at the time the policy was obtained.

___a___ 4. Marvin purchased a standard form of life insurance on Lisa's life, naming himself as beneficiary. The policy contains a clause granting a thirty-day grace period, but the policy is silent regarding the insurer's right to modify the policy. Premiums are due June 1. Under these facts:
   a. Marvin cannot enforce the policy unless he had an insurable interest in Lisa's life at the time he purchased the policy.
   b. Marvin cannot enforce the policy unless he has an insurable interest in Lisa's life at the time of her death.
   c. If Marvin fails to pay the premium on June 1, the insurer can immediately cancel the policy.
   d. The insurer can unilaterally modify the policy whenever it chooses to do so.

___d___ 5. A contract of insurance is subject to which of the following:
   a. According to statutes in most jurisdictions, the policy must be in writing.
   b. Statutes sometimes specify not only the size, but also the style, of type that must be used in printing insurance policies.
   c. The application for the insurance policy is often attached to and made part of the policy when the policy is issued.
   d. All of the above.

CASE PROBLEM

Answer the following problem, briefly explaining your answer.

Mario owned a fire insurance policy on a building used in his business. In the policy, Mario agreed to a coinsurance term that required him to insure the building for 80 percent of its value. The value of the building was $100,000. However, Mario only insured the building for $60,000. A fire broke out in the attic of the building causing a $10,000 loss. In addition, Mario is considering selling the business and building to Janet. He wants to assign the fire insurance policy to Janet.

(a) Who has the burden to prove whether or not the fire was covered by the policy? (b) Must Mario have an insurable interest in the building in order to enforce the policy? (c) If the loss was covered, what effect does Mario's failure to carry the required insurance have on his right to recover under the policy? (d) How much can Mario recover? (e) Can Mario assign the policy without the insurer's consent?

CPA REVIEW

The following questions were given on CPA examinations. The answers for these questions are the unofficial answers prepared by the American Institute of Certified Public Accountants, Inc. (AICPA). All material is reproduced with permission of the AICPA.

___ 1. Which of the following parties has an insurable interest?
  I. A corporate retailer in its inventory.
  II. A partner in the partnership property.
  a. I only.
  b. II only.
  c. Both I and II.
  d. Neither I nor II.

___ 2. To recover under a property insurance policy, an insurable interest must exist

	When the policy is issued	At the time of the casualty
a.	Yes	Yes
b.	Yes	No
c.	No	Yes
d.	No	No

___ 3. Daly tried to collect on a property insurance policy covering a house that was damaged by fire. The insurer denied recovery, alleging that Daly had no insurable interest in the house. In which of the following situations will the insurer prevail?
  a. The house belongs to a corporation of which Daly is a 50% stockholder.
  b. Daly is not the owner of the house but a long-term lessee.
  c. The house is held in trust for Daly's mother and, on her death, will pass to Daly.
  d. Daly gave an unsecured loan to the owner of the house to improve the house.

___ 4. Hart owned a building with a fair market value of $400,000. The building was covered by a $300,000 fire insurance policy containing an 80% co-insurance clause. What amount would Hart recover if a fire totally destroyed the building?
  a. $0
  b. $240,000
  c. $256,000
  d. $300,000

CHAPTER 37

5. In 1985, Ring purchased a building for $90,000 and insured it with a $90,000 fire insurance policy having a standard 80% coinsurance clause. Ring never increased the amount of the policy. In 1990, the building, worth $120,000, was destroyed by fire. What amount could Ring collect from the insurance company?
   a. $0
   b. $ 72,000
   c. $ 90,000
   d. $120,000

6. Clark Corp. owns a warehouse purchased for $150,000 in 1990. The current market value is $200,000. Clark has the warehouse insured for fire loss with Fair Insurance Corp. and Zone Insurance Co. Fair's policy is for $150,000 and Zone's policy is for $75,000. Both policies contain the standard 80% coinsurance clause. If a fire totally destroyed the warehouse, what total dollar amount would Clark receive from Fair and Zone?
   e. $225,000
   f. $200,000
   g. $160,000
   h. $150,000

7. One of the primary purposes of including a coinsurance clause in a property insurance policy is to
   a. Encourage the policyholder to insure the property for an amount close to its full value.
   b. Make the policyholder responsible for the entire loss caused by some covered perils.
   c. Cause the policyholder to maintain a minimum amount of liability insurance that will increase with inflation.
   d. Require the policyholder to insure the property with only one insurance company.

8. Long purchased a life insurance policy with Tempo Life Insurance Co. The policy named Long's daughter as beneficiary. Six months after the policy was issued, Long died of a heart attack. Long had failed to disclose on the insurance application a known pre-existing heart condition that caused the heart attack. Tempo refused to pay the death benefit to Long's daughter. If Long's daughter sues, Tempo will
   a. Win, because Long's daughter is an incidental beneficiary.
   b. Win, because of Long's failure to disclose the pre-existing heart condition.
   c. Lose, because Long's death was from natural causes.
   d. Lose, because Long's daughter is a third-party donee beneficiary.

CHAPTER 38
AGENCY-- CREATION AND TERMINATION

CHAPTER OUTLINE

A. **NATURE OF THE AGENCY RELATIONSHIP**

1. **DEFINITIONS AND DISTINCTIONS**

   GENERAL RULES. ▸ An agency is a relationship that is based on an express or implied agreement by which an agent is authorized to negotiate or make contracts for a principal with a third party. ▸ Example: general manager; sales representative. ▸ An agent should be distinguished from:

   - *Employee*: ▸ An employee is a person who is hired to do a service that does not involve making contracts for the employer. ▸ Example: college professor; machine operator.
   - *Independent contractor*: ▸ An independent contractor is a person who is hired to perform a task; the employer has the right to dictate the result, but not the method or manner by which the result is obtained. ▸ Example: Homeowner hires a contractor to replace a roof.
   - *Real estate broker or bailee*: These persons do not usually have authority to contract for another.

   LIMITATIONS. ▸ A party may be hired to act as both an agent and an employee. Example: A clerk sells goods and stocks shelves. ▸ An independent contractor may be treated as an employee if the party is extensively controlled by an employer, or the party's separate identity is concealed.

   STUDY HINTS. ▸ A principal is liable on contracts that are made on its behalf by an agent who has actual or apparent authority to act for the principal. ▸ The authority to make contracts is what distinguishes an agent from an employee. ▸ The right to control the manner or method by which work is to be performed is what distinguishes an employee from an independent contractor.

2. **PURPOSE OF AGENCY**

   With rare exception (e.g., making a will), an agency can be created to carry out most legal tasks.

3. **WHO MAY BE A PRINCIPAL**

   Any competent person may be a principal. If a principal lacks capacity, the agency and contracts made by the agent are voidable or void to the same extent as if made directly by the principal.

4. **WHO MAY BE AN AGENT**

   Anyone (even incompetents) may be an agent. A partnership or corporation can be an agent.

5. **CLASSIFICATION OF AGENTS**

   - *Special agent*: ▸ A special agent is authorized to represent a principal regarding a specific transaction or a specific contract. ▸ Example: attorney authorized to make a lease for a client.
   - *General agent*: ▸ A general agent is authorized to represent a principal regarding all contracts of a business or all business conducted at a location. ▸ Example: general manager of a shoe store.
   - *Universal agent*: ▸ A universal agent is authorized to represent a principal regarding all matters that can lawfully be delegated. ▸ Example: unlimited power of attorney to make any contract.

6. **AGENCY COUPLED WITH AN INTEREST**

   ▸ *Interest in the authority*: agent paid consideration for right to exercise authority. *Interest in the subject matter*: agent has an interest in the property in question (e.g., security interest in collateral).

B. CREATING THE AGENCY

7. AUTHORIZATION BY APPOINTMENT

GENERAL RULE. A principal can expressly create an agency either in writing or orally.
LIMITATIONS. ▸ In a majority of states, appointment of agents to buy or sell an interest in land must be written. ▸ One spouse is not automatically authorized to act as an agent of the other spouse.
STUDY HINT. A written authorization is a power of attorney; the agent is an attorney in fact.

8. AUTHORIZATION BY CONDUCT

The following conduct by a principal may create authority sufficient for an agent to bind a principal:

- *Principal's conduct as to agent*: ▸ A principal's words or conduct that causes a person to believe that he or she can act as an agent for the principal creates an agency. ▸ A party who permits another to act as an agent is held to have authorized the other person's action. Example: Byron tells his mother that he is calling a repair technician on her behalf to fix her furnace and she does not object. ▸ Effect: principal's words or conduct *in relation to the agent* creates actual authority.

- *Principal's conduct as to third person (apparent authority)*: ▸ Apparent authority arises when, by words or conduct, a principal misleads a third party into reasonably believing that an agent has authority to act for the principal. ▸ Example: Principal appointed Kim as general manager of a store. General managers can customarily hire employees, but Principal told Kim not to do so. Kim then hired a new employee who was unaware of Principal's secret limitation. Kim had apparent authority to hire the new employee. ▸ Effect of apparent authority: (1) the principal and third party are bound to the contract; and (2) the agent is liable to the principal for losses suffered by the principal because the agent made the contract. ▸ Limitations: (1) apparent authority cannot be based on an agent's statements; (2) the third party's belief must be reasonable; (3) merely giving property to another person does not create apparent authority to sell the property.

- *Acquiescence by principal*: ▸ If an agent repeatedly performs certain acts and a principal knows of such acts but does not object, the agent is viewed as having authority to perform these acts. ▸ Example: Agent repeatedly accepts checks without authority to do so, and Principal is aware of Agent's actions but never objects. ▸ Effect: a principal's acquiescence creates actual authority.

9. AGENCY BY RATIFICATION

- *Intention to ratify*: ▸ In general, a principal may ratify any unauthorized action by an agent. A principal may ratify a contract by express words or by conduct indicating an intent to ratify. ▸ Examples: With knowledge of a contract, Principal: (1) performs the contract; (2) accepts or keeps contract benefits; (3) enforces the contract; or (4) fails to disavow the contract.

- *Requirements for ratification*: (1) Intent to ratify; (2) agent contracted for an identified principal; (3) principal had capacity to contract; (4) ratification occurs before the third party withdraws; (5) contract is legal; and (6) the principal has full knowledge of all facts to the extent desired.

- *Form of ratification*: In general, a ratification may be written or oral or arise by conduct. However, if a contract must be written, then a ratification of the contract must also be written.

- *Effect of ratification*: ▸ A ratified contract is treated as if it were actually authorized. ▸ When a contract is ratified, the principal and third party are bound by the contract, but the agent is not.

10. AGENCY BY OPERATION OF LAW

▸ A minor child may buy necessaries and charge them to his or her parents. ▸ An agent may have emergency power to make a contract if (1) the agent cannot communicate with the principal, and (2) failure to act will cause the principal a substantial loss.

11. PROVING THE AGENCY RELATIONSHIP

The party who will benefit from proof that an agency existed must prove such relationship.

C. TERMINATION OF AGENCY

12. TERMINATION BY ACT OF PARTIES

- *Expiration of contract*: An agency contract terminates on the date stated in the contract.
- *Agreement*: A principal and agent can agree to cancel an agency contract.
- *Option of a party*: A contract may give one party the unilateral right to cancel an agency.
- *Revocation of principal*: ▸ *Power*: A principal has the power to terminate an agency at any time, even if termination is a breach of contract. ▸ *Legal right*: (1) If an agency contract does not have a fixed duration (agency at will), a principal has the right to terminate the agency whether the agent has acted properly or not. (2) If an agency contract has a fixed duration, a principal has the right to revoke the agency only if the agent is guilty of misconduct; otherwise, a principal is liable for damages. ▸ A termination or revocation must be clear and unequivocal to be effective.
- *Renunciation by agent*: An agency is terminated if an agent refuses to continue to serve as agent. The rules regarding a principal's power and right to terminate an agency also apply to the agent.
- *Rescission*: An agency contract can be rescinded to the same extent that other contracts can be.

13. TERMINATION BY OPERATION OF LAW

▸ An agency terminates *immediately* upon the death of a principal or agent. ▸ An agency is also terminated by: (1) insanity or bankruptcy (but not mere insolvency) of a principal or agent; (2) destruction of the subject matter, change in law, or other event that makes it impossible to perform the agency; or (3) war between the countries in which the principal and agent reside.

14. DISABILITY OF THE PRINCIPAL UNDER THE UDPAA

GENERAL RULE. The Uniform Durable Power of Attorney Act (UDPAA) allows a principal to create a power of attorney: (1) that is not affected by the principal's disability or incapacity; or (2) that comes into existence only upon the principal's disability or incapacity.

LIMITATION. The UDPAA requires that a power of attorney be (1) written, (2) designate an attorney in fact, and (3) state a principal's intent to create one of these types of powers of attorney.

15. TERMINATION OF AGENCY COUPLED WITH AN INTEREST

A principal cannot terminate an agency coupled with an interest before expiration of the interest.

16. PROTECTION OF AGENT FROM TERMINATION OF AUTHORITY

- *Exclusive agency*: Agent may be given the exclusive right to sell a product for a principal in which case the agent is entitled to commissions for all sales, regardless of who makes the sale.
- *Secured transaction*: Security interest in property may secure payment of an agent's commission.
- *Payment from fund or third person*: An escrow fund, letter of credit, or guarantees by third parties may be used to assure payment of commissions.

17. EFFECT OF TERMINATION OF AUTHORITY

▸ *Between a principal and agent*, an agent's authority is not terminated until the agent is given notice of termination. ▸ If a principal voluntarily ends an agency, an agent has *apparent authority* to bind the principal after termination until: (1) actual notice of termination is given to third parties who have dealt with the agent; or (2) constructive notice (newspaper ads) is given to the public.

REVIEW OF TERMS AND PHRASES

MATCHING EXERCISE

Select the term or phrase that best matches a statement or definition stated below. Each term or phrase is the best match for only one statement or definition.

Terms and Phrases

a. Agent
b. Apparent authority
c. Attorney in fact
d. Employee
e. Exclusive agency
f. General agent
g. Independent contractor
h. Power of attorney
i. Principal
j. Special agent
k. UDPAA
l. Universal agent

Statements and Definitions

__h__ 1. Written appointment and authorization of an agent.

__l__ 2. Agent who is authorized to perform all acts that can be delegated lawfully to an agent.

__d__ 3. Party who is employed to do a task that does not involve making or negotiating contracts on behalf of the employer.

__b__ 4. Authority of an agent that arises due to the words or conduct of a principal that reasonably misled a third party into believing that an agent has authority to act on behalf of the principal.

__c__ 5. Agent who is appointed and given authorization by a written power of attorney.

__e__ 6. Agency that grants an agent the sole right to sell goods or services for a principal.

__g__ 7. Person who is hired to do a task and who retains control over the method for completing the task.

__f__ 8. Agent who is authorized to represent a principal regarding an entire business.

__k__ 9. Uniform law adopted by many states that enables a principal to create a power of attorney that is unaffected by the principal's subsequent disability or incapacity.

__j__ 10. Agent who is authorized to represent a principal regarding only a specific business transaction.

__i__ 11. Party on whose behalf an agent is authorized to negotiate and make a contract.

__a__ 12. Any party authorized to make a contract on behalf of a principal with a third party.

COMPLETION EXERCISE

Fill in the blanks with the words that most accurately complete each statement. Answers may or may not include terms used in the matching exercise. A term cannot be used to complete more than one statement.

1. An ~~Agent~~ _Agency_ is a relationship pursuant to which one party negotiates and makes contracts on behalf of another party.

2. Robert hired Nell to negotiate and make contracts on his behalf. Robert is a _principal_ and Nell is an _agent_.

3. Larry hired AAA Tax Service to prepare his personal tax returns. AAA has complete control over how it will prepare the returns. AAA is an _independent contractor_.

4. Tosco Corp. lent $50,000 to Acme Co., and Acme gave Tosco the authority to collect rents from a shopping center Acme owned and to apply these rents towards repayment of this loan. In this case, Tosco has an _interest in the subject_ _Authority_ that entitles it to collect these rents.

5. Rick was leaving the U.S., and he authorized his father to transact all business and to do all acts on Rick's behalf that Rick could lawfully do. Rick's father is a _universal_ agent.

6. Lee lent $6,000 to Ron, and Ron granted Lee a mortgage on some land to secure repayment of the loan and the authority to sell the land if he failed to repay it. In this case, Lee's authority is coupled with an interest because he has an _interest_ _in the subject matter_.

7. _Apparent_ _Authority_ is created if a principal misleads a third party into reasonably believing that an unauthorized agent has authority to represent the principal.

8. _Ratification_ is a principal's express or implied approval or adoption of an unauthorized contract.

REVIEW OF CONCEPTS

Write **T** if the statement is true, write **F** if it is false.

_T_ 1. In general, an agency is based on an express or implied agreement of a principal and an agent.

_F_ 2. An employer generally controls the method used by an independent contractor to perform a task.

_T_ 3. An employee is a person who is hired to perform a task that does not involve negotiating or making contracts on behalf of the employer.

_F_ 4. A person cannot be both an agent and an employee.

_F_ 5. A person can appoint another person as an agent for the purpose of signing a will or voting.

_T_ 6. In a majority of states, an authorization of an agent must be in writing if it authorizes the agent to buy land for a principal.

F 7. A husband is automatically the authorized agent of the wife for purposes of signing any contract.

T 8. An agent has authority to represent a principal only if a principal expressly authorizes an agent to act on his or her behalf.

T 9. If a principal knows that an agent repeatedly engages in certain conduct and the principal does not object, such acquiescence may create authority for the agent to engage in this conduct.

F 10. If a principal ratifies a contract, then both the principal and agent are liable on the contract.

T 11. If a contract must be in writing, then a ratification is also generally required to be in writing.

T 12. An agent's action is treated as if it were originally authorized if the principal ratifies the action.

T 13. By law, a minor child may have the authority to buy necessaries and charge them to his or her parents.

F 14. A principal always has the burden to prove that a person was or was not the principal's agent.

T 15. An agency automatically terminates on the expiration date stated in the agency contract.

F 16. If an agent contracted to act as a principal's agent until January 1, 1998, then the agent does not have the power to terminate the agency prior to that date.

F 17. The UDPAA does not require that a power of attorney be in writing.

F 18. The UDPAA prohibits any clause in a power of attorney that states that the power of attorney shall be unaffected by the principal's subsequent disability or incapacity.

T 19. If an agent has an exclusive agency to sell a principal's product but the principal personally sells the product to a buyer, the agent is entitled to be paid a commission on the sale by the principal.

T 20. After an agent is terminated, the agent may still have apparent authority to bind the principal.

REVIEW OF CHAPTER - APPLICATION OF CONCEPTS

MULTIPLE CHOICE QUESTIONS

d 1. Yankee Manufacturing Co. hired Roadways Inc. to build a new road at Yankee's plant. Roadways was obligated to build the road in accordance with certain plans. Roadways was to use its own tools, employees, and construction methods; Yankee did not have the right to control the manner or method by which Roadways built the road. In this case, Roadways is Yankee's:
   a. Agent.
   b. Principal.
   c. Employee.
   d. Independent contractor.

c 2. Perry, a minor, in writing authorized Allied Corporation to contract to sell certain land belonging to Perry. Pursuant to this authorization, Allied made a contract on Perry's behalf to sell the land to Don. Under these facts, the contract between Perry and Don is:
   a. Void. An agent cannot be authorized to sell land on behalf of a principal.
   b. Void. A corporation cannot be an agent.
   c. Voidable. Perry is a minor, and he can disaffirm the contract.
   d. Valid. Allied was properly authorized, and Allied had the capacity to contract.

3. Rozwell Heating Co. hired Dawn as a district sales manager for Rozwell's Midwest division. Dawn was authorized to negotiate and make all contracts to sell Rozwell's heating equipment in Ohio, Michigan, Indiana, and Illinois. Under these facts, Dawn is a:
   a. Special agent.
   b. General agent.
   c. Universal agent.
   d. Employee.

4. In which situation did Paula have authority to make the contract in question on behalf of Rod?
   a. Rod signed a written power of attorney that authorized Paula to make a contract to sell his car. On Rod's behalf, Paula signed a contract for the sale of Rod's car.
   b. Without Rod's knowledge or consent, Paula entered into a contract on Rod's behalf to sell his sailboat.
   c. Paula was authorized to sell goods for Rod. Paula was not expressly authorized to sell goods on credit. However, for several years Paula has repeatedly sold goods on credit, and Rod knew of these sales and never objected. Paula has now made another contract to sell goods on credit.
   d. a and c.

5. Without authority to do so, Avery contracted to buy a printer on behalf of P&P Printing Inc. The printer was delivered to P&P. Avery only told P&P the price and credit terms regarding the purchase; P&P indicated that it was not concerned regarding the other terms of the contract. P&P accepted and kept the printer, and P&P used it in its business. At all relevant times, P&P was capable of contracting and the contract was legal. Under these facts:
   a. The contract is binding on P&P because P&P ratified the contract.
   b. The contract is not binding on P&P because P&P did not expressly ratify the contract.
   c. The contract is not binding on P&P because P&P did not know all of the contract terms.
   d. The contract is not binding on P&P because Avery did not initially have authority to make the contract.

6. Principal hired Alex as general manager for a fixed two-year term. One year has now passed, and Principal no longer wants Alex to be general manager. However, Alex has properly performed all of his contractual and agency duties. Under these facts:
   a. Principal has the legal right and power to terminate Alex as general manager.
   b. Principal has the legal right, but not the power, to terminate Alex as general manager.
   c. Principal has the power, but not the legal right, to terminate Alex as general manager.
   d. Principal does not have the legal right or the power to terminate Alex as general manager.

7. Pam, a world-famous actress, hired Arnie as her agent to negotiate and make acting contracts on her behalf. The parties' agency relationship would *not* be terminated by operation of law if:
   a. Pam was subsequently killed while making a film.
   b. Pam was subsequently discharged in bankruptcy.
   c. The movie industry subsequently caused Arnie to become permanently insane.
   d. Pam subsequently indicated to Arnie that she thought his services were unsatisfactory and that she was considering hiring a new agent.

CASE PROBLEMS

Answer the following problems, briefly explaining your answers.

1. Carl hired Aurora as manager of Carl's auto parts store. Managers of auto parts stores customarily have the authority to order inventory. However, Carl told Aurora not to order any inventory without his prior approval. One day, a parts supplier asked Carl if he wanted to buy any inventory. Carl replied: "Go see Aurora, my manager. She will handle this entire matter." Reasonably believing that Aurora had authority to order parts for Carl, the supplier contacted Aurora. Without Carl's consent, Aurora contracted to buy parts from the supplier in violation of Carl's instructions to her.

    (a) Did Aurora have express authority, apparent authority, or no authority to contract on Carl's behalf with the parts supplier? (b) Is Carl legally obligated to perform the contract with the parts supplier?

    _____
    _____
    _____
    _____

2. Bill and Mary are an elderly married couple. Bill and Mary want to be certain that, should either of them become incapacitated, the other spouse can contract on behalf of the incapacitated spouse. They want to know: (a) Do Bill and Mary, as husband and wife, automatically have the authority to contract on behalf of each other? (b) What should they do to assure that one spouse can act on behalf of the other spouse who may become incapacitated? (c) In many states, what uniform law governs this matter?

    _____
    _____
    _____
    _____

3. Haskins Inc. hired Robin as vice president of purchasing. Robin was authorized to make contracts to buy materials on behalf of Haskins and to take delivery of such materials. On numerous occasions, Robin contracted on behalf of Haskins to buy materials from Sun Co. On June 1, Haskins sent a notice to Robin informing her that she was terminated. Robin received the notice on June 8. On June 10, Robin contracted on behalf of Haskins to buy additional materials from Sun Co. Robin took delivery of the materials, which she wrongfully kept. Sun Co. did not know that Robin had been terminated by Haskins. On June 15, Haskins gave written notice to Sun Co. that Robin had been terminated.

    (a) When was Robin's *express authority* to act for Haskins effectively terminated? (b) Did Robin have any authority to make the June 10 contract with Sun Co.? If so, what type of authority did she have? (c) Is Haskins obligated to perform the June 10 contract? (d) What should Haskins have done differently?

    _____
    _____
    _____
    _____

CPA REVIEW

The following questions were given on CPA examinations. The answers for these questions are the unofficial answers prepared by the American Institute of Certified Public Accountants, Inc. (AICPA). All material is reproduced with permission of the AICPA.

____ 1. Thorp was a purchasing agent for Ogden, a sole proprietor, and had the express authority to place purchase orders with Ogden's suppliers. Thorp placed an order with Datz, on Ogden's behalf after Ogden was declared incompetent in a judicial proceeding. Thorp was aware of Ogden's incapacity. Which of the following statements is correct concerning Ogden's liability to Datz?
   a. Ogden will be liable because Datz was not informed of Ogden's incapacity.
   b. Ogden will be liable because Thorp acted with express authority.
   c. Ogden will not be liable because Thorp's agency ended when Ogden was declared incompetent.
   d. Ogden will not be liable because Ogden was a nondisclosed principal.

____ 2. Bolt Corp. dismissed Ace as its general sales agent and notified all of Ace's known customers by letter. Young Corp., a retail outlet located outside of Ace's previously assigned sales territory, had never dealt with Ace. Young knew of Ace as a result of various business contacts. After his dismissal, Ace sold Young goods, to be delivered by Bolt, and received from Young a cash deposit for 20% of the purchase price. It was not unusual for an agent in Ace's previous position to receive cash deposits. In an action by Young against Bolt on the sales contract, Young will
   a. Lose, because Ace lacked any implied authority to make the contract.
   b. Lose, because Ace lacked any express authority to make the contract.
   c. Win, because Bolt's notice was inadequate to terminate Ace's apparent authority.
   d. Win, because a principal is an insurer of an agent's acts.

____ 3. Kent, without authority, contracted to buy computer equipment from Fox Corp. for Ace Corp. Kent told Fox that Kent was acting on Ace's behalf. For Ace to ratify the contract with Fox,
   a. Kent must be a general agent of Ace.
   b. Ace must know all material facts relating to the contract at the time it is ratified.
   c. Ace must notify Fox that Ace intends to ratify the contract.
   d. Kent must have acted reasonably and in Ace's best interest.

____ 4. Starr is an agent of a disclosed principal, Maple. On May 1, Starr entered into an agreement with King Corp. on behalf of Maple that exceeded Starr's authority as Maple's agent. On May 5, King learned of Starr's lack of authority and immediately notified Maple and Starr that it was withdrawing from the May 1 agreement. On May 7, Maple ratified the May 1 agreement in its entirety. If King refuses to honor the agreement and Maple brings an action for breach of contract, Maple will
   a. Prevail since the agreement of May 1 was ratified in its entirety.
   b. Prevail since Maple's capacity as a principal was known to Starr.
   c. Lose since the May 1 agreement is void due to Starr's lack of authority.
   d. Lose since King notified Starr and Maple of its withdrawal prior to Maple's ratification.

CHAPTER 38

_____ 5. When a valid contract is entered into by an agent on the principal's behalf, in a nondisclosed principal situation, which of the following statements concerning the principal's liability is correct?

	The principal may be held liable once disclosed	The principal must ratify the contract to be held liable
a.	Yes	Yes
b.	Yes	No
c.	No	Yes
d.	No	No

_____ 6. Pell is the principal and Astor is the agent in an agency coupled with an interest. In the absence of a contractual provision relating to the duration of the agency, who has the right to terminate the agency before the interest has expired?

	Pell	Astor
a.	Yes	Yes
b.	No	Yes
c.	No	No
d.	Yes	No

_____ 7. Wok Corp. has decided to expand the scope of its business. In this connection, it contemplates engaging several agents. Which of the following agency relationships is within the statute of frauds and thus should be contained in a signed writing?
   a. A sales agency where the agent normally will sell goods which have a value in excess of $500.
   b. An irrevocable agency.
   c. An agency which is of indefinite duration but which is terminable upon one month's notice.
   d. An agency for the forthcoming calendar year which is entered into in mid-December of the prior year.

_____ 8. Red entered into a contract with Maple on behalf of Gem, a disclosed principal. Red exceeded his authority in entering into the contract. In order for Gem to successfully ratify the contract with Maple,
   a. Gem must expressly communicate his intention to be bound.
   b. Gem must have knowledge of the relevant material facts concerning the transaction.
   c. Red must not have been a minor.
   d. Red must have acted reasonably and in Gem's best interest.

CHAPTER 39
PRINCIPAL AND AGENT

CHAPTER OUTLINE

A. AGENT'S AUTHORITY

1. **SCOPE OF AGENT'S AUTHORITY (AND TYPES OF AUTHORITY)**

   GENERAL RULE.   When an agent acts on behalf of a principal, the agent may be acting pursuant to one of the following types of authority or the agent may be acting with no authority.

   - *Express authority*: ▸ Express authority arises when a principal orally or in writing authorizes an agent to do an act. ▸ Example: Principal tells Nate to purchase a chair on behalf of Principal.
   - *Incidental authority*: ▸ It is implied that an agent has incidental authority to do acts that are reasonably necessary to carry out the agent's express authority. ▸ Example: Principal expressly authorizes Jerry to manage the financial operations of a shopping center. In this case, Jerry has incidental authority to receive rent checks from tenants of the shopping center.
   - *Customary authority*: ▸ It is implied that an agent has customary authority to do any act that is customarily done by this type of agent in the community in question. ▸ Example: Roger is the general manager of a restaurant. If it is customary in Roger's community that restaurant managers can hire necessary cooks, then Roger would have customary authority to hire a cook.
   - *Apparent authority*: ▸ An agent has apparent authority when, by words or conduct, a principal misleads a third party into reasonably believing that the agent has authority to do an act. ▸ Example: Principal tells Nanette, who is applying for a job, that Agent has complete responsibility for hiring decisions, which is not true. If Agent hires Nanette on behalf of Principal, then Agent acted with apparent authority.
   - *No authority*: ▸ A person acts with no authority when the person purports to act for another, but the person has no express, incidental, customary, or apparent authority to do so. ▸ Example: Alex indorsed a check on behalf of Fred, a complete stranger who did not authorize Alex to indorse the check. In this case, Alex had no authority to act for Fred.

   STUDY HINT.   An agent has "actual authority" when the agent has express, incidental, or customary authority to act.

2. **EFFECT OF PROPER (AND IMPROPER) EXERCISE OF AUTHORITY**

   GENERAL RULE.   ▸ If an agent contracts on behalf of a disclosed principal with actual authority to do so: (1) the principal and third party are liable to one another on the contract; and (2) the agent is not a party to, nor liable on, the contract. ▸ Example: Paul authorized Alice to buy a snowmobile on his behalf from Wanda, and Alice did so. If Paul fails to pay, Wanda can sue Paul for breach of contract, but she cannot sue Alice because Alice was not a party to the contract.

   STUDY HINTS.   ▸ If an agent has only apparent authority: (1) the principal and third party are liable to one another on the contract; and (2) the agent is liable to the principal for exceeding the agent's actual authority. ▸ If an agent has no authority: (1) the principal and third party are not liable on the contract; and (2) the agent is liable to the third party for damages. (See Chapter 40)

3. DUTY TO ASCERTAIN EXTENT OF AGENT'S AUTHORITY

GENERAL RULES. ▸ A third party cannot rely on an agent's statements regarding the extent of the agent's authority. ▸ Third parties deal at their own risk with an agent whose authority is limited to a special purpose. This is because such an agent can bind a principal only if the agent has actual authority to do so.

STUDY HINTS. ▸ Typically, an attorney is retained for a special purpose. Thus, an attorney cannot settle a client's claim without the client's consent. ▸ If a third party observes an agent acting against a principal's interests, the third party deals with the agent at the third party's own risk. ▸ If a contract is made by a third party and an agent with authority to contract on behalf of a principal, the contract is not invalidated or otherwise affected by the third party's subsequent death.

4. LIMITATIONS ON AGENT'S AUTHORITY

GENERAL RULES. ▸ A third party who knows of a limit on an agent's authority cannot ignore that limitation. ▸ If a third party knows that an agent's authority is based on a writing, then the third party is charged with knowledge of limitations stated in the writing. ▸ A third party is charged with knowledge of obvious limits on authority that are inherent in certain agencies. Example: The authority of government officials is commonly restricted.

LIMITATION. A third party's right to hold a principal liable on a contract is not affected by secret limits that the principal may have placed upon an agent's authority.

STUDY HINT. If a third party knows that an agent's authority is subject to certain limits, the third party cannot hold the principal liable for the agent's actions that exceed such limits.

5. DELEGATION OF AUTHORITY BY AGENT

GENERAL RULE. In general, an agent cannot delegate (transfer) to another person authority that the agent was given by a principal. This is especially true if a duty involves discretion or judgment.

LIMITATION. An agent can authorize a subagent to do an act if: (1) the act is mechanical or clerical in nature; (2) a custom permits the use of a subagent; (3) an emergency requires a delegation and it is impossible to contact the principal; or (4) the principal expressly or impliedly agrees to a delegation or appointment of subagents.

B. DUTIES AND LIABILITIES OF PRINCIPAL AND AGENT

6. DUTIES AND LIABILITIES OF AGENT DURING AGENCY

(a) Loyalty

GENERAL RULES. ▸ During the agency relationship, an agent owes a duty to be loyal and faithful to a principal. ▸ An agent cannot: (1) make or retain secret profits derived from the agency; (2) buy property from, or sell property to, a principal without disclosing the agent's interest; (3) accept secret benefits from a third party relating to an agency transaction; (4) aid or provide confidential information to a principal's competitors; or (5) represent both a principal and third party without disclosing such representation and obtaining the consent of both parties.

STUDY HINTS. ▸ A principal can avoid a contract that was made by an agent who failed to disclose his or her interest in the matter. ▸ A principal can sue an agent for any secret or improper profits or commissions that the agent made in connection with a transaction that was undertaken with or on behalf of a principal. ▸ A contract is voidable if the principal did not know that the agent also represented the other contracting party.

(b) Obedience and performance

▸ An agent must: (1) obey all lawful instructions of a principal; and (2) perform all agency duties for the time and in the manner agreed upon. ▸ An agent is liable to a principal for damages caused by a failure to obey instructions even if the agent acted in good faith and with the intent to benefit the principal.

(c) Reasonable care

An agent must perform duties with the care that a reasonable person would use. If an agent possesses a special skill, the agent must use such skill.

(d) Accounting

An agent must account for, and keep separate, the principal's money and property.

(e) Information

An agent must inform a principal of all facts relevant to the agency that may affect the principal's interests, including all facts relating to the desirability of a transaction.

7. DUTIES AND LIABILITIES OF AGENT AFTER TERMINATION OF AGENCY

After termination of an agency: (1) an agent's duties continue only to the extent necessary to complete prior obligations; and (2) an agent can compete against a former principal (unless a valid covenant not to compete restricts such right).

8. ENFORCEMENT OF LIABILITY OF AGENT

▸ Damages caused by an agent's breach of duty can be deducted from money owing the agent, or damages may be recovered by suing the agent. ▸ If an agent makes a secret profit, a principal can recover the profit from the agent and the agent forfeits any right to compensation. ▸ A contract may require that a shortage of money in an agent's account be deducted from the agent's pay.

9. DUTIES AND LIABILITIES OF PRINCIPAL TO AGENT

(a) Employment according to terms of contract

▸ A principal does not have the right to terminate an agent prior to the time stated in a contract unless: (1) the principal has just cause, i.e., the agent materially breaches the contract; or (2) this right is granted by the contract. ▸ A principal cannot allow another person to represent the principal if an agent has been given exclusive right to represent the principal. ▸ During the term of the agency, agents often have the right to receive commissions on repeating transactions, such as the right to continue to receive commissions on renewals of insurance policies. But agency contracts typically eliminate any right to continue to receive such commissions once the agent has been terminated.

(c) Reimbursement

▸ In general, a principal must reimburse an agent for expenses that are incurred by the agent at the principal's request or that are incurred in order to carry out the agent's duties. ▸ However, a principal need not reimburse for an expense that resulted from the agent's misconduct or negligence.

(d) Indemnity

A principal must indemnify (pay) for losses suffered by an agent due to the agency unless the losses were the result of the agent's fault.

REVIEW OF TERMS AND PHRASES

Select the term or phrase that best matches a statement or definition stated below. Each term or phrase is the best match for only one statement or definition.

Terms and Phrases

a. Actual authority
b. Apparent authority
c. Customary authority
d. Express authority
e. Incidental authority
f. No authority

Statements and Definitions

__d__ 1. Authority created by oral or written instructions given by a principal to an agent.

__c__ 2. Implied authority to perform acts that a particular type of agent can ordinarily perform.

__b__ 3. Authority created by a principal's words or conduct that mislead a third party into reasonably believing that an agent has authority to do an act when this is not true.

__e__ 4. Implied authority to perform acts that are reasonably necessary to carry out an agent's express authority.

__a__ 5. Authority that includes express, incidental, and customary authority.

__f__ 6. Status of having no express, incidental, customary, or apparent authority to act for a principal.

REVIEW OF CONCEPTS

Write **T** if the statement is true, write **F** if it is false.

__T__ 1. If an agent with express authority makes a contract for a disclosed principal, the agent is not a party to, or liable on, the contract.

__F__ 2. In general, a third person is entitled to rely on an agent's representations regarding the extent of the agent's authority.

__F__ 3. Third persons who deal with an agent who is retained for a special (limited) purpose are responsible for finding out the extent of the agent's authority.

__T__ 4. A contract made by a third person and an agent who had authority to make the contract on behalf of a principal is not terminated if the third person dies after the contract is made.

__F__ 5. A third party cannot be bound by limitations on an agent's authority that are stated in a writing unless the third party actually reads such writing.

__F__ 6. A third party is bound by all limitations that a principal places on an agent's authority, even if the third party is not informed of such limitations.

__T__ 7. An agent can represent both parties to a transaction if the agent fully discloses this fact to the parties and they consent to the agent's representation of both parties.

__T__ 8. An agent can generally delegate duties that merely entail performing mechanical or clerical tasks.

T 9. If necessary to protect a principal's interest, an agent may appoint subagents in an emergency.

F 10. If an agent pays a fair price, an agent can purchase property from a principal without disclosing that the agent is the buyer.

T 11. If an agent commingles the principal's property with the agent's property and they cannot be separated, the principal is entitled to all of the commingled property.

F 12. An agent has no duty to disclose information to a principal unless the principal expressly requests disclosure of such information.

T 13. An agent who has a special skill must exercise that skill in performing an agency.

T 14. In general, a contract of employment can authorize a principal to deduct shortages in an agent's account from the amount of compensation that is payable to the agent.

T 15. Unless otherwise agreed, a former agent is free to deal with and may compete against a former principal.

REVIEW OF CHAPTER - APPLICATION OF CONCEPTS

MULTIPLE CHOICE QUESTIONS

1. Kyle was sales manager of Mango Co., a fruit wholesaler. Kyle's authority was stated in a written statement of authority, which stated that he could make sales for only $10,000 or less. But it was customary for agents, such as Kyle, to have authority to make sales for up to $50,000. Kyle made a $20,000 sale to Acme. Acme was unaware of the statement of authority and the limit on Kyle's authority. Kyle told Acme that he had authority to make the sale. In this case:
   a. Mango is bound by this sale because it misled Acme into believing that Kyle had authority to make the sale, and Acme is not charged with knowledge of the statement of authority.
   b. Mango is bound by this sale because Acme was entitled to rely on Kyle's statements regarding the extent of his authority.
   c. Mango is not bound by this sale because Acme is charged with knowledge of the limits on Kyle's authority that are stated in the statement of authority.
   d. a and b.

2. Jill is the human resources manager of Preset Cement Co., a large cement manufacturer. Jill is responsible for all employment matters, including interviewing and hiring employees. In which situation did Jill improperly delegate her authority?
   a. Jill delegated to a subagent the task of signing letters that announced job openings.
   b. Jill delegated to a subagent the task of interviewing and hiring a new general manager.
   c. Jill delegated to a subagent the task of doing initial interviews for secretaries. It is customary that an agent, such as Jill, can delegate this type of task to a subagent.
   d. Jill delegated to a subagent the task of hiring a new shop foreman. Preset Concrete Co. expressly authorized Jill to delegate this task.

3. Duke was an agent of R&K Inc. On behalf of R&K, Duke contracted to sell one of R&K's businesses to Buyer. Unknown to R&K, Duke also represented Buyer and Buyer paid him a $5,000 commission for his services in connection with the transaction with R&K. In this case:
   a. Duke violated his duty of loyalty to R&K.
   b. R&K can recover the $5,000 commission that Duke was paid by Buyer.
   c. R&K can elect to set aside the contract with Buyer.
   d. All of the above.

CHAPTER 39

a 4. Juan was the new car sales manager for Rev Car Sales. Juan was authorized to sell Rev's cars, but he was told not to accept promissory notes as payment. In good faith and with the intent to benefit Rev, Juan sold a car to Buyer in exchange for Buyer's promissory note. Buyer subsequently failed to pay the note, and Rev suffered a $3,000 loss. Under these facts:
   a. Juan is liable to Rev for $3,000 because he breached his duty of obedience when he accepted the promissory note from Buyer.
   b. Juan is not liable to Rev because Juan acted in good faith in accepting the note.
   c. Juan is not liable to Rev because Juan intended to benefit Rev when he accepted the note.
   d. Juan is not liable to Rev because an agent can disobey a principal's instructions if the agent believes that it is in the principal's best interest to do so.

c 5. Lisa was a sales agent for DRG. By contract, DRG agreed to pay Lisa a $1,500 monthly salary plus a commission equal to 10 percent of the price of goods that she sold. Lisa's contract stated that she was not entitled to commissions on sales made after her discharge. Prior to her discharge: (1) Lisa was owed one month's salary; (2) Lisa sold $10,000 worth of goods for DRG to Rork Co.; and (3) Lisa incurred a $50 phone charge in making various sales. After Lisa's discharge, DRG sold an additional $20,000 worth of goods to Rork Co. How much does DRG owe Lisa?
   a. $1,500
   b. $1,550
   c. $2,550
   d. $4,550

6. In which situation is Pat (the principal) liable on the contract in question?
   a. Pat signed a written power of attorney, authorizing an agent to sell his house. On Pat's behalf, the agent contracted with a third party for the sale of the house.
   b. An agent signed a contract to sell Pat's car, but Pat had not authorized this sale. Later Pat decided to accept the contract as written and signed it.
   c. An agent purchased supplies from a third party on behalf of Pat, just as the agent had done many times before. Pat had never expressly authorized the agent to make these purchases, but Pat was aware that the agent had been making these acquisitions and never objected.
   d. All of the above.

CASE PROBLEM

Answer the following problem, briefly explaining your answer.

George is general manager of a Hardi Hardware store in Pelican City. Hardi authorized George to buy inventory for the store and to manage the store's ordinary business. Hardi did not say anything regarding hiring employees or making extraordinary purchases. In Pelican City it is customary for agents, such as George, to hire employees, but it is not customary for them to make extraordinary purchases. On behalf of Hardi, George: (a) contracted to buy some saws for inventory; (b) hired Dan as a clerk; and (c) contracted to buy all of the assets of a competitor.

What type of authority, if any, did George have to make the foregoing contracts? Is Hardi legally obligated to perform these contracts?

_____
_____
_____
_____

CPA REVIEW

The following questions were given on CPA examinations. The answers for these questions are the unofficial answers prepared by the American Institute of Certified Public Accountants, Inc. (AICPA). All material is reproduced with permission of the AICPA.

_____ 1. Ogden Corp. hired Thorp as a sales representative for nine months at a salary of $3,000 per month plus 4% of sales. Which of the following statements is correct?
   a. Thorp is obligated to act solely in Ogden's interest in matters concerning Ogden's business.
   b. The agreement between Ogden and Thorp formed an agency coupled with an interest.
   c. Ogden does not have the power to dismiss Thorp during the nine-month period without cause.
   d. The agreement between Ogden and Thorp is not enforceable unless it is in writing and signed by Thorp.

_____ 2. Frost's accountant and business manager has the authority to
   a. Mortgage Frost's business property.
   b. Obtain bank loans for Frost.
   c. Insure Frost's property against fire loss.
   d. Sell Frost's business.

_____ 3. Ace engages Butler to manage Ace's retail business. Butler has the implied authority to do all of the following, except
   a. Purchase inventory for Ace's business.
   b. Sell Ace's business fixtures.
   c. Pay Ace's business debts.
   d. Hire or discharge Ace's business employees.

_____ 4. Simmons, an agent for Jensen, has the express authority to sell Jensen's goods. Simmons also has the express authority to grant discounts of up to 5% of list price. Simmons sold Hemple goods with a list price of $1,000 and granted Hemple a 10% discount. Hemple had not previously dealt with either Simmons or Jensen. Which of the following courses of action may Jensen properly take?
   a. Seek to void the sale to Hemple.
   b. Seek recovery of $50 from Hemple only.
   c. Seek recovery of $50 from Simmons only.
   d. Seek recovery of $50 from either Hemple or Simmons.

CHAPTER 39

_____ 5. Borg is the vice-president of purchasing for Crater Corp. He has authority to enter into purchase contracts on behalf of Crater provided that the price under a contract does not exceed $2 million. Dent, who is the president of Crater, is required to approve any contract that exceeds $2 million. Borg entered into a $2.5 million purchase contract with Shady Corp. without Dent's approval. Shady was unaware that Borg exceeded his authority. Neither party substantially changed its position in reliance on the contract. What is the most likely result of this transaction?
   a. Crater will be bound because of Borg's apparent authority.
   b. Crater will not be bound because Borg exceeded his authority.
   c. Crater will only be bound up to $2 million, the amount of Borg's authority.
   d. Crater may avoid the contract since Shady has not relied on the contract to its detriment.

_____ 6. Ritz hired West for six months as an assistant sales manager at $4,000 a month plus 3% of sales. Which of the following is correct?
   a. The employment agreement must be in writing and signed by the party to be charged.
   b. The agreement between Ritz and Wes formed an agency coupled with an interest.
   c. West must disclose any interests he has which are adverse to Ritz in matters concerning Ritz's business.
   d. West can be dismissed by Ritz during the six months only for cause.

_____ 7. An agent will usually be liable under a contract made with a third party when the agent is acting on behalf of a(an)

	Disclosed principal	Undisclosed principal
a.	Yes	Yes
b.	Yes	No
c.	No	Yes
d.	No	No

CHAPTER 40
THIRD PERSONS IN AGENCY

CHAPTER OUTLINE

A. LIABILITY OF AGENT TO THIRD PERSON

1. **ACTION OF AUTHORIZED AGENT OF DISCLOSED PRINCIPAL**

   An agent is not personally liable on a properly executed contract that is made for a disclosed principal if the agent has actual authority or the principal ratifies the contract.

2. **UNAUTHORIZED ACTION**

   GENERAL RULES. ▸ An agent impliedly warrants to a third party that the agent has authority to bind a principal to the contract. ▸ If an agent acts with no authority: (1) the principal is not liable on the contract; and (2) the agent is personally liable to the third party for any loss the third party suffers.
   STUDY HINT.   An agent's good faith mistake regarding his or her authority is not a defense.

3. **NO PRINCIPAL WITH CAPACITY**

   An agent impliedly warrants to a third party that there is a principal who has capacity to contract.

4. **DISCLOSURE OF PRINCIPAL**

   - ***Disclosed principal***: ▸ A disclosed principal exists if an agent discloses: (1) the principal's existence and identity; and (2) that the agent is acting for a principal. ▸ Liability: agent is not liable on the contract.
   - ***Partially disclosed principal***: ▸ A partially disclosed principal exists if an agent discloses the existence, but not the identity, of the principal. ▸ Liability: agent is liable on the contract to third party.
   - ***Undisclosed principal***: ▸ An undisclosed principal exists if an agent does not disclose: (1) the existence or identity of the principal; or (2) that the agent is acting as an agent. ▸ Liability: agent is liable on the contract.

5. **WRONGFUL RECEIPT OF MONEY**

   GENERAL RULE.   An agent is liable to a third party for money paid to the agent if: (1) the agent illegally took the money; or (2) the money is an overpayment or is paid when no money is owed.
   LIMITATION.   An agent is not liable for an overpayment if the agent: (1) acted in good faith; (2) was unaware that payment was improper; and (3) gave the money to the principal.

6. **ASSUMPTION OF LIABILITY**

   An agent may agree to be personally liable on a contract made between a principal and a third party.

7. **EXECUTION OF CONTRACT**

   ▸ Between an agent and third party, an agent can avoid liability on a contract made in the agent's name by proving that it was actually intended to be a contract between a principal and the third party. ▸ An agent's signature should (1) state the principal's name, (2) "by" or "per" the agent. When signed in this manner, a principal is disclosed and an agent is not liable on the contract.

8. **FAILURE TO OBTAIN COMMITMENT OF PRINCIPAL**

   An agent may owe a duty to a party to assure that a principal makes a contract (e.g., insurance).

9. **TORTS AND CRIMES**

   An agent is liable for any tort or crime committed by the agent, even while acting for a principal.

B. LIABILITY OF THIRD PERSON TO AGENT

10. **ACTION OF AUTHORIZED AGENT OF DISCLOSED PRINCIPAL**

    In general, a third party is not liable to an agent for breach of a contract made by the agent on behalf of a disclosed principal, unless the agent is also a party to or liable on the contract.

11. **UNDISCLOSED AND PARTIALLY DISCLOSED PRINCIPAL**

    GENERAL RULE.   A third party is liable to an agent for breach of contract if the contract was made by the agent on behalf of a partially disclosed or undisclosed principal.
    STUDY HINT.   A partially disclosed or undisclosed principal can also hold the third party liable on the contract, unless the contract is commercial paper and the principal was undisclosed.

12. **AGENT INTENDING TO BE BOUND**

    An agent can sue a third party for breach of contract if the agent is legally bound by the contract.

13. **EXECUTION OF CONTRACT**

    If an agent is liable on a contract to a third party, then the third party is liable to the agent.

14. **AGENT AS TRANSFEREE**

    An agent can hold a third party liable on a contract if the contract has been assigned to the agent.

C. LIABILITY OF PRINCIPAL TO THIRD PERSON

15. **AGENT'S CONTRACTS**
    - *Simple contract with principal disclosed*: A disclosed principal is liable if (1) an agent had actual authority or (2) the principal ratified the contract. The agent is not liable on the contract.
    - *Simple contract with principal partially disclosed*: If a principal is partially disclosed, the principal and agent are liable on the contract, and the third party must elect which one to hold liable.
    - *Simple contract with principal undisclosed*: ▸ An undisclosed principal is liable if an agent had actual authority to contract. ▸ *Election of remedies rule*: In some states, a third party must elect whether to hold the agent or undisclosed principal liable on a contract. (2) *Modern rule*: In some states, a third party can hold the agent and the undisclosed principal jointly and severally liable on a contract.
    - *Commercial paper*: Traditionally, an undisclosed principal has no legal obligation to pay commercial paper (e.g., a check) that is executed by an agent in the agent's own name.

16. **PAYMENT TO AGENT**

    ▸ Payment to an agent with actual authority to accept payments is deemed payment to a principal, even if the principal does not receive the money. ▸ Payment to an agent who has no authority to accept money is not valid payment unless the money is received by the principal.

17. AGENT'S STATEMENTS

A principal is bound by statements made by an agent while acting within the scope of authority.

18. AGENT'S KNOWLEDGE

A principal is bound by an agent's knowledge of most facts acquired while the agent is acting within the scope of authority, but a principal is not bound by knowledge of facts unrelated to the agency.

D. LIABILITY OF PRINCIPAL FOR TORTS AND CRIMES OF AGENT

19. VICARIOUS LIABILITY FOR TORTS AND CRIMES

GENERAL RULES. ▸ *Respondeat superior*: Traditionally, an employer has vicarious liability for the negligence of an employee who is acting within the scope of employment. Under the modern rule, an employer is also liable for an employee's intentional tort, fraud, or violation of a government regulation that is committed within the scope of employment. ▸ The same rules make a principal liable for torts committed by an agent who is acting within the scope of authority.
LIMITATION. There is no vicarious liability for: (1) a tort if an employee is not acting within the scope of employment; or (2) an intentional tort committed by an employee for a personal reason.
STUDY HINT. An employee is acting within the scope of employment if the employee's action is intended to further the employer's interests (even if the employee is violating a work rule).

20. NEGLIGENT HIRING AND RETENTION OF EMPLOYEES

An employer is liable for an employee's tort (including intentional tort) due to the employer's negligence in hiring or retaining the employee if (1) the employer knew or should have known that the employee posed an undue risk to others (2) regarding the harm that the employee actually caused to a third party.

21. AGENT'S CRIMES

▸ In general, a principal is liable only for an agent's crimes that the principal authorized or ratified.
▸ Some modern government regulations make an employer criminally liable for employee crimes that are committed within the scope of employment. Examples: environmental laws; liquor sales laws.

22. OWNER'S LIABILITY FOR ACTS OF AN INDEPENDENT CONTRACTOR

GENERAL RULE. An owner is generally not liable for an independent contractor's torts.
LIMITATIONS. ▸ An owner is liable for an independent contractor's tort if: (1) the owner controls the independent contractor's actions; or (2) the fact that a party is an independent contractor is not disclosed.
▸ Trend: An owner is liable for an independent contractor's tort if the assigned work: (1) is inherently dangerous; or (2) involves a heightened risk that a tort may be committed.

23. ENFORCEMENT OF CLAIM BY THIRD PERSON

A person can sue the employer or employee or both parties, but the person can recover only once.

E. TRANSACTIONS WITH SALES PERSONNEL

24. SOLICITING AND CONTRACTING AGENTS

▸ An order given to a soliciting agent is only an offer; it is not a contract until accepted by a principal.
▸ But, an acceptance of an order by a contracting agent forms a contract.

REVIEW OF TERMS AND PHRASES

Select the term or phrase that best matches a statement or definition stated below. Each term or phrase is the best match for only one statement or definition.

Terms and Phrases

a. Contracting agent
b. Disclosed principal
c. Election of remedies rule
d. Federal Tort Claims Act
e. Inherently dangerous work
f. Partially disclosed principal
g. *Respondeat superior*
h. Soliciting agent
i. Undisclosed principal
j. Vicarious liability

Statements and Definitions

____ 1. Principal whose existence and identity are disclosed to the third party at time of contracting.

____ 2. Liability imposed upon an employer or principal for a wrong that was committed by an employee or agent.

____ 3. Ultrahazardous activity that cannot be performed with total safety.

____ 4. Principal whose existence, but not identity, is disclosed to the third party at time of contracting.

____ 5. Principal whose existence and identity are not disclosed to the third party at time of contracting.

____ 6. Sales agent (salesperson) who does not have authority to accept a customer's order.

____ 7. Agent who has authority to accept a customer's order, thereby forming a contract.

____ 8. Federal law that imposes vicarious liability on the U.S. government for federal employees' torts that are committed while employees are driving motor vehicles in the course of employment.

____ 9. Doctrine that imposes vicarious liability on an employer for a tort that was committed by an employee while the employee was acting within the scope of employment.

____ 10. Rule followed in some states that requires a third party to choose whether to hold an agent or undisclosed principal liable on a contract.

REVIEW OF CONCEPTS

Write **T** if the statement is true, write **F** if it is false.

____ 1. In general, an agent of a disclosed principal is liable to a third party if the principal fails to perform a contract.

____ 2. An agent can generally avoid liability for breach of the implied warranty of authority by providing the third party with a copy of the writing that defines the agent's authority.

____ 3. An agent cannot be held liable for an improper payment or overpayment that is paid to the agent.

____ 4. An agent may agree to be personally bound by a contract that the agent made on behalf of a principal.

_____ 5. If an authorized agent signs the principal's name without indicating the agent's name or identity, then the signature generally operates as the signature of the principal.

_____ 6. In a lawsuit between an agent and a party to a contract, parol evidence may be admitted to prove whether the agent or a principal was intended to be the other party to the contract.

_____ 7. An employee is not personally liable for a tort or crime that the employee commits if the employee was acting within the scope of employment.

_____ 8. An agent can hold a third party liable on a contract if the third party could hold the agent liable.

_____ 9. Payment by a third party to an authorized agent discharges the party's liability to the principal.

_____ 10. A principal is bound by an agent's knowledge of facts that are within the scope of the agency.

_____ 11. A principal is criminally responsible for all crimes that are committed by an agent.

_____ 12. Under a modern trend, an owner may be vicariously liable for a tort that was committed by an independent contractor who was performing an inherently dangerous task for the owner.

_____ 13. Under the modern rule, a principal may be liable for fraud that is committed by an agent who was acting within the scope of authority.

_____ 14. Placing an order with a soliciting agent creates a contract between the customer and principal.

_____ 15. An employer is liable for an employee's intentional tort if the employer knew that the employee had a criminal record for committing this type of wrong and the relationship between this type of wrong and the employee's job created an unreasonable risk of harm to others.

REVIEW OF CHAPTER - APPLICATION OF CONCEPTS

MULTIPLE CHOICE QUESTIONS

_____ 1. Select the correct answer.
   a. Barry is manager of A&A Clothing Store, and he is authorized to buy inventory for the store. On behalf of a fully disclosed A&A, Barry bought a shipment of shirts from Seller. In this case, Barry is personally liable to Seller if A&A fails to pay for the shirts.
   b. Ali is manager of Bea's Candy Store. With no authority to do so, Ali made a contract on behalf of Bea's to buy a store from Seller. In this case, Bea's is not bound by the contract, but Ali is liable to Seller because Ali breached an implied warranty of authority.
   c. Fred contracted to sell land to Buyer on behalf of Pam, a minor. Buyer was unaware that Pam was a minor. Pam now refuses to perform the contract because she is a minor. In this case, Fred is not liable to Buyer for losses that Buyer may suffer because Pam is a minor.
   d. a and b.

_____ 2. Rosa was an agent for Saxon Inc. On behalf of Saxon and with actual authority to do so, Rosa contracted to buy a business from Seller. Rosa is not personally liable on the contract if:
   a. The existence and identity of Saxon was disclosed to Seller at time of contracting.
   b. The existence and identity of Saxon was disclosed to Seller soon after the contract was made.
   c. The existence, but not the identity, of Saxon was disclosed to Seller at time of contracting.
   d. Rosa did not intend to be personally bound on the contract. Rosa's disclosure or failure to disclose Saxon's existence and identity would not affect her liability on the contract.

_____ 3. On behalf of Wendy (a disclosed principal), Yen contracted to sell a patent to Ted. Yen had actual authority to sell the patent and to accept payment for the patent. Ted paid the price to Yen, who wrongfully kept the money. Under these facts:
   a. Yen is personally bound by the contract.
   b. Wendy is not personally bound by the contract.
   c. Wendy is bound by the contract, and Ted's payment to Yen discharged his liability to Wendy.
   d. Wendy is bound by the contract, and Ted's payment to Yen did not discharge his liability to Wendy.

_____ 4. With actual authority to do so, Susan contracted to lease a town house from Lessor on behalf of Birch. Susan made the contract in her personal name, without disclosing to Lessor the existence or identity of Birch or that Susan was acting only as an agent for Birch. Under these facts:
   a. Birch cannot be bound by the contract because Birch was an undisclosed principal.
   b. Birch cannot be bound by the contract because Birch was a partially disclosed principal.
   c. Birch cannot be bound by the contract because her name and identity were not expressly stated in the contract.
   d. Birch is bound by the contract once Lessor learns of her identity. But, under the traditional rule followed in some states, Lessor must elect whether to hold Susan or Birch liable.

_____ 5. Todd is an employee of C&C Car Sales. During working hours, Todd committed the torts described below. Under these facts, C&C may be vicariously liable for which torts?
   a. Todd intentionally hit Jim because Jim was dating Todd's girlfriend.
   b. While making a delivery for C&C, Todd negligently damaged Kip's car. Todd was speeding at the time of the accident, a violation of a work regulation adopted by C&C.
   c. Todd secretly abandoned his work and, while he was driving to see a friend thirty miles away, Todd negligently caused an accident with Helen.
   d. All of the above.

CASE PROBLEM

Answer the following problem, briefly explaining your answer.

Donna hired Pace Remodeling Co. to remodel her house for $30,000. Pace was required to remodel the house in accordance with certain plans, and Pace was to complete the work by May 1. Pace had the exclusive right to control the manner and method for performing the work, including the right to select the workers and tools to be used. One day, a Pace employee was picking up a bathtub to be installed in Donna's house. While loading the tub into a truck, the employee negligently dropped the tub, injuring Roger, a passer-by.

(a) What is the relationship between Donna and Pace? (b) Is Donna vicariously liable for Roger's injury? (c) Is Pace vicariously liable for Roger's injury?

CPA REVIEW

The following questions were given on CPA examinations. The answers for these questions are the unofficial answers prepared by the American Institute of Certified Public Accountants, Inc. (AICPA). All material is reproduced with permission of the AICPA.

____ 1. Easy Corp. is a real estate developer and regularly engages real estate brokers to act on its behalf in acquiring parcels of land. The brokers are authorized to enter into such contracts, but are instructed to do so in their own names without disclosing Easy's identity or relationship to the transaction. If a broker enters into a contract with a seller on Easy's behalf,
   a. The broker will have the same actual authority as if Easy's identity had been disclosed.
   b. Easy will be bound by the contract because of the broker's apparent authority.
   c. Easy will not be liable for any negligent acts committed by the broker while acting on Easy's behalf.
   d. The broker will not be personally bound by the contract because the broker has express authority to act.

____ 2. Which of the following rights will a third party be entitled to after validly contracting with an agent representing an undisclosed principal?
   a. Disclosure of the principal by the agent.
   b. Ratification of the contract by the principal.
   c. Performance of the contract by the agent.
   d. Election to void the contract after disclosure of the principal.

____ 3. North, Inc. hired Sutter as a purchasing agent. North gave Sutter written authorization to purchase, without limit, electronic appliances. Later, Sutter was told not to purchase more than 300 of each appliance. Sutter contracted with Orr Corp. to purchase 500 tape recorders. Orr had been shown Sutter's written authorization. Which of the following statements is correct?
   a. Sutter will be liable to Orr because Sutter's actual authority was exceeded.
   b. Sutter will not be liable to reimburse North if North is liable to Orr.
   c. North will be liable to Orr because of Sutter's actual and apparent authority.
   d. North will not be liable to Orr because Sutter's actual authority was exceeded.

____ 4. When an agent acts for an undisclosed principal, the principal will not be liable to third parties if the
   a. Principal ratifies a contract entered into by the agent.
   b. Agent acts within an implied grant of authority.
   c. Agent acts outside the grant of actual authority.
   d. Principal seeks to conceal the agency relationship.

CHAPTER 40

_____ 5. Able, as agent for Baker, an undisclosed principal, contracted with Safe to purchase an antique car. In payment, Able issued his personal check to Safe. Able could not cover the check but expected Baker to give him cash to deposit before the check was presented for payment. Baker did not do so and the check was dishonored. Baker's identity became known to Safe. Safe may not recover from
   a. Baker individually on the contract.
   b. Able individually on the contract.
   c. Baker individually on the check.
   d. Able individually on the check.

_____ 6. A principal will not be liable to a third party for a tort committed by an agent
   a. Unless the principal instructed the agent to commit the tort.
   b. Unless the tort was committed within the scope of the agency relationship.
   c. If the agency agreement limits the principal's liability for the agent's tort.
   d. If the tort is also regarded as a criminal act.

_____ 7. Neal, an employee of Jordan, was delivering merchandise to a customer. On the way, Neal's negligence caused a traffic accident that resulted in damages to a third party's automobile. Who is liable to the third party?

	Neal	Jordan
a.	No	No
b.	Yes	Yes
c.	Yes	No
d.	No	Yes

_____ 8. If an agent has, within the scope of the agency relationship, committed both negligent and intentional acts resulting in injury to third parties, the principal
   a. May be liable even if the agent's acts were unauthorized.
   b. May effectively limit its liability to those third parties if the agent has signed a disclaimer absolving the principal from liability.
   c. Will be liable under the doctrine of respondeat superior only for the intentional acts.
   d. Will never be criminally liable unless it actively participated in the acts.

CHAPTER 41
REGULATION OF EMPLOYMENT

CHAPTER OUTLINE

A. THE EMPLOYMENT RELATIONSHIP

1. CHARACTERISTICS OF RELATIONSHIP

An employee is a person who is hired to perform a service subject to the control of an employer. An employee is different from an agent and an independent contractor. (See Chapter 38)

2. CREATION OF EMPLOYMENT RELATIONSHIP

GENERAL RULES. ▸ Both the employer and the employee must consent to the creation of an employment relationship. ▸ Most employment relationships are made pursuant to employment contracts that may be either express or implied (e.g., one accepts services for which there is an expectation of payment). ▸ Contracts may be: (1) individual contracts negotiated with each employee; or (2) collective bargaining contracts relating to fundamental employment terms that are negotiated by a representative of all employees.
STUDY HINT. Collective bargaining contracts typically include terms relating to work assignments, wages and benefits, promotion and layoff, management's rights, and grievance procedures.

3. DURATION AND TERMINATION OF EMPLOYMENT CONTRACT

- *Employment-at-will doctrine*: Under the employment-at-will doctrine, an employment contract that does not state a fixed duration may be terminated by either party at any time, and for any reason or for no reason. However, a contract that states a fixed term can be terminated only for just cause.
- *Developing exceptions to employment-at-will doctrine*: The right to fire an employee at will is limited *in some states* by: (1) statutes; (2) public policy exceptions that forbid discharging an employee for refusing to do an illegal act, filing a worker's compensation claim, or reporting illegal activities in the workplace; (3) duty to act in good faith and deal fairly which prevents an employee's discharge if done only to benefit an employer (for instance, an employer cannot fire an employee just to avoid paying pension benefits); or (4) employer statements in personnel policies or employee handbooks that are viewed as part of the employment contract, thereby limiting the power to discharge an employee.
- *Justifiable discharge*: A contract that can be terminated for only "just or good cause" may be terminated because of an employee's: (1) nonperformance of duties; (2) fraud in obtaining the employment; (3) disobedience of proper orders; (4) disloyalty; (5) theft or other dishonesty; (6) illegal drug use; (7) misconduct; or (8) incompetency.

4. DUTIES OF THE EMPLOYEE

GENERAL RULE. An employee must (1) perform his or her contractual duties and (2) not disclose or use an employer's confidential trade secrets (whether this is expressly forbidden or not).
STUDY HINT. Unless otherwise agreed, an employee owns an invention that he or she makes. But an employment contract can legally state that the employer owns any invention made by the employee.

5. **RIGHTS OF THE EMPLOYEE**

- ■ *Compensation*: Employees have a right to be paid agreed wages, earned vacation pay, and bonuses. ▸ Unless otherwise agreed, a discharged employee has a right to be paid to the end of the pay period.
- ■ *Federal wage and hour law*: ▸ The Fair Labor Standards Act (Wage and Hour Act) provides that most workers cannot be paid less than a specified minimum wage. Executive, administrative, and professional employees and outside salespersons are exempt from the minimum wage and overtime provisions of this Act. Other provisions of this Act: (1) *subminimum wage*: certain persons may be paid less than the minimum wage; (2) *wage deductions*: deductions from wages for cash or merchandise shortages cannot reduce wages below the minimum wage; (3) *overtime pay*: an employee must be paid time and one-half for all hours worked in excess of forty hours per week; and (4) *child labor*: restrictions for hours of work and work assignments are stated for minors under sixteen.

B. **LABOR RELATIONS LAWS**

6. **THE NATIONAL LABOR RELATIONS ACT (NLRA)**

The NLRA established the right of employees to bargain collectively with employers. This Act also prohibits certain employer and employee actions as unfair labor practices and authorizes the National Labor Relations Board to enforce this Act.

7. **THE NATIONAL LABOR RELATIONS BOARD (NLRB)**

▸ Important functions of the NLRB, a federal agency, include (1) investigating and enforcing unfair labor cases and (2) conducting union representation elections and decertification elections (i.e., elections to remove a union as representative of a bargaining unit). ▸ The NLRB will certify a union as the exclusive representative of all employees within a given bargaining unit if a majority of the employees vote in favor of union representation.

8. **ELECTION CONDUCT**

▸ During the pre-election period, the NLRA prohibits: (1) employer interference or coercion of employees and threats of reprisals or promises of benefits. ▸ The "24-hour rule" forbids unions and employers from making speeches to captive audiences for twenty-four hours prior to a union election.

9. **UNION ACTIVITY ON PRIVATE PROPERTY**

GENERAL RULES. Employers can generally forbid union solicitation during working hours and prohibit all nonemployees, including nonemployee union officials, from soliciting on the employer's premises.
LIMITATION. An employer cannot deny access to nonemployee union officials during nonworking time unless legitimate efficiency or safety concerns exist.

10. **FIRING EMPLOYEES FOR UNION ACTIVITY**

▸ An employer cannot directly or indirectly punish or fire an employee for lawful union activities or for supporting unionization. ▸ In a "dual-motive" case, an employer fires an employee for violation of a valid company rule and for union activity. To recover in this case, the employee must prove that the union activity was a motivating factor for the discharge. If this is proven, the employer is liable unless the employer can prove that the employee would have been fired for legitimate reasons without considering the union activity.

11. **DUTY OF EMPLOYER TO BARGAIN COLLECTIVELY**

GENERAL RULE. Once a union is elected and then certified by the NLRB, an employer must bargain in good faith with the union regarding all mandatory subjects of bargaining including: (1) working conditions; (2) wages; (3) hours; (4) seniority; (5) promotions; (6) layoff terms; and (7) grievances.
LIMITATION. An employer may, but is not required to, bargain regarding permissive subjects of bargaining, such as internal union affairs and benefits for already retired workers.

12. RIGHT TO WORK

Twenty-one states have adopted right-to-work laws that forbid agreements which deny a person employment because he or she is not a member of a union or does not pay union dues.

13. STRIKE AND PICKETING ACTIVITIES

- *Rights of strikers*: ▸ Employees can strike if: (1) an employer fails to agree to a union's demands (employees are "economic strikers"); or (2) an employer engages in unfair labor practices (employees are "unfair labor practice strikers"). ▸ Once a strike is over, economic strikers can require reinstatement to their former jobs only when positions become available; employers are *not* required to fire permanent replacements who filled the strikers' jobs. But, employers must immediately reinstate unfair labor practice strikers even if permanent replacements have been hired.
- *Picketing*: ▸ Legal picketing includes: (1) primary picketing, i.e., placing persons outside the site of a labor dispute; and (2) product picketing, i.e., picketing neutral retail stores and asking shoppers not to buy the employer's product. ▸ Illegal picketing includes: (1) mass picketing, i.e., massing many picketers in order to shut down entrances to a job site; and (2) secondary picketing, i.e., picketing an employer's customers or suppliers in order to persuade them not to do business with the employer.

14. REGULATION OF INTERNAL UNION AFFAIRS

The Labor-Management Reporting and Disclosure Act (LMRDA) imposes many standards in connection with union elections, such as secret ballots in local elections, to assure that union elections are democratic.

C. PENSION PLANS AND FEDERAL REGULATION

15. ERISA

▸ Employees Retirement Income Security Act (ERISA) requires: (1) administrators of pension funds to handle funds so as to protect employees' interests; (2) vesting of pension rights within 5 to 7 years; and (3) actuarially-established employer contributions. ▸ ERISA established the Pension Benefit Guaranty Corp. which guarantees that pension benefits will be paid if an employer goes out of business.

D. UNEMPLOYMENT BENEFITS, FAMILY LEAVES, AND SOCIAL SECURITY

16. UNEMPLOYMENT COMPENSATION

- *Benefits*: States provide unemployment benefits for most laid-off employees. However, agricultural, domestic, and state and local government employees are generally not covered.
- *Eligibility*: In most states, benefits are denied if an employee: (1) is unavailable for work in a similar job; (2) refuses similar work for comparable pay; (3) quits without cause; or (4) is fired for misconduct, such as theft or refusal to complete an alcohol treatment program.
- *Funding*: Employers are taxed for unemployment benefits based on their experience rating.

17. FAMILY AND MEDICAL LEAVES OF ABSENCE

GENERAL RULE. Family and Medical Leave Act of 1993 (FMLA) entitles male or female employees to twelve weeks of unpaid leave during any twelve-month period: (1) due to birth or adoption of the employee's child; (2) to care for the employee's spouse, child, or parent who has a serious health problem; or (3) due to a serious health problem of the employee that makes the employee unable to perform his or her job.

LIMITATION. To be eligible for this leave, an employee must (1) be employed by the employer for at least 12 months and (2) have worked at least 1250 hours during the twelve months preceding the leave.

18. SOCIAL SECURITY

Employers and employees are required to pay social security taxes that provide employees insurance protection for: (1) retirement benefits; (2) disability benefits; (3) life insurance; and (4) health insurance.

E. EMPLOYEES' HEALTH AND SAFETY

19. STANDARDS (OCCUPATIONAL SAFETY AND HEALTH ACT)

Under the Occupational Safety and Health Act (OSHA), the Secretary of Labor may create safety standards to protect employees from "significant" health risks. Standards must be economically feasible and can be adopted only after hearings and publication.

20. EMPLOYER DUTIES

▸ Employers have a general duty to keep a workplace safe from hazards likely to cause death or serious injury. ▸ OSHA requires employers to keep records of serious occupational illnesses or injuries.

21. ENFORCEMENT

▸ OSHA can inspect a workplace if there is a complaint or serious accident, but an employer can demand a warrant before inspection. ▸ OSHA may issue a citation for violation of safety or health regulations. An employer may contest the citation before the Occupational Safety and Health Review Commission, an independent commission. ▸ Employers cannot retaliate against employees for refusing to work in dangerous conditions, testifying in OSHA proceedings, or filing complaints.

22. STATE "RIGHT-TO-KNOW" LEGISLATION

Many states require employers to notify an employee's doctor, local public and fire officials, and neighborhood residents regarding hazardous substances used or maintained at the workplace.

F. COMPENSATION FOR EMPLOYEE'S INJURIES

23. COMMON LAW STATUS OF EMPLOYER

GENERAL RULES. ▸ Workers' compensation laws typically do not apply to certain employers, such as employers of agricultural, domestic, or casual workers. ▸ If workers' compensation laws do not apply, the common law requires an employer: (1) to provide a reasonably safe workplace, safe tools, and sufficient, capable coworkers; and (2) to warn of unusual dangers.

LIMITATION. Under common law, an employer is not liable for an employee's injury if (1) the employee was to any extent negligent, (2) the injury was caused by a fellow employee, or (3) the injury was caused by an ordinary work hazard.

24. STATUTORY CHANGES

GENERAL RULES. ▸ Workers' compensation pays medical benefits, a portion of lost wages for a stated number of weeks, and death benefits if an employee suffers work-related injuries or certain occupational diseases. ▸ Compensation is provided whether or not the employer or employee is negligent.

LIMITATIONS. ▸ An employee cannot sue an employer under tort law for damages for a work-related injury; workers' compensation is the employee's exclusive remedy. ▸ Typically, no compensation is provided for willful, self-inflicted injuries or injuries received while the employee was intoxicated.

H. EMPLOYER-RELATED IMMIGRATION LAWS

30. EMPLOYER LIABILITY

The Immigration Reform and Control Act (IRCA) establishes civil and criminal penalties for employers who knowingly hire aliens who have illegally entered the United States.

31. EMPLOYER VERIFICATION

When an employer hires someone, IRCA requires the employer to verify that the employee is legally entitled to work in the U.S. This is done by confirming that the employee has certain documentation.

REVIEW OF TERMS AND PHRASES

Select the term or phrase that best matches a statement or definition stated below. Each term or phrase is the best match for only one statement or definition.

Terms and Phrases

a. Collective bargaining contract
b. Dual-motive case
c. Economic striker
d. Employment-at-will doctrine
e. Family and Medical Leave Act
f. ERISA
g. Fair Labor Standards Act
h. Just (good) cause for job termination
i. Mandatory subjects of bargaining
j. National Labor Relations Act
k. National Labor Relations Board
l. OSHA
m. Permissive subjects of bargaining
n. Right-to-know laws
o. Unfair labor practice striker
p. Workers' compensation law

Statements and Definitions

____ 1. An employee's theft, failure to perform duties, or other serious misconduct.

____ 2. Federal law that established employees' right to collectively bargain with employers.

____ 3. Agreement negotiated between an employer and a representative of that employer's employees.

____ 4. State law that requires an employer to notify an employee's doctor, community residents, and local officials regarding hazardous substances maintained at the employer's workplace.

____ 5. Legal principle that generally authorizes an employer at any time and for any reason to discharge an employee who is not hired for a fixed term.

____ 6. Administrative agency that enforces federal laws relating to health and safety in the workplace.

____ 7. Federal law requiring full vesting of employee pension rights after five to seven years of service.

____ 8. State law that provides benefits for work-related injuries and certain occupational illnesses.

____ 9. Employment matters regarding which an employer must negotiate with the employees' collective bargaining representative.

____ 10. Federal law that requires employers to pay most employees at least a specified minimum wage.

____ 11. Employer discharges an employee for violating a valid work regulation and engaging in union activities.

____ 12. Federal administrative agency that is responsible for investigating unfair labor practices.

____ 13. Employment matters that an employer may, but is not required to, negotiate about with the employees' collective bargaining representative.

____ 14. Employee who is striking because an employer would not agree to a union's economic demands.

____ 15. Federal law that creates the right of certain employees to take up to twelve weeks of unpaid leave in certain situations.

____ 16. Employee who is striking because an employer has engaged in unfair labor practices.

REVIEW OF CONCEPTS

Write **T** if the statement is true, write **F** if it is false.

_____ 1. In general, an employment relationship cannot be created without the consent of both the employer and the employee.

_____ 2. In some states, public policy would prohibit discharging an employee at will if the reason for the discharge is because the employee refused to do an illegal act.

_____ 3. An employment-at-will contract is one that states a fixed term of employment, such as one year.

_____ 4. An employer has "good cause" to fire an employee if the employee committed fraud in obtaining employment or if the employee disobeys proper orders of the employer.

_____ 5. Absent a binding nondisclosure agreement, an employee can disclose an employer's confidential information and trade secrets after termination of employment.

_____ 6. Unless otherwise agreed, an employee generally owns any invention that the employee creates even if the employee used the employer's time and equipment in order to create this invention.

_____ 7. An employee who is terminated may be entitled to be paid for earned, but unused, vacation time.

_____ 8. The Fair Labor Standards Act requires that all employees, including executive and administrative employees, be paid a specified minimum wage.

_____ 9. The Fair Labor Standards Act restricts the hours of work and work assignments for employees who are under the age of sixteen.

_____ 10. In most states, an employee is ineligible for unemployment benefits unless the employee is available and willing to take a similar replacement job for comparable pay.

_____ 11. Safety standards established by the Secretary of Labor under the Occupational Safety and Health Act do not need to be economically feasible.

_____ 12. Under common law, an employer is not liable to an employee for work-related injuries that were caused by the employee's own negligence.

_____ 13. Agricultural and domestic workers are frequently not covered by workers' compensation laws.

_____ 14. Under workers' compensation laws, an employee who suffers a work-related injury is entitled to receive payment for only medical expenses and, if the employee dies, death benefits.

_____ 15. Under IRCA, an employer may be subject to civil and criminal penalties for knowingly hiring an alien who is not legally entitled to work in the United States.

REVIEW OF CHAPTER - APPLICATION OF CONCEPTS

MULTIPLE CHOICE QUESTIONS

____ 1. Marlene has been a full-time employee of Garland Corp. for two years. Marlene recently became pregnant and gave birth to a son. Garland Corp. is subject to the Family and Medical Leave Act of 1993. Under these facts:
   a. Marlene is entitled to receive one year of paid leave so she can care for her son.
   b. Marlene is entitled to receive twelve weeks of paid leave so she can care for her son.
   c. Marlene is entitled to receive twelve weeks of unpaid leave so she can care for her son.
   d. Marlene is not entitled to receive any paid or unpaid leave so she can care for her son.

____ 2. Ben's employment contract with Employer states that Ben can be terminated only for "good cause." Under these facts, Ben *cannot* be fired for which of the following reasons?
   a. Ben used illegal drugs during working hours.
   b. Ben participated in lawful union activities.
   c. Ben disclosed his employer's confidential customer list to a competitor.
   d. Ben falsely stated on his employment application that he had a required college degree.

____ 3. In most states, which individual would be eligible to receive unemployment benefits?
   a. Mary quit her job because it was boring.
   b. Jim was laid off from his job as a carpenter due to a recession in the building industry.
   c. Frank cannot find work because he is a full-time student and is unavailable for work.
   d. Elizabeth was fired because she was embezzling money from her employer.

____ 4. Teresa filed a safety complaint with OSHA against her employer, Bayside Industries. Teresa has alleged that there are serious safety hazards at Bayside's plant. OSHA has indicated that it wants to inspect Bayside's plant. Under these facts:
   a. OSHA has the authority to inspect Bayside's plant, and Bayside cannot require OSHA to obtain a warrant prior to inspecting its plant.
   b. OSHA has no authority to inspect Bayside's plant. OSHA has only the power to adopt health and safety regulations.
   c. OSHA can issue a citation against Bayside if it finds safety violations at Bayside's plant, but Bayside can contest the citation if it chooses to do so.
   d. Bayside can discharge Teresa for filing the complaint with OSHA.

____ 5. Sharon was injured while working for Ajax Corp. Sharon's accident and resultant injuries were the result of her negligence and the negligence of Ajax Corp. Also, Ajax alleges that the accident was due to Sharon's intoxication, which claim she denies. Under these facts:
   a. Sharon cannot recover workers' compensation because her negligence caused the accident.
   b. Sharon can forego workers' compensation, and she can instead elect to sue Ajax under tort law for all damages caused by Ajax's negligence.
   c. If Sharon was intoxicated, this fact would not affect her right to workers' compensation.
   d. If Sharon was not intoxicated, she can recover workers' compensation for medical benefits and a portion of her lost wages.

CASE PROBLEMS

Answer the following problems, briefly explaining your answer.

1. Weiss Co. employs 70 nonunion factory workers pursuant to contracts that do not state a fixed period of employment. Weiss also employs 10 management employees pursuant to two-year employment contracts.

    Weiss Co. has experienced financial difficulties and is considering these actions: (1) discharge Henry, a factory worker, even though he has properly done his work; (2) discharge Ellen, a factory worker, because she has filed a claim for workers' compensation; and (3) discharge Karen, a management employee, even though she has properly performed her work. Which of the foregoing actions may Weiss Co. legally do?

2. The assembly line employees of Sheridan Company are represented by Union Local 482. The company and union have been unable to agree upon a wage increase for the employees. Also, the company refuses to bargain with the union regarding internal management policies that do not relate to the employees. The union has called a strike because the company failed to agree to the union's requested wage increase for the employees.

    Under these facts: (a) Was the company legally required to negotiate with the union regarding the wage increase and/or internal management policies? (b) Is the union legally entitled to call a strike because the company refuses to agree to the wage increase? (c) Can the union picket the company's work site? (d) If the company hires replacement workers, must it fire them and rehire striking employees once the strike is over?

3. Isabel has been a full-time employee of Pell Corp. for ten years during which time Pell Corp. has had a pension plan for its employees. The plan is subject to all ERISA regulations. Isabel is concerned that she may be discharged, thereby depriving her of her pension benefits. She is also concerned that the pension fund may not have sufficient assets to pay her benefits when she retires, or that Pell Corp. may become insolvent thereby depriving her of her pension benefits.

    (a) What federal law regulates this pension fund? (b) When must Isabel's right to pension benefits vest? (c) What guarantee does Isabel have that she will receive her pension benefits if Pell Corp. goes out of business?

CPA REVIEW

The following questions were given on CPA examinations. The answers for these questions are the unofficial answers prepared by the American Institute of Certified Public Accountants, Inc. (AICPA). All material is reproduced with permission of the AICPA.

____ 1. Which of the following payments are deducted from an employee's salary?

	Unemployment compensation insurance	Worker's compensation insurance
a.	Yes	Yes
b.	Yes	No
c.	No	Yes
d.	No	No

____ 2. Which of the following provisions is basic to all workers' compensation systems?
   a. The injured employee must prove the employer's negligence.
   b. The employer may invoke the traditional defense of contributory negligence.
   c. The employer's liability may be ameliorated by a co-employee's negligence under the fellow-servant rule.
   d. The injured employee is allowed to recover on strict liability theory.

____ 3. Under which of the following conditions is an on-site inspection of a workplace by an investigator from the Occupational Safety and Health Administration (OSHA) permissible?
   a. Only if OSHA obtains a search warrant after showing probable cause.
   b. Only if the inspection is conducted after working hours.
   c. At the request of employees.
   d. After OSHA provides the employer with at least 24 hours notice of the prospective inspection.

____ 4. Under the Federal Fair Labor Standards Act, which of the following would be regulated?

	Minimum wage	Overtime	Number of hours in the workweek
a.	Yes	Yes	Yes
b.	Yes	No	Yes
c.	Yes	Yes	No
d.	No	Yes	Yes

CHAPTER 41   355

CPA REVIEW

_____ 5. Kroll, an employee of Acorn, Inc., was injured in the course of employment while operating a forklift manufactured and sold to Acorn by Trell Corp. The forklift was defectively designed by Trell. Under the state's mandatory workers' compensation statute, Kroll will be successful in

	Obtaining workers' compensation benefits	A negligence action against Acorn
a.	Yes	Yes
b.	Yes	No
c.	No	Yes
d.	No	No

_____ 6. An unemployed CPA generally would receive unemployment compensation benefits if the CPA
  a. Was fired as a result of the employer's business reversals.
  b. Refused to accept a job as an accountant while receiving extended benefits.
  c. Was fired for embezzling from a client.
  d. Left work voluntarily without good cause.

_____ 7. Nix, an employee of Fern, Inc., was injured in the course of employment while operating a drill press manufactured and sold to Fern by Jet Corp. It has been determined that Fern was negligent in supervising the operation of the drill press and that the drill press was defectively designed by Jet. If Fern has complied with the state's mandatory workers' compensation statute, Nix may
  a. Not properly commence a products liability action against Jet.
  b. Not obtain workers' compensation benefits.
  c. Obtain workers' compensation benefits and properly maintain a products liability action against Jet.
  d. Obtain workers' compensation benefits and properly maintain separate causes of action against Jet and Fern for negligence.

_____ 8. Farr, an employee of Sand Corp., was involved in an accident with Wohl, an independent contractor. Wohl was making a delivery for Byrd Corp. when Farr negligently passed through a red light resulting in the accident and injuries to Wohl and Farr. The accident occurred during Farr's regular working hours and in the course of Farr's employment. If Sand and Byrd have complied with the state's workers' compensation laws, which of the following is correct?
  a. Farr will either be denied workers' compensation benefits or have his benefits reduced due to his negligence.
  b. Farr will be denied workers' compensation benefits since Sand was free from any wrong-doing.
  c. Wohl will be denied workers' compensation benefits under Sand's or Byrd's workers' compensation policy.
  d. Wohl will be denied workers' compensation benefits due to the fellow-servant rule.

CHAPTER 42
EQUAL EMPLOYMENT OPPORTUNITY LAW

CHAPTER OUTLINE

A. TITLE VII OF THE CIVIL RIGHTS ACT OF 1964, AS AMENDED

Title VII seeks to eliminate discrimination against job applicants and employees on the basis of race, color, national origin, religion, and sex.

1. THEORIES OF DISCRIMINATION

A discrimination claim may be based on disparate treatment or disparate impact.

- *Disparate treatment*: A disparate treatment claim exists when an employer intentionally treats a job applicant or employee less favorably because of his or her race, color, national origin, religion, or sex.

- *Disparate impact*: Disparate impact exists when a neutral employment practice has a significantly different, negative impact on a protected group.

2. THE EQUAL EMPLOYMENT OPPORTUNITY COMMISSION (EEOC)

- *Procedure*: ▸ The EEOC administers Title VII and other federal antidiscrimination laws. A charging party (job applicant or employee) must first file a claim with a state or local EEO agency if one exists. If there is no such state agency, then the EEOC may attempt to resolve the dispute through conciliation. If this is unsuccessful, the EEOC may file suit or it may give the charging party a "right-to-sue" letter, entitling the party to file suit in federal court within ninety days.

- *Damages*: Victims of discrimination may recover damages, including back pay.

B. PROTECTED CLASSES AND EXCEPTIONS

3. RACE AND COLOR

▸ Discrimination based on a person's race or color is prohibited by Title VII. "Race" applies to all members of the following four major racial groups: black, white, Native American, and Asian-Pacific.

4. RELIGION

GENERAL RULES. ▸ Employers cannot discriminate against persons on the basis of their religion or religious beliefs. ▸ Employers must try to reasonably accommodate job applicants' and employees' religious beliefs and practices.
LIMITATIONS ▸ Employers are not required to violate a collective bargaining agreement or to go to great expense to hire a replacement to accommodate an employee's religious requirements for days off.
▸ Religious societies and schools may give preference to members of their religion.

5. **SEX**

   GENERAL RULES. ▸ It is illegal for employers to discriminate against male or female employees on the basis of their sex. ▸ The Pregnancy Discrimination Act requires that an employer treat pregnancy and related conditions in the same manner that other disabilities are treated.
   LIMITATION. Sex refers only to a person's gender (i.e., male or female). Therefore, Title VII does not prohibit discrimination because of a person's sexual orientation.
   STUDY HINT. If a particular employment requirement, such as the height, weight, or physical strength, has a disparate impact on women or another protected group, then the employer must be able to show that the requirement is actually job related.

6. **SEXUAL HARASSMENT**

   There are two types of sexual harassment for which an employer may be held liable under Title VII.

   - *Quid pro quo sexual harassment*: This type of harassment occurs when an employer or supervisor requests sexual favors from an employee in return for job benefits, such as a raise or promotion.
   - *Hostile working environment harassment*: ▸ This type of harassment occurs if the workplace becomes poisoned with sexual conduct. It may result from unwelcome sexual propositions, insults, suggestive pictures, and/or physical contact. ▸ Whether a work environment is "hostile" is determined by the facts of each case. ▸ Remedies may include an injunction, attorney's fees, and compensation for economic losses caused by an employee's job loss from the hostile environment.

7. **NATIONAL ORIGIN**

   GENERAL RULE. Title VII forbids discrimination based on a person's national origin.
   STUDY HINTS. ▸ Physical standards, such as height, must be justified as a "business necessity" if they tend to exclude persons of a particular nationality. ▸ English language skills can be considered in employment decisions only when it is clearly necessary for successful job performance. ▸ An employer can consider a person's accent only if it impairs his or her ability to communicate effectively.

8. **TITLE VII EXCEPTIONS**

   - *Bona fide occupational qualification (BFOQ) exception*: ▸ An employer can hire an employee on the basis of religion, sex, or national origin if this consideration is a BFOQ that is reasonably necessary to the normal operation of a particular enterprise. ▸ There is no BFOQ for race or color. ▸ A fetal protection policy that is intended to protect unborn children of women cannot be defended as a BFOQ.
   - *Testing and educational requirements*: ▸ Title VII allows professionally developed ability tests that are not designed, intended, or used to discriminate. Employers must prove that these tests and educational requirements are job related. ▸ The Civil Rights Act of 1991 forbids "race-norming," i.e., adjusting test scores or cutoff points to assure that minorities are considered for employment.
   - *Seniority systems*: Title VII allows differences in employment terms and compensation that are the result of a bona fide seniority system, so long as there is no intention to discriminate.

9. **AFFIRMATIVE ACTION AND REVERSE DISCRIMINATION**

   GENERAL RULE. An affirmative action plan (AAP) can undertake special efforts to hire, train, and advance women and minorities and, in appropriate cases, can extend preferences to them if necessary.
   LIMITATIONS. ▸ An AAP should: (1) have a plan; (2) be justified as remedial; (3) be voluntary; (4) not unnecessarily limit the interests of whites; and (5) be temporary. ▸ If an AAP is not justified or unreasonably limits the interests of whites, it is "reverse discrimination" and it is illegal.

C. OTHER EEO LAWS

10. EQUAL PAY

GENERAL RULE. The Equal Pay Act requires that employers must pay male and female employees the same wage for jobs that are substantially equal.

LIMITATION. Differences in pay for male and female employees are permissible if they are the result of: (1) a seniority system; (2) a merit system; (3) a pay scale based on quality or quantity of production; or (4) any factor other than the sex of the employees.

11. AGE DISCRIMINATION

- The Age Discrimination in Employment Act (ADEA) prohibits employers, unions, and employment agencies from discriminating against persons over forty years of age on the basis of their age. Twice the amount of damages can be recovered if age discrimination is willfully undertaken.

- The Older Workers Benefit Protection Act of 1990 prohibits age discrimination in connection with employee benefits unless the employer can prove that the cost of benefits for older workers is more than for younger workers.

12. DISCRIMINATION AGAINST PERSONS WITH DISABILITIES

GENERAL RULES. ▸ The Americans with Disabilities Act (ADA) prohibits discrimination against persons with disabilities who are qualified, with or without reasonable accommodation, to perform the essential functions of a job. Employers must make reasonable accommodations for employees with disabilities including: (1) making existing facilities accessible to and usable by persons with disabilities; and (2) restructuring jobs, modifying schedules, and acquiring or modifying equipment or devices.

LIMITATIONS. ▸ Employers are not required to make accommodations that would cause them an "undue hardship." ▸ The following conditions are not protected disabilities under the ADA:

(1) current, illegal use of drugs;
(2) transvestitism;
(3) transsexualism;
(4) pedophilia;
(5) exhibitionism;
(6) compulsive gambling;
(7) kleptomania;
(8) pyromania; or
(9) psychoactive substance disorders resulting from current illegal drug use.

STUDY HINTS. ▸ In certain cases, persons with contagious diseases may be protected from discrimination. Persons with AIDS are protected under the ADA and must be treated the same as anyone else with a disability.

D. EXTRATERRITORIAL EMPLOYMENT

GENERAL RULE. The Civil Rights Act of 1991 provides that U.S. citizens employed by American companies in foreign countries are protected by Title VII and the Americans with Disabilities Act.

LIMITATION. U.S. employers doing business in other countries are not required to comply with Title VII or the ADA if this action would violate the law of the host country.

REVIEW OF TERMS AND PHRASES

MATCHING EXERCISE

Select the term or phrase that best matches a statement or definition stated below. Each term or phrase is the best match for only one statement or definition.

Terms and Phrases

a. Affirmative action plan
b. Age Discrimination in Employment Act (ADEA)
c. Americans with Disabilities Act (ADA)
d. Bona fide occupational qualification (BFOQ)
e. Discrimination
f. Disparate impact
g. Disparate treatment
h. EEOC
i. Equal Pay Act
j. Hostile work environment harassment
k. Quid pro quo harassment
l. Race
m. Reasonable accommodation
n. Reverse discrimination
o. Seniority system

Statements and Definitions

_____ 1. Discrimination resulting from a neutral employment practice that has a disparate effect on a protected class.

_____ 2. Conduct against a person based on the person's race, color, religion, sex, or national origin.

_____ 3. Defense that allows an employer to hire a person on the basis of sex, religion, or national origin when necessary for normal operations of the business.

_____ 4. Law that forbids paying male and female employees different wages for substantially equal work.

_____ 5. Law that prohibits discrimination against persons over forty years of age.

_____ 6. Sexual harassment resulting from unwelcome sexual conduct that poisons the workplace.

_____ 7. Plan that may allow an employer to provide job preferences for women and minorities.

_____ 8. Law that prohibits discrimination against qualified persons with disabilities.

_____ 9. Federal agency that administers Title VII and other federal antidiscrimination laws.

_____ 10. Protected class under Title VII that includes blacks, whites, Native Americans, and Asian-Pacific individuals.

_____ 11. Employment program that benefits workers who have worked the longest time for an employer.

_____ 12. Sexual harassment that involves an employer's request for sexual favors in exchange for employment benefits.

_____ 13. Employer action required by the ADA to make a workplace accessible to employees with disabilities.

_____ 14. Discrimination that exists when an employer intentionally discriminates against a person on the basis of the person's race, color, religion, sex, or national origin.

_____ 15. Discrimination against whites resulting from an invalid affirmative action plan.

REVIEW OF CONCEPTS

Write **T** if the statement is true, write **F** if it is false.

_____ 1. Disparate treatment exists when a neutral employment practice has a disproportionate, negative impact on a protected class.

_____ 2. Title VII prohibits discrimination against males and whites.

_____ 3. An employee's religious practices must always be accommodated, even if accommodation requires violation of a collective bargaining agreement.

_____ 4. A religious society may refuse to hire a person who practices a different religion.

_____ 5. A combination of severe and widespread sexual intimidation, propositions, and the displaying of nude pictures in the workplace may constitute sexual harassment.

_____ 6. The sex (gender) of an employee may constitute a BFOQ in certain situations.

_____ 7. The race of an employee may constitute a BFOQ.

_____ 8. Title VII absolutely prohibits the use of tests in the hiring process.

_____ 9. An affirmative action plan can legally provide that only women or minorities will be considered for jobs.

_____10. In general, it is a violation of the Equal Pay Act for an employer to pay a male employee more than a female employee for performing the same job.

_____11. It is not a violation of the Equal Pay Act to pay different wages to male and female employees if the difference is due to a bona fide seniority system.

_____12. The ADA requires employers to provide reasonable accommodation for employees who use illegal drugs.

_____13. The ADA generally protects U.S. citizens who are employed by U.S. companies in foreign countries.

_____14. The ADA requires an employer to reasonably accommodate an employee who has a disability if the employee can perform the essential job functions with such accommodation.

_____15. Under the ADA, persons with AIDS are treated the same as persons with other disabilities.

CHAPTER 42

REVIEW OF CHAPTER - APPLICATION OF CONCEPTS

MULTIPLE CHOICE QUESTIONS

____ 1. The Johnson Trucking Company is a national trucking firm that is owned by four black women. The company hires only women and minorities because the owners are prejudiced against all other persons. Under these facts, this hiring practice:
   a. Violates Title VII.
   b. Violates the ADA.
   c. Violates the ADEA.
   d. Does not violate any laws because it is a valid affirmative action plan.

____ 2. ABC Sporting Goods International fired John as a salesperson because he is homosexual and is infected with the AIDS virus. Under these facts:
   a. ABC's discrimination against John because he is homosexual violates Title VII.
   b. ABC's discrimination against John because he is infected with the AIDS virus violates the ADA.
   c. ABC's conduct does not violate Title VII or the ADA.
   d. a and b.

____ 3. Mary was recently hired by XYZ Company to work as a stocker in the warehouse. Mary's male coworkers made a couple of sexual jokes in front of Mary. Mary was highly offended by these jokes and she quit. A reasonable person would not have been offended by these jokes, nor would a reasonable person have found the workplace to be hostile. Under these facts:
   a. XYZ would be liable to Mary for quid pro quo sexual harassment.
   b. XYZ would be liable to Mary for hostile working environment harassment.
   c. XYZ would not be liable to Mary for any type of sexual harassment.
   d. a and b.

____ 4. Mega Corporation is a U.S. firm that engages in substantial international business. Nancy, a U.S. citizen, applied for a job as a mechanic at Mega Corporation's Paris plant. Nancy was refused employment because the company has traditionally considered women only for secretarial positions at this plant. Under these facts:
   a. Mega Corporation has violated Title VII.
   b. Mega Corporation has not violated Title VII because Title VII does not apply outside the U.S.
   c. Mega Corporation has not violated Title VII because a U.S. company can discriminate in another country if it has traditionally done so.
   d. Mega Corporation has not violated Title VII because Title VII does not prohibit sex discrimination.

____ 5. The Christian Academy refused to hire Paul for a teaching position because he is Muslim. Instead, the Academy hired a Christian who had less experience than Paul. Under these facts:
   a. The Academy committed religious discrimination in violation of Title VII.
   b. The Academy committed religious discrimination in violation of the ADA.
   c. The Academy did not violate Title VII or the ADA.
   d. a and b.

_____ 6. Dr. Kathy Payne advertised for an "experienced receptionist, females preferred." Payne is a gynecologist and she believes that her patients feel more comfortable when greeted by a female receptionist than when greeted by a male receptionist. Bill, a highly qualified job applicant applied for the advertised job, but was rejected because of his gender. Under these facts, Payne has:
   a. Violated Title VII.
   b. Violated the ADA.
   c. Violated the ADEA.
   d. Not violated any federal antidiscrimination law.

_____ 7. Julio was born in Mexico and now lives in the United States. Julio is not yet a U.S. citizen. He applied for an analyst position at the Intelligence Research Center (IRC), a private firm that provides intelligence analysis for the government. Analysts must have top secret security clearance, which is impossible to obtain without U.S. citizenship. IRC refused to hire Julio because he did not have the required clearance. Under these facts IRC has:
   a. Violated Title VII.
   b. Violated the ADA.
   c. Violated the ADEA.
   d. Not violated any federal antidiscrimination law.

_____ 8. Ames Fire Department requires its firefighters to be able to lift 250 pounds because, on rare occasion, a firefighter may have to lift this amount of weight. Chris applied for a job as fire fighter and she was qualified to perform the duties of the job. Chris and all other female applicants were rejected, however, because they could not lift this weight. Fifty percent of the qualified applicants were women. Has the Ames Fire Department violated Title VII?
   a. Yes, it has committed a disparate treatment violation.
   b. Yes, it has committed a disparate impact violation.
   c. Yes, it has committed a sexual harassment violation.
   d. No, this requirement is a protected BFOQ.

_____ 9. Joe Wiper is the head custodian at Blinker High School. Joe told Maria, a school custodian, that her job may be in jeopardy because of cutbacks in the janitorial force. However, he told her that he could protect her job if she agrees to have sex with him. Has Blinker High School violated Title VII?
   a. Yes, it has committed a disparate treatment violation.
   b. Yes, it has committed a disparate impact violation.
   c. Yes, it has committed a sexual harassment violation.
   d. No, Blinker High School is not responsible for Joe's conduct.

_____ 10. Todd is a lawyer, and he is blind. Todd applied for a job as associate lawyer with a large, national law firm. Todd met all qualifications of the job. He also could perform all of the duties of the job if the firm occasionally provided a reader to help him with his legal research. The law firm rejected Todd's application, arguing that he is not qualified for the job. Under these facts, did the law firm violate the ADA?
   a. No, because Todd is blind, a condition that is not protected by the ADA.
   b. No, because Todd is not qualified to perform the job in question.
   c. Yes, because the ADA requires employers to hire all persons with a disability, whether they are qualified or not.
   d. Yes, because Todd is qualified to perform the job in question, if the law firm provides reasonable accommodation.

CASE PROBLEM

Answer the following problem, briefly explaining your answer.

Kim Pak was born in Korea and she recently became a U.S. citizen. Kim speaks fluent English, but she has a mild Korean accent. Her accent does not interfere with her ability to communicate with others. Kim applied for the job of manager at the Jasper Hotel, a large hotel in Minneapolis. However, Kim was not hired for this position.

Explain whether the following reasons are proper reasons for not hiring Kim. (a) Kim speaks with a slight Korean accent. (b) Kim is fifty years old, and she may not work for as many years as someone younger. (c) Kim has a hearing disorder and the hotel would have to spend $250 to purchase a special telephone for her.

CPA REVIEW

The following questions were given on CPA examinations. The answers for these questions are the unofficial answers prepared by the American Institute of Certified Public Accountants, Inc. (AICPA). All material is reproduced with permission of the AICPA.

____ 1. Under the provisions of the Americans With Disabilities Act of 1990, in which of the following areas is a disabled person protected from discrimination?

	Public transportation	Privately operated public accommodations
a.	Yes	Yes
b.	Yes	No
c.	No	Yes
d.	No	No

____ 2. Under Title VII of the 1964 Civil Rights Act, which of the following forms of discrimination is not prohibited?
   a. Sex.
   b. Age.
   c. Race.
   d. Religion.

____ 3. Under the Federal Age Discrimination in Employment Act, which of the following practices would be prohibited?

	Compulsory retirement of employees below the age of 65	Termination of employees between the ages of 65 and 70 for cause
a.	Yes	Yes
b.	Yes	No
c.	No	Yes
d.	No	No

364　　CHAPTER 42

CHAPTER 43
FORMS OF BUSINESS ORGANIZATIONS

CHAPTER OUTLINE

A. **PRINCIPAL FORMS OF BUSINESS ORGANIZATIONS**

  1. **INDIVIDUAL (SOLE) PROPRIETORSHIPS**

   - ■ *Definition*: An individual (sole) proprietorship is a business that is owned and controlled by one person, the proprietor.
   - ■ *Advantages*: ▸ *Formation*: There is no expense to form a sole proprietorship, and nothing is generally required to establish this business. ▸ *Control*: The owner controls all business decisions. ▸ *Profits*: The proprietor is entitled to all profits of the business. ▸ *Taxation*: Profits of the business are not subject to corporate income tax. Instead, profits are taxed only as personal income.
   - ■ *Disadvantages*: ▸ *Liability*: A proprietor has unlimited personal liability for debts of the business. ▸ *Capital*: The capital (financial resources) of the business is limited to the owner's personal assets. ▸ *Duration*: The business of a sole proprietorship commonly terminates on the death or disability of the owner.

  2. **PARTNERSHIPS**

   - ■ *Definition*: A partnership is an association of two or more persons who combine their financial resources and business skills to carry on a business for profit as co-owners.
   - ■ *Advantages*: ▸ *Formation*: A partnership does not require a formal organizational structure. Consequently, little or no expense is required to form a general partnership. ▸ *Capital*: The multiple ownership of a partnership permits individuals to combine their financial resources.
   - ■ *Disadvantages*: ▸ *Liability*: Each partner has unlimited personal liability for partnership debts. ▸ *Duration*: The duration of a partnership is potentially unstable because the death of any partner and numerous other events may cause a partnership to dissolve.

  3. **CORPORATIONS**

   - ■ *Definition*: ▸ A corporation is an artificial legal entity that may be created by permission of the government. ▸ The shareholders are the owners of a corporation, and they elect a board of directors who manage the corporation's business.
   - ■ *Advantages*: ▸ *Liability*: A shareholder's liability is limited to the amount of capital invested. ▸ *Capital*: A corporation can obtain investments from many individuals in order to raise significant capital. ▸ *Duration*: Corporations may enjoy perpetual (continuous) existence because a shareholder's death does not cause a dissolution of a corporation. ▸ *Transferability of ownership*: Shareholders are free to transfer shares.
   - ■ *Disadvantages*: ▸ *Formation*: Creating a corporation requires an expenditure of time and money. ▸ *Taxation*: A corporation pays income tax on its profits and shareholders are taxed on dividends paid to them, creating "double taxation."

B. SPECIALIZED FORMS OF ORGANIZATIONS

4. JOINT VENTURES (JOINT ADVENTURES)

- *Definition*: ▸ A joint venture is an association of two or more persons who pool their resources in order to engage in a single business undertaking, with profits and losses being shared equally unless otherwise agreed. ▸ Example: Texas Oil Corp. and Ramon Oil Corp. combine their resources to jointly build and operate an oil pipeline that will serve their respective oil fields.

- *Nature of relationship*: A joint venture is quite similar to a general partnership. The primary distinction is that a joint venture is typically formed to accomplish a single enterprise whereas a partnership is usually intended to operate an ongoing business.

- *Duration*: ▸ A joint venture terminates at the time stated in the joint venture agreement. ▸ If a fixed term is not stated, a joint venture can typically be terminated at any time by any party.

- *Liability to third persons*: A member of a joint venture has unlimited personal liability for obligations of a joint venture, including liability for torts committed by other venturers.

- *Controlling law*: In general, a joint venture is governed by general partnership law.

5. UNINCORPORATED ASSOCIATIONS

- *Definition*: ▸ An unincorporated association is a group of two or more persons who come together in order to further a common (and typically nonprofit) purpose. ▸ Social clubs and fraternal orders are common types of unincorporated associations. ▸ Example: Mary Jean, Tanya, and Diana agree to perform free singing recitals for residents of local retirement communities.

- *Nature of relationship*: ▸ An unincorporated association is not a separate legal entity, and no formal organization is required. An association may result from any conduct or agreement to work together for a common purpose. ▸ Rights of parties are governed by ordinary contract law. Consequently, members cannot be expelled except for reasons expressly agreed upon.

- *Liability*: ▸ An unincorporated association cannot sue or be sued. ▸ An association member is generally not liable for an obligation of the association unless the member authorized or ratified the contract or action in question. ▸ If a member is liable for an association obligation, the member has unlimited personal liability for the obligation.

6. COOPERATIVES

- *Definition*: ▸ A cooperative is an association of two or more independent parties that cooperate with one another in order to accomplish a common objective. ▸ Examples: farmers collectively sell their crops; consumers collectively own and operate a food cooperative (i.e., grocery store).

- *Nature of relationship*: State laws frequently require that the profits of a cooperative must be shared by cooperative members. These laws commonly require that excess funds or profits be distributed to members in proportion to the volume of business that each member has done with the cooperative.

- *Incorporated cooperatives*: Statutes often provide special rules for incorporation of cooperatives.

- *Antitrust law exemption*: The Capper-Volstead Act of 1922 exempts normal activities of farmers' and dairy farmers' cooperatives from the Sherman Antitrust Act that prohibits price fixing. This exemption applies as long as the subject cooperatives do not conspire to fix prices with outsiders.

C. THE FRANCHISE BUSINESS FORMAT

7. Definitions and types of franchises

- ***Definitions***: ▸ A franchise is a business arrangement by which the owner of a trademark, trade name, or copyright licenses a franchisee to sell goods or services utilizing such mark, name, or copyright. ▸ A franchisor is the party who grants a franchise. ▸ A franchisee is the party to whom a franchise is granted.

Nature of (franchisor-franchisee) relationship

- ***Nature of relationship***: ▸ A franchise is a business relationship between separate businesses that is governed by a franchise contract. A franchisor and franchisee are independent contractors. ▸ The word "franchise" does not have to be used in order to create a franchise. A relationship is treated as a franchise if it meets the applicable legal test for a franchise. An element that is frequently required in order to satisfy this test is that a party has been granted the right to use another party's trademark, trade name, or logo.

- ***Duration and termination***: ▸ The franchise contract generally determines the duration of a franchise and the reasons for which it can be terminated. Contracts often allow termination upon a franchisee's death, bankruptcy, failure to make payments, or failure to meet sales quotas. ▸ Laws restrict termination of some franchises. Examples: (1) In some states, prior notice of termination is required. (2) The federal Automobile Dealers' Franchise Act forbids termination of auto dealership franchises for failure to comply with unreasonable demands.

- ***Regulation***: ▸ UCC Article 2 applies to a franchise if its primary purpose is the sale of a franchisor's goods. ▸ Antitrust law forbids an agreement between a franchisor-manufacturer and franchisee-distributor that fixes the resale price for the franchisor's goods. If a franchise is terminated because a franchisee violates this type of agreement, the franchisor is liable for treble damages. ▸ FTC rules require a franchisor to give a franchisee a disclosure statement ten days before signing a franchise contract or paying for a franchise. A franchisor may be fined for up to $10,000 if a franchisor knows or should know of this duty but fails to comply.

(c) The franchisor and third persons

GENERAL RULE. ▸ In general, a franchisor is not liable for the contracts or torts of a franchisee. ▸ Example: Acme Corp. grants Boswell a franchise to sell Acme's equipment. Boswell leases a store for its business. If Boswell defaults on the lease, Acme Corp. is not liable on the lease and it does not have to pay the rent.

LIMITATION. A franchisor may be liable to a third party in connection with a franchisee's business if: (1) the franchisor controls (or appears to control) the franchisee's business, and the franchisee is not (or does not appear to be) an independent contractor, but instead the franchisee is (or appears to be) an employee or agent; (2) the third party is injured due to the franchisor's negligence; or (3) the third party is injured by products made or supplied by the franchisor.

STUDY HINT. To avoid liability for a franchisee's acts, franchisors often require franchisees to give public notice that they are independent businesses, distinct from the franchisors.

(d) The franchisee and third persons

▸ A franchisee is liable to third persons for its contracts and torts to the same extent that the franchisee would be liable had there been no franchise. ▸ Example: Al has a franchise to sell ovens. While delivering an oven, Al negligently injured Pat. Al is personally liable to Pat.

REVIEW OF TERMS AND PHRASES

Select the term or phrase that best matches a statement or definition stated below. Each term or phrase is the best match for only one statement or definition.

Terms and Phrases

a. Cooperative
b. Double taxation
c. Franchise
d. Franchisee
e. Franchisor
f. Individual (sole) proprietorship
g. Joint venture
h. Partnership
i. Proprietor
j. Unincorporated association

Statements and Definitions

__b__ 1. Multiple taxation that occurs when a corporation is taxed on its profits, and shareholders are also taxed when corporate profits are distributed to the shareholders as dividends.

__j__ 2. Unincorporated group of two or more persons who come together to further a common, and frequently nonprofit, goal.

__d__ 3. Person to whom a franchise is granted.

__g__ 4. Association, similar to a general partnership, whereby two or more persons combine their resources in order to accomplish a single business undertaking for profit.

__c__ 5. Business arrangement whereby an owner of a trademark, trade name, or copyright licenses a person or business to sell or distribute goods or services using such mark, name, or copyright.

__h__ 6. Association of two or more persons to carry on a business for profit as co-owners.

__e__ 7. Person who grants a franchise to another person.

__f__ 8. Business that is owned and operated by one person.

__a__ 9. Association of two or more independent persons or businesses who cooperate with one another in order to accomplish a common objective.

__i__ 10. Owner of an individual (sole) proprietorship.

REVIEW OF CONCEPTS

Write **T** if the statement is true, write **F** if it is false.

__F__ 1. A proprietor does not have personal liability for the debts of an individual (sole) proprietorship.

__T__ 2. A disadvantage of a sole proprietorship is that its capital is limited to the owner's personal assets.

__T__ 3. In general, a franchisor is not liable for the contracts and torts of a franchisee.

__F__ 4. A franchise contract cannot define a franchise's duration; statutes determine this matter.

T___ 5. A franchise contract can legally permit a franchisor to terminate a franchise if a franchisee fails to make required franchise payments or if the franchisee fails to meet reasonable sales quotas.

T___ 6. Federal antitrust laws prohibit a franchisor and franchisee from agreeing on the price for which the franchisee will resell the franchisor's products.

T___ 7. FTC regulations require that a franchisor make certain disclosures to a franchisee at least ten days prior to signing a franchise contract or accepting money for a franchise.

F___ 8. A partnership is typically formed to only accomplish a specific undertaking whereas a joint venture is typically formed to engage in an ongoing business.

T___ 9. Unless otherwise agreed, the profits of a joint venture are shared equally by the venturers.

F___ 10. A joint venture is legally treated as a corporation and is governed by corporation law.

T___ 11. An informal bridge club is an example of an unincorporated association.

T___ 12. An unincorporated association is not a separate legal entity that is distinct from its members.

F___ 13. Statutes typically require that a cooperative's profits must be divided among cooperative members equally.

F___ 14. Cooperatives cannot be incorporated.

T___ 15. The Capper-Volstead Act declares that farmers' cooperatives violate the Sherman Antitrust Act because such cooperatives involve price fixing by the farmers who belong to the cooperative.

REVIEW OF CHAPTER - APPLICATION OF CONCEPTS

MULTIPLE CHOICE QUESTIONS

a___ 1. Alex intends to start a for-profit construction business. Alex wants to control the entire business, he does not wish to pay any expenses in order to create the business organization, and he wants to receive the entire net profits from the business. These are Alex's only considerations. Under these facts, which form of business organization is most appropriate for Alex?
   a. Individual (sole) proprietorship.
   b. Partnership.
   c. Corporation.
   d. Joint venture.

b___ 2. Betty and Dan intend to jointly establish and operate a for-profit catering business. Betty and Dan wish to use a form of business organization that: (1) will permit them to pool their respective personal assets for the purpose of conducting this business; and (2) will not entail any organizational fees to establish the business organization. These are the sole considerations of the parties. Under these facts, which form of business organization is most appropriate?
   a. Individual (sole) proprietorship.
   b. Partnership.
   c. Corporation.
   d. Franchise.

_C_ 3. Kelly, Pinky, and Bill are planning to start a for-profit manufacturing firm. It is important to the parties that they not have personal liability for obligations of the business, and that the business will continue even if one of the parties dies. These are the sole considerations of the parties. Under these facts, which form of business organization is most appropriate?
   a. Individual (sole) proprietorship.
   b. Partnership.
   c. Corporation.
   d. Joint venture.

_d_ 4. Nexus Computer Co. and Tracer Computer Co. are competing computer manufacturers. However, Nexus and Tracer have pooled their resources for the sole purpose of engaging in a business undertaking to develop a particular type of computer chip. Nexus and Tracer each have an equal right to control the business of this limited undertaking. Under these facts:
   a. Nexus' and Tracer's business is a joint venture.
   b. Nexus and Tracer each have unlimited liability for obligations arising out of this business.
   c. The parties' rights relating to this business are generally governed by partnership law.
   d. All of the above.

_a_ 5. Betsy, Peter, and Katie organized and operated a not-for-profit shelter for abandoned cats called "Nine Lives Shelter." The parties did not incorporate their undertaking. On behalf of the Nine Lives Shelter, Betsy purchased $500 worth of cat food on credit from Seller. Peter and Katie did not know of or consent to this purchase. Seller was never paid. Under these facts:
   a. Nine Lives Shelter is an unincorporated association.
   b. Peter and Katie are personally liable for the purchase price of the cat food.
   c. Seller can sue Nine Lives Shelter for the purchase price of the cat food.
   d. All of the above.

CASE PROBLEM

Answer the following problem, briefly explaining your answer.

Sugarland Co. granted Carlos the right to sell Sugarland's candy products and to use Sugarland's trademark and trade name in connection with selling its products. One day, Sue purchased a piece of Sugarland candy from Carlos. The candy made Sue ill because the candy was made with a toxic substance, giving rise to a claim for product liability. Also, the next day Tom slipped while walking in Carlos' store. Tom slipped because Carlos had negligently left a spilled drink on the floor.

(a) What is the business relationship between Sugarland and Carlos? Describe the nature of this relationship. (b) In general, is Sugarland liable for Carlos' contract and tort obligations? (c) Is Sugarland liable to Tom and/or Sue? Why or why not? (d) Is Carlos liable to Tom?

CPA REVIEW

The following questions were given on CPA examinations. The answers for these questions are the unofficial answers prepared by the American Institute of Certified Public Accountants, Inc. (AICPA). All material is reproduced with permission of the AICPA.

__b__ 1. A general partnership must
   a. Pay federal income tax.
   b. Have two or more partners.
   c. Have written articles of partnership.
   d. Provide for apportionment of liability for partnership debts.

__c__ 2. In a general partnership, the authorization of all partners is required for an individual partner to bind the partnership in a business transaction to
   a. Purchase inventory.
   b. Hire employees.
   c. Sell goodwill.
   d. Sign advertising contracts.

__d__ 3. Rivers and Lee want to form a partnership. For the partnership agreement to be enforceable, it must be in writing if
   a. Rivers and Lee reside in different states.
   b. The agreement cannot be completed within one year from the date on which it will be entered into.
   c. Either Rivers or Lee is to contribute more than $500 in capital.
   d. The partnership intends to buy and sell real estate.

__d__ 4. Grey and Carr entered into a written partnership agreement to operate a hardware store. Their agreement was silent as to the duration of the partnership. Grey wishes to dissolve the partnership. Which of the following statements is correct?
   a. Unless Carr consents to a dissolution, Grey must apply to a court and obtain a decree ordering the dissolution.
   b. Grey may not dissolve the partnership unless Carr consents.
   c. Grey may dissolve the partnership only after notice of the proposed dissolution is given to all partnership creditors.
   d. Grey may dissolve the partnership at any time.

_b_ 5. With respect to the following matters, which is correct if a general partnership agreement is silent?
   a. A partnership will continue indefinitely unless a majority of the partners votes to dissolve the partnership.
   b. Partnership losses are allocated in the same proportion as partnership profits.
   c. A partner may assign his interest in the partnership but only with the consent of the other partners.
   d. A partner may sell the goodwill of the partnership without the consent of the other partners when the sale is in the best interest of the partnership.

_d_ 6. A joint venture is a(an)
   a. Association limited to no more than two persons in business for profit.
   b. Enterprise of numerous co-owners in a nonprofit undertaking.
   c. Corporate enterprise for a single undertaking of limited duration.
   d. Association of persons engaged as co-owners in a single undertaking for profit.

_a_ 7. Noll Corp. and Orr Co. are contemplating entering into an unincorporated joint venture. Such a joint venture
   a. Will be treated as a partnership in most important legal respects.
   b. Must be dissolved upon completion of a single undertaking.
   c. Will be treated as an association for federal income tax purposes and taxed at the prevailing corporate rates.
   d. Must file a certificate of limited partnership with the appropriate state agency.

_b_ 8. Which of the following is a correct statement concerning the similarities of a limited partnership and a corporation?
   a. Both are recognized for federal income tax purposes as taxable entities.
   b. Both can only be created pursuant to a statute and each must file a copy of its certificate with the proper state authorities.
   c. Both provide insulation from personal liability for all of the owners of the business.
   d. Shareholders and limited partners may both participate in the management of the business and retain limited liability.

CHAPTER 44
CREATION AND TERMINATION OF PARTNERSHIPS

CHAPTER OUTLINE

A. NATURE AND CREATION

1. DEFINITION

▸ A partnership is a voluntary association of two or more persons to carry on as co-owners a business for profit. ▸ A partner is an agent of a partnership. A partner is not an employee even while the partner is performing work for the partnership.

2. CHARACTERISTICS OF A PARTNERSHIP

▸ A partnership is a voluntary relationship that is established to conduct a business for profit. ▸ Partners contribute capital or services, or both, and they are co-owners of partnership assets. ▸ A partnership is not a separate entity under the Uniform Partnership Act (UPA), but it is considered an entity under the UCC and by some courts.

3. RIGHTS OF PARTNERS

Partners' rights are determined by the partnership agreement. If an agreement is silent regarding a matter, the parties' rights may be determined by the UPA.

4. PURPOSES OF A PARTNERSHIP

A partnership may engage in any lawful business for profit. Illegal partnerships are void.

5. FIRM NAME

GENERAL RULE. A partnership may adopt a firm name, although it is not usually required to do so.
LIMITATIONS. ▸ A name (1) cannot be the same as or deceptively similar to another firm's name and (2) in some states, a name cannot use the words "and company" unless it indicates an additional partner. ▸ If a fictitious name is used, most states require registration of the name.

6. CLASSIFICATION OF PARTNERS

▸ *General partner*: partner publicly known as a partner who participates in partnership business. ▸ *Silent partner*: partner publicly known as a partner who does not participate in the business. ▸ *Secret partner*: partner not publicly known as a partner who actively participates. ▸ *Dormant partner*: partner not publicly known as a partner who does not participate. ▸ *Nominal partner*: person who holds himself or herself out, or permit others to hold him or her out, as a partner when this is untrue.

7. WHO MAY BE PARTNERS

▸ Any competent person can be a partner. Minors may be partners, but they can disaffirm and withdraw.
▸ Common law: corporation cannot be a partner; modern law: corporation can be a partner.

8. CREATION OF A PARTNERSHIP

GENERAL RULE. A partnership may be expressly agreed upon or it may be implied from conduct.
STUDY HINT. A partnership may be implied even if a business is not called a partnership.

9. PARTNERSHIP AGREEMENT (ARTICLES OF PARTNERSHIP)

GENERAL RULE. In general, a partnership agreement may be oral or written.
LIMITATION. A writing is required if a partnership's term is stated to be more than one year.

10. DETERMINING THE EXISTENCE OF A PARTNERSHIP (IMPLIED PARTNERSHIPS)

GENERAL RULES. ‣ A partnership may be implied. If a business has the characteristics of a partnership, it will be treated as a partnership. ‣ Important factors: (1) intent to do business as a partnership; (2) each party has a right to control the business; and (3) parties share profits and losses.
LIMITATION. Factors that do *not* establish a partnership: (1) profits are paid as wages or rent, or as payment for a debt; (2) gross income is shared; (3) parties merely co-own property and share the rentals from the property; or (4) a party is paid a fixed sum for his or her services.

11. PARTNERS AS TO THIRD PERSONS (NOMINAL PARTNERS)

A party (nominal partner) is liable to third persons: (1) if the party misleads, or permits others to mislead, third persons into falsely believing the party is a partner; and (2) third persons, to their detriment, extend credit to or transact business with the partnership in reliance on this misrepresentation.

12. PARTNERSHIP PROPERTY

GENERAL RULE. Partnership property generally includes: (1) property contributed by partners; (2) property acquired in the partnership's name; and (3) property acquired with partnership funds.
STUDY HINTS. ‣ Property that a partner agreed to contribute is partnership property even if title is not held in the partnership's name. ‣ Property bought with partnership funds is presumed to be partnership property unless a party can prove that it was intended to belong to an individual partner.

13. TENANCY IN PARTNERSHIP

GENERAL RULE. Partners hold title to partnership property by tenancy in partnership. This means: (1) each partner has an equal right to use the firm's property for partnership business; (2) a partner does not own, and cannot sell or mortgage, a divisible interest in specific items; (3) one partner's creditor cannot force a sale of specific properties; and (4) on a partner's death, title vests in the other partners.
STUDY HINT. An individual partner's creditor can obtain a charging order against a partner's interest in a partnership. A charging order entitles the creditor (1) to receive the partner's share of partnership profits when paid and (2) to force a sale of the partner's interest in the partnership.

14. ASSIGNMENT OF A PARTNER'S INTEREST

A partner can assign a partnership interest without the other partners' consent. An assignee does not become a partner; an assignee is only entitled to a partner's share of profits, and assets upon dissolution.

B. DISSOLUTION AND TERMINATION

15. EFFECT OF DISSOLUTION

GENERAL RULES. ‣ Dissolution is a change in the purpose of a partnership from that of pursuing a business to concluding the business. ‣ Upon dissolution, a partner has actual authority to contract only to the extent necessary (1) to wind up partnership affairs and (2) to complete existing contracts.
LIMITATION. A dissolution does not terminate a partnership. A partnership continues to exist during the winding-up process. A partnership terminates when its affairs are wound up.
STUDY HINT. Dissolution does not terminate the liabilities of partners.

16. DISSOLUTION BY ACT OF THE PARTIES

GENERAL RULE.   A partnership is dissolved by any of the following events:

- *Agreement*: expiration of the time or fulfillment of the purpose stated in the agreement, or unanimous consent of partners.
- *Expulsion*: expulsion of a partner by the other partners, whether the expulsion is proper or not.
- *Withdrawal*: partner's withdrawal, whether withdrawal violates a partnership agreement or not.

LIMITATION.   A sale or assignment of a partner's interest does not cause a dissolution.

STUDY HINTS.   ▸ If a partnership does not have a fixed duration, a partner may withdraw at any time and for any reason without liability. ▸ If a partner wrongfully withdraws from a partnership, the partner is liable to the other partners for any damages caused by the withdrawal.

17. DISSOLUTION BY OPERATION OF LAW

These events automatically cause a dissolution: (1) death of any partner; (2) bankruptcy (but not insolvency) of the partnership or any partner; or (3) the partnership business becomes illegal.

18. DISSOLUTION BY DECREE OF COURT

A partner may obtain a judicial dissolution of a partnership if: (1) any partner is judicially declared mentally incompetent or is indefinitely incapable of performing his or her duties; (2) any partner engages in serious misconduct (e.g., habitual drunkenness or repeated violations of the partnership agreement); (3) continuous, serious disagreements among partners make it impractical to continue business; (4) business cannot be continued except at a loss; or (5) other equitable reasons justify dissolution.

19. NOTICE OF DISSOLUTION

- *Notice to partners*: A partnership and each partner is liable for contracts made by a partner who was unaware of a dissolution that was caused by the death, bankruptcy, or act of another partner.
- *Notice to third persons*: ▸ A dissolved partnership is liable to a third party on a contract made by a partner without actual authority if: (1) dissolution was caused by an act of a partner; and (2) the third party did not have notice of the dissolution. ▸ Required notice: (1) Actual notice must be given to a third party who has previously dealt with a partnership. (2) Constructive notice, such as publication in a newspaper, is sufficient if a third party has not previously dealt with a partnership. (3) Notice is not required if a partnership is dissolved by operation of the law.

20. WINDING UP PARTNERSHIP AFFAIRS

GENERAL RULE.   Unless otherwise agreed, surviving or remaining partners have the right and obligation to wind up the business of a partnership following a dissolution.

LIMITATIONS.   ▸ Winding up only permits partners to take actions and make contracts that are necessary to conclude the partnership's business; partners cannot indefinitely continue the business.
▸ Partners who are winding up must account for the share of a partner who has withdrawn, been expelled, or died. If remaining partners wrongfully continue the business, the former partner (or estate) is entitled to the partner's share of partnership assets, *plus interest or a share of the profits.*

21. DISTRIBUTION OF ASSETS

Partnership assets are distributed in the following order: (1) payment of debts owing to third party creditors; (2) payment to partners for loans or advances; (3) return of capital contributions to partners; (4) remaining assets, if any, are divided among partners as profits.

22. CONTINUATION OF PARTNERSHIP BUSINESS

By agreement, a partnership's business is often continued by remaining partners after dissolution.

REVIEW OF TERMS AND PHRASES

... the term or phrase that best matches a statement or definition stated below. Each term or phrase is the best match for only one statement or definition.

Terms and Phrases

a. Articles of partnership
b. Charging order
c. Dormant partners
d. General partners
e. General partnership
f. Nominal partners (partners by estoppel)
g. Secret partners
h. Silent partners
i. Tenancy in partnership

Statements and Definitions

g 1. Partners who actively participate in a partnership, but who are not publicly known as partners.
e 2. Partnership that is formed for the purpose of generally conducting an ongoing business.
c 3. Partners who do not participate in a partnership and who are not publicly known as partners.
a 4. Agreement between partners that establishes the partners' rights and obligations.
d 5. Partners who actively engage in a partnership and who are known to the public as partners.
b 6. Court decree directing that a partner's share of profits be paid to the partner's individual creditor.
h 7. Partners who do not actively participate in a partnership, but who are publicly known as partners.
f 8. Persons who hold themselves out, or permit others to hold themselves out, as partners in a partnership when in fact they are not partners.
i 9. Ownership rights of a partner in specific items of partnership property.

REVIEW OF CONCEPTS

Write **T** if the statement is true, write **F** if it is false.

T 1. A partner is treated as an agent of a partnership, not as an employee.
T 2. To be a partnership, the business must be created by a voluntary, consensual association of two or more persons to carry on as co-owners a business for profit.
T 3. In many states, a fictitious partnership name must be registered with a designated public office.
F 4. A partnership cannot be created unless parties specifically call their relationship a partnership.
F 5. A partnership agreement cannot be enforced unless it is in writing.

T 6. The fact that parties share profits earned by a business is *prima facie* evidence that the parties' business relationship is a partnership.

T 7. A nominal partner is liable for all debts of a partnership, including debts owed to creditors who were not aware that the nominal partner had been misrepresented as being a partner.

T 8. Property may be partnership property even if title is held in the name of an individual partner.

T 9. In general, property that is acquired with partnership funds is presumed to be partnership property.

F 10. Upon an assignment of a partner's partnership interest, the assignee automatically becomes a partner in the partnership and is entitled to participate in the management of the partnership.

F 11. A dissolution of a partnership immediately ends the partnership's existence.

T 12. If a partnership does not have a definite duration or purpose, then any partner is legally entitled to withdraw at any time.

F 13. Bankruptcy of a partnership causes a dissolution, but bankruptcy of only one partner does not.

F 14. If a partnership is dissolved due to a partner's death, surviving partners can indefinitely continue the partnership business and they do not have to pay the estate for the deceased partner's interest.

T 15. Creditors of a partnership have priority to partnership assets over creditors of individual partners. (pg 860)

REVIEW OF CHAPTER - APPLICATION OF CONCEPTS

MULTIPLE CHOICE QUESTIONS

c 1. In which situation does a partnership probably exist between Felix and Art?
   a. Felix owed $10,000 to Art. Felix agreed to pay 10 percent of his company's profits to Art as partial payment of the $10,000 debt.
   b. Felix owns an insurance agency. As compensation, Felix pays Art 5 percent of the gross premiums paid on insurance policies that are sold by Art.
   c. Felix and Art co-own a grocery store. Felix and Art jointly control the business and they share the net profits and losses derived from the store.
   d. All of the above.

b 2. Cal, Oscar, and Len are partners. Cal's creditor has obtained a charging order against Cal's partnership interest. Oscar wants to sell his interest in a truck that is owned by the partnership. Len wants to use the partnership's computer to prepare partnership tax returns. In this case:
   a. Cal's creditor can force a sale of Cal's interest in specific items of partnership property.
   b. Cal's creditor is entitled to Cal's share of partnership profits when they are distributed.
   c. Oscar can sell his interest in the partnership truck.
   d. Len cannot use the computer without first obtaining the other partners' approval.

CHAPTER 44

__a__ 3. Bruce, Mark, and Erwin are partners in B-MER Partnership. The agreement states that the partnership will continue until January 1, 2001. Which event would *not* cause a dissolution?
   a. On May 1, 1999, Bruce assigns his partnership interest to Reginald.
   b. On May 1, 1999, Mark is declared bankrupt.
   c. On May 1, 1999, Erwin withdraws in violation of the partnership agreement.
   d. On May 1, 1999, Mark is expelled from the business for a reason authorized in the agreement.

__b__ 4. Lee and Mindy are partners in L&M Partnership. The partnership agreement states that the partnership will continue until June 1, 2000. In which situation can Lee properly request a court to enter a decree dissolving the partnership prior to June 1, 2000?
   a. Mindy made an ordinary contract on behalf of the partnership with authority to do so, but Lee objects to the contract.
   b. Mindy has embezzled partnership funds and she refuses to perform her partnership duties.
   c. The partnership is not quite as profitable as it was in the past.
   d. Lee cannot obtain a decree of dissolution; a court cannot dissolve a partnership.

__d__ 5. Jim and Ray were partners in a partnership that bought and sold medical supplies. The partnership was dissolved due to Jim's proper withdrawal, and Ray was notified of the withdrawal. After dissolution, Ray contracted on behalf of the partnership to buy a shipment of supplies from Manufacturer who had previously dealt with the partnership. Manufacturer did not know of the dissolution. Ray intended to sell the supplies to new customers that he hoped to solicit on behalf of the partnership. Under these facts:
   a. Ray acted properly in making the contract on behalf of the partnership.
   b. Ray did not act properly in making the contract on behalf of the partnership.
   c. The partnership is liable on the contract.
   d. b and c.

CASE PROBLEM

Answer the following problem, briefly explaining your answer.

Clay, Bonnie, and Tess were partners in a partnership, and they equally shared partnership profits. The partnership has dissolved due to Clay's death. The partnership has $90,000 cash. The partnership owes $20,000 to Rosco, an outside creditor, and it owes Tess $10,000 for an advance she made to the partnership. Clay contributed $15,000 to the partnership, Bonnie contributed $10,000, and Tess contributed $5,000. The partnership agreement is silent regarding the partners' rights upon the death of a partner.

(a) Can Bonnie and Tess indefinitely continue the partnership business or must they wind up the partnership's business? (b) In general, who is entitled to wind up the affairs of a partnership? (c) If the partnership in this case is wound up, to whom and in what order will the partnership assets be distributed?

CPA REVIEW

The following questions were given on CPA examinations. The answers for these questions are the unofficial answers prepared by the American Institute of Certified Public Accountants, Inc. (AICPA). All material is reproduced with permission of the AICPA.

 1. Which of the following requirements must be met to have a valid partnership exist?
   I. Co-ownership of all property used in a business.
   II. Co-ownership of a business for profit.
   a. I only.
   b. II only.
   c. Both I and II.
   d. Neither I nor II.

Questions 2 and 3 are based on the following:

Downs, Frey, and Vick formed the DFV general partnership to act as manufacturers' representatives. The partners agreed Downs would receive 40% of any partnership profits and Frey and Vick would each receive 30% of such profits. It was also agreed that the partnership would not terminate for five years. After the fourth year, the partners agreed to terminate the partnership. At that time, the partners' capital accounts were as follows: Downs, $20,000; Frey, $15,000; and Vick, $10,000. There also were undistributed losses of $30,000.

 2. Which of the following statements about the form of the DFV partnership agreement is correct?
   a. It must be in writing because the partnership was to last for longer than one year.
   b. It must be in writing because partnership profits would not be equally divided.
   c. It could be oral because the partners had explicitly agreed to do business together.
   d. It could be oral because the partnership did not deal in real estate.

 3. If Frey died before the partnership terminated
   a. Downs and Vick, as a majority of the partners, would have been able to continue the partnership.
   b. The partnership would have continued until the five-year term expired.
   c. The partnership would automatically dissolve.
   d. Downs and Vick would have Frey's interest in the Partnership.

 4. Cobb, Inc., a partner in TLC Partnership, assigns its partnership interest to Bean, who is not made a partner. After the assignment, Bean asserts the rights to
   I. Participate in the management of TLC.
   II. Cobb's share of TLC's partnership profits.
   Bean is correct as to which of these rights?
   a. I only.
   b. II only.
   c. I and II.
   d. Neither I nor II.

CHAPTER 44

_d_ 5. Grey and Carr entered into a written partnership agreement to operate a hardware store. Their agreement was silent as to the duration of the partnership. Grey wishes to dissolve the partnership. Which of the following statements is correct?
   a. Unless Carr consents to a dissolution, Grey must apply to a court and obtain a decree ordering the dissolution.
   b. Grey may not dissolve the partnership unless Carr consents.
   c. Grey may dissolve the partnership only after notice of the proposed dissolution is given to all partnership creditors.
   d. Grey may dissolve the partnership at any time.

_d_ 6. The partners of College Assoc., a general partnership, decided to dissolve the partnership and agreed that none of the partners would continue to use the partnership name. Under the Uniform Partnership Act, which of the following events will occur on dissolution of the partnership?

	Each partner's existing liability would be discharged	Each partner's apparent authority would continue
a.	Yes	Yes
b.	Yes	No
c.	No	Yes
d.	No	No

_a_ 7. On dissolution of a general partnership, distributions will be made on account of:
   I. Partners' capital accounts
   II. Amounts owed partners with respect to profits
   III. Amounts owed partners for loans to the partnership
   in the following order

   a. III, I, II.
   b. I, II, III.   pg 860
   c. II, III, I.
   d. III, II, I.

_d_ 8. Unless otherwise provided in a general partnership agreement, which of the following statements is correct when a partner dies?

	The deceased partner's executor would automatically become a partner	The deceased partner's estate would be free from any partnership liabilities	The partnership would be dissolved automatically
a.	Yes	Yes	Yes
b.	Yes	No	No
c.	No	Yes	No
d.	No	No	Yes

CHAPTER 45
PARTNERSHIPS, LIMITED PARTNERSHIPS, AND LIMITED LIABILITY COMPANIES

CHAPTER OUTLINE

A. AUTHORITY OF PARTNERS

1. AUTHORITY OF MAJORITY OF PARTNERS (COLLECTIVE MANAGEMENT)

GENERAL RULES. ▸ The decision of the majority of partners controls regarding ordinary matters arising in the usual course of partnership business. ▸ Transactions properly authorized by a majority of the partners are binding on the partnership and on all partners.

LIMITATION. Unanimous consent is required: (1) to amend the partnership agreement or to approve an action that conflicts with the agreement; and (2) to authorize any action that changes the nature of, or makes it impossible to carry on, the partnership business (e.g., a sale of all assets of the partnership).

2. EXPRESS AUTHORITY OF INDIVIDUAL PARTNERS

An individual partner has express authority to contract for a partnership if the contract is authorized by (1) the partnership agreement or (2) the required number of partners.

3. CUSTOMARY AUTHORITY OF INDIVIDUAL PARTNERS

GENERAL RULES. ▸ Unless expressly limited, a partner has customary authority to individually do what is needed to carry out partnership business in the usual way. Examples: (1) make ordinary contracts; (2) buy/sell inventory; (3) hire employees; (4) acquire/cancel insurance; (5) compromise and pay debts; (6) settle and receive payment of accounts; (7) make admissions and receive notice regarding partnership matters. ▸ A contract made by a partner with customary authority binds the partnership and all partners.

LIMITATION. There is no customary authority to do an act that requires unanimous approval.

STUDY HINT. A partner acting with customary authority is acting properly.

4. LIMITATIONS ON AUTHORITY (AUTHORITY DESPITE LIMITATIONS)

GENERAL RULES. ▸ Customary authority may be limited by: (1) the partnership agreement; or (2) a vote of a majority of partners. Such limits are binding on partners and third parties with notice. ▸ If a partner contracts for the partnership in violation of a limit on his or her authority, but the third party is unaware of the limitation: (1) the partnership is bound by the contract and (2) the acting partner is liable for any loss resulting from the contract.

LIMITATIONS. ▸ A third party cannot rely on a partner's statements regarding his or her authority. ▸ A third party may be charged with notice that a partner has no authority due to: (1) the nature of the partnership; (2) the transaction is outside the ordinary scope of partnership business; (3) the partnership's being dissolved; or (4) the act's being contrary to partnership interests.

5. PROHIBITED TRANSACTIONS (ACTS FOR WHICH EXPRESS AUTHORITY IS NEEDED)

GENERAL RULE. A partner cannot do the following acts without express authority: (1) any act that makes it impossible for a partnership to carry on its business; (2) contracts of surety, guaranty, or indemnity; (3) arbitration agreements; (4) confessions of judgment; (5) assignments of partnership property for the benefit of creditors; (6) contracts to pay personal debts using partnership assets.

STUDY HINT. A partnership is not bound by such acts unless a partner has express authority.

B. DUTIES, RIGHTS, REMEDIES, AND LIABILITIES OF PARTNERS

6. DUTIES OF PARTNERS

- *Loyalty and good faith*: A partner is a fiduciary of the partnership. Thus, a partner cannot: (1) misrepresent or conceal relevant facts; (2) make secret profits; (3) use partnership property for personal use; (4) take a partnership's business opportunity; or (5) compete with the partnership. These duties continue until a partner withdraws or a partnership is terminated (not just dissolved).
- *Obedience*: ‣ A partner must perform contract duties and obey restrictions imposed by (1) the partnership agreement or (2) a vote of the required number of partners. ‣ A partner must not make contracts for a partnership unless the partner has express or customary authority to do so.
- *Reasonable care*: ‣ A partner must use reasonable care in transacting partnership business. ‣ A partner is not liable for reasonable errors of judgment but is liable for negligent actions.
- *Information*: A partner must inform the partnership of all matters relating to partnership affairs.
- *Accounting*: A partner must account for all partnership property and keep appropriate records.

7. RIGHTS OF PARTNERS AS OWNERS

- *Management*: Equal right to participate in partnership's management, regardless of contributions.
- *Inspection of books*: Equal right to inspect the books and records of the partnership.
- *Share of profits*: Unless otherwise agreed, each partner is entitled to an equal share of profits, regardless of the partners' contributions or services rendered.
- *Compensation*: ‣ A surviving partner is entitled to be paid for services done in winding up a partnership. ‣ There is no right to compensation for other services unless the partners agree otherwise.
- *Repayment of loans*: Partners have a right to be repaid loans made to a partnership, with interest.
- *Payment of interest*: Contributions do not bear interest; advances (loans) by partners do.
- *Contribution and indemnity*: A partner who pays more than his or her proportionate share of a partnership debt has a right to contribution (repayment) from the other partners for their share of such debt. ‣ A partnership must indemnify (reimburse) a partner for payments made on behalf of the partnership, and personal liabilities incurred in conducting partnership business. ‣ There is no duty to indemnify if a partner acted in bad faith or negligently, or agreed to pay the expense.
- *Distribution of capital*: After payment of creditors and partner loans, a partner is entitled to repayment of contributions and a share of excess assets in accordance with percentage of profits.

8. LIABILITY OF PARTNERS AND PARTNERSHIP

- *Nature and extent of partners' liability*: ‣ Partners are jointly liable for unpaid partnership contracts. ‣ A partnership and all partners have joint and several liability for torts committed by any employee or partner while acting within the scope of the partnership business.
- *Liability for breach of duty*: If a partner breaches a duty to the partnership or another partner, then the partnership or partner may recover damages from the partner who breached the duty.
- *Liability of new partners*: A new partner has limited liability for partnership debts arising prior to the partner's admission. Unless otherwise agreed, a new partner's liability for preadmission partnership debts is limited to his or her contributions to the partnership.
- *Effect of dissolution on partner's liability*: Each partner or partner's estate remains liable for unpaid partnership obligations following the dissolution of the partnership or death of the partner.

9. ENFORCEMENT AND SATISFACTION OF CREDITOR'S CLAIMS

‣ A partnership may be sued by suing the partners doing business as the partnership. ‣ Creditors of an individual partner must first seek payment from a partner's personal assets. If such assets are insufficient to satisfy the debt, then the creditor may seek a charging order, whereby a court orders the partnership to pay the partner's share of partnership profits to the creditor until the debt is paid.

C. LIMITED PARTNERSHIPS

10. FORMATION OF LIMITED PARTNERSHIPS

- *Law*: In some states, limited partnerships are governed by the Uniform Limited Partnership Act (ULPA). In other states, the Revised Uniform Limited Partnership Act (RULPA) controls.
- *Members of a limited partnership*: A limited partnership is comprised of: (1) limited partners who contribute capital and whose liability is limited to their contributions; and (2) general partners who manage the partnership's business and have unlimited personal liability for partnership obligations.
- *Certificate of limited partnership*: ▸ A limited partnership can be created only by complying with applicable state law that requires filing a certificate of limited partnership with the appropriate government office. ▸ If a certificate is not filed, all partners are treated as general partners. However, technical defects in a certificate do not prevent formation of a limited partnership.

11. CHARACTERISTICS OF LIMITED PARTNERSHIPS

- *Capital contributions*: ▸ ULPA: A limited partner may contribute cash or property, but not services. ▸ RULPA: A limited partner may contribute cash, property, or services.
- *Firm name*: ▸ In general, a limited partner's name cannot be used in the partnership name. ▸ RULPA: A limited partnership's name must include the words "limited partnership."
- *Management and control of the firm*: ▸ General partners manage and control the partnership business, and limited partners cannot control partnership business. Limited partners forfeit their limited liability by exercising control over partnership business. ▸ RULPA: Limited partners can do these acts without losing their limited liability: (1) act as contractor or employee; (2) consult with or advise general partner; (3) act as surety; and (4) vote on extraordinary matters, such as dissolution.
- *Right to sue*: A limited partner may sue on a partnership's behalf if general partners refuse to do so.
- *Dissolution*: Dissolution and winding up are governed by rules applicable to general partnerships.

D. LIMITED LIABILITY COMPANIES

12. CHARACTERISTICS OF LLCs

- *Formation*: ▸ LLCs are a new type of business organization that are formed by filing articles of organization with the secretary of state. ▸ The name of an LLC must contain the words "limited liability company" or "LLC."
- *Capital contributions*: A "member" (owner) may buy an interest for cash, services, or property.
- *Management*: Management of an LLC is vested in its members who may delegate their authority to managers pursuant to an operating agreement. Managers are fiduciaries of an LLC.
- *Distributions*: Profits and losses are shared by members in accordance with the operating agreement.
- *Assignment*: A member can assign his or her interest, but the assignee does not become a member.
- *Dissolution*: ▸ Existence of LLCs is usually limited to thirty years. ▸ LLCs dissolve upon the consent of the members, or upon the death, bankruptcy, retirement, resignation, or expulsion of a member.
- *Technical classification*: In order to be taxed as a partnership, an LLC must meet certain tests.

13. LLCs AND OTHER ENTITIES (DIFFERENT CHARACTERISTICS)

▸ *LLC*: No limit on number of members or who may be members. ▸ *Subchapter S corporation*: This corporation is taxed like a partnership and it can have only 75 or fewer shareholders, shareholders can be only U.S. citizens or resident aliens, and shareholders cannot be corporations or partnerships. ▸ *LLC*: Members may actively participate in control of business without losing their limited liability. ▸ *Limited partnership*: Limited partners lose their limited liability if they exercise control of business.

E. LIMITED LIABILITY PARTNERSHIPS

A limited liability partnership is a special form of partnership in which a partner is not liable for torts committed by other partners or agents, unless the partner participated in or controlled the tortious conduct.

REVIEW OF TERMS AND PHRASES

Select the term or phrase that best matches a statement or definition stated below. Each term or phrase is the best match for only one statement or definition.

Terms and Phrases

- a. Articles of organization
- b. Customary authority
- c. Dissolution
- d. Express authority
- e. General partner
- f. Limited liability company
- g. Limited partner
- h. Limited partnership
- i. Manager
- j. Member
- k. Operating agreement
- l. Winding up

Statements and Definitions

__c__ 1. Change in the purpose of a partnership from pursuing an ongoing business to doing what is necessary to wind up the affairs of a partnership.

__e__ 2. Partner in a limited partnership who manages and controls the partnership business.

__a__ 3. Document that must be filed with the secretary of state in order to form a limited liability company.

__l__ 4. Following dissolution, process for concluding partnership business and distributing partnership assets in the manner required by law.

__j__ 5. Owner of a limited liability company.

__d__ 6. Authority of a partner given by the partnership agreement or by the required number of partners.

__g__ 7. Partner in a limited partnership whose liability is limited to his or her contributions and who does not control the partnership business.

__k__ 8. Document that sets forth the specific management authority of members and managers of a limited liability company.

__h__ 9. Partnership comprised of both general and limited partners.

__b__ 10. Implied authority of a partner to do those acts that are necessary to carry out the partnership business in the usual way.

__i__ 11. Person to whom members may delegate their power to manage the business of a limited liability company.

__f__ 12. New form of business organization in which anyone can be an owner, and owners may exercise control of the organization's business without losing their limited liability for business obligations.

REVIEW OF CONCEPTS

Write **T** if the statement is true, write **F** if it is false.

__T__ 1. In general, a decision by a majority of partners controls regarding ordinary partnership matters.

__T__ 2. Unanimous consent of all partners is required to authorize a transaction that will change the fundamental nature of a partnership's business.

__F__ 3. A partner's customary authority cannot be limited by the partnership agreement.

__T__ 4. Members of a limited liability company do not have unlimited personal liability for company debts.

T _____ 5. A partner must disclose any information to the partnership that relates to partnership affairs.

F _____ 6. A partner ceases to be a fiduciary of the partnership as soon as the partnership dissolves.

T _____ 7. A partner is automatically entitled to reasonable compensation for any services that the partner performs on behalf of the partnership.

T _____ 8. If a partner pays more than his or her proportionate share of partnership debts, the partner has a right of contribution entitling the partner to recover excess payments from the other partners.

F _____ 9. A partnership is not required to indemnify a partner for expenses that the partner paid on behalf of the partnership unless indemnification is expressly required by the partnership agreement.

T _____ 10. Corporations and partnerships can be members of a limited liability company but they cannot be shareholders of a Subchapter S corporation.

F _____ 11. A partnership and other partners are generally not liable for a tort that was committed by a partner who was acting within the scope of the partnership business.

T _____ 12. Partners in a limited liability partnership do not have personal liability for any type of partnership obligation.

T _____ 13. A new partner does not have unlimited personal liability for existing partnership obligations.

T _____ 14. A partnership creditor who has not been paid on a contract with the partnership must first exhaust the partnership assets before the creditor can seek satisfaction from the personal assets of partners.

T _____ 15. A general partner has unlimited personal liability for the obligations of a limited partnership.

REVIEW OF CHAPTER - APPLICATION OF CONCEPTS

MULTIPLE CHOICE QUESTIONS

C _____ 1. Don and Rene are the partners in a partnership that owns a retail paint store. Under these facts, Don does *not* have customary authority to make which contract on behalf of the partnership?
   a. Contract to purchase a case of paint.
   b. Contract to hire a salesclerk who is needed to run the store.
   c. Contract to sell the entire store.
   d. Contract to purchase fire insurance for the store.

d _____ 2. Laura is a partner in a partnership that owns a retail tire store. A partner in this type of partnership typically has customary authority to make warranties regarding tires that are sold. However, all partners agreed that no one would warrant tires without first obtaining the other partners' consent. In violation of this restriction, Laura sold tires to John and she warranted the tires against defects. The tires are defective, and John is demanding a refund that will cause a $300 loss. John was not aware of the limitation on Laura's authority. Under these facts:
   a. The partnership is not bound by the warranties made by Laura.
   b. The partnership is bound by the warranties made by Laura.
   c. Laura is liable to the partnership and the other partners for the $300 loss.
   d. b and c.

___b___ 3. Kit was a partner in a partnership that sold hospital supplies. In which situation did Kit breach a duty that she owed to the partnership or the other partners?
   a. Prior to dissolution, Kit purchased supplies for the partnership. Kit had express authority to act and she used reasonable judgment, but the partnership lost money due to the purchase.
   b. After the partnership dissolved but before it was terminated, Kit set up a new firm that purchased supplies from the partnership at discounted prices. Kit did not disclose her interest in the new firm, and she secretly profited from the firm's transactions with the partnership.
   c. After termination of the partnership, Kit opened a hospital supply company that competed with a new business that was created by her former partners.
   d. All of the above.

___b___ 4. Cooper, Tex, and Chien are the partners in CTC Partnership. Cooper contributed $50,000 to the partnership, and Tex and Chien each contributed $25,000. The partnership agreement is silent regarding management rights and allocation of profits. Under these facts:
   a. Cooper has the exclusive right to manage the partnership.
   b. Cooper, Tex, and Chien are each entitled to an equal vote regarding partnership matters.
   c. Cooper is entitled to 100 percent of the partnership profits.
   d. Cooper is entitled to 50 percent of the partnership profits.

___d___ 5. Ethel is the general partner in L&L Limited Partnership. Betty is a limited partner in the partnership. A certificate of limited partnership has been properly recorded, but the certificate has a minor technical error. Also, Betty periodically consults with Ethel regarding partnership business, although Ethel in fact controls the business. Under the RULPA:
   a. Betty has personal liability for partnership obligations because she is a limited partner.
   b. Betty has personal liability for partnership obligations because of the error in the certificate.
   c. Betty has personal liability for partnership obligations because she consulted with Ethel.
   d. Betty's liability for partnership obligations is limited to her contributions to the partnership.

CASE PROBLEM

Answer the following problem, briefly explaining your answer.

Harry and Al were the partners in a partnership that owned a drugstore. On behalf of the partnership, Harry bought inventory from Seller on credit for $5,000. Harry had customary authority to make this contract. The partnership failed to pay the contract price, and the partnership was subsequently dissolved. The partnership agreement states that Harry and Al shall each bear 50 percent of partnership losses.

(a) Is the partnership liable on the contract made by Harry? (b) Does the partnership's dissolution terminate Harry's and Al's liability for partnership obligations? (c) Does Al have personal liability for the contract price owed to Seller? (d) If Al pays the entire contract price, can Al seek contribution from Harry?

CPA REVIEW

The following questions were given on CPA examinations. The answers for these questions are the unofficial answers prepared by the American Institute of Certified Public Accountants, Inc. (AICPA). All material is reproduced with permission of the AICPA.

_____ 1. The apparent authority of a partner to bind the partnership in dealing with third parties
   a. Will be effectively limited by a formal resolution of the partners of which third parties are aware.
   b. Will be effectively limited by a formal resolution of the partners of which third parties are unaware.
   c. Would permit a partner to submit a claim against the partnership to arbitration.
   d. Must be derived from the express powers and purposes contained in the partnership agreement.

_____ 2. Acorn and Bean were general partners in a farm machinery business. Acorn contracted, on behalf of the partnership, to purchase 10 tractors from Cobb Corp. Unknown to Cobb, Acorn was not authorized by the partnership agreement to make such contracts. Bean refused to allow the partnership to accept delivery of the tractors and Cobb sought to enforce the contract. Cobb will
   a. Lose because Acorn's action was beyond the scope of Acorn's implied authority.
   b. Prevail because Acorn had implied authority to bind the partnership.
   c. Prevail because Acorn had apparent authority to bind the partnership.
   d. Lose because Acorn's express authority was restricted, in writing, by the partnership agreement.

_____ 3. Cass is a general partner in Omega Company general partnership. Which of the following unauthorized acts by Cass will bind Omega?
   a. Submitting a claim against Omega to arbitration.
   b. Confessing a judgment against Omega.
   c. Selling Omega's goodwill.
   d. Leasing office space for Omega.

_____ 4. Blake, a partner in QVM, a general partnership, wishes to withdraw from the partnership and sell her interest to Nolan. All of the other partners in QVM have agreed to admit Nolan as a partner and to hold Blake harmless for the past, present, and future liabilities of QVM. As a result of Blake's withdrawal and Nolan's admission to the partnership, Nolan
   a. Must contribute cash or property to QVM to be admitted with the same rights as the other partners.
   b. Is personally liable for partnership liabilities arising before and after being admitted as a partner.
   c. Has the right to participate in QVM's management.
   d. Acquired only the right to receive Nolan's share of QVM's profits.

CHAPTER 45

5. The partnership agreement for Owen Associates, a general partnership, provided that profits be paid to the partners in the ratio of their financial contribution to the partnership. Moore contributed $10,000, Noon contributed $30,000, and Kale contributed $50,000. For the year ended December 31, 1993, Owen had losses of $180,000. What amount of the losses should be allocated to Kale?
   a. $ 40,000
   b. $ 60,000
   c. $ 90,000
   d. $100,000

6. Which of the following statements is correct concerning liability when a partner in a general partnership commits a tort while engaged in partnership business?
   a. The partner committing the tort is the only party liable.
   b. The partnership is the only party liable.
   c. Each partner is jointly and severally liable.
   d. Each partner is liable to pay an equal share of any judgment.

7. In general, which of the following statements is correct with respect to a limited partnership?
   a. A limited partner will be personally liable for partnership debts incurred in the ordinary course of the partnership's business.
   b. A limited partner is unable to participate in the management of the partnership in the same manner as general partners and still retain limited liability.
   c. A limited partner's death or incompetency will cause the partnership to dissolve.
   d. A limited partner is an agent of the partnership and has the authority to bind the partnership to contracts.

8. Which of the following statements is correct with respect to a limited partnership?
   a. A limited partner may not be an unsecured creditor of the limited partnership.
   b. A general partner may not also be a limited partner at the same time.
   c. A general partner may be a secured creditor of the limited partnership.
   d. A limited partnership can be formed with limited liability for all partners.

CHAPTER 46
INTRODUCTION TO CORPORATION LAW

CHAPTER OUTLINE

A. NATURE AND CLASSES

1. THE CORPORATION AS A PERSON

A corporation is a separate legal entity that is given powers and created by government permission.

2. CLASSIFICATIONS OF CORPORATIONS

- ■ *Relation to public*: ▸ *Public corporation*: created to conduct government affairs. Example: municipal (city) corporation. ▸ *Private corporation*: created by individuals for private purpose. ▸ *Quasi-public corporation*: private corporation providing a basic service to the public. Example: gas company.
- ■ *Public authority*: created by government to accomplish specific purpose
- ■ *State of incorporation*: ▸ *Domestic corporation*: doing business in the state of incorporation. ▸ *Foreign corporation*: doing business in a state other than the state in which it was incorporated.
- ■ *Corporate functions*: ▸ *Special service corporation*: engages in a specialized commercial activity, such as insurance or banking. ▸ *Professional corporation*: engages in a profession, such as law. ▸ *Nonprofit corporation*: engages in charitable, educational, religious, or social activities.
- ■ *Special characteristic*: ▸ *Close corporation*: stock is owned by one or a few shareholders. ▸ *Subchapter S corporation*: shareholders elect to be treated as partners for income tax purposes.

3. CORPORATIONS AND GOVERNMENTS

- ■ *Power to create and regulate*: ▸ A corporation can be created by complying with the corporation code of the state of incorporation. (A majority of states have adopted some version of the Model Business Corporation Act (MBCA)).
- ■ *Constitutional rights*: ▸ In general, a corporation enjoys the same constitutional rights as natural persons. ▸ However, the privileges and immunities clause does not apply to corporations.

4. IGNORING THE CORPORATE ENTITY

GENERAL RULE. Shareholders, directors, and officers are not liable for corporate obligations.
LIMITATIONS. ▸ A court may "pierce the corporate veil" and hold shareholders liable for corporate obligations if necessary to avoid a fraud or an injustice. Factors that may justify this action include: (1) failure to keep corporate records and commingling of corporate and personal assets; (2) grossly inadequate capitalization; (3) diversion of corporate assets; (4) using a corporation to avoid existing obligations; (5) using a corporation to engage in fraud or illegal conduct; and (6) using a corporation to obtain an unjust benefit. ▸ Some courts also disregard the corporate shell when it is merely the "alter ego" of a person who uses it for wrongful purpose.
STUDY HINT. A court will *not* ignore a corporation's separate existence merely because: (1) two corporations have the same shareholders or are closely related (parent-subsidiary); (2) a corporation is formed to take advantage of tax benefits or to obtain limited liability for its owners; (3) a corporation cannot pay its debts; or (4) shareholders actively participate in a corporation's business.

B. CREATION AND TERMINATION OF THE CORPORATION

5. PROMOTERS

GENERAL RULES. ▸ A promoter is personally liable on a contract that the promoter made on behalf of a corporation to be formed unless: (1) the contract states otherwise; or (2) the promoter and third party intended otherwise. ▸ A corporation is not liable for a promoter's contract unless it expressly or impliedly adopts the contract. A promoter, but not a corporation, is liable for a promoter's tort.

STUDY HINT. A promoter is a fiduciary of the corporation and of prospective shareholders, and the promotor cannot make secret profits while acting on their behalf.

6. INCORPORATION

In order to create a corporation, incorporators sign appropriate forms and file them with the state.

7. APPLICATION FOR INCORPORATION (ARTICLES OF INCORPORATION)

The process of forming a corporation is ordinarily begun by filing an application for a certificate of incorporation with the secretary of state. The application typically includes articles of incorporation that must contain certain fundamental information about the corporation.

8. THE CERTIFICATE OF INCORPORATION (WHEN CORPORATE EXISTENCE BEGINS)

▸ In most states, a certificate of incorporation is issued after articles of incorporation are filed. ▸ In most states, corporate existence begins when the certificate is issued; in other states, existence begins when an organizational meeting is held. ▸ The Revised Model Business Corporation Act (RMBCA) eliminates certificates of incorporation; corporate existence begins when articles of incorporation are filed.

9. PROPER AND DEFECTIVE INCORPORATION

GENERAL RULES. ▸ A corporation legally exists if: (1) incorporation procedures are complied with perfectly or with only minor deviations (a *de jure* corporation); or (2) compliance with incorporation procedures is sufficient to warrant recognizing existence of a corporation despite substantial deviations from required procedures (a *de facto* corporation). ▸ If parties completely fail to comply with incorporation procedures: (1) a corporation is not created; and (2) persons acting for the purported corporation have the same liability for business obligations as partners would have.

LIMITATIONS. ▸ Under the corporation by estoppel doctrine followed by some states, a person who contracts with another party believing that the other party is a corporation cannot later impose personal liability on the other party. ▸ The RMBCA and many states do not deny corporate existence because of errors in following incorporation rules if the articles have been filed with the state.

10. INSOLVENCY, BANKRUPTCY, AND REORGANIZATION

A corporation experiencing financial difficulties may seek relief under bankruptcy law.

11. FORFEITURE OF CHARTER

Under the RMBCA, a state may seek to dissolve a corporation if the corporation fails to: (1) pay certain taxes; (2) file required annual reports; or (3) maintain a registered agent or office.

12. JUDICIAL DISSOLUTION

In some states, a corporation may be dissolved by judicial decree if management is deadlocked and the deadlock cannot be broken by the shareholders.

C. CORPORATE POWERS

A corporation has the powers that are authorized by its articles of incorporation in accordance with applicable law. The RMBCA and many states grant a corporation the same powers as natural persons enjoy in order to do all things that are necessary or convenient to carry out the corporation's business.

13. PARTICULAR POWERS

GENERAL RULE. Common corporate powers include the power to: (1) enjoy perpetual life (continuous existence); (2) adopt bylaws (rules governing internal affairs); (3) issue and repurchase stock; (4) make contracts; (5) borrow money; (6) execute commercial paper and issue bonds; (7) buy, sell, transfer, and mortgage property; (8) do business in another state; (9) be a general or limited partner; (10) establish and fund employee benefit plans; and (11) make charitable gifts.

LIMITATIONS. ▸ Bylaws cannot conflict with the articles of incorporation or state law. ▸ Under the RMBCA, authorized but unissued (unsold) shares may be sold for whatever price is set by the board of directors. ▸ A corporation cannot repurchase its stock if the corporation is insolvent or if the purchase would impair the corporation's capital.

STUDY HINTS. ▸ In most states, a corporation's name must contain some word indicating the company's corporate nature. ▸ With a few exceptions, a corporation need not use a corporate seal.

14. ULTRA VIRES ACTS

An action that exceeds the powers granted by the articles and applicable law is an *ultra vires* act.

D. CONSOLIDATIONS, MERGERS, AND CONGLOMERATES

15. DEFINITIONS

GENERAL RULE. Important definitions include: (1) *consolidation*: two or more corporations combine, terminating their separate existences and forming a new corporation; (2) *merger*: two or more corporations combine; one corporation continues to exist and the other corporation terminates; (3) *conglomerate*: parent corporation creates or acquires subsidiary corporations that engage in unrelated activities.

LIMITATION. If a shareholder dissents to an authorized consolidation or merger, the shareholder must be paid for his or her stock provided the shareholder returns the stock to the corporation.

STUDY HINTS. ▸ A "two-step merger" is a transaction whereby (1) an outside investor buys control of a target corporation, and (2) this control is used to approve a merger of the target corporation with a second corporation owned by the outside investor. ▸ Statutes commonly require disclosure of details of a merger or consolidation a certain number of days prior to any action on the combinations. These requirements are intended to make sure stockholders are fully informed about the nature and effect of the combinations.

16. LEGALITY

In some cases, a proposed consolidation, merger, or acquisition of assets may be prohibited by federal antitrust laws because it may substantially lessen competition in interstate commerce.

17. LIABILITY OF SUCCESSOR CORPORATIONS

- *Mergers and consolidations*: The new or continuing corporation that exists after a consolidation or merger is liable for obligations of the prior companies.
- *Asset sales*: A corporation that buys the assets of another company is not liable for the seller's debts unless the asset purchase is in effect a merger. Example: Company *A* buys all assets of Company *B*, issuing Company *A* stock as payment. This transaction will be treated as a merger.

REVIEW OF TERMS AND PHRASES

Select the term or phrase that best matches a statement or definition stated below. Each term or phrase is the best match for only one statement or definition.

Terms and Phrases

a. Articles of incorporation
b. Bylaws
c. Certificate of incorporation
d. Close corporation
e. *De facto* corporation
f. *De jure* corporation
g. Incorporator
h. Nonprofit corporation
i. Professional corporation
j. Promoter
k. Public corporation
l. Special service corporation
m. Subchapter S corporation
n. Treasury stock
o. *Ultra vires* act

Statements and Definitions

__c__ 1. Document issued by a secretary of state after appropriate application for incorporation and articles of incorporation are filed.

__b__ 2. Corporate document stating rules that govern the internal affairs of a corporation.

__e__ 3. Corporation that is created despite significant noncompliance with incorporation requirements.

__j__ 4. Person who brings together others who are interested in an undertaking, and who conceives of the idea of forming a corporation.

__f__ 5. Corporation that is created as a result of perfect or substantial compliance with incorporation requirements.

__a__ 6. Fundamental corporate document that is typically filed with a secretary of state in connection with an application to form a corporation.

__g__ 7. Person who signs and files articles of incorporation.

__i__ 8. Corporation formed to engage in a profession, such as the practice of medicine.

__n__ 9. Stock of a corporation that the corporation has issued and repurchased.

__m__ 10. Corporation whose shareholders elect to be treated as partners for federal income tax purposes.

__l__ 11. Corporation formed to carry out a specialized commercial enterprise, such as banking.

__o__ 12. Action that exceeds the lawful powers of a corporation.

__d__ 13. Corporation owned by one or a few persons.

__h__ 14. Corporation formed to carry out a charitable, educational, religious, or social activity.

__k__ 15. Corporation formed by the government to carry out governmental affairs.

REVIEW OF CONCEPTS

Write **T** if the statement is true, write **F** if it is false.

__T__ 1. A corporation is a legal entity that is separate and distinct from its shareholders.

__T__ 2. For federal income tax purposes, the profits and losses of a Subchapter S corporation are taxed to the shareholders.

__F__ 3. In general, corporations do not enjoy the constitutional rights granted to natural persons.

__F__ 4. In general, shareholders and officers are personally liable for the debts of a corporation.

___T___ 5. A parent corporation is automatically liable for the debts of a subsidiary corporation due to the close relationship between the corporations.

___T___ 6. A promoter is a fiduciary of the corporation to be formed and of prospective shareholders. Therefore, a promoter is prohibited from making secret profits at the expense of such parties.

___F___ 7. The RMBCA significantly limits the powers of a corporation, and it does not permit a corporation to exercise many of the powers enjoyed by natural persons.

___T?___ 8. Under the corporation by estoppel doctrine, a creditor cannot assert personal liability against an individual if the creditor thought that the individual was acting on behalf of a corporation.

___T___ 9. Under certain circumstances, a secretary of state may seek to dissolve a corporation if the corporation fails to pay certain taxes or if it fails to file annual corporate reports.

___F___ 10. In general, a corporation cannot repurchase its own stock.

_____ 11. Corporate bylaws do not bind shareholders unless the shareholders know of their existence.

___T___ 12. A two-step merger may be legal if it is undertaken for a legitimate corporate purpose.

___T___ 13. Minority shareholders that dissent from a proposed merger or consolidation generally have a right to compel the new or continuing corporation to buy their shares for a fair value.

___F___ 14. The new or continuing corporation that exists after a merger or consolidation is generally not liable for the obligations of the prior corporations.

___T___ 15. In general, a company that buys the assets of a second company is liable for the debts of the second company.

REVIEW OF CHAPTER - APPLICATION OF CONCEPTS

MULTIPLE CHOICE QUESTIONS

___d___ 1. Phyllis and Rod, who are cousins, are the sole shareholders of Food Inc. which was incorporated in Iowa. Food Inc. sells produce to wholesalers and the general public in Arizona. Food Inc. is a:
   a. Quasi-public corporation.
   b. Domestic corporation with regard to its business activities in Arizona.
   c. Professional corporation.
   d. Close corporation.

___c___ 2. Jim and Todd are the shareholders of J&T Inc. In which situation would a court be justified in piercing the corporate veil and imposing liability on Jim and Todd for obligations of J&T Inc.?
   a. Jim and Todd form J&T Inc. in order to obtain substantial tax benefits.
   b. Jim and Todd form J&T Inc. in order to avoid personal liability for future corporate debts.
   c. Jim and Todd form J&T Inc. in order to engage in illegal, fraudulent stock sales that would otherwise cause them significant personal liability.
   d. All of the above situations would justify piercing the corporate veil of J&T Inc.

__b__ 3. Sylvia planned to form a corporation to own and operate a shoe store. Prior to incorporation, Sylvia leased a store, signing the contract in her individual capacity and on behalf of the corporation to be formed. The corporation has now been incorporated. In most states:
   a. The corporation is liable on the contract even if it does not adopt the contract.
   b. The corporation is liable on the contract only if it adopts the contract.
   c. Sylvia was automatically released from liability on the contract when the corporation was formed.
   d. Sylvia will be released automatically from liability on the contract if the corporation adopts the contract.

__d__ 4. Polly wishes to incorporate Polly's Pets Inc. When will the corporate existence for this proposed corporation begin?
   a. The corporation will exist as soon as Polly files corporate bylaws with the Secretary of State.
   b. The corporation will exist as soon as Polly commences doing business as a corporation.
   c. Under the RMBCA, the corporation will not exist until Polly files articles of incorporation with the Secretary of State and the state issues a certificate of incorporation.
   d. In some states, the corporation will not exist until Polly files an appropriate application (with articles of incorporation) and the state issues a certificate of incorporation.

__b__ 5. The shareholders and board of directors of Acme Inc. and Belco Inc. have voted in favor of combining their respective corporations. Pursuant to this combination, Acme Inc. and Belco Inc. will terminate, and a new corporation, Cactus Inc., will be created. This combination is a:
   a. Consolidation.
   b. Merger.
   c. Two-step merger.
   d. Conglomerate.

CASE PROBLEM

Answer the following problem, briefly explaining your answer.

Ted and Alice intend to form a corporation and they are trying to determine what powers the corporation may have. Ted and Alice have asked you the following questions:

(a) If the articles of incorporation are silent regarding corporate powers, the RMBCA (and many states) will grant a corporation the right to exercise what general powers?
(b) Must the corporate name indicate that the enterprise is a corporation?
(c) Can the corporation be formed to have perpetual life?
(d) Can the corporation be empowered to buy, sell, and mortgage real and personal property?
(e) Must the corporation have a corporate seal?

CPA REVIEW

The following questions were given on CPA examinations. The answers for these questions are the unofficial answers prepared by the American Institute of Certified Public Accountants, Inc. (AICPA). All material is reproduced with permission of the AICPA.

____ 1. Rice is a promoter of a corporation to be known as Dex Corp. On January 1, 1985, Rice signed a nine-month contract with Roe, a CPA, which provided that Roe would perform certain accounting services for Dex. Rice did not disclose to Roe that Dex had not been formed. Prior to the incorporation of Dex on February 1, 1985, Roe rendered accounting services pursuant to the contract. After rendering accounting services for an additional period of six months pursuant to the contract, Roe was discharged without cause by the board of directors of Dex. In the absence of any agreements to the contrary, who will be liable to Roe for breach of contract?
   a. Both Rice and Dex.
   b. Rice only.
   c. Dex only.
   d. Neither Rice nor Dex.

____ 2. Under the Revised Model Business Corporation Act, which of the following must be contained in a corporation's articles of incorporation?
   a. Quorum voting requirements.
   b. Names of stockholders.
   c. Provisions for issuance of par and non-par shares.
   d. The number of shares the corporation is authorized to issue.

____ 3. The corporate veil is most likely to be pierced and the shareholders held personally liable if
   a. The corporation has elected S corporation status under the Internal Revenue Code.
   b. The shareholders have commingled their personal funds with those of the corporation.
   c. An ultra vires act has been committed.
   d. A partnership incorporates its business solely to limit the liability of its partners.

____ 4. Under the Revised Model Business Corporation Act, a merger of two public corporations usually requires all of the following except
   a. A formal plan of merger.
   b. An affirmative vote by the holders of a majority of each corporation's voting shares.
   c. Receipt of voting stock by all stockholders of the original corporations.
   d. Approval by the board of directors of each corporation.

_____ 5. Assuming all other requirements are met, a corporation may elect to be treated as an S corporation under the Internal Revenue Code if it has
   a. Both common and preferred stockholders.
   b. A partnership as a stockholder.
   c. (Seventy-five) or fewer stockholders.
   d. The consent of a majority of the stockholders.

_____ 6. Which of the following must take place for a corporation to be voluntarily dissolved?
   a. Passage by the board of directors of a resolution to dissolve.
   b. Approval by the officers of a resolution to dissolve.
   c. Amendment of the certificate of incorporation.
   d. Unanimous vote of the stockholders.

_____ 7. Generally, a merger of two corporations requires
   a. That a special meeting notice and a copy of the merger plan be given to all stockholders of both corporations.
   b. Unanimous approval of the merger plan by the stockholders of both corporations.
   c. Unanimous approval of the merger plan by the boards of both corporations.
   d. That all liabilities owed by the absorbed corporation be paid before the merger.

_____ 8. A parent corporation owned more than 90% of each class of the outstanding stock issued by a subsidiary corporation and decided to merge that subsidiary into itself. Under the Revised Model Business Corporation Act, which of the following actions must be taken?
   a. The subsidiary corporation's board of directors must pass a merger resolution.
   b. The subsidiary corporation's dissenting stockholders must be given an appraisal remedy.
   c. The parent corporation's stockholders must approve the merger.
   d. The parent corporation's dissenting stockholders must be given an appraisal remedy.

CHAPTER 47
CORPORATE STOCK AND BONDS

CHAPTER OUTLINE

A. CORPORATE STOCK

1. NATURE OF STOCK

GENERAL RULE. Stock (shares) represents a fractional ownership of a corporation and its assets.
LIMITATION. A shareholder does not own an interest in specific corporate assets.
STUDY HINTS. ▸ Stock is issued with a par value or with no par value. ▸ *Book value*: value of assets divided by outstanding shares. ▸ *Market value*: price for which stock is sold on open market.

2. CERTIFICATES OF STOCK AND UNCERTIFICATED SHARES

Ownership of stock is typically represented by a certificate of stock (share certificate). In some states, uncertificated shares (shares not represented by a stock certificate) may be sold.

3. KINDS OF STOCK

▸ A corporation typically issues common stock; it may also issue preferred stock. ▸ *Common stock*: right to vote on certain matters; no preference to dividends or distributions. ▸ *Preferred stock*: nonvoting; preference to dividends and/or distributions on dissolution. ▸ *Cumulative preferred*: dividends accrue for each year that dividends are not paid. Unless otherwise stated, it is frequently presumed that dividends for preferred stock accumulate if a surplus was available for payment of dividends but they were not declared. ▸ *Participating preferred*: preferred stock shares equally with common stock in extra dividends/distributions that are paid after all shareholders first receive equal dividends/distributions.

B. ACQUISITION OF SHARES

4. NATURE OF ACQUISITION

Shares may be acquired from a corporation or from a shareholder of the corporation.

5. STATUTE OF FRAUDS

▸ Contract to sell stock must be evidenced by a signed writing that describes the stock and states the number of shares sold and the price. A writing is not needed for stockbroker-client transactions.
▸ The 1994 version of UCC Article 8 dispenses with the writing requirement for sales of securities.

6. SUBSCRIPTION

- *Definition*: A stock subscription is a contract to buy an amount of shares when they are issued.
- *Preincorporation subscription*: ▸ In many states, a preincorporation subscription is merely an offer to buy stock; a contract is not formed until the corporation accepts the offer. ▸ Under the RMBCA, a preincorporation subscription is irrevocable for 6 months unless otherwise stated.
- *Subscription after incorporation*: A subscription is an offer; an acceptance is needed to form a contract. Typically, a subscriber is a shareholder as soon as a subscription is accepted.

7. TRANSFER OF SHARES

GENERAL RULE. In general, a shareholder can transfer stock to anyone the shareholder chooses.
LIMITATION. Shareholders may agree to reasonable restrictions on stock transfers. (Restrictions are not binding on transferees unless they are stated on a certificate or transferees know about them.)

8. **MECHANICS OF TRANSFER**

   When stock is represented by a certificate, it is transferred by an owner's indorsing the certificate and delivering it to a transferee. But, a transfer of a certificate to a transferee without an indorsement is still effective between the parties.

9. **EFFECT OF TRANSFER**

   GENERAL RULE. UCC Article 8: A good faith buyer of stock for value (1) receives the seller's title to the stock and (2) takes it free from many defenses that could be asserted against the seller.
   STUDY HINTS. ▸ A corporation views the owner of stock as being the shareholder of record (person who is registered as the owner on corporate books). ▸ A corporation may refuse to register a transfer if: (1) the transfer was wrongful; or (2) the outstanding certificate is not surrendered.

10. **LOST, DESTROYED, AND STOLEN SHARE CERTIFICATES**

    ▸ The owner of a lost, destroyed, or stolen certificate can request a new certificate if the owner posts an appropriate bond. ▸ In certain cases, an owner's rights to lost or stolen stock may be inferior to the rights of a good faith purchaser who purchased the lost or stolen stock for value.

C. RIGHTS OF SHAREHOLDERS

11. **OWNERSHIP RIGHTS**

    ▸ In general, shareholders may sell shares to whomever they wish and for any price they can obtain.
    ▸ A shareholder, even a director or officer, may sell shares at a premium, i.e., more than market price.

12. **RIGHT TO VOTE**

    - *Who may vote*: Common stockholders who are shareholders of record are usually entitled to vote.
    - *Matters entitled to vote upon*: (1) Election of board of directors; (2) extraordinary matters requiring shareholder approval, such as changing a corporation's capital, mergers, or a sale of all corporate assets; and (3) matters submitted by the board of directors for shareholder approval.
    - *Straight voting*: Shareholders may cast one vote per share on each matter that is voted upon.
    - *Cumulative voting*: ▸ Type of voting that may be used for electing directors. It is mandatory in approximately one-half of all states; it is optional in the other states. ▸ A shareholder has a number of votes equal to the number of shares owned multiplied by the number of directors being elected. Votes may be cast for one candidate or they may be allocated among several candidates.
    - *Voting by proxy*: By written proxy, a shareholder may authorize anyone to vote his or her shares.
    - *Voting agreements and trusts*: Shareholders may agree how they will vote their shares as a group.

13. **PREEMPTIVE OFFER OF SHARES**

    GENERAL RULE. If a corporation increases the authorized amount of common stock that it may sell, a preemptive right gives existing shareholders a right to buy a pro rata share of the new stock.
    LIMITATION. RMBCA: There are no preemptive rights unless this right is stated in the articles.

14. **INSPECTION OF BOOKS**

    ▸ In most states, a shareholder can inspect corporate books if it is done in good faith and for a proper purpose. Proper purposes include: (1) determining the value of stock; (2) investigating management's conduct; and (3) determining a corporation's financial condition. Improper purposes are:
    (1) harassment; (2) idle curiosity; (3) to obtain information to aid competitors. ▸ RMBCA requires a corporation to furnish an annual financial statement to shareholders.

15. DIVIDENDS

- ***Funds available for declaration of dividends***: ▸ Dividends can ordinarily be declared only to the extent a corporation has earned surplus (retained earnings). ▸ Exception: Wasting asset corporations can pay dividends out of current net profits and, in a few states, so can other types of corporations.
- ***Discretion of directors***: The board of directors has broad discretion to determine whether to declare a dividend; it need not declare a dividend even if there are funds available to pay a dividend.
- ***Form of dividends***: Dividends may be paid in cash, property, or in shares of the corporation.
- ***Effect of transfer of shares***: ▸ Cash dividend: Unless otherwise agreed, if stock is transferred, the owner on the record date (date fixed by board) receives a cash dividend, regardless when it is paid. ▸ Stock dividend: Owner on the date the dividend is distributed is entitled to the dividend.

16. CAPITAL DISTRIBUTION

▸ Upon dissolution, shareholders are entitled to corporate assets that remain after payment of creditors. ▸ Preferred shareholders typically have a limited preference to distributions of these assets.

17. SHAREHOLDERS' ACTIONS

▸ A shareholder may bring a derivative lawsuit on behalf of a corporation if the corporation improperly refuses to sue. In a derivative action, any monetary recovery is paid to the corporation.
▸ Shareholders bringing a derivative suit must show that they "fairly and adequately" represent the interests of other "similarly situated" shareholders.

D. LIABILITY OF SHAREHOLDERS

18. LIMITED LIABILITY

A shareholder's liability for corporate obligations is generally limited to the capital contributed by the shareholder. Ordinarily, a shareholder does not have personal liability for corporate debts.

19. EXCEPTIONS TO LIMITED LIABILITY

- ***Wage claims***: In some states, shareholders may be liable for wages owed to corporate employees.
- ***Unpaid subscriptions***: If a corporation is insolvent and money is needed to pay creditors, a shareholder is liable to the corporation and/or creditors for the amount owed for stock. Liability may exist if the par value for stock was not paid or if stock was paid for with overvalued property.
- ***Unauthorized dividends***: Subject to certain limitations in some states, if a dividend is improperly paid from capital, shareholders are liable to creditors for the amount of the improper dividend.

20. THE PROFESSIONAL CORPORATION

▸ A shareholder in a professional corporation is liable for his or her own torts committed while acting for the corporation. ▸ Depending on state law, a shareholder may or may not be personally liable for torts, such as malpractice, committed by other shareholders while acting for a corporation.

E. BONDS

21. CHARACTERISTICS OF BONDS

▸ A bond is an instrument, secured by corporate assets, promising to repay a loan to a corporation.
▸ The relation between a bondholder and corporation is that of creditor-debtor. ▸ Principal is paid on the maturity date, and interest is paid periodically. ▸ Bondholders have no right to vote.

22. TERMS AND CONTROL

Rights are stated in the loan contract (bond indenture/deed); indenture trustee represents bondholders.

REVIEW OF TERMS AND PHRASES

Select the term or phrase that best matches a statement or definition stated below. Each term or phrase is the best match for only one statement or definition.

Terms and Phrases

a. Bond
b. Book value
c. Certificate of stock
d. Common stock
e. Cumulative preferred stock
f. Derivative (secondary) action
g. Outstanding stock
h. Participating preferred stock
i. Par value
j. Preferred stock
k. Principal
l. Proxy
m. Stock subscription
n. Surplus (earned)
o. Voting trust

Statements and Definitions

_i_ 1. Minimum price for which certain designated stock may be initially sold by a corporation.

_a_ 2. Instrument promising to repay a loan to a corporation, which is often secured by corporate assets.

_n_ 3. Funds from which dividends can ordinarily be paid.

_j_ 4. Class of stock which typically is nonvoting, but which has a preference to dividends and/or distributions upon dissolution of a corporation.

_b_ 5. Stock valuation computed by dividing value of corporate assets by number of outstanding shares.

_h_ 6. Preferred stock that shares in excess dividends (distributions) paid after common stockholders receive dividends (distributions) equal to those already paid to preferred stockholders.

_m_ 7. Written offer to purchase a corporation's stock when the stock is issued by the corporation.

_c_ 8. Document evidencing a shareholder's ownership of stock.

_l_ 9. Writing that authorizes another person to vote one's stock.

_g_ 10. Stock that has been issued by a corporation and is owned by a shareholder.

_d_ 11. Class of stock that generally has voting rights, but no preferences to dividends or distributions.

_o_ 12. Agreement whereby shareholders transfer stock to a trustee who votes the shares in accordance with the parties' agreement.

_e_ 13. Preferred stock for which unpaid, past dividends accrue.

_f_ 14. Lawsuit filed by shareholders on behalf of a corporation.

_k_ 15. Amount of loan that a bond promises to repay.

REVIEW OF CONCEPTS

Write **T** if the statement is true, write **F** if it is false.

_F_ 1. Shares of stock cannot be issued without a par value.

_F_ 2. In general, a purchaser of stock is not a shareholder until a certificate of stock has been issued.

_T_ 3. Preferred stock is often presumed to be cumulative unless otherwise stated.

T 4. In general, a contract for the sale of stock must be evidenced by a writing to be enforceable.

F 5. In virtually all states, a preincorporation subscription agreement is deemed to be automatically binding on the subscriber and the corporation as soon as the corporation is incorporated.

T 6. In general, ownership of stock that is represented by a certificate is transferred by the delivery of a properly indorsed certificate to a buyer or other transferee.

T 7. A good faith buyer who purchases stock for value may take the stock free from certain defenses that could have been asserted by a third party against the seller.

___ 8. A secured party perfects a security interest in stock by taking possession of the stock certificate.

F 9. Cumulative voting enables a minority shareholder to elect a majority of the board of directors.

F 10. A shareholder cannot authorize another person to vote his or her shares.

T 11. Under the RMBCA, shareholders do not have preemptive rights unless this right is stated in the articles of incorporation.

F 12. Under no circumstance can a shareholder file a lawsuit on behalf of a corporation.

F 13. In all states, a shareholder in a professional corporation has personal liability for malpractice that is committed by another shareholder while acting on behalf of the corporation.

T 14. Bondholders are creditors of a corporation. Bondholders do not own an interest in a corporation.

F 15. Bondholders typically have the same right as shareholders to vote on corporate matters.

REVIEW OF CHAPTER - APPLICATION OF CONCEPTS

MULTIPLE CHOICE QUESTIONS

d 1. Axco Inc. has two classes of stock: common stock and cumulative preferred stock. In 1998, the board of directors of Axco did not declare a dividend even though there was a surplus sufficient to do so. In 1999, the directors intend to declare a dividend. Under these facts:
   a. Preferred stock must be paid a dividend for 1998 before common stock is paid a dividend.
   b. Preferred stock must be paid a dividend for 1999 before common stock is paid a dividend.
   c. Common stock must be paid a dividend before preferred stock is paid any dividends.
   d. a and b.

b 2. Ed was a majority shareholder of MED Inc. In a shareholder agreement, Ed and the other shareholders agreed not to sell their stock to anyone else without first offering it to each other. This restriction was not stated on the stock certificates. In violation of this agreement, Ed sold and transferred his stock to Hank who bought it in good faith and without knowledge of the restriction. Hank paid Ed a premium for his interest in the corporation. Under these facts:
   a. Ed was legally entitled to sell his stock to Hank because it is illegal to restrict stock transfers.
   b. Ed was not legally entitled to sell his stock to Hank, and the transfer to Hank can be set aside.
   c. Ed was not legally entitled to sell his stock to Hank, but the transfer to Hank cannot be set aside.
   d. The sale of stock to Hank was illegal because Hank paid Ed a premium for his stock.

__b__ 3. Roger is a minority shareholder in Neco Inc. Roger has demanded to inspect the records of the corporation. *In most states*, is Roger entitled to inspect the corporation's records?
   a. No. Shareholders have no right to inspect corporate records.
   b. Yes, if Roger intends to inspect financial records in order to compute the value of his stock.
   c. Yes, if Roger intends to obtain confidential corporate data in order to aid a competitor.
   d. Yes. Roger is entitled to inspect the records for any purpose; shareholders have an absolute right to inspect corporate records.

__c__ 4. KLZ Corp. had a $2 million earned surplus, and its board of directors declared a $1 million cash dividend. The record date for the dividend was March 1, and the payment date was May 1. On April 1, Todd sold and transferred shares of KLZ Corp. stock to Bob. In this case:
   a. The dividend was illegal. Only shareholders can declare a dividend.
   b. The board of directors was legally required to declare the dividend. A board of directors must declare a dividend if a corporation has earned surplus sufficient to pay the dividend.
   c. Todd was legally entitled to the dividend that was paid on the shares he sold to Bob.
   d. Bob was legally entitled to the dividend that was paid on the shares he bought from Todd.

__b__ 5. Benito is a shareholder in Wren Corp. Benito purchased 10,000 shares of $10 par-value common stock from Wren Corp. for $10 per share. Benito paid the corporation $50,000 for the stock. Wren Corp. subsequently paid Benito a $5,000 dividend out of capital at a time when it was insolvent and it owed $200,000 to Ace Finance Co. The corporation never paid Ace Finance Co. Under these facts, Benito has personal liability to the corporation and/or Ace Finance Co. for:
   a. $0
   b. $5,000
   c. $55,000
   d. $200,000

CASE PROBLEM

Answer the following problem, briefly explaining your answer.

ABC Inc. issued common and preferred stock. Earl owns 60,000 shares of ABC common stock and Antonio owns the remaining 40,000 shares of common stock. Trisha owns 200,000 shares of ABC preferred stock, which has typical rights and preferences. At its annual meeting, the shareholders are to elect a board of directors comprised of three directors. The articles of incorporation require cumulative voting for electing the board of directors. Each shareholder has three candidates that he or she would like to be elected to the board.

(a) Who is entitled to vote? (b) How many directors can Earl, Antonio, and Trisha elect? (c) Could Earl authorize Ann, a third party, to vote his shares? If so, how would he do this? (d) If the shareholders were voting on another type of corporate matter, what type of voting would be used? Describe this type of voting.

CPA REVIEW

The following questions were given on CPA examinations. The answers for these questions are the unofficial answers prepared by the American Institute of Certified Public Accountants, Inc. (AICPA). All material is reproduced with permission of the AICPA.

____ 1. Which of the following actions may a corporation take without its stockholders' consent?
  a. Consolidate with one or more corporations.
  b. Merge with one or more corporations.
  c. Dissolve voluntarily.
  d. Purchase 55% of another corporation's stock.

____ 2. Which of the following rights is a holder of a public corporation's cumulative preferred stock always entitled to?
  a. Conversion of the preferred stock into common stock.
  b. Voting rights.
  c. Dividend carryovers from years in which dividends were not paid, to future years.
  d. Guaranteed dividends.

____ 3. Price owns 2,000 shares of Universal Corp's $10 cumulative preferred stock. During its first year of operations, cash dividends of $5 per share were declared on the preferred stock but were never paid. In the second year, dividends on the preferred stock were neither declared nor paid. If Universal is dissolved, which of the following statements is correct?
  a. Universal will be liable to Price as an unsecured creditor for $10,000.
  b. Universal will be liable to Price as a secured creditor for $20,000.
  c. Price will have priority over the claims of Universal's bond owners.
  d. Price will have priority over the claims of Universal's unsecured judgment creditors.

____ 4. A corporate stockholder is entitled to which of the following rights?
  a. Elect officers.
  b. Receive annual dividends.
  c. Approve dissolution.
  d. Prevent corporate borrowing.

CHAPTER 47

_____ 5. Opal Corp. declared a 9% stock dividend on its common stock. The dividend
   a. Requires a vote of Opal's stockholders.
   b. Has no effect on Opal's earnings and profits for federal income tax purposes.
   c. Is includable in the gross income of the recipient taxpayers in the year of receipt.
   d. Must be registered with the SEC pursuant to the Securities Act of 1933.

_____ 6. A stockholder's right to inspect books and records of a corporation will be properly denied if the stockholder
   a. Wants to use corporate stockholder records for a personal business.
   b. Employs an agent to inspect the books and records.
   c. Intends to commence a stockholder's derivative suit.
   d. Is investigating management misconduct.

_____ 7. The corporate veil is most likely to be pierced and the shareholders held personally liable if
   a. The corporation has elected S corporation status under the Internal Revenue Code.
   b. The shareholders have commingled their personal funds with those of the corporation.
   c. An ultra vires act has been committed.
   d. A partnership incorporates its business solely to limit the liability of its partners.

_____ 8. Which of the following securities are corporate debt securities?

	Convertible bonds	Debenture bonds	Warrants
a.	Yes	Yes	Yes
b.	Yes	No	Yes
c.	Yes	Yes	No
d.	No	Yes	Yes

CHAPTER 48
SECURITIES REGULATION

CHAPTER OUTLINE

A. STATE REGULATION

1. STATE BLUE SKY LAWS

GENERAL RULE. Every state has adopted "blue sky laws" to regulate intrastate sales of securities. Regulations include: (1) antifraud rules; (2) broker-dealer licensing; and (3) registration of securities.
LIMITATION. Blue sky laws do not apply to interstate sales of securities.

2. UNIFORM SECURITIES ACT

States may adopt provisions of the Uniform Securities Act which includes alternatives of the foregoing three types of regulations for sales of securities in intrastate commerce.

B. FEDERAL REGULATION

3. FEDERAL LAWS REGULATING THE SECURITIES INDUSTRY

- *Securities Enforcement Remedies and Penny Stock Reform Act*: gives the SEC new remedial powers to prevent anyone from violating federal securities laws, including the power to issue cease and desist orders and to seek injunctions and monetary penalties.
- *Securities Acts Amendments of 1990*: authorizes sanctions against SEC-regulated persons for violating foreign laws. *Market Reform Act of 1990*: gives the SEC new powers to deal with instability in the securities markets.

4. DEFINITION OF SECURITY

GENERAL RULES. ▸ Federal securities laws apply only to interstate transactions involving a security. ▸ The term "security" is interpreted broadly, and it generally includes any financial instrument that is sold as an investment. ▸ Examples: stocks, bonds, notes, and "investment contracts," which include certain investments in oil, cattle, minerals, and other enterprises. ▸ The Supreme Court defines an investment contract as: (1) an investment of money (2) in a common enterprise (3) with an expectation of future profits (4) to be derived primarily from the efforts of others.
STUDY HINT. Under the "family resemblance" test, factors that may indicate an instrument is a security include: (1) a party's reason for entering into the transaction (the buyer wants to earn a profit from the instrument); (2) plan of distribution (the instrument is commonly sold to the public for investment purposes); (3) reasonable expectations of the investing public (the public regards the instrument as an investment); and (4) absence of other factors that would reduce the potential risk of the investment.

5. SECURITIES ACT OF 1933

- ***Applicability***: Regulates initial sale of any security in interstate commerce by an issuing company.
- ***General requirements***: Prior to sale, an issuer must: (1) file a registration statement with the SEC; and (2) provide a prospectus to each potential purchaser of offered securities.
- ***The registration process***: ▸ *Prefiling period*: Prior to filing a registration statement with the SEC, an issuer cannot offer for sale or sell any securities. ▸ *Waiting period*: During the period following the filing of a registration statement but prior to its becoming effective, securities may be advertised and preliminary prospectuses may be distributed. ▸ *Posteffective period*: After a

registration statement has become effective, sales of securities may be completed.

- **Regulation A offerings**: This regulation provides a simplified "mini registration" process for sales of up to $5 million of securities within a twelve-month period.
- **Registration exemptions**: ▸ *Intrastate offering*: A sale may be exempt from registration under the Securities Act if securities are offered only to residents of the state in which the issuing company is incorporated and does business. ▸ *Regulation D*: Also exempt are: (1) sales of securities of any amount made to only accredited investors or (2) sales that meet the following requirements:
  - ▸ *Rule 504 exemption*: (1) Securities for $1 million or less may be sold (2) in a one-year period (3) to any number of accredited or unaccredited investors. No special information is required to be provided to purchasers, and there are no restrictions on the resale of the securities.
  - ▸ *Rule 505 exemption*: (1) Securities for a total price of less than $5 million may be sold (2) in a one-year period (3) to any number of accredited buyers and less than thirty-five nonaccredited investors (unsophisticated investors not meeting a certain test). A public offering of securities is prohibited, and certain information must be disclosed if any offeree is nonaccredited.
  - ▸ *Rule 506 exemption (private placement exemption)*: (1) Securities for any amount may be sold (2) to any number of accredited investors and less than thirty-five nonaccredited investors, but (3) nonaccredited investors must have sufficient business or financial experience to adequately evaluate the investment. Certain information must be disclosed if any offeree is nonaccredited.
- **Liability for violations**: ▸ Section 11 imposes civil liability on an issuer for making materially false or misleading statements in a registration statement, or for omitting required facts. ▸ Section 12 imposes liability on parties who fraudulently offer or sell a security. ▸ Willful violations may also be criminally punished.

6. **SECURITIES EXCHANGE ACT OF 1934**

    - **Registration requirements**: ▸ Brokers, dealers, and exchanges dealing in securities in interstate commerce or on any national exchange must register with the SEC. ▸ The 1934 act imposes certain reporting requirements on (1) companies whose securities are traded on a national stock exchange, and (2) other companies with both assets greater than $3 million and 500 or more shareholders.
    - **Antifraud provisions**: ▸ Section 10(b) of the 1934 act and SEC Rule 10(b)-5 generally prohibit the use of any manipulative, deceptive, or fraudulent scheme or device in connection with the initial issuance or resale of securities in interstate commerce. Important concepts include:
      - ▸ *Scope of application*: The 1934 act's antifraud provisions apply to an offer to sell or sale of any security (registered or not) involving the use of the mail, interstate commerce, or a national stock exchange. The 1934 act applies to both sellers and buyers of securities. The SEC, but not private investors, can sue aiders and abettors under Section 10(b).
      - ▸ *Rule 10(b)-5 violation*: ▸ Important elements needed to prove a Rule 10b-5 violation include: (1) an untrue statement of "material" fact or a failure to state a "material" fact that is needed to make a statement not misleading; (2) reliance; and (3) a resultant injury. ▸ "Material" means a substantial likelihood that a reasonable investor would consider the matter important in making an investment decision. Materiality is determined on a case-by-case basis. ▸ Whether preliminary merger talks are material and must be disclosed depends on (1) the probability that a merger will occur and (2) the importance that the merger will have to the issuer of the security. ▸ The Litigation Reform Act of 1995 recognizes certain "safe harbors" (defenses) to Section 10(b) liability.

7. **TRADING ON INSIDER INFORMATION**

    - **General duty**: ▸ Insiders and other persons identified below have a duty to either (1) disclose material nonpublic information before trading in a security, or (2) abstain from trading in the security. ▸ This duty applies to the purchase or sale of any security in interstate commerce.

- **Parties subject to duty**: ▸ *Insiders*: directors, officers, and other corporate employees. ▸ *Temporary insiders*: outside attorneys, accountants, or other professionals who have access to material nonpublic information due to their employment by a company. ▸ *Tippees*: persons who receive material nonpublic information from (1) an insider or temporary insider (2) who breaches a fiduciary duty by improperly disclosing the information to the tippee (3) if the tippee knows or should know that disclosure is a breach of duty. ▸ *Misappropriators*: persons who steal data or wrongfully take information in breach of a fiduciary duty to their employer.
- **Disclosure to tippee**: ▸ Disclosure of information to a tippee is a breach of duty if an insider derives a personal or financial gain as a result of the disclosure. ▸ A tippee may act on information if disclosure of the information to the tippee did not breach an insider's duty.
- **Remedy**: Investors who bought or sold stock during a time that wrongful insider trading was occurring may recover damages from any insider who traded on the undisclosed information.
- **Other federal law**: The Insider Trading Sanctions Act of 1984 authorizes the SEC to bring an action against a person trading on material nonpublic information and authorizes persons suing for insider trading to recover a penalty for up to three times the wrongful gain.

8. **DISCLOSURE OF OWNERSHIP AND SHORT-SWING PROFIT (1934 ACT)**

- **Section 16(a)**: Directors or officers who own securities in a company, and shareholders who own more than 10 percent of a class of stock, must file a statement disclosing their stock ownership.
- **Section 16(b)**: The parties described above must pay to the corporation any short-swing profits (profits made by buying and selling securities in the company within a six-month period). This duty does not require proof of fraud.

9. **TENDER OFFERS**

- **Defined**: A cash tender offer is an offer made to all shareholders of a corporation to buy their shares at a specified price provided that a minimum number of shares are tendered for sale.
- **Williams Act - disclosure requirement**: Any person making a tender offer must file documents with the SEC disclosing certain information regarding the tender offer and related matters.
- **Williams Act - antifraud provision**: ▸ Fraudulent, deceptive, or manipulative conduct is prohibited in relation to tender offers. ▸ Tender offers must remain open for at least twenty business days. ▸ A violation requires proof of an actionable misrepresentation or other misconduct.

10. **REGULATION OF ACCOUNTANTS BY THE SEC**

▸ Accountants are subject to liability under most provisions of the 1933 act relating to registration statements and prospectuses, and may have liability under Section 10(b) of the 1934 act.

▸ SEC Rule 2(e) regulates accountants practicing before the SEC. An accountant practicing before the SEC may be disciplined if the accountant is unqualified, unethical, or violates federal law.

C. **INDUSTRY SELF-REGULATION**

11. **ARBITRATION OF SECURITIES DISPUTES**

Many firms that sell securities include an arbitration clause in customer contracts. This clause makes it mandatory that the firm and customer arbitrate a dispute instead of suing in court. A court will set aside an arbitrator's award only if (1) the arbitrator exceeded his or her power or (2) the arbitration process was seriously flawed.

REVIEW OF TERMS AND PHRASES

Select the term or phrase that best matches a statement or definition stated below. Each term or phrase is the best match for only one statement or definition.

Terms and Phrases

a. Accredited investor
b. Blue sky law
c. Insider
d. Misappropriator
e. Prospectus
f. Registration statement
g. Regulation D
h. SEC
i. Securities Act of 1933
j. Securities Enforcement Remedies Act
k. Securities Exchange Act of 1934
l. Short-swing profit
m. Tippee
n. Uniform Securities Act
o. Williams Act

Statements and Definitions

___d___ 1. Person who obtains information by theft or by breach of a fiduciary duty owed to an employer.
___a___ 2. Investor (such as a bank, insurance company, investment company, or director of an issuing company) to whom a security may be sold without registration under the 1933 act.
___e___ 3. Disclosure document required by the 1933 act to be provided to prospective buyers of securities.
___g___ 4. Regulation that exempts certain offerings from the registration requirements of the 1933 act.
___b___ 5. State law regulating the intrastate sale of securities.
___f___ 6. Disclosure document required by the 1933 act to be filed with the SEC.
___m___ 7. Person to whom an insider discloses material nonpublic information.
___i___ 8. Federal law that generally regulates the initial sale of securities by an issuing company.
___j___ 9. Federal law that gives new remedial powers to the SEC, enabling it to prevent anyone from violating federal securities laws.
___o___ 10. Federal law that generally regulates tender offers.
___k___ 11. Federal law that generally regulates the resale of securities in interstate commerce.
___l___ 12. Profit made by officers, directors, and certain shareholders by buying and selling securities in their company within a six-month period.
___c___ 13. Director, officer, or other corporate employee who has access to material nonpublic information.
___h___ 14. Federal agency that enforces federal securities laws.
___n___ 15. Uniform law that proposes rules for state regulation of sales of securities.

REVIEW OF CONCEPTS

Write **T** if the statement is true, write **F** if it is false.

___F___ 1. State blue sky laws generally regulate both the intrastate and interstate sale of securities.
___T___ 2. If a contract between a securities firm and customer contains an arbitration clause, then the firm and customer must arbitrate a dispute instead of suing in court.
___T___ 3. In general, federal securities laws only apply if a transaction involves a security.
___T___ 4. The term "security" generally includes any instrument that is bought as a financial investment.

T 5. An issuer's compliance with the registration requirements of the 1933 Act does not necessarily mean that a security is a good investment.

T (F) 6. During the waiting period, a preliminary prospectus ("red herring" prospectus) may be distributed to prospective investors, and "tombstone" ads may be published.

T (F) 7. A sale of stock made solely to residents of the state in which the issuing company is incorporated and primarily does business may be exempt from the 1933 act registration requirements.

F 8. Accountants cannot be held liable for misstatements or omissions that were made in registration statements that they helped prepare. (only)

T 9. The 1933 act may impose both civil and criminal penalties for its violation.

? F 10. The 1934 act imposes reporting requirements on all companies that issue securities.

F 11. Under Rule 10b-5, the only parties prohibited from engaging in insider trading are insiders.

T 12. Under the Litigation Reform Act of 1995, an issuer does not have private liability for erroneous, forward-looking statements if the statements were made innocently and were accompanied by meaningful cautionary statements indicating that the statements might ultimately prove to be incorrect.

F 13. A cash tender offer is an offer that is made to a corporation to buy all of the corporation's assets. *certain # of shares*

F 14. The Williams Act outlaws the making of tender offers in interstate commerce.

T 15. The SEC cannot prohibit an accountant from practicing before that agency.

REVIEW OF CHAPTER - APPLICATION OF CONCEPTS

MULTIPLE CHOICE QUESTIONS

 C 1. Mayfield Corp. is selling a variety of instruments and property in order to raise capital. Which instrument or property would *not* be a security within the meaning of federal securities laws?
   a. A share of common stock in Mayfield Corp.
   b. A ten-year corporate bond issued by Mayfield Corp. that pays 15 percent annual interest and that is sold to the general public as an investment.
   c. A 100 acre parcel of land.
   d. Investment interests in a shrimp farm operated by Mayfield Corp., with investors sharing in the profits made by the farming enterprise.

d 2. R&V Limited Partnership is planning to issue limited partner interests and to publicly offer these securities for sale in interstate commerce. What must R&V do to comply with the 1933 act?
   a. R&V has no duties under the 1933 act. R&V is only required to comply with blue sky laws in the states in which the securities are offered.
   b. R&V is only required to file a registration statement with the SEC.
   c. R&V is only required to provide a prospectus to prospective investors.
   d. Unless it fits within an exemption, R&V is required to both file a registration statement with the SEC and provide a prospectus to prospective investors.

C 3. Nassau Inc. plans to issue and sell $10 million worth of preferred stock. The stock will be sold to (1) forty-five banks, investment companies, and other accredited investors; and (2) fifteen nonaccredited investors who have sufficient financial and business experience to evaluate the merits and risks of the investment. There will be no general solicitation or public offering of the stock. Is this offering exempt from the registration requirements of the 1933 act?
   a. Yes. Rule 504 of Regulation D exempts this offering.
   b. Yes. Rule 505 of Regulation D exempts this offering.
   c. Yes. Rule 506 of Regulation D exempts this offering.
   d. No. This offering is not exempt from the registration requirements of the 1933 act.

d 4. Pepco Inc. has just received a secret medical report that conclusively establishes that Pepco's only product causes cancer. As a result, the company may be liable to thousands of persons who contracted cancer due to their use of this product. Under these facts, which party is engaging in insider trading in violation of Rule 10b-5?
   a. Tom, a Pepco director, sells his Pepco stock without disclosing the report.
   b. Bonnie, an outside financial analyst who was retained by Pepco to assess the financial impact of this report, sells all of her Pepco stock without disclosing the report.
   c. Faye, a janitor, steals the report and sells her Pepco stock without disclosing the report.
   d. All of the above.

d 5. Frye Co. is subject to all provisions of the 1934 Act. Dick is a director of Frye Co., and he owns 5 percent of the company's common stock. Bonnie owns 15 percent of the company's common stock. Sally owns 4 percent of the company's common stock. Under Rule 16 of the 1934 act:
   a. If Dick buys and sells stock in Frye Co. within a six-month period, thereby earning a profit, Dick must pay the profit to the company even if he did not trade on inside information.
   b. Dick, Bonnie, and Sally must each file disclosure statements with the SEC.
   c. Dick, Bonnie, and Sally are each exempt from filing disclosure statements with the SEC.
   d. a and b.

CASE PROBLEM

Answer the following problem, briefly explaining your answer.

Midas Inc. owns several gold mines. Unknown to the public, Midas engineers have just discovered a massive new gold deposit. After this discovery, the Midas board of directors made several public announcements denying that the company had made any new discoveries. Without knowledge of the secret discovery, Tom sold his Midas stock for $10 a share. One week later, Midas stock went to $20 per share when the Midas board announced the new discovery.

(a) What federal securities act governs this case? (b) What elements must Tom prove to establish a Rule 10b-5 violation by the Midas board of directors? (c) In all likelihood, did the board violate Rule 10b-5?

CPA REVIEW

The following questions were given on CPA examinations. The answers for these questions are the unofficial answers prepared by the American Institute of Certified Public Accountants, Inc. (AICPA). All material is reproduced with permission of the AICPA.

____ 1. Which of the following are exempt from the registration requirements of the Securities Act of 1933?
   a. All industrial development bonds issued by municipalities.
   b. Stock of a corporation offered and sold only to residents of the state in which the issuer was incorporated and doing all of its business.
   c. Bankers' acceptances with maturities at the time of issue ranging from one to two years.
   d. Participation interests in a money market fund that consists wholly of short-term commercial paper.

____ 2. Acme Corp. intends to make a public offering in several states of 250,000 shares of its common stock. Under the Securities Act of 1933,
   a. Acme must sell the common stock through licensed securities dealers.
   b. Acme must, in all events, file a registration statement with the SEC because the offering will be made in several states.
   c. Acme's use of any prospectus delivered to an unsophisticated investor must be accompanied by a simplified explanation of the offering.
   d. Acme may make an oral offer to sell the common stock to a prospective investor after a registration statement has been filed but before it becomes effective.

____ 3. While conducting an audit, Larson Associates, CPAs, failed to detect material misstatements included in its client's financial statements. Larson's unqualified opinion was included with the financial statements in a registration statement and prospectus for a public offering of securities made by the client. Larson knew that its opinion and the financial statements would be used for this purpose.
   Which of the following statements is correct with regard to a suit against Larson and the client by a purchaser of the securities under Section 11 of the Securities Act of 1933?
   a. The purchaser must prove that Larson was negligent in conducting the audit.
   b. The purchaser must prove that Larson knew of the material misstatements.
   c. Larson will not be liable if it had reasonable grounds to believe the financial statements were accurate.
   d. Larson will be liable unless the purchaser did not rely on the financial statements.

____ 4. In order to raise $375,000, Penn Corp. is offering its securities under Rule 504 of Regulation D of the Securities Act of 1933. Under Rule 504, the offering
   a. Must be sold to accredited investors.
   b. Can not be sold to more than 35 non-accredited investors.
   c. Can be sold to an unlimited number of accredited and non-accredited investors.
   d. Will not subject the issuer to the antifraud provisions of the Securities Act of 1933.

CHAPTER 48

5. Dart Corp. engaged Jay Associates, CPAs, to assist in a public stock offering. Jay audited Dart's financial statements and gave an unqualified opinion, despite knowing that the financial statements contained misstatements. Jay's opinion was included in Dart's registration statement. Larson purchased shares in the offering and suffered a loss when the stock declined in value after the misstatements became known.

   If Larson succeeds in the Section 11 suit against Dart, Larson would be entitled to
   a. Damages of three times the original public offering price.
   b. Rescind the transaction.
   c. Monetary damages only.
   d. Damages, but only if the shares were resold before the suit was started.

6. Rice, Inc. is a reporting company under the Securities Exchange Act of 1934. The only security it has issued is its voting common stock. Which one of the following statements is correct?
   a. Any person who owns more than 5% of Rice's common stock must file a report with the SEC.
   b. Rice need not file its proxy statements with the SEC because it has only one class of stock outstanding.
   c. It is unnecessary for the required annual report (Form 10-K) to include audited financial statements.
   d. Because Rice is a reporting company, it is not required to file a registration statement under the Securities Act of 1933 for any future offerings of its common stock.

7. Which of the following statements is correct with respect to the Securities Exchange Act of 1934?
   a. Issuers whose securities are registered under the Act are required to comply with its reporting requirements.
   b. The Act applies only to issuers whose securities are traded on a national securities exchange.
   c. The Act subjects all issuers of securities to its registration requirements if the issuer has more than $2.5 million of assets or more than 250 shareholders.
   d. The antifraud provisions of the Act do not apply to issuers of securities that are exempt from the Act's registration requirements.

8. Under the provisions of Section 10(b) and Rule 10b-5 of the Securities Exchange Act of 1934, which of the following activities must be proven by a stock purchaser in a suit against a CPA?
   I. Intentional conduct by the CPA designed to deceive investors.
   II. Negligence by the CPA.
   a. I only.
   b. II only.
   c. Both I and II.
   d. Neither I nor II.

CHAPTER 49
MANAGEMENT OF CORPORATIONS

CHAPTER OUTLINE

A. SHAREHOLDERS

1. EXTENT OF MANAGEMENT CONTROL BY SHAREHOLDERS

GENERAL RULE. Shareholders have a right to vote regarding: (1) amendments of articles or bylaws; (2) elections of directors; (3) shareholder resolutions; and (4) extraordinary matters, including a merger, dissolution, or sale of all corporate assets not in the regular course of business.
LIMITATION. Shareholders do not directly manage the business of a corporation.

2. MEETINGS OF SHAREHOLDERS

- *Requirement*: In general, shareholder action is effective only if taken at a valid meeting.
- *Regular meetings*: Time and place is stated in articles or bylaws; notice is generally not required.
- *Special meetings*: Meetings are called by directors or, sometimes, by holders of sufficient shares of stock. For special meetings, notice that states the proposed business must be given to shareholders.
- *Quorum*: A valid shareholder meeting requires the presence of a minimum number of shareholders.
- *Required approval*: Unless otherwise required by statute or by the articles or bylaws, an affirmative vote of a majority of shares present at a meeting is sufficient to authorize a matter.

3. ACTION WITHOUT MEETING

The RMBCA and numerous states permit an action to be taken by shareholders without holding a meeting if a written consent to the action is signed by all shareholders who were entitled to vote.

B. DIRECTORS

4. QUALIFICATIONS (AND REQUIRED NUMBER)

- *Qualification*: Unless otherwise required, anyone (minor or nonshareholder) may be a director.
- *Minimum required number of directors*: ▸ Most states: number fixed by bylaws. ▸ Many states require at least three directors. ▸ Some states allow a corporation to have one or more directors. ▸ In some states, professional corporations may have one or two directors.

5. POWERS OF DIRECTORS

GENERAL RULES. ▸ The board of directors manages the business of a corporation. ▸ A board can: (1) authorize any transaction necessary to carry out the corporation's business; (2) appoint or remove officers; and (3) appoint directors to an executive committee to act for the board between meetings.
LIMITATIONS. ▸ A board cannot: (1) authorize extraordinary corporate matters; or (2) delegate to an officer or executive committee total control of a corporation or the power to make unusual contracts. ▸ A court may interfere with a board's management of a corporation if the board approves illegal or fraudulent actions.

413

6. CONFLICT OF INTEREST

GENERAL RULES. ▸ A director cannot vote on a matter in which he or she has an undisclosed personal interest. ▸ A corporation may avoid an action if a director is subsequently disqualified due to a conflict.
LIMITATION. In some states a transaction is proper and cannot be avoided if a director discloses his or her interest in the transaction, and the transaction is fair and reasonable to the corporation.

7. MEETINGS OF DIRECTORS

▸ In most states, a board can act either (1) at a duly called meeting or (2) without a meeting, if a written consent to an action is signed by all directors. ▸ In general, a director cannot vote by proxy.

8. LIABILITY OF DIRECTORS

(a) The business judgment rule--liability of director

GENERAL RULES. ▸ A director is a fiduciary of a corporation, and a director owes a high duty of trust and loyalty to a corporation. ▸ *Business judgment rule*: Directors are not personally liable for unprofitable or erroneous decisions if such decisions were made: (1) on an informed basis (i.e., a director did not act with gross negligence); (2) in good faith; and (3) with an honest belief that the action was in the best interest of the corporation.
LIMITATION. Traditionally, a director's decision is presumed to be made on an informed basis, in good faith, and with a belief that it is in a corporation's best interest. A party claiming that a director is liable due to a corporate decision must prove one of these elements is missing.
STUDY HINT. State laws often permit stockholders to approve indemnification of directors against liability for their gross negligence if directors did not: (1) act in bad faith; (2) breach their duty of loyalty to the corporation; or (3) obtain improper personal benefits from their acts.

(b) Removal of director

GENERAL RULE. Shareholders can typically remove directors. The RMBCA allows removal with or without cause by a majority vote of the shareholders unless the articles state otherwise.
STUDY HINT. In some states, a board may remove and replace one of its own members.

C. OFFICERS, AGENTS, AND EMPLOYEES

▸ A corporation typically has officers consisting of a president, at least one vice president, a secretary, a treasurer, and frequently a chief executive officer (CEO). Officers are appointed by the board of directors and their duties are stated in the bylaws. ▸ Officers ordinarily hire the employees and agents of a corporation.

9. POWERS OF OFFICERS

- *Officers as agents*: ▸ Officers are agents of a corporation and their authority is generally controlled by agency law. ▸ An officer's implied authority to act for a corporation is not increased simply because the officer is also a major shareholder. ▸ Third parties are charged with knowledge of limits on officers' authority that are stated in recorded articles of incorporation.
- *President*: ▸ According to some authorities, a president has the implied authority to act for a corporation regarding any matter in the normal course of the corporation's business (especially if the president is also general manager). ▸ A president does not have implied authority to: (1) do acts requiring board authorization; (2) authorize out-of-the-ordinary contracts; (3) execute guarantees or commercial paper; (4) release claims; or (5) obligate the corporation to repurchase its own stock. If a corporation has both a president and CEO, the CEO typically has broad decision-making authority and the president has the power to implement corporate decisions.

10. LIABILITY RELATING TO FIDUCIARY DUTIES

▸ An officer is liable to a corporation for: (1) secret profits made in connection with any corporate transaction; and (2) profits obtained by personally taking a business (corporate) opportunity in which the corporation may have had an interest. ▸ An officer who breaches his or her fiduciary duty to a corporation may also forfeit the right to be paid salary and other compensation by the corporation.

11. AGENTS AND EMPLOYEES

The authority, rights, and obligations of corporate agents and employees are generally governed by agency law.

D. LIABILITY

12. LIABILITY OF MANAGEMENT TO THIRD PERSONS

Officers, directors, and executive employees are typically not liable to third parties for any indirect effect that their good faith management decisions may have had on such parties.

13. CRIMINAL LIABILITY

GENERAL RULES. ▸ Officers, directors, and agents are personally liable for their crimes, even if they were acting for a corporation. ▸ Officers and directors may be guilty of some federal or state crimes if they fail to prevent commission of the crimes and they are a "responsible corporate officer." ▸ A corporation may be convicted of a crime committed by an officer or agent who was acting within the scope of authority. ▸ A corporation and its officers may be criminally liable under the Foreign Corrupt Practices Act for bribing foreign officials. ▸ Under federal guidelines, corporations that have effective programs to detect and prevent corporate crimes and that voluntarily disclose those crimes to the government are subject to much lower fines than corporations without such programs.
STUDY HINT. The corporation itself may be guilty of a crime involving specific intent, such as theft of property, that is committed by an agent if (1) the agent was trying to serve the corporation's interests and (2) corporate management authorized, tolerated, or ratified the criminal act.

14. INDEMNIFICATION OF OFFICERS, DIRECTORS, EMPLOYEES, AND AGENTS

▸ The RMBCA allows a corporation to indemnify persons who actED on its behalf if: (1) they acted in good faith; (2) with a reasonable belief that they acted in the firm's interest; and (3) they had no reason to believe that their conduct was unlawful. ▸ Some states require indemnification of officers and directors for expenses incurred in defending against unfounded suits brought by shareholders.

15. LIABILITY FOR CORPORATE DEBTS

GENERAL RULE. Officers, directors, and agents are not liable for corporate obligations, even though their acts created the debts.
LIMITATION. In some states, if the corporation improperly does business, the officers and directors can be held liable.

16. PROTECTION OF SHAREHOLDERS

Shareholders who disapprove of board actions may: (1) remove directors; (2) elect new directors at the next annual meeting; or (3) bring a derivative action (when appropriate).

17. CIVIL LIABILITY OF THE CORPORATION

A corporation is liable for contracts made or for torts committed by officers and agents acting within the scope of authority.

REVIEW OF TERMS AND PHRASES

Select the term or phrase that best matches a statement or definition stated below. Each term or phrase is the best match for only one statement or definition.

Terms and Phrases

a. Business judgment rule
b. Directors
c. Executive committee
d. Extraordinary corporate matters
e. Foreign Corrupt Practices Act
f. Gross negligence
g. Officers
h. Organizational Federal Sentencing Guidelines
i. Quorum

Statements and Definitions

__c__ 1. Directors who are appointed by the board to act on its behalf regarding certain limited matters.

✗ __g__ 2. Persons appointed by a board of directors to manage the day-to-day affairs of a corporation.

__b__ 3. Persons who have the legal right to collectively manage the business of the corporation.

✗ __d__ 4. Transactions that require shareholder approval, such as a merger, dissolution, or sale of all assets of a corporation not in the regular course of business.

__i__ 5. Minimum number of shares or shareholders required to be represented at a shareholder meeting in order to have a valid meeting.

__e__ 6. Federal law that holds a corporation and its officers liable for illegally bribing a foreign official.

__h__ 7. Basis for subjecting corporations to fines for criminal convictions.

__f__ 8. Conduct for which a director may be held personally liable.

✗ __a__ 9. Principle that directors are not liable for business decisions made while acting on an informed basis, in good faith, and with an honest belief that their acts are in the corporation's best interest.

REVIEW OF CONCEPTS

Write **T** if the statement is true, write **F** if it is false.

__T__ 1. The board of directors of a corporation is generally elected by the shareholders.

__F__ 2. In general, notice to shareholders must be given in order to hold a valid regular meeting.

__T__ 3. Some states permit shareholders to act without holding a meeting if a written consent to an action is signed by all shareholders who are entitled to vote regarding that action.

__T__ 4. Many states require that a corporation have a board comprised of at least three directors.

__F__ 5. The board of directors can delegate total control of a corporation to an individual officer or to an executive committee.

__T__ 6. In general, a director cannot vote by giving a proxy to another person to vote in his or her place.

__F__ 7. Directors, but not officers, are fiduciaries of the corporation.

__T__ 8. Typically, the board of directors appoints officers of a corporation.

__T__ 9. Officers are agents of a corporation and their authority is largely governed by agency law.

__F__ 10. An officer of a corporation is personally liable to a corporation if the officer personally takes a corporate opportunity without first offering it to the corporation.

__T__ 11. An officer may forfeit the right to be paid salary and other compensation during the time that the officer was acting in violation of his or her fiduciary duties to a corporation.

__F__ 12. State statutes do not permit stockholders to approve plans that indemnify directors from liability resulting from their gross negligence.

__T__ 13. In general, an officer is not liable for harm that a third party may indirectly suffer as a result of a good faith decision that the officer made on behalf of a corporation.

__F__ 14. A corporation cannot be convicted of a criminal offense that is committed by a corporate officer.

__F__ 15. Corporate directors and officers are personally liable for corporate debts.

REVIEW OF CHAPTER - APPLICATION OF CONCEPTS

MULTIPLE CHOICE QUESTIONS

__C__ 1. Hee Haw Inc. owns and operates a fun house. Which transaction can be authorized by the Hee Haw Inc. board of directors without obtaining shareholder approval?
   a. A merger of Hee Haw Inc. with Fun Inc., a separate corporation.
   b. An extraordinary sale of the fun house and all other assets of Hee Haw Inc.
   c. Purchase of a new building for the fun house and the granting of a mortgage on the building.
   d. The board cannot authorize any of the foregoing transactions without shareholder approval.

__C__ 2. A special meeting of the shareholders of Camco Inc. was called to vote on a proposed amendment of the corporation's bylaws. Notice of the meeting and the proposed business was given. The corporation has 100,000 shares of outstanding common stock. At the meeting, owners of 70,000 shares are represented. The articles state that a meeting requires the presence of at least a majority of all shares entitled to vote. The articles and state law do not expressly state what percentage of shares must vote in favor of an amendment of a corporation's bylaws. In this case:
   a. Notice of the meeting was not required. Notice is only required for regular meetings.
   b. A quorum is not present at the meeting because all shareholders are not present.
   c. Assuming that the meeting is valid, an affirmative vote by shareholders owning 35,001 or more shares would typically be required to approve the amendment of the bylaws.
   d. Assuming that the meeting is valid, an affirmative vote by shareholders owning 50,001 or more shares would typically be required to approve the amendment of the bylaws.

d. 3. Terra Inc. is considering buying land from Piedmont Co. Unknown to the Terra board of directors, Piedmont is owned by Roger, a director of Terra. In a number of states:
   a. Roger can vote on the proposed purchase as a director of Terra without disclosing his interest in the transaction.
   b. Terra cannot under any circumstance purchase the property. A corporation cannot agree to a transaction that may involve a conflict of interest with a director of the corporation.
   c. A contract to buy the land from Piedmont is valid and cannot be set aside if it is approved by the Terra board, even if the board is not informed of Roger's interest in the transaction.
   d. A contract to buy the land from Piedmont is valid and cannot be set aside if Roger first discloses his interest in the transaction, and the transaction is fair and reasonable to Terra.

a. 4. Carmen is president of Acme Corp., a manufacturing firm with assets worth $2 million. Carmen is expressly authorized to manage the day-to-day business affairs of Acme Corp., and she enjoys the customary and incidental authority normally associated with this position. Under these facts, Carmen has authority to take which action on behalf of Acme Corp.?
   a. Employ A&A Accounting Service to prepare the corporation's tax returns.
   b. Agree to repurchase $500,000 worth of the corporation's outstanding stock.
   c. Execute a guarantee by the corporation, guaranteeing payment of another company's debt.
   d. Remove and replace the board of directors of Acme Corp.

c. 5. Jay is president of Hawk Co., and he did the acts described below on behalf of the corporation. Jay was authorized by the corporation to do these acts. Select the correct answer.
   a. Jay contracted to buy a truck on behalf of the corporation, but the corporation failed to pay for the truck. In this case, Jay is liable for the contract price.
   b. Jay refused to buy goods for the corporation from Winn Co. As a result, Winn Co. suffered a loss. In this case, Jay is liable to Winn Co. for its loss.
   c. Jay bribed a city official in order to obtain a contract for the corporation. Bribery is a crime. In this case, Jay is guilty of the crime even though he acted on behalf of the corporation.
   d. All of the above.

CASE PROBLEM

The board of directors of Ameri Finance Inc. approved a loan to L&K Co. for $1 million. The loan was secured by collateral. Prior to approving the loan, the Ameri board reviewed (1) a credit report that showed L&K to be solvent and (2) an appraisal valuing the collateral at $2 million. Subsequently, L&K defaulted on the loan and the collateral was sold for $600,000, causing a $400,000 loss. Minority shareholders in Ameri filed a derivative suit alleging that the Ameri directors are personally liable for the loss because they failed to exercise proper care in approving the loan.

(a) Who has the burden to prove whether the Ameri board acted properly or not? (b) What test is used to determine the liability of the Ameri directors? (c) Are the Ameri directors personally liable for the loss?

CPA REVIEW

The following questions were given on CPA examinations. The answers for these questions are the unofficial answers prepared by the American Institute of Certified Public Accountants, Inc. (AICPA). All material is reproduced with permission of the AICPA.

____ 1. Which of the following actions may a corporation take without its stockholders' consent?
  a. Consolidate with one or more corporations.
  b. Merge with one or more corporations.
  c. Dissolve voluntarily.
  d. Purchase 55% of another corporation's stock.

____ 2. Generally, a merger of two corporations requires
  a. That a special meeting notice and a copy of the merger plan be given to all stockholders of both corporations.
  b. Unanimous approval of the merger plan by the stockholders of both corporations.
  c. Unanimous approval of the merger plan by the boards of both corporations.
  d. That all liabilities owed by the absorbed corporation be paid before the merger.

____ 3. Which of the following statements is correct regarding the fiduciary duty?
  a. A director's fiduciary duty to the corporation may be discharged by merely disclosing his self-interest.
  b. A director owes a fiduciary duty to the shareholders but not to the corporation.
  c. A promoter of a corporation to be formed owes no fiduciary duty to anyone, unless the contract engaging the promoter so provides.
  d. A majority shareholder as such may owe a fiduciary duty to fellow shareholders.

____ 4. Absent a specific provision in its articles of incorporation, a corporation's board of directors has the power to do all of the following, except
  a. Repeal the bylaws.
  b. Declare dividends.
  c. Fix compensation of directors.
  d. Amend the articles of incorporation.

CHAPTER 49

_____ 5. Davis, a director of Active Corp., is entitled to
   a. Serve on the board of a competing business.
   b. Take sole advantage of a business opportunity that would benefit Active.
   c. Rely on information provided by a corporate officer.
   d. Unilaterally grant a corporate loan to one of Active's shareholders.

_____ 6. Under the Revised Model Business Corporation Act, which of the following statements is correct regarding corporate officers of a public corporation?
   a. An officer may not simultaneously serve as a director.
   b. A corporation may be authorized to indemnify its officers for liability incurred in a suit by stockholders.
   c. Stockholders always have the right to elect a corporation's officers.
   d. An officer of a corporation is required to own at least one share of the corporation's stock.

_____ 7. Generally, officers of a corporation
   a. Are elected by the shareholders.
   b. Are agents and fiduciaries of the corporation, having actual and apparent authority to manage the business.
   c. May be removed by the board of directors without cause only if the removal is approved by a majority vote of the shareholders.
   d. May declare dividends or other distributions to shareholders as they deem appropriate.

_____ 8. Knox, president of Quick Corp., contracted with Tine Office Supplies, Inc. to supply Quick's stationery on customary terms and at a cost less than that charged by any other supplier. Knox later informed Quick's board of directors that Knox was a majority stockholder in Tine. Quick's contract with Tine is
   a. Void because of Knox's self-dealing.
   b. Void because the disclosure was made after execution of the contract.
   c. Valid because of Knox's full disclosure.
   d. Valid because the contract is fair to Quick.

CHAPTER 50
REAL PROPERTY

CHAPTER OUTLINE

A. NATURE OF REAL PROPERTY

1. DEFINITIONS

▸Real property includes land, buildings, fixtures, and rights in land of others, such as easements and profits. ▸ Land is soil, water, minerals, oil, gas, things fixed to land, and airspace above land. ▸ Profits are the right to take a part of the soil (minerals) or produce of the land.

2. EASEMENTS

- ***Definitions***: ▸ *Easement*: right to use another's land for limited purpose. ▸ *Dominant tenement*: land benefitted by (entitled to use) easement. ▸ *Servient tenement*: land subject to an easement.
- ***Creation***: ▸ An easement is an interest in land that is created by: (1) deed; (2) implication (implied in connection with a conveyance of land); (3) estoppel (unfair conduct gives rise to an easement); or (4) prescription (adverse use of land). ▸ Oral easements are not binding.
- ***Termination***: ▸ An easement is terminated if it is not used and there is an intent to abandon the easement. ▸ An easement cannot be revoked without the consent of the owner of the easement.

3. LICENSES

▸ A license is a personal, revocable privilege to do an act on another's land. Example: right to camp overnight. ▸ A license is not an interest in land. A license may be terminated at anytime by the licensor.

4. LIENS

▸ A lien is a security interest in realty. ▸ Examples: mortgages, tax liens, and mechanics' liens.

5. DURATION AND EXTENT OF OWNERSHIP

A leasehold estate is an ownership interest for a specified period of time. A freehold estate is an ownership interest with no fixed duration when created, and it may be either:

- ***Fee simple estate***: ▸ Ownership lasts forever. ▸ Ownership may be transferred during an owner's life or upon an owner's death. ▸ Ownership is subject to rights of surviving spouse and creditors.
- ***Life estate***: A life estate is an ownership of land that lasts only for the life of a person.

B. FIXTURES

6. DEFINITION

A fixture is personal property that is attached to land or a building in such a manner that it is legally viewed as being part of the real property. Example: a furnace is made a permanent part of a house.

7. TESTS OF A FIXTURE

Unless otherwise agreed, one of the following tests may be used to determine whether property is a fixture:

- ***Annexation test***: ▸ Property is a fixture if its removal would materially damage the real property or would destroy the attached property. ▸ Example: lumber that is used to construct a building.
- ***Adaptation test***: Property is a fixture if specially made for realty. Example: custom-made door.
- ***Intent test***: Property is a fixture if, at time of affixing, the property owner intended it to be a fixture.

8. MOVABLE MACHINERY AND EQUIPMENT

▸ Movable machinery and equipment is personal property and not fixtures. ▸ Example: a dryer.

9. TRADE FIXTURES

Tenants can usually remove trade fixtures (tenants' equipment that is used to conduct a business).

C. LIABILITY TO THIRD PERSONS FOR CONDITION OF REAL PROPERTY

10. STATUS-OF-PLAINTIFF COMMON LAW RULE

Under common law, an occupier of land owed the following duties to persons coming upon the land:

- *Trespasser*: Duty not to intentionally harm known trespassers, but no duty to warn or to protect.
- *Attractive nuisance doctrine*: Under an exception to the rule for trespassers, an occupier of land is liable if an injured trespasser is a child who was attracted onto the land by a dangerous condition.
- *Licensee*: ▸ A licensee is a person who is on premises with the occupier's permission. ▸ Duty to warn a licensee of nonobvious dangers known to occupier, but no duty to discover unknown dangers.
- *Invitee*: ▸ An invitee is a person on premises at the invitation of the occupier or for the occupier's benefit. ▸ Duty to reasonably discover and to warn an invitee about or correct dangerous conditions.

11. NEGLIGENCE RULE

Some courts ignore the foregoing common law distinctions regarding the status of an injured person and hold an occupier of land liable according to ordinary negligence standards.

12. INTERMEDIATE RULE

Some courts impose upon an occupier of land the same duty to both licensees and invitees.

13. RECREATIONAL USE STATUTES

In most states, a landowner owes no duty to warn of dangers or to keep property safe for persons who are allowed to use the property for recreational purposes without charge.

D. CO-OWNERSHIP OF REAL PROPERTY

14. MULTIPLE OWNERSHIP

Several persons may simultaneously own interests in the same real property. If jointly owned property is sold, the proceeds are held in the same tenancy as the property was held by the parties.

15. CONDOMINIUMS

- *Ownership*: Common areas are co-owned; separate condominium units are individually owned.
- *Control*: State laws allocate management, control, and expenses among owners in various ways.
- *Liens*: A lien may be imposed against an owner's unit if the owner fails to pay required expenses.
- *Tort liability*: A few states allow one injured in common areas to sue only the condo association.
- *Cooperatives distinguished*: A cooperative is usually a corporation that owns a building and stockholders rent units in the building, whereas condominium owners actually own their units.
- *Advantages of condominium ownership*: ▸ Owners are not liable for debts of condo enterprise. ▸ Tax deduction for mortgage interest and taxes. ▸ Ownership of units may be transferred.

E. TRANSFER OF REAL PROPERTY BY DEED

16. DEFINITIONS

▸A deed is an instrument or writing by which an owner (grantor) conveys an interest in land to a new owner (grantee). ▸ A deed is required to convey real property, whether the conveyance is made in connection with a sale or gift. ▸ Consideration is not required for a deed to be valid.

17. CLASSIFICATION OF DEEDS

▸ A *quitclaim deed* does not specify a particular interest being conveyed; it transfers only what interest, if any, that a grantor may have. ▸ A *warranty deed* transfers a specified interest and it guarantees that the interest is conveyed. ▸ A *common law deed* is a long form that states the details of a conveyance. ▸ A *statutory deed* is a short form that merely states that a conveyance is made between named parties.

18. EXECUTION OF DEEDS

▸A deed must be signed or sealed by the grantor. ▸ A grantor must have capacity. ▸ A deed may be set aside for a grantee's fraud. ▸ To record a deed, laws often require that two or more witnesses sign a deed, and that it be acknowledged by a grantor before a notary public. ▸ A deed is binding between a grantor and a grantee even if it is not acknowledged or recorded.

19. DELIVERY AND ACCEPTANCE OF DEEDS

▸A deed is not effective and title does not pass until the deed is delivered to a grantee with an intent to transfer ownership. ▸ Delivery includes mailing a deed to a grantee. ▸ If a deed is given to a third party to give to a grantee only after conditions are met (a delivery in escrow), title passes only when the conditions are met. ▸ Delivery may be symbolic. Example: Grantor gives Grantee a key to a locked box containing the deed, with the intent to make a present transfer of title.

20. RECORDING OF DEEDS

GENERAL RULES. ▸ Recording is not needed to make a deed effective, but it provides notice to the public. ▸ A buyer takes land: (1) subject to valid previously recorded deeds; but (2) free from unrecorded deeds or claims if the buyer was unaware of such deeds or claims when acquiring title.

LIMITATION. A grantee who holds title under a recorded deed may lose to another party who claims ownership if: (1) the other party has superior title; (2) the grantee had notice of the other party's claim when title was acquired; (3) a party claiming land by adverse possession occupies the land; (4) the grantee took the land only as a gift; or (5) the grantee acquired the land by fraud.

21. ADDITIONAL PROTECTION OF BUYERS

Buyers may protect themselves by purchasing title insurance, which insures good title, or an abstract of title, which reports all recorded transfers of title and recorded claims against the property.

22. CANCELLATION OF DEEDS

A grantor may cancel a deed under the same circumstances that would justify avoiding a contract.

23. GRANTOR'S WARRANTIES

- *Warranties of title*: ▸ *Common law deed*: A grantor may expressly warrant various matters.
  ▸ *Statutory deed*: Laws typically provide that a grantor under a statutory (short form) deed makes certain warranties that include: (1) grantor owns land conveyed; (2) grantor has the right to convey the land; (3) land is not encumbered by third party rights, such as liens; (4) grantor will not disturb grantee's possession; and (5) grantor will execute additional necessary documents.
- *Fitness for use*: In most states, courts hold that a warranty of fitness for use (habitability) is implied in a sale of a new house by a builder or real estate developer. Some courts may permit subsequent purchasers to enforce the warranty against the contractor for a reasonable time.

24. GRANTEE'S COVENANTS

▸A grantee's promise in a deed that directly relates to the land "runs with the land," i.e., it binds future owners who acquire the grantee's land, and it can be enforced by future owners of the grantor's land. ▸ Restrictive covenants forbid acts by a grantee. Examples: building restrictions; nondiscriminatory resale limitations. ▸ Affirmative covenants require a grantee to do something.

F. OTHER METHODS OF TRANSFERRING REAL PROPERTY

25. EMINENT DOMAIN

By eminent domain, the government may take (purchase) property from private parties for a public use.

26. ADVERSE POSSESSION

One may acquire title to land by taking possession of the land if possession is (1) actual, (2) visible and notorious, (3) exclusive, (4) hostile, and (5) continuous for the period of time required by statute.

G. MORTGAGES

27. CHARACTERISTICS OF A MORTGAGE

▸ A mortgage is a security interest in real property that is given by a mortgagor to a mortgagee. ▸ A mortgagee can enforce a mortgage by foreclosure. ▸ A mortgagor may redeem (recover) property after foreclosure. ▸ A mortgagee's interest ends when the secured debt is paid.

28. PROPERTY SUBJECT TO MORTGAGE

Any interest in real property can be mortgaged.

29. FORM OF MORTGAGE

In general, no particular language is required to create a mortgage. However, a mortgage must be written, and it must express the parties' intent to create a mortgage.

30. RECORDING OR FILING OF MORTGAGE

An unrecorded mortgage binds the parties and their heirs and donees; it does not bind a good faith land buyer or creditor who acquires an interest for value and without knowledge of the mortgage.

31. RESPONSIBILITIES OF THE PARTIES

- *Repairs*: ▸ Unless otherwise agreed, a mortgagor has no duty to make improvements or to repair premises that are damaged without the mortgagor's fault. ▸ A mortgagee in possession must make reasonable, necessary repairs but is entitled to reimbursement for such expenses.
- *Taxes, assessments, and insurance*: ▸ The mortgagor must pay taxes and assessments. ▸ Unless otherwise agreed, neither party is required to insure the property.
- *Impairment of security*: A mortgagor may be liable to the mortgagee if the mortgagor damages the mortgaged property, thereby impairing the value of the property.

32. TRANSFER OF INTEREST

▸ Typically, a mortgagor may transfer property without a mortgagee's consent. But, a mortgagor remains liable for the debt unless the mortgagee agrees otherwise. ▸ Unless otherwise agreed, a buyer of mortgaged property takes the property subject to a recorded mortgage, but the buyer is not personally liable to the mortgagee to pay the secured debt. ▸ A mortgagee can assign a mortgage.

33. RIGHTS OF MORTGAGEE AFTER DEFAULT

If a mortgagor defaults, a mortgagee may (1) declare the entire debt due (even if only a part is in default), and foreclose on and sell the land. Foreclosure eliminates a mortgage and a buyer is not subject to the mortgage. But foreclosure does not end the debt, and a mortgagor is liable for any deficiency.

34. RIGHTS OF MORTGAGOR AFTER DEFAULT

▸ In certain cases, a mortgagor may obtain a stay of a foreclosure to prevent undue hardship. ▸ In many states, a mortgagor has a right of redemption after a foreclosure sale, which entitles the mortgagor to recover the property by paying a required sum within a specified time.

REVIEW OF TERMS AND PHRASES

MATCHING EXERCISE

Select the term or phrase that best matches a statement or definition stated below. Each term or phrase is the best match for only one statement or definition.

Terms and Phrases

a. Deed
b. Delivery in escrow
c. Dominant tenement
d. Easement
e. Fee simple estate
f. Fixture
g. License
h. Mortgage
i. Profits
j. Quitclaim deed
k. Servient tenement
l. Warranty deed

Statements and Definitions

__f__ 1. Property that is affixed to land or buildings and is legally considered part of real property.

__a__ 2. Writing or instrument used to convey real property.

__g__ 3. Revocable privilege to perform an act or acts on land belonging to another.

__j__ 4. Deed that only transfers whatever interest, if any, that a grantor holds in property.

__d__ 5. Irrevocable right to use land belonging to another.

__c__ 6. Land that is benefitted by an easement.

__h__ 7. Lien that is voluntarily given by a property owner to secure performance of an obligation.

__b__ 8. Delivery of a deed by a grantor to a third person pursuant to an agreement that the deed is to be delivered to the grantee upon satisfaction of certain conditions.

__k__ 9. Land that is subject to an easement.

__l__ 10. Deed that conveys a specified interest in property and guarantees that such interest is transferred.

__e__ 11. Complete and absolute real property ownership interest that lasts forever.

__i__ 12. Right to take a part of the soil or produce from land belonging to another.

COMPLETION EXERCISE

Fill in the blanks with the words that most accurately complete each statement. Answers may or may not include terms used in the matching exercise. A term cannot be used to complete more than one statement.

1. __Real property__ includes land, buildings, fixtures, and rights in land.

2. Business equipment that is attached to a rented building by a tenant is commonly called a __Trade Fixtures__.

3. Martin transferred title to a ranch to Tami for the duration of Tami's life and, upon Tami's death, title was to pass to Beth. Tami's interest in the ranch is a __life__ __interest__.

4. A restrictive covenant in a recorded deed that directly relates to the land is binding on future owners of the land because the covenant __runs__ __with the land__.

CHAPTER 50

5. _eminent domain_ is the power of a government body to take title to the property of a private person for a public purpose.

6. A party may acquire title to property by _adverse possession_ if the party takes possession of the property, and such possession is actual, visible, notorious, exclusive, hostile, and continuous for the legally required period of time.

7. _Foreclosure_ is the procedure by which a mortgagee enforces its rights under a mortgage.

REVIEW OF CONCEPTS

Write **T** if the statement is true, write **F** if it is false.

_T_ 1. A landowner's ownership of airspace is subject to reasonable use by aircraft flying overhead.

_F_ 2. An oral easement is legally enforceable.

_T_ 3. In general, a license can be revoked by the person granting the license.

_T_ 4. Whether property is a fixture or not largely depends on the intent of the party affixing the property to the land or building.

_F_ 5. In general, movable machinery and equipment are fixtures.

_F_ 6. Under common law, an occupier of land must protect trespassers from known dangers.

_T_ 7. By statute in most states, a landowner has no duty to warn or protect persons who are permitted to use his or her land for recreational purposes without charge.

_F_ 8. A condominium and a cooperative are the same thing.

_T_ 9. In a condominium project, individual owners own their respective condominium units and all of the unit owners co-own the common areas.

_F_ 10. A deed is not valid unless consideration is given for the deed.

_T_ 11. In general, a deed is not effective and does not transfer title unless the grantor effectively delivers the deed to the grantee with an intent to convey the grantor's interest in the property.

_T_ 12. A deed may be delivered by placing it in a box and giving the grantee a key to the box if this is done with the intent to presently transfer ownership of the property.

_T_ 13. Statutes commonly hold that a grantor who conveys land by a statutory (short form) warranty deed warrants that the grantor owns the land and that the land is not subject to any liens.

_F_ 14. A restrictive covenant prohibiting an owner from selling to certain racial groups may be enforced.

_T_ 15. A purchaser for value and in good faith generally takes real property free from an unrecorded mortgage if the purchaser was unaware of the mortgage.

REVIEW OF CHAPTER - APPLICATION OF CONCEPTS

MULTIPLE CHOICE QUESTIONS

b 1. Joseph owns a farm. In a signed writing, Joseph granted Fran the irrevocable right to use a road on his farm so that Fran could more easily reach her own property. What kind of interest in land did Joseph grant to Fran?
   a. License.
   b. Easement.
   c. Lien.
   d. Profit.

b 2. Shanti leased a building. Shanti installed a stove and a boiler in the building. Upon expiration of the lease, Shanti intends to remove the stove, but not the boiler. The stove can be removed easily without harming anything. Removal of the boiler, however, will seriously damage both the building and the boiler. Are the stove and boiler fixtures?
   a. The stove and boiler are both fixtures.
   b. The stove is not a fixture, but the boiler is a fixture.
   c. The stove is a fixture, but the boiler is not a fixture.
   d. Neither the stove nor the boiler is a fixture.

d 3. Jean owns a unit in the Essex Condominiums. This condominium complex is managed by the Essex Condo Association which is comprised of Jean and the owners of the other units in the complex. A swimming pool is located in the common area of the complex. Disputes have arisen regarding this pool and certain other matters. In many states:
   a. Jean does not have a right to use the swimming pool.
   b. Jean does not have any right to participate in the management of the association.
   c. Jean cannot sell her unit without the approval of the association.
   d. Jean is obligated to pay a share of the taxes and other expenses of the complex, and she can take a tax deduction for property taxes and mortgage interest that she pays.

c 4. Margaret contracted to sell a seaside cottage to Lex. Margaret executed a deed to convey title to Lex, three witnesses signed the deed, and the deed was acknowledged. Pursuant to the contract, Margaret delivered the deed to an escrow company, with instructions to deliver the deed to Lex when he delivered the purchase price to the escrow company. Under these facts:
   a. Title passed to Lex when Margaret signed the deed.
   b. Title passed to Lex when Margaret delivered the deed to the escrow company.
   c. Title will pass to Lex when he makes the required payment and the escrow company delivers the deed to him.
   d. Title will not pass to Lex until he makes the required payment, the escrow company delivers the deed to Lex, and Lex records the deed.

a 5. Sheena borrowed money from Ace Finance and she executed a written mortgage on her home as security for the loan. Ace Finance inadvertently neglected to record the mortgage. Subsequently, the home was damaged by hail, and property taxes for the home came due. The mortgage is silent regarding duties to repair and taxes. Under these facts:
   a. The mortgage is enforceable against Sheena even though it was not recorded.
   b. As mortgagor, Sheena has a general obligation to Ace Finance to repair the hail damage.
   c. As mortgagee, Ace Finance is obligated to pay the property taxes.
   d. None of the above is correct.

CHAPTER 50   427

CASE PROBLEMS

Answer the following problems, briefly explaining your answers.

1. Dee purchased a meal at a cafe owned by Maxwell. While Dee was eating her meal, the stool she was sitting on collapsed, injuring her. The stool collapsed due to a defective stand. The defect could have been discovered easily by a simple inspection. However, Maxwell did not know that the stool was defective because he never inspected the premises. Dee sued Maxwell for her injuries.

    (a) Under common law, what is Dee's status? (b) Under common law, what duty did Maxwell owe to Dee? (c) Under common law, is Maxwell liable to Dee for her injuries? (d) What alternative rule may some courts apply to determine if Maxwell is liable to Dee?

2. Martha sold her home to Dylan for $50,000. Martha executed and delivered a statutory warranty deed to Dylan, but Dylan failed to record the deed. Later, Martha sold the same property for value to Sandra. Sandra purchased the property in good faith and she was unaware of the prior conveyance to Dylan. Martha executed and delivered a warranty deed to Sandra, and Sandra recorded the deed.

    (a) Who has superior title to the home? (b) Did Martha breach any warranties to Dylan?

3. Helen obtained a loan from Bank to help finance her daughter's education. Helen granted Bank a mortgage on her home as security for the loan, and the mortgage was duly recorded. The loan agreement and mortgage are silent regarding Helen's right to sell the home. Helen subsequently sold the home to Bryson. Bryson did not expressly assume or agree to pay the loan. Bank did not expressly approve or disapprove of the sale, nor did it expressly agree to release Helen from liability for the loan.

    (a) Was Helen entitled to sell the home even though it was subject to the mortgage? (b) Is Helen still liable for the loan? (c) Is Bryson personally obligated to pay the loan? (d) If the loan is not repaid, can Bank foreclose on the home even though it has been sold to Bryson?

CPA REVIEW

The following questions were given on CPA examinations. The answers for these questions are the unofficial answers prepared by the American Institute of Certified Public Accountants, Inc. (AICPA). All material is reproduced with permission of the AICPA.

___ 1. Which of the following warranties is (are) contained in a general warranty deed?
   I. The grantor has the right to convey the property.
   II. The grantee will not be disturbed in possession of the property by the grantor or some third party's lawful claim of ownership.
   a. I only.
   b. II only.
   c. I and II.
   d. Neither I nor II.

___ 2. Which of the following is a defect in marketable title to real property?
   a. Recorded zoning restrictions.
   b. Recorded easements referred to in the contract of sale.
   c. Unrecorded lawsuit for negligence against the seller.
   d. Unrecorded easement.

___ 3. For a deed to be effective between a purchaser and seller of real estate, one of the conditions is that the deed must
   a. Be recorded within the permissible statutory time limits.
   b. Be delivered by the seller with an intent to transfer title.
   c. Contain the actual sales price.
   d. Contain the signatures of the seller and purchaser.

___ 4. On May 1, 1991, Chance bought a piece of property by taking subject to an existing unrecorded mortgage held by Hay Bank. On April 1, 1992, Chance borrowed money from Link Finance and gave Link a mortgage on the property. Link did not know about the Hay mortgage and did not record its mortgage until July 1, 1992. On June 1, 1992, Chance borrowed money from Zone Bank and gave Zone a mortgage on the same property. Zone knew about the Link mortgage but did not know about the Hay mortgage. Zone recorded its mortgage on June 15, 1992. Which mortgage would have priority if these transactions took place in a notice-race jurisdiction?
   a. The Hay mortgage because it was first in time.
   b. The Link mortgage because Zone had notice of the Link mortgage.
   c. The Zone mortgage because it was the first recorded mortgage.
   d. The Zone and Link mortgages share priority because neither had notice of the Hay mortgage.

CHAPTER 50

___ 5. Wilk bought an apartment building from Dix Corp. There was a mortgage on the building securing Dix's promissory note to Xeon Finance Co. Wilk took title subject to Xeon's mortgage. Wilk did not make the payments on the note due Xeon and the building was sold at a foreclosure sale. If the proceeds of the foreclosure sale are less than the balance due on the note, which of the following statements is correct regarding the deficiency?
   a. Xeon must attempt to collect the deficiency from Wilk before suing Dix.
   b. Dix will not be liable for any of the deficiency because Wilk assumed the note and mortgage.
   c. Xeon may collect the deficiency from either Dix or Wilk.
   d. Dix will be liable for the entire deficiency.

Questions 6 through 8 are based on the following:

On February 1, Frost bought a building from Elgin, Inc. for $250,000. To complete the purchase, Frost borrowed $200,000 from Independent Bank and gave Independent a mortgage for that amount; gave Elgin a second mortgage for $25,000; and paid $25,000 in cash. Independent recorded its mortgage on February 2 and Elgin recorded its mortgage on March 12.

The following transaction also took place:

- On March 1, Frost gave Scott a $20,000 mortgage on the building to secure a personal loan Scott had previously made to Frost.
- On March 10, Scott recorded this mortgage.
- On March 15, Scott learned about both prior mortgages.
- On June 1, Frost stopped making payments on all the mortgages.
- On August 1, the mortgages were foreclosed. Frost, on that date, owed Independent, $195,000; Elgin, $24,000; and Scott, $19,000.

A judicial sale of the building resulted in proceeds of $220,000 after expenses were deducted. The above transactions took place in a notice-race jurisdiction.

___ 6. What amount of the proceeds will Scott receive?
   a. $0
   b. $ 1,000
   c. $12,500
   d. $19,000

___ 7. Why would Scott receive this amount?
   a. Scott knew of the Elgin mortgage.
   b. Scott's mortgage was recorded before Elgin's and before Scott knew of Elgin's mortgage.
   c. Elgin's mortgage was first in time.
   d. After Independent is fully paid, Elgin and Scott share the remaining proceeds equally.

___ 8. Frost may redeem the property before the judicial sale only if
   a. There is a statutory right of redemption.
   b. It is probable that the sale price will result in a deficiency.
   c. All mortgages are paid in full.
   d. All mortgagees are paid a penalty fee.

CHAPTER 51
ENVIRONMENTAL LAW AND COMMUNITY PLANNING

CHAPTER OUTLINE

A. PREVENTION OF POLLUTION

1. STATUTORY ENVIRONMENTAL PROTECTION

GENERAL RULES. ▸ To protect the environment, Congress adopted the National Environmental Policy Act (NEPA) in 1969, and it later adopted other laws to address specific problems. ▸ States also regulate the environment, and many have adopted laws similar to federal environmental laws.
LIMITATION. State laws cannot conflict with federal law or unduly burden interstate commerce.

2. WASTE CONTROL

GENERAL RULES. ▸ Federal and state laws have been adopted to protect citizens from harmful wastes. Example: federal Comprehensive Environmental Response, Compensation and Liability Act of 1980 (CERCLA). ▸ CERCLA establishes (1) a national inventory of inactive hazardous waste sites and (2) a Hazardous Waste Fund (Superfund) to help pay for cleaning up such sites. The Environmental Protection Agency (EPA) is authorized to sue responsible persons to recover the cost for cleanup operations.
STUDY HINT. Government agencies can require a license to handle hazardous wastes, and they can make persons who dispose of wastes contribute to a fund used to pay for hazardous waste spills.

3. ENVIRONMENTAL IMPACT STATEMENTS

GENERAL RULES. ▸ Any federal action (including passage of new laws) that may significantly affect the quality of the human environment requires an environmental impact statement (EIS). An EIS analyzes: (1) the impact of a proposed action; and (2) practical and feasible alternatives to such action. ▸ Some states require an EIS for (1) government projects and/or (2) large, private construction projects. ▸ Courts may prohibit a project for failure to submit an adequate EIS.
LIMITATION. A federal EIS must be revised or supplemented as new information is obtained.
STUDY HINT. At least one court has held that an EIS must consider a project's impact on the character of the surrounding neighborhood and its effect on local residents and businesses.

4. REGULATION BY ADMINISTRATIVE AGENCIES

Most environmental regulation is accomplished through the adoption and implementation of regulations by administrative agencies, such as the EPA.

5. LITIGATION

GENERAL RULES. ▸ A private party can sue a polluter for damages or for an injunction to stop pollution if the party can prove damages different from those suffered by the public. ▸ In some cases, only a particular government agency can bring suit for violation of environmental laws.
LIMITATIONS. ▸ Federal law lets a private party sue to stop a violation of air, water, or noise pollution standards. ▸ Organizations are increasingly allowed to sue on behalf of their members.

6. CRIMINAL LIABILITY

GENERAL RULES. ▸In general, it is a crime to knowingly violate an environmental protection statute. ▸ It is not a defense that (1) a party did not intend to violate the law, (2) that the party was not negligent, or (3) that the party was acting in the same manner as others act.

LIMITATION. A party's lack of intent to violate the law and other extenuating circumstances may be considered in determining the appropriate punishment for violating environmental laws.

B. COMMUNITY PLANNING

7. RESTRICTIVE COVENANTS IN PRIVATE CONTRACTS

GENERAL RULES. ▸ A real estate developer who subdivides and sells land may undertake private community planning by including restrictive covenants (restrictions and duties regarding the use of land) in deeds. Such covenants are binding on a buyer. Any subsequent owner is also bound by a valid restrictive covenant that: (1) is stated in a recorded deed; or (2) is known to the buyer. ▸ Example: Seller conveyed land to Buyer. Seller duly recorded a deed that prohibited any buildings more than fifty feet in height. This covenant is binding on Buyer and all future owners. ▸ An owner of land in a development that is subject to restrictive covenants may sue any other owner in the development who is violating the development's restrictive covenants.

LIMITATIONS. ▸Restrictive covenants are interpreted narrowly to allow the greatest use of land. ▸ A restrictive covenant that violates a law or public policy is invalid and unenforceable.

STUDY HINT. Restrictive covenants are interpreted using standard rules of contract interpretation, and words are given their ordinary meaning.

8. PUBLIC ZONING

GENERAL RULES. ▸Zoning is government-imposed restrictions on the use that may be made of land. ▸ Example: Cedar City adopted a zoning ordinance that permitted the construction of only single-family houses in a designated portion of the city. ▸ Zoning is used to plan future community growth and to ensure reasonable, orderly development. ▸ A governmental body, such as a city or county, can adopt zoning ordinances to promote public health, welfare, and safety, or to control population density. ▸ Ordinarily, a person does not have a right to use property in a manner prohibited by a valid zoning ordinance.

LIMITATIONS. ▸ A zoning ordinance is invalid if it violates a person's constitutional rights. ▸ In certain cases, a property use that conflicts with a zoning ordinance may be permitted due to:

- *Nonconforming use*: ▸ A nonconforming use is an existing use of property that conflicts with a newly adopted zoning ordinance. ▸ In general, a nonconforming use has a constitutional right to continue. ▸ However, if an owner discontinues a nonconforming use, the owner loses the right to this use through abandonment, and the nonconforming use cannot be resumed at a later time.

- *Variance*: ▸ A variance is an exception granted by an administrative agency that permits a use of property that is inconsistent with an existing zoning ordinance. ▸ An agency may grant a variance if the desired use for the property is harmonious with the character of surrounding areas. ▸ Variances are not frequently granted because they defeat the purpose of zoning. Variances are not granted if: (1) doing so would result in inequality that would likely be condemned by the courts; (2) a variance is requested merely to avoid a hardship that the owner is responsible for having created (for example, an owner bought land for a purpose that was not permitted by an existing zoning ordinance); or (3) a variance is requested solely to produce more income for the owner.

C. NUISANCES

9. DEFINITION OF NUISANCE

GENERAL RULES. ▸A nuisance is conduct that unreasonably interferes with the enjoyment or use of land. ▸ Examples: noise and dust from a mining operation that unreasonably impairs the ability of persons to live on neighboring property; emissions from a plant that damages neighboring buildings. ▸ Persons affected by a nuisance may sue for (1) damages and (2) an injunction stop the offending conduct. ▸ A nuisance may be classified according to: (1) who is harmed; or (2) the nature of the offending activity. Types of nuisances include:

- *Public nuisance*: Nuisance that affects the community or public at large.
- *Private nuisance*: Substantial and unreasonable interference with the use of property of one or a few persons.
- *Criminal nuisance*: A criminal nuisance is a location or business where criminal acts repeatedly occur. ▸ Example: establishment illegally selling liquor or where illegal prostitution takes place.
- *Permanent and continuing nuisances*: ▸ A permanent nuisance is a single act causing permanent harm to a plaintiff. ▸ A continuing nuisance is a series of related acts or continuing activity.
- *Nuisance per se and nuisance in fact*: ▸ A nuisance per se is an act, occupation, or building that always is a nuisance, regardless of the circumstances. ▸ A nuisance in fact is an activity or place that may be a nuisance in light of the surrounding circumstances. ▸ Example: Noise is typically a nuisance in fact because whether or not noise is a nuisance depends on the facts of each case.

LIMITATIONS. ▸ A minor interference with the enjoyment of land by others is not a nuisance. ▸ Mere inconvenience or annoyance with another's use of property is not a nuisance.

STUDY HINTS. ▸An activity or business that is conducted in accordance with applicable laws may nonetheless be a nuisance, depending on the effect that the activity or business has on others. ▸ To determine whether an activity is a nuisance, courts balance the social utility of the plaintiff's interest and the severity of the harm to the plaintiff, with the social utility of the defendant's activity. ▸ The fact that a defendant did not intentionally or negligently create a nuisance is not a defense.

10. THE TECHNOLOGICAL ENVIRONMENT OF THE LAW OF NUISANCE

▸ Real property law and the law of nuisance continue to change in order to keep in step with new technologies. ▸ Example: In an appropriate case, a property owner may be prevented from positioning a home on his or her property in a certain manner if doing so will unreasonably interfere with a neighbor's solar heating system.

11. THE COMPUTER AS A NUISANCE

Operation of a computer may be a nuisance if it interferes with another's use of private property. A nuisance caused by using a computer may exist even if the computer user is not negligent.

REVIEW OF TERMS AND PHRASES

Select the term or phrase that best matches a statement or definition stated below. Each term or phrase is the best match for only one statement or definition.

Terms and Phrases

a. Abandonment
b. CERCLA
c. Environmental impact statement (EIS)
d. NEPA
e. Nonconforming use
f. Nuisance
g. Restrictive covenant
h. Variance
i. Zoning

Statements and Definitions

____ 1. Study that examines the effect that a proposed action may have on the environment and the practical alternatives to such action that may exist.

____ 2. First significant federal environmental law, adopted in 1969.

____ 3. Zoning ordinance exception that is granted by an administrative agency and that permits a property use inconsistent with existing zoning laws.

____ 4. Major hazardous waste law that created the Superfund to clean up inactive hazardous waste sites.

____ 5. Government restrictions on land use that are used to plan community growth and development.

____ 6. Privately created land use restriction that is stated in a recorded deed.

____ 7. Forfeiture of the right to make a nonconforming use of property; occurs if an owner discontinues using the property for the nonconforming purpose.

____ 8. Property use that is constitutionally protected even though it conflicts with a newly adopted zoning ordinance.

____ 9. Conduct that unreasonably interferes with another's enjoyment or use of land.

REVIEW OF CONCEPTS

Write **T** if the statement is true, write **F** if it is false.

____ 1. In general, a state can adopt a water pollution law that conflicts with a federal clean water statute.

____ 2. The federal Superfund is designed to aid in cleaning up inactive hazardous waste sites.

____ 3. Some states require an environmental impact statement for large, private construction projects.

____ 4. An EIS must consider all alternatives to a project, whether the alternatives are feasible or not.

____ 5. Environmental protection laws are primarily adopted and enforced by administrative agencies.

____ 6. Under certain environmental laws, a private citizen can sue a polluter only if the citizen suffers a special harm that is different from the harm that is suffered by the general public.

____ 7. In general, a party may be criminally prosecuted for violating an environmental law even if the party did not intend to violate the law.

____ 8. An owner of a home in a development that has restrictive covenants can sue another homeowner in the development for violating one of the development's restrictive covenants.

____ 9. A party may discontinue a nonconforming use for up to five years without abandoning the right to resume the nonconforming use.

___10. A zoning variance may be granted if the intended use is in harmony with surrounding property.

___11. Landowners commit a nuisance whenever they use their land in a way that reduces the value of adjoining property.

___12. All interferences with another's enjoyment or use of his or her land are nuisances.

___13. A party affected by a nuisance may recover damages in addition to obtaining an injunction.

___14. Noise is a nuisance per se, not a nuisance in fact.

___15. Courts have refused to change traditional real property law in order to keep abreast of technological changes in society.

REVIEW OF CHAPTER - APPLICATION OF CONCEPTS

MULTIPLE CHOICE QUESTIONS

___1. The U.S. Army Corps of Engineers (a federal agency) proposes building a large dam. The dam will affect the environment, and it will require abandonment of several towns. In this case:
   a. The U.S. Army Corps of Engineers must prepare an EIS before it builds the dam.
   b. An EIS must consider the impact that the dam may have on residents and businesses in the towns that must be abandoned if the dam is built.
   c. An EIS must consider feasible, practical alternatives to the dam.
   d. All of the above.

___2. The U.S. government filed criminal charges against Martin Co. for discharging residue wastes into a river in violation of federal environmental law. Martin Co. knew that it was discharging wastes into the river. However, Martin Co. did not intend to violate the law, it did not act negligently, and it did not discharge more wastes than other similar companies. In this case:
   a. Martin Co. is probably guilty.
   b. Martin Co. is probably not guilty because it did not intend to violate the law.
   c. Martin Co. is probably not guilty because it did not act negligently.
   d. Martin Co. is probably not guilty because it did not discharge more wastes than other firms.

___3. Richard bought an existing home from Kim. The home is located in a planned development that is governed by restrictive covenants. The covenants are publicly recorded and they were noted on all deeds. In violation of a covenant, Richard built a fence around the home. In this case:
   a. Richard's neighbor can sue him for violation of the restrictive covenant.
   b. Richard is not bound by the covenants because restrictive covenants are unconstitutional.
   c. Richard is not bound by the covenants because he did not buy the home directly from the developer who imposed the restrictive covenants.
   d. Richard is not bound by the covenants because a person's use of property can only be restricted by zoning laws.

___4. Azores Co. held a permit to operate a gravel pit within Pine City, and it had operated a gravel pit within the city for five continuous years. Then Pine City adopted a new zoning ordinance which prohibited gravel pit operations within the city limits. Under these facts:
   a. Azores must stop its gravel pit operation on the date the zoning ordinance becomes effective.
   b. Azores' gravel pit operation is a nonconforming use, and Azores can continue such use.
   c. Azores may stop its gravel pit operation without losing the right to renew such use at a later date.
   d. b and c.

CASE PROBLEM

Answer the following problem, briefly explaining your answer.

Hank owns and operates a factory that employs 100 people. Hank built the factory next to a quiet residential neighborhood. There are no restrictive covenants or zoning ordinances that prohibit or restrict the factory's operations. However, two neighbors have sued him, asserting that the factory is a nuisance because the noise and traffic generated by the factory interferes with their enjoyment of their property.

(a) What will a court consider in determining whether the factory is a nuisance? (b) Is it possible for a lawful activity, such as Hank's factory, to be a nuisance? (c) If the factory is a nuisance: would it be a nuisance per se or a nuisance in fact; would it be a private nuisance or a criminal nuisance?

CPA REVIEW

The following questions were given on CPA examinations. The answers for these questions are the unofficial answers prepared by the American Institute of Certified Public Accountants, Inc. (AICPA). All material is reproduced with permission of the AICPA.

____ 1. Under the Comprehensive Environmental Response, Compensation, and Liability Act (CERCLA), commonly known as Superfund, which of the following parties would be liable to the Environmental Protection Agency (EPA) for the expense of cleaning up a hazardous waste disposal site?
   I. The current owner or operator of the site.
   II. The person who transported the wastes to the site.
   III. The person who owned or operated the site at the time of the disposal.
   a. I and II.
   b. I and III.
   c. II and III.
   d. I, II, and III.

____ 2. Which of the following remedies is available against a real property owner to enforce the provisions of federal acts regulating air and water pollution?

	Citizen suits against the (EPA) to enforce compliance with the laws	Citizen suits against violators	State suits against violators
a.	Yes	Yes	Yes
b.	Yes	Yes	No
c.	No	Yes	Yes
d.	Yes	No	Yes

CHAPTER 52
LEASES

CHAPTER OUTLINE

A. CREATION AND TERMINATION

1. DEFINITION AND NATURE

▸ A lease is a relationship and agreement whereby one party (a lessee) is permitted to possess real property belonging to another (a lessor or landlord). ▸ Modern law focuses on the contractual nature of the lease relationship. Consequently, contract concepts, such as warranties, often apply to leases.

2. CREATION OF THE LEASE RELATIONSHIP

GENERAL RULES. ▸ A lease is created by an express or implied contract. ▸ Under common law, an oral lease is valid. ▸ In many states today, leases for more than three years must be in writing. In other states, leases for more than one year must be written.
LIMITATIONS. ▸ Statutes in many states prohibit lessors from discriminating on the basis of race, religion, national origin, or color. ▸ Some states prohibit unconscionable terms in leases.
STUDY HINTS. ▸ A covenant is a promise or an obligation. ▸ A covenant in a lease is called a condition if its breach justifies termination of the lease.

3. ESSENTIAL ELEMENTS

These elements are needed to create a landlord-tenant relationship: (1) landlord consents to tenant's occupation of property; (2) tenant's occupation is subject to landlord's rights; (3) tenant has present possession of the property; and (4) property reverts to the landlord after termination of the lease.

4. CLASSIFICATION OF TENANCIES

▸ *Tenancy for years*: lease is for definite duration (not necessarily a year). ▸ *Tenancy from year to year*: lease is for indefinite duration; rent is paid periodically; proper notice is required to terminate. ▸ *Tenancy at will*: lease is for indefinite duration, and it may be terminated at any time by either party. ▸ *Tenancy by sufferance*: If a tenant holds over without permission, the tenant is a tenant by sufferance until the landlord decides whether to treat the party as a tenant or as a trespasser.

5. TERMINATION OF LEASE

GENERAL RULE. Leases are terminated by: (1) proper notice (either notice required by lease or notice required by statutes if lease is a tenancy from year to year); (2) expiration of lease term in a tenancy for years (notice not required); (3) landlord's acceptance of tenant's surrender of premises; (4) forfeiture of tenant's interest due to tenant's breach (if termination is allowed by lease); (5) destruction of premises; (6) fraud; or (7) tenant being transferred (if termination allowed by lease).
LIMITATION. A lease is generally not terminated by the death, insanity, or bankruptcy of either party unless (1) the lease is a tenancy at will or (2) the lease provides otherwise.

6. NOTICE OF TERMINATION

▸ If a party's intention to terminate is clear, no special words must be used in order to give notice of termination. ▸ Unless statutes require otherwise, an oral notice is sufficient to terminate a lease.

7. RENEWAL OF LEASE

▸ Parties may renew an expired lease. ▸ If a lease requires notice to renew, renewal cannot occur without notice. ▸ A lease may provide that it automatically renews unless a party states otherwise.

B. RIGHTS AND DUTIES OF PARTIES

8. POSSESSION

GENERAL RULES. ▸A tenant has a right to possession of leased premises on the date the lease begins. ▸ A tenant has the right to exclusive possession of leased premises, and may exclude a landlord from the premises unless otherwise agreed. ▸ A tenant can sue a landlord for wrongfully evicting the tenant.
  ▸ Evictions may be: (1) actual; (2) constructive (landlord acts or fails to act, intending to substantially deprive a tenant of the use and enjoyment of premises); or (3) partial.
LIMITATION. A lessee cannot remain in leased premises and claim a constructive eviction.
STUDY HINT. Most written leases contain a covenant of quiet enjoyment. This clause expressly protects the tenant from interference by the landlord (but not from interference by third parties).

9. USE OF PREMISES

▸ A lease may state permissible uses of property; any different use may create a right to terminate a lease. ▸If no particular use is specified, any lawful use contemplated by the parties is permitted. ▸ A lease may allow a landlord to make reasonable, binding regulations. ▸ A lease may forbid pets.

10. RENT

GENERAL RULES. ▸ A tenant must pay the agreed rent. ▸ If a tenant assigns a lease, the original tenant and assignee are both liable for rent. ▸ If premises are sublet, the original tenant is liable for rent; a sublessee is not liable to a lessor for rent unless liability is imposed by the sublease or by law. ▸ Rent must be paid (1) at the time stated in a lease or (2) if not stated, at the end of the lease term.
LIMITATION. Government regulations (e.g., rent controls) may limit rent that may be charged.
STUDY HINT. Leases may include escalation clauses that automatically increase rent.

11. REPAIRS AND CONDITION OF PREMISES

GENERAL RULES. ▸Unless otherwise agreed, a tenant has no duty to make repairs (although a tenant is liable for willful or negligent damage). ▸ Housing laws may require a landlord to maintain premises in a habitable condition. ▸ At common law, a landlord did not warrant the habitability of a residence. But in most states today, a landlord is held to impliedly warrant the habitability of residences. Moreover, if premises are unfit, a tenant may sometimes withhold rent or pay rent into an escrow account, or the rent may be reduced to reflect the actual rental value of the premises.
STUDY HINT. A landlord cannot enter and inspect premises unless given this right by a lease.

12. IMPROVEMENTS

▸ Unless otherwise agreed, neither a tenant nor a landlord is required to make improvements.
▸ If a lease requires either party to make improvements, failure to comply is an actionable breach.

13. TAXES AND ASSESSMENTS

▸ Unless otherwise agreed, a landlord pays taxes and assessments. ▸ Tax increases resulting from a tenant's improvements are paid: (1) by the landlord if the improvements remain with the property; or (2) by the tenant if the improvements can be removed by the tenant.

14. TENANT'S DEPOSIT

▸A landlord may require a tenant to pay a deposit to protect against the tenant's default. ▸ Some states treat a deposit as a trust fund, requiring a landlord: (1) to tell the tenant where the money is deposited; and (2) to pay a penalty if the deposit is used prior to a breach of the lease by the tenant.

15. PROTECTION FROM RETALIATION

Modern laws prohibit a landlord from evicting a tenant or otherwise retaliating because a tenant (1) exercises a legal right or (2) reports the landlord for violating housing codes.

16. REMEDIES OF LANDLORD

- *Landlord's lien*: Lessor has no lien for unpaid rent unless lien is given by a lease or statute.
- *Suit for rent*: If a tenant fails to pay rent, a landlord may sue for the rent that is due.
- *Distress*: The common law remedy of distress, which allowed a landlord to seize and hold a tenant's property until the rent was paid, has been abolished or modified in most states.
- *Recovery of possession*: ▸ Leases often allow a landlord to recover possession of premises if a tenant defaults. ▸ At common law and in many states, a landlord has a right of re-entry (right to retake premises without legal proceedings). ▸ But, some modern cases do not permit a lessor to lock out a tenant for nonpayment of rent, and legal proceedings are needed to regain possession.
- *Mitigation of damages*: A majority of states do not require a landlord to mitigate (reduce or avoid) damages by seeking a new tenant if a tenant abandons premises. A modern trend requires mitigation.

C. LIABILITY FOR INJURY ON PREMISES

17. LANDLORD'S LIABILITY TO TENANT

▸ Absent a duty to make repairs, a landlord is not liable for a tenant's injuries caused by defects in premises that are under the tenant's control or that are known to the tenant. ▸ Landlords are not liable for unforeseeable crimes committed by others. ▸ Commercial leases can excuse landlords from liability for tenants' losses; some states restrict this right in connection with residential leases.

18. LANDLORD'S LIABILITY TO THIRD PERSONS

▸In general, a landlord is not liable to a third party who is injured due to the condition of premises that are under a tenant's control. ▸ A landlord is liable for injuries caused: (1) by defective premises under the landlord's control; or (2) by a condition the landlord had a contractual duty to correct.

19. TENANT'S LIABILITY TO THIRD PERSONS

Regardless of whether a landlord is obligated to repair, a tenant in possession of property is liable for injuries to licensees and invitees that are caused by the tenant's failure to use due care.

D. TRANSFER OF RIGHTS

20. TRANSFER OF LANDLORD'S REVERSIONARY INTEREST

Lessors' interests can be voluntarily/involuntarily transferred; new owners are bound by lease terms.

21. TENANT'S ASSIGNMENT OF LEASE AND SUBLEASE

▸An assignment of a lease is a transfer of a tenant's entire interest to another. An assignee is bound by (and liable under) the original lease. Unless restricted, a tenant may assign a tenancy for years. ▸ A sublease transfers only a portion of a tenant's interest. Unless otherwise agreed, a sublessee is not liable to the lessor. ▸ A lease may restrict the right to make an assignment or sublease. ▸ An assignment or sublease does not release a lessee from the lease.

REVIEW OF TERMS AND PHRASES

Select the term or phrase that best matches a statement or definition stated below. Each term or phrase is the best match for only one statement or definition.

Terms and Phrases

a. Assignment (of lease)
b. Condition
c. Constructive eviction
d. Covenant
e. Covenant of quiet enjoyment
f. Distress
g. Escalation clause
h. Lease
i. Lessee
j. Lessor
k. Partial eviction
l. Right of reentry
m. Sublease
n. Surrender
o. Warranty of habitability

Statements and Definitions

____ 1. Eviction that results from an act or omission by a landlord that substantially deprives a tenant of the enjoyment and use of leased premises.

____ 2. Lease term that provides for automatic rent increases under certain conditions.

____ 3. Implied warranty that premises leased for residential use are fit to be lived in.

____ 4. Lessor's or lessee's obligation or promise that is stated in a lease.

____ 5. Common law right of a landlord to retake leased premises without legal proceedings.

____ 6. Party who lawfully occupies (leases) real property that is owned by another.

____ 7. Transfer of a tenant's entire interest in a lease.

____ 8. Promise by landlord not to interfere with a tenant's enjoyment and use of leased premises.

____ 9. Transfer of only a portion of a tenant's interest in a lease.

____ 10. Landlord's common law right to seize tenant's personal property as security for payment of rent.

____ 11. Promise which, if breached, entitles the other party to terminate a lease.

____ 12. Relationship or agreement by which one party lawfully occupies the property of another.

____ 13. Eviction of a tenant from a portion of leased premises.

____ 14. Party who owns real property and permits occupation of the property by another.

____ 15. Tenant's giving up of his or her interest in leased premises to a landlord.

REVIEW OF CONCEPTS

Write **T** if the statement is true, write **F** if it is false.

____ 1. In most states, landlords can discriminate on the basis of a tenant's race, religion, or color.

____ 2. One required element of a landlord-tenant relationship is that the landlord has a reversionary interest in the premises, i.e., the premises revert back to the landlord once the lease terminates.

____ 3. A tenant who holds over without permission may be treated as a trespasser by the landlord.

____ 4. A tenancy for years is automatically terminated by the bankruptcy of the tenant.

____ 5. Unless otherwise agreed, a tenant is generally entitled to exclude a landlord from leased premises during the term of a lease.

____ 6. Modern leases commonly provide that a landlord may terminate a lease if a lessee uses premises in a manner that is different from the use permitted by the lease.

____ 7. Leases can include escalation clauses, and an escalation clause may be enforceable even if it requires payment of more rent than the tenant anticipated that he or she would have to pay.

____ 8. Unless otherwise agreed, a tenant generally has a duty to make all repairs to leased premises.

____ 9. In some states, a tenant may withhold payment of rent if the premises are unfit to live in.

____ 10. A landlord is entitled to evict a tenant for reporting housing code violations to the government.

____ 11. Most states require a landlord to mitigate damages by re-renting leased premises after a tenant abandons a lease.

____ 12. A landlord is generally liable for injuries caused by the unforeseen criminal acts of third parties.

____ 13. A landlord may be liable for injuries suffered by a tenant in an area that the landlord controls.

____ 14. In general, a landlord is liable to a third party who is injured on leased premises that are under the exclusive control of a tenant.

____ 15. A tenant is liable to a third party who is injured due to the tenant's failure to exercise due care.

REVIEW OF CHAPTER - APPLICATION OF CONCEPTS

MULTIPLE CHOICE QUESTIONS

____ 1. Isako leased a home for an indefinite time. The lease requires Isako to pay rent on a monthly basis, on the first day of each month. Sixty days' prior written notice is required to terminate the lease. Under these facts, Isako's tenancy is classified as a:
   a. Tenancy for years.
   b. Tenancy from year to year.
   c. Tenancy at will.
   d. Tenancy at sufferance.

____ 2. Sara leased an apartment from Landlord. Subsequently, Landlord intentionally shut off all utilities to Sara's apartment in order to do major remodeling at the apartment complex. Landlord kept the utilities shut off for an indefinite time. As a result of Landlord's conduct, Sara had no practical choice but to move out. Landlord's conduct is best described as being:
   a. An actual eviction of Sara.
   b. A partial eviction of Sara.
   c. A constructive eviction of Sara.
   d. Permissible conduct.

____ 3. Landlord leased a home to Jack for a two-year term. Annual property taxes at that time were $1,000. Shortly after making the lease, Landlord built a garage at the home, and Jack built a movable, above-ground swimming pool at the home. Jack has the right to remove the pool when the lease expires. The annual property taxes increased $300 due to the garage, and $200 due to the pool. The lease is silent regarding taxes. How much of the property taxes must Jack pay?
   a. $0
   b. $200
   c. $500
   d. $1,500

____ 4. Lee rented an apartment to Kirk. Kirk failed to pay the rent, and Lee properly terminated the lease. The lease is silent regarding landlord liens, and the state in question does not have any statutes relating to such liens. This state recognizes the common law right of re-entry, but it has abolished the common law remedy of distress. In this case:
   a. Lee cannot sue Kirk for the unpaid rent.
   b. Lee has a landlord's lien against Kirk's personal belongings that are in the apartment, and Lee can retain possession of these belongings until the rent is paid.
   c. Lee can re-enter the apartment and evict Kirk without first utilizing legal proceedings.
   d. b and c.

____ 5. Sam leased a warehouse from Landlord. Landlord is obligated to maintain the warehouse parking lot, and Sam has exclusive control over and responsibility for the warehouse. Landlord is liable for which of the following losses?
   a. Sam's inventory was destroyed when an unknown arsonist burned down the warehouse.
   b. A third party slipped on oil that Sam negligently spilled on the warehouse floor.
   c. A third party fell in a pot hole that was negligently allowed to exist in the parking lot.
   d. b and c.

CASE PROBLEM

Answer the following problem, briefly explaining your answer.

Jackie leased several offices from Landlord pursuant to a three-year lease. Later, Jackie agreed to lease one of the offices to Kate for one year. The agreement between Jackie and Kate did not state whether it was an assignment or a sublease, and it did not address the parties' responsibility for performance of the original lease. Subsequently, Kate did not pay the rent for the office she leased from Jackie, and Landlord was not paid the rent for this office. Landlord sued Jackie and Kate for the unpaid rent for the office.

(a) Is the agreement between Jackie and Kate an assignment or a sublease? (b) Is Jackie liable to Landlord for the unpaid rent? (c) Is Kate liable to Landlord for the unpaid rent?

CPA REVIEW

The following questions were given on CPA examinations. The answers for these questions are the unofficial answers prepared by the American Institute of Certified Public Accountants, Inc. (AICPA). All material is reproduced with permission of the AICPA.

___ 1. Which of the following provisions must be included in a residential lease agreement?
   a. A description of the leased premises.
   b. The due date for payment of rent.
   c. A requirement that the tenant have public liability insurance.
   d. A requirement that the landlord will perform all structural repairs to the property.

___ 2. Which of the following forms of tenancy will be created if a tenant stays in possession of the leased premises without the landlord's consent, after the tenant's one-year written lease expires?
   a. Tenancy at will.
   b. Tenancy for years.
   c. Tenancy from period to period.
   d. Tenancy at sufferance.

___ 3. Bronson is a residential tenant with a 10-year written lease. In the absence of specific provisions in the lease to the contrary, which of the following statements is correct?
   a. The premises may not be sublet for less than the full remaining lease term.
   b. Bronson may not assign the lease.
   c. The landlord's death will automatically terminate the lease.
   d. Bronson's purchase of the property will terminate the lease.

___ 4. A tenant renting an apartment under a three-year written lease that does not contain any specific restrictions may be evicted for
   a. Counterfeiting money in the apartment.
   b. Keeping a dog in the apartment.
   c. Failing to maintain a liability insurance policy on the apartment.
   d. Making structural repairs to the apartment.

___ 5. Delta Corp. leased 60,000 square feet in an office building from Tanner under a written 25-year lease. Which of the following statements is correct?
   a. Tanner's death will terminate the lease and Delta will be able to recover any resulting damages from Tanner's estate.
   b. Tanner's sale of the office building will terminate the lease unless both Delta and the buyer consented to the assumption of the lease by the buyer.
   c. In the absence of a provision in the lease to the contrary, Delta does not need Tanner's consent to assign the lease to another party.
   d. In the absence of a provision in the lease to the contrary, Delta would need Tanner's consent to enter into a sublease with another party.

CHAPTER 52

___ 6. Lusk borrowed $20,000 from Marco Finance. The loan was secured by a mortgage on a four-unit apartment building owned by Lusk. The proceeds of the loan were used by Lusk to purchase a business. The mortgage was duly recorded 60 days after Marco loaned the money to Lusk. Six months after borrowing the money from Marco, Lusk leased one of the apartments to Rudd for $800 per month. Neither Rudd nor Lusk notified Marco of the lease. Subsequently, Lusk defaulted on the note to Marco and Marco has commenced foreclosure proceedings. Under the circumstances,
   a. Marco's mortgage is junior to Rudd's lease because the mortgage was not a purchase money mortgage.
   b. Marco's mortgage is junior to Rudd's lease because Marco failed to record the mortgage for 60 days after the closing.
   c. Rudd's lease is subject to Marco's mortgage because Marco recorded its mortgage prior to the time Rudd's leasehold interest arose.
   d. Rudd's lease is subject to Marco's mortgage because of the failure to notify Marco of the lease.

___ 7. Mack & Watts, CPAs, wishes to relocate its office. Its existing lease is for four years, with one year remaining. Its landlord is not agreeable to canceling the lease. The lease also prohibits a sublease without the landlord's consent but is silent as to an assignment. Mack & Watts has found a financially responsible and respectable prospective subtenant but is convinced that the landlord will not consent to a sublease. Which of the following statements is correct?
   a. A sublease without the landlord's consent would not be a breach of the lease.
   b. An assignment by Mack & Watts would be a breach of the lease.
   c. An assignment by Mack & Watts would not relieve it of liability under the lease.
   d. A sublease with the landlord's consent would relieve Mack & Watts of liability under the lease.

___ 8. Mini, Inc., entered into a five-year lease with Rein Realtors. The lease was signed by both parties and immediately recorded. The leased building was to be used by Mini in connection with its business operations. To make it suitable for that purpose, Mini attached a piece of equipment to the wall of the building.
   Which of the following statements is correct regarding Mini's rights and liabilities?
   a. Mini is prohibited from assigning the lease if it is silent in this regard.
   b. Mini has a possessory interest in the building.
   c. Mini is strictly liable for all injuries sustained by any person in the building during the term of the lease.
   d. Mini's rights under the lease are automatically terminated by Rein's sale of the building to a third party.

CHAPTER 53
DECEDENTS' ESTATES AND TRUSTS

CHAPTER OUTLINE

A. WILLS

1. DEFINITIONS

▸*Will*: writing that determines the distribution of a person's property upon his or her death. ▸ *Testator (testatrix)*: person who makes a will. ▸ *Testate distribution*: property distribution through a valid will. ▸ *Beneficiary*: person to whom property is left by a will. ▸ *Legacy (bequest)*: gift of personal property under a will. ▸ *Devise*: gift of real property under a will.

2. PARTIES TO WILL

- *Testator*: In general, a person (testator or testatrix) can make a valid will only if he or she: (1) is eighteen years of age or older; and (2) possesses testamentary capacity.
- *Beneficiary*: ▸ There are no special requirements for beneficiaries. ▸ A guardian may need to be appointed to administer property left to a minor unless: (1) a will directs a trustee to hold the property; or (2) property is not significant and it is paid to the minor or to the person maintaining the minor.

3. TESTAMENTARY INTENT

A valid will requires that a testator have testamentary intent (intent that action is effective only on death). This intent is present if a will: (1) transfers property on death; or (2) an executor is named.

4. FORM

▸If a will does not comply with statutory requirements, the will is invalid and a decedent's property is distributed as if no will existed. ▸ Ordinarily, a will must be written and must be signed by the testator, but it need not be dated. ▸ Most states require attestation (witnessing testator's execution of will) by two witnesses; some states require publication (testator verifies that a will is his will).

5. MODIFICATION OF WILL

▸A separate writing (codicil) may amend a will. A codicil must satisfy the requirements for making a will. ▸ A will cannot be changed by merely crossing out terms and writing in new ones.

6. REVOCATION OF WILL

▸ A testator revokes a will (or a part of it) if the testator, with an intent to revoke, tears or destroys the will or crosses out a part of it. ▸ In some cases, a will is revoked in whole or in part if a testator marries, divorces with a property settlement, or has a child after making the will.

7. PROBATE OF WILL

▸ Probate is a determination by an appropriate court or official that a will meets the statutory requirements for being a decedent's will. ▸ In general, a will has no legal effect until it is probated.

8. WILL CONTEST

Probate of a will may be refused or set aside if: (1) a testator lacked testamentary capacity; (2) a will was made as a result of undue influence, duress, fraud, or mistake; or (3) the will is a forgery.

9. SPECIAL KINDS OF WILLS

▸ *Holographic will*: unwitnessed will, entirely in a testator's handwriting. ▸ *Self-proved will*: will allowed in some states that eliminates the need for some formalities of proof if executed as set forth by statute. ▸ *Living will*: document allowing a person to state whether life-sustaining medical treatments should be used during an incurable, irreversible medical condition.

B. DISTRIBUTION UNDER THE WILL

10. LEGACIES

- ***Definitions***: ▸ *General legacy*: bequest of sum of money. ▸ *Specific legacy (devise)*: bequest of specific item of personal (real) property. ▸ *Residuary bequest*: bequest of all property of a decedent that remains after general and specific legacies have been satisfied.
- ***Abatement and ademption***: ▸ If assets are insufficient to satisfy all bequests, bequests abate (are reduced) in the following order (bequests in the same class abate proportionately): (1) residuary; (2) general; (3) specific. ▸ If property given by a specific legacy is disposed of before a testator dies, the legacy is adeemed (canceled); the beneficiary gets nothing.
- ***Antilapse statute***: Unless a testator directs otherwise, a beneficiary's children or heirs take a gift that was bequeathed to the beneficiary if the beneficiary dies before the testator dies.

11. ELECTION TO TAKE AGAINST THE WILL

A surviving spouse may ignore a will and elect to take the share he or she would have received had there been no will. Misconduct (e.g., desertion, nonsupport) may bar a right to make this election.

12. DISINHERITANCE

With two exceptions, anyone may be disinherited or excluded from sharing in an estate.

13. CONSTRUCTION OF WILL

A will is interpreted according to its ordinary meaning, and courts try to carry out all terms of a will.

C. INTESTACY

14. PLAN OF INTESTATE DISTRIBUTION

▸State laws commonly provide that property of a decedent who dies without a valid will (intestate) is distributed in the following manner after debts are paid: (1) surviving spouse takes all unless there are surviving children, in which case the spouse takes a one-third or one-half share and children take the remainder; (2) lineal (blood) descendants (children; grandchildren; etc.) take all if there is no spouse; (3) parents of a decedent take all if there is no spouse or lineal descendants; (4) collateral heirs (brothers; sisters; their descendants) take all if none of the foregoing persons survive. ▸ Property not distributed under these rules passes to the state by escheat. ▸ Distributions to two or more heirs who have equal rights to a decedent's property are distributed per capita (equal shares). ▸ Persons entitled to distribution are determined as of date of death. If a distributee dies *after* a testator, distributee's share passes to his or her estate.

D. ADMINISTRATION OF DECEDENTS' ESTATES

15. DEFINITIONS

▸ *Executor (executrix)*: party named in will to administer estate. ▸ *Administrator (administratrix)*: party appointed by court to administer estate. ▸ *Personal representative*: executor or administrator.

16. WHEN ADMINISTRATION IS NOT NECESSARY

No administration is required if: (1) the decedent owned no property at death; or (2) all property was owned jointly with another person who takes the property by right of survivorship.

17. APPOINTMENT OF PERSONAL REPRESENTATIVE

▸ To represent an estate, personal representatives must first be appointed by a court or appropriate official. Appointment is made by letters testamentary for executors, and letters of administration for administrators. ▸ An administrator is appointed only if an executor is not named or appointed.

18. PROOF OF CLAIMS AGAINST THE ESTATE

Most states provide that a creditor's claim is barred unless filed with an estate within a certain time.

E. TRUSTS

19. DEFINITIONS

▸ *Trust*: legal device by which one person (trustee) holds property (trust corpus or res) in trust for another (beneficiary or cestui que trust). ▸ *Settlor*: person who creates a trust. ▸ *Inter vivos (living) trust*: trust that takes effect during a settlor's lifetime. ▸ *Testamentary trust*: trust created by a will, and the trust is effective upon the death of the settlor. ▸ *Trust agreement*: writing creating a trust.

20. CREATION OF TRUSTS

GENERAL RULE. Typical requirements to create a trust: (1) any lawful purpose (a trust to defraud creditors is invalid); (2) in writing if the trust relates to land, is created by will, or takes effect on death; (3) designation of a beneficiary, the trust purpose, and the trust property; and (4) the trust intends to and does give the trustee an active duty to manage the trust.
LIMITATION. A trust does not require consideration, and capacity of a beneficiary is irrelevant.
STUDY HINT. A trustee is presumed to accept a trust unless he or she renounces it. If a trustee is not named or a trustee renounces an appointment, a court will appoint a trustee.

21. NATURE OF BENEFICIARY'S INTEREST

▸ A trustee holds legal title to trust property; a beneficiary holds equitable title. ▸ With the exception of a spendthrift trust, a beneficiary's creditors may reach trust property to satisfy claims.

22. POWERS OF TRUSTEE

A trustee can exercise only powers that are conferred by the trust or by law or that are judicially implied.

23. DUTIES OF TRUSTEE

▸ A trustee must (1) try to protect a trust from losses; (2) defend the trust in court if its validity is questioned; (3) manage it to yield income; (4) administer it according to the terms of the trust; and (5) make periodic accountings of trust affairs. ▸ A trustee cannot delegate personal duties. ▸ A trustee must use reasonable skill and care, and a trustee is liable for losses caused by the trustee's failure to do so.
▸ A trustee cannot personally profit from being trustee, except for allowable compensation.

24. REMEDIES FOR BREACH OF TRUST

A trustee's breach of a trust may result in: (1) a money judgment and/or injunction against a trustee; (2) criminal prosecution of a trustee; (3) removal of a trustee; (4) suit against a surety on a trustee's bond; (5) suit against third parties who participated in the breach of trust; and (6) recovery of trust property from a transferee unless the party paid value and took property without notice of a breach.

25. TERMINATION OF TRUST

A trust may terminate: (1) according to its terms; (2) if a trust's stated object is impossible to obtain; (3) if a settlor properly revokes the trust; (4) if all interests merge in the same person; or (5) if all beneficiaries request termination and there is no express purpose that requires continuation.

REVIEW OF TERMS AND PHRASES

Select the term or phrase that best matches a statement or definition stated below. Each term or phrase is the best match for only one statement or definition.

Terms and Phrases

a. Abatement
b. Ademption
c. Antilapse statute
d. Codicil
e. Devise
f. Holographic will
g. Inter vivos trust
h. Intestate succession
i. Lineal descendants
j. Living will
k. Personal representative
l. Probate
m. Testamentary capacity
n. Testamentary intent
o. Testator/testatrix

Statements and Definitions

__c__ 1. Law providing that a beneficiary's children take a legacy if the beneficiary dies before the testator and the testator did not state an alternative disposition in the event that the beneficiary died first.

__g__ 2. Trust that takes effect during a settlor's lifetime.

__i__ 3. Blood descendants of a person (i.e., children, grandchildren, and their descendants).

__d__ 4. Separate writing that amends a will.

__a__ 5. Loss of all or a portion of a bequest if an estate has insufficient property to fulfill the bequest.

__o__ 6. Person who makes a will.

__k__ 7. Executor or administrator who administers a decedent's estate.

__b__ 8. Cancellation of a specific legacy if the bequeathed property is disposed of before the testator dies.

__e__ 9. Bequest of real property made in a will.

__h__ 10. Distribution of property of a person who dies without a valid will.

__m__ 11. Testator's ability to understand (a) that a writing is a will (i.e., it disposes of property upon death), (b) who the testator's family and friends are, and (c) nature and extent of his property.

__f__ 12. Will that is written entirely in a testator's handwriting and that is made without witnesses.

__j__ 13. Document by which a person indicates whether life-sustaining medical treatment should be used in the event the person suffers an irreversible, incurable illness.

__l__ 14. Act by which a court or official accepts a will and determines that it meets the requirements for being the will of a testator or testatrix.

__n__ 15. Intent that a disposition of property be effective only upon the death of the party.

REVIEW OF CONCEPTS

Write **T** if the statement is true, write **F** if it is false.

__T__ 1. Property of a person who dies without a will or with an invalid will is distributed according to intestate succession.

__T__ 2. Attestation is the act of having a will witnessed by a required number of witnesses, whereas publication is the act of a testator or testatrix acknowledging that a will is his or her will.

F 3. Most states do not require attestation of a will.

F 4. In general, a will is not required to be in writing to be enforceable.

T 5. A will is revoked if a testator burns or destroys the will with the intent to revoke the will.

T 6. In some states, a will is automatically revoked, in whole or in part, if the testator marries, or has additional children (by birth or adoption) after making the will.

F 7. Probate of a will is typically an optional procedure; a will is generally effective without probate.

T 8. In general, a spouse can elect to forego what is bequeathed by a will, thereby electing to take what the spouse would have received had there been no will.

F 9. Under the intestate succession laws in most states, a surviving spouse takes all of a decedent's estate even if there are surviving children.

F 10. If a distributee is entitled to receive property from a decedent's estate by intestate distribution and the distributee dies *after* the decedent, the distributee's right to receive a share of the decedent's estate is forfeited; the right to receive the property does not pass to the distributee's estate.

T 11. A decedent's debts must be paid by an estate prior to distributions to legatees, devisees, or heirs.

T 12. In many states, a creditor forfeits the right to be paid if the creditor fails to file a claim with a decedent's estate within the time required by law.

F 13. A trust may be created to fraudulently keep property away from a settlor's creditors.

T 14. Consideration is not required to create a valid trust.

T 15. A valid trust cannot be created without sufficiently designating a beneficiary.

REVIEW OF CHAPTER - APPLICATION OF CONCEPTS

MULTIPLE CHOICE QUESTIONS

C 1. Sabrina made a will leaving everything to her daughter. Two years later, Sabrina decided she wanted to change her will in order to leave some jewelry to her best friends. Under these facts:
   a. Sabrina can change her will only by first destroying the will and then making a new one.
   b. Sabrina can change her will by crossing out undesired bequests and writing in new bequests.
   c. Sabrina can change her will by signing a codicil that is properly attested and published.
   d. Sabrina cannot change her will; a person is legally prohibited from changing an executed will.

b 2. Harvey drank heavily for years. Due to his drinking, Harvey suffered permanent mental impairment, and he could not recall to whom he was related or what he owned. Nonetheless, Harvey executed a properly attested and published will. The will left everything to Bob, a recent acquaintance; nothing was left to Harvey's son whom Harvey had forgotten about. In this case:
   a. The will is invalid because a testator cannot disinherit a child.
   b. The will is invalid because Harvey did not have testamentary capacity.
   c. The will is valid. A testator may disinherit a child, and a will is valid if it is properly signed, attested, and published.
   d. a and b.

C 3. Matilda died leaving all of her property to various nieces and nephews. She bequeathed her stamp collection to Richard; $5,000 each to Sue and John; and her residuary estate to Marty. However, after payment of debts and expenses, the only remaining assets of Matilda's estate were the stamp collection and $5,000. Under these facts:
   a. The stamp collection will be sold for cash. Then, Richard, Sue, John, and Marty will each receive one-fourth of the assets of the estate.
   b. Richard will receive the stamp collection, and Marty will receive the $5,000.
   c. Richard will receive the stamp collection, and Sue and John will each receive $2,500.
   d. Richard will receive the stamp collection; Sue, John, and Marty will equally divide the $5,000.

b 4. Ladd died without a will. He is survived by his wife, two children, and his mother and father. Under typical intestate succession rules, how will Ladd's property be distributed?
   a. Ladd's wife will receive all of the property.
   b. Ladd's wife will receive one-third or one-half of the property, and his children will each receive equal portions of the remaining property.
   c. Ladd's children will equally share all of the property.
   d. Ladd's wife, children, and parents will each receive one-fifth of his property.

a 5. Hector is trustee of a trust. The trust beneficiaries are Hector's nephews. The trust has $50,000 cash. In most states, what would Hector be permitted to do as trustee?
   a. Hector can invest the cash in U.S. Treasury bonds and corporate stocks.
   b. Hector can make an interest-free loan of the trust's cash to his business.
   c. Hector can delegate all of his duties under the trust to his wife.
   d. a and c.

CASE PROBLEM

Answer the following problem, briefly explaining your answer.

Settlor validly created a charitable trust. The trust designated Mona as trustee, and the trust agreement stated that Settlor reserved the right to terminate the trust at any time. Mona never formally accepted her appointment as trustee, but she did serve as trustee for one year. During this time, she irresponsibly invested the trust assets in speculative investments, causing significant losses of the trust corpus.

(a) Is Mona the trustee even though she never formally accepted her appointment? (b) Can Settlor revoke the trust? (c) Did Mona breach any duty? (d) What remedies may be available in light of Mona's conduct?

CPA REVIEW

The following questions were given on CPA examinations. The answers for these questions are the unofficial answers prepared by the American Institute of Certified Public Accountants, Inc. (AICPA). All material is reproduced with permission of the AICPA.

____ 1. A decedent's will provided that the estate was to be divided among the decedent's issue, per capita and not per stirpes. If there are two surviving children and three grandchildren who are children of a predeceased child at the time the will is probated, how will the estate be divided?
  a. ½ to each surviving child.
  b. ⅓ to each surviving child and 1/9 to each grandchild.
  c. ¼ to each surviving child and 1/6 to each grandchild.
  d. 1/5 to each surviving child and grandchild.

____ 2. Generally, an estate is liable for which debts owed by the decedent at the time of death?
  a. All of the decedent's debts.
  b. Only debts secured by the decedent's property.
  c. Only debts covered by the statute of frauds.
  d. None of the decedent's debts.

____ 3. A personal representative of an estate would breach fiduciary duties if the personal representative
  a. Combined personal funds with funds of the estate so that both could purchase treasury bills.
  b. Represented the estate in a lawsuit brought against it by a disgruntled relative of the decedent.
  c. Distributed property in satisfaction of the decedent's debts.
  d. Engaged a non-CPA to prepare the records for the estate's final accounting.

____ 4. Rita Tyan died leaving a will naming her children, John and Dale, as the sole beneficiaries. In her will, Rita designated John as the executor of her estate and excused John from posting a bond as executor. At the time of Rita's death, she owned a parcel of land with her sister, Ann, as joint tenants with right of survivorship.
  With respect to Rita's interest in the land, it will pass to
  a. John and Dale outside Rita's estate by operation of law.
  b. John and Dale through Rita's estate after the will is probated.
  c. Ann through Rita's estate after the will is probated.
  d. Ann outside Rita's estate by operation of law.

____ 5. Colt's will created a testamentary trust for the benefit of Colt's spouse. Colt's sister and Colt's spouse were named as co-trustees of the trust. The trust provided for discretionary principal distributions to Colt's spouse. It also provided that, on the death of Colt's spouse, any remaining trust property was to be distributed to Colt's children. Part of the trust property consisted of a very valuable baseball card collection. After Colt's death, which of the following statements would be correct?
   a. The co-trustees must use the same degree of skill, judgment, and care in managing the trust assets as reasonably prudent persons would exercise in managing their own affairs.
   b. The co-trustees must employ an investment advisor to manage the trust assets.
   c. Colt's sister may delegate her duties as co-trustee to the spouse and thereby not be liable for the administration of the trust.
   d. Under no circumstances could the spouse purchase the baseball card collection from the trust without breaching fiduciary duties owed to the trust and Colt's children.

____ 6. Cord's will created a trust to take effect on Cord's death. The will named Cord's spouse as both the trustee and personal representative (executor) of the estate. The will provided that all of Cord's securities were to be transferred to the trust and named Cord's child as the beneficiary of the trust. Under the circumstances,
   a. Cord has created an inter vivos trust.
   b. Cord has created a testamentary trust.
   c. The trust is invalid because it will not become effective until Cord's death.
   d. Cord's spouse may not serve as both the trustee and personal representative because of the inherent conflict of interest.

____ 7. In a written trust containing no specific powers, the trustee will have all of the following implied powers except
   a. Sell trust property.
   b. Pay management expenses.
   c. Accumulate income.
   d. Employ a CPA to prepare trust tax returns.

____ 8. A trustee's fiduciary duty will probably be violated if the trustee
   a. Invests trust property in government bonds.
   b. Performs accounting services for the trust.
   c. Sells unproductive trust property.
   d. Borrows money from the trust.

CHAPTER 53

EXERCISE 1

HOW DO I CLOSE ON A HOUSE WHEN I'M OUT OF THE COUNTRY?
POWERS OF ATTORNEY

Text References: Chapters 38 and 39

Nancy Travis, a photographer for *National Geographic*, lives in Scarsdale, New York. The National Geographic Society has just given Nancy an assignment in the Andes that will run from June 1, 1998 until July 14, 1998. Nancy will depart on May 29, 1998 for South America.

Nancy is single and has just purchased a house. The closing on her house is scheduled for June 15, 1998 and because of title searches and mortgage paperwork, she has learned that this date is the earliest she can expect for the closing. In addition, Nancy will be receiving an inheritance of 22,000 shares of IBM stock from her late uncle's estate which is scheduled for a final distribution hearing on June 20, 1998.

Nancy is concerned because she can't handle all of these personal transactions when she is out of the country working. "But, they'll need my signature on documents for the closing and the stock transfer. And the papers aren't even completed yet so I can't sign them in advance. There won't even be an papers for the stock until the judge signs them after the hearing. How can I sign for the shares then?"

Jake Truitt, a life-time friend of Nancy's, has offered to help in whatever way he can to handle the transactions while Nancy is gone but notes, "I just can't see that they will accept my signature."

Review the materials on agency in Chapters 38 and 39. Then turn to the Quicken Business Law Partners Program and refer to the power of attorney documents.

1. What authority does a general power of attorney give?

_____

_____

_____

_____

_____

2. According to the agreement, is Jake entitled to compensation? _____

3. Can Jake serve under the power of attorney without compensation? _____

_____

4. Can Nancy revoke the power of attorney? _____

_____

Refer to the special power of attorney in the Quicken business law partners documents.

5. What is the distinction between this document and the general power of attorney?

_____

_____

6. Is the agent entitled to compensation? _____

_____

INSTRUCTOR ASSIGNED EXERCISES:

Can you help Nancy with her dilemma? Explain the pros and cons of a power of attorney to Nancy.

Using the information you have been given, draft a power of attorney for Nancy.

NOTE: Exercises 2 through 8 are based on the following fact pattern.

EXERCISE 2
THEY SCRATCHED MY WIDE-SCREEN TV, NOW WHAT?
BREACH OF CONTRACT AND WITHHOLDING PAYMENT

Text References: Chapters 8, 18 and 33

David and Joan Woods contracted with Tolleson Carpet for the purchase and installation of carpet in their home for a total price of $4281. While the installers were moving the furniture in the Woods' family room in order to remove the old carpet and install the new, one worker swung a roll of carpet around in such a way that it hit the screen of the Woods' wide-screen television. Joan Woods witnessed the screen being scraped by the roll of carpet but could not get close enough to inspect the television screen when it happened.

After the carpet installation was complete, both David and Joan noticed a scratch on their wide-screen television. Joan told David, "That's just where that worker scraped the roll of carpet when they were moving the furniture." The Woods' television was two months old at he time of the carpet installation. The Woods had a repair service examine the screen. Replacement cost for the screen, including labor, was estimated at $671.

Joan called Tolleson's manager, Frank Fairbanks and explained the problem with the television screen. "Look," Fairbanks responded, "you can't prove we did that. That's not our problem. Besides, read your contract, it says right in there that we have no liability for any damages to your house or furniture that occurs while we're installing your carpet." Joan hung up and told David, "I guess I could put it all in writing and maybe the company could respond.

Refer to the BBB/Attorney General Letter of Complaint provided in the Quicken Business Law Partner documents.

1. What details will Joan and David need to fill in to draft the complaint?

_____

_____

2. What documents do you think they should attach to their complaint?

_____

_____

QUICKEN EXERCISES

3. Can you think of means of alternative dispute resolution that might help Joan and David and Tolleson to resolve their differences?

_____

_____

_____

INSTRUCTOR ASSIGNED EXERCISE:

Help Joan draft a letter of complaint using the form provided in the Quicken Business Law Partner documents. Do you have all the information you need?

EXERCISE 3

WE NEED TO GET THAT CHECK BACK
STOP PAYMENT ORDERS

Text Reference: Chapter 33

David has just given Tolleson a check for $2,281, the balance due on the carpet contract. "I wonder if there is anything I can do to get my money back until this issue with the television screen is resolved," wondered David.

Review Chapter 33 in the text and determine whether David can take any action with the check to Tolleson. Refer to the Quicken Business Law Partner credit documents, the stop payment on a check form, and answer the following questions:

1. Can the Woods rightfully stop payment on the check to Tolleson?

2. Must the drawer give a reason for the stop payment?

3. According to the stop payment form, who will pay the costs and fees for stopping payment?

4. Will the bank be held liable if the stop payment order should not have been requested by the drawer?

5. Who will be held liable if the stop payment order was wrongfully issued?

INSTRUCTOR ASSIGNED EXERCISES:

Review Chapters 8 and 13 and discuss the validity of Tolleson's disclaimer for damages that occur while they are installing carpet.

What information would the Woods need to stop payment on the check?

Draft a stop payment order for the Woods and be sure to customize it for their fact circumstances.

EXERCISE 4

THE SAGA OF THE WIDE-SCREEN TV CONTINUES
NOTICE OF DISHONOR

Text Reference: Chapter 33

After Tolleson deposited the Woods' check, it is notified that the check has been dishonored by the Woods' bank. Review Chapter 33 and determine Tolleson's rights. Answer the following questions:

1. Is Tolleson required to notify the Woods of the bank's dishonor of the check?

_____

Turn to the Quicken Bad Check Notice under the credit document section, and answer the following questions:

2. According to the notice, what will happen if payment is not made immediately?

_____

_____

3. Is interest accruing?_____

INSTRUCTOR ASSIGNED EXERCISE:

Help Tolleson by also drafting a follow-up letter to the Woods with a demand for payment.

EXERCISE 5

COLLECTION EFFORTS FOR THE CARPET BEGIN
COLLECTION ACTIVITIES

Text Reference: Chapter 29

With no response from the Woods, Tolleson has referred the matter to a collection agency. The collection agency has contacted the Woods and demanded payment. The letter from the collection agency includes the following paragraph:

Tolleson Carpet has made repeated demands for payment on your carpet contract. Please pay the amount due ($2281.00) today so that your credit rating is not affected by your non-payment of this binding obligation.

If payment is not received within 10 days, we shall proceed with all rights and remedies afforded Tolleson by law.

Review Chapter 29 and the Quicken Business Law Partners Credit Documents and answer the following questions:

1. Has the collection agency violated any laws with it demand letter?

_____

_____

2. What rights could Woods assert?

_____

_____

INSTRUCTOR ASSIGNED EXERCISE:

Help the Woods respond to the collection agency's demand for payment. What rights could the Woods assert? Has the collection agency violated any laws with its demand letter?

QUICKEN EXERCISES

EXERCISE 6

NOW THE SCREEN SCRATCH MIGHT AFFECT MY CREDIT RATING
CREDIT REPORTS

Text Reference: Chapter 29

The Woods are concerned that their problems with Tolleson may have resulted in a blemish on their previously flawless credit report. Review Chapter 29 and the Quicken Business Law Partner Credit Documents. Refer to the request for a credit report and answer the following:

1. What must be included with a request for a credit report in order for the report to be furnished?

_____

_____

2. Why would the inclusion of a social security number be important?

_____

_____

INSTRUCTOR ASSIGNED EXERCISES:

Help the Woods make the appropriate request.

Be sure to list any additional information you would need in order to make the request.

EXERCISE 7

THE LAW SUIT FOR THE CARPET PAYMENT
SMALL CLAIMS COURT

Text References: Chapters 1 and 18

Suppose that the Woods still have not paid the remaining balance for the carpet and Tolleson wishes to proceed with a suit to recover the amount due from the Woods. Refer to the Quicken Business Law Partners Credit Documents and the small claims worksheet and answer the following questions:

1. Go to the list of state small claims limits in the document. Does the claim against the Woods qualify for small claims court in your state? Suppose that the Woods have paid all but the $671 for the television screen, would the Tolleson suit then qualify for small claims court in your state?

_____

_____

2. What additional information do you need to complete the checklist?

_____

_____

3. Who is the plaintiff in this suit? Who is the defendant?

_____

4. Which state has the highest small claims court maximum?

_____

INSTRUCTOR ASSIGNED EXERCISE:

Complete the small claims checklist for Tolleson.

EXERCISE 8

THE SUIT FOR THE TELEVISION SCREEN SCRATCH
FILING A LAW SUIT

Textbook Reference: Chapters 1 and 18

Suppose that the Woods make the $2,281 payment to Tolleson and then file suit against Tolleson to collect the $671 for the repair of their television screen. Refer to the Quicken Business Law Partners Credit Document and the portion on Defending A Lawsuit - Business and answer the following questions:

1. In this situation, who is the plaintiff? Who is the defendant?

___

2. What additional information do you need to complete the form?

___

___

INSTRUCTOR ASSIGNED EXERCISE:

Complete the checklist as thoroughly as you can for Tolleson with the information you have been given.

EXERCISE 9

CREDIT APPLICATIONS AND DENIAL

Text References: Chapter 29

Assume you have been denied a loan for the purchase of a car. Refer to Chapter 29 and the Challenge to a Denial of Credit in the Quicken Business Law Partners program.

What requests for information are made in the letter?

___

___

EXERCISE 10

THE DEFECTIVE APARTMENT

Textbook Reference: Chapter 52

The heating in your apartment does not work, and it is February in North Conway, New Hampshire. Refer to Chapter 52 and the Complaint to the Landlord in Quicken Business Law Partners.

1. What two things does the note to the landlord accomplish?

_____

_____

2. What rights do tenants have generally regarding the conditions of their leased premises?

_____

_____

INSTRUCTOR ASSIGNED EXERCISE:

Draft a letter of complaint for a problem in your own apartment.

EXERCISE 11

COMMERCIAL REAL ESTATE LEASES

Textbook References: Chapter 52

Refer to Chapter 52 and the Real Estate Lease-Commercial in the Quicken Business Law Partners and answer the following questions:

1. When is the rent due under the lease?

2. Who is responsible for insurance on the property?

3. How does either party give notice to the other according to the lease?

4. What happens if a portion of the lease agreement is unenforceable?

QUICKEN EXERCISES

EXERCISE 12

RESIDENTIAL LEASES

Textbook Reference: Chapter 52

Refer to the Residential Lease in the Quicken Business Law Partner and Chapter 52 and answer the following questions:

1. What provisions do you see in the residential lease that are not found in the commercial lease?

_____

_____

2. What is the habitability clause and what does it do for the tenant?

_____

_____

EXERCISE 13

RENTAL APPLICATION

Textbook Reference: Chapter 52

Refer to the Rental Application in the Quicken Business Law Partner and answer the following questions:

1. What happens if a tenant submits an application and is approved by the landlord and then fails to rent the premises?

_____

2. Will the landlord be permitted to do a credit check?_____

_____

3. List the grounds on which the landlord can't discriminate.

_____

_____

4. What rights does the tenant have if rejected by the landlord?

_____

_____

INSTRUCTOR ASSIGNED EXERCISE:

What problem questions do you see in the application?

EXERCISE 14

THE RENTAL PROPERTY INSPECTION

Textbook Reference: Chapter 52

Refer to the Renter's's Inspection Worksheet in the Quicken Business Law Partners and answer the following questions:

1. What are the general standards for the condition of the premises that the parties confirm through sign-off on this inspection sheet?

_____

_____

2. What effect does this checklist have on termination rights of the tenant?

_____

_____

3. What defects does the tenant assume the risk for?

_____

4. What does the tenant agree to do with respect to the smoke detector? _____

_____

EXERCISE 15

BILL OF SALE

Textbook References: Chapters 25 and 27

Refer to the Bill of Sale in the Quicken Business Law Partner and answer the following questions:

1. What does property sold "AS IS" mean?

2. What does a bill of sale do?

3. Is a bill of sale different from a document of title?

EXERCISE 16

BILL OF SALE FOR MOTOR VEHICLES

Textbook References: Chapters 25, 27 and 29

Refer to the Bill of Sale-Motor Vehicles in the Quicken Business Law Partner and answer the following questions:

1. What differences are there between the bill of sale and the bill of sale for motor vehicles?

_____

_____

2. What happens if the seller makes a false statement regarding the vehicle's mileage?

_____

3. What promise does the seller make in the bill of sale about the vehicle's odometer?

_____

_____

EXERCISE 17

EQUIPMENT LEASE

Textbook References: Chapters 20 and 22

Refer to the Equipment Lease in the Quicken Business Law Partner and answer the following question:

1. When is the rent due?

    _____

2. Who has the risk of loss or is responsible for damage to the equipment?

    _____

3. Can the lessee make alterations to the equipment?_____

4. Who pays for repairs to the equipment?_____

5. Can the lessor see the equipment during the term of the lease?_____

    _____

6. What options are given to the lessee when the lease ends?

    _____

    _____

7. Does the lessor make any warranties about the property?_____

8. Is the lessor's disclaimer valid?_____

    _____

9. Can the lessee assign the lease?_____

10. How will disputes be settled?_____

    _____

QUICKEN EXERCISES

EXERCISE 18

THE ROLE OF GUARANTORS

Textbook References: Chapter 35

Refer to chapter 35 and the Guaranty in the Quicken Business Law Partner and answer the following questions:

1. What type of guaranty is this?_____

_____

2. How long does the guaranty last?_____

_____

3. Does the creditor have to notify the guarantor if the debtor defaults?_____

4. Does the creditor have to notify the guarantor if he loans more money to the debtor?

_____

5. Does the creditor have to show diligence in collection before turning to the guarantor?

_____

6. What can the creditor change without notice to the guarantor?

_____

7. Is the guarantor released if the creditor does change terms?_____

EXERCISE 19

A LICENSE AGREEMENT

Textbook References: Chapter 21

Refer to Chapter 21 and the License Agreement in Quicken Business Law Partner and answer the following questions:

1. What types of arrangements would this agreement cover?

   _____

2. What is the compensation under the agreement?

   _____

EXERCISE 20

PROMISSORY NOTES

Text Reference: Chapter 30

Refer to the Promissory Note in the Quicken Business Law Partner documents and answer the following questions:

1. How are payments applied?

_____

2. In what currency is the note payable?

_____

3. Review Chapter 30. Is it possible to have a negotiable promissory note in the United States when the note is not payable in U.S. currency?

_____

_____

EXERCISE 21

ARTICLES OF INCORPORATION

Text References: Chapters 46 and 49

Review the Articles of Incorporation in the Quicken Business Law Partner and answer the following questions:

1. List the information needed for incorporation using this document.

   _____   _____

   _____   _____

   _____   _____

2. Is this same information required under the MBCA? Refer to Chapter 46

   _____

   _____

3. Will the corporation provide indemnity for its officers and directors?

   _____

4. Refer to Chapter 49. What does indemnity for officers and directors mean?

   _____

   _____

INSTRUCTOR ASSIGNED EXERCISE:

Draft your own articles of incorporation.

QUICKEN EXERCISES

EXERCISE 22

CORPORATE BYLAWS

Text References: Chapters 46 and 49

Review the Corporate Bylaws in the Quicken Business Law Partner and answer the following:

1. How often will meetings of shareholders be held?

   _____

2. Who can call a special meeting?_____

   _____

3. When must notice of a meeting be given?_____

   _____

4. What constitutes a quorum for meetings?_____

   _____

5. Can a quorum be met with proxy representation?_____

6. Can a director be removed without cause?_____

7. List the offices provided by the bylaws.

   _____   _____

   _____   _____

8. Who elects the officers?_____

9. How are the bylaws amended?_____

   _____

10. Can you own shares in the corporation without actually having stock certificates?

    _____

EXERCISE 23

CORPORATE PROXY

Text Reference: Chapter 49

Review the corporate proxy in the Quicken Business Law Partner and answer the following:

1. Does this proxy revoke prior proxies? _____

2. Review Chapter 29 and explain why a proxy might be necessary. _____
   _____

3. Is there a provision for designating votes? _____
   _____

QUICKEN EXERCISES

EXERCISE 24

EMPLOYMENT/AGENCY
CONFIDENTIALITY AGREEMENT

Text References: Chapters 21 and 38

Review the Confidentiality Agreement in the Quicken Business Law Partner and answer the following:

1. What is the definition of confidential information given?

    _____

    _____

2. What kinds of information would you list as being confidential? Refer to Chapters 21 and 38.

    _____   _____

    _____   _____

    _____   _____

EXERCISE 25

EMPLOYMENT/AGENCY
CONSULTING AGREEMENT

Textbook References: Chapters 38, 39, 40 and 41

Review the Consulting Agreement in the Quicken Business Law Partner and answer the following:

1. Will the consultant be an independent contractor or an employee?

_____

2. Why is this distinction important? What differences exist between hiring an independent contractor and hiring an employee? Refer to Chapters 39-41.

_____

_____

_____

_____

EXERCISE 26

EMPLOYMENT/AGENCY
EMPLOYMENT AGREEMENT

Text References: Chapters 38 and 41

Review the Employment Agreement in the Quicken Business Law Partner and answer the following:

1. How long will the employment last?

2. Is an employment of this length legal?

3. How are the parties to the agreement to give notice?

EXERCISE 27

EMPLOYMENT/AGENCY
LETTER OF ACCEPTANCE

Text References: Chapters 10 and 38

Review the Quicken Business Law Partner Letter of Acceptance under Employment and answer the following:

1. Prior to the time of the use of this document, what interaction had the parties had regarding employment?

2. How would a letter like this help the employee? Be sure to review Chapters 10 and 38.

EXERCISE 28

NON-COMPETE AGREEMENT
ANTITRUST AND EMPLOYMENT

Text References: Chapters 4, 21 and 38

Review the Non-Compete Agreement in the Quicken Business Law Partner and answer the following:

1. What types of activities does the agreement prohibit?

    _____   _____

    _____   _____

2. What remedies are given for violation of the agreement?

    _____

3. Refer to Chapter 21 and discuss why and when this type of an agreement would be necessary.

    _____

    _____

    _____

    _____

EXERCISE 29

CONSIGNMENT AGREEMENT
SALES - UCC ARTICLE 2

Text References: Chapters 22 and 25

Review the Consignment Agreement in the General Business document section of Quicken Business Law Partner and answer the following:

1. What is a consignment arrangement? _____

   _____

2. Who is the consignee? _____

3. Who is the consignor? _____

4. How will the consignee be compensated for the sale of the goods? _____

   _____

5. Who has title to the goods during the consignment? _____

6. Who has the risk of loss during the consignment? _____

7. What is the difference between a bailment and a consignment? _____

   _____

   _____

EXERCISE 30

COPYRIGHT APPLICATION
INTELLECTUAL PROPERTY

Text References: Chapter 21

Review the Copyright Application in the Quicken Business Law Partner and answer the following:

1. List the types of works that can be copyrighted.

2. If a book is written by an employee during the course of employment, who has the right to the copyright?

EXERCISE 31

GENERAL CONTRACT - PRODUCTS
SALES/ARTICLE 2

Text References: Chapters 24, 25, 26, 27 and 28

Review the General Contract-Products in the General Business documents of Quicken Business Law Partner and answer the following:

1. What happens in the buyer fails to make a payment?

2. What is the time given for delivery?

3. Who pays the costs if improper packaging produces damages to the goods?

4. Who pays the taxes in this transaction?

5. What are the inspection rights under the contract?

6. Are these inspection rights different from those given under the UCC?

7. What is force majeure?

8. Give examples listed as force majeure.

QUICKEN EXERCISES

_____   _____

_____   _____

_____   _____

9. What do the parties agree to do in the event there is a dispute between them?

_____

_____

_____

10. What is the pledge of confidentiality?_____

_____

11. Is an assignment of this contract permitted?_____

EXERCISE 32

TRADEMARK VIOLATION
INTELLECTUAL PROPERTY/TRADEMARKS

Text References: Chapters 1 and 21

Review the Trademark Violation letter in the Quicken Business Law Partner and answer the following:

1. What is the demand made in the letter?_____

_____

2. If the recipient of the letter complies with its demands, what will happen?_____

_____

INSTRUCTOR ASSIGNED EXERCISE:

See if you can, through observation, find a trademark violation in the newspaper, on television, in ads or in business names. Describe it, the appropriate remedy and why it is important for the owner of the trademark to take action.

EXERCISE 33

GOVERNMENT RECORDS

Text References: Chapters 3 and 5

Review the Request for FBI and CIA Records in the Government section of the Quicken Business Law Partner and answer the following:

1. If you used this letter request, what would you obtain? _____

_____

_____

2. If the agency indicates it will withhold the records you have requested, what information must the agency give?

_____

INSTRUCTOR ASSIGNED EXERCISE:

Write and make a request for your own records.

EXERCISE 34

FREEDOM OF INFORMATION REQUEST
ADMINISTRATIVE LAW

Text Reference: Chapter 5

Review the FOI Request in the Quicken Business Law Partner and answer the following:

1. What information does the requestor need to provide to the agency?

_____

_____

2. What does the letter request if your request is not addressed to the proper agency?

_____

EXERCISE 35

EMPLOYMENT LAW
REGULATION OF EMPLOYMENT

Text Reference: Chapter 41

Review the Social Security-Earnings Benefit Request in the Quicken Business Law Partner and answer the following:

1. What information is this request designed to obtain for you?

_____

_____

2. What are the penalties for making a request to obtain this information on someone other than yourself without their permission?

_____

INSTRUCTOR ASSIGNED EXERCISE:

Write and obtain your own SS-Earnings benefit statement.

EXERCISE 1 - ANSWERS

1. A general power of attorney gives Jake full authority to run Nancy's business affairs. He can open, maintain and close bank accounts and securities accounts. He is given full access to safe deposit boxes. He can sell, exchange, buy, invest, and reinvest assets. He can purchase insurance and collect debts. He can enter into binding contracts on Nancy's behalf. He can exercise her stock options, employ help and sell, mortgage and lease property. If Nancy had any kind of business operations, he could run them with full authority. He can prepare, sign and file government documents on Nancy's behalf.

    This general power of attorney is an enormously broad one that gives Jake full and complete authority over any of Nancy's property and legal issues. In this case, a general power of authority may be more than Nancy wishes to give to Jake.

2. Yes, Jake is entitled to reasonable compensation plus reimbursement for expenses.

3. Yes, Jake could serve as a gratuitous agent but this form entitles him to compensation. Because jake is helping Nancy as a friend, they will need to change this portion of the form. Remember, forms are not customized for individual needs and there are legal issues and implications for each clause.

4. Yes, Nancy can revoke the power of attorney at any time. Nancy may want to put a time limitation on the power of attorney. Nancy could also put a transaction limitation on it in that she could direct the transactions for which Jake has authority.

5. The special power of attorney in the Quicken Business Law Partner requires that the specific matters for which there is authority be spelled out; the power of attorney is limited in scope in that transactional limitations are placed on the delegated authority.

6. Yes, Jake is again entitled to compensation. Jake can serve as a gratuitous agent but the clause on compensation would need to be deleted from the document.

EXERCISE 2 - ANSWERS

1. Joan and David will need to tell their story in their letter as it is reflected in the facts. They will need to spell out their issues about the carpet layers and the television screen.

2. Copies of the documents Joan and David should attach are: the carpet contract; the purchase contract for the television (to show it was a relatively new purchase at the time of the carpet problem); and the estimate for the repair. Joan and David could attach affidavits from people who had seen the screen before the installation (including themselves) that attest to the fact the screen was not scratched prior to the installers' conduct.

3. Joan and David and the Tollesons could sit with a mediator and try and work out a fair solution such as perhaps at least splitting the cost of the screen repair. They could also try arbitration in which the arbitrator could propose a solution.

EXERCISE 3 - ANSWERS

1. Yes, the Woods can stop payment on the check. Stopping payment on the check is not a final determination for the contract rights that might exist between the parties. Stopping payment on the check is simply a means for the Woods to gain leverage in terms of resolution of the dispute. By stopping payment, they are not in the position of having to seek money from Tolleson. Tolleson will be forced to deal with the issues the Woods have raised in order to obtain payment.

2. Yes, the drawer must give a reason for the stop payment order. In this case, the Woods would simply explain that they are stopping payment because of a contract dispute.

3. The drawer bears the cost of stopping payment on a check.

4. No, the bank is not liable because the bank has no way of knowing whether the contract complaint is legitimate. The bank puts a clause in its stop payment forms to protect it — the bank stops the payment at the customer's direction but does not agree to assume the liability if the bank is wrong.

5. The drawer has full liability to the payee for a wrongful stop payment order. This liability rests where it should because the stop payment order is the result of a dispute between the drawer and the payee. To the extent the drawer is wrong, the parties' contractual liability will take over and determine damages.

EXERCISE 4 - ANSWERS

1. Yes, Tolleson is required to notify the Woods because the primary party, or at least the first party for presentment of the instrument, the bank, has refused to pay. In order to attach liability of the secondary party (the drawer), the payee must give notification of dishonor.

2. If payment of the amount of the check is not made immediately, Tolleson will make an additional charge and there will be no further credit extended to the Woods.

3. Yes, interest does accrue during the entire time that Tolleson attempts to collect the amount due from the Woods.

EXERCISE 5 - ANSWERS

1. The collection agency has not violated any of the provisions of the Fair Debt Collections Practices Act assuming that the notice is given privately. The notice contains a classic collector's hedge in that it does not threaten a suit directly in case the creditor or the agency decides not to proceed with such action. The notice is broad enough that any additional action could be taken, but not so specific that the agency would be making a threat it would not carry out which is a violation of the FDCPA.

2. The Woods could respond that they wish to have no further contact from the collection agency and the contact would have to stop. If the Woods do assert their rights to no further contact, the issue about the scratched screen will come to a head because it is intertwined with the issue of payment and any legal action by Tolleson to collect the amount due will enable the Woods to respond with their claim for damages to their TV.

EXERCISE 6 - ANSWERS

1. Personal ID (copy), the appropriate fee, social security number and addresses for the last five years.

2. The social security number is included because mix-ups between individuals with the same names can be avoided when the SS# is used. Also, phoney requests are at least reduced because the SS# is more difficult to come by than a name and address. The additional information on addresses is also requested to match persons with reports correctly. Because of numerous lawsuits over the past few years of mix-ups in identification, credit reporting agencies take additional precautions with respect to data and the released of credit reports.

EXERCISE 7 - ANSWERS

1. Simply review the chart provided in the Quicken small claims worksheet and match it to your state. In most states the $671 qualifies for small claims court.

2. To complete the small claims checklist, you will need an address for Tolleson as well as its business status, i.e., is it a corporation or sole proprietorship, etc.

3. Tolleson is the plaintiff and the Woods would be the defendants.

4. Florida and Delaware, with a maximum of $15,000 have the highest small claims court jurisdiction.

EXERCISE 8 - ANSWERS

1. In this factual situation, the Woods will be the plaintiffs and Tolleson will be the defendant.

2. Tolleson will need to check with its employees or contractors who installed the carpeting to see what happened. Tolleson will need to find and provide any documentation it has with respect to the incident.

EXERCISE 9 - ANSWERS

1. The information requested in the Quicken form is whether a consumer reporting agency was used, and, if so, which one. The letter also requests a description of the nature of the investigation conducted.

An important tip in checking a credit denial is to be certain that the creditor had the information on you — did the have the right credit report and the right person?

EXERCISE 10 - ANSWERS

1. The letter serves two very important purposes: the landlord is put on notice of a heating problem in the apartment: and the landlord is given a time within which to solve the problem

2. Most states gives residential tenants a warranty of habitability which means that the premises are fit and habitable at the time of the lease. The Uniform Residential Landlord Tenant Act (URLTA) also provides tenants with rights in the event the basic essentials of habitation (such as heat, water, and, in some circumstances, air conditioning) cease to work. Those rights include the right to make a demand for repair (which is what this Quicken letter is designed to do), and then the right to self-help or making the repairs themselves and then billing the landlord or deducting that amount from their rent. However, all these rights begin with the notice to the landlord of the problem.

EXERCISE 11 - ANSWERS

1. The rent is due on the first day of each month.

2. Both the landlord and the tenant are responsible for carrying insurance on their respective properties. Tenants would have to carry their own insurance, for example, on their furniture. Landlords would carry an owner's policy on the property.

3. Notice must be given in writing.

4. If one portion of the lease is unenforceable, it is to be struck from the lease so that the remainder can be enforced.

EXERCISE 12 - ANSWERS

1. Some of the provisions in the residential lease not found in the commercial lease include the condition of the dwelling unit, absences for extended periods of the tenant from the property, and the rights and obligations with respect to the keys.

2. The habitability clause simple puts into the official language of the lease the rights most tenants have in most states: that the premises are in habitable condition at the commencement of the lease.

EXERCISE 13 - ANSWERS

1. The tenant whose application is approved by the landlord and who fails to enter into a lease agreement will lose his or her application fee. The reason for such damages is that the landlord does expend time and effort (and in some cases fees for the credit report) in processing an application.

2. Yes, the application form authorizes the landlord to do a credit check.

3. The grounds on which a landlord can't discriminate are race, religion, national origin, age, and disability.

4. If the applicant makes a written request for the reason for rejection of the application, the landlord has 60 days within which to respond to the applicant.

EXERCISE 14 - ANSWERS

1. The general standards that the checklist is intended to confirm are that the premises are in good, clean, sanitary order and in good condition and repair.

2. The tenant, by signing off on the inspection sheet, agrees to return the premises to the landlord in the same condition as when the inspection occurs.

3. The tenant assumes the risk for any defects in the rental property that he knew of or should have known of through inspection of the property.

4. The tenant agrees to test the smoke detector at least every other week and to be certain that it has an alkaline battery that is in working order.

EXERCISE 15 - ANSWERS

1. When the phrase "AS IS" appears in a contract it means that both the implied warranty of merchantability as well as the implied warranty of fitness for a particular purpose are disclaimed. The goods are sold with all their defects and the buyer assumes the risk of those defects. Subsequently discovered defects cannot be a basis for suit or liability against the seller.

2. A bill of sale is evidence of a transfer of title.

3. A bill of sale is evidence of a transfer of title. It is not, however, a document of title.

EXERCISE 16 - ANSWERS

1. A bill of sale for motor vehicles has more details including a description of the car (make, model, etc) as well as the mileage.

2. A false statement about the mileage on the car is a federal offense and can result in fines and/or imprisonment.

3. The seller promises that the odometer is in good working order and that it has not been tampered with so as to affect the recorded mileage on the car.

EXERCISE 17 - ANSWERS

1. The rent on the leased equipment is due when the equipment is returned.

2. The lessee agrees to assume the risk of loss and responsibility for damage to the property.

3. No, the lessee is not permitted to make alterations to the equipment.

4. The lessee is responsible for repairs to the equipment.

5. Yes, the lessor retains the rights of inspection of the equipment during the term of the lease.

6. When the lease agreement ends, the lessee is given the option of renewing the lease agreement or purchase the leased property according to stated financial terms

7. No, the lessor specifically disclaims any warranties about the leased equipment.

8. This disclaimer may create problems since it is, in essence, an exculpatory clause that permits the lessor to lease defective property that could injure the lessee and others. It is against public policy to hold oneself immune from liability for one's own negligence. While many lease agreements contain such provisions, they can be successfully challenged on the grounds of unconscionability.

9. No, assignment by the lessee is prohibited.

10. The lease agreement provides that any disputes between the parties will be settled through binding arbitration.

EXERCISE 18 - ANSWERS

1. This is an absolute and unconditional guaranty.

2. There can be no revocation of this guaranty and it lasts until all obligations under the original credit contract are satisfied.

3. No, as is typical in most guaranty contracts, the creditor need not notify the guarantor of the debtor's default.

4. No, the creditor need not notify the guarantor if additional loans are made by the creditor to the debtor.

5. No, the creditor need not show due diligence in collection because this guaranty is an unconditional guaranty of payment. Only in a guarantor of collection situation must a creditor establish due diligence before demanding payment from the guarantor.

6. The creditor can change the payment terms of the credit agreement and release the collateral without giving notice to the guarantor.

7. No, the guarantor is not released if the creditor changes the terms.

EXERCISE 19 - ANSWERS

1. This license agreement would cover any type of use of intellectual property such as the right to use a song or software.

2. The compensation to the owner of the intellectual property will be payment of royalties which is a percentage of total sales as when a songwriter is given a percentage of record sales in exchange for the artist's right to record the song.

EXERCISE 20 - ANSWERS

1. Payments under the note are applied first to accrued interest and then to principal.

2. The note is payable in U.S. currency.

3. Yes, a note can still be negotiable even though it is payable in a currency that is foreign to the country in which the note is made or either party is located. So long as the note is payable in a medium of exchange recognized by some country, it is negotiable and valid.

EXERCISE 21 - ANSWERS

1. Under these sample incorporation documents, the information needed is the total # of shares, the registered agent for the corporation, the purpose of the corporation and the directors.

2. No, the MBCA does not require all the information noted in these articles of incorporation. These articles require more information which is permitted and possibly desirable from the standpoint of the parties' rights.

3. Yes, the corporation's officers and directors will enjoy the protection of indemnity from the corporation.

4. Indemnity means that the officers and directors can be reimbursed for the expenses they incur in defending their conduct with respect to the corporation. There can be some exceptions such as when the directors and officers engage in fraud.

EXERCISE 22 - ANSWERS

1. The shareholders will hold meetings at least once each calendar year.

2. A special meeting of shareholders can be called by the president, the board or a majority of the outstanding shareholders of voting shares.

3. Notice of a meeting must be given no later than 10 days prior to the meeting. The time can be measured from the time the notice is mailed and not when it actually is received by the shareholders.

4. A quorum is the majority of the outstanding voting shares.

5. Yes, proxies can be used to make up a quorum.

6. Yes, a director can be removed with or without cause.

7. The offices provided in these bylaws include the president, vice president, secretary and treasurer. More than one office can be held by a single person.

8. The officers are elected by the directors.

9. The bylaws can be amended by the directors or the shareholders by a majority of a quorum of voting shares.

10. Yes, you can own shares in the corporation without having to have certificates as evidence.

EXERCISE 23 - ANSWERS

1. Yes, all prior proxies are revoked.

2. Proxies are needed because the majority of shareholders are unable to attend the annual meeting yet they want to have a voice in corporate governance. They designate a representative as well as their voting choices.

3. Yes, a segment of the proxy allows the shareholder to dictate how votes should be made.

EXERCISE 24 - ANSWERS

1. The definition of confidential information given in the document is proprietary information not generally known to the public.

2. Information about customers including customer lists, new products, strategies, supply chain management techniques, planned ad campaigns, etc.

EXERCISE 25 - ANSWERS

1. The consultant will be an independent contractor.

2. This distinction is important because of wage tax issues and liability issues and worker's compensation coverage issues. For an employee, an employer must pay wage taxes, if fully liable for acts within the scope of employment and subjects the employee to worker's compensation system rules. An independent contractor pays his or her own wage taxes and is not covered by worker's compensation. The employer would also not be liable for the torts of an independent contractor.

EXERCISE 26 - ANSWERS

1. It is an "at will" agreement — it can be terminated at any time.

2. Yes, it is legal. There are some exceptions such as terminating a whistle-blower that would prevent termination because such a termination would be retaliatory in nature.

3. Notices must be given in writing.

EXERCISE 27 - ANSWERS

1. From the document, we can conclude that the parties had a conversation about a contract for employment.

2. A letter such as this would help the employee prove that some type of a contract exists. It would be contemporaneous evidence of discussions of employment. It also serves as a formal acceptance of an oral offer. Further, the failure of the employer to correct any misunderstandings about the conversation and offer of employment would allow the employee to rely on the oral promise and begin the process of terminating another job or moving.

EXERCISE 28 - ANSWERS

1. The types of activities prohibited under the agreement are: competing directly; competing indirectly; soliciting customers for business; inducing employees to leave; revealing confidential business information.

2. Monetary remedies as well as injunctive relief are afforded under the agreement.

3. This type of an agreement is necessary to prevent employees from obtaining proprietary information and then using it to start their own businesses or taking it to other employers who are competitors.

EXERCISE 29 - ANSWERS

1. A consignment is an arrangement whereby the property owner transfers property to a consignee for purposes of selling that property in exchange for a fee or a commission. For example, a consignment furniture store is filled with the used furniture of others that can be sold for a price below new and in exchange for a percentage to the consignee.

2. The consignee is the party who has possession of the property and agrees to sell it for a fee.

3. The consignor is the owner of the property who transfers possession.

4. The consignee is entitled to a fee or percentage for the sale of the goods.

5. The consignee.

6. The consignee.

7. A bailment is a temporary transfer of possession. A consignment is the transfer of possession for purposes of sale with the authority to transfer title to another. Until the terms of the consignment arrangement end, the title is held by the consignee. A bailee does not hold title in any type of bailment.

EXERCISE 30 - ANSWERS

1. The types of works that can be copyrighted are music, books, movies, television shows, magazines, newspapers, periodicals and software.

2. The employer has the right to the copyright because the employer provided the resources for its development.

EXERCISE 31 - ANSWERS

1. The failure of the buyer to make a payment is considered a material breach.

2. "Time is of the essence" is the time given for delivery — ASAP would be the standard.

3. The seller absorbs the loss if the goods are damaged due to improper packaging.

4. The buyer is to pay the taxes.

5. The inspection rights include the right to open, test and view.

6. The inspection rights afforded under the contract are about the same as those given under Article 2 with the exception that the buyer must give written notice of rejection and the reasons for such rejection.

7. A force majeure is an event that interferes with the performance of the contract that is beyond the parties' control and was not anticipated by them.

8. Examples of force majeure in the contract include: acts of God; fire; explosion; vandalism; storms; riots; military action; wars, insurrections.

9. If the matter has not been resolved in five days, they agree to go to binding arbitration.

10. A pledge of confidentiality is an agreement not to disclose the terms of the agreement or any proprietary information regarding the product.

11. No, assignment of the contract is not permitted.

EXERCISE 32 - ANSWERS

1. The demand is that the use of the trademark stop.

2. If the recipient complies, the owner of the trademark will take no further action and will not seek any damages.

EXERCISE 33 - ANSWERS

1. All information about you held by the FBI and CIA with certain exceptions such as information related to any ongoing investigations.

2. The agency must disclose why the information is being withheld.

EXERCISE 34 - ANSWERS

1. The requestor must provide what documents he/she is looking for and for what period.

2. That the request be forwarded to the proper agency.

EXERCISE 35 - ANSWERS

1. Your history of wages and applicable social security withholding as well as what benefits you could expect under SS programs.

2. Making a request for another without their permission is a violation of federal law that carries fines and/or imprisonment.